THE SELECTED LETTERS OF FLORENCE KELLEY, 1869–1931

The Selected Letters of Florence Kelley, 1869–1931

EDITED BY

KATHRYN KISH SKLAR AND

BEVERLY WILSON PALMER

Kathryn Sklar
1·26·2011

UNIVERSITY OF ILLINOIS PRESS

URBANA AND CHICAGO

Publication of this book was supported
by a grant from the National Historical
Publications and Records Commission.

Manufactured in the United States of America
C 5 4 3 2 1
∞ This book is printed on acid-free paper.

Library of Congress Cataloging-in-Publication Data
Kelley, Florence, 1859–1932.
The selected letters of Florence Kelley, 1869–1931 /
edited by Kathryn Kish Sklar and Beverly Wilson Palmer.
p. cm.
Includes bibliographical references and index.
ISBN 978-0-252-03404-6 (cloth : alk. paper)
1. Kelley, Florence, 1859–1932—Correspondence.
2. Women social reformers—United States—Biography.
3. Feminists—United States—Biography.
I. Sklar, Kathryn Kish.
II. Palmer, Beverly Wilson
III. Title.
HQ1413.K45K454 2009
303.48'4092—dc22 [B] 2008039602

The more closely the rights of purchasers are scrutinized, the more clearly it appears that they are social rights. However much they may present themselves to the mind as individual personal rights, the effort to assert them invariably brings the experience that they are inextricably interwoven with the rights of innumerable other people. In the last analysis, they cannot be asserted without the previous assertion of the claim of the weakest and most defenseless persons in the community.

—Florence Kelley, *Some Ethical Gains through Legislation,* 129

CONTENTS

ILLUSTRATIONS

ACKNOWLEDGMENTS

During our years of labor on this book, we incurred many debts. No documentary edition results from the efforts of one or two persons, but our work process drew on such sustained support from scholars, archivists and apprentice historians—graduate students and undergraduates—that we came to see it as a collective enterprise.

Grants from the National Endowment for the Humanities in 2003–2004 and the National Historical Publications and Records Commission in 2004–2006 supported our most intensive years of archival search and manuscript preparation. We thank Michael Hall at NEH and Timothy Connelly at NHPRC for their advice and guidance.

We are grateful to members of the Kelley family for permission to reproduce the letters of their celebrated ancestor.

Historians always work closely with archivists, but our search for the entire universe of Florence Kelley's correspondence required repeated visits and a steady stream of e-mail and calls to many archivists. We are especially grateful for the generous assistance of the late Mary Wolfskill, director of reader services at the Manuscript Division, Library of Congress, and her colleague, archivist Jeffery Flannery, as well as the entire Manuscripts Room staff for their help with the extensive papers of the National Consumers' League and a multitude of other collections. Special thanks also to William Stingone, Charles J. Liebman Curator of Manuscripts at New York Public Library, and his colleague, manuscript specialist Thomas Lannon, who aided us with the extensive Florence Kelley Papers and Kelley Family Papers. Tara Craig helped us with valuable collections in Butler Library's Rare Books and Manuscripts, Columbia University. Tab Lewis facilitated our work at the National Archives. Mary Pryor aided our searches in the Rockford College Archives. We are grateful to Patrizia Sione, reference archivist at the Kheel Center for Labor-Management Documentation and Archives at the School of Industrial and Labor Relations, Cornell University, for her unfailing assistance, and to Curtis Lyons, director of the Kheel Center, for making our database of almost 7,000 letters of Florence Kelley correspondence available online at the ILR DigitalCommons at http://digitalcommons.ilr.cornell.edu.

At Binghamton our project became a massive cataloging effort that moved forward at the Sklar-Dublin home in rural Pennsylvania as well as at the Center for the Historical Study of Women and Gender at SUNY Binghamton. Graduate students Sarah Boyle, Deanna Gillespie, Halle Lewis, Laura Murphy, Jennifer Tomas, and Corinne Weible organized the growing phalanx of file drawers that contained relevant research materials as well as the letters themselves. Our thanks to undergraduates Sarah Koniewicz and Frank Pantano, who began working on the project as work-study students and spent a year prior to graduate school perfecting our inventory. During 2004–2005, when the project temporarily resided at the University of Oxford, Helen Baker smoothed its path. Annette Varcoe provided essential assistance in the final stage of the book's completion.

This volume could not have been completed without the superb assistance of librarians at Bartle Library, SUNY Binghamton. Ed Shephard, history bibliographer and head of collection development and management, arranged for the purchase of related microfilm collections. Helen Insinger processed our prodigious flow of interlibrary loan requests. And Carol Clemente, head of reader services, made it possible for us to assemble an auxiliary library of related books for the project.

Work also proceeded at Pomona College in Claremont, California. Thanks to Janet Brodie, professor of history at Claremont Graduate University, a fellowship from that institution allowed Kristine Ashton Gunnell to assist in every phase of editing these letters. Ms. Gunnell ably helped transcribe, annotate, and verify facts in Florence Kelley's letters. Pomona College provided office space, computer expertise, and research support. We thank Pomona's History Department, especially former academic department coordinator Janice Ginther; Cecilia Conrad, former associate dean; Sandra Fenton, grants administrator; Brenda Briggs, assistant controller; and Denis Recendez at the Office of Information Technology. Pomona College students Anthony Forte, Rebecca Abbey, Patrick Hall, Martha Beard, Susan Hoang, Micah Ganz, and Edan Schurtzer reliably assisted in the preparation of the manuscript. At the Libraries of the Claremont Colleges, Kaia Poorbaugh and Barbara Garcia rendered extraordinary help.

We are grateful to a wide network of colleagues who generously responded to our research inquiries. Victoria Brown helped us read Jane Addams's handwriting. Independent scholar Ellen Skerrett completed crucial research in Chicago archives. John McGuire of Tompkins-Cortland Community College assisted us in charting the activism of social justice feminists in New York City. Landon Storrs of the University of Houston guided our understanding of Lucy Mason.

We are deeply indebted to colleagues who read and commented on our interpretative introductions. Anonymous readers for the University of Illinois Press provided us with insightful suggestions that guided our revisions. Many colleagues read more than one version of our introductory materials. Special thanks go to Dorothy Sue Cobble, Professor of History at the School of Management and Labor Relations, Rutgers University; Estelle Freedman, Edgar E. Robinson Professor of U.S. History, Stanford University; and Eileen Boris, Hull Professor of Women's Studies, University of California, Santa Barbara. Special thanks to William Forbath, Lloyd M. Bensten Chair in Law at the University of Texas Law School; and Nick Salvatore, Maurice and Hinda Neufeld Founders Professor in Industrial and Labor Relations, Cornell University. For multiple readings of and foundational ideas about the book's introduction, we thank Thomas Dublin and Rifa'at Abou El-Haj of the History Department at SUNY Binghamton.

We thank Joan Catapano, editor in chief and associate director of the University of Illinois Press for her generous support. Her counsel guided us at every stage of the book's development and her belief in the project fortified our own. Assistant Editor Breanne Ertmer ably processed our large collection of photographs. Managing Editor Rebecca Crist and Associate Editor Tad Ringo provided crucial support during the editing process.

We thank Kate Babbitt, independent scholar and editor, whose research skills and editorial expertise have improved every page of this book. During the last five years of our labors, and especially through her rigorous copyediting, she prompted us to chart Florence Kelley's world ever more completely.

Most of all we are grateful to one another. Bridging history and documentary editing, our collaborative efforts required each of us to see our project from the other's perspective. When that wasn't easy, our mutual respect, growing friendship, and belief in the importance of Florence Kelley's letters helped us over obstacles.

We dedicate this book to those who, following in Florence Kelley's footsteps, continue her struggle to end child labor and the exploitation of working people.

INTRODUCTION

Florence Kelley's letters are a national treasure. They carry us deep into the everyday workings of social rights campaigns during the tumultuous decades of U.S. history between 1880 and 1930 that historians call the Progressive Era. Early in that epoch the United States emerged as the world's largest economy. By 1900 an unprecedented flow of immigrants powered the world's largest industrial workforce and dozens of raw cities arose on what had been pasture land. Kelley's letters illuminate the process by which American democracy—as a set of social ideals and political practices—shaped and was shaped by this unruly economic transformation.

Kelley's reform career stretched between two iconic events. The battle of Little Big Horn took place the year she entered college in 1876. At her death in 1932, Franklin Roosevelt was poised to become his party's presidential nominee. During the half-century between those events a modern nation emerged. Florence Kelley was part of the far-flung networks of middle-class reformers, labor leaders, rank-and-file working people, women suffragists, academics, politicians, intellectuals, and businessmen who shaped the emergence of modern America in the decades before the election of Woodrow Wilson in 1912.[1]

These networks created historic transformations in American society. Drawing on the economic, political and social power of diverse groups, they supported a shared ideological commitment to "progress" that ultimately supplanted the political status quo.[2] The new era became visible around 1900. In 1901, President Theodore Roosevelt replaced William McKinley's mode of state capitalism with a new determination to curb the power of the large economic units that commanded much of the nation's wealth. Seth Low's election as mayor of New York City in 1902 symbolized the movement of reformers into offices formerly held by urban machines and bosses. Many state legislatures also underwent the sea change that carried Massachusetts, Wisconsin, and Oregon to the forefront of the Progressive movement.[3]

Three streams of Progressive reform reconfigured American life. One focused on the economics of trust-busting. Another supported good-government goals that promoted citizen participation in electoral primaries, recalls, and referenda and in 1913 provided for the popular election of U.S. senators through the Seventeenth Amendment to the U.S. Constitution.[4]

A third stream—the largest and most turbulent—sought social change. Spilling over into political and economic change, it addressed "the labor question," "the social question," and "the woman question," attracting reformers from overlapping and interacting social movements.[5] Florence Kelley joined other social justice feminists in that stream who built cross-class alliances and drew on the economic strength of women consumers and the political strength of the woman suffrage movement to promote social rights for working people.[6]

Historian Dorothy Sue Cobble defines "social rights" as "the social supports necessary for a life apart from wage work, including the right to care for one's family." She notes that after 1940, labor feminists built on the achievements of Florence Kelley and her generation of reformers.[7] Kelley sought changes in the workplace that would change life outside it: the abolition of child labor to give children in wage-earning families greater access to education, limits on the length of the legal working day to give adult women more hours for their personal and community lives, and a living wage for working women sufficient to support them "in health."[8]

Yet Kelley also sought workplace rights as a form of social rights that maintained human dignity at work. The *Oxford English Dictionary*'s definition of "rights" helps us probe deeper into Kelley's construction of social rights. It defines "rights" as "the standard of permitted and forbidden action within a certain sphere."[9] That definition fits Kelley's work well, since "permitted and forbidden action" invokes moral judgments similar to those she used. For her, rights were infused with ethical concepts that regulated relationships between individuals. Beginning with the conscience and actions of individuals, Kelley extended "permitted and forbidden action" to include social groups. Her notion of rights derived from social justice rather than the ownership of private property; words like "ethical," "moral," and "decent" were central to her reform discourse.[10]

The *OED*'s definition of "rights" as involving "standards" fits Kelley's persistent focus on the exact standards to which employers would be held accountable. Her closest allies sometimes considered her fanatical when she refused to accept legislative wording that would permit lower standards than those she thought employers should be required to maintain. Exact standards were a crucial part of her work precisely because they measured what was "permitted" and "forbidden."

The *OED* definition is also appropriate for Kelley because she always pursued "action within a certain sphere," focusing on particular settings—schooling for children, homework in tenements, hours worked in laundries, wages in poorly paid occupations. These settings permitted specific, achievable goals, the attainment of which could be measured and the necessity for which could be defended in courts. For Kelley, then, "social rights" were legislated standards of permitted and forbidden action for particular groups in particular work-related settings.

Kelley's reforms focused on extending the benefits of industrialization to working people, particularly in the forms of leisure and a higher standard of living. She wanted "toilers" to become "citizens." Her main means of achieving her goals was organizing consumers to promote legislation that regulated the industrial workplace. Like other Progressive Era reformers, she combined social science evidence and moral arguments. Her training as a social scientist and an attorney was central to her reform career but so too was her Protestant ethnicity; for her, "rights" and "righteous" were closely related.[11]

Kelley and her allies were severely disadvantaged by the absence of any explicit provision for social rights in the United States Constitution. This absence meant that courts usually interpreted the Constitution as protecting individual rights—through the first ten Amendments, or "the Bill of Rights," and the Fourteenth Amendment, which prohibits state laws from depriving persons of "life, liberty or property, without due process."

The power of the Supreme Court to overturn laws passed by Congress or state legislatures further handicapped advocates of social rights.[12] No written constitution constrained the enactment of social rights in Great Britain or Germany, the two political cultures that Kelley and her allies consulted for examples of social rights policies—such as laws to protect the public's health, limitations on the length of the working day, legislation to guarantee workplace safety, and laws to provide old age pensions and set a minimum wage. Parliament's law was supreme in England, unrestricted by common law or courts. In the United States, social rights moved forward only when championed by social movements that brought together constituencies capable of defending those rights in the courts. Kelley and her American allies were part of an international movement that established social rights throughout the industrializing nations of Europe and North America, but their strategies were shaped by American circumstances.[13]

The power of the judiciary in American political institutions permitted opponents of social rights to use courts to defend employers' property rights. Kelley and her allies not only had to overcome constitutional interpretations biased against social rights, they also had to struggle against well-funded employers' organizations that opposed workplace regulation as un-American and unnecessary. Public opinion was crucial in this never-ending battle. Between 1890 and 1920 Kelley helped create a positive public view of workplace regulation, and after 1920 she struggled against those who sought to turn the tide of public opinion away from Progressive reform.[14]

The chronology of Kelley's career paralleled that of social justice reform in the Progressive Era, emerging in the 1890s and cresting before World War I. She first exercised power in Chicago in the 1890s, when, as chief factory inspector of Illinois, she implemented path-breaking labor legislation that she herself drafted and successfully lobbied to enact. After 1899, in New York City as general secretary of the National Consumers' League (NCL), she forged her own alliance of dozens of local consumer leagues that brought together middle-class and wage-earning women and men on a platform that championed both the rights of consumers and the rights of producers.

By 1915 she and the NCL had successfully campaigned for the passage of child labor laws in most states and a federal law that prohibited child labor nationally. By 1917 they had obtained the enactment of minimum wage laws for women in eleven states and effectively defended wage legislation in its first review by the Supreme Court. In the 1920s she helped establish state and federal responsibility for maternal and infant health and ferociously defended her achievements against right-wing critics who supported Warren Harding's call for "normalcy."[15] After her death in 1932 the younger generation in her network moved into positions of federal power with the election of Franklin Roosevelt. In 1933 FDR appointed her protégé, Frances Perkins, as secretary of labor, the first woman presidential cabinet member. Perkins forged a solid link between Kelley's agenda in the Progressive Era and the legislative program of the New Deal.[16]

Kelley entered public life at a moment when the shift from a rural to an industrial economy had already created a higher standard of living for middle-class families but unskilled immigrants still worked long hours for low pay and gained little from the wealth that they helped create. Like other Progressive Era reformers, she envisioned a revitalized nation-state in which the industrial workplace was more humane. Her unique contribution was to join the power of middle-class consumers with working-class groups to promote workplace rights through legislation. As head of the National Consumers' League, she generated rights discourses that made the league a major force in American political culture. Her voice was decisive on three kinds of rights for working people—the child's right to an education, the adult wage-earner's right to leisure, and the adult worker's right to wages adequate "to supply the necessary cost of living and to maintain the workers in health."[17] Eventually incorporated in the Fair Labor Standards Act of 1938, these social rights were foundational to the "American standard of living" and post-1940 consumer society.[18]

Kelley's goals were not easily secured. In a political culture that valued individualism, she championed social rights and collective responsibility. In a constitutional polity that gave courts the power to nullify state and federal legislation, she shaped legal arguments that validated social legislation. In a society with a growing gap between rich and poor, she promoted strategies that redistributed wealth. At a time when production and consumption were growing ever more distinct, she showed how they were connected. In an economy that rarely regulated capital, she convinced businessmen of the value of humane standards in the workplace.

To realize her goals Kelley often sought gendered labor legislation. Necessitated by the bias of American courts against social legislation and the fiction that men should be "free" to contract their labor on any terms, her strategy argued that the state's interests were served by laws that protected women against exploitation in the workplace. She sought labor legislation for women as an end in itself but also as an entering wedge to establish protections for men and women. This gendered strategy was a well-established trade-union expedient that had first succeeded with textile workers in Massachusetts in 1873, when state law limited women's working day to ten hours. This indirectly limited men's hours because men left the factories when women did.[19]

Kelley greatly expanded this gendered "wedge" strategy. After she and the NCL succeeded in obtaining the U.S. Supreme Court approval for state ten-hour-day laws for women in 1908 in *Muller v. Oregon,* they achieved a similar court victory in 1917 for state maximum-hours laws for men in *Bunting v. Oregon.* Her success in promoting state minimum wage laws for women led to the inclusion of a federal minimum wage law for men and women in the Fair Labor Standards Act of 1938. Her strategies used gender-based arguments and politics to achieve results that in Britain and elsewhere were accomplished by class-based arguments and politics.[20] Using gender as a surrogate for class, she became one of the most powerful agents of change in modernizing America.

Historians have included Kelley's gender-based labor legislation in the pantheon of "maternalist" reforms that dominated women's activism in the Progressive Era, defining "maternalist" as "ideologies that exalted women's capacity to mother and extended to society as a whole the values of care, nurturance, and morality."[21] In a cascade of scholarship on social welfare policies in the United States, such as mothers' pensions and juvenile courts, historians have found that social provisions for mothers and children often fell short of achieving social rights.[22] Until recently, historians who have written about labor legislation for women adopted this maternalist framework, emphasizing that legislation's gendered strategies and slighting the workplace rights it achieved.[23]

Yet Kelley was more than a maternalist. Maternalism was but one of her many discourses. In an 1897 article written for a German periodical, she critiqued both the limitations of and the need for gendered claims about the rights of American working people.

> It is much easier to find approval by appealing to the sympathy of the masses for the welfare of helpless working women and children than to find it by suggesting absolutely necessary measures to protect the lives, bodies and health of men, who are the fathers, husbands, and breadwinners of the same women and children. It is not easy to gain the sympathy of the whole population for these male workers, because it is assumed that they can protect themselves and that they can achieve what they need by virtue of their right to vote, without appealing to the support of public opinion.[24]

Thus, for Kelley, maternalism was a strategy to obtain social rights for all workers. Although many middle-class women may have supported her agenda out of a maternalist concern for the welfare of women and children rather than an interest in the welfare of working people generally, for Kelley the result was the same—she deployed gendered arguments and strategies to establish social rights that in other political cultures were advanced by more robust labor movements and class-based strategies.[25]

The best lens for viewing Florence Kelley's social rights agenda is her 1905 book *Some Ethical Gains through Legislation.* Written to explain social rights to her middle-class constituency, her book argued that everyone was a consumer, that consumers were linked to producers in a web of social rights, and that these rights could be sustained only through legislation. "In any given community every person is directly or indirectly a purchaser," she wrote. "[W]orkers exist to supply the demand that is incarnate in their friends and fellow citizens, acting as the purchasing public. All of us, all the time, are deciding what industries shall survive, and under what conditions." Purchasers were connected to workers ethically as well as economically. "The most obvious right of the purchaser," she said, is "to have his goods as they are represented, and to have food pure," but "most important, to be free from participating indirectly, through the purchase of his goods, in the employment of children and of the victims of the sweating system."[26]

This ethical connection occurred within a system of social rights. As she put it,

> The more closely the rights of purchasers are scrutinized, the more clearly it appears that they are social rights. However much they may present themselves to the mind as individual personal rights, the effort to assert them invariably brings the experience that they are inextricably interwoven with the rights of innumerable other people. In the last analysis, they cannot be asserted without the previous assertion of the claim of the weakest and most defenseless persons in the community.[27]

Kelley challenged the Social Darwinist claim that the future belonged to the strong. She explained that the "sacrifice of the weak and the defenseless to the search for cheapness" was an ethical distortion created by competition among employers in an unregulated marketplace. For her the future belonged to the community that cared for all its members.[28]

The pressure of competition in the marketplace meant that "the highest ethical level possible to our social life can be reached only through legislation." Social rights and the community's ethical values could only be realized "by comprehensive statutes sustained by decisions of the highest courts, and enforced by endless effort of the purchasers and the wage-earners defending their interests together." In this way, she noted, human rights became legal rights: "The right to leisure is a human right in process of recognition as a statutory right."[29]

Kelley's book also described how she relied on middle-class women's activism to transform abstract human rights into concrete statutory rights. Middle-class women were ethically obliged to assist working women, she argued.

> Since the leisure of prosperous women is due largely to the labor of young wage-workers (who are engaged chiefly in the food and garment trades, the textile industries and that retail commerce which lives by the patronage of home-keeping women), it behooves the fortunate to assume their full share of the duty of making and enforcing laws for the protection of these young wage-workers.[30]

She also argued that middle-class women buttressed their own claims to full citizenship when they campaigned for wage-earners and that to do that work they needed to "perform all the duties of citizenship, voting and serving on public boards and commissions when elected or appointed to them." Finally, she wrote, women's perspective was needed in public life because they were different from middle-class men: "It is because women are less under the stress of competitive business, because they do, in fact, represent children and youth, that their vote is needed."[31]

Kelley's book repeatedly insisted that statutory social rights were necessary for the creation of "enlightened self-governing citizens": "An unfailing test of the ethical standards of a community is the question, 'What kind of citizens are being trained here?'"[32] Similarly, she argued that "assured daily leisure" was essential to adult citizenship: "Excessive fatigue precludes the possibility of well-conducted meetings of classes, lodges, cooperative societies and all other forms of organized effort for self-improvement." Without regular leisure "there can be no sustained intelligence in the voting constituency."[33] Thus, social rights shaped life inside and outside the workplace.

Kelley's letters highlight the multiple strategies she used to create new social rights. They take us into the interstices of her struggles, accenting her sophisticated understanding of American politics, her belief in the positive power of government, and her fierce commitment to social justice. Outlining alternatives, tracking opportunities, and marking dangers, her letters vividly recreate her radical perspective on these decades of profound transition in American life. Her scathing humor and scholarly attention to detail show us that modern America was built by human emotions and probing intelligence as well as by machines and markets.

Kelley's impact was immediate and enduring. Felix Frankfurter, who worked closely with her from 1916 to 1930 before becoming a U.S. Supreme Court justice in 1939, said that she "had probably the largest single share in shaping the social history of the United States during the first thirty years of this century." He thought her legacy was twofold. First, "hers was no doubt a powerful if not decisive role in securing legislation for the removal of the most glaring abuses of our hectic industrialization following the Civil War." In addition, he said, "we owe her an even deeper and more enduring debt for the continuing process she so largely helped to initiate, by which social legislation is promoted and eventually gets on the statute books."[34] For Frankfurter and other Progressive Era reformers, Kelley not only created social rights, she created an enduring path for rights-seeking activity.[35]

Kelley's understanding of the process of social reform—and the process of creating social rights—had four stages, the first of which was to investigate and create social data. The second was to educate with that data. Then legislate, then enforce. Thus for her the process of rights-seeking activity involved social data, popular support, political will, and governmental power. It was and is a challenging quartet to master. Through her letters we can learn about that process as well as its various outcomes.

Florence Kelley's letters offer a vital and fascinating window on her work, but important dimensions of her career occurred elsewhere. For example, her prodigious flow of writings, which established her as one of the leading public voices of her time, is largely invisible in this volume. From 1899 through 1931 she authored over 300 articles. Her literary output at its peak between 1903 and 1916 maintained an astonishing rate of more than one major article a month. These included scholarly social science interpretations of data in *Annals of the American Academy of Political and Social Science,* cogent definitions of legislative strategies in the reform-oriented *Survey,* and descriptions of her agenda in union publications such as *Machinists' Monthly Journal,* political journals such as the *New Republic,* and women's magazines such as *Women's Home Companion.*[36] Kelley's letters occasionally refer to her publications, but they do not fully convey the priority she gave them.

The rich and voluminous minutes of NCL board and council meetings constitute another important absence. Discussions, disagreements, and digressions in those meetings provide historians with front-row seats in the theater of progressive reform. They appear here occasionally in annotations that clarify references in Kelley's letters, but their story remains to be told.

The peripatetic movement of the NCL offices is a story in itself. The league's stationery shows that it nestled with other reform groups in the United Charities Building at 105 East 22nd Street from 1900 to 1912. That stately structure with a side entrance on Park Avenue brought Kelley and her staff into constant interaction with the growing number of reform groups that were headquartered in New York City. In 1912 the league moved three blocks away, closer to Union Square, the site of the first Labor Day parade in 1882. Their offices migrated for a few months in 1915 to the Craftsman Building on East 39th Street, a site offering public lectures, a library, and club rooms, not far from the lavish department stores of Fifth Avenue. Then, for a four-year stretch until 1919 the NCL conducted business at 289 Fourth Avenue, alongside the offices of the Congregational Church. In the postwar years between 1919 and 1923, Kelley and her staff worked at 44 E. 23rd Street, close to Madison Square. During her final years, the league resided at 156 Fifth Avenue, very close to and in a building that closely resembled its original location in the Charities Building.

Yet while Kelley's letters do not depict all aspects of her world, they connect us with its immediacy and complexity as she lived it—moment by moment.

More akin to a hand-held video camera than a film with high production values, they take us to unexpected places as well as familiar venues, zoom in on some relationships and frame others more distantly. They capture her complaints when the NCL was low on money and she received no paycheck. They express the vitality of her relationships with friends and family. And above all they convey the energy of someone who strongly believed that her work was creating a more humane and just society.

Selections of Kelley's letters are arranged here in eight chapters that depict her personal engagement in that struggle. Each chapter also contains a brief introduction. The letters are supplemented by annotations, chronologies in the front of the volume, and a biographical directory in the back. Kelley's surviving letters chronicle her youth, early career, and mid-career, but the best-documented era of her life is her mature struggle to defend and extend her achievements in the 1920s.[37] Our chronological distribution of letters across the book's chapters reflects their relative scarcity in the years before 1916 and their relative abundance thereafter. The first four chapters contain letters dating from 1869 through 1916, taking her from age ten to age fifty-seven. Letters in the last four chapters date from 1917 to 1931, portraying her from age fifty-eight to age seventy-two.

Chapter 1, "The Wrong to the Working People," covering the years 1869–1891, embraces Kelley's girlhood and youth and the beginning of her reform career. It chronicles her close relationship with her politically powerful father, William Darrah Kelley. It also offers glimpses of her bonds with her family on her mother's side, which proudly continued Unitarian and Quaker dissenting traditions. She was a serious student at Cornell and went to Europe for postgraduate study. There she broke with her family, translated a classic work by Frederick Engels, and returned to the United States in 1886 as one of the most knowledgeable English-speaking students of German socialist writings about industrial capitalism. In Europe she married a Russian Jew and then gave birth to three children in three years. In New York City in the late 1880s she assiduously sought a place in the Socialist Labor Party, but despite (and partly because of) her friendship with Frederick Engels, that door remained shut.

Kelley's receptivity to German socialism in the 1880s was rooted in her childhood encounters with the working poor. "Florrie's" father taught her to read from a book that depicted the brutality of contemporary child labor in British brickyards. As a schoolgirl she passed "little skinny girls waiting on the sidewalk" by a Philadelphia textile mill. Her great-aunt, Sarah Pugh, who served for almost forty years as president of the Philadelphia Female Antislavery Society, was a close friend of Lucretia Mott. Pugh corresponded in the 1860s with British reformers Richard Cobden and John Bright about their campaign to repeal corn laws that allowed elites to profit from taxes on poor people's food. Sarah Pugh boycotted products derived from slave labor, especially sugar and cotton, modeling in the "free produce" movement an antecedent of the consumers' leagues of the Progressive Era.[38]

When Kelley joined the German socialist party in Zurich in the mid-1880s, she self-consciously drew on her great-aunt's free-thinking example; her connection with European socialism made her more, not less, independent in her reform strategies. As a woman, she was relatively unmentored in her post-graduate studies at Zurich and perhaps for that reason affiliated more strongly with German socialism than did other Americans who studied in Germany, including Richard Ely and W. E. B. Du Bois.[39] Moreover, as a woman, she was excluded from academic employment and therefore not forced to recant her socialist convictions as Richard Ely did in the 1890s. Kelley's gender identity—as well as her Yankee ethnicity, forceful personality, and independent ideas—contributed in 1887 to her suspension from the Socialist Labor Party in New York (whose membership was almost entirely German-speaking), and thereafter she remained skeptical of organized socialism in the United States. Four years later, she ended her troubled marriage and fled with her children to Chicago.[40]

Chapter 2, "This Beloved Hull House," covering 1892–1899, depicts the remarkable opportunities that opened up for Kelley at the nation's leading social settlement, where she lived collectively with other women reformers. A circle of talented peers, Jane Addams preeminent among them, supplanted her long-distance alliance with Frederick Engels. She worked for the Illinois Bureau of Labor Statistics and the U.S. Department of Labor Statistics. In 1893 she became one of the most powerful women public officials in the western world when she became chief factory inspector of Illinois, responsible for enforcing path-breaking labor legislation that she had drafted and successfully lobbied to enact. That legislation launched her historic strategy of lobbying for the passage of laws that regulated women's working conditions as a opening wedge for regulating working conditions for women and men.

Abraham Bisno, a union organizer in the Chicago garment industry in the 1890s, witnessed the blossoming of her robust leadership in the mid-1890s in Chicago. He recalled the gusto with which Kelley applied to Chicago's sweatshops the knowledge she had gained as a student of German socialism. "The world of the rebel and the student was her world completely," Bisno later wrote. "Her criticism of the present order was sharp, bitter, vigorous, with a finely developed sense of humor always present, as well as enormous erudition." She worked independently of the socialist movement in Chicago; Bisno described her as an "English" socialist. "She believed in the development of the labor movement along the lines of what she called English socialism, namely, the realization of socialism step by step, that as industry developed, the labor movement would develop, and through that force, laws would be enacted in the interests of labor." Bisno valued her friendship as well as her ideas, remembering that "[s]he talked with me as though I were her equal. The fact that she was a Yankee and I a Jew seemed to make no difference to her."[41]

Kelley's self-identification as a socialist was a political extension of her commitment to social science and social data as a basis for social change. Remembered by scholars as an economist, she pursued social data as though it held the keys to a social justice kingdom.[42] Her path-breaking maps of income and ethnicity in her 1890s Chicago neighborhood mark a high point in the history of American social science during her lifetime, and her ongoing critique of social data collected (or not collected) by government agencies made her an effective watchdog for the interests of social reform.[43]

Kelley's letters for this period reveal the patchwork efforts by which she and her allies wove a new social fabric, with all its gaps and limitations. No inexorable forces drove this process. Rather, a new consensus gradually emerged from dissenting campaigns that embraced union halls, church sanctuaries, civic clubs, college classrooms, state legislatures, and courts. And despite her formidable aptitude, there was nothing inevitable about Kelley's accomplishments. Although her expertise expanded when she completed a law degree at Northwestern University in 1895, a new governor dismissed her in 1897 and her public power evaporated. She fell back upon the network of women and women's organizations connected with Hull House, especially the Illinois Consumers' League, which led to her appointment as general secretary of the National Consumers' League in 1899.

Chapter 3, "The Power and Responsibility of the Purchasers," covers the years 1900–1907 and follows Kelley in her new life as the leader of the National Consumers' League in New York City. Initially she lived with her children in a midtown annex of Lillian Wald's Henry Street Nurses Settlement, but she soon moved into the settlement's main building on the Lower East Side. During her first years as secretary of the NCL, she assiduously cultivated local consumers' leagues. She also developed a national agenda of labor legislation to protect child and women wage earners. Particularly effective was the consumers' White Label, which educated league members and their communities about local working conditions. The league was also part of the coalition that obtained the passage of the Pure Food and Drug Act in 1906.[44] To promote these activities, she spent half her time traveling. Kelley's encouragement of local leagues endeared her to their members. One league reported on the effects of her leadership in 1903:

> [She] can travel from one end of the Continent to the other without losing her hold upon local problems in State Leagues the farthest removed from her bodily presence, stirring our zeal and opening new fields for our activity by letters, which are prompt and full as if letter writing were the chief occupation of her day. Mrs. Kelley gives us service which it is impossible to overestimate.[45]

Much of Kelley's power flowed from the growing potency of women as a force in American civil society after 1870. The suffrage movement and its many related expressions of political activism informed her agenda and sustained her success. She drew on the support of hundreds of women reformers, both middle class and working class, especially those affiliated with the social settlement and trade union movements.

Yet while Kelley depended on gendered constituencies within American political culture, her protean energy was never contained within any one group, even those that she created. The pan-Progressive ties she forged across gender, class, and ethnic differences were crucial to her achievements. The NCL included men as well as women members, as did the National Child Labor Committee and the New York Child Labor Committee, both of which she helped found, in 1902 and 1904, respectively. She was present at the first meeting of the American Association for Labor Legislation after it moved to New York City in 1906. She worked closely with male reformers such as John Graham Brooks and Democratic Party leaders such as Newton Baker, both of whom served as NCL presidents, a position that, during her lifetime, was held only by men. She recruited the support of leading academics such as John Commons, who also served as an NCL president. In 1910, the NCL letterhead listed as honorary vice-presidents prominent economists and sociologists Arthur Hadley of Yale University, Frank Taussig of Harvard University, E. R. A. Seligman of Columbia University, J. W. Jenks of Cornell University, H. C. Adams of the University of Michigan, C. R. Henderson of the University of Chicago, S. M. Lindsay of Columbia University, and Richard T. Ely of the University of Wisconsin.[46]

Chapter 4, "The Fight to Extend the Labor Law," traces Kelley's campaigns in legislatures and courts for state hour and wage statutes during the period 1908–1916. That fight engaged the full range of her talents and expanded her networks. The favorable U.S. Supreme Court decision in *Muller v. Oregon* (1908), which upheld state laws regulating women's working hours, deepened Kelley's commitment to labor legislation for women as an opening wedge for general workplace protections. Her assistant, Josephine Goldmark, wrote the "Brandeis brief" that defended the Oregon law with social data rather than abstract legal arguments, creating a precedent that did much to shape American judicial history in the twentieth century. With the legality of women's state hours laws established, Kelley and the NCL initiated a successful campaign for the passage of state minimum wage laws for women, which in 1938 became the basis for the federal minimum wage law for men and women.

Drawing on her family's deep roots in the pre–Civil War anti-slavery movement, Kelley also crossed race lines. She was present at the founding of the National Association for the Advancement of Colored People in New York City in 1909 and served for twenty years on its executive board, often acting as an important intermediary between W. E. B. Du Bois—the association's chief founder and editor of its periodical *The Crisis*—and his critics in the organization.[47] A visit in April 1908 to Atlanta University, where Du Bois was professor of history and sociology, brought her into his world.[48] She had written him earlier to express admiration for his 1903 book, *Souls of Black Folk,* which passionately challenged Booker T. Washington's policy of advancing the economic status of African Americans without advancing their civil rights.[49]

During this period, Kelley spent more time in Washington, D.C., joining allies there who were building the capacity of the federal government to serve the needs of average people, especially through the U.S. Children's Bureau, which was created in 1912.[50] The bureau lent vital institutional support to Kelley's campaigns against child labor, resulting in the first federal child labor act in 1916. The NCL became a watchdog that promoted the enforcement of the Pure Food and Drug Act.[51] During this last decade before World War I, Kelley made two trips to Europe, in 1908 to attend the International Congress of Women and the first International Conference of Consumers' Leagues and in 1913 to attend the International Association for Labor Legislation and the International Conference of Consumers' Leagues.

Chapter 5, "The Work of the Nation," views Kelley's letters during and immediately after World War I. These years began with the league's success in obtaining positive Supreme Court rulings on state laws that regulated men's hours and an initial favorable ruling on minimum wage laws for women. But increasingly Kelley and the NCL became central players in an emerging struggle between Congress and the Supreme Court over Congress's right to enact social legislation. A series of court rulings beginning in 1918 overturned federal child labor legislation, sparking new strategies for Kelley in the decades ahead.

During the war Kelley sought to enforce labor standards in federal contracts for army clothing and exposed violations of the Pure Food and Drug Act by the meatpacking industry. After the war she traveled with Jane Addams to the Women's International Congress for Permanent Peace in Zurich in 1919 and in 1921 to the first meeting of the Women's International League for Peace and Freedom in Vienna. For the twentieth anniversary of the founding of the NCL she launched a new initiative on occupational toxins, especially radium. In 1920 she began to concentrate on what became the centerpiece of her reform career, the Sheppard-Towner Act, passed by Congress in November 1921. Administered by the Children's Bureau, the act allocated federal funds for clinics and conferences to improve maternal and infant health.

Chapter 6, "Necessary Protection for Women," surveys Kelley's burgeoning agenda when great success mixed with crushing setbacks in the years 1922–1924. Anticipating in 1920 the adoption of the Nineteenth Amendment and its guarantee of women's right to vote throughout the United States, Kelley helped create the League of Women Voters and the Women's Joint Congressional Committee. The latter served as an expanded base of support for her agenda in Washington, particularly for continued funding of the Sheppard-Towner Act. But that power base was challenged by right-wing attacks on the WJCC, the women's peace movement, and Kelley herself. With popular support for Progressive reform diminishing, the Supreme Court ruled unconstitutional a second federal child labor law, necessitating (in Kelley's view) a child labor amendment to the constitution.

Most devastating was the decision by Alice Paul and the National Woman's Party to oppose Kelley's agenda of labor legislation for women. Representing professional women who did not benefit from such laws, the NWP proposed an equal rights amendment to the U.S. Constitution that called for women and men to be legally treated the same. Kelley fought the amendment and proposed legislation that remedied discrimination on an issue-by-issue basis and took account of women's and men's different circumstances. She lost the first round of this struggle over differing views of women's rights in the 1923 Supreme Court decision in *Adkins v. Children's Hospital,* which ruled unconstitutional the minimum wage law of the District of Columbia, which the NCL had drafted.

Chapter 7, "No Good Decision Seems Secure from Reversal," considers Kelley's letters during the crisis of the period 1925–1927, when right-wing attacks crested and the power of her allies waned. She remained creative, collecting data about children's injuries that she found in state workmen's compensation records, promoting a petition campaign for the child labor amendment, and seeking support for state minimum wage laws that continued to function despite the *Adkins* decision. To counter attacks on her patriotism, she wrote a series of autobiographical articles for *Survey,* the era's leading reform periodical, where she was an associate editor. She vigorously campaigned against the NWP and increasingly saw its members as aligned with her chief enemy, the National Association of Manufacturers.

Chapter 8, "How to Keep the Interest of the Careless Public Alive," gathers Kelley's letters from her last years of public life. Her remarkable vitality and optimism pushed the NCL agenda forward in the South, where in future decades the league provided valuable support for union organizing efforts. She revived the NCL's white list strategy as a means of establishing minimum wages, beginning with the candy industry. She moved the NCL further into the new territory of occupational disease. On the NAACP board she initiated a standing committee against discrimination in education. She refused to accept the end of Sheppard-Towner funding and continued to mobilize support for its extension. And in women's organizations where the NWP was making headway, she campaigned for her perspective on women's rights. One of Kelley's last letters in this volume, written to Lucy Mason, who later replaced her as NCL general secretary, deftly criticized Mason's draft of a pamphlet on *Standards for Workers in Southern Industry,* advising Mason to maintain her own voice and not become dull like authors at the Women's Bureau or garbled like those at the National Child Labor Committee.[52] Never dull or garbled, Kelley's letters illuminate American politics from a vanguard that she created and defended for forty years.

Representing her talents as an organizer, politician, and social scientist, Kelley's letters also depict her utopian rebellion against the status quo. Intellectually, politically, and personally, she refused to accept the world as it was. Her rebellion dug a deep channel forward that often led the way toward significant reform but sometimes left her isolated. Her letters navigate the tension between her practical understanding of the possible and her visionary reach for justice. That tension was profoundly creative but it also created a ceaseless urgency in her life and work that left her chronically unsatisfied.

Yet she never gave up her vision. As a student in Zurich, she had adopted the intellectual tools of "scientific-materialistic criticism," which gave her a lifelong framework for critiquing the effects of industrialization. This standpoint assumed that unskilled workers were paid only part of the value that they produced, the rest being pocketed by owners and investors. More important, that ethical framework valued people as ends in themselves, not the means used by others in the marketplace.[53] Kelley's socialism reinvigorated the social justice values that she inherited from her family, informed the social science methods that pervaded her work and writings, empowered her political vision, and emboldened her personal style.

Yet she worked in a context in which socialism did not build a labor party. Bitter sectarian struggle within and between socialist groups marginalized their political effectiveness. The power of German socialism within socialist groups in American cities recreated there even more intensely the German conflict between advocates of trade-union organizing and proponents of political parties. That conflict led to Kelley's suspension from the Socialist Labor Party in New York in 1887. Rather than a coalition that combined trade union and political party strategies, socialist groups had formed by 1895 what one scholar has called "a mutually reinforcing culture of factional conflict."[54]

The absence of a labor party in the American political economy shaped debates over working women's social rights during Kelley's lifetime and thereafter. If a labor party had developed in the United States between 1880 and 1910, as it did in other industrializing democracies, the debate over wage-earners' social rights would almost certainly have been absorbed into that party's agenda and would not have been conducted so fiercely and independently by women's political culture. Women like Kelley would have exercised less control over the debate, but they might have worked in coalitions that gained more ground for social rights generally.[55]

Why did a labor party not emerge in the United States? This question has long engaged the interest of historians, whose writings on the topic have identified the absence of a labor party as one of the salient characteristics of American politics during Kelley's lifetime. That absence made it much more difficult for Kelley to overcome the constitutional bias in favor of individual and against social rights. Yet it created windows of opportunity that she exploited throughout her career, enabling her leadership in the National Consumers' League to accomplish many of the social rights that in Britain were achieved by labor activists and reformers associated with the Independent Labour Party (founded 1893) and the Labour Party (founded 1906).[56]

Historians' interpretations of the factors that account for the absence of a labor party in the United States help us understand the context of Kelley's achievements as well as the limitations she encountered. Earlier interpretations argued that the combination of high wages, social mobility, and a multiplicity of cultural backgrounds discouraged working-class men from mobilizing to assert their class interests in American politics.[57] More recently, historians have emphasized the ability of the two-party system to absorb working-class activism, particularly since that system was in place before industrialization gave rise to an urban proletariat. Working-class men were drawn into both parties, neither of which made their interests a top priority.[58] Scholars have also argued that the power of the courts to overturn labor legislation discouraged unions from pursuing political channels to achieve their goals.[59]

The darker side of this history has recently been explored by William Forbath and others, who have shown how state and federal officials, closely allied with employers, systematically used court injunctions—enforced by police, state militias, and federal troops—to repress industrial unions.[60] In other countries industrial unionism, or the "new unionism" that united skilled and unskilled workers, became the basis for labor parties because it could generate more popular support than craft unions.[61] When industrial unions were crushed in the United States, particularly in the railroad and steel industries, a divide emerged between the social rights of skilled workers and unskilled laborers that was not overcome until after the 1935 Wagner Act, which offered much-needed protection of the rights of industrial unions and fostered the rise of the Congress of Industrial Organizations.[62] During Kelley's heyday, between 1890 and 1930, court injunctions in the United States generated more violence and less arbitration than was the case in Britain or Europe and created an environment that deprived Eugene Debs and other industrial labor leaders of the popular base that might have evolved into a labor party.

The potency of religion in American politics also eroded that popular base. Robin Archer has argued that Protestant and Catholic religious identities fortified workingmen's loyalties—Protestants to the Republican Party and Catholics to the Democratic Party—causing labor leaders to fear the destructive effect on unions of political agendas that challenged those loyalties. Reflecting the Irish ethnicity of most of its members, the Knights of Labor was predominately Catholic, as were many craft union members of the American Federation of Labor. As AFL skilled unions became stronger in the 1890s and replaced the Knights of Labor's more inclusive form of unionism, rank-and-file AFL Catholics found a comfortable home in the Democratic Party. But native-born rank-and-file union members allied with the Republican Party, which favored their Protestant culture. As a Jewish immigrant from Britain and head of the AFL, Samuel Gompers chose not to challenge these ethno-cultural political differences, which, while not important among union leaders, had powerful divisive potential among ordinary wage earners.[63]

As these factors were narrowing possibilities for the emergence of a labor party in the United States, they were also fundamentally shaping Florence Kelley's career options. Her suspension from the sectarian-ridden Socialist Labor Party in 1887 propelled her formidable energies into the mainstream of women's political culture. There her emphatic invocation of Protestant discourse about "righteousness" hastened her rise to power and sustained her continued prominence, as did her close alliance with Jews and Catholics. Her work with the NCL's middle-class constituency directly counteracted anti-labor ideology. That work began soon after she witnessed the violent repression in Chicago of the 1893 strike of American railway workers; she raised bail money for her imprisoned friend Eugene Debs, a Jeffersonian democrat whom the government labeled a dangerous radical.[64]

Although she understood the weakness of organized socialism, the importance of religious differences in working-class culture, and the power of government repression, Florence Kelley did not forgive the AFL and other groups of male allies for their timid unwillingness to support social rights legislation for working people. "[T]he unfortunate policy of Mr. Gompers and his colleagues through nearly half a century in relation to women, non-English speaking immigrants, and Negroes," she declared in 1925, "injured" all those groups.[65] In the same year that her star was rising with the 1908 Supreme Court decision in *Muller,* the AFL joined forces with the Democratic Party, where, as one voice among many, they were never able to dominate the party's agenda. The "Rights of Labor" plank of the 1908 Democratic Party platform (which was duplicated in 1912) was anchored in the individual rights of wage earners to work under terms they agreed to. Rather than calling for legislated rights, it upheld "the right of wage earners and producers to organize for the protection of wages and the improvement of labor conditions" and endorsed only the mildest limitations on court injunctions.[66]

The closest the AFL came to advocating statutory social rights in these years was its endorsement of legislation that gave federal workers an eight-hour day, which the 1908–1912 Democratic Party platform ignored. The AFL vehemently opposed the passage of the Adamson Act in 1916, which established an eight-hour day for railroad workers and was passed to avoid a national strike by a coalition of unions that included skilled and unskilled workers.[67] Finding itself aligned with anti-labor opinion in the Adamson case, the national AFL became more flexible thereafter, but it had long since ceded the leadership of social rights campaigns to reformers, women trade unionists, and independent unions.[68]

One of Kelley's most effective adaptations to the absence of a labor party was her use of the emerging power of consumers as a tool to promote her vision of the rights of working people. Through the NCL she educated middle-class consumers, who had been evolving as the vanguard of consumer society for nearly a century, about their obligations to the producers of the goods and services they purchased.[69] In her writings, Kelley argued that because neither employers nor the state had responded to workers' needs, the moral mandate for promoting change fell on their shoulders.

Kelley also understood the potential of wage earners as a purchasing group. She reminded employers that social rights for working people, including the right to a living wage, would create more consumers to purchase their goods. Historians are only beginning to study the inclusion of working people in the evolution of consumer society between 1890 and 1930.[70] Kelley's letters help us understand that process, especially the struggle to extend to unskilled workers the two basic components of their entry into consumer society: leisure time and adequate wages.

Kelley and her NCL colleagues energetically sought minimum wage legislation for theoretical and practical reasons. From a theoretical perspective, wages measured the value of labor and therefore constituted a crucial feature of every market economy. In practical terms, wages defined whether working people could support themselves decently or had to supplement their wages with public relief or private charity. Socialist and laissez-faire economists had long debated what factors were most important in determining wages, but not until the British anti-sweatshop campaigns of the 1890s did a theoretical framework and a practical solution unite to prevent employers from paying less than what their employees needed to live on. The theory of "parasitic trades," as explained by Beatrice and Sidney Webb in 1902, held that employers who paid wages "insufficient to provide enough food, clothing, and shelter to maintain [workers] in health" obtained "a supply of labor-force which it does not pay for."[71] Because their workers had to supplement their wages with relief or charity, such employers were parasites on others and competed unfairly with employers who were not parasitic. The practical solution for parasitic employers was state regulation of wages in poorly paid occupations. In New Zealand in 1896 and Britain in 1909, national wage boards began to set wages in those occupations, some but not all of which were dominated by women.[72]

Although the theoretical explanation of parasitic employers fit the United States as well as Great Britain, the practical solution of wage regulation was much more difficult to achieve. In 1909, Florence Kelley and the NCL led the way by launching a campaign for state minimum wage legislation for women.[73] Deterred by previous court decisions from focusing on all workers in poorly paid occupations, the NCL continued the American pattern of enacting legislation for women as an entering wedge for protections for all poorly paid women and men.[74] Although leaders in the American Association for Labor Legislation initially shunned the campaign because they thought that wage regulation would never pass court scrutiny in the United States, they halfheartedly endorsed wage laws in 1915, by which time laws were already in place in eleven states.[75] Working with local coalitions of women's organizations, labor unions, and reform groups, the NCL had successfully promoted the passage of minimum wage laws for women in sixteen states by 1923.[76]

After their first victory in Massachusetts, Kelley's colleagues celebrated the theoretical dimensions of their achievement, saying that wage laws "pierce[d] to the heart the classic claim that industry is a purely private affair."[77] Kelley and her allies applied the theoretical framework of "parasitic trades" to urban wage-earning women, the great majority of whom were twenty-five years of age or younger and unmarried. Most lived at home; worked in unskilled or semiskilled, sex-segregated jobs; and did not earn enough to support themselves.[78] Early in the campaign Kelley explained, "The well-nigh universal requirement that girl employes shall live at home betokens the parasite nature of the industry which intends to extract from their families a share of the support of the girls."[79] Kelley's campaign acknowledged young women as permanent feature of the paid labor force and sought to provide them with wages sufficient to live independently of their families.

Although the U.S. Supreme Court declared the District of Columbia minimum wage law for women unconstitutional in 1923, some state laws remained intact. The success of minimum wage laws for women became a crucial basis for the minimum wage provision for men and women in the Fair Labor Standards Act of 1938.[80] A decade later, the United States was well on its way to becoming a consumer society that included working people—one in which "citizenship" was increasingly defined as access to an "American standard of living."[81] Social justice perspectives continue to inform campaigns against sweatshops globally. The National Consumers' League remains a leader in those campaigns in the United States, struggling with a complex set of social, economic, legal, and gendered questions reminiscent of the complicated issues that Florence Kelley tackled.[82]

Kelley's campaigns for wage earners' social rights filled an important gap in American political culture. She never accepted the hegemony of two fundamental features of the American political economy—the power of courts to overturn popular legislation and the political weakness of labor that flowed from the absence of a labor party.

Yet Kelley's legacy has been contentious. Until recently, feminist legal scholars and many historians of women have distanced themselves from her vision of gender-based social rights. The split that began in the 1920s between "difference" and "sameness" as paths to equality for women distorted feminist options until the late 1980s. Rather than a united feminist strategy that embraced "different from men" and "same as men" as two viable paths to women's equality, one appropriate in some settings, one in others, the options became mutually exclusive, their proponents resentful antagonists. That split, which began in the 1920s in the struggle between Florence Kelley and Alice Paul over the ERA, was shaped by class differences between poorly paid women who benefited from state protection and professional women who did not. The conflict deepened from 1930 to 1960, when many advocates of "sameness" and the ERA aligned closely with anti-labor opinion and advocates of "difference" sought to remedy women's gendered circumstances in the paid labor force.[83] Although women wage earners in 1960 were no longer predominately young and unmarried, the overwhelming majority still worked in sex-segregated occupations, where employers benefited by paying lower wages for work comparable to that done by men in other occupations.[84] Dorothy Sue Cobble has shown that labor feminists between 1930 and 1960 supported both sameness and difference as paths to equality for working women, advocating gendered labor legislation when such laws sustained women's access to employment, as was often the case in hours legislation. Even women in male-dominated occupations endorsed women's labor laws "because of their loyalty to 'protecting' their low-paid sisters in other unions."[85]

Yet middle-class advocates of sameness strategies sought to eliminate difference as a path to women's equality. The same class lines that fractured women's solidarity in the 1920s appeared again in 1963. That year, seeking to revive wartime legislation that had raised wages in occupations dominated by women, trade union women championed proposed legislation that called for equal pay "for work of comparable character." They were bitterly disappointed when ERA supporter and Republican congresswoman Katharine St. George amended the bill so as to require equal pay "for equal work." St. George explained, "Equal implies no difference."[86]

This view of "equal" as meaning "no difference" in policies pertaining to women wage earners dominated feminist legal activism in the transformative decades between 1960 and 1990. The new feminist movement mobilized around the ERA and archaic features of labor legislation for women were joyously dismantled.[87] Yet while gendered labor legislation virtually disappeared from the law books, women continued to experience the labor force as a gendered system. Responding to that reality in the 1980s, some feminist legal activists began to draw on Kelley's legacy of gendered social rights. A pivotal battle between difference and sameness as strategies for women's rights came to the Supreme Court in 1987 in *California Federal Savings and Loan v. Guerra*. In that case, the National Organization for Women (NOW) and many feminist legal activists allied with the bank against a woman teller who wanted to reclaim her job after time off for childbirth. Because California law provided job protection for pregnancy but not for other health-related absences, NOW and the ACLU Women's Rights Project argued against any special privilege for pregnant people. Their position against the woman teller marked a high point of "sameness" as an abstract principle of women's equality. A small vanguard, led by members of the ACLU of Southern California, submitted an amicus brief that argued for the acknowledgement of women's social difference as a means of advancing their individual rights. The Supreme Court decision, written by Thurgood Marshall, drew on the amicus brief to uphold the California law, arguing: "By 'taking pregnancy into account,' California's pregnancy disability-leave statute allows women, as well as men, to have families without losing their jobs."[88] Legal scholar Christine Littleton later noted that this decision "signaled a truce" between the advocates of different and similar treatment because it showed that the California statute provided for equal treatment by recognizing difference. The real issue became how and when "difference" should be recognized.[89]

In keeping with the post-1987 truce, the National Organization for Women offered a new version of the ERA in 1995, renamed the Constitutional Equality Amendment. It "incorporated all of the concerns that have arisen out of a two year study of the ERA which reviewed the history of the amendment from 1923 until the present." Section 3 of the new proposed amendment prohibits pregnancy discrimination and Section 4 "prohibits discrimination through the use of any facially neutral criteria which have a disparate impact based on membership in a class protected under this article." Thus, the new version of the ERA recognizes gender difference and the inability of gender-neutral legislation alone to provide women with full equality.[90]

Kelley's letters help us understand the passionate origin of the divergent paths of women's rights-seeking activity and why the melding of sameness and difference took so long. Responding to American political structures, especially the power of courts to define the rights of working people, she used central features of her political economy—the growing power of consumers and of women's organizations—to advance social rights for the working poor. Lacking the support of a labor party, she used gender to achieve class-delineated rights.

Kelley's father told her that his generation's duty "was to build up great industries in America so that more wealth could be produced for the whole people." He said that the duty of her generation "will be to see that the product is distributed justly."[91] Florence Kelley worked with others in her generation to make the benefits of industrialization more widely available in American society. Crossing class, gender, and race boundaries, her path of rights-seeking activity helped create new possibilities for future generations. Kelley's letters give us an extraordinary opportunity to study the emergence of social rights in the United States during the half century before 1930. Those rights were incompletely achieved at her death in 1932 and they remain so today, but this volume makes her tools and her example newly accessible.

NOTES

1. Recent overviews of the Progressive Era include Dawley, *Struggles for Justice;* McGerr, *A Fierce Discontent;* Rauchway, *Murdering McKinley;* Sanders, *Roots of Reform;* Diner, *A Very Different Age;* and Clemens, *The People's Lobby.*

2. Thus, the Progressive movement resembled what Antonio Gramsci called a "historical bloc." See Forgacs, *An Antonio Gramsci Reader,* 190, 192–193, 197, 220.

3. Rauchway, *Murdering McKinley.* For Seth Low, see McCormick, *From Realignment to Reform.* For Progressive reform in Wisconsin, see Unger, *Fighting Bob La Follette.*

4. See Freyer, *Regulating Big Business;* and Mattson, *Creating a Democratic Public.*

5. For "the labor question," see Currarino, "The Politics of 'More.'" Marx referred to "the social question" in the 1840s; Marx, "The *Kölnische Zeitung* on the Elections," 8:286–289. By 1900, "the social question" had become a popular term that embraced both ethical and economic issues related to the fact that the needs of working-class people were not being met by contemporary economic and political institutions. See Peabody, *Jesus Christ and the Social Question.* For an ongoing discussion of the social question, see Judt, "The Social Question Redivivus." For "the woman question," see Schofield, "Rebel Girls and Union Maids."

6. "Social justice" is a term that arose within Christian socialism during the last three decades of the nineteenth century. Whereas Marx constructed scientific arguments to discuss the exploitation of labor by capital, Christian socialists drew on moral arguments and spoke

of social justice. In Great Britain, Europe, and the United States, this moral discourse appealed to middle-class constituencies. Between the time that the term "feminism" came into use in the United States around 1910 and was preempted by others around 1920, progressive women reformers applied it to their own efforts, along with the term "social justice." Social justice feminists were therefore advocates for women's rights who also supported social justice movements. See Sklar, Schüler, and Strasser, *Social Justice Feminists,* 4–7. Linda Gordon defined feminism as "a critique of male supremacy, formed and offered in the light of a will to change it, which in turn assumes a conviction that it is changeable." Gordon, "What's New in Women's History," 29.

7. Cobble, *The Other Women's Movement,* 3–4. Cobble describes "labor feminists" as "a multi-class group of women closely associated with the labor movement" (232n13).

8. See, for example, FK to Lavinia Dock, 24 November 1923, below.

9. *Oxford English Dictionary.* A useful review of Anglo-American rights traditions is Waldron, *Theories of Rights.*

10. For examples, see Letter 122, FK to Katherine Philips Edson, 16 April 1914; and Letter 129, FK to Myrta Jones, 21 September 1915, both below.

11. For the word "righteous" in FK's discourse, see Letter 58, FK to Henry Demarest Lloyd, 14 October 1899, below. In contrast to the Keynesian economics that dominated public policy after 1930 and pursued its goals by manipulating the economy, Kelley advanced her aims through the older discourse of moral economy. For the history of Anglo-American moral economy traditions see Thompson, *The Making of the English Working Class.*

12. For this bias in interpretations of the Constitution, see Hart, *Bound by Our Constitution;* Fink, "Labor, Liberty, and the Law"; and Forbath, "Caste, Class, and Equal Citizenship."

13. For international networks among Kelley's male contemporaries, see Rodgers, *Atlantic Crossings;* for American women's networks with German women, see Sklar, Schüler, and Strasser, *Social Justice Feminists.*

14. See Wilson, *The Women's Joint Congressional Committee and the Politics of Maternity,* 110–132.

15. For Harding's use of "normalcy," see McGerr, *A Fierce Discontent,* 311.

16. See Ware, *Beyond Suffrage;* and Ware, *Partner and I.*

17. FK, "Minimum Wage Laws," 1000.

18. See Cohen, *A Consumers' Republic,* 129–133; and Glickman, *A Living Wage.*

19. See Sklar, "'The Greater Part of the Petitioners Are Female.'"

20. See Hart, *Bound by Our Constitution,* 39–62.

21. Koven and Michel, "Womanly Duties," 1079.

22. This extensive literature includes Koven and Michel, "Womanly Duties"; Skocpol, *Protecting Soldiers and Mothers;* and Fraser and Gordon, "Contract versus Charity." See also Sklar, "The Historical Foundations of Women's Power in the Creation of the American Welfare State, 1830–1930." These writings build on and critique T. H. Marshall's 1950 essay, "Citizenship and Social Class," which analyzed the development of social rights as emerging from eighteenth-century civil rights and nineteenth-century political rights. He defined social rights as the provisions needed "to live the life of a civilized being according to the standards prevailing in the society"—especially the right to schooling, housing, and health care. Marshall, *Citizenship and Social Class,* 8. Yet because social welfare provisions for women—especially mothers' pensions—were not established as rights in the United States, scholars have emphasized the inadequate basis such provisions provided for women's equality.

23. For a review of historical writings on social provision and workplace rights, see Boris, "On the Importance of Naming."

24. FK, "Die weibliche Fabrikinspektion in der Vereinigten Staaten," 142; translated and reprinted as "Women Factory Inspectors in the United States" in Sklar, Schüler, and Strasser, *Social Justice Feminists,* 95–104, quote on page 103.

25. A more complete statement of this argument is in Sklar, "The Historical Foundations of Women's Power in the Creation of the American Welfare State, 1830–1930."
26. FK, *Some Ethical Gains through Legislation,* 209, 229.
27. FK, *Some Ethical Gains through Legislation,* 229.
28. FK, *Some Ethical Gains through Legislation,* 230, 229.
29. FK, *Some Ethical Gains through Legislation,* 229–230, 168.
30. FK, *Some Ethical Gains through Legislation,* 205.
31. FK, *Some Ethical Gains through Legislation,* 205.
32. FK, *Some Ethical Gains through Legislation,* 30.
33. FK, *Some Ethical Gains through Legislation,* 108.
34. Felix Frankfurter, "Foreword," in Goldmark, *Impatient Crusader,* v.
35. For examples of the rights that flowed from child labor legislation, see Messer-Kruse, "Technology and the Decline of Child Labor." For the rights achieved through hours legislation, see Steinberg, *Wages and Hours.* For the rights gained by minimum wage legislation see Prasch, "American Economists and Minimum Wage Legislation during the Progressive Era," 169–171; and Card and Krueger, *Myth and Measurement.*
36. A complete bibliography of FK's writings after 1889 will appear in Sklar, *Florence Kelley and the Struggle for a New Social Contract in Modernizing America, 1900–1930* (forthcoming, Yale University Press, 2011).
37. For more on our selection process, see "Editorial Principles," below.
38. Sklar, *Florence Kelley and the Nation's Work,* 1–49.
39. Daniel Rodgers concluded that among American students studying in Europe, "only Florence Kelley . . . actually threw in her lot with working-class socialism"; Rodgers, *Atlantic Crossings,* 88. See Letter 16, FK to Frederick Engels, 29 March 1888, below.
40. Sklar, *Florence Kelley and the Nation's Work,* 295.
41. Bisno, *Abraham Bisno, Union Pioneer,* 116. In 1893, Bisno became one of FK's deputy inspectors in Illinois.
42. Dimand, Dimand, and Forget, *A Biographical Dictionary of Women Economists,* 230.
43. Kelley's maps are reprinted in Bulmer, Bales, and Sklar, *Social Survey in Historical Perspective,* between pages 12 and 13. For an example of FK's work as a watchdog, see FK, "Measuring the Health of Working Children." See also Sklar, "Hull-House Maps and Papers."
44. Johnson, *Governing the American State,* 86.
45. NCL, Fourth Annual Report [1903], 37–39, Box A5, NCL Records, DLC.
46. For an example of NCL letterhead from this period, see FK to Josephine Goldmark, 12 October 1910, Goldmark Papers, MCR-S.
47. See Letter 124, FK to Joel Spingarn, 27 July 1914, below.
48. See Letter 106, FK to NK, 8 April 1908, below.
49. See Letter 89, FK to W. E. B. Du Bois, 30 October 1906, below. In an eloquent memorial tribute to Kelley after her death, Du Bois said that she "dared to see the plight of the American Negro as an integral part of the problem of American democracy." W. E. B. Du Bois, "Florence Kelley" in Herbert Aptheker, ed., "Du Bois on Florence Kelley," *Social Work: Journal of the National Association of Social Workers,* Vol. II, No. 4 (Oct. 1996), 98–100, quote on 99.
50. Muncy, *Creating a Female Dominion,* 42–48.
51. Johnson, *Governing the American State,* 107.
52. Storrs, *Civilizing Capitalism,* 65–106.
53. Letter 15, FK to Engels, 29 December 1887, below.
54. Archer, *Why Is There No Labor Party in the United States?* 223.
55. For the history of feminists working with men in trade unions and labor parties to advance women's protective labor legislation between 1890 and 1930, see Hagemann, "Protection or Equality?" (Norway); Howe, "A Paradise for Working Men but Not for Working Women" (Australia); and Thane, "Visions of Gender in the Making of the British Welfare State" (Britain).

56. See Thane, "Visions of Gender in the Making of the British Welfare State."
57. For a summary of this historiography, see Archer, *Why Is There No Labor Party in the United States?* 259n15.
58. Oestricher, "Urban Working-Class Political Behavior and Theories of American Electoral Politics."
59. Forbath, *Law and the Shaping of the American Labor Movement,* 37–58.
60. Forbath, *Law and the Shaping of the American Labor Movement,* 59–127. See also Schneirov, Stromquist, and Salvatore, *The Pullman Strike and the Crisis of the 1890s.*
61. For the broad base of industrial unionism, see Brody, *Labor in Crisis.*
62. For the Congress of Industrial Organizations, see Brody, *Labor Embattled,* 46–51.
63. Archer, *Why Is There No Labor Party in the United States?* 177–232; and Fones-Wolf, *Trade Union Gospel,* 84–155.
64. Sklar, "Florence Kelley Tells German Readers about the Pullman Strike, 1894," 127–147.
65. Letter 208, FK to John A. Fitch, New York, 26 March 1925, below.
66. The 1912 Democratic Party Platform is available online at *The American Presidency Project,* http://www.presidency.ucsb.edu/showplatforms.php?platindex=D1912. Not until 1912 did the AFL influence the Democratic Party to speak to the needs of working men beyond the AFL membership. Greene, *Pure and Simple Politics,* 276–277.
67. Greene, *Pure and Simple Politics,* 257–258. See also Kolko, *Railroads and Regulation,* 219–230.
68. Fink, *Workingmen's Democracy,* 228–230.
69. For the strength of consumer culture among middle-class American women by 1880, see Garvey, *The Adman in the Parlor,* 16–50.
70. Historian Sue Benson has shown that while some families of skilled workers might have joined consumer society in the 1920s, most working-class families still struggled to pay basic food and housing costs and almost none had cash or credit for discretionary use. The income gap between unskilled and skilled workers remained stark until 1930, as did the political gap in the access those groups had to the benefits of citizenship. Benson, *Household Accounts,* 18–21.
71. Webb and Webb, *Industrial Democracy,* 751–752.
72. Hart, *Bound by Our Constitution,* 14–62.
73. Sklar, "Two Political Cultures," 36–51; Hart, *Bound by Our Constitution,* 66–107.
74. Kelley, "Status of Legislation in the United States," 487.
75. Sklar, "Two Political Cultures," 61; Brandeis, "Labor Legislation," 502–503.
76. Brandeis, "Labor Legislation," 503.
77. Elizabeth Glendower Evans, quoted in FK to Edwin V. O'Hara, 28 October 1914, "The Minimum Wage Law: Scrapbook of Edwin V. O'Hara," Oregon Historical Society.
78. For an analysis of the age, marital status and residence of wage-earning women in 1910, see Claudia Goldin, "The Work and Wages of Single Women, 1870–1920," 81–89.
79. FK, "Minimum Wage Boards," 150. See also Letter 119, FK to Katherine Philips Edson, 22 November 1912, below. For FK's characterization of industries that paid less than a minimum wage to workers as parasitical, see Letter 181, FK to Felix Frankfurter, 26 May 1923, below.
80. For a summary of legal scholars' positive view of state minimum wage legislation for women before 1938, see Brandeis, "Labor Legislation," 689–690.
81. Cohen, *A Consumers' Republic,* 18–165.
82. Boris, "'Social Responsibility on a Global Level.'"
83. For the anti-labor activism of NWP members, see Storrs, "Civilizing Capitalism," 76–88.
84. On the continuing importance of sex-segregated occupations after 1960, see Rose and Hartmann, *Still a Man's Labor Market.*

85. Quoted in Cobble, *The Other Women's Movement,* 187.
86. Quoted in Cobble, *The Other Women's Movement,* 165.
87. For labor feminists' opposition to the dismantling of beneficial state laws, see Cobble, *The Other Women's Movement,* 186–190.
88. *California Fed. S. & L. v. Guerra,* 479 U.S. 272 (1987).
89. Littleton, "Review: Whose Law Is This Anyway?" 1568. For the *Cal. Fed.* case and the 1987 "equality crisis" in feminist legal theory, see Littleton, "Reconstructing Sexual Equality." For the reintroduction of "difference" in feminist legal theory, see Fineman, "Feminist Theory and Law."
90. The text of the current equal rights amendment is available at the Web site of the National Organization for Women, http://www.now.org/issues/economic/cea/draft.html.
91. FK, "My Philadelphia," 8.

EDITORIAL PRINCIPLES

SEARCH, SELECTION, AND ORGANIZATION

Although individual letters by Florence Kelley are cited frequently in scholarly studies of the Progressive Era, no previous edition of her correspondence exists.[1] Our search for Florence Kelley's letters began over twenty-five years ago when Kathryn Sklar gathered materials for *Florence Kelley and the Nation's Work* (1995), the first volume of Sklar's two-volume biography of Kelley. Sklar collected all the known Florence Kelley (hereafter FK) letters at the two largest collections, the National Consumers' League (hereafter NCL) Records at the Manuscript Division of the Library of Congress, and the Florence Kelley Papers at the New York Public Library, and she mined collections at major archives such as the University of Chicago, Columbia University, and the International Institute of Social History in Amsterdam. To supplement her work here, we conducted a nationwide search for FK letters, writing every archival collection that we thought might possibly hold correspondence to or from Florence Kelley. We eventually compiled a database of incoming and outgoing FK correspondence (not including many family letters) of almost 7,000 letters. This database will be published as "The Correspondence of Florence Kelley, 1865–1932" on the Web site of the Kheel Center for Labor-Management Documentation and Archives at Cornell University's Industrial Labor Relations School.

From the approximately 3,100 letters FK wrote, we have selected 275. Our goal has been to record FK's career as a social reformer by including letters to prominent allies such as Jane Addams, W. E. B. Du Bois, Frederick Engels, Julia Lathrop, and Lillian Wald. To capture the full range of her efforts, we also include correspondence with scores of other contemporaries who were less well known. Our selections also reflect the chronological distribution of FK's surviving correspondence—we recovered relatively few letters from the 1890s but found voluminous correspondence from the 1920s.

We made three decisions about FK's extensive correspondence with her family. We decided to include a strong representation of her letters to her son Nicholas, with whom she sometimes corresponded daily in letters that often described her reform work most vividly and completely, especially in the crucial years from 1899 through 1907. Second, since we recovered very few letters to her daughter Margaret and her son John (although we found hundreds from them to her), we decided to include a high proportion of them because they illuminated her relationship with her younger children. Third, except for a few letters to her parents and three to her brother Albert, we decided not to include any of FK's extensive correspondence with other family members because these letters did not add to our understanding of her public life or her immediate family.

Within this framework our selection strategy eliminated letters that simply arranged meetings, or accepted or declined appointments. FK often dictated letters with similar passages to several recipients; from those we chose examples that most fully expressed her intentions. Since most of FK's letters went deeply into specific reform issues, most of our selections do too, offering examples that expressed her thoughts, strategies, or coalition building related to particular reforms. Yet whenever possible we include the rare letters that summarized her reform agenda. When space considerations prevented us from including letters we deemed important, we often refer to or quote from them in our notes. Similarly, our notes include (when available) comments and quotations from the incoming correspondent.

All the letters included in our volume are from FK, and their arrangement is chronological in eight chapters reflecting different stages of her life and career.

TRANSCRIPTION

Many of FK's letters were handwritten. We have transcribed these handwritten letters as written—including misspellings, numbers, symbols, and erratic punctuation and paragraphing. All superscripts have been lowered, e.g. 5th to 5th, or $100.^{00}$ to 100.00. We have reproduced text that FK crossed out unless the word is simply a repetition (e.g., "town ~~town~~"). In cases where it is difficult to determine whether a word is capitalized (e.g., "state" vs. "State") we follow standard rules for capitalization.

FK began typing letters in 1894; after 1911 almost all her typewritten letters were typed by a secretary. FK's handwritten additions or corrections to any typed letter are indicated by italics, as is her signature. We have silently corrected obvious typographical errors, for example "papers" for "papaers." In typed letters we also corrected punctuation (e.g., deleting a misplaced comma) and irregular spacing. However, we have not changed the original syntax or made changes that affect the meaning. We have not corrected capitalization, errors of usage, inconsistent tenses, misspelled proper names, or common spelling conventions of the time (e.g., "employe"). We have added notes to designate any unusual features in typed letters, such as when handwritten additions and/or corrections made by someone (presumably a secretary) other than FK. We also note when FK's editing of a draft is unusually complex.

If the recipient's copy cannot be located, we have transcribed the carbon copy. FK routinely corrected the original version of letters typed by secretaries, and we have shown her editing using italic typeface for her handwritten corrections and instructions. Occasionally FK added a note or signed the carbon, and these additions are included, in italics. For the occasional printed letter to newspaper editors, special printed features such as a salutation in capitals or italics are retained, but obvious printer's errors are silently corrected.

Illegible words are noted, underscored: [illegible]. If the manuscript is torn so that parts are unreadable, we indicate with: [ms. damaged]. If we guess at a word, we put it in brackets with a question mark, as: [illustrious?]. When we have completed a word in instances where letters are cut off by photocopying, we have added the text in brackets without underscoring: the demand fo[r] school buildings. When we have added copy that adds factual information to a letter, such as a person's full name, we have underscored it within brackets: Josephine [Goldmark]. When FK omitted a letter in a word that is necessary for clarity of meaning, we have added it, underscored within brackets: Hear[s]t Hall. Material marked with an asterisk or other symbol and added elsewhere in the letter is inserted in the text of the letter in brackets preceded by "inserted in margin" to reflect FK's thought process.

We have added, underscored and in brackets, quotation marks or parentheses that FK omitted. We have added annotations to describe the arrangement of words that FK added above the line. We have converted brackets FK used to parentheses to avoid confusion between editorial interventions and her punctuation. Underlined unbracketed copy indicates FK's underlining in the text of the letter; double underlined unbracketed copy indicates FK's double underlining. Occasionally FK drew a line to indicate a new topic in her letter; these have been preserved.

We have not reproduced letterhead addresses of stationery of hotels FK stayed at while traveling. However, we have reproduced the letterhead addresses of the NCL and other major reform institutions and the letterhead on FK's personal stationery. Dates and FK's location are standardized and placed at the top of the letter, below the letterhead if there is one, as is the address of the recipient, placed at the beginning of the letter just above the salutation. Also standardized are the placement of the complimentary close and FK's signature. We have supplied the name of the state when it is missing from the letter, underscored in bracketed text.

After each letter, whether a selection that we print in full or a letter that we refer to in an annotation, we cite the abbreviated name of the collection and the Library of Congress MARC code for the archive where the letter can be found; the key to the MARC codes we use is provided below. For letters in large collections of FK materials we provide more information. For example, we give box numbers and folder titles of letters drawn from the massive collection of NCL Records at the Library of Congress. And for letters in the large collection of Florence Kelley Papers (FKP) at the New York Public Library we identify the series. The FKP (Mss Col 6303) have recently been catalogued into two series: Series 1A, General Correspondence; and Series 1B, Family Correspondence. Within those series items can easily be located in folders identified by year in the General Correspondence (e.g., 1910–1914), or by correspondent and year in the Family Correspondence (e.g., FK to John Bartram Kelley, 1898–1932). The guide to the FKP is available online at the New York Public Library's Web site.

If an envelope survives, we add to this information "Env" along with the address. Most of the enclosures FK mentions have not been recovered; when enclosures to the letter have survived, we have noted them, marked "Enc:" and, if significant, described or reproduced them.

ANNOTATIONS AND ENDNOTES

Annotations following each letter identify individuals, provide background for FK's comments (frequently from correspondence immediately before or after her letter), and refer readers to other relevant letters to or from FK. Family members and individuals appearing frequently throughout the volume, such as Nicholas Kelley or Lillian Wald, are identified in the biographical directory. Other persons are normally identified at their first mention in a letter in the volume. Persons mentioned only in the annotations are not fully identified.

Sources of readily available information, such as the *American National Biography, Biographical Dictionary of the American Congress, Notable American Women,* other standard encyclopedias, and electronic resources such as Lexis-Nexis, are not cited. Generally we have not supplied notes for references to names or events in the letters that cannot be identified.

Titles of works in the endnotes to introductions and annotations to letters fall into three categories. When a publication is mentioned in the text of the letter, we cite the source fully in a letter annotation. When we cite works in notes and annotations that we consulted as part of research for this book, we use short citations in annotations and notes and provide the full citation on the bibliography. When we mention titles of publications as part of our identification of individuals mentioned in letters, we provide only the title and date of the work in annotations and do not cite it fully in this book. Regardless of which of these categories they belong to, FK's writings are cited fully in the bibliography.

NOTE

1. The only previously printed collection of FK letters appear as excerpts in Dorothy Blumberg, "'Dear Mr. Engels': Unpublished Letters, 1884–1894, of Florence Kelley (Wischnewetzky) to Friedrich Engels" (*Labor History* 5 [spring 1964]: 103–133).

ABBREVIATIONS

DOCUMENT DESCRIPTIONS

ALDft	autograph letter draft
ALS	autograph letter signed
AN	autograph note (inserted in typed letter)
CC	carbon copy
Enc	enclosure
Env	envelope included
Inc	incomplete letter or letter with a page torn or otherwise damaged
PL	printed letter
TEL	telegram
TDft	typed draft
TL	typed letter (no handwriting on letter)
TLS	typed letter with either FK's typed or handwritten signature

PEOPLE

AK	Albert Kelley
CBK	Caroline Bonsall Kelley
FK	Florence Kelley
JA	Jane Addams
JK	John Kelley
LW	Lazare Wischnewetsky
MK	Margaret Kelley
NK	Nicholas Kelley
WDK	William Darrah Kelley

ORGANIZATIONS

AALL	American Association for Labor Legislation
ACLU	American Civil Liberties Union
ACWA	Amalgamated Clothing Workers of America
AFL	American Federation of Labor
C. B. & Q.	Chicago, Burlington & Quincy Railroad
CL	Consumers' League (in a proper name)
DAR	Daughters of the American Revolution
ERA	Equal Rights Amendment
GFWC	General Federation of Women's Clubs
GPO	Government Printing Office
IALL	International Association for Labor Legislation
ICW	International Congress of Women
ILGWU	International Ladies Garment Workers Union
ILO	International Labour Organization
IWW	Industrial Workers of the World
LID	League for Industrial Democracy
LWV	League of Women Voters
MP	Member of Parliament
NAM	National Association of Manufacturers
NCL	National Consumers' League
NCM	National Congress of Mothers
NWP	National Woman's Party
NWTUL	National Women's Trade Union League
NYCLC	New York Child Labor Committee
PTA	Parent Teacher Association
SLP	Socialist Labor Party
WCTU	Woman's Christian Temperance Union
WILPF	Women's International League for Peace and Freedom
WJCC	Women's Joint Congressional Committee
WJLC	Women's Joint Legislative Conference
YMCA	Young Men's Christian Association
YWCA	Young Women's Christian Association

FREQUENTLY CITED WORKS

Cong. Rec.	*Congressional Record*
NYT	*New York Times*

ARCHIVAL COLLECTIONS

AALL Papers	American Association for Labor Legislation Records, 1905–1943, Kheel Center, Martin P. Catherwood Library, Cornell University, Ithaca, New York
Abbott Papers	Edith and Grace Abbott Papers, 1870–1967, Special Collections, Archives, University of Chicago Library, Chicago, Illinois
Addams Collection	The Jane Addams and Hull House Collection, Howard Colman Library Archives, Rockford College, Rockford, Illinois
ACWA Records	Amalgamated Clothing Workers of America Records, 1914–1980, Kheel Center, Martin P. Catherwood Library, Cornell University, Ithaca, New York
Altgeld Correspondence	John Peter Altgeld Correspondence, 1893–1897, Illinois State Archives, Springfield, Illinois
Baker Papers	Papers of Newton Diehl Baker, ca. 1898–1962, Manuscript Division, Library of Congress, Washington, D.C.
Berger Papers	Victor L. Berger Papers, Archives Division, State Historical Society of Wisconsin, Madison, Wisconsin
Bourne Papers	Papers of Randolph Silliman Bourne, ca. 1910–1966, Rare Book & Manuscript Library, Columbia University, New York, New York
Brandeis Papers	Papers of Louis Dembitz Brandeis, Louis D. Brandeis School of Law, University of Louisville, Louisville, Kentucky
Brooks Papers	Papers of John Graham Brooks, 1845–1938, Schlesinger Library, Radcliffe Institute for Advanced Study, Cambridge, Massachusetts
Catt Papers	Papers of Carrie Chapman Catt, 1848–1950, Manuscript Division, Library of Congress, Washington, D.C.
CB Records	Records of the Children's Bureau, 1912–69, RG 102, National Archives at College Park, College Park, Maryland
Chicago City Club Records	City Club of Chicago Records, 1903–1978, Chicago Historical Society, Chicago, Illinois
CLM Records	Records of the Consumers' League of Massachusetts, 1891–1955, Schlesinger Library, Radcliffe Institute for Advanced Study, Cambridge, Massachusetts
Colby Papers	Papers of Clara Dorothy Bewick Colby, 1882–1914, The Huntington Library, Art Collections and Botanical Gardens, San Marino, California
Crane Collection	Caroline Bartlett Crane Collection, 1843–1945, Western Michigan University Archive & Regional History Collections, Kalamazoo, Michigan
Dewson Papers	Papers of Molly Dewson, 1893–1962, Schlesinger Library, Radcliffe Institute for Advanced Study, Cambridge, Massachusetts
Du Bois Papers	W. E. B. Du Bois Papers, 1803–1999, Special Collections and Archives, W. E. B. Du Bois Library, University of Massachusetts, Amherst, Massachusetts

Edson Papers	Katherine Philips Edson Papers, 1870–1933, Department of Special Collections, UCLA Library, Los Angeles, California
Ely Papers	Richard T. Ely Papers, Archives Division, State Historical Society of Wisconsin, Madison, Wisconsin
Factory Investigating Commission Correspondence	Correspondence of the New York State Factory Investigating Commission, 1912–1916, New York State Archives, Albany, New York
FKP	Florence Kelley Papers, 1832–1967, Manuscripts and Archives Division, New York Public Library, New York, New York
Frankfurter Papers	Papers of Felix Frankfurter, 1846–1966, Manuscript Division, Library of Congress, Washington, D.C.
Goldmark Papers	Papers of Josephine Clara and Pauline Dorothea Goldmark, 1886–1962, Schlesinger Library, Radcliffe Institute for Advanced Study, Cambridge, Massachusetts
Hamilton Family Papers	Hamilton Family Papers, 1818–1976, Schlesinger Library, Radcliffe Institute for Advanced Study, Cambridge, Massachusetts
Lloyd Papers	Papers of Henry Demarest Lloyd, Archives Division, State Historical Society of Wisconsin, Madison, Wisconsin
JA Papers	Jane Addams Papers, 1838–1935, Swarthmore College Peace Collection, Swarthmore, Pennsylvania
Joel Spingarn Papers	Joel Elias Spingarn Papers, 1875–1939, Manuscript Division, Moorland-Spingarn Research Center, Howard University, Washington, D.C.
Kellogg Papers	Paul U. Kellogg Papers, 1891–1952, Social Welfare History Archives Center, Elmer L. Andersen Library, University of Minnesota, Minneapolis, Minnesota
Kent Papers	William Kent Family Papers, 1768–1961, Sterling Memorial Library, Yale University, New Haven, Connecticut
KFP	Kelley Family Papers, 1681–1936, Rare Book & Manuscript Library, Columbia University, New York, New York
La Follette Papers	Papers of Robert M. La Follette, 1879–1910, Manuscript Division, Library of Congress, Washington, D.C.
Lathrop Papers	Julia C. Lathrop Papers, Archives, Howard Colman Library, Rockford College, Rockford, Illinois
Lippmann Papers	Walter Lippmann Papers, 1900–1974, Manuscripts and Archives, Yale University Library, New Haven, Connecticut
Lloyd Papers	Henry Demarest Lloyd Papers, 1847–1903, State Historical Society of Wisconsin, Madison, Wisconsin
LWV Records	League of Women Voters (U.S.) Records, 1884–1986, Library of Congress, Washington, D.C.
Manny Papers	Frank Addison Manny Papers, 1868–1954, Michigan Historical Library, University of Michigan, Ann Arbor, Michigan
Marx/Engels Papers	Karl Marx/Friedrich Engels Papers, International Institute of Social History, Amsterdam, Netherlands

NAACP Board Minutes	Minutes of the Meeting of the [NAACP] Board of Directors, 1909–1959, Glenn G. Bartle Library, State University of New York at Binghamton
NAACP Papers	Papers of the NAACP, Manuscript Division, Library of Congress, Washington, D.C.
NAWSA Records	Records of the National American Woman Suffrage Association, 1839–1961, Manuscript Division, Library of Congress, Washington, D.C.
NCL Records	Records of the National Consumers' League, 1882–1986, Manuscript Division, Library of Congress, Washington, D.C.
NCLC Records	Records of the National Child Labor Committee, U.S., 1904–1953, Manuscript Division, Library of Congress, Washington, D.C.
NWP Records	Records of the National Woman's Party, 1850–1975, Manuscript Division, Library of Congress, Washington, D.C.
NYCLC Records	New York Child Labor Committee, Records, 1903–1941, Manuscripts and Special Collections, New York State Library Albany, New York
Papers of Eleanor Roosevelt	Papers of Eleanor Roosevelt, Franklin D. Roosevelt Presidential Library and Museum, Hyde Park, New York
Perkins Papers	Papers of Frances Perkins, ca. 1895–1965, Rare Book & Manuscript Library, Columbia University, New York, New York
Rubinow Papers	Papers of I. M. Rubinow, 1895–1936, Kheel Center, Martin P. Catherwood Library, Cornell University, Ithaca, New York
Stanton Papers	Papers of Elizabeth Cady Stanton, 1814–1946, Manuscript Division, Library of Congress, Washington, D.C.
TR Papers	Papers of Theodore Roosevelt, 1759–1993, Manuscript Division, Library of Congress, Washington, D.C.
Wald Papers	Papers of Lillian D. Wald, 1895–1936, and Papers of William D. Wald, 1889–1957, Rare Book & Manuscript Library, Columbia University, New York, New York
WDK Correspondence	Correspondence of William Darrah Kelley, 1814–1890, Historical Society of Pennsylvania, Philadelphia, Pennsylvania
WJCC Records	Records of the Women's Joint Congressional Committee, Manuscript Division, Library of Congress, Washington, D.C.
WTUL Papers	Papers of the Women's Trade Union League and Its Principal Leaders, 1855–1964, Schlesinger Library, Radcliffe Institute for Advanced Study, Cambridge, Massachusetts

LIBRARY OF CONGRESS MARC CODES FOR REPOSITORIES OF COLLECTIONS

CLU-SC	Department of Special Collections, University of California, Los Angeles
CSmH	Huntington Library, San Marino, California
CtY	Sterling Memorial Library, Yale University, New Haven, Connecticut

DHU-MS	Moorland-Spingarn Research Center, Howard University, Washington, D.C.
DLC	Library of Congress, Washington, D.C.
I-Ar	Illinois State Library, Archives Division
ICHi	Chicago Historical Society, Chicago, Illinois
ICU	University of Chicago Library, Chicago, Illinois
IRoC	Rockford College, Rockford, Illinois
KyLoU-L	Louis D. Brandeis School of Law Library, University of Louisville, Louisville, Kentucky
MCR-S	Schlesinger Library, Radcliffe Institute for Advanced Study, Cambridge, Massachusetts
MdCpNA	National Archives at College Park, College Park, Maryland
MiKW	Western Michigan University, Kalamazoo, Michigan
MiU-H	Michigan Historical Library, University of Michigan, Ann Arbor, Michigan
MnU-SW	Social Welfare History Archives Center, Elmer L. Andersen Library, University of Minnesota, Minneapolis, Minnesota
MU	W. E. B. Du Bois Library, University of Massachusetts, Amherst, Massachusetts
N	New York State Library, Albany, New York
N-Ar	New York State Archives, Albany, New York
NBiSU	Bartle Library, Binghamton University, Binghamton, New York
NCC-RB	Rare Book and Manuscript Library, Columbia University, New York, New York
NHyF	Franklin D. Roosevelt Presidential Library and Museum, Hyde Park, New York
NL-AmISG	International Institute of Social History, Amsterdam, Netherlands
NN	New York Public Library, New York, New York
NNCorI	ILR Library, Kheel Center, Cornell University, Ithaca, New York
PHi	Historical Society of Pennsylvania, Philadelphia, Pennsylvania
PSC-P	Swarthmore College Peace Collection, Swarthmore, Pennsylvania
WHi	State Historical Society of Wisconsin, Madison, Wisconsin

CHRONOLOGY OF SELECTED EVENTS IN FLORENCE KELLEY'S LIFE

1859	12 September: Born in Philadelphia
1859–1871	Loses five sisters in infancy
1869–1875	Attends private schools in Philadelphia sporadically and reads widely in her father's library
1882	Earns B.A. at Cornell University
	December: travels to Europe with brother WDK Jr.
1883	Studies at University of Zurich
1884	October: marries LW in Zurich
	Joins German Social Democratic Party
1885	Translates Engels's *Condition of the Working Class* (published 1887)
	July: gives birth to NK
1886	October: returns to United States with LW and NK
	November: gives birth to MK
1887	FK and LW are suspended from the New York chapter of the Socialist Labor Party
1888	Translates Marx's *Free Trade*
	January: gives birth to JK
1890	WDK dies
1891	December: leaves LW and moves to Chicago with NK, MK, and JK
1892	Awarded custody of children, who take Kelley as their last name
1893	Drafts legislation that becomes the Factory Inspection Act for Illinois
1893–1897	Chief factory inspector for state of Illinois
1894	Writes brief for *Ritchie* case and uses social data in ways that anticipate the 1908 Brandeis brief
1895	Earns LL.B. at Northwestern Law School
1897–1899	Works at Crerar Library in Chicago
1899	Appointed general secretary of NCL and moves to New York
1899–1927	Lives at Lillian Wald's Henry Street Settlement
1900–1904	Travels widely to promote the creation of local consumers' leagues

1900	Divorces LW
	Begins advocating for a federal department devoted to needs of children; promotes a wide range of state labor legislation for women and children
1902	Helps found NYCLC with Lillian Wald
1903	Becomes associate editor at *Charities* (after 1909, *The Survey*)
1904	Helps found NCLC
1905	Vice-president of NAWSA
	September: MK dies of heart failure
	October: publishes *Some Ethical Gains through Legislation*
1906	Helps found Intercollegiate Socialist Society (precursor of LID)
	CBK dies
1907	Buys farmhouse in Brooklin, Maine; takes possession in 1909
1908	July–September: attends ICW and first international meeting of consumers' leagues in Geneva
	Joins the Socialist Party of America
1909	Helps found NAACP
	Begins promoting state minimum wage laws
1913	Publishes *The Present Status of Minimum Wage Legislation*
	September: attends IALL meeting in Basel, Switzerland, and International Conference of Consumers' Leagues in Antwerp
1914	Participates in the peace movement protesting World War I
1915	Joins American League to Limit Armament (later American Union Against Militarism, the precursor of the ACLU)
1918	August 1917–January: Serves on federal Board of Control for Labor Standards in Army Clothing
1919	May: attends woman's peace conference in Zurich, Switzerland
	November: resigns from NCLC
1920	December: helps found the WJCC and serves as first chair of Sheppard-Towner Maternity and Infancy Bill subcommittee
1921	July: attends first meeting of WILPF in Vienna
	Reorganizes the NCL, establishing a Board of Directors with more authority over NCL affairs
1923	Critiques the Sterling education bill, which allowed southern states to allocate federal money in public schools
1925	Begins collecting statistics on injuries to child workers as recorded in state workmen's compensation boards
1925–1927	Conducts covert petition campaign for ratification of child labor amendment in New York State
1927	April: joins Society of Friends
	February–June: publishes autobiographical articles in *Survey*
1931	September: hospitalized in Germantown Hospital with colon cancer
1932	17 February: dies in Germantown, Pennsylvania

CHRONOLOGY OF SELECTED EVENTS RELATED TO FLORENCE KELLEY'S POLITICAL AGENDA AT THE NATIONAL CONSUMERS' LEAGUE

1899	FK becomes general secretary of NCL
	NCL begins using White Label in garment industry
1899–1904	Sixty new local consumers' leagues form in twenty states
1905	*Lochner v. New York* rules ten-hour–day law unconstitutional (U.S.)
1906	Pure Food and Drug Act
1908–1912	NCL promotes enforcement of Pure Food and Drug Act
1908	U.S. Supreme Court upholds ten-hour–day law for women in *Muller v. Oregon;* Josephine Goldmark and Louis Brandeis prepare Brandeis brief
1908	NCL publishes *Child Labor Legislation*
1909	NCL publishes *The Consumers' Control of Production*
1911	FK and NCL promote minimum wage boards in Minnesota, Wisconsin, and Massachusetts
1912	Congress creates U.S. Children's Bureau
	Massachusetts passes nation's first minimum wage law
1913	NCL publishes *Modern Industry in Relation to the Family, Health, Education, Morality*
1915	U.S. Supreme Court upholds California's eight-hour law for women workers in *Miller v. Wilson*
	NCL publishes *What Women Might Do with the Ballot: The Abolition of Child Labor*
1916	Congress passes the Keating-Owen Child Labor Act
	NCL publishes *The Eight Hours Day for Working Women*
1917	U.S. Supreme Court upholds Oregon ten-hour working day for men in *Bunting v. Oregon*
	U.S. Supreme Court affirms Oregon's minimum wage law for women workers in *Stettler v. O'Hara*
	FK and NCL work with NWTUL on eight-hour laws for women; help submit bills to eleven state legislatures

1918	U.S. Supreme Court invalidates Keating-Owen Child Labor Act in *Hammer v. Dagenhart*
1919	Children's Bureau adopts minimum standards of child welfare that include minimum age of sixteen for employment in most occupations, eight-hour day, 44-hour week, compulsory education until age sixteen, and employment certificates
	Congress passes the Child Labor Tax Law
1920	NCL announces its second ten-year program, which focuses on the eight-hour day, elimination of night work for women, minimum wage commissions, publicity about industrial poisons, and pure food
	Congress approves creation of Women's Bureau as part of U.S. Department of Labor
	Nineteenth Amendment, extending suffrage to women, ratified
1921	Congress passes Sheppard-Towner Maternity and Infancy Act
	National Women's Party proposes Equal Rights Amendment
	NCL personnel and Felix Frankfurter prepare brief for *Adkins* case in lower court
1922	NCL begins its support of the Dyer Anti-Lynching bill
	In *Bailey v. Drexel Furniture Co.*, U.S. Supreme Court invalidates the 1919 Child Labor Tax Law
	NCL publishes *Twenty Questions about the Federal Amendment Proposed by the National Woman's Party*
1923	U.S. Supreme Court overturns decision of D.C. lower court in *Adkins v. Children's Hospital,* invalidating minimum wage in District of Columbia
	NCL publishes *Progress of Labor Legislation for Women*
1924	Congress passes child labor amendment to the U.S. Constitution; it goes to states for ratification
	Massachusetts court declares its minimum wage law constitutional
	NCL publishes *State Minimum Wage Laws in Practice*
	Spider web chart published in *Dearborn Independent*
1924–1925	Only five states ratify the child labor amendment
1925	NCL begins campaign against poisoning of workers in radium dial-painting industry
	FK edits and publishes *The Supreme Court and Minimum Wage Legislation*
1926	NCL publishes *Children's Compensation for Industrial Accidents*
	FK and other women reformers attacked in *Woman Patriot;* attack on FK read into *Congressional Record*
1927	NAM issues employment standards that allow employers to hire children at age fourteen; NCLC supports the NAM program
	FK denounces NAM program in *Survey*

1929	NCL publishes first Candy White List as strategy to promote minimum wage
	FK works with NAACP to protest discrimination in federal funding for education
	Sheppard-Towner funding ends
1931	WJCC defeats President Hoover's plan to dismantle the Children's Bureau
	Following strikes of women workers in southern textile areas, FK successfully pressures the Cotton Textile Institute to institute policies prohibiting night work for women and girls
1938	Fair Labor Standards Act prohibits child labor in most industries, sets a national minimum wage for women and men; sets a 40-hour work week; and mandates time and a half for overtime

Florence Kelley, 1880. Courtesy of Florence Kelley Papers, Rare Books and Manuscripts Division, New York Public Library, Astor, Lenox and Tilden Foundations.

1 1869 – 1891

"The Wrong to the Working People"

INTRODUCTION

Florence Kelley's childhood and early adulthood letters depict her unusual family background, her close friendships with a few women, and the relationships she cultivated with powerful men. Her storybook childhood included the Olympian example of her politically powerful father and the women activists in her mother's Unitarian-Quaker family. A trip to Los Angeles in 1872 taught her about the vast scale of the nation when the frontier was still a reality and Custer's last stand had not yet occurred.

The impact of her father's example would be hard to exaggerate. Her sickly childhood kept her at home, so William Darrah Kelley taught her to read and she educated herself in his library. She began to correspond with him when she was ten. On the eve of her departure for college and later at college, she wrote him about her interest in public affairs. Although her mother, Caroline Bonsall Kelley, provided a more long-lived parental tie, her relationship with her father was more intense—and more problematic.

A founding member of the Republican Party who represented a working-class district in the U.S. House of Representatives for thirty years before his death in 1890, William Kelley passionately urged that Congress act against the terrorism that sought to restore white supremacy after the Civil War: "A government that cannot protect the humblest man within its limits, that cannot snatch from oppression the feeblest woman or child, is not a government. . . . Will [congressmen] never learn that the object of government is not to protect the strong, who can care for themselves, but to protect the weak, the ignorant, and those who are degraded because they have been made to suffer in the past?"[1] Through such speeches William Kelley earned a reputation for eloquent language and independent thought.

Yet soon after Florence's thirteenth birthday, her father's reputation suffered when he became involved in the Crédit Mobilier scandal. He and other congressmen had accepted payments from the fiscal agent of the Union Pacific Railroad in exchange for agreeing to halt investigations of the railroad's colossal profits from the use and sale of public lands. Although William Kelley avoided official censure and his daughter's adolescent letters did not comment on the scandal, it almost certainly informed her 1885 view of her father as a member of the "privileged class" and her critique of the "Capitalist system."[2]

In the 1870s, William Kelley supported industrialization in the North and West by promoting high tariffs that protected American labor and capital from foreign competition. But his political power diminished in the 1880s when he lost faith in that cross-class strategy, broke with his party's alliance with business and the gold standard, and championed a pro-labor greenback fiscal policy.[3] His legacy to his daughter at his death in 1890 was a vision of high national purpose, loyalty to his working-class constituency, and a dogged capacity for independent action.

Florence Kelley viewed her studies at Cornell as preparation for a political career; an 1878 letter to her father described her work as appropriate for "future editors statesmen and lawyers."[4] She lived with her father in the District of Columbia while working on her senior thesis at the Library of Congress. After graduation she co-founded in Philadelphia the New Century Working Women's Guild, which encouraged self-supporting women to come together "for mutual help, enjoyment, and encouragement in high endeavour." There she taught history courses and developed a vanguard library in social science. Drawing on her experience with women wage earners at the Guild, her article "Need Our Working Women Despair?" championed protective legislation as the cure for women's oppression in industry.[5] Transformative as the school might have been for the 500 women who enrolled in its courses, Kelley wanted more for herself, and when the University of Pennsylvania declined to admit her to graduate study in 1884, she traveled to study government and law at the University of Zurich.[6]

Accompanied by her mother and younger brother, she joined a lively community of Americans studying abroad in Zurich. Her distraught response to the death of her college friend, Margaret Hicks, suggested deep currents of discontent beneath her otherwise calm exterior. "I cannot conceive of my life without her," she wrote William Kelley. But finding consolation in her studies in political economy, she befriended a group of Russian socialist émigrés in whose company she began to attend political meetings led by exiled German socialists.[7] The idealism of those meetings reminded her of Quaker meetings she had known in Philadelphia. By May 1884 she was beginning to find her own political voice—one informed by the perspective of German socialism. That year she joined the German Social Democratic Party, a membership she retained through much of her life.[8]

Lazare Wischnewetzky, a Jewish Russian who shared her interest in political economy, probably accompanied her to socialist meetings that winter. A medical student from Taganrog, Russia, a Black Sea seaport 400 miles east of Odessa, he began to court her in January 1884 with an enthusiasm that verged on harassment. In October she shocked friends and family in Zurich and Philadelphia by marrying Wischnewetzky.[9] Their three children were born in the next three years.

The marriage embodied Kelley's profound discontent with the limited opportunities available to her in the United States, which she expressed in letters to May Lewis, a friend from her days with the New Century Working Women's Guild. Those letters also show how her relationship with Lazare accelerated her involvement with European socialism and sharpened her view of herself as a scholar of political economy. Having brushed aside an invitation by Susan B. Anthony to dedicate herself to the woman suffrage movement, she focused on women and child workers, an interest she had developed earlier under her father's tutelage. And, prompted by her contact with German socialists in exile in Zurich, she began to translate the writings of Frederick Engels.[10]

Florence Kelley Wischnewetzky's translation of Engels's *The Condition of the Working Class in England in 1844* became her most important intellectual achievement during her years abroad. Completed during her first pregnancy, hers was the first English translation of that classic work and remains the English version that scholars still prefer.[11] Engels, as a manager of his father's textile factory in Manchester, wrote authoritatively about how owners and investors derived wealth from the process by which wage earners and machines turned raw materials into commercial products. His path-breaking book drew on parliamentary reports, accounts of agitation for the Ten-Hour Bill in the 1830s, and evidence of the need for further factory regulations—sources and goals familiar to Kelley from her research on her Cornell honors thesis and her father's political milieu.[12]

Kelley's translation work drew her into the intellectual workshop of German socialism. Her correspondence with Engels shows that she defended her place there despite prejudice against her gender, youth, and elite origins. Her Philadelphia friend, Rachel Foster, corresponding secretary of the National Woman Suffrage Association and Susan B. Anthony's chief financial backer, financed the publication and distribution of her translation.[13] Anticipating her return to the United States, she wanted to make "the best of our literature" available to American workers, believing those writings could help workers understand "the source and meaning of the evils that beset them" and direct their energy toward effective solutions rather than random violence. She deplored "the sad want of a scientific literature" and offered to translate other socialist works and arrange for them to be published. And she roundly denounced competitors of socialism among compromised trade union leaders, utopian socialists, college professors, and political leaders. After her return to the United States in 1886, she oversaw the distribution of *The Condition.* Yet Engels's tone in letters to her was abrupt and condescending.[14]

Florence and Lazare arrived in New York City with their son Nicholas a few months before the November 1886 birth of their second child, Margaret, named after Margaret Hicks. Upon their return, Florence ended a year-long hiatus in her communication with her parents, but rather than ask them to finance the creation of her new household, she borrowed $700 from Helen Campbell, a successful reform-minded author whom she had met at the New Century Working Women's Guild.[15] The Wischnewetzkys' social life revolved around Katharine and Friedrich Sorge, who had emigrated from Germany in 1852 and lived in Hoboken, representing the Marxist remnant of the First International.[16] A generation older than Florence and Lazare, the Sorges became their surrogate parents and served as godparents at the christening of their third child, John, born in January 1888.

During her five-year residence in New York City, FK failed to find a home for her political views. She buoyantly believed that her translation of Karl Marx's pamphlet, *Free Trade,* would banish working-class support for her father's tariff policies, not because Marx advocated free trade but because he demonstrated the unimportance of the tariff issue compared to the exploitation of workers and the extraction of surplus value from their labor.[17] Yet when *Free Trade* was published with an introduction by Engels in the fall of 1888, the pamphlet was ignored by those she had hoped to convert, even within the Socialist Labor Party.

FK and Lazare had joined that German-speaking party soon after their arrival in New York City, but bitter clashes with party officials led to their expulsion in April 1887.[18] Engels's prefaces to her translations harshly criticized the party's ethnic isolation and its lack of contact with the American trade union movement. Party leaders responded by boycotting her translations. By the spring of 1888 she had begun her own study of child labor, drawing on American sources, as she wrote Engels, from "statistics of State Bureaus, State Board of Education reports, census, Factory Inspectors' Reports, etc."[19] A year later she completed a hard-hitting attack on the capitalist exploitation of child labor, published as a pamphlet by the Woman's Temperance Publication Association.[20] Meanwhile, Lazare's medical practice languished, and her last letter to her dying father appealed for financial support.

FK's turn to American issues and source materials drew her into correspondence with Richard T. Ely in 1890. Although she had earlier denounced Ely as a "false prophet," in 1888 she attended the annual meeting in Philadelphia of his new organization, the American Economic Association, where she met him and his wife.[21] Founded to advocate positive government as an antidote to the power of great corporations, the American Economic Association welcomed Christian socialists and women to its ranks. Ely went further and asked FK to comment on his current work. Writing from her precarious perspective as an American representative of Marxian socialism, her tone was nevertheless comfortable and congenial. In her correspondence with Ely, she finally returned to America.

Whatever progress Florence and Lazare had made toward establishing a home in New York City was shattered early in 1891 when he began beating her. She later testified that he struck her "in the face so as to disfigure her and cause her confinement to her room for two or three weeks." At the end of that year, when he "spat in her face" and walked out the door, she borrowed money from an English governess she had met in a local park and with six-year-old Nicholas, five-year-old Margaret, and three-year-old John boarded a train to Chicago.[22]

NOTES

1. WDK, *The Enforcement of the Fourteenth Amendment Essential to the Prosperity of the South,* 339–340.
2. See Letter 9, FK to Mary Thorne Lewis, 19 March 1885, below.
3. Sklar, *Florence Kelley and the Nation's Work,* 43.
4. See Letter 5, FK to WDK, 2 December 1878, below.
5. Sklar, *Florence Kelley and the Nation's Work,* 75.
6. Sklar, *Florence Kelley and the Nation's Work,* 82–86.
7. Sklar, *Florence Kelley and the Nation's Work,* 83–84; see Letter 6, FK to WDK, 2 January 1884, below.
8. Sklar, *Florence Kelley and the Nation's Work,* 87. The party adopted its present name, Social Democratic Party, in 1891. When Kelley joined, it was called the German Socialist Workers' Party (Sozialistische Arbeitspartei Deutschlands). Because antisocialist laws banned the party in Germany until 1890, Zurich became one of its headquarters in exile.
9. Sklar, *Florence Kelley and the Nation's Work,* 93–94.
10. On the diverse spellings of Engels's first name, see Sklar, *Florence Kelley and the Nation's Work,* 350.
11. Engels's book was originally published in German in 1845 as *Die Lage der arbeitenden Klasse in England, Nach eigener Anschauung und authentischen Quellen* (*The Condition of the Working Class in England, from Personal Observation and Authentic Sources*). For more on FK's translation and her relationship with Engels, see Sklar, *Florence Kelley and the Nation's Work,* 100–139.
12. Sklar, *Florence Kelley and the Nation's Work,* 101–105. Engels's book was foundational to Karl Marx's analysis of capitalism in *Das Kapital,* which was published in German in the 1850s but in 1885 was not yet available in English. From Engels's volume Marx developed his analysis of the relationship between capitalist development and working-class formation: the mechanization of production would create a proletariat, which would inevitably produce revolution as workers came together to live and work in larger groups while capitalists remained captive to their own needs.
13. Sklar, *Florence Kelley and the Nation's Work,* 118–119, 129.
14. See Letter 12, FK to Engels, 9 June 1886, below.
15. Sklar, *Florence Kelley and the Nation's Work,* 122.
16. See Letter 16, FK to Frederick Engels, 29 March 1888, below; and Sklar, *Florence Kelley and the Nation's Work,* 122–123.
17. See Letter 15, FK to Engels, 29 December 1887, below.
18. See Letter 16, FK to Engels, 29 March 1888, below; and Sklar, *Florence Kelley and the Nation's Work,* 129.
19. See Letter 16, FK to Engels, 29 March 1888.
20. FK, *Our Toiling Children* (Chicago: Woman's Temperance Publication Association, 1889). See Sklar, *Florence Kelley and the Nation's Work,* 151.
21. See Letter 9, FK to May Thorne Lewis, 19 March 1885; and Sklar, *Florence Kelley and the Nation's Work,* 88, 367.
22. Sklar, *Florence Kelley and the Nation's Work,* 167–168, 181.

1. To William Darrah Kelley

Germantown [Pennsylvania]
Jan. 12-69

Dear Papa

I am a great deal better and come downstairs to all my meals and Grandma says I like mutton-chops and every thing else that is good.[1]
Mama brought little Anna out in all the storm they came out in the twelve oclock and stayed till six.[2] Will came over to see me on saturday he came in the nine train and went in at eleven. I was out a good deal in the fine weather and hope to be in town on sunday to meet you. good bye Dear Papa

Your loving child
Florie

ALS, FKP, NN

1. Elizabeth Kay Pugh (d. 1894) and her husband Isaac Pugh (1799–ca. 1884), a wallpaper manufacturer, adopted FK's mother, Caroline Bonsall, in 1838 at the age of nine, when her father died. FK recalled spending much time at "their peaceful home in Germantown" (FK, *Notes of Sixty Years*, 35–36).
2. "Little Anna" was FK's sister, Anna Caroline Kelley (1865–1871).

2. To Elizabeth Kay Pugh and Isaac Pugh

Pico House, Los Angeles
Aug. 7/72

Dear Grandpa and Grandma

I received Grandma's letter on Monday morning about one hour before starting and was equally surprised and delighgted at the news it contained.[1] Seventy one dollars would indeed be a great assistance in my undertaking.

You spoke of the sum being made up to one hundred dollars. I thank you more than I can tell you, for the help that you have already given me and for your kind intentions, but I think that Mama would rather that nothing should be said among our friends about the project. She seems sensitive about having the subject made public. I thank dear Grandpa a thousand times for his kind offer to add four dollars to the English money, but I would much rather that, unless it is perfectly convenient, he would not trouble his mind about it, when you have so many uses for money.[2]

We left San Francisco on Monday morning by steamer 'Pacific,' for this place, and arrived here at about two o'clock to-day. We had not a very pleasant voyage because Mama and Mary were both so sick as scarcely to be able to raise their heads, until this morning, and Will was sick till yesterday noon.[3] Papa, Bertie, and I, were the well ones of the party, which was fortunate for if either one of us had been sick the other two would have fared badly.

We are beautifully situated here. Mama and I have a large, light, well ventilated bedroom with a beautiful parlor attached. The furniture is the most handsome that I have ever seen in a hotel.

We are very much pleased, on the whole.

Papa was taken possession of immediately upon our arrival, and has gone riding already without even waiting for dinner. He is not so well as he was among the mountains and we are anxious to get him back to Laramie.

Papa thinks that this travelling will be worth very nearly a whole years school to me, and I am very nearly of his opinion, although it robs me of the pleasant fall I had hoped to spend at the dear old place with you.[4] To-day is a great day with the Chinese. They are holding various solemn ceremonies for the repose of the dead. While at dinner we saw several of their Priests in scarlet robes, holding banners of scarlet cloth, fringed with orange and white cord.

Last Sunday we went to a mission school for the Chinese boys, and were very much interested in them. One of them played the melodeon, while the others sang. Some of them spoke quite good English and read and wrote well. One of the Teachers gave Mama a letter signed "Dear Chen," which was well worded and written, and which you shall see as soon as we get home.

Mama and Mary recovered as soon as we landed, so we are all quite well now.

With much love from all, to all, and to yourselves in particular, I remain

Your affectionate granddaughter,
Florrie

ALS, FKP, NN

1. FK was traveling through the western United States with her family. They had already visited Denver, Salt Lake City, and Laramie (FK, "My Philadelphia," 57; see also Sklar, *Florence Kelley and the Nation's Work,* 43–44).
2. Although no record remains of the content of FK's "project," her fund-raising skills seem to have been well developed at the age of twelve.
3. Mary was most likely a caretaker for FK's brother Albert, then two years old.
4. Although FK had little formal schooling, she had attended "a delightful little school in Germantown" (FK, *Notes of Sixty Years,* 40).

3. To William Darrah Kelley

Germantown [Pennsylvania]
July 27/76

My Dear Father

How can I thank you for your valuable gift! I think it will just fill a vacancy which I have begun to feel in this exposition.[1] If I ask an exhibitor a question about anything, except the jewelry in the Italian dept, he usually stares surprisedly at me, as though wondering what a girl of sixteen can possibly want to know, and answers in monosyllables with a bored air, or, which is still more discouraging, treats me as a Russian exhibitor did; saying to me "I know nothing whatever about the subject" and then turning to an old gentleman near by volunteered a quantity of information on the very topic about which I had asked him, doing it in a way which made it impossible for me to stay and get the benefit of his explanations. Now a great many of the objects about which I want to learn something, were exhibited at Vienna and will therefore be mentioned in this report, so that I can gain from it what information I want.

Have you heard anything of preparations making in France for an exposition in 1878?[2] There is a good deal said about it here, but I have not heard that it will be international.

What a country Russia must be! True, I do not know very much about its commercial importance, (except that like our own country it exports wheat) but it seems to me that internal improvement is written everywhere in its exhibit. How I wish we could study together in this great American kindergarden for children of a little larger growth! for I think there must be things here which will surprise you in spite of your knowledge of the relative industrial importance of the different countries.

By the way Papa, one thing has set me wondering a good deal. What reason do you suppose there is for the fact that our American porcelain china and pottery are inferior not only in texture but still more in design. With our ideas of English clumsiness it is disagreeable to find their designs beautifully delicate

William Darrah Kelley, ca. 1860. Courtesy of Kelley Family Papers, Rare Book and Manuscript Library, Columbia University.

and ours coarse and badly colored. But enough of those things. The family is flourishing, but Bertie is so thin that his bones almost come through. Will wrote yesterday and Mamma is writing today, so I need not enclose messages from them.

I'm very busy, studying for my fall reexamination and must close, hoping that your cold may soon be cured and that you will believe me as ever your loving daughter[3]

Florrie

Hon. W. D. Kelley

ALS, FKP, NN

1. WDK had sent FK a printed guide to the 1873 Vienna Exposition (Sklar, *Florence Kelley and the Nation's Work,* 49). The Centennial Fair in Philadelphia (10 May–10 November 1876) celebrated the 100th anniversary of the signing of the Declaration of Independence.
2. France held its third world's fair, the Exposition Universelle, in Paris in 1878.
3. FK was studying for exams for admission to Cornell (FK, *Notes of Sixty Years,* 45–46; Sklar, *Florence Kelley and the Nation's Work,* 48–49). She did well; WDK congratulated FK on "your success at the examination of which I never entertained a doubt. Your position at the university will be a proud one and if health and strength be given you you will maintain it to the end" (WDK, Washington, D.C., to FK, 22 June 1876, WDK Correspondence, PHi).

4. To Caroline Bonsall Kelley

Ithaca [New York]
Sept. 29/1876

My Dear Mother,

Give me a good long credit mark!! I resisted the temptation to go to a German[1] last night—the first of a series of Gymnasium germans to be given on Saturday evenings,—the boys paying for the music one week, we the next. Of course, they will be great fun and it is considered a little peculiar not to take any part in them. They are the least objectionable things of the kind imaginable. Mrs. Kinney chaperones the girls and the dancing begins at 6.15 and the lights are out and even the most determined late-stayer is gone by ten o'clock. Still with twenty two hours of University work there is very little time left even on Saturday evening which I can afford to spend on anything but Latin and I should not feel justified (even by the training in small talk) in hurting my eyes by subjecting them to the lights of the gymnasium or in risking cold by running heated from the Gymnasium to the main hall along the piazza.

Also another credit mark, for, when the first of the month comes and with it the fresh installment of allowance, I shall have clear accounts showing myself out of debt (except to you most lenient creditor!) and able to use my money for legitimate purposes. I cannot tell you how proud I feel to have kept out of debt this first term.

Caroline Bonsall Kelley, ca. 1860. Courtesy of the Florence Kelley Papers, Rare Books and Manuscripts Division, New York Public Library, Astor, Lenox and Tilden Foundations.

Now there is one confession which I must make which will disgust you I'm afraid, namely that after all my previous preparation in German I got only a creditable examination the other day. My shame, rage, and disgust ever since have been too great to be borne. However there are several weeks yet before the end of the term in which to make up, and I may possibly still get into the honor section. All those students who pass examinations more finely than is required to receive an honorable mark, form a class, choose their own professor, and their own books for the next term and, being relieved of the burden of the stupids, make much greater headway than under other circumstances they could do. Out of the hundred and fifty German scholars usually about twelve form this class, so you see it's rather ambitious on my part to attempt to work for it, and my only encouragement lies in the fact that Louisa attained it last year.

Again, Mother darling, you failed to mention your health and I think you cannot know ~~how~~ with what interest I watch in each letter for some tidings of improvement. About my books, I think you will find some or all of them in the following places. viz; the bureau in the room back of Berties the bookcase in the little room in front of the dining room; in a box back of the piano or in the wardrobe of Papa's room. Will you please keep a carefully open eye for the examination papers lent me by C.W.A. and N.A.R.?[2] I never was more uncomfortable about a small thing in my life than about those. My only hope is that you may in looking for other things through the boxes at Sarah's come across them. You cannot realize with what eagerness I look forward to Xmas. With reference to clothes as well as everything else. It is the custom for the girls who live any where near here to go home about this time and get their outfits somewhat freshened up, a process of which I'm rather in need inasmuch as going out in all weathers and writing a great deal as well as studying with one's arms on the table, a bad habit of mine which I think you may remember from the Miss Longstreth days are not calculated to benefit clothing.[3] Still by means of that pretty black dress I can get along nicely through this term. As green will be the color through the winter, perhaps I can match my green silk and so use the skirt and overskirt now utterly useless, as the foundation of a cloth and silk suit. I don't remember the cloth at Sharplesses unless it was some to make an overskirt for my rough grey plaid suit. But my impression was that that came from Haffleigh's. I am exceedingly sorry that Papa is overworking so for many reasons. I'm afraid too that he is likely to have a very hard winter.[4]

You don't know how I rejoice in the thought of going home to the Pinckney House at Xmas, as well as in the thought that you're settled for the winter in such pleasant quaters. I like my room more and more; and, when I get rocking chairs, table cover, pincushion, window curtains, books, pictures, and bookshelves (as I probably shall, about graduating time) I shall consider myself quite satisfactorily placed. I'm already making a list of things to bring back with me at Xmas and think I shall need your Saratoga trunk as well as Wills and mine to contain all my possessions. This letter is wretchedly full of myself, but really nothing happens which I can relate in such a way as to give you the least interest and yet when I have a little leisure I can't resist the temptation to talk to you even if I've no better theme than myself and my doings. If I only could describe my Latin lessons to you!!!! They are alternately delightful, and mortifying beyond measure, because for one I have plenty of time to prepare for the next very little. One half of them I shall always remember with keen delight, the other half I wish to forget as soon as possible. If only Will could share them with me I should have nothing more to desire, for I think he would now really enjoy the exquisite beauty of "De Amicitia" and the quiet fun of Cicero's letters.[5]

How can he get time to leave the office two whole days? If we "cut" an hour, (as I haven't done yet) it is an offence to be atoned for, not to the authorities but to ~~your~~ our own selves when examination comes; and frequently the loss of two lectures will cause one to be conditioned at, least, so say those who having tried the experiment are certainly competent to judge. Professor Corson read Tennyson's Maud to us in the Botannical Lecture room on Friday evening and I think has rather made me admire it, a state of affairs which I had always supposed impossible, disliking Tennyson as I do. I read his Oenone, too, with a good deal of pleasure, in connection with the Ecologues of Virgil which are copied from the same verses of Theocritus, so I think I'm getting bravely over the orthodox Freshman hatred of Tennyson.[6]

Hoping that you can report progress towards good health next time and that everything may go well with Papa and the boys, I remain my dear Mother your affectionate

Florrie

ALS, KFP, NCC-RB

1. In the fall of 1876, FK lived in Sage College, a women's dormitory completed in 1875, ten years after the founding of Cornell University (Conable, *Women at Cornell*, 71–84). A "German" was a folk dance. For FK's education at Cornell, see FK, *Notes of Sixty Years*, 49–53; and Sklar, *Florence Kelley and the Nation's Work*, 50–63.

2. Charles W. Ames (1855–1921) was a Cornell friend (class of 1878); he later managed the West Publishing Co. in St. Paul, a publisher of law books. "N. A. R." probably referred to Nathaniel Archer Randolph (b. 1858), Cornell class of 1875 (Hewett, *Cornell University*, 4:72, 452).

3. When she was thirteen, FK attended a Quaker girls' school in Philadelphia for about six months run by Mary Anna Longstreth (Sklar, *Florence Kelley and the Nation's Work*, 30).

4. For William D. Kelley's congressional career, see Sklar, *Florence Kelley and the Nation's Work*, 35–43. In 1875, WDK broke with the Republican Party and supported the greenback-labor movement.

5. Cicero's *De Amicitia* (*On Friendship*) was written in 44 B.C.E. and his *Familiar Epistles* between 62 and 43 B.C.E.

6. Hiram Corson (1828–1911) was professor of English literature at Cornell. Alfred Tennyson published "Maud" in 1855 and "Oenone" in 1833. Virgil wrote his *Ecologues* from 42 to 37 B.C.E. Theocritus, a Greek poet, wrote around 270 B.C.E.

5. To William Darrah Kelley

Ithaca [New York]
Dec. 2nd 1878

My Dear Father,—

I should have written more promptly to acknowledge your letter and its enclosure,—but for the fact that every moment has been crowded to the utmost.

I thought of you all, on Thanksgiving day, wondering how you were spending it, and, when I received first Will's letter, then yours, then one from Grandma, all mentioning the dear boy's success,—I was seized with such a longing to go home and express my feelings that I could hardly bear seeing Charles [Ames] and Archer [Randolph] depart without me. However, a fortnight more will bring us all together again. I never looked forward so eagerly to a vacation.

You can hardly conceive of a life so uneventful as mine,—there is absolutely nothing in it of the excitement which penetrates even life in sleepy Philadelphia.

Perhaps you may be interested, however, in knowing that we students have formed a Social Science club which avows its intention of discussing "all live questions social, moral and political." I have the honor to be secretary thereof and there are three or four professors who come very regularly, and, once in a while, take part in the debate. Last time we had a very heated argument over Kearneyism in general and Kearney in particular; and you would have been very much pleased, I think, with the rational tone of the whole performance.[1]

I am heartily interested in my work this term. I have, as regular university work, eight lessons of an hour each with a Greek professor every week and to that I give my most careful study. Besides this, I have wonderfully fine lectures on Modern European History from President White who speaks admirably just so long as he confines himself to History which is properly his "last" and does not fly off into discussions of monetary questions.[2] He keeps very close to the line of his work which is the "Development of Rationalism in Europe."

Then, distributed through the week, there are lectures on Literature and lessons in Italian. On Monday evenings, Prof. Corson reads us Shakespeare;—and, on Saturday, four of us,—Misses Clements, Hicks, Mills, and Kelley—meet him in his library and he reads us Robert Browning's "Ring and the Book".[3] Then too, every fortnight we write an essay on English History. That is the most satisfactory work of my college course. The subjects for this term have been (1.) ["]The Political Institutions of the Saxons in Germany" (2.) The Effect of the Norman Conquest on Anglo Saxon Institutions" 3. "Magna Charta; Its Origin and Results". 4 "Growth of Parliament down to Henry VII" and "Suspension of Parliament under the Tudors." Next term we shall seven more essays concerning American Constitutional History down to 1860. Isn't that good work for future editors statesmen and lawyers? In reading for them we get a knowledge of the style and methods of all the best historians English and American.

I owe you an apology for boring you with all this account of myself and my avocations,—but it is hard to remember that what most interests me is not necessarily of exciting import to those I love.

Mr. Haight's account of Bertie delighted me greatly and added to my homesickness.[4]

Hoping to find you well as the end of a fortnight and thanking you for your great thoughtfulness for my comfort.

I am as ever simply
FMK[5]

ALS, FKP, NN

1. In 1877, Denis Kearney organized the Workingmen's Party of California, which targeted Chinese laborers and their employers. Kearney was imprisoned in 1877 and 1878, and in 1878 traveled to the East to solicit support for white California workingmen (Hart, "The Sand Lot and Kearneyism").
2. Andrew D. White (1832–1918), co-founder and president of Cornell University from 1865 to 1885, served as U.S. minister to Germany from 1879 to 1881.
3. These Cornell classmates are Gabrielle DeVaux Clements, B.S. 1880; Margaret Hicks, B.A. 1878; and Harriet May Mills, B.Lit. 1879. FK is listed as receiving a B.Lit. in 1882 (Hewett, *Cornell University* 4:155, 289, 395, 326). Robert Browning's *Ring and the Book* was published in 1868–1869.
4. Mr. Haight may have been a relative of FK's college friend, James Haight (see Letter 180, FK to James A. Haight, 19 May 1923, below).
5. This is one of the few occasions on which FK invoked her middle name, Molthrop.

6. To William Darrah Kelley

Zürich [Switzerland]
Jan. 2nd. 1883[1884]
9 P.M. Wednesday evening

My dear Father,

Your delightful letter came last night, and a sweet, cheery, affectionate one from Willy has just completed our enjoyment of the holidays. We are all well, now, and have had as lovely a Christmas week, I think, as any family in Zürich.[1] I promised to be truthful about our health; and, so, I assure you, on my conscience, that I do not remember a time in my life when Mother was so rigorously, cheerfully, muscularly well, as at present. She sleeps well, eats well, takes good care of the eyes, which only need rest, and takes tremendous walks without fatigue. Could you desire more? She enjoys every day! Bert is not growing so fast as through the summer, and has had a single brief return of his eruptive trouble. Otherwise, he also leaves nothing to be desired; is affectionate, gentle, seems to have conquered his temper once for all, after a couple of sharp battles with it in the early Fall; and has grown quite naturally into "taking care of his family" doing errands etc. Altogether he is a constant pleasure and a decided blessing. Conscience compels me to confess that the sad news from Karl threw me into a high fever which lasted one night, Dec. 18th, Tuesday, and alarmed good Dr. Heine a good deal.[2] The next morning, however, after a night of mustard plasters on my feet and ice on my head, I was free from fever and only weak. On Wed. Dec. 19th, I sat up; on Thurs., the 20th, I had a short drive and walk; on the 21st. a whole day in the sharp cold, air which completed the work of bracing me; so that, on Saturday, when there was a great Xmas ball in the pension, I was able to sit a two hours dinner through, to which we had invited the Byers family, and to watch the dancers an hour or two. The doctor dismissed me then, putting me on dyspeptics' diet, however, in the hope of permanently curing my lifelong dyspepsia. By way of making assurance doubly sure, she forbade my reading heavy books or writing for a fortnight (so mother wrote the Xmas letter for the Tribune,[3] bless her!); and that is the reason that you have not received this volume earlier. I am now, if possible, stronger than before my brief illness; for my dyspeptics' diet gives me such a sense of being well nourished as I do not remember ever having had. I am back at work in a pleasant leisurely way, reading and making notes, writing long German translations, and waiting impatiently for lectures to re-begin next week.

I think mother told you of my our homelike Christmas dinner at the Byers; of the three couples of children dancing by the light of the Xmas tree the next afternoon in our little salon; of our prowls about the town, through the week, watching the peasants in their holiday. But she cannot have told you of our happy New Year's day. Some of the people in the pension watched the New

Year in rather noisily, after the custom of the country, and kept us awake until the bells rang midnight. So we slept late on New Year's morning, and then were busy sorting the debris of the Christmas tree (which had just been successfully banished ~~from~~ (through the window!) when Mr. Wishnawitsky came to make his first call, on New Year's Morning. This is a charming Russian gentleman who has been very kind in bringing me books on the National Economy lectures that we both hear. He has access to a private library of rare books, and has taken a good deal of trouble for my benefit; but this was the first time that he had called. He was as well bred and friendly as usual, and spirited away all embarassment over the by no means ugly disorder of the salon; and went away leaving us the pleasant conviction that our first caller was one whose acquaintance we shall value increasingly as the year wears on. Mr. Wischnawitzky was scarcely gone when Mr. Byers came with Mr. Feérie an American whom we have met pleasantly several times. Mr. Byers had received a call from a gentleman whose name he could not remember, who had just come from America and had been present when you called upon Mr. Arthur and talked about Col. Shaw.[4] This episode gave me much pleasure and so did the sweet, friendly letter that came later from the Shaws, with New Year's cards and greetings. Later in the day, came Dr. Dibble a Michigan man whom we like; and good Herr Krüger the tutor with long, cordial, good wishes for the New Year and a bundle of brochures on the Labor Question, the only New Year's gift which his limited student-funds permitted; and what is a German New Year's call without a little gift? When Herr Krüger bowed his huge frame and brightly-colored beard out of our little salon, there came a stiff, silent youth from Wisconsin with Miss Dean, his betrothed, also a student, and the only one among the young women whose acquaintance I have felt moved to cultivate. This youth is one of the tedious men, from whose strong, cleanly cut, firm features, rectitude looks sternly forth upon a world which the youth's presence always seems to accuse of frivolity. But Miss Dean is so delightful that she makes up for her fiancée's want of social qualities; and the last call of the day was almost as nice as the first.

Today we went to a pleasant coffee-party at Frau Hauptmann Bloest's and met some nice German and Swiss people; and came home in high spirits to find Willy's welcome letter. The only things which have in anywise marred the pleasure of our simple Xmas amusements, were the fact that our dearest ones were not sharing them, (and this was palliated by the reflection that their occupations were, after all, as congenial to them as could be) and the thought of the mourning household in Cambridge. Margaret's death is not yet a reality to me. I cannot conceive of my life without her. But poor Karl's grief is deeply stamped upon my thoughts; and I keep myself very busy lest, through this medium, my own realization of my loss should come, at last. It will be time enough for that when I go home. And yet it is unreasonable to call Karl unhappy, for knowing my own year with Margaret, I believe that Karl is richer in possession of his memory of his youth of pure unselfish love for Margaret, and his single married year of absolute devotion to her in her long, painless weakness, than anyone in a thousand of the men who, after a youth spent as men ordinarily spend the years which he spent in Margaret's companionship, count themselves happily married.

I received, several days ago, a pleasant note from Herr Platter asking your address, and whether you read German, and mentioning, with pleasure "your Fathers literary works which he has kindly sent me, in which I find so many excellent thoughts that I feel urged to thank him heartily for his valuable gift."[5] I gave him the address, assured him that you could get his note translated and would value it. What would I not give to have such a man in an American university! Just, candid, thoughtful, earnest, learned, enthusiastic, I regret daily that his class is not made up of Americans; whereas, so far as I can see, Mr. Wischnawitsky and I are the only students upon whom his teaching takes a deep hold. However, it would not be labor lost if the Russian were the only one. And I mean to make this year's teaching tell in my later work—unless something which I cannot now foresee breaks up my plans again. However, after the supreme surprise of being able to carry out this beautiful plan it would be thankless to cherish any doubts about the remaining modest ones.

The speeches which you sent I read with fresh pride and pleasure in the light of my recent study. Then Mr. Cabot a young Harvard man who happened to see them, in calling, begged for one "Reasons for Abandoning Free Trade."[6] As he is of a stiff-necked generation and was not converted by the first one I shall lend him another when he comes back from Dresden after the holidays. He is a fine, upright, thoughtful, fellow, clear headed and possessed of strong convictions—worth the trouble of discussing things with. I can't tell you how I sympathize with you in the loss of your colleague. I remember the respect with which you always spoke of Mr. Haskell.[7] I trust that his death may not make your own burden of work dangerously heavy.

The authorities, here, have done me the honor to take me into consultation and beg me to write to you and to General Eaton concerning the abuse of ~~Dr.~~ Zürich medical degrees.[8] It seems that a number of persons have recently been discovered, who have forged degrees and are practicing in America with them. Others, who failed to pass the examination have taken false oaths, swearing to possession of the degree which had been refused them. They have used various pretexts for not producing the degrees. Three of these persons have written from New York City alone. The following are the names of two fraudulent practitioners who are published in the New York State Medical Register as Zürich-Doktors, whose names do not appear in the University register as having received the degree;———Seyde MacKrieyrxy 80 St. Marks Place New York City. (He claims to have made his degree in 1854); and E. B. Lyons 220 W. 24th Street New York City. (claims Zürich degree 1865) Others have written to the Beadle that they have been obliged to change name and occupation in apprehension of being prosecuted in consequence of his publication of the Statistics. They wrote in the hope of bribing him; but he stupidly did not preserve the first batches of letters. The university authorities are indignant that Zürich degrees are not properly investigated, and their integrity protected in America; and the American students are mortified and indignant at this further development of the futility of our state administrations. The authorities beg ~~that~~ the Bureau of education ~~will~~ to scatter copies of the Zürich statistics among the State Boards of Health or Registering Bureaus (or whatever other anomalous state bodies are charged with the duty of investigating the registry of physicians;), and ~~will~~ to call the attention of the state legislatures to the need of more stringent legislation. I know how busy you are and I hesitated to undertake to trouble you about a matter which does not properly come within your own domain; but I feel so grateful to the authorities here for their liberal bestowal of opportunities which my own state refuses me, that I could not bring my mind to refuse the only service which I shall probably ever be able to render the University of Zürich. Moreover, the question of collegiate degrees is one which lies near my heart as I have already proved to General Eaton; and I should be profoundly thankful if anything could be done to lead the State Administrations to assume the responsibility for all medical degrees. I won't write a homily on the subject, because I've done that already for the Tribune.[9]

I am waiting for Tribunes of Nov. 5th. and 12th. and December 13th. with which to finish my English series; when I shall promptly mail to you my little packet of material. It will be a crude little book; but if it can be published in very cheap form it may fall into hands in which it will not be less useful for its crudity. But I do not wish to publish it unless Mr. Houghton feels sure it will pay for itself.[10] I am glad Captain Lemon likes the idea.

Please thank Mr. Ripley for his pleasant letter; and, when he has copied the University-business portion of this one, please let him forward it to Grandmama unless you wish, for any reason, to keep it by you. I wish Mr. Lemon would make an editorial on the medical degree business. All the statistics that could be wanted to set all the state administrations on the track of reform, could not cost the Bureau thirty dollars!

I hope your holidays have been as happy as ours and that you and Willy are as well as you represent yourselves! With warmest love from us all,

Your ever loving daughter
Florence

ALS, KFP, NCC-RB

1. FK had traveled to the French Riviera in December 1882 to accompany and care for her brother WDK, Jr., who was stricken with temporary blindness. Thereafter she traveled in England with CBK and AK and enrolled in a graduate program at the University of Zurich, studying government (Sklar, *Florence Kelley and the Nation's Work*, 80–83).
2. FK's close friend at Cornell, Margaret Hicks Volkmann, had recently died. Margaret's husband, Arthur Ludwig Karl Volkmann (A.B. 1877 and B.Arch. 1878, Cornell), later headed a school in Brookline, Massachusetts (Hewett, *Cornell University*, 4:289, 565); see Letter 77, FK to NK, 29 August 1905, below.

3. In 1883–1885, FK wrote a series of letters to the *Washington National Tribune* and two leading suffrage periodicals, the *Woman's Tribune* and the *Woman's Journal* (Sklar, Schüler, and Strasser, *Social Justice Feminists,* 81–90). The *Tribune* letter referred to here is probably the one titled "The Light Fantastic and How It Is Tripped at the Balls of Zurich" (*Washington National Tribune,* 17 January 1884, 3).

4. FK probably was referring to Albert D. Shaw, U.S. consul at Manchester, whom WDK and FK visited in the summer of 1883 (FK, *Notes of Sixty Years,* 65).

5. Julius Platter (1844–1923), a professor of economics from Tyrol, taught three of the four courses FK took in her first year at the university (Sklar, *Florence Kelley and the Nation's Work,* 83). William D. Kelley's *Speeches, Addresses and Letters on Industrial and Financial Questions* (Philadelphia: Henry Carey Baird, 1872) conveyed his eloquent style as well as his political ideas.

6. This Harvard student could be either Edward Twistleton Cabot (d. 1893) or Henry Bromfield Cabot. WDK's speech was delivered in the House of Representatives on 1 May 1872 (42nd Cong., 2nd sess., *Cong. Rec.,* Appendix, 301–308).

7. Congressman Dudley C. Haskell (b. 1842, Republican, Kansas, 1877–1883) died on 16 December 1883.

8. Former brigadier general John C. W. Eaton (1829–1906) was U.S. commissioner of education from 1870 to 1886.

9. In her letter to the *Washington National Tribune* titled "Forged Diplomas: The Latest Scandal in Swiss Medical Circles" (21 February 1884, 4), FK declared, "Grave as is the importance of the assumption by the State of the work of guarding completely the integrity of medical degrees, this is yet only one of a wide range of functions which the central government administers in the older civilized countries; which the State governments in America must sooner or later administer."

10. FK probably referred to her *Washington National Tribune* articles, "A Novel Benefaction: Some Further Facts as to the Manchester Museum" (1 November 1883, 2), "Plans for the Poor: The Manchester Movement for Bettering the Condition of Working People" (15 November 1883, 6), and "England of To-Day: And Why It Is More Like Than Unlike America" (13 December 1883, 4). Henry O. Houghton (1823–1895) founded the publishing company Houghton Mifflin & Company in 1880.

7. To Susan B. Anthony[1]

Zürich, [Switzerland,] Jan. 21st 1884

Dear Miss Anthony,

It makes me glad and proud that you remembered me, and wish for the feeble help that I could give you in your noble work.

But when you ask me to "say the word that will stir my Father and the other Congressmen up to go to work for Woman's Emancipation," you ask a double impossibility. I can not speak the word which will stir my Father up to go to work for the Emancipation of Women, because he was already at that work before I was born, has continued at it in three fold wise throughout my life, and is as firm in his conviction, and as ready in his action now, as always.[2]

I think that my father's judicial decisions upon marriage questions before the war, his labor for enabling all American working people, whether men or women, to emancipate themselves, a labor which has extended throughout his whole Congressional life; and his recent vigorous effort to secure the opportunities of higher education for Women in Pennsylvania, would prove that he needs no word of mine to urge him forward, even if he had not been steadily proving this truth for many years, by presenting every suffrage resolution which has come up from the suffrage societies of Pennsylvania.

Unhappily, my Father stands far in advance of his constituency upon this question. Neither the men nor the women of Pennsylvania support him to any helpful extent in carrying forward liberal measures for the Emancipation of Women.

In the second place, I am far from able to write eloquently. I wish profoundly for the franchise for every woman in America. I am humiliated that my country does not confer upon me a responsibility to which I feel myself adequate, just as I am mortified that the Universities of America are closed to me.[3] But I cannot write eloquently about it.

When my student life is over, I shall give myself to work for the best interests of the working women of America, as my Father has given himself to work for the best interests of the country, as far as he has seen his way clearly. Meanwhile, I am only a student, not yet a teacher.

I wish I could be in America for the Convention;[4] but otherwise, I am thankful to be here in Zürich, accepting from this little Swiss canton, instruction which the University of my own state, would on principle refuse me, if, in practice, it had such instruction to bestow.

With an earnest hope that the Convention may be rich in that eloquence to which I cannot contribute, I am now and always with profound respect,

Sincerely Yours,
Florence Kelley

Miss Susan B. Anthony

ALS, FKP, NN

1. FK had met women's rights leader Susan B. Anthony (1820–1906) in 1882 when Anthony visited WDK in London. See FK, *Notes of Sixty Years,* 62.
2. For WDK's work for woman suffrage, see FK, *Notes of Sixty Years,* 61–62; and Sklar, *Florence Kelley and the Nation's Work,* 46–47.
3. FK unsuccessfully sought admission to the University of Pennsylvania after she graduated from Cornell in 1882 (Sklar, *Florence Kelley and the Nation's Work,* 66–67).
4. The annual convention of the National Woman's Suffrage Association took place on 4–7 March 1884 in Washington, D.C.

8. To William Darrah Kelley[1]

[Zurich, Switzerland, ca. May 1884]

I could wish for a more vigorous handling of the eight-hour law, which seems to me almost as valuable a measure as the tariff itself.[2] As I look at our American working people from this distance, it seems to me that before the war their interest harmonized more or less with that of the American capitalist in general. The whole country—working classes pre-eminently—needed the industrial development of our resources, the development of capital in general.

Then came a time when, in the struggle against slave labor, Northern capital and Northern labor stood, perforce, side by side against the South and the slave, in identity of interest; against the foreign capitalist and the foreign pauper, and to a rapidly diminishing extent this remains to-day. But how rapidly this identity is melting out of sight and existence under the influence of internal conflict I think I see better from this distance than I should if I were in the midst of it. It is not only pauper labor in Europe, but the labor of women and children and imported contract laborers and ever-improving man-superseding machinery in America that the American workingman must ever more and more compete with, as our industry develops home competition under a fostering tariff. And the same policy which shields him against European capital and European pauper competition to-day must do what it can to support his manhood for his growing struggle with American capital and American pauperism, if it is to be true to itself as a workingmen's policy, and not, as the free-traders claim, work more in the interest of the American capitalist than the American laborer. And the eight-hour law seems to me, from this point of view, not a possibility of the future, but a need of to-day.[3]

PL, 48th Cong., 1st sess., *Cong. Rec.*, 3 June 1884, 4774

1. On 3 June 1884, in the course of a debate in the House on a bill to prevent foreign corporations from unlawfully occupying public lands, WDK read into the *Congressional Record* part of a letter, now unrecovered, from FK, whom he described as a "young but profound student of political science." WDK argued that immigrant laborers, who would work for lower wages and thus displace American workers, should be denied entry into the United States. He also argued that the federal government should set aside public lands for the benefit of working men (48th Cong., 1st sess., *Cong. Rec.*, 3 June 1884, 4768–4769, 4774).

2. During his congressional career WDK championed tariffs as a means of achieving higher wages for American workingmen. He also supported the movement for shorter hours (48th Cong., 1st sess., *Cong. Rec.*, 3 June 1884, 4774). The first eight-hour law in the United States was passed by the federal government in 1868, covering federal employees who were laborers, workmen, and mechanics. For more on FK and the movement for shorter hours, see Sklar, "'The Greater Part of the Petitioners Are Female.'"

3. WDK had praised the British government for enacting legislation prohibiting women from working in coal mines and any child under fourteen "who has not passed the fifth standard in a public school" from working "in any shop or factory" (48th Cong., 1st sess., *Cong. Rec.*, 19 June 1884, 5355; see also Sklar, *Florence Kelley and the Nation's Work*, 89).

9. To Mary Thorne Lewis[1]

Heidelberg Germany
March 19th. 1885

My dear May;

Thank you very much for your good letter, compact and sweet, like a large nut. Times change! Three years ago the club would not let me talk suffrage; and now, to escape the labor question, it takes refuge behind the ballot![2] However, that is a very good and wholesome place for it to be in, and I am glad to have been instrumental in getting it there even for one afternoon! It is very good of you to take so much trouble about my essay. I am delighted to have it read before the Political Science club (or any other); and have sent a line to Mr. Curtis asking him to forward it to the Woman's Journal if Harper will [have] none of it, as will doubtless be the case. After all, the Popular Science Monthly might have taken it![3] If by chance, you have not sent it to Mr. C. on receiving this, will you kindly try the P.S.M. first?

If it bores you to have me ride my hobby, say so as Grace Soper and Charles Ames have done, and I'll dismount without being offended.[4] Meanwhile, I'll take the questions and suggestions of your present letter seriatim. I have the more pleasure in doing so because I advanced them all, in pretty much the same order, in a correspondence with Lazare, just a year ago, to make it clear to him (I being in Italy and he in Zürich for the vacation) that to stay in Europe and work at and for Socialism was utterly preposterous and out of the question and that I could not possibly think of marrying him.[5]

I admit that my view is one sided; but then yours is other-sided—the national American view, limited by the absence of the German literature, and the excessive poverty of the Anglo-American literature, which contains but two works upon the subject, Hyndman's Historical Basis of Socialism in England; and Gronlund's Cooperative Commonwealth, neither of which is brilliant, profound, or strictly scientific, though both are worth reading in the absence of better things.[6]

Next as to the democratic government making different remedies necessary. Switzerland is in two aspects a more advanced form of democratic government than ours. It has outgrown the Presidential stage and simply has its executive head elected by the two houses of the Federal Government, so getting rid of our fourth years' meaningless turmoil; and second it has a great deal of its legislation submitted to popular vote as our state-constitution-amendments are submitted. Now I have lived a year in the town which is regarded as the brain of Switzerland, following the political and social movements of town, canton, and Federation with the closest observation; and I am perfectly convinced that the purer the democracy, the more highly developed the political form of any [given?] country,—the more speedy the development of capital and of the enslavement of labor, and the more inevitable the break up of the capitalist form of production and of society. Nowhere is legislation more at the mercy of the rich than in the little republic, and nowhere is the conviction of the more thoughtful working men firmer, that only through their united political action can they save their class from total deterioration. Acting upon this belief they have carried a maximal working-day-law; an employers'-liabilities-law; a compulsory school law, a factories inspection law for the whole country; and cantonal hailstorms insurance, home insurance, phylloxera insurance[7] for several cantons, and township free kindergartens in untold townships. But only by enormous exertion for the propagation of socialist teachings can they rouse enough working men and peasants to vote for such self-defensive measures. Ordinary, non-socialized workers let themselves be hoodwinked by Free-Trade and Protection professional politicians just as our own native workingmen do.

Now so far as I can see, every one of these measures (except phylloxera and hail insurance) is just as necessary in Phila. as in Zürich and can be attained in the same way and in no other—viz by the socialized workingmen uniting to force the law giving bodies.

You say "Here, we are free to believe in and labor for the perfectability of human nature." I thought so to, and tried it. I wrote a book (<u>this strictly between ourselves</u>) and Houghton Mifflin and Co. undertook to publish it, offering me most flattering terms. They delayed work nearly a year (to bring it out before the election, as I learned later) and I outgrew it meanwhile. It was a collection of letters about the English working people. I found that it could be used for advocating Mr. Blaine and Protection and I believe in neither.[8] I therefore wrote a final letter making clear the impossibility of any <u>thorough</u> improvement in the condition of the English people under our present system, and the points of resemblance between our own workers' condition and theirs. I offered to pay the cost of the addition out of the profits if the book should be successful, out of my pockets if it should be a failure, or to pay the whole cost of the wasted work if H. M. Co. preferred to suppress the whole rather than print this chapter. They suppressed the whole and I paid the costs. So much for the American freedom of speech! My Father wanted the book for campaign purposes and has made my suppression of it—in spite of my elaborate explanations that I could not publish what I no longer believe—the cause of profound unhappiness for four months past. And finally, the whole American and Americo-European scandal-press has published a rumor that Lazare forbade me to publish the poor little worthless book for fear of the Russian authorities (!) whence we became unhappy and I had left him to return to my family![9] I do not find myself free to work for the perfectability of human nature if this [<u>illegible word crossed out</u>] differing from my publisher and my father and refusing to publish my motives in the daily press.

As to a workingmens' party. The workingman may become a capitalist—once in ten thousand cases—if he ceases to be a working man. My father would never have become a member of Congress if he had stuck to his printing or his diamond setting; but he abandoned his craft and became a lawyer i.e. entered the privileged class. The only fortune he possessed—embarrassed land—he obtained from the investment of lawyers' fees in land—two forms of possession possible only to members of the privileged class. So the example does not fit. My brother [WDK, Jr.] would not have become assistant-city-solicitor in a thousand years without the paternal name and fame—upon his own exertions; so he does not answer either. Your brother probably did not live exclusively upon his wages during his machine shop experience, had a tolerable certainty of help in securing promotion, and the infinite advantage of preliminary education. So had Arthur Hale. They are no working men, any more than my father. A few real workingmen undoubtedly emerge from their class—fewer with every decade of intensifying centralization; but the infinite majority live and die "hands."

Ours are good, (I should go on working in ours if I returned to America tomorrow,) but they have no effect upon financial crises, want of work, wages-reductions, increasing pauperism, crime, prostitution and insanity. These are inherent evils, chronic diseases of our method of production and distribution, and they can only be cured when the cause is removed, i.e when organized labor takes the place of mad, wild, blind competition.

Begging his pardon, I do not think Mr. Ames opinion valid.[10] (He, too, left his handicraft to enter the privileged salaried class by the way.) ~~But~~ I do not believe he has read five economic works in his life, even the English ones; and I question his competence to judge the German school. A physician scouts at a layman who discussed the relative merit of medical hypotheses, and recommends him to enter a medical school and we all agree with him. But every minister arrives at Social Science via Theology and Philanthropy, and it incenses me to hear one talking Politics or Political Economy. I always wish to propound some statement in Theology for the sake of being snubbed and saying tu quoque![11]

There are three little American books which every American who honestly regrets the evils and sufferings of American society is in duty bound to read (ministers especially!) They are Henry George's Progress and Poverty, his Social Problems and Godwin~~s~~ Moody's Land and Labor.[12] I think they answer your analogy of osmosis.

I cannot write or talk of indifferent things. If I am right, then the wrong to the working people, all the world over, is a question as~~o~~ much graver than our slavery question was, as the working class is greater than the number of our slaves. And [several words illegible]fort upon this work they are robbed of, are bound to make restitution and to help them recover their own. This I believe, and to act on this belief seems to me as imperative as the agitation for the freeing of the negroes seemed to the early anti-slavery workers. And to ignore the question seems to me to be shirking the highest duty that our powers and education lay upon us.

Lazare is writing his thesis to make his Doktor, in May, and then we go to Zürich to wait until I make mine. I have never been so well, nor worked so steadily, nor had such efficient, on-spurring help as in these past five months. I have but one ungratified wish in the world—I want a foreign correspondence-ship of an American paper, and that will probably come in the course of time. Thank you again; and with love to your Mother and a warm kiss to Mrs. Turner.[13] I am

Yours affectionately
Florence Kelley Wischnewetzky

P.S. I have overlooked one little sentence "I think that, seeing as we all do, the great need for profound and conscientious study of social problems—you do not see how much is being done in that direction." Now, I watch and read all the new publications upon the subject, follow the Nation and the reviews and Putnam's lists of authorities (which are atrocious), and the programs of the scores of Congresses met to discuss special branches of the subject; and it all implies a great deal of conscientious work but very little that is profound. Old theses are discussed as new, that had their day and were disposed of in Germany from fifteen to forty years ago. Professors publish dilutions of the English classic economists as contributions to present investigations à la Perry and Sumner, or they condense Carey à la Thompson, or they pervert the German's à la [Richard T.] Ely, and the result is probably the [worst literature?] of Social Science now to be had in any civilized country.[14] I am not simply growling; I am looking at things as they are, and waiting impatiently for Dr Aveling's translation of Marx, and my own translation of Engels, to confront the Ely tribe and force them to stop their role of false prophets.[15] If they would use their knowledge of German for making honest translation they could enable their conscientious countrymen to bring their economic studies down to date i.e. some twenty years further than the point which leading American publicists have reached at present. Meanwhile the American industrial development strides onward with seven league boots and the blind continue to lead the blind, and to us it looks as though the ditch were not far off.

Noch einmal,[16]

Yours affectionately,
Florence Kelley Wischnewetzky

Env: Miss Mary Thorn Lewis, 2224 Green Street, Philadelphia, Pennsylvania, Vereinigte Staaten, Amerika

ALS, FKP, NN

1. Mary Thorne Lewis (1854–1952) earned a certificate of proficiency in chemistry in 1880 from the University of Pennsylvania. Active with FK in the New Century Club and the New Century Working Women's Guild in Philadelphia in 1881, she later married William Chan-

ning Gannet, a Unitarian minister (University Archives and Records Center, University of Pennsylvania, "Women at Penn").

2. The New Century Club of Philadelphia discussed social problems as well as literary topics. It declined to hear FK's essay, "American Women Students in Zurich" (Sklar, *Florence Kelley and the Nation's Work,* 115–116).

3. George William Curtis (1824–1892) was editor of *Harper's Weekly Magazine. Woman's Journal,* founded in Boston 1870 as the chief publication of the American Woman Suffrage Association, featured articles on woman suffrage and temperance along with reminiscences and short fiction. *Popular Science Monthly* was founded in 1872 (Mott, *A History of American Magazines,* 3:108, 495–499).

4. Grace Weld Soper, a Cornell classmate, received her A.B. in 1882 (Hewett, *Cornell University,* 4:512).

5. In fact, FK married LW on 14 October 1884.

6. Henry M. Hyndman (1842–1921), author of *The Historical Basis of Socialism in England* (London: K. Paul, Trench & Co., 1883), was an early British convert to Marxism. Laurence Gronlund (1846–1899), author of *Cooperative Commonwealth: An Exposition on Modern Socialism* (Boston: Lee and Shepherd, 1884), was a Danish immigrant living in Chicago.

7. Phylloxera is a destructive plant lice.

8. On FK's *Washington Tribune* letters, see Letter 6, FK to WDK, 2 January 1884, above. James G. Blaine (1830–1893), Republican congressman, ran for U.S. president on a protectionist platform in 1884.

9. In February 1885, FK had telegraphed instructions her father to stop publication of the proposed volume (Sklar, *Florence Kelley and the Nation's Work,* 109–110). Earlier the *New York Times* had carried a report that "a New-York paper" had published a statement from WDK that LW had demanded that FK withdraw the volume. The *Times* reported that WDK "denounces the statement as false in every particular"; he and CBK had wholeheartedly approved of the marriage, he said. WDK stated that FK had decided not to submit the book because of "the publishers declining to modify certain chapters in accordance with her wishes" (*NYT,* 21 January 1885, 3).

10. Charles Gordon Ames (1828–1912), who began his career as a printer, was minister of the Unitarian Church in Germantown in the 1870s and was the father of FK's classmate, Charles W. Ames.

11. Latin: "You also."

12. Henry George (1839–1897) wrote *Progress and Poverty* (San Francisco, Calif.: W. M. Hinton, 1879) and *Social Problems* (Chicago: Belford, Clarke, 1883). (For FK and Henry George, see Sklar, *Florence Kelley and the Nation's Work,* 123–124.) William Godwin Moody wrote *Land and Labor* (New York: Scribners, 1883).

13. Eliza Sproat Randolph Turner (1826–1903), a suffrage leader, co-founded the New Century Club in 1877. She was the mother of FK's Cornell classmate, Nathaniel Archer Randolph.

14. *The Nation,* published weekly, was founded in 1865; *Putnam's Monthly* in 1853. Yale economist William Graham Sumner (1840–1910) favored laissez-faire and opposed trade unions. Philadelphia economist Henry C. Carey (1793–1879) had been an advocate of the protective tariff since the 1850s.

15. Edward B. Aveling (1851–1898) was the translator of Karl Marx's (1818–1883) *Capital: A Critical Analysis of Capitalist Production* (London: S. Sonnenschein, 1887). For FK's translation of Frederick Engels's work, see Letter 11, FK to Engels, 10 January 1886, below.

16. German; "Once again."

10. To *Woman's Tribune* Editor[1]

Heidelberg, Germany
[ca. April 1885]

Dear Mrs. Colby:

I thank you very much for the specimen of the WOMAN'S TRIBUNE which came yesterday. I had not seen it before. I like the tone of the TRIBUNE immensely and wish it all success. I hope our best energies in the West may be let to concentrate upon it; it is so very necessary to have two or three organs clear in tone and rich in substance.[2]

I have one subject heavily upon my mind. If I had been in America I should have brought all the vigor I possess, to bear, in bringing this subject before the convention. At present I am hammering upon it in the Woman's Journal and in my whole private correspondence.[3] We need a program. Our platform of one plank the ballot is not enough. The maxim Equality before the Law is not enough, though it is good as far as it goes.[4] (For instance, neither of them has any immediate bearing upon the question of equal pay for equal work.) We want a formulated program defining our general objects first and our immediate practical demands second: In my work, for instance, I am constantly hampered for want of it. If, for instance, I want to criticize the action of the German Working Men's Party, here in Germany, in any given case, I have their program at hand, a program adopted sixteen years ago, modified at succeeding annual conventions and freely ratified every year. Candidates are elected on pledges to support this program, organs are conducted in accordance with it, speeches of representatives in the superial parliament are criticized with it as a standard, and friends defend and enemies attack a set of principles clearly formulated and universally acknowledged as the principles of the party.

But when I want to defend our movement against some wild charge, when I want confidentially to affirm what it is pledged to do, in general, and what it demands for today and tomorrow while working for the ballot, I have to hunt up some single resolution of some single convention, or some good word of a known leader, or the motto of some organ: and it is most unsatisfactory. I am in danger of quoting some momentary piece of political tactics for an eternal principle of the movement, and some transitory observation as part of the creed.

At present, in writing an elaborate criticism upon Mr. Lawrence Gronlund's chapter on Woman, in his "Co-operative Commonwealth," I feel this disadvantage sorely. It is as clear as daylight what he wants; but when he says what the Suffragists want (besides suffrage), he has me at an infinite disadvantage for he can assert what he pleases and I have no formulated declaration of general principles and special demands with which to confront him. I must bring up our whole array of reports of conventions, resolutions, arguments, petitions, etc., where half a dozen lines ratified by successive national conventions as the principles of the party would be worth the whole collection.

It is no slight task to prepare such a program. If every one concerned should begin to think about it now, and discuss it personally until the next Washington convention,[5] I think it would still take three days of debate to make such a program as would stand here, year after year, as this program of the German Workingmen's Party does.

For we have the interests of more than half the nation to represent, and times have changed so infinitely that the old general demand for equality of the sexes is not comprehensive enough. At the close of the war [it] answered very well, but then the inequality of the sexes was the greatest that there was, even outweighing the inequality between the Blacks and the Whites, now that is all past. The inequality between the millionnaire capitalist and his employe on the verge of pauperism, on the verge of starvation, is greater than the difference between the millionaire and his wife, and the employe and his wife though the employe may have a vote (which he must use as commanded) and the fashionable lady none. To make the employe's wife the equal and leave her there is cruel disregard of her human needs, and to make the millionnaire's wife his equal is to add almost nothing to her present power. While to make the employe's wife the equal of the millionnaire himself, neither the ballot nor any contemplated law can do any more than it can make hungry employe and millionnaire equal. The mere demand for equality of the sexes is good as far as it goes; but to make the working women the mere equal of the working man in these days of wages reductions, lockouts, short-time, voting to order, and the rest of the workingman's hardships, is a task which will not arouse much enthusiasm among thinking people. Our demand must be more comprehensive, it must prove that we represent the working women or our movement is proved to have fallen behind the need of the times; and this will prove the toughest point in the preparation of the program when ever come to prepare a program, as prepare one we must, sooner or later, I believe. I wonder whether I have made my idea clear. In the absence of a program, the first principle of suffragists that occurs to one's mind is always the equality of the sexes. But, at present, the inequality of men among themselves is so frightful, that to make each woman (rich or poor) merely equal to the men of her family, or her class, is to leave the sum total of inequality now cursing society almost unchanged, and that is a bad outlook. Moreover, it is so easily proved that it would make a program whose chief principle should be mere equality of the sexes a laughing stock.

In this convention I have another thing upon my mind. When I want to learn anything definite about the status of working women in America, I have to turn my back to our organs after searching them in vain; and I find full particulars in the "New York Volkszeitung," the organ of the German Workingmen and the "Sozialist" the central organ of the Socialistic Workingmen's Party.[6] For instance the bill for prohibiting the manufacture of cigars in N.Y. tenement houses affecting chiefly women and children. The non-enforcement of the compulsory education act and the consequent employment of little girls in factories in Brooklyn, the strike of a thousand or more women and girls in the Yonkers carpet-mills; the bill for prohibiting the employment of children and restricting the mill hours of women in Michigan are all carefully registered or perhaps thoroughly discussed in my workingmen's organs. It seems as if we were indifferent to the interests of the majority of our fellow country-women and cared only for the minority when we fight married women's property acts through the legislatures and the factory acts that protect unmarried, non-property-holding workinggirls to the workingmen to take care of and not even discuss them, sometimes fail even to record their passage. In this respect we are far behind the English suffrage movement, which, while concentrating to attention upon that fraction of the ballot which it has the best chance of getting, i.e., for property holding women, never loses a chance of lending a hand to the working women, watches new laws, criticizes old ones, investigates the manner in which beneficial ones are embraced and has succeeded in suspending that most corrupt law which exists in some of our own states, licensing prostitution that is fostering vice chiefly at the cost of the women of the working class.[7]

I cannot judge from the convention number of the WOMAN'S TRIBUNE,[8] whether it differs in this respect from our other organs, and I am waiting with great interest for the next number. With greatest respect, very truly yours,

Florence Kelley Wischnewetzky

[The above was the first communication received from our German correspondent. Although it was laid aside to make room for other interesting letters, yet it contains valuable suggestions and criticisms which make it timely for any issue.—Editor.]

PL, *Woman's Tribune* 2, no. 11 (September 1885): 1; previously published in part in Sklar, Schüler, and Strasser, *Social Justice Feminists*, 81–85).

1. Clara Bewick Colby (1846–1916) helped found the Nebraska Woman Suffrage Association in 1881 and established the weekly *Woman's Tribune* in 1883 in Beatrice, Nebraska. Colby moved the *Tribune,* the organ of the National Woman Suffrage Association, to Washington, D.C., in 1888.

2. Italics in original.

3. In 1885, the *Woman's Journal* published a series of letters from FK on child labor and European workingmen's support for the rights of working women (e.g., "European Workingmen for Woman Suffrage," 28 February 1885, 72; "Will Working Women Vote Wisely?" 23 March 1885, 162; "A New Book about Women," 4 July 1885, 210).

4. "Equality Before the Law" was printed on the *Woman Tribune*'s masthead.

5. The annual meeting of the National Woman Suffrage Association.

6. The *New Yorker Volkszeitung* (1878–1932), owned not by a party but by an independent board, was the most prestigious and influential German-American socialist newspaper. *Der Sozialist* was the national weekly paper of the Socialist Labor Party, which was headquartered in New York.

7. In 1874, the National Society for Women's Suffrage, headquartered in Manchester, England, proposed a bill to Parliament that would have extended suffrage to widows and unmarried women but explicitly excluded married women. In 1884, strategies supporting limited forms of woman suffrage were renewed during parliamentary debates over the expansion of male suffrage. Many politically active middle-class British women supported the Women's

Protective and Provident League, which formed in 1874. The public regulation, hence legal recognition, of prostitution through the Contagious Diseases Acts (passed 1864–1869) was repealed in Parliament in 1886 after vigorous lobbying by Josephine Butler (1828–1906) and the Ladies Association Against the Contagious Diseases Act.

8. The March issue of the *Woman's Tribune* was devoted to coverage of the National Woman Suffrage Association meeting in Washington, D.C., 20–22 January 1885.

11. To Frederick Engels

Zürich [Switzerland] Pension Liefman
Steinwiesstr. 6 Hottingen
Jan. 10th 1886

My dear Sir,

I am very thankful indeed to you for promising to lose no time in looking over the translation,[1] the more so as I received an urgent letter yesterday from my friend in America who wishes to take passage on the steamer of Feb. 16th begging me to forward her before that date, if not the mss. at least an approximate estimate of the number of words in preface and appendix or which ever you decide to publish, if but one.[2] That is, however, less important than her being able to place a part of the ms. in the printers hands for stereotyping.

I am especially glad to have the book appear in this way and am quite indemnified for the much fruitless correspondence with publishers, for Miss Foster, who has undertaken to bear the expense, is the very active secretary of the National Woman Suffrage Ass'n. and will see to it that the book is placed

Frederick Engels, ca. 1888.
Source: John Spargo, *The Marx He Knew* (Chicago: C. H. Kerr, 1909).

in all the many libraries of that Assn. and so within reach of a very large body of young workingwomen, teachers etc. as well as of the thousands of women for whome their movement has hitherto offered chiefly political interest, and has, perhaps, been of little value except in the way of drawing them beyond the narrow range of their own firesides. Miss Foster is ready too, to go on publishing socialist works as fast as I translate them. I prefer, however, not to publish anything further, until after the appearance of the English translation of das Kapital, as I felt very strongly the want of a standard of equivalent terms for many technical words and phrases.

I think it will be a very good thing that die Lage and das Kapital will appear in the same year in English, as each helps to the comprehension of the other, as I know from personal experience.[3]

As to the American belief that America is economically "not as other men",[4] it is unfortunately true that the reports of the statistical bureaus of labor have been favorite sources from which the politicians of both the old parties have drawn material by skillful perversions of which they have persuaded the workingmen of the correctness of their assertion. And that great masses of workingmen believe today in this exemption, our comrades who are most active among them will, I am sure, agree with me, in asserting.

Yours very truly
Florence Kelley Wischnewetzky

ALS, Marx/Engels Papers, NL-AmISG

1. FK approached Engels in December 1884 with her translation of his original preface to *The Condition of the Working Class in England in 1844,* proposing that she translate *The Condition* from German into English. She asked him to write a new English-language preface as a substitute for the original German one (FK, Heidelberg, Germany, to Engels, 6 February 1885, Marx/Engels Papers, NL-AmISG). Engels wrote that he welcomed the translation because economic conditions in Germany and the United States resembled those he had described in *The Condition.* He outlined the topics he would cover in his new preface, particularly "the impending change for the worse which must necessarily follow the breakdown of the industrial monopoly of England in consequence of the increasing competition in the markets of the world" (Engels, London, to FK, 10 February 1885, in Marx and Engels, *Letters to Americans,* 144–145). In December 1885, FK sent her translation to Engels for his review; Engels replied that he would try to get to the manuscript quickly (FK, Zürich, Switzerland, to Engels, 28 December 1885, Marx/Engels Papers, NL-AmISG; Engels, London, to FK, 7 January 1886, Marx and Engels, *Letters to Americans,* 148; see also Sklar, *Florence Kelley and the Nation's Work,* 100–106, 117–119).

2. FK was not able to convince G. P. Putnam's Sons to publish the translation of *The Condition,* but she secured an agreement to publish from Rachel Foster, later Avery (1858–1919), who had met FK in 1885 while studying at the University of Zurich.

3. FK's English translation of Engels's *The Condition* and Aveling's translation of Marx's *Capital* both appeared in 1887.

4. Engels wrote that Americans who considered "their country exempt from the consequences of fully expanded capitalist production" were unaware of the existence of "evidence to the contrary" in published statistics from labor bureaus in states such as Massachusetts, New Jersey, and Ohio (Engels, London, to FK, 7 January 1886, in Marx and Engels, *Letters to Americans,* 148).

12. To Frederick Engels

Zürich [Switzerland]
June 9th. 1886

Dear Mr. Engels

Your letter and the preface came duly on Saturday and I mailed the whole package of proof on Monday to New York.[1]

Your letter gave me great pleasure, the more so as it formulated what I have been thinking. But just because the movement is so sudden and so mighty is the need of a suitable literature so urgent. Think of the whole accessible literature at such a time as this, limited to the works of Henry George, Gronlund's wretched, would-be-popular-at-all-costs Cooperative Commonwealth, and the translation of Bebel's Frau.[2] (And the last named will hardly find prompt circulation among the workers. At present I have, myself, succeeded in getting it a public by exploiting the organs of the suffrage movement, but this consists chiefly of bourgeoises among whom one can only hope to win one or two, here and there. I do not think that the book finds many readers even among workingwomen.)—And what the Anglo American workingmens' press offers in the way of confusion you doubtless know as well as I.

The whole drama that is playing itself out before our eyes, with its hundred thousands of workingmen pushed by the development of the Capitalist System to act directly in the spirit of Socialism and to make demands of our present society made by the enlightened workers of Germany for instance, while the Americans are still so little enlightened that they revile and repudiate everything that bears the name Socialism;—what a commentary upon the old cry that one still hears now and then from the idealogues in our own ranks "If Lassalle Marx and Engels had not been Germans, if the Soz. Dem. agitators had never been born, there would never have been a Social Democracy in Germany"![3]

In America there is no scientific literature. The mangled plagiarisms from Böhmert and Mehring which Professor [Richard] Ely offers a hungry public as his own investigations, and the drivellings of Professors James and Adams do but prove the sad want of a scientific literature. As to the leaders, to whom one may almost say that millions of workers listen (though late events have made Mr. Powderly's followers somewhat sceptical), their calibre is shown in their still undiscouraged preaching of the harmony between capital and Labor.[4] And the masses, themselves, are in a state of confusion incredible if it were not proved at every election. The whole presidential campaign that created so much discussion, two years ago, turned upon no principle whatsoever.[5] The sole question was, "who is the least of a rascal?" That was all the enlightenment that the whole struggle between the old parties offered the workers; and fancy in a state so highly developed, industrially, as my native Pennsylvania, a constituency of workingmen electing for the fourteenth time to the twenty-eighth consecutive year of service, as their representative in Congress my Father whose sole wisdom is praise of American protective tariff. And even now, when he admits in tête-a-tête conversation, that he no longer believes in the effectiveness of his panacea, the workingmen of his district give him ten to thirty thousand majority every second year. And the same men naturally elect my brother, a militiaman [WDK, Jr.], who is among the first at the shooting down "rioters" in every disturbance—to be assistant city solicitor. And this morning's American mail brought, in my bourgeois daily, an announcement of a mass meeting called by the Knights of Labor in Philadelphia to demand a change in the wool duties![6] Free Trade and or[7] Protection is the burden of the song of the politicians, and workingmen take up the chorus now in the midst of their own movement, so far from clear are they, as to the source and meaning of the evils that beset them. And how should they be clear, with no literature, with unenlightened leaders, such political training, and a capitalist press perhaps yet more corrupt than the English?

When, under such circumstances, the development of the Capitalistic System forces an organization and an activity that terrifies the ruling class, the movement incarnates the Marxist theory in a way that might be instructive not only for the bourgeoisie that attributes the whole "disturbance" to "foreign Anarchists, Socialists, Communists, Nihilists and Atheists" but for some of our German leaders, too, who still dream of moulding, or at least of determining the pace of, the general movement.

The capitalists have taken to organizing, en gros,[8] (though they too preach with increasing energy through press and pulpit, the harmony of interest of Capital and Labor) and have, as I am told, formed a federation of the largest Iron, Sugar, and Textile interests for common protection. Their common fund was reported some time ago as having reached ~~three~~ two and a half million dollars. The textile manufacturers of Philadelphia have a paid up fund of one and a half millions for common use, and for the especial support of small firms in resisting the demands of the organized worker. (And in the teeth of this Pope Powderly promulgates Harmony in every encyclical!) The bourgeoisie shows no want of class consciousness, and it must have been a puzzle for many an Anarchist when the bourgeois "radical" democrat Lawlor, recommended on the floor of Congress, among the shouts applause and laughter of his colleagues, that Gould be hung to the nearest lamppost as the man whose recklessness had brought the country to the verge of civil war (by pointing out unmistakably the chasm that separates the interest of Capital and Labor)[9] Of course the action of the bourgeoisie arouses further the class consciousness of the workers, but it does not enlighten them as they need to be enlightened and I am convinced that much crude action and wasted energy might be spared if we could make the best of our literature available for them.

I am glad "die Entwickelung" is under way, and if you think there is need of "Lohnarbeit and Kapital" in a second translation, I can make it now and it can be in readiness until you have time to look it over. I see the Sozialist offers in its list of English pamphlets "Marx, Karl,—Wages Labor and Capital, price

10 cents." In the same way, if no one has "den Ursprung["] in hand and you are willing for me to translate it I shall gladly do so during the summer and it can be at your disposal.[10] You will be interested to know that a large section of the Suffrage Association in Iowa, took for the subject of its ~~winter~~ discussions through the winter, Morgan's works, especially his Ancient Society. The money for publishing whatever of yours or Marx' I may translate, is in readiness at anytime, having been placed at my disposal.[11]

Yours very truly
Florence Kelley Wischnewetzky

As I shall be in America for a time, I can doubtless make better publishing arrangements for all future work. The address which I stupidly gave you without comment, is my permanent address wherever I may be whether in Zürich or New York.

F.K.W.

The current North American has an especially interesting essay from Powderly, worth looking up.[12]

ALS, Marx/Engels Papers, NL-AmISG

1. Earlier in June, Engels had sent the proofs with his corrections of FK's translation of *The Condition of the Working Class in England in 1844* (Engels, London, to FK, 3 June 1886, in Marx and Engels, *Letters to Americans,* 157).
2. Engels wrote that "the American working class is moving, and no mistake." He regarded the "appearance of the Americans upon the scene" as "one of the greatest events of the year" (Engels to FK, 3 June 1886). August Bebel's *Woman in the Past, Present and Future,* trans. H. B. Adams Walther (London: The Modern Press) was published in 1885.
3. Ferdinand Lassalle (1825–1864) founded the first German labor party in 1863 with the goal of increasing socialist participation in electoral politics. The party later became the German Social Democratic Party (SPD).
4. Franz Mehring (1846–1919) was a journalist and historian of the SPD (Marx and Engels, *Letters to Americans,* 300). Edmund J. James (1855–1925) became the director of the first collegiate business school, the Wharton School at the University of Pennsylvania, in 1881. Henry Carter Adams (1851–1921) was professor of political science at Cornell from 1883 to 1887. Terence Powderly (1849–1924) was head of the Knights of Labor from 1879 to 1893.
5. The 1884 presidential campaign pitted Benjamin F. Butler of the National Greenback-Labor Party against Republican James G. Blaine and Democrat Grover Cleveland.
6. The Knights of Labor evolved from a fraternal organization to a labor union in the mid-1870s, opening its ranks to all workers, skilled and unskilled. By 1886, the Knights had over 700,000 members and were advocating an eight-hour working day, boycotts, and arbitration.
7. The word "or" is inserted above the line.
8. French: "wholesale."
9. The House of Representatives had recently debated whether to establish arbitration procedures for the 1886 strike of workers against railroads controlled by industrialist Jay Gould (1836–1892). Frank Lawler (1842–1896; Democrat, Illinois, 1885–1891) stated that workers were unhappy with the 57 cents a day paid "under the Gould system." Lawler declared that "if Jay Gould were hanged from a lamp-post in New York it would be a blessing to the United

States. [Laughter.]" He held Gould responsible for the "thousands of deaths" in the United States as a result of the strike (49th Cong., 1st sess., *Cong. Rec.*, 2 April 1886, 3040).

10. Engels told FK that Edward Aveling was translating his *Entwicklung* (*Socialism: Utopian and Scientific*) but that he would be pleased to have her translate Marx's *Lohnarbeit und Kapital* (*Wage Labor and Capital*). He wrote that he considered *Der Ursprung* (*The Origin of the Family, Private Property and the State*) more challenging than *The Condition* but that he would approve FK's proposal as long as he closely supervised her translation (Engels, London, to FK, 25 February 1886; Engels, Eastbourne, to FK, 13 August 1886, both in Marx and Engels, *Letters to Americans,* 151, 158).

11. American ethnologist Lewis H. Morgan (1818–1881), was the author of *Ancient Society, or Researches in the Lines of Human Progress from Savagery through Barbarism to Civilization* (London: Macmillan, 1877). For Rachel Foster Avery's financial support for FK's translations, see the introduction to this chapter.

12. The Wischnewetzkys, with their infant son Nicholas, moved to New York City in October 1886; see Sklar, *Florence Kelley and the Nation's Work,* 122. FK was referring to Powderly's "Strikes and Arbitration," *North American Review* 142 (May 1886): 502–506.

13. To Frederick Engels

110 E. 76th St. New York City
June 6th. 1887

Dear Mr. Engels,

Your card of May 28th came this morning. I am greatly mortified at the delay in your receipt of copies of die Lage and was really not to blame, they having been the first that I ordered sent. Mr. Lovell inanely kept them back to send a Morocco bound copy with them. I hope you have a good number by this time.[1]

I ordered one copy sent Mr. Kautzky and eighteen to Zürich. Mr. L reversed the order sending but one to schlueter where 12 should have gone to the Volksbuchhandlung and six to friends in Zürich.[2] I saw Mr. L. this morning and he undertook to make good his blunder by sending off 17 copies from here for Zürich to day; and writing Trübner to take off Mr. Kautzky's hands whatever Mr. K. may have left. Mr. Lovell has sent Trübner 50 copies. As to T's being a Bismarckian, that unfortunately cannot be helped. However, the Bismarckians are fond of driving a bargain where they can, even in the matter of socialism, and, so far as I have been able to learn, Trübner is no exception to the rule. So I can but hope he may do his best for the book—for the sake of his pocket.[3]

The book is getting well noticed in the press—as one of the most dangerous publications of recent years! Mr. Lovell is keeping the notices for me and if there is anything worth while among them, I shall forward it to you.[4]

I shall acknowledge the receipt of the ms. immediately.

I hope that your eyes are recovering and I am

Yours very truly
Florence Kelley Wischnewetzky

ALS, Marx/Engels Papers, NL-AmISG

1. Engels wrote from London that he had not yet received a copy of the preface or published copies of *The Condition* (Engels to FK, 7 May 1887, in Marx and Engels, *Letters to Americans,* 187). After Engels objected to Foster's agreement to have the Socialist Labor Party publish the English translation of *The Condition,* John W. Lovell of New York took on the work. Meanwhile, FK had arranged to have 20,000 copies of Engels's preface printed in a pamphlet edition (FK, New York, to Engels, 25 April and 26 April 1887, Marx/Engels Papers, NL-AmISG; see also Sklar, *Florence Kelley and the Nation's Work,* 128–129, 359n16).

2. SDP member Karl Kautsky (1854–1938) was editor of *Die Neue Zeit.* German socialist Hermann Schluter (d. 1919) emigrated to New York in 1889 and edited the *Volkszeitung* (Marx and Engels, *Letters to Americans,* 298, 302).

3. Trübner was possibly a brother of Nicholas Trübner (1817–1884), who had established a publishing firm in London around 1855. Otto von Bismarck (1815–1898) was prime minister of Prussia from 1862 to 1873 and was the first chancellor of newly unified Germany from 1871 to 1890. Supporters endorsed his policies of enacting social legislation while at the same time repressing the SDP.

4. Engels replied that he was "greatly amused" by the press reviews (Engels, n.p., to FK, 20 July 1887, in Marx and Engels, *Letters to Americans,* 189). For reception of *The Condition,* see Blumberg, *Florence Kelley,* 80–82.

14. To Caroline Bonsall Kelley

New York City
Dec. 20th, 1887

My dear Mother,

I reached home last night tired and stiff but very happy. I hasten to write this morning and use a pencil because I am on duty in the nursery where ink is out of the question. The menagerie is exceedingly animated as both my small animals are squealing at the top of their lungs.[1] However, they are well and happy and the happy tone in their voices makes up for the lack of musical quality While I was gone L. was called at midnight to a croupy child between Park and Madison Avenues. And last night towards <u>one</u> an anxious father from across the street called L. again to another croupy baby. The attack passed each time quickly and satisfactorily, and L. is established as family doctor in two more families, making eight in this one street several of them wealthy American families through which he has already some Fifth Avenue cases.

The only other episode here during my absence was funny. A pipe burst in the kitchen while the Sunday dinner was cooking; and the fire had to be put out at once. The plumber who was summoned was a good friend of the cook in no. 118; and before L. had an inkling as to what was being done, his turkey was whisked off to be roasted at a neighbor's whome we know ~~whether~~ neither by name nor by sight.

I have always forgotten to tell you how much pleasure the picture papers gave in which you packed my dresses. We never see them as they do not come in the line of business and are one of the luxuries that can be dispensed with. When we had done with them we sent them to some friends in Zürich.

Now as to the special points of your letters in their order. Thanks very much for the potted beef recipe. We shall try it tomorrow. I convinced myself that father's lamp is by no means bad while the one which L. had in mind for him needs home care. The wretched Mongrins finally got the kirsch to Washington. I was not thinking of the bloom of the greenhouse so much as the "greens." In city surroundings our eyes get fairly hungry for the sight of plants or meadows and the latter being out of the question the thought of the greenhouse is refreshing.

It is too bad that Father's sec'y who seemed a very intelligent and obliging one should have had to leave and Father was without anyone yesterday.[2]

The threadlace collar is still a mystery.

We basely opened the Christmas packet while I was in Washington. Had father kindly undertook to keep the presents under lock and key until he should come away tomorrow. They are delightful.

I shall look up the half flannel which you mention. I did know about it. You would scoff at the flannels which Ko and Margaret wore and which were rarely a whole day in use without washing.

I thought of the [M.?] C. after the letters had gone. I won't write it again.

I think with pleasure of your quiet days, though I fancy that you need the rest as rest perhaps even more than I do. It is a standing joke of ours that a confinement is a "resting spell" to be looked forward to with a sense of relief![3]

I have the paper to prepare for the Social Science club meeting here tomorrow night; and as it is far from complete I must close, send the babies out and set about preparing it.[4]

With a handshake for Willie and another for Bert in case he reaches you while this is still fresh, I am

Your loving daughter
Florence

Lazare is off to his dispensary or he would join me in sending greetings.

ALS, KFP, NCC-RB

1. NK was then two and a half years old, MK thirteen months.
2. FK had recently reconciled with her father; see Sklar, *Florence Kelley and the Nation's Work*, 135–136. H. J. Weirick was WDK's secretary (Blumberg, *Florence Kelley*, 109).
3. John Bartram Kelley was born 31 January 1888.
4. Founded in 1880 as one of several state affiliates of the American Social Science Association (founded 1865), the New York Social Science Association brought together women and men reformers who valued an interdependent view of society (see Leach, *True Love and Perfect Union*, 292–345). Kelley's paper may have focused on child labor; she later contributed to "White Child Slavery: A Symposium" (*The Arena* 1 [December 1889]: 589–603) and wrote *Our Toiling Children* (Chicago: Woman's Temperance Publication Association, 1889), a hard-hitting attack on capitalism.

15. To Frederick Engels

110 E. 76th St. New York
Dec. 29th. 1887

Dear Mr. Engels;

Your postal card of Dec. 2nd. and letter of Dec. 3d. came duly. The terms which Mr. Reeves proposes seem to me satisfactory though I do not see why the book should be a whole shilling dearer in London than in the retail trade here.[1] I will see that all future copies are sent unbound. I am delighted that Mr. Reeves is to render his accounts to you. It simplifies matters for me and I have had so much bother with correspondence about both book and pamphlet that I dreaded the thought of beginning afresh with a transatlantic publisher.

I shall indeed, notify you early of all projected future publications.

As to the English reprint of the Labor movement in America, I suppose there will be no guaranty against reprints so long as there is no international copyright law.[2] I do not understand Mr. [Karl] Kautzky's having to pay anything on the books when Mr. [John] Lovell prepaid them here.

The pamphlets too, were prepaid. Please deduct for Mr. Kautzky and yourself the sums laid out, when the first account is rendered.

I thank you very much for the copy of Commonweal and the other papers. As to the preface for the Free Trade, I am not at all uneasy.[3] All that I want is that you make its use as a protectionist document utterly impossible. As it stands, today, it can be used as such in the present of state of things here.

When I tried to give you an inkling of the manner in which the protectionist press here snaps at everything which can be pressed into its service, it was not with the thought of your undertaking to meet such practices. There is no escape from them in any case. But the great mass of workingmen here are full of ~~Free Trade and still more~~ Protectionist sophistry and the Free Trade speech as it stands is not explicit enough upon the latter subject. The protectionist Weltanschaŭŭng is gaining ground wherever it is not already supreme. The workingmen do not regard it as a passing question of financial or administrative measures; but as a permanent theory of social and economic development.

We see a good deal of some of the more wide awake, progressive and influential men among the English speaking organizations (for instance [Samuel] Gompers president of the Federation of Labor with its 600000 members[)]. He is perfectly fuddled upon the subject and so are most of the rest of them. It is not a question of polemic against the protectionists but of your defining your position explicitly towards protection.

The workingmen have been known to go through a whole campaign for a labor candidate and then, at the last moment, vote for the regular bourgeois old party man because he happened to be a better protectionist. It is nothing new, the Free Trade-Protection ding-dong has been clanged and droned into the workingmen's ears for generations.

It is the workers whom I wish the preface to meet not the penny-a-liners.

This is just the time for the pamphlet, when Congress and the press are absorbed in the fight between the protectionists and Free Traders, and the relative merits of reducing import duties and abolishing internal revenue duties obscure all else.

I wonder whether you noticed the Sozialists' list of especially recommended Xmas books. The treatment of die Lage by the ring here, amounts to a boycott. It would be a joke if it were not so pitiful.

The violence of the reaction among the workers themselves is surprising. The Federation of Labor held its annual convention in Baltimore a short time ago. It voted in favor of maintaining the internal taxes upon cigars; upon improvement in the methods of oyster culture and other equally urgent matters; but of the improvement of the Factory Acts, prohibition of the employment of children etc. not one word could I find. The Congress voted against the resumption of the Eight Hour Movement; and against independent labor politics; and against a strike funds.[4] Thanks to Bloch a N.Y. Socialist they adopted a resolution against—the tyranny of the police![5] A resolution very well in its way for Trades Unions in Germany or Russia but in America!

A stray article in the Volkszeitung gave a chance for a communication pointing out the fact that the German Socialist press here does nothing in the way of discussing or recommending the English editions of Capital or die Lage. To my surprise, the Volkszeitũng published such a communication from me. Of course it was translated to suit the editor who made the most of the chance for self glorification claiming that no paper had done so much as the Volkszeitũng for popularizing the teachings of Marx and Engels. On that point I beg leave to differ, certainly as to the quality of the popularization. And so doubtless do all who watch the Socialist press on both sides of the ocean.

The main beauty of the Volkz. half column of reply to my strictures was this;—I had insisted upon the duty of the press to the English editions and Jonas[6] stretched my words to cover the Am. Soc. press in its relation to Socialist teachings Marx-Engels' scher Richtung überhaũpt.[7] I had been clear enough for him who runs to read, and let the thing go without farther dispute. The fact remains that the German Socialist press might contribute largely to the circulation of standard Socialist literature in English if it cared to do so.

It is pitiful to see Capital and die Lage persistently kept dark while the Sozialist forces Rosenberg's Tantalus into the foreground week by week and the Volkszeitũng devotes column long articles to puffing such a mediocre production as Grönlund's Ça Ira or Danton in the French Revolution.[8] It is a feebly idealogisch "history" in which Grönlund professes to carry forward Marx' work in the direction of "constructive criticism" (!) He has tried to trick out Socialism mixing in "the power behind Evolution" and "the Will of God" to suit the peculiarities of the Anglo Saxon habit of thought. He insists at some length that revolutions are made by books.

And this confused stuff, calculated to do anything else rather than promote earnest thought among our Americans, is puffed to the skies by the German Socialist press here in the face of shameful neglect of the now accessible literature of scientific-materialistic criticism. Perhaps you have seen Ça Ira. But I fancy your time is too precious to admit of your wading through it.

I took the liberty of sending my friend Mrs. Helen Campbell[9] a card to you. She is good and warm hearted and gets at everything from the side of strongly humane feeling. But my countrywomen will not study. So they come home and decide that what is admirable for Germany or England will not do at all for America—and Socialism remains for them a European product.

You will see from the enclosed, how great a role personal contact has played in her case. That is characteristic, too, for the America of today where we have almost no English speaking Socialists worthy of consideration or capable of influencing anyone favorably.

With the best wishes for the New Year from Dr. Wischnewetzky and myself, I am

Very truly yours
F. K. Wischnewetzky

ALS, Marx/Engels Papers, NL-AmISG

1. London publisher of socialist literature William Reeves had assumed distribution of the translation of *The Condition* in England (Blumberg, *Florence Kelley,* 82).

2. Engels's preface to *The Condition* was published as a pamphlet in the United States in 1887 by Lewis Weiss with the title *The Labor Movement in America* (Blumberg, *Florence Kelley,* 75)

3. FK wrote Engels that she was spending as much time as she could spare from her "daily hack work" on translating Karl Marx's *Free Trade: A Speech Delivered before the Democratic Club, Brussels, Belgium, January 9, 1848.* Engels had agreed to write a preface to FK's translation (FK, Gloucester, Mass., to Engels, 28 August 1887, Marx/Engels Papers, NL-AmISG; Engels, London, to FK, 3 December 1887, in Marx and Engels, *Letters to Americans,* 193; see also Sklar, *Florence Kelley and the Nation's Work,* 130).

4. FK's criticism highlighted the AFL's limited support for the eight-hour–day movement. The 1887 AFL convention, which met in Baltimore on 13–17 December, took the limited step of resolving to work to "secure the enactment by Congress of laws that will reduce the hours of labor" (*New York Times,* 17 December 1888, 2). Although the federation briefly supported an eight-hour movement from 1888 to 1891, thereafter the movement was advanced primarily by local unions (Kaufman, *The Samuel Gompers Papers,* 2: xvi–xvii, 163–164; see also Sklar, *Florence Kelley and the Nation's Work,* 137–138).

5. A resolution proposed by George G. Block (1848–1925), secretary of the Journeymen Bakers' National Union, to denounce police interference with labor meetings was approved after "prolonged debate" between socialist and conservative delegates (*NYT,* 18 December 1887, 9; see also Kaufman, *Samuel Gompers Papers,* 2:434).

6. German-American socialist Alexander Jonas (1834–1912), had edited the *Volkszeitung* since 1885 (Marx and Engels, *Letters to Americans,* 298).

7. German; "of the Marx-Engels type generally."

8. Engels replied that he was used to having his works "boycotted" and believed that the New York German Socialists' "efforts to boss the American movement as they have done with the German-American one must fail miserably. The masses will set all that right when

once they move" (Engels, London, to FK, 22 February 1888, in Marx and Engels, *Letters to Americans,* 196–197). Gronlund's *Ça Ira! Or Danton in the French Revolution* (Boston: Lee and Shepard) was published in 1888.

9. Helen Stuart Campbell (1839–1918), an advocate of better wages for working women, wrote *The Problem of the Poor* (1882) and *Prisoners of Poverty* (1887) (see Sklar, *Florence Kelley and the Nation's Work,* 143–145).

16. To Frederick Engels

110 E. 76th St.—N.Y.
March 29th 1888

Dear Mr. Engels;

The enclosed speaks for itself. The letters referred to, were notes calling attention to 1.) the defiance of all discipline involved in the Executive's appealing to the N.Y. section against the decision of the Supervisory Com.; 2) its the Executive's[1] dragging our names into print in the reports of the meetings when the object of the appointment of the Com. by the Buffalo Congress was the avoidance of public scandal; and 3.) the ridiculous executive demand for an investigation after the Supervisory Committee had unconditionally reinstated us. What the Executive will do next, remains to be seen. The beauty of their publishing their own decisions was that they ignored and suppressed the Supervisory Committee's decisions uniformly.[2]

I enclose a scrap showing the situation in Chicago to day.[3] This strike promises to be as important as the famous strike of two years ago on the Gould Southwestern System. But in one respect it means even more than that one, for it has already proved the nullity of the Inter State Commerce Law—from which such wonders were promised in the prevention of strikes and enforcement of the responsibility of railroads for the performance of their duties as common carriers—i.e. uninterrupted transportation of persons and freight!

I am working on the subject of Child Labor (and Compulsory Education) using statistics of State Bureaus, State Board of Education reports, census, Factory Inspectors' Reports, etc. In this volume I shall use exclusively American official data. Later I shall work out a second volume based on European official data for comparison.[4] The German and Swiss I can get from Messrs. [Hermann] Schlueter and Grenlich. Can you tell me to whom to apply for English official data?

The ms. has not yet come.[5]

As you know, the Sorge's came back to Hoboken (and by the way, they have cheered up since their return to Hoboken to such an extent that they are scarcely to be recognized).[6] Three days after their return, we had a fine christening (March 19th), when we named our second son, born Jan. 31st.,—John Brown. The Sorge's (who formed the entire company), acted as godfather and godmother, and the occasion was celebrated with the help of a "Tüchtige Bowle,"[7] the three babies, Nikolai Margaret and John forming a lively and delightful circle of their own. (The eldest, Nikolai will be three years old in July!) We are all delighted at the return of the Sorge's.

With best wishes from us both for your continued good health, I am

Yours sincerely
F. K. Wischnewetzky

P.S. Please give me exact instructions as to the publication of the preface. Shall it appear in an English (N.Y.) morning paper in advance of the pamphlet form? I think I can accomplish this. Or have you any reason for preferring not to have it so appear? Shall it appear in the Volksz. (wh. will want it of course). If so, would it not be well for you to send the preface in German along with the English copy?

Of course I have no other means of preventing German papers from making their own translations. If, however, you will send a German version with the English one, I will make a number of ms. copies of it, and send them to most of the German Soc. sheets so preventing bad translations.

Yours truly
F. K. W.

ALS, Marx/Engels Papers, NL-AmISG

1. The words "the Executive's" are inserted above the line after the word "its."
2. In April 1887, FK had described to Engels how she and LW had been "suspended" from the New York chapter of the SLP for "incessant slander" (see Sklar, *Florence Kelley and the Nation's Work,* 129). Among the causes in this complicated conflict was Engels's stern criticism of the party in his preface to *The Condition.* At the SLP's national convention in Buffalo in September, a committee was formed to review the charges. In March 1888, FK told Engels that the "Supervisory Committee, upon the recommendation of a com. appointed by the Buffalo Congress (Jonas and Gronlund) to adjust the differences between us and the party, has unconditionally reinstated us, acting over the heads of the Executive and in spite of the frantic protest of the N.Y. section" (FK, New York, to Engels, 26 April 1887, 28 August 1887, and 11 March 1888; all in Marx/Engels Papers, NL-AmISG). See also Sklar, *Florence Kelley and the Nation's Work,* 125–129; and Blumberg, *Florence Kelley,* 64–67, 71–74, 82–83, 93–95. Engels wrote from London that he was pleased to hear of "your success against the Executive as far as it goes" (Engels, London, to FK, 11 April 1888, in Marx and Engels, *Letters to Americans,* 199).
3. Engineers and firemen struck against the Chicago, Burlington & Quincy Railroad on 27 February 1888, but switchmen and brakemen did not join them. Despite fears in early March that the strike would spread to other western railroads, on 21 March the *New York Times* reported that the C.B. & Q. was functioning with new employees and that the strike had ultimately failed (Foner, *History of the Labor Movement,* 2: 249–250; *NYT:* 1 March 1888, 1; 6 March 1888, 1; and 21 March 1888, 1).
4. Out of this work FK published "Child Labor," in *Fifth Annual Report of the Bureau of Labor Statistics of the State of Connecticut for the Year Ending November 30, 1889* (Hartford: Case, Lockwood & Brainard, 1890), 14–55; and "Evils of Child Labor," *Frank Leslie's Illustrated Newspaper* 60 (March 1, 1890): 84 (Sklar, *Florence Kelley and the Nation's Work,* 410). See also Letter 14, FK to CBK, 20 December 1887, above.
5. Engels replied that because of poor eyesight and other pressing obligations, he was un-

able to complete the preface to FK's translation of *Free Trade* right away; he sent corrections to FK's translation on 2 May and promised his preface soon after (Engels, London, to FK, 11 April and 2 May 1888, in Marx and Engels, *Letters to Americans,* 198, 199–200).

6. Friedrich Sorge (1827–1906), German-American socialist, emigrated to the United States in 1852 with his wife Katharine and founded the Socialist Labor Party in 1877 (Sklar, *Florence Kelley and the Nation's Work,* 122–123). In an earlier letter to Engels, FK had written of the Sorges' previous isolation in "a remote nest in a 'suburb'" near Rochester, New York (FK, New York, to Engels, 8 January 1887, in Marx/Engels Papers, NL-AmISG).

7. German: "punchbowl."

17. To Frederick Engels

41 St. and Parrish Sts. Phila. Pa.
[ca. July 1888]

Dear Mr. Engels,

I have been prevented from writing you first by Dr. Wischnewetzky's long and terrible illness, and of late,—by sheer mortification.[1]

On receiving the preface and revised ms. I immediately set about getting the preface published The North American Review wrote me through Redpath that "Mr. Rice thought it not advisable to consider the ms."[2]

Mr. Metcalf of the Forum said to me in my own house "I do not doubt Mrs. Wischnewetzky that the article is all you describe. But I cannot afford to stampede my audience." Appleton's pamphlet department said "The name is enough! We don't want it." Mr. [John] Lovell said of the pamphlet "Indeed, Mrs. Wischnewetzky, even when you pay all the costs of publication, it's a burden upon any library. I cannot sell ten copies of works of that character." And Lee and Shepard returned me the whole ms. unread.[3] One man said "Engels, Engels? Ah! Yes, the man that was hung in Chicago!" (!)

Now, however, after all this loss of time and untold refusals, I have got Lee and Shepard to reconsider and they will have the pamphlet out in first rate shape by Aug. 15th. They send 500 copies to the press. I will forward to you for [William] Reeves as directed. In case you are not in London, I can only hope that some of our friends may be willing to make the necessary arrangements with Reeves under your direction.

The pamphlet will sell here to perfection. Lee and Shepard themselves are convinced of it——now that they have read it.

Yours sincerely
Florence Kelley Wischnewetzky

ALS, Marx/Engels Papers, NL-AmISG

1. See Letter 16, 29 March 1888, above, for FK's most recent letter to Engels.

2. James Redpath (1833–1891) and Allen Thorndike Rice (1853–1889) edited the *North American Review.*

3. Lorettus Sutton Metcalf (b. 1837) founded *The Forum* in 1886. William H. Appleton founded D. Appleton & Co. in 1838. Lee and Shepard was a Boston firm.

18. To William Darrah Kelley

78 W. 72nd. St. [New York City]
Dec 11th 1889

My dear Father,

Your beautiful present reached me yesterday, and I beg you to accept my sincere thanks for it.

In the absence of news for several days, I feel very anxious about you and venture to beg Mr. [H. J.] Weirick for a triweekly bulletin.

We are all well. We had a very pleasant call upon Miss Tyler and the trio, Willy, Carrie, and Emily are to dine here on Thursday evening.[1]

L. writes that Dr. Hardwill of Baltimore spent the summer in Stockholm and obtained for the Johns Hopkins University the exclusive right for Baltimore. That, too, is a good card for the professional brethren. I'll keep you posted as to the contents of every letter. He is most anxious for the purchase of the land in order to have Hardenbergh begin the work of building. But the requisite $20.000 if borrowed from an outsider would involve surrender of the monopoly (partial if not complete) to the lender and carry the enterprise beyond the limits of the family and that neither you nor he desire. Yet the loss of time is greatly to be deplored. He is much disturbed thereat, and asks me to lay the matter before you.[2] I have mailed to Mr. Nicholson a verbatim translation of my letter from L. and he will doubtless forward it to you if you feel well enough to trouble your mind with the matter.[3]

Clearly, the understanding is a superb one and every day's loss of time a great loss. I have a little St. Vitus' Dance patient waiting for treatment now.

Mother joins me in sending love and asks to have all invitations and cards from Philadelphia friends which may drift to you, forwarded to her. The chicks are well and jolly and rosy and looking forward to the first snow with more eagerness than their seniors.

With kind regards to Mr. Weirick and a longing to hear that you are feeling better,[4] I am

Your loving daughter
Florence

ALS, KFP, NCC-RB

1. Emily Tyler was possibly a sister of WDK, Jr.'s, wife, Caroline Tyler Kelley (d. 1946).
2. Since their arrival in New York City, LW had found it difficult to establish a viable medical practice. FK had asked her father for funds to establish LW's Mechanico-Therapeutic and Orthopedic Zander Institute (Sklar, *Florence Kelley and the Nation's Work*, 163–164).
3. William R. Nicholson (d. 1927), president of Philadelphia Land Title & Trust Co., was the Kelley family's financial advisor.
4. WDK died in Washington, D.C., on 9 January 1890. A codicil to his will provided for additional funds for the Zander Institute, a bequest that WDK, Jr., contested (Sklar, *Florence Kelley and the Nation's Work*, 164, 167).

19. To Richard T. Ely

78 W. 72[1] [New York City]
[after December 11, 1890]

Dear Mr. Ely

Please accept my sincere thanks for the volume which I find on my return home after an absence of several days.

I have read the first edition and shall read this with added interest.[2]

I shall be very glad to read the Independent articles consecutively, pen in hand, and shall be grateful if you will send me a full set, as I do not see the paper regularly.[3] But I must warn you that my friends think my criticisms more candid than kindly, and must beg you to make allowance for an inborn brusqueness which has brought me much trouble. But then—perhaps I may not find any thing to differ seriously from and this may be all borrowed in vain.

My Néué Zeit has been packed away beyond my reach so that I could not send you the promised articles. The one by Engels on Rodbertus was back at the close of 1884 or the beginning of 1885.[4]

I do not know of any work dealing with agriculture under Socialism and cannot see how such a work could very well be undertaken at the present stage. I imagine that Paul Lafargue's articles contain the best criticism of the present status of agriculture from the Socialist standpoint.[5]

You see, it is really only the [Laurence] Grönlund sort who undertake to lay down a Socialist scheme at all. The rest of us can only examine the present and the past, and try to ascertain which way we are moving and how fast we are going. But we don't venture say how things will be done a hundred years hence,—for how can we foresee the technical changes and the discoveries in the domain of applied natural science which may intervene?

The only thing we feel sure of is this, that the minority cannot go on forever exploiting the majority, and that exploitation can be abolished only by removing the means of production from the irresponsible few to the responsible servants of all; and that this can come only when the economic conditions and the intelligence of the masses sufficiently ripen. But how any branch of industry may be carried on we have to leave to Messrs. Bellamy and Grönlund to divine.[6]

Meanwhile Lafargue's articles are suggestive! The only English one of them that I know of, was published in To-Day in 1885. But he is always at it in French, and I think his things come out through the regular book trade and could be found by reference to a good bibliography.

With very kind regards to Mrs. Ely.[7]

Yours sincerely
Florence Wischnewetzky

Prof. R. T. Ely

ALS, Box 14, Ely Papers, WHi

1. Penciled address not in FK's hand.

2. Publisher Thomas Y. Crowell published revised and expanded editions of two of Richard Ely's books in 1890: *The Labor Movement in America* (1886) and *Problems of To-Day: A Discussion of Protective Tariffs, Taxation, and Monopolies* (1888).

3. Ely, "Socialism (Its Nature, Its Strength, and Its Weakness)," *Independent* 43 (5 February–2 July 1891). When revised, these twenty-one weekly articles became Ely's *Socialism: An Examination of Its Nature, Its Strength, and Its Weakness, with Suggestions for Social Reform* (New York: Thomas Y. Crowell & Co., 1894); see Rader, *The Academic Mind and Reform*, 250.

4. In an unrecovered letter, Ely presumably asked FK to send him Engels's article, which FK had mentioned to him in December (FK, New York, to Ely, ca. 11 December 1890, Box 14, Ely Papers, WHi). In that 1885 article, Engels refuted charges that Marx had plagiarized his concept of surplus value from the work of German economist Johan Karl Rodbertus (1805–1875) (Blumberg, *Florence Kelley*, 114).

5. French Marxist Paul Lafargue (1842–1911) married Laura Marx, daughter of Karl Marx. He helped organize the French Workers' Party in 1879 (Marx and Engels, *Letters to Americans*, 298; Kapp, *Eleanor Marx*, 1:71–75).

6. Edward Bellamy (1850–1898) was the author of *Looking Backward, 2000–1887* (Boston: Ticknor & Co., 1888), a visionary novel about the future that generated a proto-socialist movement known as "Bellamy nationalism."

7. Anna Morris Anderson (d. 1923) married Richard Ely in 1884.

20. To Richard T. Ely

78 WEST 72ND STREET
NEW YORK

Feb. 4th 1891

Dear Sir,

Pray accept my sincere thanks for so promptly sending the prize essays. After I wrote you, the missing Columbia Library copy turned up, but mine seems hopelessly gone.

Do you know of any contributions to the literature of the hygiene of occupation besides those of Drs. Azel Ames and Roger Tracy?[1]

Of course there [is] any amount of foreign data, but I mean American writers.

We have a bill in the legislature for placing messenger boys and cash girls under the factory acts and reducing the working day of minors to eight hours.[2]

Jay Gould having just bought up our whole rapid transit scheme, streets, tunnels, franchises, legislature, aldermen and a good share of the rights of the New York Central, I think there will be a sudden impulse given to the municipalization of transportation.

I am interested in watching the preparations for the miners' strike.[3] It seems to me that Mr. Bellamy might flank their movement, if he would, by urging the immediate nationalization of the mines.

But the New Nation is not a very vigorous sheet and Mr. B's policy is not very impressive I'm afraid.[4]

Again thanking you I remain

Yours very truly
F. K. Wischnewetzky

ALS, Box 3, Ely Papers, WHi

1. Azel Ames, Jr., *Sex in Industry: A Plea for the Working Girl* (Boston: J. R. Osgood & Co., 1875); Roger S. Tracy (1841–1926), *The Essentials of Anatomy, Physiology and Hygiene* (N.Y.: D. Appleton & Co., 1884).
2. The New York legislature did not pass this bill, known as the Ainsworth bill, which the New York Working Women's Society had sponsored. In 1895, however, a commission was formed to look into working conditions in New York factories (Blumberg, *Florence Kelley,* 115; see also Sklar, *Florence Kelley and the Nation's Work,* 142).
3. Employees of the Tennessee Coal Mining Company were striking because the company had hired convict workers (Blumberg, *Florence Kelley,* 116).
4. The *New Nation,* founded in 1891 by Edward Bellamy, ceased publication in 1894.

21. To Richard T. Ely

April 23d 1891
78 West 72nd St. N. Y. City

In re Ely's Socialism & Social Reform
Dear Sir

Pray accept my thanks for the budget upon Socialism which came this morning.[1]

So far I have had time to read only number 1 and I find myself joining issue already. For you say

> "but it entertains no peculiar notions concerning the family as a social institution."

If Socialists may speak for Socialism it certainly does entertain the notion that the family ~~life~~ of today belongs to the industrial system of today; and that its economic foundation i.e. the economic dependence of the wife upon the husband, passes away with the rest of the economic dependence of one person upon another.

To say nothing of the Utopists from Plato to Fourier, every Socialist writer (except [Ferdinand] Lassalle and [Johan Karl] Rodbertus who did not handle this part of the subject) has taken this ground I'll look up the references and send them in a few days. One which is fresh in my mind is Marx' historic sneer in the Communist Manifest at the bourgeois panic because, having never seen in women any thing more than a means of production, the bourgeois forthwith jumped to the conclusion that they too, were to be held in common. But Lewis Morgan's Ancient Society culminates in the inference that the present form of the family is merely transitional.

Engels' Ursprung der Familie des Privateigentumes und des Staats hinges upon the transitory nature of the present form of the family.

[August] Bebels' book in its first edition is one continuous broadside fired into the present form of the family.

Morris, Bax and the Avelings are all explicit upon this point, and if they may be thought too strongly Marxist to represent English opinion fairly, there is George Bernard Shaw with his anti Marxist Socialism and his anti marriage-as-it-is to-day novels; and Karl Pearson with his morals under Socialism[2]

Even our own Bellamy both in Looking Backward and in the New Nation frees the wife from the economic thralldom which is the essential feature of marriage to-day.[3] Therefore, while the statement "Socialism is not free love" is true in a sense, I differ radically from all that follows down to "Most Socialists will claim that" etc. And again, I differ from the assertion that "Socialism has no connection with views about marriage." For I cannot conceive how, with the means of production the property of the community, any wife could be dependent upon her husband. And with the abolition of dependence there would remain solely inclination and affection to bind husband and wife, even the tie of common duty towards the future material welfare of their own children which now holds so many couples together would fall away, and there would remain, as stated before, solely affection for each other and their children.

To-day, the duty of providing for beings dependent upon him, determines the life of the average married man; and the duty of providing for her children makes life an endless petty economy for the average wife. And each endures the yoke by reason of the sense of duty, in untold numbers of cases in which respect and affection have fled. Hence, if you remove the economic dependence you do make love free. And all who have thought their Socialism out to its logical end—not only those whom I have mentioned above but a lot of lesser lights—such as Mrs. Besant and others are unanimous in arriving at this conclusion.[4]

So much for no. 1. I'll write again when I come to anything which strikes me as misleading.[5]

Yours sincerely
F. K. Wischnewetzky

You see, I take you at your word and write with the utmost frankness

ALS, Box 3, Ely Papers, WHi

1. This "budget" was an early draft of Ely's *Socialism: An Examination of Its Nature, Its Strength and Its Weakness, with Suggestions for Social Reform,* possibly in the form of lectures published as *Socialism: Syllabus of a Course of Six Lectures* (Madison, Wisc.: University Extension Department, 1892). See Bloomberg, *Florence Kelley,* 113–118; and Sklar, *Florence Kelley and the Nation's Work,* 167–168.

2. British artist William Morris (1834–1896) founded the arts and crafts movement. He wrote *News from Nowhere, or an Epoch of Rest* (Boston: Roberts, 1890) and edited the prominent socialist publication *The Commonweal.* British socialist Ernest Belford Bax (1854–1926) was a co-editor of *The Commonweal.* Eleanor Marx Aveling (1855–1898), daughter of Karl Marx, edited writings by her father and Frederick Engels, most notably Friedrich Engels and Karl Marx, *Revolution and Counter-Revolution in Germany in 1848* (London: S. Sonnenschein, 1851). With her husband Edward Aveling, she wrote several works, including *The Woman*

Question (London: Sonnenschein, 1886) and *The Working Class Movement in America* (London: Sonnenschein, 1891). George Bernard Shaw (1856–1950) edited *Essays in Fabian Socialism* (1889). British mathematician and socialist Karl Pearson (1857–1936) wrote *The Ethics of Freethought* (1888), a collection of his essays and lectures.

3. In *Looking Backward: 2000–1887*, Edward Bellamy attacked the existing social system and advocated a government-run socialist society.

4. British birth control advocate Annie Wood Besant (1847–1933) was a Fabian socialist.

5. On Ely's use of FK's comments, see Sklar, *Florence Kelley and the Nation's Work*, 168; and Blumberg, *Florence Kelley*, 118–119.

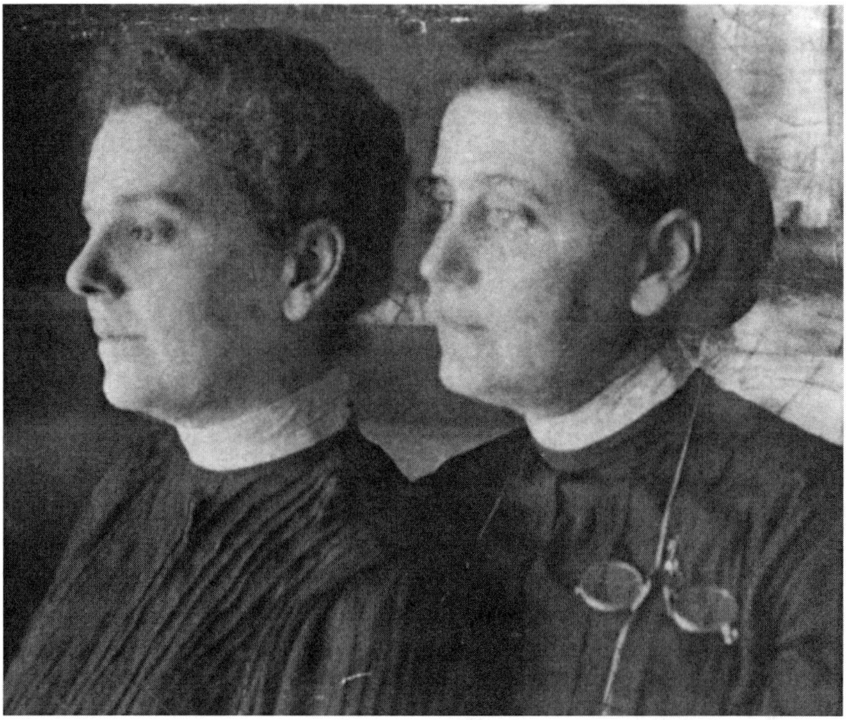

Jane Addams and Mary Rozet Smith, 1896. Courtesy of the Swarthmore College Peace Collection, Jane Addams Collection.

2 1892 – 1899

"This Beloved Hull House"

INTRODUCTION

Florence Kelley's letters in the 1890s depict her personal and professional transformation at Hull House in Chicago. She went first to the Woman's Temple, the twelve-story building in downtown Chicago that served the office and hotel needs of the Woman's Christian Temperance Union, a monument to the Union's colossal success among midwestern women. There she sought aid from the editor of her 1890 child labor pamphlet, who promptly directed her to Hull House. Although in 1891 Kelley had found the young women callow when she lectured on economics at the University Settlement on Rivington Street in Manhattan's Lower East Side, at Hull House she instantly trusted Jane Addams and wholeheartedly joined the community.[1] Addams helped her arrange for Ko, Margaret, and John to live in suburban Winnetka with the family of Jessie Bross Lloyd and Henry Demarest Lloyd. Partly because the children were so well provided for there, Kelley's attorney successfully defended her custody of the children when Lazare challenged her in court.[2]

She wrote her mother soon after arriving: "[I]n the few weeks of my stay here I have won for the children and myself many and dear friends whose generous hospitality astonishes me."[3] As an activist with an independent agenda, Kelley flourished there. Hull House made it possible for her to grow from a municipal to a state and national political leader on questions related to the rights of working people. Jane Addams later wrote that Kelley "galvanized us all into more intelligent interest in the industrial conditions around us."[4]

During the 1890s, the United States became the world's biggest industrial economy. Calculated in terms of steel production, the American economy grew from being about equal to that of Britain in 1880 to being almost as large as that of Britain and Germany combined in 1900. Kelley's residence at Hull House made her an expert witness of the effects of this industrialization on working-class life. About a million immigrants a year entered the United States from 1880 to 1914, far more than ventured to Brazil or Argentina, two other nations where immigrants sustained industrial development.[5]

Because this new group came mostly from eastern and southern Europe, replacing the former dominance of immigrants from western and northern Europe, they introduced new cultural differences into American cities. Kelley lived alongside orthodox Russian Jews and Serbian Orthodox Catholics rather than the assimilated German Jews and French Canadian Catholics that had once populated the nation's poorer neighborhoods. Along with continuing streams of immigrants from China and Japan, these new ethnicities threatened to become an unassimilated class of industrial workers that was politically as well as socially alien.

The "Haymarket massacre" in Chicago in 1886 became an iconic event in American popular opinion that associated large labor rallies with anarchist violence. At a rally where 200 skilled and unskilled workers had gathered to support the eight-hour day, a bomb exploded, killing a policeman. Six other policemen later died from gunshot wounds (apparently having fired on one another with their own guns in the confusion). About sixty other rally participants and bystanders were wounded by the bomb and the guns. The presence of anarchists at the rally led to the arrest and conviction of a group of anarchists, four of whom were hanged.[6] This event made it more difficult for skilled workers to forge unions that included unskilled laborers and for unskilled wage earners to elect leaders from their ranks to serve in state legislatures. Yet at the same time, the ongoing need for remedies for the poverty of unskilled workers—many of whom were women—created opportunities for Florence Kelley and other middle-class women reformers.

The growth of the settlement movement expanded those opportunities. Settlements had diverse sources of funding. Many were affiliated with Protestant religious denominations, an expression of the Social Gospel and the growing concern clergy and laity felt about their moral responsibility to the working poor. Nonsectarian women's settlements in New York, Boston, and Philadelphia attracted residents and financial support from women's colleges. Others, like Hull House, relied on local philanthropists for support.[7] In the three years preceding Florence Kelley's arrival, Jane Addams had spent over $10,000 of her own money to fund Hull House—a small fortune at that time and a large portion of her family inheritance. This fiscal autonomy gave her settlement its unique character and independence. Soon after Kelley's arrival, Mary Rozet Smith became the settlement's chief benefactor, followed by Louise de Koven Bowen, who generously supported Jane Addams's vision of thinking globally and acting locally.[8]

Although American settlements were modeled on Toynbee Hall and other British predecessors that sought to give young men at Oxford and Cambridge the opportunity to learn about modern industrial life by living in working-class neighborhoods, the American movement attracted more women than men; by 1905, women settlement house residents outnumbered men by about four to one and three-fourths of settlement heads were women. This numerical dominance made it easier for women to integrate men into space that they controlled, and Hull House began to accept male residents in 1893.[9]

The dominance of the settlement movement by men in Great Britain and by women in the United States helps us understand differences in the gendered channels of political opportunity in the two cultures. Britain's more activist state and effective civil service meant that British settlements became a training ground for civil servants. In the United States, where access to governmental influence flowed through party patronage, young men did not crowd women out of the settlement movement. In the United States, settlement work focused on immigrants, but despite a steady flow of immigrants into London's East End, the British settlement movement focused on British-born working people. Perhaps for this reason, British settlements remained loyal to the assumptions of middle-class charities, while Jane Addams, working outside the boundaries of her ethnic culture, led the American movement toward a new view of "social democracy" that envisioned immigrants as a source of democratic renewal.[10] In that spirit, in 1892 Florence Kelley taught a night school with "sixty pupils, Greeks, French, Germans, Austrians, Poles, Russians, Bohemians" and thought the "most open-minded" group were "the Russian Hebrew Immigrants."[11]

As one of the nation's fastest-growing industrial cities and the site of its most sustained industrial strife in the 1890s, Chicago facilitated the fullest development of Kelley's political talents. Her supportive environment at Hull House brought her into interaction with a wide range of politically active groups. She witnessed the bloody repression of the National Railway Union's strike in 1894 and organized support for an imprisoned Eugene Debs.[12] Most important, she generated practical legislative solutions for seemingly insoluble problems and worked productively to gain popular support. Aided by Clarence Darrow and other reformers, in 1892 she drafted (and Hull House supporters helped enact) path-breaking legislation that established an eight-hour day for women workers, curbed child labor, and created a robust factory inspector's office to enforce the legislation. When Illinois reform governor John Peter Altgeld appointed her as chief factory inspector, she made the most of the opportunity, enforcing the new law in an area two-thirds the size of Prussia.

Kelley assembled a staff of eleven zealous deputies, half of whom were required by the legislation to be women and most of whom were trade-union socialists, then she vigorously enlisted public support and steadily informed employers of her intention to enforce the law. By 1895, Illinois had become the site where the struggle to solve the "social question" through legislation for women and children was most powerfully engaged. That year, she added to her reform muscle by completing a law degree at Northwestern University.

In 1895, an Illinois Supreme Court decision gave manufacturers the first victory what became Kelley's lifelong battle to establish and defend laws regulating the industrial workplace. Because her goals could be trumped in courts by briefs sponsored by manufacturers' associations, she needed more than the power of a chief factory inspector. When John Altgeld lost his bid for reelection in 1896 and his successor fired Kelley, she did not immediately find a new path to political power. But by 1899, her work with consumers' leagues, which predated her arrival in Chicago and had steadily expanded there, drew her (albeit reluctantly) into accepting the offer of the newly founded National Consumers' League to serve as their general secretary. In 1899, she moved to New York and entered the national stage as one of the most ferocious and capable defenders of the rights of wage-earning women and children.[13]

NOTES

1. For FK in New York settlements, see Sklar, *Florence Kelley and the Nation's Work,* 156.
2. Sklar, *Florence Kelley and the Nation's Work,* 180–181; *Chicago Tribune,* 26 March 1892.
3. See Letter 23, FK to CBK, 24 February 1892, below.
4. Addams, *My Friend, Julia Lathrop,* 116.
5. For immigration statistics, see the introduction to Dublin, *Immigrant Voices.*
6. For the Haymarket massacre, see Green, *Death in the Haymarket.*
7. See Sklar, *Florence Kelley and the Nation's Work,* 170–205.
8. Sklar, "Who Funded Hull House?"
9. Sklar, *Florence Kelley and the Nation's Work,* 202–205.
10. Addams, *Democracy and Social Ethics,* 168–171.
11. See Letter 28, FK to Engels, 27 November 1892, below; and Letter 24, FK to Engels, 7 April 1892, below.
12. See Letter 39, FK to Lloyd, 18 July 1894, below. For speculation about FK's part in converting Debs to socialism, see Sklar, "Florence Kelley Tells German Readers about the Pullman Strike, 1894."
13. See Letter 57, FK to Lillian Wald, 23 March 1899, below. See also Sklar, *Florence Kelley and the Nation's Work,* 237–315.

22. To Henry D. Lloyd[1]

161 La Salle St.,
cf. Miss M. A. West [Chicago]
Jan. 4th 1892

Dear Sir,

Although I had not the pleasure of meeting you when you were in New York, I avail myself of the privilege of being one of the friends of your sister, Miss Caro Lloyd, and one of the interested readers of your valuable Strike of Millionaires, to ask you to grant me the favor of an interview at your earliest convenience.[2]

Yours very truly
Florence Kelley Wischnewetsky

ALS, Box 4, Lloyd Papers, WHi

1. Lloyd was an early supporter of Hull House and lectured there frequently (Brown, *Education of Jane Addams,* 243; Destler, *Henry Demarest Lloyd,* 252–253).
2. Caroline A. Lloyd (b. 1859), later Strobell, published a biography of her brother in 1912 (*Henry Demarest Lloyd, 1847–1903*). Lloyd's *Strike of Millionaires against Miners: The Story of Spring Valley* (Chicago: Bedforte-Clarke, 1890) attacked a coal-mining company in northern Illinois for its lockout of miners in 1889 (see Destler, *Henry Demarest Lloyd,* 226–232, 234–237). Shortly after FK wrote this note, Lloyd and his wife, Jessie Bross Lloyd (ca. 1845–1904), took the three Kelley children into their home in Winnetka, Illinois. The children "spent the rest of their first western winter, well and happy under Mrs. Lloyd's wise, unwearied kindness and exhilarated by unimagined experiences of country freedom," Kelley later wrote. (FK, *Notes of Sixty Years,* 82; see also Sklar, *Florence Kelley and the Nation's Work,* 178–179.)

Henry Demarest Lloyd, ca. 1893. Courtesy of the Wisconsin Historical Society.

23. To Caroline Bonsall Kelley

Hull House
335 S. Halsted St
Feb. 24th 1891[1892]

My dear Mother,

Your loving letter has just reached me for, since Friday I have been in hiding. Dr. Wischnewetzky and Mr. Wakeman have been here. Dr. W. went back on Sunday but Mr. Wakeman is still here. They wanted to get habeas corpus writs and try the case at once for the custody of the children. But there is no danger now of their doing so, for my counsel has made it clear that I should ruin Dr. W. if I made merely the baldest statement of my reasons for my action.[1]

Thank Willy with all my heart for his generosity and tell him that I have at last resumed possession of my conscience which I handed over, seven years ago, for "safe" keeping. And that hence forth if he cares to have any thing to do with me he will have to do with a woman who has come to her senses completely.

We are all well, and the chicks are happy. I have fifty dollars a month and my board and shall have more as soon as I can collect my wits enough to write. I have charge of the Bureau of Labor of Hull House here, and am working in the lines which I have always loved. I do not know what more to tell you except this, that in the few weeks of my stay here I have won for the children and myself many and dear friends whose generous hospitality astonishes me.[2]

There is no reason for us to maintain exaggerated secresy. It will be all right henceforth for you to write to me as Mrs. Kelley or Mrs. Florence Kelley, Hull House 335 S. Halsted Chicago. It is understood that I am to resume the maiden name and that the children are to have it. John is henceforth John Bartram[3] I have decided to do nothing to inj [ms. damaged] injure Dr. W. financially, so long as he leaves me in peace. For he is earning a great deal of money and when he has paid the most urgent debts and has some money there may be something for the chicks.

Don't try to send me anything but as much kindly feeling as my years of cruel ingratitude may have left possible. I am living in real comfort in this beloved Hull House and am better off than I have been since I landed in New York since I am now responsible myself for what I do.

I brought two trunks crammed with clothing for myself and chicks; and, now Clara the faithful girl who has had care of them since Maria left, is here also with another trunk full of toys and clothes; so there is no need to spend any money for some time to come upon clothes[.]I am thankful that you are enjoying peace and quiet and that you can read and write.

Sometime, somehow, I shall succeed in being of some use and comfort to you. And if you all prefer to wait and see and not waste any more faith upon me———why that would only be reasonable of you all.

If you think Will and Carrie [Kelley] would care for my scrawls, please forward them if you care to do so. Do as you feel like doing about everything concerning me.

I write to ~~k~~no one except Mary Forster the English governess who gave me the money to come away.

Your loving daughter
Florence

I cannot be with the chicks just now lest I betray their whereabouts. But they are in excellent hands!

ALS, FKP, NN

1. Thaddeus B. Wakeman (1834–1913), a New York lawyer, was the secretary of LW's Zander Institute. FK's attorneys were Messrs. Weckershaw and Gilbert (*Chicago Tribune:* 26 March 1892, 7, and 27 March 1892, 3).
2. FK was put in charge of a small experimental employment office for working girls and women. "We were welcomed as though we had been invited," she later wrote (FK, *Notes of Sixty Years,* 77–80, quote on 77; see also Sklar, *Florence Kelley and the Nation's Work,* 177, 182–195).
3. JK was originally named John Brown Kelley (Sklar, *Florence Kelley and the Nation's Work,* 136).

24. To Frederick Engels

Hull House Chicago Ill.
335 S. Halsted St.
Apr. 7th 1892

Dear Mr. Engels;

I have asked my friend Miss Ellen Gates Starr[1] to call upon you and carry you tidings of me.

I hope she may have done so already. You will see from the change of address and signature, the change which has been forced upon my life.

I have found friends and an opportunity for work for the support of my little children; and I hope to be able to resume work among the wage earners.

We have a colony of efficient and intelligent women living in a working men's quarter with the house used for all sorts of purposes by about a thousand persons a week. The last form of its activity is the formation of unions of which we have three, the cloak makers the shirt makers and the book binders. Next week we are to take the initiative in the systematic endeavor to clear out the sweating dens. There is a fever heat of interest in that phase of the movement just at present; Senator Sherman Hoar is travelling about the country poking into the dens at night and unattended.[2] The Trades Assembly is paying the expenses of weekly mass meetings; and the sanitary authorities are emphasizing the impossibility of their coping, unaided, with the task allotted to them.[3] So we may expect some more palliative measures pretty soon.

But, so far as my limited observation goes, I find more "root and branch Socialism" among men and women of the prosperous class than I do among our native American and Irish American wage earners, who seem to me the most shallow beings both in mind and heart, that come in my way. And the most open minded workers seem to me to be the Russia Hebrew Immigrants.

But my range is limited. I am living in the colony mentioned above, conducting a bureau of women's labor and learning more in a week, of the actual conditions of proletarian life in America than in any previous year.

I fear that the remittance of royalty, and the specimen copy of the English edition of the book, must have gone to New York and so been lost to me.[4] The address at the head of this letter will be my permanent one, as I have cast in my lot with Misses Addams and Starr for as long as they will have me. With sincere regard

Yours faithfully
Florence Kelley

ALS, Marx/Engels Papers, NL-AmISG

1. Ellen Gates Starr (1859–1940), co-founder of Hull House, was traveling in England and Italy (FK, Chicago, to CBK, 16 March 1892, KFP, NCC-RB).
2. In February, the U.S. House of Representatives had authorized Sherman Hoar (1860–1898; Democrat, Massachusetts, 1891–1892) to head a committee to investigate sweatshops. Hoar stated that the "great labor organizations of the country and the merchants themselves are urging Congressional investigation" (52nd Cong.,1st sess., *Cong. Rec.*, 13 February 1892, 1116–1117; see also Sklar, *Florence Kelley and the Nation's Work,* 381n25). For authorization for Hoar's investigation, see *Report of the Committee on Manufactures on the Sweating System.*
3. Founded in the 1870s, the Chicago Trade and Labor Assembly was an umbrella group that represented many of the city's mainstream trade unions.
4. Engels wrote describing a new contract with Swan Sonnenschein & Co. to publish FK's translation of *The Condition* with a new preface by him tailored to a British audience. (Engels, London, to FK, 28 January 1892; the full text of the letter is printed in Blumberg, *Florence Kelley,* following page 121.)

25. To Frederick Engels

STATE OF ILLINOIS
BUREAU OF LABOR STATISTICS

Hull House 335 S. Halsted St.
Chicago Ill. May 27th 1892

Dear Mr. Engels,

I cannot remember whether I acknowledged the receipt of your letter enclosing a draft for Ł5, 10 and 6d. If not please pardon the neglect, in view of the heavy strain under which I have been working for the past half year.

The Illinois courts have now finally awarded me the custody of my three little children;—and I can begin once more to live and act somewhat methodically.[1]

I am now in receipt of your note of May 11th and have received a notification of the safe arrival of the books at the N.Y. Custom House. I dare say they may come by any mail or express delivery now. I thank you very much, indeed, for taking so much trouble about them.

As you will see from the heading of this sheet, I have been made special agent for the Bureau. I enclose a schedule thinking that it may interest you.[2] For a full schedule, I receive the munificent compensation of fifty cents. This is piece work for the government with no regular salary. It remains to be seen how many I can fill in a month. The greater part of the investigation is now completed and there remain 1000~~0~~ schedules to be filled by "sweaters' victims" in the clothing trades. They are Poles, Bohemians, Neapolitans Sicilians and Russian Hebrews, almost excluding all other nationalities.

The work consists in shop visitation followed by house to house visitation and I find my polyglot acquisitions invaluable. The fact of living directly among the wagesearners is also an immense help. The municipal arrangements are so wretched that the filth and overcrowding are worse than I have seen outside of Naples and the East Side of New York. In the ward in which I live, the Nineteenth, with 7000 children of school age, (6–14 inclusive), there are but 2579 school sittings and everything municipal is of the same sort. This aggravates the economic conditions greatly, making possible child labor in most cruel forms and rendering the tenement house manufacture of clothing a deadly danger to the whole community. The Irish Catholics "run" the city government in the interest of the Church and their own pockets, and the Trade and Labor Assembly is as corrupt and as stupid as the City Council.

The general public is absorbed in the World's Fair and has no interest in the municipality; and when all the world and his wife come to look at the Fair, they will see the richest, filthiest, ugliest aggregation of houses, streets and people to be called a city, that Carlyle's worst dyspepsia could have conjured up.[3] The Socialists are active but practically unorganized, and very few at best.

The best visible work is doing, at the present moment, by a lot of women who are organizing tradesunions of men and women.

Yours faithfully
Florence Kelley

ALS, Marx/Engels Papers, NL-AmISG

1. On 25 March 1892, LW initiated a suit in the Chicago courts to obtain custody of their three children. Testimony from both FK and LW focused on each parent's financial ability to care for the children. While LW testified that he "had never struck her intentionally," FK insisted that LW had treated her cruelly and failed to support the family adequately. On 26 March, Judge Frank Baker awarded FK custody of the children. The *Tribune*'s account con-

cluded, "After a painful parting with the children the doctor left the court without glancing at his wife" (*Chicago Tribune:* 26 March 1892, 7, and 27 March 1892, 3; Sklar, *Florence Kelley and the Nation's Work,* 180–181).

2. With the help of some "wirepulling" from JA, FK was appointed on 23 May as a special agent to research and report on sweatshop conditions in Chicago, especially as they affected working women. On the schedule she enclosed, FK recorded the conditions she found in the sweatshops (FK, Chicago, to CBK, 16 March 1892, KFP, NCC-RB; see also Sklar, *Florence Kelley and the Nation's Work,* 206–216, 222).

3. Chicago's Columbian Exposition, which was popularly known as the Chicago World's Fair, celebrated the 400th anniversary of Columbus's discovery of America. It ran from 1 May to 30 October 1893. British historian and philosopher Thomas Carlyle (1795–1881) was known for his conservative critiques of "progress."

26. To Caroline Bonsall Kelley

[Chicago]
[ca. June 2, 1892]

[Continuation of missing portion of letter] Hull House at present.

I expect to earn very well, as I have been doing during the present week, though as it is all piece work, (so to speak,) everything depends upon my success from week to week.

When Bert marries you must come to me———or when L. goes back to Russia I'll come to you!

The treasures of the box are a delight. I did not know of the existence of the little thimble. Puss [MK] sews in a tentative way, and will do so very nicely.

The wrapper is a delight; the basque will be a beautiful present for Clara and the scrapbook for Ko—, and the trousers for both boys.

Give my best love to the boys. Do not worry about my finances, I'll keep you posted. And I think I can manage them myself. I shall not go to any friend. I have not done so. But I told W. of Mr. Straus' offer and he approved of it.[1] I have made no debts but those of which you know and shall make none.

I think I have been most fortunate to keep perfectly well and my nerves in good order in spite of all the strain of the trial, which was terrific.

And if I were a little blue and apprehensive, now and then, it would not be surprising particularly as we never see the sun and have had January weather ever since I came here except a few bright Sundays.

The horrors of the slums settle down upon my spirits but only for a few moments at a time. Then I am all right again.

But your loving letters and my exquisite bairns are enough to keep any one braced up and cheerful. The children are so beautiful physically and so loving and frank, that I have never dreamed of anything like them.

Yours lovingly
Florence

I was with the chicks on Decoration Day, and the older ones went for an hour to the village school for the patriotic exercises.[2] John decided to learn to read during their absence.

ALS, FKP, NN

1. In March, FK had told her mother about Mr. Straus's offer to testify against LW and his offer of funds to offset any financial difficulties FK might face (FK, Chicago, to CBK, 16 March 1892, KFP, NCC-RB).

2. The Kelley children remained with the Lloyds in Winnetka throughout the spring. FK later wrote CBK that she missed them "with a perennial heartache. In the Autumn, I must try to have them within reach, in my own interest, though I really think they are far better off in the country" (FK, Chicago, to CBK, [July 1892], FKP, NN).

27. To Henry D. Lloyd

STATE OF ILLINOIS
BUREAU OF LABOR STATISTICS

[Chicago]
June 30th, 1892
Dear Mr. Lloyd,

I had mercy upon you for a fortnight, but news items are accumulating so that I can't refrain any longer from posting you a little.

First as to ourselves. I know that you and Mrs. Lloyd will be glad to know that the chicks are well and continue to like their quarters; and that in the month from May 23d when my Bureau work began to June 23d, I earned $78.00 from the Bureau and $12.00 from the Signal. (They held over so much of my ms. that the payments for the month were only $3.00, $4.00, and $5.00). Nothing came of the Inter-Ocean work for some unexplained reason. However, my current expenses are only $64.00 per month, so that I came out well ahead, so far.[1]

Next as to the "Cause," I mail, herewith, the first instalment of the report of Commr. Ware of the Health Department.[2] A lot of shops have moved into better quarters.

I had a two hours' interview with Marshall Field a week ago.[3] He says he cannot deprive worthy widows of the chance of working at home with their children! The only one I have yet found working for him, earned $9.37 in 13 weeks and we fed her children meanwhile!

On Monday morning I told 64 Congregational Ministers about our neighbors of the cloak trade. One minister preaches to Henry W. King.[4] He was woe begone when I insisted that H. W. K. is a prop of the system.

Yesterday six ministers came over to see for themselves. Bisno devoted the afternoon to four of them. When he finished they felt in their vest pockets for tips for him! He slunk away from them insulted beyond words.

He is working at the Athenaeum and will enter the Law School in the Fall.

Dr. Bayard Holmes will pay his tuition. Alexander McCormick comes over every Wed. eve. to give him some extra coaching.[5]

Bessie Nahinsky comes two evenings a week to read English with me (and with a class of twelve of her compatriots). She is going to a Grammar School next year, living with her brother meanwhile. Pascha some thingorother, her pretty blonde cousin——Shapira, with all her brothers and cousins are laboring through the third reader with me and when they have finished I mean to have them read William Morris' News from Nowhere and More's Utopia and then Engels' Development of Socialism from a Utopia to a Science.[6] They are really intellectual, the whole dozen, and it is delightful to teach them.

Miss Addams is at Rockford with the Summer School, Miss Starr at Chicopee, Misses Lathrop and Brockway with Miss Addams, and I am here with Miss Farnsworth seriously ill, Miss Mason the visiting nurse about to leave, and no one to do anything but the housekeeper and Cray (who won't have anything to do with me!).[7]

So, as the neighborhood takes no vacation (except as we send the children through the Fresh Air Fund, and college extension students go to Rockford) there is an ample sufficiency of occupation.

All the lawsuits seem to be slumbering over the summer holidays and my horizon continues serene and cheerful.

The Sweating System pamphlet is exhausted and a number of people are begging for more.[8] I have gone through various states of mind about it. First, I wanted a new edition immediately. Then I wished to await action of Mr. Ware. Then I wanted an enlarged pamphlet. Now I want to wait, include Mr. Ware's data, the ordinances we spoke of, the latest enactments of Massachusetts and New York, and make a rousing campaign document of it for use when the legislature first meets.

What do you think about it? Don't you think its just as well to let Mr. Ware investigate and the preachers preach, and then when their energies begin to flag, return to the charge ourselves, and make the proper authorities do some practical thing about it?

It rains, every single day. It is rarely uncomfortably hot, but a trifle depressing.

With love to Mrs. Lloyd and kind regards to Frl. Stahlbohm,[9] I am, with grateful affection

Faithfully yours
Florence Kelley

Mr. Henry D. Lloyd

ALS, Box 4, Lloyd Papers, WHi

1. The Lloyds had left Winnetka for their summer home, Watch House, in Little Compton, Rhode Island, and the Kelley children had moved to Hull House for the summer. Payment from the *Union Signal* was most likely for FK's article "Household Labor," published in its

4 February 1892 issue. The *Inter Ocean,* a Chicago weekly, advertised itself as "radically Republican" (Sklar, *Florence Kelley and the Nation's Work,* 219, 410; Blumberg, *Florence Kelley,* 129).

2. [John D. Ware], *Report of the Department of Health of the City of Chicago for the Year 1892* (Chicago: Morris, 1893). Ware, a physician who had worked at Cook County Hospital, was appointed health commissioner of Chicago in May 1891. He favored the appointment of women sanitary inspectors and worked closely with them (*Chicago Tribune:* "Preparing to Take Charge," 1 May 1891, 2; and "Appointments to be Made," 2 May 1891, 3).

3. Marshall Field (1834–1906) opened a department store in Chicago in 1865.

4. Kelley's meeting with the ministers was covered in "Ministers Take a Summer Vacation" (*Chicago Daily Tribune,* 28 June 1892, 9), where she was described as "a Special Agent of the Illinois Bureau of Labor Statistics" who was "gathering facts and figures" to present to the state legislature in support of legislation to regulate sweatshops. Wages were constantly going lower and lower, she said, and "the most prominent and wealthiest dry-goods houses patronized these establishments."

Henry W. King (1828–1898) was a prominent leader of Chicago charities and the owner of "the largest clothing business in the United States" with retail stores in fifteen cities. At hearings conducted by U.S. congressmen on Chicago sweatshops in April 1892, King testified that his firm maintained its garment factory in New York City because skilled labor was cheaper there than in Chicago, since immigrants were "inclined to stay there, and the result was lower wages" (*Chicago Daily Tribune,* 14 April 1898, 10, and 5 April 1892, 1).

5. Abraham Bisno (1866–1929) was an organizer of women textile workers (see Sklar, *Florence Kelley and the Nation's Work,* 220–221). Bayard Holmes (1852–1924) was a prominent surgeon on the faculty of both the Postgraduate Medical School of Chicago and the University of Illinois College of Medicine. Alexander McCormick (b. 1863) wrote *A Study of Cook County* (1914).

6. William Morris, *News from Nowhere, or an Epoch of Rest* (Boston: Roberts, 1890); Thomas More (1478–1535), *Utopia* (1516; reprint, New York: Alden, 1887); Engels, *Development of Socialism from a Utopia to Science* (New York: The People's Educational Library, 1892).

7. Wilfreda Brockway taught kindergarten at Hull House and later married Frederick Deknatel (for more about Deknatel, see Letter 52, FK to CBK, 24 July 1898, note 6, below); Anna Farnsworth, whom FK described as "an agreeable woman of leisure and means," acted as a hostess and counselor at Hull House (Bryan and Davis, *100 Years at Hull House,* 58–59; FK, *Notes of Sixty Years,* 78). Cray was probably a housecleaner; FK was sometimes harshly critical of housecleaners' methods (Sklar, *Florence Kelley and the Nation's Work,* 223.)

8. Bureau of Statistics of Labor of Illinois [Florence Kelley], "The Sweating System of Chicago," 357.

9. Caroline Stallbohm, a former nurse to the Lloyds' son Will, was Lloyd's secretary (Destler, *Henry Demarest Lloyd,* 209).

28. To Frederick Engels

Hull House 335 S. Halsted St.
[Chicago]
Nov. 27th 1892

Dear Mr. Engels,

I thank you with all my heart for the remittance of Ł5.14.10 which I received, enclosed in your kind note of Nov. 9th. The increase in sales is most encouraging and the money very welcome indeed.

The increased discussion of Socialism here is very marked, though the study of book's and requests for lectures come almost exclusively from people of the prosperous middle class. Thus I have been asked to speak twice before the Secular Union and five times in churches in Chicago and its suburbs, and the more radically I speak the more vigorous the discussion in all these meetings. But in the workingmen's meetings, Socialists are regarded as bores, nuisances and professional promoters of discord, not only between working men and capitalists, but especially among workingmen. And certainly the local Socialist agitators, Morgan and the Germans, faithfully earn the dislike with which they are regarded.[1] The Irish American trades-unionists as a rule seem never to read anything but a democratic or republican newspaper. Moreover Chicago is "booming" and everybody gets some share of the general prosperity and hopes for more next year.

It is characteristic that Whitelaw Reid's Tribune's "scab" reputation, influenced the trades-unionists to vote for the democrats far more than any interest in the question of Free Trade or Protection, and the Tribune's deathbed conversion to Trades Union principles only strengthened the determination of the men to punish its long life of sins against organized labor. Now the more radical Irish-American leaders are turning towards the People's Party for the local Spring elections.[2]

I am teaching a night school in one of the foreign regions of the city. I have sixty pupils, Greeks, French, Germans, Austrians, Poles, Russians Bohemians, dividing the work of teaching them with a German American lady who has the more advanced pupils. In the same school there is an Italian who has some fifty Italian pupils, learning English. I taught a volunteer class throughout the summer. The present school is regularly carried on every winter by the city. It would be hard to duplicate this prosperous, polyglot workingmen's school, I think, outside of Chicago. There is one family in which father mother two adult sons and a little daughter are all at work side by side over their first readers. They are recent immigrants from Bohemia.

The Fair, next year, will be magnificent in its scope and beautiful in location and buildings. I have seen several World's Fairs, but never anything comparable to the beauty of the City by the Lake which has sprung up, as if by magic, during the past year. I hope you may come to see it; and if you do, come early, not later than June 15th here in Chicago, for the crowds and the weather in August and September will be intolerable.[3]

Please say to Mrs. Kautzky that I will answer her interesting note very soon.[4]

Yours very truly
Florence Kelley

ALS, Marx/Engels Papers, NL-AmISG

1. Thomas J. Morgan (1847–1912) was secretary of the Machinists' Union and a Chicago SLP leader.

2. In 1883, in protest of a wage cut, Typographical Union No. 6, one of the strongest unions

in the country, initiated a boycott of the *New York Tribune* that lasted for nine years. Editor Whitelaw Reid (1837–1912), who had ordered the wage cut, was the Republican Party candidate for vice-president in 1892. During the campaign, Reid was accused of buying off the union at the *Tribune* (Foner, *History of the Labor Movement,* 2:49; *NYT,* 13 August 1892, 5). In the 1892 presidential election, the Democrats returned Grover Cleveland to the White House and assumed control of both houses of Congress. The People's Party (also known as the Populist Party) was formally organized in St. Louis on 22 February 1892. Its election platform included government control of all transportation, a shorter working day, and a graduated income tax.

3. On the Columbian Exposition, see FK, *Notes of Sixty Years,* 86–87; and Sklar, *Florence Kelley and the Nation's Work,* 242–243. In early 1893, Lloyd invited Engels to the exposition, but he declined (Engels, London, to Lloyd, [March 1893], in Marx and Engels, *Letters to Americans,* 251–252).

4. Louise Strasser Kautsky (1860–1950), first wife of Karl Kautsky, had been Engels's secretary since 1890 (biographical entry in Marx and Engels, *Letters to Americans,* 298).

29. To Henry D. Lloyd

327 W. Harrison St.
[Chicago]
Nov. 28th, 1892 [and Dec. 2]

Dear Mr. Lloyd,

I have swarmed off from Hull House into a flat near by, with my mother and my bairns, and I don't get my mail promptly. So the delightful skit at the Carnegie Mahatma has only now reached me.[1]

I wished all last Spring that you felt as warmly with the workingmen, on a basis of personal contact, as you feel against the robbers in spite of the acquaintance of the most decent of them. And now I wish it more than ever.

There is such urgent need of a leader now; and the men at the helm are such sorry steersmen.

We are getting a constantly improving body of men to make the House their headquarters; and now that the ground is actually broken and the foundation is laid for the Coffee House and the lease secured for land for a great meeting hall, the nucleus cannot fail to grow into a larger mass of thinking, active workingmen.[2]

Now, if some turn of the wheel of Fortune had only sent you to the Nineteenth, instead of the prosperous regions, here's your garden ready to your hand, awaiting cultivation.[3]

Friday night. Since I wrote the foregoing Miss Starr has given me the good tidings that you are to speak at the House on Sunday afternoon, and Bisno announced on Tuesday that you w'd. speak tonight at Schwarz Hall. It is too bad that I'm going to Geneva on Sunday to speak on Child Labor to the Unity Club; and tonight I had my night school. I seem destined not to hear you speak! Now comes your letter today which makes me long to plunge into the anti-sweaters agitation at once. But——I am teaching in the Polk Street nightschool Monday to Friday evening inclusive. By day I am a "temporary expert" in the employ of the Department of Labor—Carroll D. Wright[4]—and, on Dec. 4th (Sunday) I go to Geneva, Dec. 11th to Madison to tout for Hull House under the auspices of Mr. [Richard] Ely, and Dec. 17th and 18th to Oak Park to speak on Hull House and the Sweating System on Sat. and Sunday eves.

Me voila! There is only a limited amount of me at best; and, such as it is, it works twelve hours on weekdays for "grub and debts" and on Sundays it goes out of town to tell the outlying public how life looks in the Nineteenth. By way of consoling the small fry for these absences I take one with me. Puss [MK] is going to Geneva and Ko to Madison with me.

I want very much to see Mrs. Lloyd and the chicks beg me to take them to see "the Lloyds" indiscriminately. But I seem to have no time for living of late. So I don't see how I, personally, can agitate at all before Xmas.

But the Trades Assembly would snap at the chance to hold the meeting you propose. You would do best to go ahead as if I were in New York, and if later I can lend a hand, so much the better

Certainly the work begun in May ought to go on now that the legislature is coming into session.[5]

Yours always with cordial regard
Florence Kelley

ALS, Box 4, Lloyd Papers, WHi

1. On the new arrangement for the Kelley children, see Sklar, *Florence Kelley and the Nation's Work,* 223–224. At the Chicago Sunset Club, as part of an entertainment skit, Lloyd read a letter purportedly from Andrew Carnegie (1835–1919), which he introduced as a letter from a "new Mahatma, Mahatma Carnegie," a satirical reference to Carnegie's aspiration to be perceived as an intellectual leader with his book *Gospel of Wealth* (1889). The supposed letter stated that Carnegie was retiring into the mountains to establish a "Millionaire's paradise" where the "Almighty Dollar" would rule (Destler, *Henry Demarest Lloyd,* 247).

2. On Hull House improvements, see Sklar, *Florence Kelley and the Nation's Work,* 198.

3. In the 1890s, 50,000 people representing eighteen nationalities lived in deplorable conditions in Chicago's Nineteenth Ward, where Hull House was located (see Sklar, *Florence Kelley and the Nation's Work,* 172).

4. In *Notes of Sixty Years,* FK described her new responsibility of heading the Chicago section of a federal inquiry into city slums directed by Commissioner of Labor Carroll D. Wright (1840–1909). FK's team gathered data on working and living conditions in the square mile surrounding Hull House (FK, *Notes of Sixty Years,* 80–81; Sklar, *Florence Kelley and the Nation's Work,* 228–229).

5. Abraham Bisno, Bayard Holmes, Lloyd, and FK spoke on 8 May 1892 at the Trade and Labor Assembly meeting at Bricklayers Hall to protest the sweatshop system. FK declared that "the children who work in Chicago are in worse condition than I have seen on the east side of New York. . . . If the people would notify Marshall Field, Henry King, and others that they would buy from them no clothing made in sweat shops the evil would be stopped." The group named FK, Lloyd, and several others to a committee to seek solutions to the sweatshop problem from Illinois gubernatorial candidates (*Chicago Tribune,* 9 May 1892, 6).

30. To Henry D. Lloyd

U.S. DEPARTMENT OF LABOR

[Chicago] July 13th, 1893

Dear Mr. Lloyd,

I'll learn what I can about the unions and send you whatever I can learn.

Governor Altgeld made my boy a good birthday present without knowing it, when he mailed yesterday the commission which assures us four years of permanent useful employment.[1]

I only hope I may have the insight to make the most of the huge opportunity he has given me.

Any gray matter that you're willing to squander might be profitably employed by way of suggestions!

Yours with the profoundest satisfaction
Florence Kelley

ALS, Box 4, Lloyd Papers, WHi

1. Democrat John P. Altgeld (1847–1902), former justice of the superior court in Cook County, was elected governor of Illinois in 1892. FK's appointment as chief factory inspector resulted from the Illinois legislature's enactment in June 1893 of a bill that she had helped draft. The bill created a state factory inspector's office with a staff of eleven, five of whom had to be women. Altgeld first offered the position to Lloyd, who declined and recommended FK (*Chicago Tribune,* 13 July 1893, 5; Sklar, *Florence Kelley and the Nation's Work,* 234–236).

31. To Richard T. Ely

STATE OF ILLINOIS
OFFICE OF FACTORY INSPECTOR
247 W. POLK ST.
CHICAGO

Aug. 20th 1893

Dear Mr. Ely,

Don't laugh, please at the meagre beginning of a collection of constitutions which accompanies this. I'll send more as fast as I can get them.

The papers are so savage in their onslaughts upon us that I think we must be doing fairly good work.[1]

We have had no prosecutions yet under the new law, of which I enclose a copy; but I am preparing for a long series of them to begin next week and continue for a month or more.[2] Meanwhile the large manufacturers are obeying promptly and the little employers are bumptious just in proportion to the badness of their shops.

I hope to see you during the Labor Congress.[3]
With very kind regards to Mrs. [Anna] Ely

Yours Sincerely
Florence Kelley

ALS, Box 6, Ely Papers, WHi

1. For example, the *Chicago Tribune* editorialized that the new factory inspectors went into shops they had no authority to enter and attempted to enforce regulations that applied to other trades. The *Tribune* was concerned that these state employees were "trying everywhere to organize unions among employees." An article in the German-language *Illinois Staats-Zeitung* characterized FK as "an extreme socialist agitator who hardly differs from an anarchist" (*Chicago Tribune,* 31 July 1893, 4) FK responded in a letter to the editor (Sklar, *Florence Kelley and the Nation's Work,* 237–238.)

2. The bill establishing the factory inspector's office limited the workday for women and children to eight hours and set fourteen as a minimum working age. It also authorized inspectors to search tenement houses for possible disease and required employers to compile lists of those working in sweatshops (FK, *Notes of Sixty Years,* 82; Sklar, *Florence Kelley and the Nation's Work,* 234–235) For the text of the bill, see Document 13 in Sklar and Tyler, "How Did Florence Kelley's Campaign against Sweatshops in Chicago in the 1890s Expand Government Responsibility for Industrial Working Conditions?"

3. The International Labor Congress met at the site of the Columbian Exposition from 28 August to 4 September. Speakers included U.S. labor leader Samuel Gompers and British Fabian socialists Beatrice and Sidney Webb. Ely, then a professor of economics at the University of Wisconsin, spoke on "Public Ownership of Agencies to Supply Public Needs" (Destler, *Henry Demarest Lloyd,* 259).

32. To Henry D. Lloyd

STATE OF ILLINOIS
OFFICE OF FACTORY INSPECTOR
247 W. POLK ST.
CHICAGO

Oct. 10th, 1893

Dear Mr. Lloyd,

Can you grant M. Genoud's request? He seemed to be a remarkably thoughtful, able man, about whom it might be worth while to take some trouble.

I am going to make a personal endeavor to enlist the clergy again actively in the agitation[x] I have neglected them, thinking them absorbed by the Fair. But they must be in need of subjects now and then, and I'll furnish them taking ones.

Out of sixty five names of children sent to the Board of Education in our first month of notifying it when we turned children under 14 yrs. of age out of factories, twenty one were immediately returned to school and several others are known to be employed as nursegirls and cashgirls i.e. in non-prohibited occupations. This is good co-operation.

The Boards of Health and Education, the medical profession, and the Herald, Inter Ocean and Record are all co-operating now, satisfactorily, and you doubtless saw the flamboyant resolutions of the Women's Alliance.[1] Governor Altgeld is doing everything in his power to back the law, and has authorized me to engage counsel for continuous prosecutions. I have engaged counsel and am gathering testimony and hope to begin a series of justice court cases this week.

We are weighing and measuring factory children at a great rate and shall publish photographs of deformed children found in the cutlery trade where every boy yet found has shown the same deformity of the right shoulder and one youngster, having worked from his 11th birthday, is now, at 15 an actual monstrosity unfit for work for the rest of his life! I think the medical chapter of this report will start a new line of activity for medical men and factory inspectors both.

Give my love to Mrs. Lloyd and believe me

Yours sincerely
Florence Kelley

ALS, Box 4, Lloyd Papers, WHi

1. Like the *Inter Ocean*, the *Herald* and the *Record* were Republican papers (Grossman, Keating, and Reiff, *The Encyclopedia of Chicago*, 569). The Illinois Woman's Alliance, formed in 1889, brought together women from a variety of class backgrounds to protect women and children in the workplace, promote public health, and oversee "the management of public institutions as they affect women and children." After the Chicago Trade and Labor Assembly opposed the Alliance's activist support for women inspectors in 1891, the Alliance began to lose momentum. By 1893, it was better at issuing resolutions than leading effective action. See Sklar, *Florence Kelley and the Nation's Work*, 211–216, 221, 243, 263–264; see also Tax, *The Rising of the Women*, 66–67.

33. To Frederick Engels

STATE OF ILLINOIS
OFFICE OF FACTORY INSPECTOR
247 W. POLK ST.
CHICAGO

Nov. 21st 1893

Dear Mr. Engels,

I am very much obliged, indeed, for the royalty-remittance received from Mr. [Friedrich] Sorge this morning. I am only sorry that the sales have fallen of[f] since last year.

I find my work as inspector most interesting; and as Governor Altgeld places no restrictions whatever upon our freedom of speech, and the English etiquette of silence while in the civil service is unknown here, we are not hampered by our position and three of my deputies and my assistant are outspoken Socialists and active in agitation.

I am at work upon my first report due Dec. 15th. When it is finished I shall take great pleasure in sending you a copy.[1]

I read with much interest of your reception in Zurich and Vienna.[2]

With kind regards to Mrs. [Louise] Kautzky

Yours Sincerely
Florence Kelley

ALS, Marx/Engels Papers, NL-AmISG

1. See Letter 34, FK to CBK, 31 December 1893, below.
2. Engels traveled there and to other European cities from 1 August to 29 September 1893. In Zurich he delivered a speech at the close of the International Social Congress; in Vienna he spoke to the Social Democratic Party on the increasing influence of socialists (Draper, *The Marx-Engels Chronicle,* 279).

34. To Caroline Bonsall Kelley

STATE OF ILLINOIS
OFFICE OF FACTORY INSPECTOR
247 W. POLK ST.
CHICAGO

Dec. 31st 1893

My dear Mother,

I never before felt so imperatively the desire to write you at the end of the last day of the year. I think every month unites me more tenderly with the loving heart that you kept so warm for me when I did not deserve it. It has been, in every way, a good year for me, personally. Good health, good children, good work, good friends and as much of your presence as it was at all reasonable to ask for. What more could a woman wish, who has survived the illusions of youth without bittern[ess].

I finished at 3 o'clock this afternoon all my part of the wearisome report. A little clerical work remains for Mrs. Stevens and then it goes to His Excellency who will promptly order it published, I trust.[1]

I begin to think that February will see me in Hoboken, for the work here is in almost perfect shape and can well be left with Mrs. Stevens while I reconnoitre the situation of the clothing trades in New York City. You will readily understand that I shall sleep in N[ew] Jersey and my work will lie in the obscure streets of the East Side of New York so that I have no fear of having any papers served upon me. And of course you will see me either by joining me or by my joining you. So there is a pleasant prospect for the near future.

Love to the boys. I go to the chicks by the early train for N. Years and must write the rough draft of two circulars before I go to bed. So Good night and good New Year to you.

Your Florence

ALS, KFP, NCC-RB

1. FK's *First Annual Report of the Factory Inspectors of Illinois for the Year Ending December 15, 1893* (Springfield, Ill.: State Printers, 1894) described conditions in 704 sweatshops. The report emphasized workers' injuries and the harm children suffered from lack of schooling. (FK, "Recommendations," Document 18 in Sklar and Tyler, "How Did Florence Kelley's Campaign against Sweatshops in Chicago in the 1890s Expand Government Responsibility for Industrial Working Conditions?"; see also Sklar, *Florence Kelley and the Nation's Work,* 250–252, 389n34, 389n35.) Alzina Parsons Stevens (1849–1900) was the first president of Working Woman's Union Number 1 in Chicago in 1877. After organizing women for the Knights of Labor in Toledo in the 1880s, Stevens moved to Chicago and organized several unions there before becoming FK's assistant factory inspector (Sklar, *Florence Kelley and the Nation's Work,* 238).

35. To John P. Altgeld

STATE OF ILLINOIS
OFFICE OF FACTORY INSPECTOR
247 W. POLK ST.
CHICAGO

Jan. 9th, 1894

Hon. John P. Altgeld
Governor of Illinois
My dear Governor;

Will you kindly sign the enclosed requisitions and start them on their way to the printer? And did the printer's copy of our law in the form for posting, finally reach you?

The case against the Chicago Stamping Co. (charged with employing a girl under sixteen years of age, without posting the required notice of hours of work required of her) comes up this week in Justice Kersten's court. I am told that counsel for the defendant is Adolph Kraus.[1] It is strange that he permitted his name to be used as in the enclosed circular, while he was still corporation counsel for the City of Chicago, is it not?

To me this seems <u>almost</u> as inappropriate as for Mr. Moloney or Mr. Kern to do a similar thing in relation to a State law.[2] This is gossip of course, but closely connected with the duties of the office. The circular was sent me by a trades union in its present battered state.

I am sending copies of the enclosed warning circular to all employers of large numbers of girls under 16 yrs. of age, and am preparing to follow it up with prosecution if necessary.[3]

Yours very truly
Florence Kelley

ALS, Altgeld Correspondence, I-Ar

1. George Kersten (1853–1934) was a Chicago police magistrate and justice of the peace (1883–1903). Adolph Kraus (1850–1928) was a member of the Chicago Board of Education (1881–1887).
2. Maurice T. Maloney (1849–1917) was Illinois attorney general from 1893 to 1897. Charles Kern (1831–1897), a leading Democrat, was treasurer of Cook County from 1890 to 1894.
3. See Letter 36, FK to Rand McNally and Company, 9 January 1894, below.

36. To Rand McNally and Company

STATE OF ILLINOIS
OFFICE OF FACTORY INSPECTOR
247 W. POLK STREET
CHICAGO

Jan. 9th 1894
Rand McNally and Co.[1]

Gentlemen;

In view of the present depressed condition of manufactures, and the very large number of women consequently unemployed, it becomes doubly the duty of this office to call to the attention of employers the provisions of the law touching the hours of work of women and girls in factories and workshops in the State.

Sections Five and Six of the law, of which a marked copy is enclosed herewith, specify that the hours between which work is required of women and girls shall be posted in every room in which such help is such employed, and limit those hours to eight per day.[2]

While many employers of women and girls have given this law prompt obedience and loyal support, yet the complaint of female employes that they are required to work more than eight hours per day is so constant that it is needful to urge once more upon employers the duty of strict compliance with these sections, not only because obedience to the law is the duty of the citizen, but also to the end that overworked women and children may be relieved of excessive toil, and a portion, at least, of the unemployed may find work to do.

Very truly yours,
Florence Kelley

ALS, Altgeld Correspondence, I-Ar

1. Founded in 1856, Rand McNally and Company printed maps, atlases, and textbooks.
2. "Factories and Workshops," in *Laws of the State of Illinois, Passed by the Thirty-Eighth General Assembly* (Springfield, Ill.: H. W. Rokker, 1893), 99–102, Document 13 in Sklar and Tyler, "How Did Florence Kelley's Campaign against Sweatshops in Chicago in the 1890s Expand Government Responsibility for Industrial Working Conditions?"

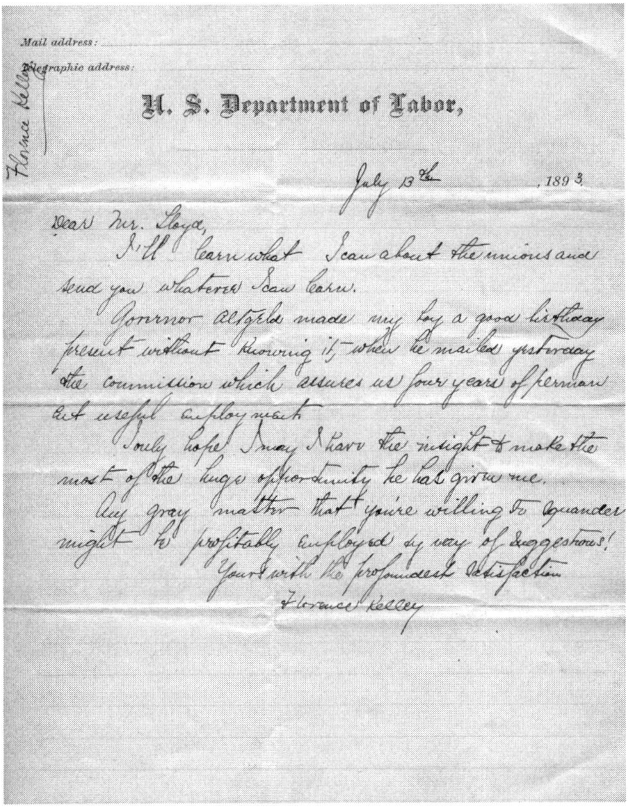
Mail address:
Telegraphic address:

U. S. Department of Labor,

July 13th, 1893

Dear Mr. Lloyd,
I'll learn what I can about the unions and send you whatever I can learn.
Governor Altgeld made my boy a good birthday present without knowing it, when he mailed yesterday the commission which assures us four years of permanent useful employment.
I only hope I may have the insight & make the most of the huge opportunity he has given me.
Any gray matter that you're willing to squander might be profitably employed by way of suggestions!
Yours with the profoundest satisfaction
Florence Kelley

Florence Kelley

Florence Kelley to Henry Demarest Lloyd, 13 July 1893. Courtesy of the Henry Demarest Lloyd Papers, Wisconsin Historical Society.

37. To Richard T. Ely

STATE OF ILLINOIS
OFFICE OF FACTORY INSPECTOR
247 W. POLK ST.
CHICAGO

June 21st, 1894

Dear Dr. Ely,

I have abandoned the idea of either method of publication of my Hull House essays in advance of the book.[1]

But for my own use strictly, I am desirous of having a copy of each. If the essays have not yet been forwarded, can you have a copy of each made for me?

I am reading Socialism and Social reform with much interest but I do not think the U.S. now have the opportunity which Dr. Meyer thought Germany had twenty years ago.[2]

The concentration of wealth has gone too far, and the instinctive Socialism of the vast body of wageearners now struggling so actively to get together, is too vital to be calmed by any reform however comprehensive, short of the collective administration of land and industrial capital.

I personally participate in the work of social reform because part of it developes along Socialist lines, and part is an absolutely necessary protest against the brutalizing of us all by Capitalism. Not because our Hull House work alone would satisfy me.

Yours Sincerely
Florence Kelley

ALS, Box 7, Ely Papers, WHi

1. In 1892, Ely became editor of the Crowell Library of Economic and Political Science, which in 1895 published *Hull-House Maps and Papers* (Rader, *The Academic Mind and Reform*, 128). FK refers here to her two essays that were published in *Hull House Maps and Papers,* "The Sweating System" and "Wage Earning Children," the latter written with Alzina Stevens (see Letter 41, to Richard T. Ely, 14 November 1894, below).

2. German American mining engineer Siegfried Meyer (1840–1872) helped found the General German Working Men's Union of New York (biographical entry in Marx and Engels, *Letters to Americans,* 300).

38. To John P. Altgeld

STATE OF ILLINOIS
OFFICE OF FACTORY INSPECTOR
247 W. POLK ST.
CHICAGO

July 15th, 1894

Hon. John P. Altgeld
Governor of Illinois,
My dear Governor;

I sent, this morning, the final pages of the smallpox-sweatshop report.[1]

We have a rough copy of it here.

Shall I have copies of this ms. type-written and send them to the judges of the Supreme Court? Or is the State Printer so short of work that he will get this report out in a few days? And shall I wait and send a printed copy to each of them?

The reports concerning the decision of the Supreme Court which have leaked out so far, are rather harrowing.[2]

Thomas Hall told me that a judge (name not mentioned) had told him that he, the judge, had written the opinion and sustained the law in all essential points.[3]

The next day, however, Carl Meyer told Mrs. Powell that the decision as submitted was rejected by the court and—if I understand aright—reassigned to Judge Bailey[4] who is a partner (in a city law school) of Moran who was counsel for the mfrs. Ass'n. and argued the case before the full bench, against the law.

From all this conflicting hearsay one thing is clear; that the Court certainly did not hand down its decision in June as it promised counsel on both sides that it would do. And the natural inference is that the court is not unanimous and there is room for the smallpox report to do its work.

Mrs. [Alzina] Stevens typewrites well and quickly and we can send out the six typewritten copies quickly if you think well of it. Pending your approval of the report, we naturally wait to hear from you.[5]

Yours very truly
Florence Kelley

ALS, Altgeld Correspondence, I-Ar

1. *First Special Report of the Factory Inspectors of Illinois, on Small-Pox in the Tenement House Sweat-Shops of Chicago, July 1, 1894* (Springfield, Ill.: H. W. Rokker, 1894).
2. In 1893, a group of manufacturers formed the Illinois Manufacturers' Association to combat the eight-hour law for women. In May 1894, paper-box manufacturer W. C. Ritchie & Co. appealed this portion of the 1893 factory law to the Illinois Supreme Court in *Ritchie v. People of Illinois* (*Chicago Tribune*, 31 January 1894, 5). For FK's role in the defense, see Sklar, *Florence Kelley and the Nation's Work*, 255–260.
3. Thomas Cuming Hall (1858–1936) was then minister of the Fourth Presbyterian Church in Chicago.
4. Belle Matteson Powell was a deputy factory inspector (Sklar, *Florence Kelley and the Nation's Work*, 239). Joseph M. Bailey (1833–1895) was an Illinois Supreme Court justice (1888–1895). Thomas A. Moran (1839–1904), a former judge, resumed private practice in 1892 (Ffrench, *Biographical History of the American Irish in Chicago*, 684–687).
5. Governor Altgeld presumably discouraged FK from distributing the report (Sklar, *Florence Kelley and the Nation's Work*, 393n7). However, she asked Colonel William F. Dose to mail copies of the sweatshop report to the seven Illinois supreme court justices (FK, Chicago, to William F. Dose, 6 August 1894, Altgeld Correspondence, I-Ar).

39. To Henry D. Lloyd

STATE OF ILLINOIS
OFFICE OF FACTORY INSPECTOR
247 W. POLK ST.
CHICAGO

July 18th, 1894

Dear Mr. Lloyd,

Debs is in jail and his courage, while not failing, needs all the bracing it can get. And the length of his imprisonment may, perhaps, be modified by the degree of public interest shown in the present injunction outrage. Fancy an injunction that makes it a crime "to attempt to induce by persuasion any person to refrain from handling a freight car"![1] Yet I read this injunction containing these words, posted in the Rock Island yards.

So I am trying to arrange a Central Music Hall meeting and Darrow will speak and, I hope, Bemis and Zeublin and Dr. Holmes.[2] I do not yet know who else. It is a national calamity that you are away from Chicago now when the public mind is seething and the time is ripe for such farreaching action.

However, I suppose you cannot come on.

Can you write a letter to the meeting? The date is not fixed but the fact that there will be such a meeting is certainly determined. Probably next Thursday week. It will be a meeting of Citizens of Chicago to protest against Government by injunction and rifles.[3]

Give my love to Mrs. [Jessie] Lloyd and my boy and your boys.[4] I have had moments of longing to get away from my slum and my drudgery. But I would not be out of Chicago today for a thousand dollars an hour.

Yours Sincerely
Florence Kelley

ALS, Box 5, Lloyd Papers, WHi

1. Eugene V. Debs (1855–1926) was president of the American Railway Union. On 26 June 1894, protesting recent wage cuts, the union boycotted all trains with Pullman cars, creating a national disruption in railroad traffic. Illinois courts issued an injunction on 2 July ordering the union to stop aiding the boycott. Despite Governor Altgeld's objections, President Grover Cleveland sent federal troops to Chicago on 4 July to enforce this ruling. On 10 July, Debs and three others were indicted on charges of conspiracy. After being released on bail, the four were rearrested on 17 July for contempt of court and sent to Cook County Jail, where they remained until 25 July. Their trial was set for 5 September. For FK's view of the Pullman strike, see FK, "Ein Ruckblick auf den Pullman-Strike" ("Looking Back on the Pullman Strike"); Sklar, *Florence Kelley and the Nation's Work,* 269–274; and Sklar, "Florence Kelley Tells German Readers about the Pullman Strike, 1894."

2. Clarence Darrow (1857–1938), Altgeld's former law partner, defended Debs against conspiracy charges. In 1894, Edward W. Bemis (1860–1930) was associate professor of economics at University of Chicago, where Charles E. Zueblin (1866–1924) taught sociology.

3. The protest meeting never took place. Lloyd subsequently contributed to Debs's defense fund (FK, Chicago, to Lloyd, 1 August 1894, Lloyd Papers, WHi; Constantine, *Letters of Eugene V. Debs,* 1:70–75).

4. NK was spending the summer with the Lloyds in Little Compton, Rhode Island. FK refers to the Lloyds' sons, William Bross Lloyd (1875–1946), Henry D. ("Hal") Lloyd (1878–1964), and John ("Jack") Lloyd (b. ca. 1886).

40. To Miss Williams[1]

STATE OF ILLINOIS
OFFICE OF FACTORY INSPECTOR
247 W. POLK ST.
CHICAGO

Sept. 1st 1894

Dear Miss Williams:

I send herewith copies of my two reports.[2] We are very soon to begin work upon the third, unless the Supreme Court pronounces us unconstitutional as it may do in October. It is my ambition to make the most thorough***ly*** specialized study of the statistics of child labor that has ever been made; and I am employing all the resources of my position to do this. A very intelligent assistant, a first rate lawyer to prosecute offenders; eight unusually active and faithful deputies and, in addition to all this, a Governor who is as much interested as I am, and eager to help in every way. All these things would seem to facilitate the enterprise very greatly. ~~Had~~ ***And*** one standard work upon the subject will compel all others who deal with it to treat it more scientifically than has yet been done. It has never yet been shown how far the exploitation of children contributes to the concentration of the people in cities and to a number of other ~~the~~ ***phenomena*** of your present life. I hope you will write me often.

Yours sincerely
Florence Kelley

CC, CLM Records, MCR-S

Note: handwritten changes in this copy are not in FK's hand.

1. Although Miss Williams is not mentioned as having any part in the organization that became the CL of Massachusetts in 1897, she was probably connected in some way, since two letters to her from FK are in that organization's files.

2. For FK's *First Annual Report,* see Letter 34, FK to CBK, 31 December 1893, above; for the smallpox report, see Letter 38, FK to John P. Altgeld, 15 July 1894, above.

41. To Richard T. Ely

STATE OF ILLINOIS
OFFICE OF FACTORY INSPECTOR
247 W. POLK ST.
CHICAGO

Nov. 14th, 1894

DEAR DR. ELY:

I sen***t*** ~~herewith~~ ***today to Crowell and Co.*** the corrected proof of the two chapters on The Sweating System and Wage-Earning Children.[1] The bibliography which is to follow the latter does not appear in the proof. I have sent you copy for it three times, and trust ~~you have not lost~~***that*** all the copies ***are not lost.*** ~~If you have,~~ ***Please*** let me know and I will forward still another, as I am anxious to have it appear in connection with that chapter.

I am, of course, disappointed at the delay in getting out the book, after I held back my essays from the Archiv fur Soziale Gesetzgebung (which pays liberally and promptly), because you wrote me in May that the book would be in the market last September.[2]

But the disappointment over the delay is trivial in comparison with the dismay which I felt when you suggested cutting the maps. This I positively decline to permit.

The charts are mine to the extent that I not only furnished the data for them but hold the sole permission from the U.S. department of labor to publish them. I have never contemplated, and do not now contemplate, any form of publication except as two linen-backed maps or charts, folding in pockets in the cover of the book, similar to Mr. Booth's charts.[3]

If Crowell and Co. do not contemplate this, it will be well to stop work at once, as I can consent to no use of my charts in any other form.

I shall be glad of an answer, at your earliest convenience, containing a definite acceptance or rejection of this proposition, as I am ~~no longer~~ unwilling to hold back my essays longer upon any uncertainty.[4]

Yours Very Truly,
Florence Kelley

TLS, Box 8, Ely Papers, WHi

1. Both essays were published in [Residents of Hull-House], *Hull-House Maps and Papers* (Boston: Thomas Y. Crowell, 1895).

2. This periodical printed FK's "Die Fabrik-Gesetzgebung der Vereinigten Staaten" ("Factory Legislation in the United States") in 1895, "Die weibliche Fabrikinspektion in der Vereinigten Staaten" ("Women Factory Inspectors in the United States") in 1897, and other FK essays in 1898, 1899, and 1901 (see Sklar, *Florence Kelley and the Nation's Work,* 410–411).

3. Charles Booth (1840–1916) published his "Descriptive Map of London Poverty" in volume 2 of *Life and Labour of the People of London* (London: Williams and Norgate, 1891). The color-coded maps in *Hull-House Maps and Papers* were modeled on the maps in Booth and revealed the extent and depth of poverty in Chicago. FK's maps depicted moral relationships—the concentration of certain ethnic groups in certain blocks and the relationship between poverty and race, between the isolated brothel district and the rest of the ward, and between the very poor who lived in crowded, airless rooms in the rear of tenements and those with more resources in the front (Sklar, "Hull-House Maps and Papers," 123–129, 136–138). For further analysis of the maps' significance, see Sklar, *Florence Kelley and the Nation's Work,* 277–278, 396n33.

4. Crowell published the maps to her specifications.

42. To Miss Williams

STATE OF ILLINOIS
OFFICE OF FACTORY INSPECTOR
247 W. POLK ST.
CHICAGO

November 18th, 1894

Dear Miss Williams:

I have your note of Nov. 3rd and cannot think of anything on the subject except the Joseph[***ine***] Butler Anti-Contagious Diseases Acts Agitation tracts which you doubtless know; and Bebel's Woman in the Past Present and Future; and Parent-Duchatelets French work.[1] Certainly the attempts to legalize prostitution ought to be fought tooth and nail; but I think the effort should not stop there; but that a persistent ten-years' effort to enlighten women upon the medical and ethical aspects of syphilis is quite as much needed. While physicians permit their syphilitic patients to marry without clear instruction as to the probable consequences; and while girls marry in ignorance of their physical danger, the mere restraint of injurious legislation seems to me a most inadequate aim.

Dr. Heegar, one of the best of the German gynaeoclogists, announces a work on the Geschlechtstrict[2] which is strongly recommended by Heinrich Bram's [Braun's] [Sozialpolitisches Centralblatt] for its great social value.[3] The N. Y. Medical Record recently contained an article by a physician in good standing asking for data concerning the inheritance of syphilis; and another in review of a work on the infection of the innocent. This makes me think that you can get valuable clues by searching the files of the Record for a year or two past. The Academy of Medicine of New York recently adopted some resolutions adverse to the legalization of prostitution but I have not seen the text thereof.[4]

I believe, however, that prostitution is the inevitable accompaniment of monogamy and that we shall never be rid of it until the relations of wife, spinster, and prostitute have become mere historical expressions and the designations of the categories of women are reduced to maid and mother with the choice of motherhood and its responsibilities left absolutely with each woman. Of course it is a long, long, look ahead to such a change. But the dissolution of the family is going on so fast, and the old vilification of the woman who asserts her claim to motherhood without the slavery of marriage is dying out so fast, that we shall doubtless live to see a very widespread modification of public opinion upon the subject. And nothing is helping more effectively than the spread of knowledge of syphilis among women physicians, nurses and educated women generally. This, with the daily increasing economic self-dependence of women is greatly under-mining the status of marriage. And marriage is of course the strongest bulwark of prostitution. Perhaps this may sound to you very crude and brutal. But it is the result of much observation and painful thinking. And I find it a hopeful outlook. For the present excessive sexual life of the prostitute and repression of the spinster are alike unnatural. And the sex which accepts both cannot command the respect of the men who, though they share the suffering of the excess, have, at least, never (even when living in legal celibacy) seriously undertaken any general repression of the of human instincts for themselves. Of course I shall not mention the sec'y until you authorize me to do so.

Yours
Florence Kelley

CC, CLM Records, MCR-S

Note: Unfortunately, no ALS has been recovered. Spaces left in this transcription are probably terms the transcriber was unable to decipher; in one instance probable wording is supplied.

1. On Butler and the Contagious Diseases Acts, see Letter 10, FK to *Woman's Tribune,* ca. April 1885, above. Alexandre-Jean Bapiste Parent-Duchatelets (1790–1836) wrote *De la prostitution dans la ville de Paris* (Prostitution in the City of Paris) (Paris: J. B. Bailliere, 1837).

2. German; "sexual instinct."

3. Heinrich Braun (1854–1927) published *Sozialpolitsches Centralblatt,* for which FK wrote several articles (Sklar, *Florence Kelley and the Nation's Work,* 390n43).

4. FK probably learned about this resolution from her good friend Dr. Mary Putnam Jacobi, a member of the New York Academy of Medicine.

43. To Jessie Bross Lloyd

~~STATE OF ILLINOIS~~
~~OFFICE OF FACTORY INSPECTOR~~
~~247 W. POLK ST.~~
~~CHICAGO~~

Leland Hotel
Springfield [Illinois]
~~Chicago~~ March 2nd 1895

Dear Mrs. Lloyd,

Hon. Wm. A. Mussett[1] has introduced in the Senate (Springfield) two bills, one regulating the employment of minors and one to protect the public health and safety. He is not getting endorsements for them except from Chicago working people.

I think it would cheer him, in the path of duty, if you would write him a line and ask him for the text of his bills, (of course not referring to me, whose interest he probably already finds rather much.)

We are not publishing the bills yet, because we want to get them out of Committee before the editorial column raises its voice in defense of the infant newsboy and the toddling "cash," who will both come under its provisions.

I have been here three weeks, getting my report out, and starting these bills, and it looks as though it might be three weeks more before the last one passes first reading.[2]

Ever since October I've been dreaming of a day at Wayside, but I guess its an ignis fatuus.[3]

Love to the Household.

Yours
Florence Kelley

ALS, Box 6, Lloyd Papers, WHi

1. Republican William A. Mussett represented Edwards County in the Illinois senate from 1893 to 1896 (*The Illinois Fact Book and Historical Almanac*, 251–253).
2. FK was working on the publication of her *Second Annual Report of the Factory Inspectors of Illinois for the Year Ending December 15, 1894* (Springfield, Ill.: State Printers, 1895).
3. Wayside was the Lloyds' Winnetka home. *Ignis fatuus* is Latin for will-o'-the-wisp.

44. To Richard T. Ely

STATE OF ILLINOIS
OFFICE OF FACTORY INSPECTOR
247 W. POLK ST.
CHICAGO

Aug 22nd 1895

Dear Mr. Ely,

We are going to begin the work of getting out of our third annual report of the Illinois Factory Inspectors, in about six weeks.[1]

I am very desirous of making these reports valuable to students. We have issued two annual (and one special) reports, and have sent them to all the Reviews with which I am acquainted, hoping that we might receive some criticism which might enable us to make the next ones better. But not one word have we had, though the contents of the reports have been pretty widely reproduced by the publication of extracts.

In default of this more public criticism, may I beg you to do me the favor of looking over the reports (of which I have ordered copies sent you) and making any suggestions which may occur to you?

I know that you are very busy, and that this is asking no small thing. But I think the official reports ought to be made of the highest possible value, and feel sure that you will be willing to lend a hand.

Yours very truly
Florence Kelley

ALS, Box 9, Ely Papers, WHi

1. *Third Annual Report of the Factory Inspectors of Illinois for the Year Ending December 15, 1895* (Springfield, Ill.: Ed. F. Hartman, 1896). On 14 March 1895, in *Ritchie v. People of Illinois,* the Illinois Supreme Court had unanimously declared unconstitutional section five of the 1873 factory act, the eight-hour law for women. Although the court expressed doubt about the legality of the salaries paid to factory inspectors, the state continued to pay them (*Chicago Tribune,* 15 March 1895, 1). See the following documents in Sklar and Tyler, "How Did Florence Kelley's Campaign against Sweatshops in Chicago in the 1890s Expand Government Responsibility for Industrial Working Conditions?": Document 15, "Opinion of the Supreme Court of Illinois, Filed March 18, 1895, *Ritchie vs. the People,*" 128–138; Document 18, FK, "Recommendations," 23; and Document 20, FK, "Factory and Workshop Law," 4.

FK denounced the court's decision in her 1895 report (Sklar, *Florence Kelley and the Nation's Work,* 283; for an analysis of all four annual reports, see 389nn34–39).

45. To Henry D. Lloyd

STATE OF ILLINOIS
OFFICE OF FACTORY INSPECTOR
247 W. POLK ST.
CHICAGO

March 3rd 1896

Dear Mr. Lloyd,

Won't you write the resolutions for the Sunday meeting at Central Music Hall?[1]

The garment trade is perfectly dead; when it should be approaching the height of the season It is killed by the refusal of the Manufacturers to arbitrate. Thousands of men, women and children, (certainly not less than ten thousand,) are therefore unemployed. The poorer ones have nothing laid by, for the season, last year, ended at Thanksgiving and they have earned nothing since.

The meeting, of course, is a protest against the Sweating System, but the sufferings of the garment workers under that system are sorely aggravated by the strike and we cannot ignore the strike, of course.

If you still do not think it wise for the purpose in hand that you should speak, there is no reason you should not write the resolutions.

I think myself that your speaking would vastly strengthen the meeting.[2]

Yours Sincerely
Florence Kelley

ALS, Box 7, Lloyd Papers, WHi

1. Hull House residents were organizing an 8 March 1896 meeting to call for federal regulation of sweatshops (*Chicago Tribune,* 9 March 1896, 9).

2. No reply from Lloyd has been recovered. Apparently he did not attend the meeting, at which FK, JA, and others spoke. FK described how clothing manufacturers created more sweatshops and "now employ 500 more girls." The meeting approved a resolution that called on Illinois senators and representatives to support the congressional bill to regulate sweatshops (*Chicago Tribune,* 9 March 1896, 9).

46. To Frank A. Manny[1]

STATE
OFFICE OF FACTORY INSPECTOR
247 W. POLK ST.
CHICAGO

April 18th 1896

Mr. F. A. Manny
Principal Moline High School

My dear Sir;

My terms for speaking outside of Chicago are $25.00 and my travelling expenses. I could go to Moline for any day and evening between May 3d and 17th or after Monday May 18th. I am obliged to be in Chicago on May 3d and 18th.

I should be very glad to speak to the Tri-City Labor Union, or to any other body of citizens upon our working children, or the Sweating System or upon the work of Hull House——these being the three Social subjects with which I am acquainted. Begging the favor of a prompt reply as to whether or not you wish ~~you~~ me to come, in order that I may arrange the dates of visits arising under the factory [act] so as not conflict with the appointment I remain

Yours very truly
Florence Kelley[2]

ALS, Manny Papers, MiU-H

1. Frank A. Manny (1868–1954) was principal of Moline (Iowa) High School (1894–1896) and assistant in pedagogy at the University of Chicago (1896–1897).
2. FK thanked Manny for his check and told him that she would use the money to help pay NK's expenses while he stayed with the Lloyds in Rhode Island (FK, Chicago, to Manny, 26 May 1896, Manny Papers, MiU-H). Manny arranged for FK to speak at least once more in Indianapolis (FK, Chicago, to Manny, 29 November 1897, Manny Papers, MiU-H). On FK's speaking skills, see Sklar, *Florence Kelley and the Nation's Work,* 217–218.

47. To Henry D. Lloyd

[Chicago]
June 18th, 1896

My dear Mr. Lloyd,

I have been thinking over the question which you asked me last evening, in regard to going to the convention at St. Louis.[1] I had not given the subject any previous attention and was not prepared to reply out of hand. What I do think, is this; that the present Socialist organization in this country, is a most undesirable one. The practise of expelling everyone who can speak English from the Socialist Labor Party, while not literally followed, is so nearly universal, that the party is very largely a bunch of greenhorns. If there could be segregated from the Popul*i*st party a body, however small, of Socialists of American nationality and traditions, *t*his seems to me worth a very great sacrifice indeed.

Such a body could win followers. This the Socialist Labor ~~Part~~ Party under its present leadership, and followin*g* its present policy, can never do. I hold to the whole platform of the Socialist labor party the world over; that is, the International Socialist Party. But it had not occurred to me, until after my conver*s*ation with you last evening, that this may be the opportunity to obtain a nucleus of Americans to adopt that platform, who yet woul*d* never, of their own accord, enter the Socialist Labor Party as at present constituted. I am such an American. I could never affiliate with any party which made Silver the burden of its cry.[2] But I cannot stand the scurrility of the People, the organ of the Socialist Labor Party. Nor do I approve of the policy of splitting trades unions which is one of the favorite activities of the present leadsers ***of the S.L.P.*** But I would make a ***g***ood deal of sacrifice, for the ***s***ake of working with a party of American Socialists.

It does ***n***ot seem to me at present, as thou***g***h any thing less than an attempt at gettin***g*** the remnant of the Populists to undertake such a movement, were worth taking much trouble about.[3]

Yours Sincerely
Florence Kelley

[ms. damaged] ***safe and sound. He had waited*** [ms. damaged] ***for me. F. Kelley***

TLS, Box 7, Lloyd Papers, WHi

1. The Populist Party held its convention in St. Louis on 22 July 1896.
2. FK and others tried to persuade Lloyd to attend the Populists' convention to represent socialist interests. To relieve debtors and stimulate the economy, Democrats were campaigning for free coinage of silver at a ratio of sixteen ounces of silver to one ounce of gold. Lloyd and his allies believed that the government should go further and own major industries, including silver mining (Destler, *Henry Demarest Lloyd,* 286).
3. At their convention, much to Lloyd's disappointment, the Populists endorsed Democrat William Jennings Bryan for president. Lloyd was prevented from presenting his agenda for government ownership of monopolies and subsequently abandoned party politics. Lloyd wrote that convention delegates deserted their reform interests "to do what the miners and the Democrats and the traders wanted them to do" (Lloyd, "The Populists at St. Louis," 303; Destler, *Henry Demarest Lloyd,* 286–287; see also Sklar, *Florence Kelley and the Nation's Work,* 395n26).

48. To Henry D. Lloyd

STATE OF ILLINOIS
OFFICE OF FACTORY INSPECTOR
247 W. POLK ST.
CHICAGO

October 1st 1896

My dear Mr. Lloyd,

We miss you very much in the campaign. Things are badly muddled, and Governor Altgeld's friends seem few, indeed, in this time of need. The Socialists and the labor skates are knifing him alike. The Silver populists and the straight trades-union vote seem to be his main hope besides the farmers.[1] And if the working people allow him to be defeated now, in the face of his record, surely they deserve to have no other friend until this generation dies out and another and better one takes its place.

I wonder whether any candid friend has told you that the disreputable end of the Populists have nominated you and are using your name for Lieutenant Governor. On this ticket there was no nomination made for Governor. If the ticket had been made in good faith, to help Governor Altgeld's election, his name would have been put on it, of course.

This week, a new lot of bolters have come out, calling themselves Silver-Republicans. It is among the possibilities that these may take your name for the first place on their ticket.

So long as you do not come out for Governor Altgeld; or do not, at least, formally declare yourself out of the race, your name will continue to be used to fool workingmen.[2] And it carries great weight with thousands of them.

I do not know whether you want Governor Altgeld re-elected——everything is so confused this year that I don't feel certain of much in any direction! But if you do——he needs every bit of help, of every kind, that every friend can give him until election day.

Yours faithfully
Florence Kelley[3]

ALS, Box 8, Lloyd Papers, WHi

1. "Badly muddled" aptly described the 1896 presidential and gubernatorial elections in Illinois. Some Republicans deserted their party because of its opposition to free silver, while a group of Populists merged with Democrats to form a Popocrat party, an organization with which many Populists refused to cooperate. Meanwhile, Governor Altgeld broke with the Democrats and their presidential candidate, William Jennings Bryan, and separated his candidacy from that of other Populists and Popocrats on the Illinois ticket. (*NYT,* 26 September 1896, 2; *Chicago Tribune:* 29 September 1896, 1, 3, 4; 30 September 1896, 2; and 1 October 1896, 3.)

2. Lloyd remained in Rhode Island during the fall; he did not return to Chicago until 2 November, when he issued a statement that asserted his surprise that his name was on the ballot as the Populist candidate for lieutenant governor: "This use of my name was made without consultation with me in the first place, and against my protest" (*NYT,* 3 November 1896, 2; Destler, *Henry Demarest Lloyd,* 287–288).

3. FK wrote Lloyd two weeks later that she feared that Altgeld would be defeated, which would result in "the turning back of the labor movement in Illinois" (FK, Chicago, to Lloyd, 15 October 1896, Box 8, Lloyd Papers, WHi). In a letter to the *New York Journal* that was reprinted in Illinois newspapers, Lloyd defended the governor but to no avail. Altgeld lost the election by over 118,000 votes (Destler, *Henry Demarest Lloyd,* 288–289; *Chicago Tribune,* 7 November 1896, 12).

49. To Agnes Hamilton[1]

STATE OF ILLINOIS
OFFICE OF FACTORY INSPECTOR
247 W. POLK ST.
CHICAGO

12-8-96

My dear Miss Hamilton,

I put your letter of inquiry aside to be answered fully, in detail,—and so delayed it much longer than I meant to do.

As to the demand for factory-made goods. It is true that hitherto, manufacturers have not been urgently asked to guarantee their garments not to have been in tenement houses. No manufacturer can afford to give a fraudulent guarantee. Nearly all retail clerks, however, are entirely ready to give a prompt verbal assurance that any given garment is factory made without any knowledge whatever of the facts of the case. The difference between the mfrs.' guarantee and the clerk's assurance is all the difference between a penal offense if the former is fraudulent and a peccadillo to be settled with the clerk's conscience in the latter case.

There are, so far as I have been able to learn, no goods now in the market guaranteed not tenement made. The point is to clamor for a guaranty until some firm can be induced to give it; and then use it as an entering wedge.

Women's tailors use the sweating system to a great extent whether they make goods to order or otherwise.

I do not know anything of Haas' Bros. in New York.

Nearly all merchant tailors use the sweating system in having men's ordered garments made.

Women's underclothes are made chiefly in penal and reformatory institutions. Some are made by footpower machine in tenement houses and a small quantity are made in factories. Direct sweating is, I think, not found in that branch.

Fur goods are very largely made under the sweating system.

I am urging the starting of a consumers' league which should add to the functions of the New York one the demand for guaranteed garments.[2]

I shall hope for more questions on Monday.

Yours Sincerely
Florence Kelley

ALS, Hamilton Family Papers, MCR-S

1. Agnes Hamilton (1868–1961) was a cousin and close friend of Alice Hamilton. FK had recently met her in Fort Wayne, Indiana. Attracted to the possibility of working with FK, in the fall of 1897 Agnes considered joining the Hull House community. In 1902, she began work at the Lighthouse, a Philadelphia settlement (Sicherman, *Alice Hamilton,* 21, 115–116).

2. In 1897, members of the Chicago Association of Collegiate Alumnae organized a consumers' league. Within the league, a committee, headed by FK, investigated the working conditions of department store clerks and distributed shopping guidelines that would improve the Christmas season for sales clerks. FK considered this part of her "regular winter occupations" for two years (Sklar, *Florence Kelley and the Nation's Work,* 307–308).

50. To Henry D. Lloyd

STATE OF ILLINOIS
OFFICE OF FACTORY INSPECTOR
247 W. POLK ST.
CHICAGO

8-19-97

My dear Mr. Lloyd,

Far be it from me to defend the Supreme Court! For the moment, however, our youngsters are better off, in spite of the Supreme Court, because they cannot work even eight hours during the first two of the three years in which the Czar limits the hours of work of his children.[1] But we have sunk low, indeed, when the comparison has to be made with Russia.

Perhaps, in view of this encouraging symptom, you'll be less stern towards my conviction that Napoleon's vision is fulfilled and Europe is Cossack. I think we are living to see the assimilation of West and East as far as the borders of India. But most of us are missing the drift of the drama, in spite of the fact that the long perspective ought to make it peculiarly intelligible to us Americans.

I would give a good deal for a glimpse of the bloom of Ko.[2]

Dear love to the Missus——the Lady of the Watch House Rocks.

Yours
Florence Kelley

ALS, Box 8, Lloyd Papers, WHi

1. FK was apparently responding to a comment in an unrecovered Lloyd letter. In 1882, Russia enacted a law that made it illegal for children under twelve to work and limited the workday for children from twelve to eighteen to eight hours (Glickman, *Russian Factory Women*, 74).
2. NK was once again spending the summer with the Lloyds in Rhode Island (NK, Sakonnet, R.I., to FK, 28 June 1896 and 1 July 1896, FKP, NN).

51. To Elizabeth Cady Stanton[1]

HULL-HOUSE
335 SOUTH HALSTED ST.
CHICAGO

May 24th. 1898

My dear Mrs. Stanton,

I was very sorry, indeed, not to be able to avail myself of Mrs. Lawrence's kind invitation to call upon you during my brief stay in New York. I was leaving the next day, after the Consumers' League meeting and was only able to go with my mother, who is very lame, to her train for Philadelphia, and then catch my own train for Chicago.[2] It would have been a great pleasure to see you; and I have always remembered with pleasure a little visit which I made to you several years ago. I have read with great interest your expression of my own opinion about the war.[3] It is most extraordinary how melo-dramatic the good people do get over this episode in our history! Although my young brother has undergone some acute hardships with his battery, already, they do not seem to me to compare with the strain of effort for even a little amelioration of our social conditions. That long, steady, disappointing effort which we all have to make for civil improvements has none of the charm and excitement of the war; but how infinitely more vital it is! I think my brother stated the just attitude as to the war when he wrote to a friend who was begging him not to go with the battery: "I understand that there is, down below Tampa, a nuisance which must be abated at once. When it is abated, I'll come home and talk it over with you."[4]

When I next come to New York, I shall hope to stay longer than four days, and shall count upon seeing you then.[5]

Yours sincerely
Florence Kelley

TLS, Stanton Papers, DLC

1. FK knew Elizabeth Cady Stanton (1815–1902) through her father's long association with Stanton and Susan B. Anthony in the struggle for woman suffrage.

2. Margaret Stanton Lawrence (1852–1930) was Stanton's daughter. On 17 May 1898, the CL of New York City sponsored a meeting of consumers' leagues from across the country. As one of the featured speakers, FK told the group how "the greatest consumer league in existence" had brought about improved working conditions in Chicago's cigar-manufacturing sweatshops (*NYT:* 15 May 1898, 13, and 18 May 1898, 4). For FK's earlier contact with the CL of New York, see Sklar, *Florence Kelley and the Nation's Work,* 146–148; for her participation in the formation of the NCL in 1898, when she was a representative from Illinois to the national organization, see Sklar, *Florence Kelley and the Nation's Work,* 308–310; and Blumberg, *Florence Kelley,* 168–169.

3. The United States formally declared war against Spain on 25 April 1898 to free Cuba from Spanish rule. Stanton contrasted the suffering of poor workers with the glory accorded to U.S. soldiers: "I have no sympathy with all the sentimental outpouring about our boys in blue, when I consider the wrongs going on everywhere in our industrial system." She warned that strikes and the "sullen discontent of the masses . . . are so many declarations of war between capital and labor" and "far more dangerous to our republic than war with Spain" (Stanton, "War or Peace, Competition or Co-operation?").

4. After brief stints at the University of Pennsylvania in 1888 and its law school in 1892, AK worked as a law clerk in Philadelphia (University of Pennsylvania Alumni Records; AK, Philadelphia, to CBK, 7 November 1892, 7 March 1893). Joining the navy in the Spanish-American War, he later wrote FK from a ship stationed in Newport News, Rhode Island, "I do not believe that our captain wants to go to the front and I think he is using every influence to keep us back. There is much dissatisfaction and several of us are trying for commissions in something that will give us active service" (AK, Newport News, Va., to FK, 3 July 1898, KFP, NCC-RB).

5. A note to an unidentified recipient appended to this letter says "I send my article that grew out of my letter to you. If you had not suggested to me to write on the war, the world would not have had this letter so highly [complimented?]. Read & return enclosed letter. in haste E. C[.] S[.]"

52. To Caroline Bonsall Kelley

HULL-HOUSE
335 SOUTH HALSTED ST.
CHICAGO

July 24th. (Monday) aft. 1898

Mother darling,

The enclosed letter tells its own happy tale, and I need add nothing on that score. I have not written during the week; because I have been hoping to have some extra good news to send you; but it does not come, and I shall wait no longer. I received an intimation from Mr. Gage, Secretary of the Treasury that Mr. McKinley might be induced to consider the subject of an appointment for me for the Industrial commission which he is to appoint; and which carries a salary of $36,00~~0~~ (three thousand, six hundred dollars) a year for two years.[1] Miss Addams and I only waited to get some letters, and posted off, on Thursday for Washington, returning on Saturday and reaching home on Sunday evening. We saw Mr. McKinley, and he was very non-committal, but left us with just a ray of hope. He then expected to make the announcement of the appointments on Friday of this past week. But Friday has come and gone and the announcements are not yet made, and we are at a loss to know what he is going to do. Of course, I shall let you know as soon as I know myself, but by watching the papers for the announcement of the Industrial Commission, you will know as soon as I do. The Phila. papers are a great comfort. I learn from them much which our Chicago papers suppress. We have the city papers again as usual, the strike having been a dead failure.[2] But I think they omit more than they print.

I have no letters from John, but there is no doubt that he is well and happy. The weather has been even better than it usually is in the early summer, but it is not yet the beginning of August, and the tug of war is not yet begun. I am very well indeed, and working satisfactorily to myself on a paper for my German quarterly. I am just starting for a call upon Mrs. Henrotin, whom I am desirous of having address a letter to Mr. McK.[3] About the appointment. He actually had tears in his eyes when he talked about Father. But I suppose that is not difficult for him to accomplish; and may mean notheing at all.

Miss Addams is at Rockford; Miss Lathrop sails for home, August 20h[4] The shanty where the creche used to be, is being torn down while I am writing, to make room for the new Jane Club, a beautiful four story-club house, for which Miss Sarah Smith has given the money; and Mary has bought the land.[5] The work upon it will begin at once. Mrs. [Alzina] Stevens, Miss Giles and I are the only women in residence; and Mr. Ball, Mr. Swope, Mr Blount, Mr. Deknatel hold the fort in the Butler Gallery. Mr. Hooker is going to England with his sister as soon as she is recovered enough from a long illness, to bear the voyage.[6] Altogether, the House is quiet and pleasant enough to make work very agreeable.

I long for a letter from Pussy [MK] though I well know I do not deserve one; but it is very hard to do one's duty as a correspondent, when one is earning a livelihood by the help of the pen and type-writer.[7] Stanley is gone to Rockford with his Aunt,[8] and there is little of interest for Marmie [MK] here, except an occasional Sunday afternoon on the North Shore when all the residents break away and go a picknicking; but that is only once on two or three weeks.

Hoping very much indeed, to have some really good news to send you in the course of the week;[9] I am your loving daughter,

F. K.

I don't quite understand what you say about Bert. Is he trying to get discharged?[10] Or did I misread your last letter?

TLS, KFP, NCC-RB

1. Lyman J. Gage (1836–1927) was secretary of the treasury from 1897 to 1902 in the administration of President William McKinley (1843–1901).
2. Stereotypers struck against Chicago newspapers from 1 to 8 July 1898. Their strike failed when the Chicago Typographical Union did not support them (*NYT:* 6 July 1898, 12, and 10 July 1898, 11).
3. For FK's contributions to the *Archiv für Soziale Gesetzgebung und Statistik,* see Sklar, *Florence Kelley and the Nation's Work,* 297–299; and Letter 41, FK to Richard T. Ely, 14 November 1894, above. Ellen Martin Henrotin (1847–1922), wealthy society matron and labor reform activist in Chicago, was president of the General Federation of Women's Clubs from 1894 to 1898 and, in 1898, president of the newly formed CL of Illinois (Sklar, *Florence Kelley and the Nation's Work,* 308).
4. Julia Lathrop was traveling in Scotland and Belgium investigating asylums for the mentally ill (JA, *My Friend, Julia Lathrop,* 103).
5. Established by JA and Mary Kenney, the Jane Club served as a boardinghouse for young working women (FK, *Notes of Sixty Years,* 80). Sarah Smith was the sister of Mary Rozet Smith.
6. Rose Marie Gyles (1867–1949) was in charge of women's sports; Frank H. Ball directed manual training. Gerard Swope (1872–1957) had trained as an engineer but taught mathematics and science at Hull House. Ralph E. Blount (b. 1865) was an educator and writer; Frederick H. Deknatel, former head of a small hardware firm, supervised the boys' clubs. George E. Hooker (1861–1939), a city planning expert, worked on improving the Hull House neighborhood (Bryan and Davis, *100 Years at Hull House,* 59, 130)
7. MK spent June and July with CBK in Philadelphia (FK, Chicago to CBK, 2 June and 6 August 1898, both in KFP, NCC-RB). After her dismissal as chief factory inspector in August 1897, FK supported herself and her children by working in the Crerar Library, teaching occasionally, speaking, and writing articles for German periodicals (Sklar, *Florence Kelley and the Nation's Work,* 286–291).
8. Upon the death of her sister Mary Addams Linn in 1894, JA became the legal guardian and second mother of Mary's four children, the youngest of whom was Stanley Linn (b. ca. 1883) (Brown, *Education of Jane Addams,* 287).

9. The "really good news" never came. FK wrote CBK: "President McKinley has announced his appointments; and it is needless to say that I am not among them. Happily I never fix my mind upon the matter, but ask for the chance to do work for which I know I am fitted, and then, if I do not get it, there is no harm done. The Commission is a disgraceful one, and I shall probably live to thank my lucky star that I am not connected with it responsible for its shams" (FK, Chicago, to CBK, 21 September 1898, KFP, NCC-RB, see also Sklar, *Florence Kelley and the Nation's Work,* 292).

10. Apparently AK's army service was ending, for in August FK expressed her pleasure to CBK that he was back in his office (FK, Chicago, to CBK, 4 August and 17 August 1898, KFP, NCC-RB).

53. To Henry D. Lloyd

HULL-HOUSE
335 SOUTH HALSTED ST.
CHICAGO

September, 26th. 1898

Dear Mr. Lloyd,

It is pleased and proud that I am, to own a copy of Labor Copartnership with the compliments of the author.[1] I think it must prove a very valuable contribution, indeed, to the labor movements in these days of need of positive effort. I have recently read, with a good deal of care, the Webb's criticism of the movement;[2] and so far as I can see, they are quite right in saying that labor copartnership is not, in itself, socialism; but since ***it*** never claimed to be socialism, and does not wish to be socialism, I cannot see what that has to do with the matter, unless some Fabians may have been claiming that it was socialism without knowing ***it,*** as Sidney Webb, himself, once claimed that peddlers' licenses were preliminary symptoms of socialism! There is no doubt in my mind, that this is the best field for the education of the mass of the people for self-government in industry; but it is a little discouraging that, here in America, we are not even entering upon this primary-school.

A propos of primary-schools, we have at last succeeded in getting the Board to pass and the Council to authorize the purchase of fifty feet front (120 feet deep) on Harrison street, for an addition to the Dore school, which may accommodate 600 children, and will certainly accommodate 400. Although this is much less than we asked for, and not where we wanted it, and must be regarded as a not altogether satisfactory compromise,—it i***s,*** nevertheless, a distinct victory over Powers and the Jesuits, for they have fought this extension directly and indirectly for seven years.[3]

Ko reached home safely on Saturday afternoon, and is in school this morning.[4] Neither he nor I can ever thank you and Mrs. [Jessie] Lloyd for the present pleasure and the permanent benefit which you have given him, in all these years of loving kindness. He looked actually handsome, in his coating of brown, with his little blue eyes so clear and rested! He will write Mrs. Lloyd this evening; he was pretty well tired from his journey and the change from cool salt air to hot freshwater smells from the river and the Stockyards. He also opined that "Little Caroline needs some stiff discipline about as badly as any kid I've met lately."

It is always cause for rejoicing when the approach of October brings the promise of early return of the owners of the Wayside; and we are looking forward to seeing you soon.

Yours always sincerely
F.K.

TLS, Box 9, Lloyd Papers, WHi

1. In his *Labor Copartnership: Notes of a Visit to Co-operative Workshops, Factories and Farms in Great Britain and Ireland* (New York: Harper & Brothers, 1898), Lloyd advocated workers' profit-sharing and the consumer cooperative movement in the United States (Destler, *Henry Demarest Lloyd*, 388–394).
2. Sidney Webb (1859–1947) joined the Fabian Society, initially a socialist debating group, in 1885 and wrote several tracts for it that argued for larger government responsibility in managing the economy. With other Fabian Society members he founded the London School of Economics in 1895. In 1892, Webb married Beatrice Potter (1858–1943), author of *The Co-operative Movement in Great Britain* (1891) and later co-author with him of a series of books that lent scholarly authority to Fabian socialism. They visited Hull House in May 1898.
3. Since 1895, Hull House residents had fought John Powers, the representative of Chicago's nineteenth ward on the city council, in an effort to improve living conditions in the ward (see Sklar, *Florence Kelley and the Nation's Work*, 300–303). FK was referring to Jesuits who staffed the Holy Family Church and St. Ignatius College on Twelfth Street. St. Ignatius was the forerunner of Loyola University; it is now known as St. Ignatius College Prep (see Skerrett, "The Irish of Chicago's Hull-House Neighborhood," 22–63).
4. NK had been with the Lloyds in Rhode Island since 16 June 1898 (FK, Chicago, to CBK, 2 June 1898, KFP, NCC-RB).

54. To Caroline Bonsall Kelley

HULL-HOUSE
335 SOUTH HALSTED ST.
CHICAGO

[ca. 15 December 1898]

[Continuation of missing portion of letter]

Next day.—We had a delightful lunch, our old friend Marianna Gay, Mrs. Smoot, Mrs. [Ellen] Henrotin and myself.[1] We transacted a lot of Consumers' League business in the most agreeable way, in front of the open fire and over the lunch table; then the hostess ran off to a lunch of her own somewhere else, and I went over to a meeting of the teachers and parents of the children at Lewis Institute.[2] It was very pleasant to receive the congratulations and compliments about Ko; and everyone seemed to have perceived the sudden spurt of growth. Then came the library with the daily drudgery, which is not at all disagreeable.

It is only fair to say that I do not know how else one could earn a salary with less disagreeable work.

I wish I knew what day the children are coming home.[3] I suppose it will be the day before Christmas, but it may be the week before, for all the information that I have been able to extract, from either of them.

I am most grateful for the promised gift for all of us. But I do not think Margaret ought to have her share unless she behaves better about acknowledging her birthday presents.

I am going to stop this letter now and write her a serious appeal.

Your loving
F. K.

This envelope is one which she left here, at the end of vacation, a reminiscence of good intentions!

TLS, KFP, NCC-RB

1. Mrs. Kenneth Smoot had helped organize the CL of Chicago in 1897 (Blumberg, *Florence Kelley*, 166).
2. In February 1897, NK passed entrance exams and enrolled in the Lewis Institute, a progressive school located a few miles west of Hull House (FK, Chicago, to CBK, 12 February 1897 and 16 February 1897, NKP, NN; Sklar, *Florence Kelley and the Nation's Work*, 288).
3. MK and JK attended the Hillside Home School in Hillside, Wisconsin, which was run by sisters Jane and Ellen Lloyd-Jones, cousins of Henry Demarest Lloyd.

55. To Caroline Bonsall Kelley

HULL-HOUSE
335 SOUTH HALSTED ST.
CHICAGO

Dec. 26th, 1898

Mother Darling,

May we all be together next year! And may we have many happy returns of the day—You and Bert and the chicks and I. The box came on Friday, and so did the children. On Saturday Ko came in for the day, and we opened the box. It is splendid! We have munched candy and turnovers within an inch of our lives. And the children like the handiwork immensely. Ko looked at the mufflers and said "To be given to whom Ko pleases,—I guess I'll give them to Ko." And he wore them out to Winnetka to skate in. Margaret has not brought her mind to part with any of the articles of your sewing.

I have a cheque from Mary Smith for a hundred dollars, for my own Christmas present. I am asking Mr. [William] Nicholson to invest it for Ko's college money because I have never been able to keep the children's money in bank; but have had to borrow it sooner or later. So I am taking no risks this time. I am putting it beyond my reach. It is an immense comfort to me to think that, in case of the boy's not getting to Annapolis, this will start him at college and keep him until he can get work or a scholarship to carry him through.[1] And, if he should get to Annapolis, it will be laid by for the first year after. Miss Addams and Mary Smith, jointly, have given Margaret a beautiful new dress. The skirt is a splendid, Irish poplin, plaid. The shirt waist is scarlet silk and Mrs. Coates is coming to-morrow to make it up. The child is delighted. I am giving Ko a set of Dickens ($6.00).

The children were never so handsome, and so altogether satisfactory. Ko and John are like twins. Charles Ames and his Margaret came to call between trains on Christmas eve, on their way back from Jamaica.[2] My chicks were a perfect picture show,—so well and rosy and handsome.

Miss Addams and Mary Smith, jointly, gave me a most beautiful large photograph of Ko, framed in brown wood. It is like the beautiful picture of Margaret and John, of last year, but much larger. I send, herewith, but in a separate package, the lease of which I wrote[.] In one way it seems a meagre Christmas present; but in another it is interesting, and it is by far the most valuable possession I have. So I can say like Peter:—"The best that I have, give I thee." I wish it were everything that I could wish to give.

There is likely to be another conference in New York at the end of January. I shall try to arrange to get to Philadelphia for a day. I have poor Mrs. Allen, from Madison, whose darling son drowned himself this last summer, here, to tide her over this first Christmas. That is the first reason of my not having acknowledged the delightful box earl-[ms. damaged] the second reason is that the Deweys ***Fred and Evelyn*** are here, with the children, and I have to keep the peace.[3] Mayor Samuel Jones of Toledo and Governor Altgeld took lunch with us, to-day. They were very interesting. If Bert is as useful to his country as our ill-famed Governor, he can die happy when his time comes. The governor is going to run for Mayor on the platform of government ownership to try to rid us of our friend Yerkes who manages our cars as you well remember.[4]

Give my love and Christmas wishes to Bert, and believe me now and always

your loving daughter
Florence Kelley

TLS, KFP, NCC-RB

1. FK wrote Henry D. Lloyd that a congressman had promised her to "throw open the Annapolis appointment to competitive examinations"; NK would be eligible in July 1900 (FK, Chicago, to Lloyd, 8 December 1898, Box 9, Lloyd Papers, WHi).
2. "His Margaret" refers to his wife, Margaret Ames (1885–1956) (Hewett, *Cornell University*, 4:72).
3. Frederick A. (1887–1967) and Evelyn R. (1889–1965) Dewey were the children of philosopher John Dewey and his wife Alice. John Dewey chaired the philosophy department at the University of Chicago from 1894 to 1904.

4. Samuel M. Jones (1846–1904), a progressive Republican, was mayor of Toledo from 1897 to 1904 (Gille, *Encyclopedia of Ohio*, 223). Charles T. Yerkes (1837–1905) ran Chicago's street-railway system (Bryan and Davis, *100 Years at Hull House*, 54). Advocating city ownership of streetcars, Altgeld ran unsuccessfully for mayor of Chicago in 1899 as an Independent.

56. To Lillian D. Wald

HULL-HOUSE
335 SOUTH HALSTED ST.
CHICAGO

Jan 24th. 1899

Dear Miss Wald,

Here I am at my desk, in my rut, as if I had never scrambeled out of it for a day with you and my old dream of enforcing the factory law in Manhattan. I traveled comfortably home to Philadelphia with my wild hopes, and my new pocket-book, and a conscience burdened with wondering how long it might take you to pick up all the stitches I had caused you to drop; and also rather wondering whether, perhaps, I had hurt Leonora's feelings in my absorption in my letter to Teddy. I hope not![1]

I am writing to Mr. Riis, some addenda; and I'm sending Governor Roosevelt the Hull-House Maps and Paper with a line. And then I'm going to drop the matter and trust to Providence and Teddy's whims. But nothing has seemed to me since I was twenty years old so great an opportunity for social usefulness as the position of Factory Inspector of New York State. And now thinking of it, with Teddy's fearlessness to back up the Inspector makes it seem impossible that anyone else should have <u>that</u> opportunity.

You see there are so few people who know how to inspect inspectors! And that is what a Chief is for. It is not a question of caring, or meaning well, or sympathising with Labor (though I do that with all my heart). It is a question of knowing when a man is working honestly; and how to make the most of each one's qualities; and keeping track of what has been done, and of which industries are especially difficult, and all the technical points of keeping a staff going along uniformly attending to its duties without spurts or laggings. And that is what I had spent four years in learning when I was cut off in my prime!

Miss Addams is away up in Wisconsin, somewhere, lecturing. And Miss Lathrop is here, and it is too bad that you do not know her; for she is the best of all except the Chief.

Chicago looks a little less black and muggy than usual this morning; for the air is cold and the sun shining brightly. Ko went off in high feather to school so frankly pleased to have me at home again that it makes me sentimental!

Here's hoping that I may see you soon again on the heath of your adoption! But that then I shall not leave my hair-brush; nor make you break engagements or rise betimes after going to bed about the same hour!

Yours affectionately
F.K.[2]

TLS, Wald Papers, NN

1. Leonora Barry (1849–1930), was a union organizer with the Knights of Labor with whom Kelley had worked closely in Philadelphia in the late 1880s. See Sklar, *Florence Kelley and the Nation's Work,* 140–141.

Largely at the instigation of newspaperman and reformer Jacob Riis (1849–1914), New York's governor Theodore Roosevelt (1858–1919) had recently endorsed a bill adding more factory inspectors to the state's staff. FK wrote Henry D. Lloyd, "I have asked Governor Roosevelt to appoint me Chief Factory Inspector of New York. I am becoming a professional office-seeker. . . . I am persuaded that no else now in the field would work so effectively against the sweating-system as I could" (FK, Chicago, to Lloyd, 31 January 1899, Box 10, Lloyd Papers, WHi). She and JA had traveled to New York in hopes of an interview but missed seeing Roosevelt. In a letter sent in care of Wald, Roosevelt replied to FK's letter of 21 January (unrecovered), regretting that he had missed seeing them. He felt that FK's Illinois residence would preclude her appointment as factory inspector in New York but still hoped to meet her (Roosevelt, [New York], to FK, 23 January 1899, copy, TR Papers, Series 2, Reel 316, DLC; Blumberg, *Florence Kelley,* 172).

2. FK wrote Mary Rozet Smith, "Lady Jane is to see Teddy at his house on the 17th. in New York. I have abandoned all hope because Teddy has not answered my letter or taken any notice of my existence. He has, however, written Jacob Riis that while he Teddy has no prejudices, the community would object to an Altgeld appointee, which, of course, may be true and is certainly polite and a tenable position. However, we know the persuasive qualities of the Lady on her native heath. It remains to be seen whether they do better at N.Y. than at Washington" (FK, Chicago, to Mary Rozet Smith, 4 February 1899, JA Papers, PSC-P). JA's visit to Roosevelt proved unsuccessful; the governor appointed John Williams, an Albany elevator operator, to the position (Sklar, *Florence Kelley and the Nation's Work,* 292–294, 400; see Letter 92, FK to Lillian Wald, 3 February 1907, note 2, below).

Florence Kelley, ca. 1900.
Courtesy of National Consumers' League Records, Prints and Photographs, Library of Congress.

57. To Lillian D. Wald

HULL-HOUSE
335 SOUTH HALSTED ST.
CHICAGO

March 23d. 1899

Dear Miss Wald,

I have virtually accepted the position of Secretary to the National Consumers' League in spite of your advice and Miss Addams' and Miss Lathrop so I feel like a rash young thing rushing forth into the great world without the family blessing![1]

I now expect, unless something wholly unforesee[n] turns up, to come to New York about May First. I wa[nt] to come into your neighborhood, and write to ask whet[her] there is another such safe harbor as Miss Thomas has found.[2] I want to live in the cheapest possible way an[d] in the closest proximity to the clothing shops for a while. But I do not feel at liberty to undertake any [di]rect Settlement work, nor do I feel sure that it wo[uld] be best to settle in any one spot for any length o[f] time at least until the [Fall?] [ms. damaged]

TL, Inc, Wald Papers, NN

1. On 20 January 1899, John Graham Brooks, president of the NCL, traveled to Chicago to offer FK the position of corresponding secretary of the League at an annual salary of $1,500 plus expenses. FK deferred accepting until she learned that she would not be appointed as the New York State factory inspector (Sklar, *Florence Kelley and the Nation's Work*, 310–311; Blumberg, *Florence Kelley*, 171, 175).
2. Elizabeth H. Thomas was a Hull House resident and secretary of the Dorcas Federal Labor Union, a union of representatives of all Chicago unions that included women in their membership (Bryan and Davis, *100 Years at Hull House*, 61).

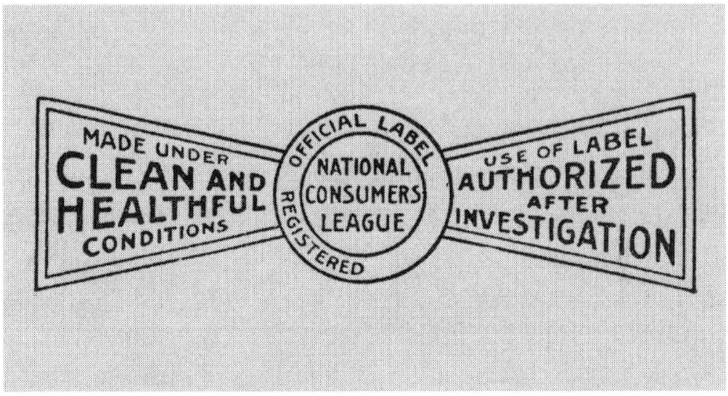

National Consumers' League White Label. Courtesy of National Consumers' League Records, Library of Congress.

3 1899 – 1907

"The Power and Responsibility of the Purchasers"

INTRODUCTION

When Florence Kelley became general secretary of the National Consumers' League in 1899, she joined an early expression of consumer culture that was less than a decade old. The first department store was established in 1876, but not until the 1890s did the production of goods and their merchandising and marketing launch the consumer culture that came to dominate the twentieth century. Parallel to this trajectory, consumers' leagues were formed with the goal of channelling consumer consciousness toward political action in the early 1890s. In New York, Boston, Philadelphia, and Chicago, their main strategy for creating better conditions under which goods were produced and sold was to create a "White List" of department stores.[1] To maintain the accuracy of their list, they needed expert assistance capable of evaluating stores' claims that they met league standards. In 1898, when local leagues combined to create the NCL, their first goal was to hire an "inspector" who could help them enforce league standards, a position for which Kelley was the leading candidate, based on her expertise as chief factory inspector for Illinois from 1893 and 1897 and her work as co-founder of the Chicago consumers' league.

Patterns of mass consumption had grown steadily in North America between 1750 and 1890 as middle-class families became an engine of economic growth through their consumption of commodities such as tea, cotton textiles, and the balloon-frame home. After the completion of transcontinental railroads in the 1870s, a vast internal market came to dominate American economic development, linking stove manufacturers in Illinois and sweatshops in New York with farm families on Iowa prairies and city dwellers in California. That market opened new political and economic opportunities. The National Consumers' League stepped into that new political space.[2]

Florence Kelley was forty years old in 1899. Her letters reveal a person in her prime whose skills at mobilizing the conscience of middle-class consumers carried her to the center of a growing network of politically active groups. By 1907, she commanded a key sector of Progressive reform: labor legislation for children and women.

Kelley rose to power within Progressive reform just as that loose coalition of diverse organizations, experimental ideas, and vivid personalities began to take shape as the second great wave of reform in American history. In the decades before the Civil War, the first wave of reform had addressed the problem of slavery. Now attention focused on problems arising from rapid industrialization, urbanization, and massive immigration. Like Kelley in the 1880s, many of her prominent peers, including Jane Addams and Theodore Roosevelt, experienced thwarted ambitions but became politically effective in the 1890s and emerged as national leaders around 1900.

Kelley exemplified her generation's success at mobilizing support through voluntary associations that worked independently of political parties. Her skill at promoting cross-class coalitions on social justice issues made her one of the most influential voices of her time. In 1902 she helped found the New York Child Labor Committee and in 1904 the National Child Labor Committee. After the founding of the Women's Trade Union League in 1903, she remained in close contact with that its leaders, especially Mary Kenney O'Sullivan, who had served as a factory inspector with her in Chicago. In 1906, she established contact with W. E. B. Du Bois, a relationship that soon flowered into her decades-long affiliation with his innovative work at the National Association for the Advancement of Colored People.

Kelley's letters help us see how she developed three reform networks. Her headquarters in New York City situated her within the nation's leading group of public intellectuals, allying her closely with peers such as Lillian Wald, at whose settlement she lived on the Lower East Side. Local consumers' leagues constituted the second network, which she promoted through wide travel and through which she promoted the NCL agenda. Her travels also connected her with a third network of politically active people across the nation, many of whom she drew into her reform efforts.

Most of Kelley's letters from these years of hectic activity have not survived. Our chief window on her activism comes from letters to her son Nicholas ("Ko"), who by the time he turned twenty-one in 1906 had become her closest confidante. To him she described her New York City routine and her travels away from home. The vitality of Manhattan's cultural environment matched her own enthusiasm for contention and struggle. She scathingly criticized the leadership of the Russell Sage Foundation and deftly dodged "anaconda" threats from Lawrence Veiller, who hoped to absorb the NCL into his own reform empire.[3]

On the road, she successfully built a network of local consumers' leagues in cities large and small, east and west, north and south that became the NCL's main agents of change.[4] Kelley's letter to Katherine Trevett of the Oregon consumers' league in 1900 exemplified the optimism and informative detail that characterized Kelley's interaction with local leagues for more than thirty years. Local leagues promoted the NCL's "Consumers' White Label," teaching league members as well as manufacturers and retailers about the working conditions in their communities.[5] Her 1901 letter to Edward Filene conveyed the complexities of that effort, which nevertheless had great educational and publicity value and gave the league a concrete way of evaluating its progress.[6]

Kelley's travel letters allow us to chart the network of reformers, politicians, and businessmen she recruited to sustain the NCL agenda. Predictable allies emerged, such as Tom Johnson, mayor of Cleveland, as well as unpredictable ones such as a symposium of rabbis in Portland, Oregon.[7] We also see how she focused on the passage of legislation in particular states, bringing her legal expertise to bear on the technical wording of laws as well as mobilizing support for their enactment. In 1903, she wrote Ko about her triumph "whirling about Delaware," where she met with the Episcopal bishop, met with the governor and thirty members of the legislature, and finally spent a "morning with Mr. Chief Justice Lore of Delaware at his home, drafting the new child labor bill for the State."[8]

Almost immediately upon her arrival at the NCL, Florence Kelley allied her efforts with the woman suffrage movement. That movement occupied a central place in American political culture, and she quickly integrated her agenda into it. Her 1901 letter to Clara Colby, chair of the Committee on Industrial Problems Affecting Women and Children of the National American Woman Suffrage Association, shows how she planned to improve the committee's effectiveness, which she began to chair a few months later.[9] At the 1906 national woman suffrage convention, the last one attended by Susan B. Anthony, she served as a vice-president, spoke on three separate occasions, and considered herself "enlisted for the war."[10]

Kelley's letters convey the centrality of child labor legislation to the NCL's agenda and the nationalizing process behind that agenda, which constantly compared states to one another and ranked them according to their ability to keep children out of factories and in school. She traveled in the South to see ten-year-old children working in textile mills and passionately insisted that the "human right of the child" was the same in Georgia as in Ohio or Oregon.[11]

By 1906, a new frontier of child labor legislation opened when Senator Albert Beveridge proposed a federal law, which she energetically endorsed as a way of establishing national standards.[12] Her understanding of the weakness of the central government in the United States as compared to those in Europe contributed to her sober recognition of the battles that lay ahead.[13] By 1907, she admitted to Ko, "[S]ometimes I get so tired talking that it seems impossible to go on doing it."[14]

This move to federal venues for child labor legislation followed a trajectory traced by many Progressive-era reforms. Pure water began as a municipal reform in the 1880s and ended in 1906 with the passage of the Pure Food and Drug Act. Coordinated by the NCL's Committee on Food, local consumers' leagues did much to support the passage of that act.[15] Suddenly it seemed that the rights of working children could become as important a public issue as tainted food.

At the same time that Kelley began to focus on federal child labor legislation, the U.S. Supreme Court issued a challenge that turned her attention to the federal judiciary. In *Lochner v. New York* the U.S. Supreme Court in 1905 ruled unconstitutional a recent New York law that limited working hours in bakeries to sixty a week. The minority and majority opinions in *Lochner* expressed the conflict in American society between those who endorsed the use of government as a tool to provide for the common welfare (the minority) and those (in the majority) who sought to limit government's ability to regulate industry. The majority opinion found the law "an illegal interference with the right of individuals, both employers and employes, to make contracts regarding labor upon such terms as they may think best."[16]

Dissenting justices in *Lochner* included Oliver Wendell Holmes, Jr., who thought the case was "decided upon an economic theory which a large part of the country does not entertain," namely the Social Darwinist theory of the survival of the fittest. The court's decision rested on the Fourteenth Amendment, which prohibits states from passing laws that deny any persons "equal protection of the laws," but Holmes insisted that "the 14th Amendment does not enact Mr. Herbert Spencer's Social Statics." The Constitution did not "embody a particular economic theory, whether paternalism. . . or *laissez faire*," he argued, concluding that a "reasonable man might think [the overturned New York law] a proper measure on the score of health. Men whom I certainly could not pronounce unreasonable would uphold it as a first installment of a general regulation of the hours of work."[17]

Kelley viewed the *Lochner* decision as a threat to all state laws regulating working hours, and, still irked by the 1895 Illinois court decision that had overturned her 1893 eight-hour law for women, she worked with her talented assistant, Josephine Goldmark, to prepare an innovative public health defense of the constitutionality of an Oregon ten-hour law for women.

Lochner overturned a New York law that had been passed primarily to extend the shorter work week of union bakeries to nonunionized shops, but it also claimed to be a public health measure that would reduce tuberculosis among bakery workers. The *Lochner* majority rejected those public health claims, but acknowledged,

> There are, however, certain powers, existing in the sovereignty of each state in the Union, somewhat vaguely termed police powers, the exact description and limitation of which have not been attempted by the courts. Those powers, broadly stated, and without, at present, any attempt at a more specific limitation, relate to the safety, health, morals, and general welfare of the public. Both property and liberty are held on such reasonable conditions as may be imposed by the governing power of the state in the exercise of those powers, and with such conditions the 14th Amendment was not designed to interfere.[18]

Kelley mobilized the NCL to test that "police power" argument related to "health, morals and general welfare of the public." She hoped that Goldmark's brother-in-law, Louis Brandeis, would join their legal team.[19]

A visit to Minneapolis in 1907 fortified her resolve. As she wrote Ko, two days in the home of Judge Charles Amidon of the Federal Circuit Court turned into an intense tutorial "about the senile fear which dominates the present Supreme Court of the United States whose average age is 74 years!" The court's goal of "denying power to the central government" through *Lochner* "has set all the state courts to work denying the powers of the states," which would produce anarchy.[20]

Although dominated by political considerations, Kelley's letters show that in many ways she remained an intellectual. To Ko she reiterated her intellectual debt to the writings of Karl Marx.[21] And she explained her faith in the science as well as the social science of progress when she told him about how a member of the NCL board had worked to make pasteurized milk available to mothers and infants in Rochester through public milk stations.[22] Letters to Jane Addams and to Ko mentioned work on her 1905 book, *Some Ethical Gains through Legislation,* especially her chapter on "the right to leisure," but her letters rarely referred to any of the sixty-four articles that she published in the first seven years of the twentieth century. Most of these appeared in *Charities,* the leading social work publication, which in 1909 became *Survey*; she began to serve as an editor of that magazine in 1903. One of her typical articles there in 1904 reviewed the *Handbook of Child Labor Legislation,* using the occasion to evaluate legislative strategies. Other articles were published in academic journals such as *Annals of the American Academy of Political and Social Science* and the *American Journal of Sociology*. Still others reached out to popular periodicals such as *Century* and *Outlook.*[23]

During these first years in New York City she lived in an uptown annex to Lillian Wald's Nurses Settlement with Ko while he attended school. She was a frequent visitor at Wald's settlement on the Lower East Side, where she moved into a room around 1904 and resided until 1927. As at Hull House in the 1890s, she benefited personally and professionally from the experience of living in a working-class neighborhood, writing Ko in the summer of 1903, "Miss Wald and I are getting a park for our ward and a street widened. It's more fun than any ordinary vacation!"[24]

Kelley's personal life in these years included brief visits with old friends such as Rachel Foster Avery, vice-president of the National American Woman Suffrage Association.[25] Within her circle of women reformers, dear friends such as Jane Addams persisted and new ones such as Emily Balch emerged. But much of her personal life remained centered at Hull House, which her two younger children continued to consider home and where contact with Jane Addams regularly renewed her energy. Her fictive kin included the Henry Demarest Lloyd family, with whom Ko spent most summers.

Kelley's letters richly depict her evolving relationship with her children in these years. Margaret's death in 1905 was a heavy blow. Friends drew close around her, and she took time away from work to recover. Ko's success at Harvard College and Harvard Law School was profoundly gratifying, but she often fretted about his health and well-being. John's academic ineptitude was an even greater source of anxiety. She felt poignantly rewarded by her ability to care for her aged mother. In 1907, Kelley bought a farm in Maine near that of the Balch sisters, which in future years became a summer retreat where she restored her energy for the struggles ahead.

NOTES

1. Only department stores that carried goods that had not been manufactured in sweatshops and that had met the NCL's standards with regard to wages and hours were included on the White List. See Sklar, *Florence Kelley and the Nation's Work*, 309–310.
2. For a review of the development of American consumer society, see Cohen, *A Consumers' Republic.*
3. See Letter 103, FK to NK, 10 November 1907, below.
4. For more on FK's national headquarters in New York and her travels, see Sklar, "Two Political Cultures in the Progressive Era."
5. For FK's label campaign, see Sklar, "The Consumers' White Label of the National Consumers' League." See also Letter 59, FK to Katherine Trevett, 25 July 1900; and Letter 61, FK to Edward Filene, 9 July 1901 (both below).
6. See Letter 61, FK to Edward A. Filene, 9 July 1901, below.
7. See Letter 93, FK to NK, 20 February 1907; and Letter 75, FK to NK, 15 July 1905 (both below).
8. See Letter 66, FK to NK, 2 February 1903, below.
9. See Letter 63, FK to Clara Colby, 27 November 1901, below.
10. See Letter 81, FK to NK, 7 February 1906, below.
11. See Letter 93, FK to NK, 20 February 1907, below.
12. See Letter 93, FK to NK, 20 February 1907.
13. For that recognition, see Letter 73, FK to NK, 18 August 1904, below.
14. See Letter 100, FK to NK, 19 October 1907, below.
15. See Letter 90, FK to Caroline Bartlett Crane, 21 January 1907, below.
16. *Lochner v. People of the State of New York*, 198 U.S. 45 (1905).
17. *Lochner v. People of the State of New York.* See also Woloch, *Muller v. Oregon*,18–20.
18. *Lochner v. People of the State of New York.*
19. See Letter 102, FK to NK, 7 November 1907, below.
20. See Letter 96, FK to NK, 1 July 1907, below.
21. See Letter 73, FK to NK, 18 August 1904, below.
22. See Letter 77, FK to NK, 29 August 1905, below
23. FK, "Handbook of Child Labor Legislation"; FK, "An Effective Child Labor Law"; FK, "Child Labor and Woman Suffrage."
24. Letter 69, FK to NK, 5 July 1903, below.
25. See Letter 100, FK to NK, 19 October 1907, below.

58. To Henry D. Lloyd

National Consumers' League
105 e. 22nd. st. N. Y. City
Oct. 14th. 1899

Dear Mr. Lloyd,

Fräulein [Stallbohm] has kindly sent me a copy of your card in the Post. I had seen the attack and the card, before; but it is a great pleasure to have a copy sent of all my own.[1] The family with which Ko and I dwell take the Times in the morning and the Post in the evening, and I have to go to the street-corner and buy my World secretly; tho' I confess that its righteous attitude in the matter of the wars has led me to brandish it of late with none of the conventional apologies for perusing it.[2]

I'm afraid that I do not agree with you as to good wealth and bad.[3] There is wealth well-used; and wealth relatively righteously accumulated; but I am afraid that I think it is all relative, just as there were humane slave-holders, who were slave-holders all the same. I'm afraid the only good wealth of the future (and almost of the present) is public wealth administered with enlightened public spirit. I'm not prepared to say that this applies wholly, at present; but I do not believe that the category Good Wealth, can be regarded as a permanent one. Perhaps it is an unconscious service that the conscienceless accumulators are rendering, in making clear the intrinsic quality of all accummulation.

Ko is having such a hard time with the rough and noisy teachers at Dr. Sachs' cramming-institution that he is more homesick than ever for Chicago and Lewis Institute.[4] That is not what one expects in returning to the effete civilizations!—To pine for the gentle humanities of the Woolly West! Otherwise we are flourishing rather more than usual. I hope the same thing is true of all the Lloyds!

With best love to the Missis and yourself,

Yours sincerely,
F. Kelley[5]

TLS, Box 10, Lloyd Papers, WHi

1. An editorial in the *New York Evening Post* criticized Lloyd's *Wealth Against Commonwealth* (New York: Harper and Brothers, 1894), his attack on monopolies in the mining, railroad, and oil industries that concentrated especially on the Standard Oil Company. The *Post* characterized many of the book's accusations as "improbable, if not false . . . and none of them is established by sufficient evidence to sustain a verdict by a jury" (*New York Evening Post,* 18 September 1899, 4). In his reply titled "A Card from Mr. Lloyd," Lloyd wrote that his study was carefully researched and was "based specifically on the verdicts of juries in civil and criminal cases, the decisions of state and federal courts, special tribunals like the Interstate Commerce Commission, and on the findings of state and national legislative investigations" (*New York Evening Post,* 26 September 1899, 4; see also Destler, *Henry Demarest Lloyd,* 293–300, 328–329).

2. As war loomed between Great Britain and the South African Republic, which was populated largely by Dutch immigrants (or Boers), over British rights in mining areas in South Africa, the *New York World* editorialized on a number of occasions that President McKinley should honor a petition from the American people urging U.S. mediation between the two countries (*New York World,* 7 October 1899, 6 and 13 October 1899, 6).

3. In his letter to the *Post,* Lloyd wrote: "If the good wealth permits the 'bad wealth' to take that leadership in business, church, education, politics, and society which it is, for obvious reasons of self-preservation, so anxious to take and to pay for most liberally in campaign contributions, pew-rents, and endowments, the day may come when the people will be so confused as not to see any difference between 'bad wealth' and 'good wealth'" (26 September 1899, 4).

4. Julius Sachs (1849–1934) established the Collegiate Institute School for Boys in 1872. It claimed to maintain rigorous standards for its pupils and serve as a model for other preparatory schools.

5. Lloyd replied that he agreed with FK about the relativity of wealth, "but after all everything is a relativity." He hoped to use wealth "that was honestly made according to the rules of the game (even though the game be a bad one ultimately) to help us smoke out and exterminate the bad wealth, which was made in violation of the rules of the game" (Henry Demarest Lloyd, Boston, to FK, 18 October 1899, Box 10, Lloyd Papers, WHi).

59. To Katherine Lucy Trevett[1]

NATIONAL CONSUMERS' LEAGUE
OFFICE: 105 E. 22ND ST.
NEW YORK CITY

[Winnetka, Illinois?]
July 25th, 1900

Dear Miss Trevett

Your letter of July 17th, having gone to the office of the League in New York, has just reached me on my travels.[2] I am very sorry for the delay and hasten to reply at once, so far as I can, at this distance from headquarters.

I have not had any correspondence with the pastor whom you mention,—but if you will kindly give me his full name and address, I shall be glad to forward to him whatever literature of the subject we have. It will also give me great pleasure to send you the same material, as soon as I reach N.Y., which will probably be about August 5th.

We now have Leagues in Mass., N.Y., Pa., Ohio, Ill., N.J., Mich., Wis., & Minnesota; and one is about to be formed in Rhode Island. The West seems really more alive to the power and responsibility of the purchasers than the East; and it ***is*** most encouraging to see how readily the organization spreads. The most favorable existing organizations seem to be the churches and the women's clubs.

One difficulty seems to lie in the opinion of intelligent people that the conditions of employment are so satisfactory in the Western States that Leagues are not needed. But the products of some of the worst factories and sweatshops in the East are sold in the West. And for improving Eastern industrial conditions it seems absolutely necessary to enlist the help of all the purchasers, however remote geographically and however well-situated industrially they may be.

I enclose the two items that I have left after a long lecturing-tour in the course of which I have distributed all the literature with whic***h*** I had provided myself; and will send you better samples of ammunition very soon.

Yours very truly
Florence Kelley

If there is a teachers' club in Portland, that is an admirable nucleus for a League.

TLS, "General Correspondence: 'T,'" Box B22, NCL Records, DLC

1. Katherine Lucy Trevett later became the recording secretary of the CL of Oregon, based in Portland and organized in July 1905. She held this position until at least 1935 and also served on the Oregon LWV board in the 1930s. (Swensen, "Pilgrims at the Golden Gate," 257; *Oregon Journal,* 15 July 1905, 5; correspondence with Janice Dilg, Portland, Oregon, 13 August 2006; Trevett, Santa Barbara, Calif., to Lucy Mason, 8 February 1935, "Chartered Leagues: Oregon," Box B9, NCL Records, DLC.)

2. FK was visiting Margaret in Winnetka on 20 July (FK, Winnetka, Ill., to CBK, 20 July 1900, KFP, NCC-RB).

60. To Caroline Bonsall Kelley

[New York City]
Jan. 19th [1901]

Mother dear,

This is just a line to reach you before Sunday, with thanks for the note in Bert's hand wh. came yesterday a.m.

It is bitterly cold, but clear and fine. We have our annual meeting on Monday afternoon, at 156 Fifth Ave., so you may imagine me arrayed in my soft black gown which the children jokingly call "spangles", addressing the multitude of the fashionable! Mr. Brooks and Mr. David Bispham form the rest of the program.[1] I tell you these details because I know how you love meetings!

Ko is off to school for an examination which he anticipated with some anxiety; in U.S. history. M. is enjoying the usual leisure of Saturday.

Miss Wald took dinner with us last evening, in high feather because she and her friends had just succeeded in getting the city to undertake a large playground in her immediate neighborhood.[2] She had been working for it for four years! I have another nice letter from John.[3] If I can find it, I'll enclose it.

As I write, the air is full of sunshine and snow—the first snow of the season—both together. It is a wonderful winter.

Margaret is looking forward to seeing you next month. She seriously means to come over for Washington's Birthday.

I trust that your general health keeps up, and that the finger keeps "inchin' along"! With much love and sympathy

Your loving
F.K.

ALS, KFP, NCC-RB

1. FK and John Graham Brooks spoke at the tenth annual meeting of the CL of New York City. David Bispham (1857–1921), American singer at the Metropolitan Opera (1896 to 1903), read "poems appropriate to the purpose of the league" (*NYT,* 22 January 1901, 3).
2. Through the Outdoor Recreation League, Lillian Wald raised funds for the improvement and upkeep of Seward Park, which was dedicated in 1903 as the first municipal playground in New York City (Duffus, *Lillian Wald,* 86).
3. John attended the Hillside Home School in Wisconsin from 1894 to 1902.

61. To Edward A. Filene[1]

NATIONAL CONSUMERS' LEAGUE
OFFICE: 105 E. 22D ST.
NEW YORK CITY

July 9th, 1901

Dear Mr. Filene,

I called at the store several months ago to thank you for the effect that your order of labeled goods had had upon the W. H. Burns Co., Mr. Burns having said that you were among those who had asked for the label and that this had in part decided him to use it.[2] To my astonishment, you replied that you were not using the label; and this was substantiated by later reports from the Massachusetts League which did not enumerate your store among those in which labeled goods were offered.

I never resumed the subject with Mr. Burns, being satisfied that he used the label, whatever his reasons for doing so;—but I naturally mentioned so strange a situation to Mrs. Nathan as one of the very active members of my Executive Committee.[3]

In regard to the Standard Manufacturing Co., 77 Bedford street, Boston, Mass., I sent them, at the request of Miss Lamb, a copy of the contra*ct* for their consideration, but have heard nothing farther from the firm thus far.[4] We are very desirous of adding to our list, as rapidly as possible, all those New England houses wh*i*ch give out no goods to be made. The New England conditions of work are so markedly superior to the best found elsewhere.[5]

Yours very truly
Florence Kelley
Secretary

TLS, CLM Records, MCR-S

1. Edward A. Filene (1860–1937) inherited his father's department store, which catered to the "carriage trade" of relatively wealthy customers. Filene wrote to FK to clear up a misunderstanding that could have cost him some business. He had just heard from Maud Nathan that FK believed that Filene was refusing to buy goods because they had the Consumers' League White Label on them. Anxious not to be on the wrong side of this issue with the Consumers' League, he wrote to ask her for details of her information so they could find out "where the error lies" (Filene, Boston, to FK, 12 July 1901, copy, CLM Records, MCR-S). Since September 1899, the NCL had been signing contracts with various manufacturers of women's goods that allowed these firms to attach labels to their goods. To meet the conditions for the label, the firms had to guarantee a) that all goods were made on the premises, not in sweatshops; b) that all state factory laws were obeyed in the manufacture of the goods; and c) that no child under sixteen was employed on their premises (*NYT,* 28 August 1899, 10).

2. Underwear manufacturer W. H. Burns Co., located in Boston and Worcester, was among a dozen or so Massachusetts manufacturers that were authorized to use the label. The firm wrote William Filene and Sons in March and December 1900 from Boston about the difficulties in carrying out the NCL guidelines (W. H. Burns Co., [Boston], to William Filene and Sons, 8 March 1900, 19 March 1900, and 15 December 1900, CLM Records, MCR-S).

3. Maud Nathan (1862–1946), a member of the NCL Executive Committee, helped organize the CL of New York City in 1890 and served as its president from 1897 until 1917.

4. Filene wrote that this underwear manufacturing company was "favorably disposed towards the Consumers League" (Edward Filene, Boston, to FK, 2 July 1901, CLM Records, MCR). Rose Lamb (1843–1927) was an editor and a member of Executive Committee of the CL of Massachusetts.

5. Filene replied that he had pressured the Burns Company to use goods with the Consumers' League Label but believed it inaccurate for the CL of Massachusetts to advertise Filene's as selling "labelled goods" because the Burns merchandise was only a small proportion of the entire Filene inventory. On 24 July, FK thanked Filene for clearing up the matter and expressed the hope that the store would continue to carry labeled goods. On 26 July, she sent him a copy of the contract the NCL used for labeling merchandise (Edward Filene, Boston, to FK, 16 July 1901, and FK, New York, to Edward Filene, 26 July 1901, both in CLM Records, MCR-S).

62. To Richard Yates [1]

NATIONAL CONSUMERS' LEAGUE
OFFICE: 105 E. 22D ST.
NEW YORK CITY

July 26th, 1901

Honorable Richard Yates
Executive Office
Springfield, Ill.
Dear Sir,

Your letter of July 3d is at hand. To one who has faithfully performed the duties of Chief Factory Inspector of the State of Illinois, the offer of the position of Assistant Chief Inspector cannot be ~~offered~~ ***presented*** otherwise than as an affront.

Yours very truly
Florence Kelley

TLS, FKP, NN

1. Richard Yates (1860–1936) was governor of Illinois (Republican) from 1901 to 1905. His wife, Helen W. Yates, telegraphed FK that she was "anxious you should talk with my husband." Although Mrs. Yates favored FK's appointment as chief factory inspector, Governor Yates wrote FK that "I have been unable to see my way clear to offer you this appointment, but I hereby offer you the position of assistant chief factory inspector, with headquarters in Chicago" (Helen W. Yates, Springfield, Ill., to FK, 16 July 1901, and Richard Yates, Springfield, Ill., to FK, 23 July 1901, both in FKP, NN).

63. To Clara Bewick Colby

NATIONAL CONSUMERS' LEAGUE
OFFICE: 105 E. 22D ST.
NEW YORK CITY

Nov. 27th 1901

Dear Mrs. Colby,

I am delighted to get your note and clippings from the Tribune. I, also, have been asking myself how we can co-operate. One way is, for the Suffrage Associations to publish two items prominently, namely, the number of women factory inspectors, and <u>their tenure of office</u>, in the different States. The other is the age at which children may begin work. If I had time to make a diagram such as were published, some years ago, with a huge black bar for the States where the age is unregulated and a tiny black bar for Massachusetts where children cannot work under 14 years, and not under 16 years unless they are attending night school etc. that would be <u>very</u> useful. But I cannot do that at present. Can you get it done?[1]

Soon, I will send you an article for the Tribune setting forth what I think we can do.

Yours sincerely
Florence Kelley

Cannot you use the literature which I send herewith?

ALS, Colby Papers, CSmH

1. Colby served from 1900 to 1903 as chair of NAWSA's Committee on Industrial Problems Affecting Women and Children. In her report to the 1902 NAWSA convention in Washington, D.C., Colby conveyed FK's request to the audience: "Mrs. Kelley asks our assistance in securing data especially concerning the number of women factory inspectors and the child labor laws in the various States. This committee would be glad of such information from any of the delegates that it may be included in the report that will be sent to Mrs. Kelley" (reprinted in the *Woman's Tribune,* 8 March 1902, 36).

64. To Nicholas Kelley[1]

105 e. 22nd street, [New York City]
March 15th, [1902]

Beloved Son,

The afternoon draws to its close, and I can hardly believe that it is already a week since my *brief* glimpse of you!

It is a gray day in March, full of the promise of Spring, so that even Grandma was stirred by it, and sallied forth after luncheon to walk across Sixteenth street, from Irving Place to Fifth Avenue, to call upon Hattie Patterson, who was gone to the country to spend Sunday.[2] We scuttled back, across Union Square sitting down in the benches to break the walk. But Grandma is pitifully bowed, and unsteady, and I think she was heartily glad when the outing came to an end.

To-morrow, I am going to hear Felix Adler preach on Child Labor, the Crime of Our Times. The next week I go again to church, in Carnegie Hall, to hear my admired Booker Washington on his one subject.[3] The rest of the time I stick to my type-writer. The first instalment of the report is remodeled in many particulars; and in the hands of the printers. I have hopes of getting the proof read before I start Westward, on the twenty-sixth.[4] It is more interesting, I think, than it was a week ago.

The enclosed letter from a boy I got from Miss Wald, to send you because you would see the point. You need not return either enclosure.

I forgot to tell you that Grandma has been so frugal of late that she has one hundred fifty dollars on her check book, and the new deposit is due in four days! So she really never worries about money any more. She has had a deadly

Nicholas Kelley, 1906. Courtesy of the Kelley Family Papers, Rare Book and Manuscript Library, Columbia University.

dull winter; but I do not see how that can be helped. She is uppermost in my mind, because she is under my care, directly again.

I stayed with Anne, in Boston, and when I spoke of getting to see Mr. Underwood, who said that he seemed to have left Hoppy, and to be in business for himself, as his card, giving an office address is published daily, in the newspapers.[5] So I abandoned that idea, but I have found a home quite near Bussey, where he would be most comfortable, e.g. John would, and I am negotiating about it.[6] I do not know whether you have met Miss Emily Balch, a friend of the Simkovitch's, and of mine. It is the home of her sisters and brother.[7]

I am wondering whether this Saturday epistle may not be delivered in your godless hole on the Sabbath. I hope it may.

Uncle Henry [Lloyd], I was interested to find, has not given up thinking pretty well of Mr. Jerome.[8]

Write me, child, write me!

Your loving
Mother

TLS, FKP, NN

1. Thanks to the efforts of AK, sixteen-year-old NK was working as an "all 'round handy lad" for the Philadelphia, Bristol and Trenton Street Railway Company in Bristol, Pennsylvania, while awaiting admission to Harvard University in the fall (AK, Philadelphia, Pa., to FK, 5 October 1901, KFP, NCC-RB). Mary Rozet Smith paid his college tuition (FK, [Boston], to NK, 5 February 1902, and NK, Hillside, Wis., to FK, 17 March 1902, both in FKP, NN.)

2. Hattie Patterson may be Hannah Jane Patterson (1879–1937), a suffrage leader then studying finance at Columbia University.

3. Felix Adler addressed the Ethical Culture Society on 16 March 1902 at Carnegie Hall. Booker T. Washington (1856–1915), founder of Tuskegee Normal and Industrial Institute for Negroes, spoke on 6 March at Carnegie Hall, describing his accomplishments at Tuskegee, which emphasized industrial education rather than civil rights. Washington exhorted northerners to recognize that the "South is not alone responsible for what is known as the negro problem. It is the Nation's problem, because the Nation as a whole was responsible for its creation" (*NYT*, 17 March 1902, 9 and 6 March 1902, 9).

4. FK's "Report of the Secretary" was published in the NCL's Third Annual Report ([1902], 7–32, Box A5, NCL Records, DLC). She left on 27 March for an extended speaking trip to Michigan; from there, she went to California to speak and organize consumers' leagues (FK, New York, to NK, 26 March 1902; FK to NK, Detroit, 3 April 1902; FK to NK, Los Angeles, 13 May 1902; and FK to NK, San Francisco, 26 May 1902; all in FKP, NN).

5. Anne Safford, an old friend, lived in Boston.

6. Fourteen-year-old JK was leaving the Hillside Home School, and while in Massachusetts FK had approached Underwood about boarding him in his home while JK attended the Bussey Institute (FK, Boston, to NK, 23 February 1902, FKP, NN). The Bussey Institute in Jamaica Plain was a small undergraduate school of agriculture and horticulture founded in 1871.

7. Mary Kingsbury Simkhovitch (1867–1951), founder in 1902 of Greenwich House, a social settlement in Greenwich Village, served on the executive committee of the NCL. Her husband Vladimir was a professor of economic history at Columbia. The sisters of Emily Greene Balch were Alice (later Stone), Anne, Elizabeth ("Bessie"), and Marion ("Maidie"); her brother was Francis Noyes Balch (Randall, *Improper Bostonian*, 462, 464).

8. William T. Jerome (1859–1934) was a reform lawyer in New York City.

65. To Nicholas Kelley

June 29th 02 [Chicago]
Hull-House, Sunday morning

Ko Darling

I am writing in the octagon. The sun is shining for the second time in three weeks. Margaret is reading the morning papers in front of the grate fire in the next room. John is at breakfast with Mr. Riddle, the very nice parole officer. After dinner, we are going to see Grandma.[1]

On July 6th, Mr. Twose and John will start for Boston together where Mr. Twose will enter John at Bussey, as a regular student if he can, otherwise as a special student.[2] They start about July 5th.

Please write me immediately on what day you are to report at Cambridge. I must know in order to arrange my engagements here. If you don't need me in Cambridge, I can go to a very important gathering in Minneapolis, to which Miss Addams and I are invited, September 23d to 26th inclusive.[3] Pres Roosevelt et hoc genus omne[4] will be there. Getting John settled thus early leaves me free for September, if Aunt Jessie [Lloyd] remains late enough to settle you, as I know she longs and means to do if she can possibly manage it.

But I need to know your dates! Have you no Harvard catalog?

Mr. Devine of the New York City Charity Organization came out this week to try to get Alice Hamilton to go to New York to serve as Secretary of the new Tuberculosis Commission. She would have $1800.00 a year to do for it what Mr. Veiller did for the Tenement House Commission. She is not going. She is working in Dr. Hektoen's laboratory investigating the bacteriology of Scarlet Fever.[5]

Miss Edith Hamilton is here. Miss Margaret [Hamilton] went last week to Mackinaw where Quint already is.[6]

Mary Smith has just come home from Europe. I wish you could see her flat! The new quadrangle is a perfect joy! The grass is so green, and the vines grow up the walls so willingly, and the residents spray the bugs with Paris Green so patiently! Mrs. Keyser has one flat and Frank and his wife have another. Mamie Sullivan had one, but she could not do the work, and has given it up to Dr. Rice whose salary as postmistress enables her both to have the flat and to eat meals in the Coffee House, which poor Mamie Sullivan could not afford! Mrs. Wilmarth and Ella Waite have flats on the Halsted Street front.[7] It is the most beautiful possible successor to the Murphys' and the Rag & Bottle Business!

Quint entered Princeton; but Mr. Carman had forgotten that logarithms were required and he had had none! So they do not yet know the result

It looks as tho' Margaret and I should be here, pretty much alone thro' July with Mr. Riddle, Mr. Tyler, (Alice Kellogg's husband)[8] and Mr. [Frederick] Deknatel.

We are drafting a child labor law, a compulsory education law, and a license law for newsboys.[9]

Your loving Mother
F.K.

ALS, FKP, NN

1. Joseph B. Riddle, probation officer for Cook County Juvenile Court, taught boys' classes at Hull House (Sicherman, *Alice Hamilton,* 149). CBK was spending the summer at the Chicago Beach Hotel (FK, [Chicago], to NK, 8 June 1902, FKP, NN).
2. George Twose, a British Hull House resident, taught woodworking and theatre there (Bryan and Davis, *100 Years at Hull House,* 40).
3. At the Convention of the Employer and Employe, FK exhorted women to boycott all clothing produced in sweatshops and to agitate for pure foods ("The Indirect Employer, the Purchaser," *Minneapolis Tribune,* 25 September 1902, 6).
4. Latin; "and all his group."
5. Edward T. Devine (1867–1948) was general secretary of the Charity Organization Society from 1896 to 1912 and edited *Charities and the Commons* (later titled *Survey*) from 1897 to 1912. Alice Hamilton, who had lived at Hull House since 1897, chose to remain there and accepted a position as a bacteriologist in Chicago at the Memorial Center for Infectious Diseases under pathologist and bacteriologist Ludwig Hektoen (1863–1951) (Sicherman, *Alice Hamilton,* 143–144). Social worker Lawrence Veiller (1872–1959) organized the Tenement House Exhibition in New York City in 1899–1900 to call attention to conditions there, a project that led to the New York State Tenement House Act of 1901.
6. Alice Hamilton's siblings, Edith (1867–1963), a classical scholar; Margaret (1871–1969), then studying anatomy at Johns Hopkins; and Arthur ("Quint") (1886–1967), later a language professor at the University of Illinois (Sicherman, *Alice Hamilton,* 12–13).
7. Frank Keyser was an engineer at Hull House; suffragist Mary Hawes Wilmarth (1837–1919) was a Hull House benefactor. Ella Waite (d. 1925) had been Hull House financial manager since 1896. (Bryan and Davis, *100 Years at Hull House,* 7, 70, 167). Working from Hull House, Harriet A. Rice had a modest medical practice (JA, Chicago, to Mary Rozet Smith, 1 October 1894, 3 February 1895, and 24 February 1895, all on Reel 2, *Jane Addams Papers*).
8. Orno J. Tyler (1853–1917) married artist Alice Kellogg (1862–1900) in 1894.
9. In March 1903, FK reported that bills proposed by the NYCLC that included these safeguards would become law in September and October 1903 (NCL, Fourth Annual Report [1903], 24–25, Box A5, NCL Records, DLC).

66. To Nicholas Kelley

105 E. 22nd St. New York City
Feb. 2nd '03

Beloved Son,

You are so delightfully regular in the matter of your Sunday letter that I looked for it this morning until it occurred to me that you doubtless imagined me still whirling about Delaware. On Tuesday, Bishop Layton Coleman came to our meeting at Wilmington. On Wednesday, Governor Hunn and thirty members of the legislature came, in Dover.[1] On Saturday, I spent the morning with Mr. Chief Justice Lore of Delaware at his home, drafting the new child labor bill for the State.[2] So it was a most flattering and delightful experience. By June, I believe we shall have a real move forward accomplished for the protection of the children.

I have a delightful letter from John, written on his birthday. Do tell him what a pleasure it is to me to get a good letter like that.

This evening I go again to Philadelphia returning to-morrow. I hope for a glimpse of Uncle Bert.[3]

Your loving mother
F.K.

ALS, FKP, NN

1. FK spoke on "Child Labor Legislation and School Attendance Laws" at the New Century Club of Wilmington on 27 January 1903. She described the long hours, poor pay, monotonous work, and unhealthy conditions children experienced in clothing, tobacco, and glass factories and urged the Delaware legislature to enact a compulsory education law for children. On a motion from Bishop Leighton Coleman (1837–1907), Episcopal bishop of Delaware from 1888 to 1907, the meeting resolved to instruct two Century Club committees to recommend to the legislature "the objects set before this meeting." FK also spoke at the Dover Century Club on 28 January, an event to which the Delaware legislature and Governor John Hunn (1849–1926) were invited (*Wilmington Every Evening:* 28 January 1903, 4; 29 January 1903, 4).

2. Charles B. Lore (1831–1911) was Delaware's chief justice from 1893 to 1909.

3. AK was working in a law office in the West End Trust Building in Philadelphia (AK, Philadelphia, Pa., to CBK, 16 September 1902, KFP, NCC-RB).

67. To Nicholas Kelley

Detroit, Mich. May 7th '03
r.r. sta. waiting room

Beloved Son,

Burn this!

If Aunt Jessie [Lloyd] asks Margaret to Sakonnet as she said in Apr. she meant to do;[1] —would you risk having her go

1. at all? & if so
2. for how long?

As I understand the standard of Demeanor for Damsels at Sakonnet requires in order to be on the White List:—

1. Perfect Punctuality at meals;
2. Exquisite Order of Room at all Hours;
3. Imperturbable affability towards

Elders	together with Distinguished	}
Domestics	Reserve towards persons of	
Bores	the male Sex.	

4. Devotion towards an Elder Brother;
5. Daily Enthusiastic Dishwashing and Bedmaking.

Do you think the lady is up to this standard?

She has as dull a summer outlook as John. But that is no reason for having too many Kelleys at Sakonnet, or for having her go there before she is up to the Standard.[2]

Your loving Ma

Letters are forwarded as usual. So keep on addressing letters to the office.

I'm not alarmed about your probation![3]

ALS, FKP, NN

1. MK wrote her mother from Hull House that she was "getting very gloomy over the Sakonnet prospect. . . . The list of requirements is somewhat appalling." She asked whether the stipulation that she must retire by 9 P.M. was because of "the great consideration of a doting Ma" (MK to FK, 8 May [1903], FKP, NN).
2. MK did not spend the summer with the Lloyds; FK wrote in response to an unrecovered letter from NK, apparently advising against the plan, that she would "find some other outing for Sister" (FK, [New York], to NK, 18 May 1903, FKP, NN).
3. FK's letters to NK continued to focus on his health and academic success; she described as "very good" his grades of A, B, C-, and C during his first term at Harvard (FK, New York, to NK, 3 January 1903, FKP, NN).

68. To Nicholas Kelley

Atlanta, Ga.,
May 10th '03

Beloved Son,

Here you are! You see you must be a righteous child, at least until after the finals.

Miss Addams says Margaret needs petting. If you are up to the strain of sending her one of your nicest letters, it will be deeply appreciated. Margaret is certainly far from well, and none of us can find out what the matter is.[1]

It is great fun rushing about with Miss Addams just as we did a year ago at Los Angeles.[2] She seems wonderfully well. Mary Smith is here and I am having a real treat.

I expect to be in New York next Sunday. An Atlanta Consumers' League has just been formed. The last was in Paris the next will be in Honolulu.[3] So you see my running about over the surface seems in no wise likely to diminish!

I spent the morning in Cotton mills where children work who are only ten years old. It is frightful!

Your loving
Mother

ALS, FKP, NN

1. JA had written FK recently about MK's health and state of mind. A teacher at the Lewis Institute was concerned about MK's "nervous condition," saying "the dear girl doesn't look well much of the time." All at Hull House were well, continued Addams, but a "fine letter to the lady from her mother would help much" (JA, Chicago, to FK, 10 April 1903, FKP, NN). For more about the correspondence between FK and MK, see Letter 76, FK to MK, 27 August 1905, note 2, below.

2. At the National Conference of Charities and Corrections, FK spoke on 11 May on "The Use and Abuse of Factory Inspection," praising the Massachusetts factory inspection system. Working conditions were strictly regulated and "the health of the purchasing public is protected." She also congratulated Illinois and Pennsylvania for removing factory inspectors who were biased toward manufacturers (*Atlanta Constitution,* 12 May 1903, 3).

3. The CL of Paris, France, was founded on 27 December 1902 (NCL, Fifth Annual Report [1904], 36, Box A5, NCL Records, DLC).

69. To Nicholas Kelley

Office [New York City], Sunday evening
July 5th '03

Beloved Son,

Our letters having crossed, you have Dr. Sachs' by now.[1] I realize the difficulty of getting enough athletics for John. But if we live with Miss Owens, in Irving Place, he will have lively walking up and down Madison or Fifth Avenue, some miles daily. And he can have his canoe on the Harlem River.

I went out to Andover and decided against it because it did not offer what John most needs, supervision. This I can give him when I am here and secure for him, I think, during my absences. He would be almost as free, at Andover, as he was at Hillside, from pressure to do daily work daily. You see, I have learned, at last, the lesson that John was not up to the freedom of this last year.

Now, as to the funds. I can spin out the savings over two years, I think, because the legacy went half to pay arrears at Hillside and half for Ferry Hall.[2]

This year, I have no arrears and John and [I] can live cheaply at Miss Owens! I shall have no lunches and carfares there.

Besides, Grandma is always willing to help, and I have made no demands upon her, whatever, except for one hundred dollars a year each year while you were at Dr. Sachs.' I feel pretty safe about finances.

Margaret is a continual pleasure, so jolly and witty.

Mrs. Prang dined with us, night before last. She is here for several months' work, reorganizing the editorial department of the publishing Company.[3] So I have a great pleasure in store, seeing her frequently.

Grandma comes to-morrow. I forget whether I told you that Mariana [Parrish] has gone to Northeast Harbor, in Maine, for two months and Bert is saving up for his wedding so he is not going on, according to present plans. The wedding seems to be set for Oct. 17th and I'm arranging my plans accordingly. But this we are told in deep—confidence.

My chief occupation is writing things for immediate publication, and this makes a poor correspondent. Miss [Lavinia] Dock goes abroad for a year, starting next month. Miss McDowell goes to Nova Scotia for a month.[4] Miss Wald and I are getting a park for our ward and a street widened. It's more fun than any ordinary vacation!

The present administration has brought down the death rate from 19.57 to 13.65 per 1000! The latest thing is

a. the appointment of nurses to take contagious cases in the tenements because the hospital accommodation is insufficient.
b. the appointment of six nurses to care for tuberculosis cases in their homes.
c. visitation by physicians, and nurses, of all babies born since Aug. 1st 1902, to make sure that their mothers are caring for them properly during the hot weather.

There was never such an administration!

The supervisor of fumigators after illness in the tenements goes about in an automobile so that he can visit, each day, all the premises fumigated and all subordinates work with the knowledge that he is coming!

Give my love to all the friends. What is Mr. [Henry D.] Lloyd writing?

I know how easy it is to be absorbed at Sakonnet. But I still clamor relentlessly for the humble minimum of one letter a week; which is 'terrible modest' for an all year 'round diet of a really doting Ma!

Your loving
F.K.

ALS, FKP, NN

1. JK did poorly at the Bussey Institute. FK was trying to place him at the Sachs Institute in New York City and was searching for a place to board him (FK, n.p., to NK, 2 June 1903; Julius Sachs, Keene Valley, N.Y., to FK, 26 July 1903, both in FKP, NN).

2. MK attended Ferry Hall in Lake Forest, Illinois, in 1902–1903, a preparatory school for the daughters of the midwestern elite that was known for its support for social justice causes (FK, Chicago, to NK, 22 July 1902, 24 July 1902, FKP, NN; MK to FK, undated letters, [1900–1902], FKP, NN). Frances Perkins taught at the school in 1904. In a letter to NK in June, FK had mentioned receiving a legacy of $500, apparently from a relative of WDK (FK, Chicago, to NK, 8 June 1902, FKP, NN).

3. FK's long association with Mary Dana Hicks Prang (1836–1927) dated back to FK's friendship at Cornell with Prang's daughter, Margaret Hicks (see Letter 6, FK to WDK, 2 January 1884, above). An art teacher before she met her second husband, Louis Prang, Mary Prang was widowed in 1909. FK was referring to the Taber-Prang company, publisher of greeting cards and art education material.

4. Lavinia Dock was a central figure at the Henry Street Settlement; Helen McDowell, daughter of Civil War Union general Irvin McDowell, owned the home that backed on the settlement (Duffus, *Lillian Wald,* 62, 66).

70. To Nicholas Kelley

105 E. 22nd St.
New York July 14th [1903]

Beloved Son,
The heat laid me low, not by actual sun-stroke but a queer, unconquerable dullness of mind and speech. Hence my failure to write for your birthday. I have recovered, with no crisis more serious than a momentary aphasia, last night, at dinner.

But please do not feel that your family forgets your birthday! It is my annual day of profound rejoicing!

Before you select next year's courses, I hope I may have a chance for a long quiet talk with you on the subject.

A wonderful piece of good fortune has come to ~~John~~ Margaret. Mrs. Glendower Evans has asked her to be Miss Fuller's successor; to live with her and go to the Latin school.[1] Ask Aunt Jessie [Lloyd] to tell you about Mrs. Evans. The invitation takes effect at the opening of school in September. You will be asked to see as much of Margaret as you choose (and expected to do the devoted brother act). Mrs. Evans has been looking for a secretary since Miss Fuller's marriage and decided on Margaret last night while visiting me at Miss Wald's. She is staying with us at the Settlement. Margaret is delighted with the idea and resumes the idea of college with fortitude. She will have her home; and will be companion and secretary. I shall keep on with her allowance for books and clothes. The work will be chiefly nominal, certainly for a good while to come. We can hardly believe our ears and eyes! There is no more interesting house in Boston! You know where it is, on the same row with the Brandeis'[2] and around the corner from Miss Rose Lamb's.

John has a written a straightforward, simple letter to Dr. [Julius] Sachs, for me to enclose. I am looking forward with much pleasure to next winter with him. He goes to Westport in a few days, to join Stanly [Linn] and Mr. Youmans.[3]

Now that my head has recovered from the heat, and this enchanting vista opens before Margaret, I'm even feeling serene about John. The Lord does certainly provide for good and diligent children when they are attractive!

I love to think of you taking Margaret to shows!

When would it be convenient for me to come, if at all? I had thought of taking Grandma and Margaret to Barton, Vermont, for August and comi[n]g down for a little while in September But I do not know what time her school begins.

Give my dear love to Aunt Jessie and accept my congratulations on the growing splendors of your Freshman record![4]

Your proud and loving
Ma![5]

ALS, FKP, NN

1. Elizabeth Glendower Evans (1856–1937) had been active in prison reform since her husband's death in 1886. She wrote FK welcoming MK and offering to help her get settled in the Brookline school (Elizabeth Glendower Evans, Boston, to FK, 27 August 1903, FKP, NN).
2. Boston attorney Louis D. Brandeis and his wife Alice Goldmark Brandeis (1866–1945) lived at 6 Otis Place, close to Evans's residence at 12 Otis Place.
3. FK may be referring to either Charles Yeomans (1877–1959) or his brother Edward (b. 1866), both Hull House residents and officials in the Yeomans Pump Company (Bryan and Davis, *100 Years at Hull House,* 68).
4. NK had earned an A in English that term (FK, New York, to NK, 29 June 1903, FKP, NN).
5. According to both parties, MK's lodging in 1903–1904 with Evans was not successful. FK wrote to NK looking for another situation for her daughter: "I cannot bear to think of M. continuing to accept food and shelter from one whom she does not love" (FK, [New York], to NK, 2 June 1904, FKP, NN). And Evans wrote at great length to FK regretting that she had "made so little headway with Margaret. She left my house more a stranger than she entered it." Evans was concerned about MK's "reserve and her manifest need,—she so young & little fitted to meet the troubles that are before her." Still, Evans was willing to continue the arrangement; she would "try another year to do better than I have done this" (Elizabeth Glendower Evans, Boston, to FK, 30 June 1904, KFP, NCC-RB).

71. To Nicholas Kelley

105 E. 22nd St.
New York City
April 30th '04

Ko Darling

Do you know any other fellows,—besides Bowie,—who have prepared for Harvard at the Hill School?[1] Uncle Bert thinks very well of it. Miss Sanford thinks they would take John for $500.00 which is what I could pay.[2] The school is not more than 200 boys, as I understand it. It is not Lawrenceville, but at Pottstown, Pa.

Will you talk about it with Bowie?

Chap I. of my book is done and gone. Chap II is seething in my mind. It is the Right to Leisure.[3] May is here, not only by the calendar, but in leaf and light, and a wood robin sings in Gramercy Park, think of that!

Mariana is so lovely that I really feel strongly reinforced by acquiring so charming a sister.[4] They liked your coming to them. I spent Thursday night in Phila. with them.

Dear Son, it is a great satisfaction to me to see you facing your difficulties with full intellectual integrity. It would be unfaithful to Uncle Henry [Lloyd]'s noble example if you held his faith simply because it was his, not because you had labored to know and understand your own grounds of belief.

There are two points, however, of which I wish to remind you,— If your present teachers set forth propositions which you cannot disprove, yet do not assent to, remember that you are fully entitled to reserve judgment pending the securing of more evidence. And, second, the fact that you cannot disprove a statement does not necessarily indicate that it is true. It may merely mean that you have, as yet, read too little.

The Marx is gone to you.[5] Soon, I shall be sending Vandervelde.[6] But I have not quite finished it yet.

The Clothing Manufacturers' Ass'n has heard of our bill and we are, therefore, taking the precaution of sending letters to Gov. Odell urging him to sign it. He will act, pro or con, tomorrow.[7]

I go to H.-H. on May 10th. But you will hear again before that.

I have never longed more keenly for anything than I long for your companionship!

We are moving to a new office at the back of the building, where Pauline [Goldmark] and I shall be alone together, leaving Comfort and Reed in 614.[8] Pauline stays here until June 1st and goes then, to the Adirondacks for the summer. In the Fall she will go either to Europe or to Southern California. I shall miss her sadly.

Your loving mother
F.K.

ALS, FKP, NN

1. Walter Russell Bowie (1882–1969, Harvard class of 1904), became a clergyman in New York City. At the Hill School (founded in 1851), students lived with the faculty in their campus homes.

2. Mary R. Sanford (ca. 1859–1947) of Bennington, Vermont, was from time to time an officer in the NCL and in 1905 was a founding member of the Executive Committee of Intercollegiate Socialist Society (*NYT,* 21 December 1947, 52). By 1905 she had become the life partner of Helen Phelps Stokes (1869–1945) (Zipser and Zipser, *Fire and Grace,* 59, 105, 225; *NYT,* 28 December 1945, 13). For more about Stokes, see Letter 145, FK to Mary R. Sanford, 14 June 1919, note 2, below.

3. In December 1902, FK contracted with Macmillan for her book *Some Ethical Gains through Legislation,* which was to be part of Richard T. Ely's Citizen Library. Because of illness and her other responsibilities, FK did not complete the manuscript as quickly as she—and Ely—desired (FK to Macmillan Company, 19 December 1902; and FK to Ely, 13 June 1900, 20 October 1902, 19 December 1902, and 1 May 1904, all in Ely Papers, WHi). Chapter I, "The

Right to Childhood," urged the enactment of effective child labor legislation. In "The Right to Leisure," which became Chapter III, FK described the process of enacting hours legislation as the best way to establish the "right to leisure" for adults.

4. Marianna Parrish (1874–1965) married AK on 6 April 1904 (FK to NK, 16 March 1904, FKP, NN).

5. Discussing his recent reading, NK asked if his mother was going to send "the Marx" (NK, Cambridge, Mass., to FK, 28 April 1904, FKP, NN). The first English translation of Karl Marx's *Capital: A Critical Analysis of Capitalist Production* (New York: Humboldt, 1886; trans. Samuel Moore, Edward Aveling, and Frederick Engels) included only the first book of *Capital.* FK and NK might have been studying an abbreviated version, Karl Marx, *Wage-Labor and Capital,* introduction by Frederick Engels (Chicago: Charles Kerr, 1891; trans. J. L. Joynes), or *The Students' Marx,* edited by Edward Aveling (London: Allen, 1891; 4th ed., London: S. Sonnenschein, 1902). For more on their discussion of Marx, see Letter 73, FK to NK, 18 August 1904, below.

6. *Collectivism and Industrial Evolution* by Emile Vandervelde (1866–1938) was published by Charles Kerr in Chicago in 1901.

7. The bill was signed into law around 2 May by Benjamin Odell, Jr. (1854–1926), Republican governor of New York (1901–1905). It transferred oversight for tenement house manufacturing from the factory inspector to the commissioner of labor and stipulated that no license could be issued if unsanitary conditions existed or tenement workers had any communicable disease. The commissioner was required to inspect tenements at least every six months (*NYT,* 4 May 1904, 3).

8. The NCL office was in the Charities Building at 105 E. 22nd Street.

72. To Nicholas Kelley

Cambridge, Mass.[1]
58 Garden St., June[July] 11th [1904]

Darling Son,

Thank you very much for your full and good letter anent John. Please pay Mrs. West out of the enclosed. She was paid from May 16th to June 15th inclusive; but this covers the time to date and, perhaps, some washing.[2] There is nothing caddish about your letter, or about inducing John to do, three months late, what he undertook to do last April. Besides, it is only three weeks until he is due to leave for the Adirondacks. It is the best of news that he seems to be well in spite of his lake-bathing sins!

Margaret and I spent Sunday at Gloucester with Miss [Mary Rozet] Smith and Miss Addams. They labored with me vigorously anent John's next winter in school. They seemed to think me fatuous to expect him to go school in the city and not go to pieces. But I mean to try him anyhow. Miss Addams will be back before the end of the month and hopes to see you at H.-H.

We are to lunch with Pauline [Goldmark] and Mrs. Oppenhym tomorrow at the Educational Union.[3]

Before John goes to the Adirondacks, I hope you will catch him as he passes through and make sure that he has enough socks and underclothes and night-clothes to keep him decent in a critical household where there may be no provision for washing for a stray guest for long periods at one time. I'll send you funds for him.

Love to Mrs. Lloyd.

You began nobly in the matter of letters. I find it hard to realize that you will be in your twentieth year when this reaches you! I think no son ever gave his mother more cause for pride and satisfaction, and less trouble and anxiety! Instead of congratulating you upon closing so good a year and opening a new one of such promise, it is I who am to be congratulated upon my eldest child.

I am having a rare privilege in the opportunity to atone somewhat, in middle life, for the selfish sins of omission and commission of my youth. I go nearly every day to see Grandma and it would be idle to pretend that this does not give her pleasure.[4]

Margaret is a most amusing and jolly companion. She and Charles Locke, a distant cousin of Miss Houghton's appear to cheer each other greatly.[5] The house is delightful, and I feel wonderfully rested after one week of vacation.

The book grows and I read Miss Addams the Chapter on The Right to Leisure. She was very encouraging about it.

If the way opens for you to be polite to Charles Arnold and his wife, do not miss any opportunity.[6] They have been more than polite, solidly friendly to us.

Please keep on in the path of virtue as to letters. Every scrap and item is of the liveliest interest to Your loving

Ma.

ALS, FKP, NN

1. FK and MK were spending the month of July (at a fee to be negotiated that would "free us both from the vague but sometimes burdensome responsibility of the relation of guest and host") with Elizabeth H. Houghton (1858–1915), who was active in Boston and Cambridge charities and was a member of the Executive Committee of the CL of Massachusetts (Houghton, Cambridge, Mass., to FK, 6 June 1904, KFP, NNC-RB).

2. From Winnetka, Illinois, where he was spending the summer with Jessie B. Lloyd and her family, NK thanked FK for the check. He had paid Mrs. West (with whom JK had been boarding near Chicago) and all of JK's debts (NK, Winnetka, Ill., to FK, 16 July 1904, KFP, NNC-RB; FK, Lake Forest, Ill., to NK, 16 May 1904, FKP, NN).

3. Mrs. Adolphe Openhym of New York City was a delegate to the 1905 NCL annual council meeting in Philadelphia.

4. CBK was staying nearby at a nursing facility in Waverley, Massachusetts (AK, Philadelphia, Pa., to FK, 14 July 1904, KFP, NCC-RB).

5. Charles Locke was a master at Hill School (FK, Cambridge, Mass., to NK, 6 July 1904, FKP, NN).

6. Charles Arnold of Winnetka, Illinois, was counsel to FK for her divorce from LW (see Letter 107, FK to NK, 19 June 1908, below). Mrs. Arnold was an officer in the CL of Illinois for many years (NCL, Annual Reports, 1903–1909, Boxes A5, A6, NCL Records, DLC).

73. To Nicholas Kelley

Balmy Beach, Toronto, Ontario,
August 18th, 1904[1]

Dearling Son,

My only regret with regard to the Marx is that I can n***o***t have the pleasure of reading it with you. I believe it to be unrivalled as a work of political economy. I have never been able to detect the Marxian fallacy;[2] and the Marxists have a cynical way of saying that any new criticism of Marx can be relied upon to secure to the critic no mere instructorship but a full ***p***rofessorship in a leading German University.

It is very difficult for me to estimate the value of the course that you propose for next year because I do not know the men who will deliver the lectures,—and that is really everything.[3] But fro***m*** my own experience I can assure you that it is most unsatisfactory to mill along through some years with so-called culture studies of various kinds and then settle down to law instead of having specialized in one subject and really learned something about it. So, in theory, I think you are doing well to take a lot of lectures in one field. The fact that it happens to be the field which I have long found the absorbing subject, may be biassing my view. You must discount that.

I do not know whether I told you that I found an old Cornell fellow-student, at Pittsfield, in the Berkshires, who is considering whether she will undertake John for two years with a view to seeing him through the high-school which gives a good fit for Harvard; and at the same time effecting a cure of his chronic and lifelong sniffles.[4] That is mountain air, life in the house with a very successful physician who knows good food and the modern methods of feeding growing lads with doubtful lungs. If she decides adversely I shall enter, literally in fear and trembling, upon another year in N. Y. City. Financially I cannot imagine where we should come out because last year used up all reserves except Margaret's lifelong savings ($175.00) which include her share of the legacy.

However, the one important thing, of course, is to keep the gain which John has made at such expense of time and money;—and if I felt confident of being able to do that, I should be less timorous about a winter in New York. But <u>how</u> to keep him away from football I do not kno***w*** when there is no other exercise to offer him. ***At Pittsfield, there is a superb country club.***

I like immensely the idea of a Dean's list, or any other list whi***ch*** will increase my glimpses of you.[5] When I come to Boston or Cambridge, the surroundings impose such constraint that I never seem to see the real you,—but merely a flesh and blood mask of you, which is better than nothing but by no means so satisfying to my human longings as those few days in April.

If my plans pull off properly, I shall be in Pittsfield to meet John on Aug.

31st, leaving here the day before,—and in New York at my desk on September first. Meanwhile the above will be my address.

Bert is convoying Mother to White Plains to-day where she will be within reach for me to spend my holidays with her,—an***d*** living somewha***t*** less expensively than at Waverley. In deepest confidence, also, there is a possibility that Bert and Marianna may come to New York to live.[6] That would be clear gain for me, of course, but for them it is a sad change,—at least for Bert certainly.

There are some points to be considered about Marx' view of revolution. Some of the expropriation takes place piecemeal,—the post-office and the public schools, public baths, parks, public-lighting, water supply etc. For the exposition of this piecemeal expropriation we might read the Fabian Essays together in the Christmas holidays. The English municipalities are deliberately taking over many forms of trading; and the Belgian and Dutch cities are feeding the children in certain grades of the public schools and looking after the food and milk supplies in ways formerly undreamed of. But in this country, the accepted maxim seems to be that the community may do all those things which cannot be ***made to yield dividends. A***lso the process is slower than he foresaw, because the East seems to be coming along through the capitalist phase. It is more really a world process than even he with all his foresight perceived or conceived. And as such it is slower, though it has proceeded with marvellous rapidity within the quarter-century that I have been watching it.

Thank you more than I can express for your kindness to John and the very great accommodation to me involved in setting him up in cloth***es*** and travelling funds.[7]

You say nothing of Mrs. [Jessie] Lloyd. Give her my love, if the way opens. I hope you may have some glimpses of Miss Addams. Taking it all in all, she is the greatest man of these times, because she puts to the test in daily life all the truth that she discerns, and her vision for the discernment of truth is singularly penetrating.

I'm wondering what will be the political echo, in the fall election, of the Colorado civil war. The real secret of the persecution of Hayward and Moyer is that they are outspoken and alarmingly effective Socialists, and their movement is for the nationalization of the mines.[8] The aim of the Peabody government is to quell that movement at all hazards; to crush the egg before the snake can hatch. But have they succeeded in doing this? The fall elections in the states in which mining interests are strong will show.[9] But it is to be remembered that for one miner there are many stockholders in mines, so that a movement which remained confined to miners, would be inevitably outvoted; and the mining states of the West have little industrial proletariat.

How do you account for the fact that the city proletariat in this country, instead of being Socialist is corruptly democratic? That is a problem which I find wholly baffling.

Now, I must write Margaret; and then get to work on my book Never again shall I fail to take a long cold summer vacation!

Your loving Mother
Florence Kelley

TLS, FKP, NN

Note: This letter and the one below to Jane Addams contain many typographical errors, no doubt a result of FK's unfamiliarity with the typewriter she used. They have been silently corrected.

1. FK was in Toronto for the General Biennial Conference of Friends, 12–18 August 1904. She spoke on "Our Duty to Neglected Children" on 13 August and answered questions on the NCL and sweatshops after her presentation (*Proceedings of the Friends' General Conference,* 95–104, 104–108).
2. From Winnetka, Illinois, NK wrote that "when you next see me, I shall be a full fledged Marxian socialist, at least if the rest of the book is like the first of it. . . . I have to admit that I can't see his mistake or the 'Marxian Fallacy' yet" (NK, Winnetka, Ill., to FK, 15 August 1904, KFP, NNC-RB). The "Marxian fallacy" might have been that of a contemporary critic who felt that Marx erred in predicting that capital would concentrate in fewer and fewer hands. He argued instead that capital was increasingly being distributed into the hands of small owners (Tcherkesoff, "The Concentration of Capital: A Marxian Fallacy").
3. NK laid out his courses for his coming year at Harvard, all in economics or history, and sought FK's advice. He hoped for honors in economics, which would qualify him for magna cum laude (NK to FK, 15 August 1904).
4. In 1904–1905, JK boarded with Dr. Alfreda Bosworth Withington (A.B. Cornell 1881), president of the CL of Pittsfield, Massachusetts, and attended the local high school (Hewett, *Cornell University,* 4:598; Letter 77, FK to NK, 29 August 1905, below; FK, New York, to NK, 27 September 1904, FKP, NN).
5. NK thought he could "probably get on the Dean's List," an achievement that would allow him to leave Cambridge occasionally. "If so, I will go down to New York and get loaded up on practical reform economics and then be able to go up and slay the honor exams" (NK to FK, 15 August 1904).
6. AK had told FK that he might relocate his insurance business (AK, Philadelphia, Pa., to FK, 6 August 1904, KFP, NCC-RB).
7. In his letter of 15 August, NK itemized funds spent on JK's clothes and travel expenses; they totaled $49.13.
8. After the strike of the United Mine Workers against Rockefeller's Colorado Fuel and Iron Company was put down, William D. Haywood (1869–1928), secretary-treasurer of the Western Federation of Miners, and Charles H. Moyer, president of the Federation, were charged with murder and inciting the riot that took place in Victor, Colorado, on 6 June.
9. James H. Peabody (1852–1917), governor of Colorado, was reelected in November. He said that labor unions had not opposed him. Rather, "a set of reckless men, both in and outside of the Republican Party" had tried to defeat him. He also noted that threats of violence and "the stirring up of strikes" had not come chiefly from the labor camp (*NYT:* 2 July 1904, 1, and 16 November 1904, 1).

74. To Jane Addams

Balmy Beach, Toronto,
August 19th, 1904

Beloved Lady,

Behold an idea which I desire to plant in the fertile soil of your mind;—and incidentally to get into clear form in the process of stating it to a friendly critic. As you know, the children cannot now leave school in New York until they are both fourteen years of age and also through with the work of class 5b, which a child should be who enters school at the age of six and misses no promotion until the age of twelve. As such children form the trivial minority, so far as I have been able to learn, this seems to be the reasonable requirement for the rank and file.

Now the enforcement of this required amount of school work brings to light the fact that an inordinate number of children do not even accomplish this by the time that they reach fourteen;—they do not make anything like the regular promotions allotted to normal children. It has occurred to me that if it were possible to have a little committee take up half a dozen schools,; say those of the nineteenth ward and make a special effort on behalf of the Children Who Fail Of Promotion, some things might be brought to light which might make it easier to get a required amount of acquisition before children can leave school in Illinois. It would be beginning at the opposite end from the New York method.

It has only recently dawned upon my dull mind that this sort of volunteer effort would afford one more reasonable reply to the ladies who ask What can we do? and then do not wish to give money for scholarships for children they do not know. I fancy it would transpire that some difficulties are inherent in the school itself—half-time sessions overcrowded classes, incompetent teachers; some in the child itself,—poor eyes, ears, adenoids, insufficient food, inappropriate clothing, cigarette-smoking, idling in the street part of the time but not enough to amount to punishable truancy; and some in the family;—quarantine of self or brothers and sisters, being kept at home to mind the baby, work as newsboys or beggars.

If it were shown that a large number of children never get beyond the third or even the second grade, for perfectly preventible causes, this would be good work, and it should pave the way for removal of those causes and for legislation in the general direction of the New York law

It has cheered me greatly to perceive even at this late day, what I should have perceived years ago, that this is one of those cases in which under the guise of co-operating with the schools and the parents, both could really be brought up pretty well by the scruff of their necks, to say nothing of the light that would be shed upon the work of B'rer Bodine and all his ilk.[1]

Such work would envolve a high-grade quality of friendly visiting, improved to the nth power. I mean where children are victims of the things enumerated above, and have failed to make a promotion, it would take work worthy of the best quality of probation officer to hold them up to the scratch and see that they not only did not fall out of school but never missed another promotion to the fourteenth birthday. But just as the probation officers began with Dr. Moore, and Mrs. Stevens, why shouldn't this begin small and work out large?[2] Something of the same idea is embodied in the work of the School-Children's Aid, but only in embryo. I wish I could tackle the job myself! So persuaded am I of the enormous field of new knowledge and help for the children that it opens up. Why, a lot of children that now get as far as the juvenile court need never even get headed towards it if they were caught immediately after their failure to be promoted, and checked, or boosted, according to the needs of the individual case. Fancy the job of getting the children in the Dante school all regularly through from the first to the second and the second to the third grade.

It has come to light in New York that a lot of boys cannot go to work at the age of fourteen, because they were troublesome when they were little fellows and were suspended or expelled and allowed to be about the streets. Now a principal is subject to strenuous discipline who suspends or expels a boy without appearing in court and preferring charges upon which he can be committed. And I fancy that the class work of a lot of conscienceless teachers would improve vastly, if they knew that every child who failed of promotion would become the object of friendly scrutiny and help on the part of persons outside the school hierarchy. I cannot imagine why I have not been pegging away at this as one important aspect of the child-labor problem. But my mind is so sadly slow! I wonder that with such a slow moving intellect, I have ever learned to speak the English language!

Of course, in the long run, when the idea took hold as the juvenile court idea has taken hold, it would involve a lot of people working at it. But I suspect that, meanwhile, the automatic improvement in reduced classes, improved teachers, improved enforcement of parental responsibility, establishment of more wards for contagious diseases, would reduce the present need of volunteer work far below the present extent.

Will you think about this, and let me know what it suggests to your fertile intellect?[3]

John is with the Goldmark's in the Adirondacks; Margaret started to-day for the Simkhovitch's at North Perry, Maine; and I am stranded here keeping my head cool until New York cools off enough for ~~in~~ me to venture thither. I came to speak to the General Biennial Conference of Friends, who have just adjourned. I have not felt so buoyantly well in years as I am this summer. I hope the same is true of you after your outing. Did you get my epistle about Stanley [Linn] and Dr. Sargent?

Your loving
F.K.

TLS, FKP, NN

1. William L. Bodine (b. 1862) was superintendent of compulsory education in Chicago (1899) and later president of the National League of Compulsory Education.
2. FK was referring either to Dr. Ernest C. Moore (1871–1955), a Hull House resident from 1896 to 1898, or his wife Dr. Dorothea Lummis Moore (ca. 1860–1942), who was also at Hull House in the 1890s (Bryan and Davis, *100 Years at Hull House,* 42, 49–53). Alzina Stevens was probation officer for Cook County from 1896 until her death in 1900.
3. No reply from JA has been recovered. She had been traveling in New England in July but returned to Chicago in August (FK, Cambridge, Mass., to NK, 17 July 1904, FKP, NN). JA had long been an advocate of education for children whose poverty limited their access to good schooling; see, e.g., JA, "The Subjective Necessity for Social Settlements," 18–19.

75. To Nicholas Kelley

Portland Oregon[1]
July 15th '05

Darling Son

Last night I made the speech of my life! It was at the Tempel Beth Israel, the most modern Jewish congregation in this country.[2] The audience was very large indeed, and very prosperous. There was to have been a symposium of rabbis on The Child. But only one arrived in time from the East. So I had thirty minutes to talk on the need of distributing immigration. The sight of all that prosperity, and the thought of the sufferings of our neighbors at home and the instinctive conviction that my listeners looked down upon them, all this had an inspiring influence, I assure you!

In some respects this is a belated old community! In arranging for speakers at the Exposition, they shut out women![3] And, although I was asked among the first by the local committee to preach to-morrow in one of the churches, it appears that the parsons are all refractory and won't have me. So I observe with malicious joy that most of the men they are counting upon are on a train which is 18 hours late and cannot keep the appointments!

This whole city is a rose garden. I cannot bear to think of Bert sweltering in New York when there is such a paradise in which he might be.

My fancy pictures you riding, playing tennis and pool (to your own great benefit) and gradually stimulating public opinion in the direction of floating that boat.[4]

The Conference begins to-day and, while the sessions last I shall be less free for writing.[5] But my greed for letters remains unabated.

Your loving old Mother
F.K.

ALS, FKP, NN

1. FK had attended the NAWSA conference in Portland, which took place 28 June–5 July 1905. She was named a first vice-president there. She told NK she had been "sitting for a week in sight of noble old Susan B. Anthony who worked with your grandfather in the anti-slavery cause fifty years ago" (FK, Portland, Ore., to NK, 11 July 1905, FKP, NN). In accepting her

appointment as vice-president at large of NAWSA, FK said, "I was born into this cause. My great-aunt, Sarah Pugh of Philadelphia, attended the meeting in London which led to the first suffrage convention in 1848. My father, William D. Kelley, spoke at the early Washington Conventions for years" (Harper, *History of Woman Suffrage*, 5:145).

2. This was the first time a woman had been invited to address this symposium of rabbis. FK's speech was entitled "The Child and Problems of Child Life." She also spoke at the First Unitarian Church on 14 July, where she endorsed plans to form a Portland consumers' league (*Oregon Journal*, 15 July 1905, 5; FK, Portland, Ore., to NK, 14 July 1905, FKP, NN).

3. The Lewis and Clark Exposition opened on 1 June (*Oregon Journal*, 23 July 1905, 1).

4. NK was spending the summer in South Orleans, Massachusetts, at the home of S. W. Winslow, where he was tutoring one of the young Winslow sons (NK, South Orleans, Mass., to FK, 16 July 1905, FKP, NN).

5. At the National Conference of Charities and Corrections, FK presided over a debate on 19 July on immigration that encouraged immigrant laborers to move from the East to the West Coast (*Oregon Journal*, 20 July 1905, 8).

76. To Margaret Kelley

HULL-HOUSE
335 SOUTH HALSTED STREET
CHICAGO

August 27th [1905]
Sunday after'n

Daughter Dear,

It is delightful to hear all the pleasant things that people are saying, about you, here among our loving friends.

Stanley [Linn] is just back from Wyoming, looking hale and hearty. Miss [Ella] Waite is well enough to have tea in her parlor where Grandma G, [Mme?] V. and I were of the party. Otherwise all the world is away.

I have to reach Boston on Sept. 1st, because my ticket expires on that date. Sept. 3d I'm to spend in Pittsfield with John. So any Boston glimpse of me will have to be snatched on the night of Sept 1st or the day of Sept. 2nd in the morning, as I take the 3 p.m. train on Sat. to spend Sunday with John whom I have not seen since May!

Write or telegraph me in care of Miss Beale 9 Pinckney St. and I'll meet your train, if you come on Sept. 2nd. a.m. I have no idea where my train will arrive on Sept. 1st. as you well know![1]

Mr. Charles Youmans [Yeomans] has just been here to say howdy.

Your loving Mother
F.K.[2]

ALS, KFP, NCC-RB

Margaret Kelley, ca. 1905. Courtesy of the Florence Kelley Papers, Rare Books and Manuscripts Division, New York Public Library, Astor, Lenox and Tilden Foundations.

1. Jessie F. Beale was corresponding secretary of the CL of Massachusetts from 1901 to 1908 (Box 1, CLM Records, MCR-S).

2. This letter is one of only four from FK to MK that have been recovered. The hundreds of letters MK wrote her mother, which frequently ended with "Please write soon," indicate an ongoing, frequent correspondence (FKP, NN).

77. To Nicholas Kelley

HULL-HOUSE
335 SOUTH HALSTED STREET
CHICAGO

Aug. 29th '05

Darling Son,

It has been a delight to receive your two letters here. My summer has been so beautiful and so fortunate that I feel as though I were closing a most delightful illustrated story. I expect to reach Boston on Friday and meet John, to see Dr. Kilburn if the latter be in Boston, and to get him (J.) some clothes in any case.

Dr. Withington's letter affords food for careful consideration.[1] It is for the sake of John's own character that I am afraid to give him still two more years of school. I fear the letting-down process in his own mind and fibre. On the other hand, I must not <u>drive</u> him into invalidism. I'm convinced that it was the fool running that really undid him, but he will never admit that. I may take him down for an interview with Knopf.[2] The mischief is that anything which lowers his vitality makes him readier for the onslaught of the bacillus.

Margaret seems to have left golden opinions here. People really love her.[3]

I think I can manage to haunt your vicinity somewhat. I trust Mr. Volkmann may raise his embargo and crown your efforts with his approval. What your kid may do under the excitement of examination is an entirely different question, of course.[4] At least, you have the soul's own reward of conscious faithfulness.

I'm haunted by two articles which I mean to write on my Sundays this year. One in relation to Congestion of Population: When does it begin? What are its chief causes? What is done to work against it consecutively and effectively?

At what stage is it an evil? i.e. Is there a normal density of population? If so what are its characteristics? How can it be arrived at?

The second will deal with infant mortality which should be called child murder or infanticide. The three sets of destroyers are 1st the milkmen, 2nd the landlords, 3rd the parents transmitting tuberculosis tendencies, syphilis etc. or feeding the children ignorantly and so killing them.

Science showed the enemy 25 years ago in the case of the milk to be the bacilli wh. can be destroyed by pasteurizing[.] Dr. Goler of Rochester applied administrative science six years ago in Rochester, and abolished the milkman, placing a hospital nurse in charge of a municipal ~~milkman~~ farm who sends sterile milk to 5 municipal nurses at milk stations in town, where the mothers get both milk and instruction.[5] He reduced the number of deaths of infants under one year sixty-five percent.

As to the landlords there is no such cheerful story.

The parents do very ill; but they have had to bear more than their share of blame hitherto. And theirs is all the sorrow and loss, while the milkmen and landlords have fattened on the profits.

These two subjects I mean to work out with as much science and "human interest" as possible and then try them on the North American. I think it might be difficult to make them sufficiently literary for the Atlantic. It is significant that the only gain thus far is made by the municipal milk supply!

Your loving old mother,
F.K.

ALS, FKP, NN

1. FK may have been referring to an undated letter from Alfreda Withington, who wrote that she was "dreadfully troubled" about JK's job and his health (Alfreda Withington, Pittsfield, Mass., to FK, [August? 1905], KFP, NCC-RB).
2. Probably Dr. S. Adolphus Knopf (1857–1940) of New York City, an authority on tuberculosis.
3. MK had earlier written her mother from Hull House, where she spent the summer, "I dote on being here and grudge every day that passes" (MK, Chicago, to FK, [July? 1905], FKP, NN).

4. NK apparently hoped that his "kid" (see Letter 75, FK to NK, 15 July 1905, above) could get admitted to the Volkmann School in Brookline.
5. Physician George W. Goler (1864–1940) was health officer in Rochester, New York, from 1896 to 1932 and a member of the NCL advisory board in 1906. He was instrumental in promoting pasteurized milk.

78. To Margaret Kelley

105 E. 22nd St.,
New York City
Sept. 20th [1905]

Daughter Dear,

It occurs to me that a brief word of greeting and affection may not come amiss in the new place.[1]

I do not believe that, among all the hundreds of your classmates, there is one who has more fairly earned the confidence of her family that she will make the most of the new opportunities; or one in whose behalf the sacrifice is more worth while which is, of course, involved when a family of small means educate all its young members.

It runs in our blood to be leaders. You will find yourself one without setting out to be one. And your jests will count. A keen wit is a terrible weapon. So don't jest with your contemporaries about serious things as you could safely do with my contemporaries.

The future of this Republic depends largely on the college student of to-day; and my children owe it to their grandfather, and to me, and to themselves, to line up on the right side now.[2]

Your loving old mother
F.K.

ALS, FKP, NN

1. In early September 1905, MK wrote about meeting FK in New York City to purchase her "college outfit" before enrolling at Smith College (MK, North Perry, Me., to FK, [ca. 5 September 1905], FKP, NN). FK wrote NK on 8 September about MK's visit to her in New York: "She is brown and rosy and so jolly that I much begrudge leaving her." MK left from New York for Smith College with an upperclass student on 20 September 1905, "thoroughly well equipped with raiment" (FK, New York, to NK, 8 September 1905 and 18 September 1905, both in FKP, NN.)
2. MK wrote on "Saturday morning" that she was one of 480 "helpless, hapless Freshmen and we are all worn out with tramping about looking up buildings, assignments, advisers and courses." She was hoping for a "few minutes peace and quite to myself . . . but I guess it is vain—There does not seem to be such a thing as peace and quiet in Northampton" (MK, Northampton, Mass., to FK, [26 September 1905?], FKP, NN).

79. To Nicholas Kelley

Oct. 4th 1905
12 Otis Place [Boston][1]

Darling Son,

I have been thinking since you left that, if it had been you instead of Margaret, the old College, and the Union, and the bandar log would all have had to stagger along without you![2] Now your first duty is to me that it shall not be you too! So please undertake the following duties, for my sake:—

1. Refuse appointments to places of responsibility;
2. Break or cancel engagements;
3. Leave~~ng~~ hulking aspirants to get their own jobs;
4 All for the purpose of being in bed nine hours every night. I do not mean merely 63 hours in the week, but nine hours every night.

If you should have any farther shock, you have no more reserve nervous energy than John, wherewith to meet it.

And my sorrowing old heart would sheer break if that blow befel me.

I'm writing at the desk here, in the upstairs library, near the telephone. I tried the Crimson, but was too early, I suppose.[3]

I have my engagement book, now, and find that I have a meeting tomorrow. So I shall spend the night with Hal and Elizabeth and go on Friday to Pittsfield to spend three days with John.[4]

It was a sad error of judgement not to carry You off for two days in the hills! I shall not forgive myself until you are rested and from cold.

Your loving old mother
Florence Kelley

ALS, FKP, NN

1. 12 Otis Place was the home of Elizabeth Glendower Evans. On 28 September 1905, Margaret Kelley died suddenly of a heart attack while awaiting a physical examination at the Smith College gymnasium. FK went immediately to Northampton and then spent several days in "a lovely quiet place" with Lillian Wald in Chesterfield, Massachusetts ("Smith College Girl's Death," 29 September 1905, unidentified clipping, FKP, NN; FK to NK, 1 October 1905, FKP, NN). FK attended a meeting of the CL of Massachusetts on 4 October and then was mostly inactive until 6 November, when she attended an executive committee meeting of the NYCLC (NCL, Seventh Annual Report [1906], 73, Box A5, NCL Records, DLC). For over a month after MK's death, condolence letters poured in from FK's Hull House and New York City friends and colleagues as well as from consumers' league members from all parts of the United States. JA telegraphed "Shall I come We are all grief stricken" (JA, Chicago, to FK, 29 September, FKP, NN). For FK's reaction to Margaret's death, see Goldmark, *Impatient Crusader,* 69–71.

2. NK was working at Prospect Union, an establishment that provided working men in the Cambridge area with vocational and liberal arts education through evening classes. He wrote his mother that he hoped she had been "resting and gaining strength" (*Harvard Crimson,* 5

October 1909; NK, Cambridge, Mass., to FK, 2 October 1905, FKP, NN). Although *Merriam-Webster Unabridged* defines "bandar-log" as "a vacuous, chattering person," FK probably referred to all of NK's various acquaintances.

3. Since 1904, NK had been on the editorial staff of the *Harvard Crimson,* the student newspaper.

4. Henry D. Lloyd II and Elizabeth Mason Lloyd had each invited FK to stay with them after Margaret's death (Henry D. Lloyd, Boston, 29 September, 1905; Elizabeth [Lloyd], Boston, 29 September 1905, both in FKP, NN).

80. To Nicholas Kelley

[Bennington, Vermont][1]
Sunday aft. Oct. 29 [1905]

Darling Son,

Richard is himself again![2] (at least more nearly than for a month past). For I have written to Mr. Sherman what I consider a convincing plea against his proposal to permit women to work at night.[3] I have worked at it an hour yesterday and two hours to-day without experiencing fatigue. That is a marked gain. Of course, I cannot tell how far his individualistic legal mind is open to conviction. I may yet have to defeat him before the legislature. But in that case, this work will not have been wasted, for the same arguments will go farther there than with him.

I'm pining for tomorrow to bring me your letter telling me your weight yesterday![4]

I liked particularly the editorial on football without insignia.[5] Keep at it!

Your loving old Ma
F.K.

ALS, FKP, NN

1. FK stayed at the home of her friend Mary R. Sanford from 23 October until approximately 1 November 1905.

2. This line from Shakespeare's *Richard III* (v.iii.28) was not in the original play but was added to Colley Cibber's (ca. 1700) popular adaptation, which was the most frequently produced Shakespearean play in nineteenth-century America (Levine, *Highbrow/Lowbrow,* 14, 43). The line occurs near the end of the play when the villainous Richard recovers from bad dreams and goes forth to battle.

3. P. Tecumseh Sherman (1867–1941) was New York State commissioner of labor from 1905 to 1907. In March 1906, FK reported that Sherman had fined two manufacturers for allowing women to work after 9 P.M. (NCL, Seventh Annual Report [1906], 21, Box A5, NCL Records, DLC).

4. NK wrote that good eating and sleeping habits were making him "one of the finest specimens of manhood that you ever saw" (NK, Cambridge, Mass., to FK, 25 October 1906, FKP, NN).

5. NK's untitled editorial in the *Harvard Crimson* encouraged Harvard students to take advantage of informal football without the "crowds, newspaper notoriety, insignia" of intercollegiate football (25 October 1905, 2).

W. E. B. Du Bois, 1920s.
Courtesy of the Library of
Congress, LC-USZ63-36176.

81. To Nicholas Kelley

1803 N. Charles St.
Baltimore Md
until Feb. 14th
[7 February 1906]

Darling Son

When you and I are cross and don't care whether school keeps, it means that we must stop the trolley and give the dynamo a chance to be re-charged. For this there is nothing like reading novels and going to bed early. People are no help, because we spend our stored energies on people.

I am gaining steadily, while working every day, because I'm in bed not less than 11 hours, and read pleasant things.

To-day begins the Suffrage convention. I've enlisted for the war! I speak on Thursday, Sat. and Monday.[1]

I'm more and more convinced that it is the worst possible economy of forces to leave the teachers and the mothers out of politics. It is not the way to have the next generation grow into strong, good, wise men and women.

I trust that you've seen a physician and begun to drink Koumyss.[2]

Your loving Mother
F.K.

ALS, FKP, NN

1. The NAWSA meetings took place from 7 to 13 February 1906. FK told NK that "the oration to Miss Susan B. Anthony last night, was the most impressive thing I have ever seen" (FK, Baltimore, Md., to NK, 9 February 1906, FKP, NN).
2. Koumiss is a distilled liquor originally made on the Russian steppes; in the United States, it was produced with cows' milk combined with yeast. NK assured his mother that his attack of grippe (influenza) was easing and he was "regular old Betty in looking after myself" (NK, Cambridge, Mass., to FK, 9 February 1906, FKP, NN).

82. To Nicholas Kelley

NATIONAL CONSUMERS' LEAGUE
OFFICE: 105 E. 22D ST.
NEW YORK CITY

[Cleveland]
Feb. 18th 1906

Darling Son,

Behold your parent staying with Senator Howe of Ohio, in a most agreeable house, over Sunday and about to be sent for (automobilewise) by Mayor Johnson to spend the late afternoon.[1] (This is in Cleveland).

In Baltimore, Miss Mary Garrett has become converted to equal suffrage for men and women and will give us a thousand dollars a month for that work.[2] This is an immediate result of the convention there. Mary Kenney O'Sullivan and I had one "industrial session" and Gertrude Barnum and I had another.[3]

Next month, I'm to go to Washington again, and some very old friends will have a parlor meeting about child labor, in a fashionable avenue, with members of Congress and senators among the guests. It will be a new sort of experience and very nice.

The hearing before the Judiciary Committee of the House of Representatives was quite fine. The gentlemen present treated me with distinguished courtesy by reason of Father.[4]

Evidently the whole movement suffers from belatedness. The women of my generation have shirked their duty and left it in the hands of the older pioneers where faces are turned to the past. Now, we are getting towards fifty and are just coming to the front when the next generation should be taking hold! However, Oregon will doubtless give the ballot to the women of that state this year; and the Charter Convention of Chicago will give women the ballot "on the same terms as men."[5] It is now sitting. So the world is moving forward a little all the time.

Your letters give me very great pleasure. I'm enchanted with the description of the secretaries' dinner.[6] That will be an ever recurring pleasure.

Charles Ames was in Baltimore for an hour and during that brief time I promised to stay with them during the week of meetings in May, in St. Paul, and, also, to visit them in Gloucester in June before, or after, Class Day.[7]

So prepare for the worst!

Your loving old Mother,
F. Kelley

ALS, FKP, NN

1. FK met with the CL of Cleveland on 17 February 1906 (NCL, Seventh Annual Report [1906], 74, Box A5, NCL Records, DLC). Frederic C. Howe (1867–1940), Ohio state senator (1906–1908), was later a progressive reformer in New York City. Tom Johnson (1854–1911), Democratic mayor (1901–1909), made Cleveland a center of Progressive reform.

2. Mary Garrett (1854–1915) was a philanthropist in women's higher education and co-founder of the Bryn Mawr School for Girls in 1885.

3. Mary Kenney O'Sullivan (1864–1943), a Hull House resident in the 1890s and a deputy factory inspector under FK, helped found the NWTUL in 1903. Gertrude Barnum (1866–1948), also a former Hull House resident, was active in the NWTUL and brought strikers' issues to national attention. At the NAWSA convention on 8 February 1906, FK, as chair of the Committee on Industrial Problems Affecting Women and Children, reported that the number of working children in New York City was so large that "no city administration in the last ten years has dared to make a school census." Despite pressure from many reform organizations in the city, Tammany Hall officials did not want to count the number of school-age children because it would "reveal the extent to which they are failing to provide for them." Citing statistics on the numbers of illiterate working American children, she urged her audience to "do something at once" about requiring schooling for them (Harper, *History of Woman Suffrage,* 5:164–165).

4. As first vice-president of NAWSA, FK headed the delegation to the Judiciary Committee hearing on 14 February and spoke of WDK's continuous but fruitless efforts for woman suffrage. She lamented the slow progress toward suffrage and asked the committee to "take a short cut . . . and ask for a Federal Amendment" (Harper, *History of Woman Suffrage,* 5:188, 190–191).

5. In June, Oregon voters rejected the women's suffrage amendment, a decision that was not reversed until 1912 (*NYT,* 6 June 1906, 1). Municipal suffrage in Chicago also proved more difficult to achieve than FK had predicted. Although by 1898 twenty-six states had enacted school suffrage for women and four states had granted them full political equality, only one had passed municipal suffrage (Anthony and Harper, *History of Woman Suffrage,* 4:314). The Chicago campaign, which was launched in 1905, crested in 1907, when eighty-seven organizations with an aggregate membership of 10,000 women petitioned for the right to vote in city elections. At the 1907 annual meeting of NAWSA in Chicago, FK spoke passionately about the municipal suffrage campaign: "It should be our immediate demand that in all matters of the life of a city we shall have a word. The greatest numbers of working people are in the cities." She added that if municipal boards could be prodded by the "lively interest of women," many working women could have "more adequate care for life and health" and their children would have more education (Harper, *History of Woman Suffrage,* 5:193, 197).

6. NK had described speaking at the annual dinner of the Association of Harvard Class Secretaries (NK, Cambridge, Mass., to FK, 10 February 1906, KFP, NNC-RB).

7. FK attended the GFWC meeting from 30 May to June 6 (NCL, Eighth Annual Report [1907], 35, Box A6, NCL Records, DLC).

83. To Nicholas Kelley

[New York City]
Thursday morning [28 March 1906][1]

Darling Son,

How I longed for you last night, at Clinton Hall![2] It was a sight to cheer the heart of any sinner! Every seat was filled. There were up-town suffragists well dressed and smug, and downtown Russian Jewish socialists, girls from the trade unions and men from the party. The speakers were Mr. [Samuel] Gompers, Mr. Edlin, a Socialist Yiddish orator, Graham Stokes and your loving Ma. But the speech of the evening was made by a little necktie maker Rose Schneiderman.[3]

Resolutions were adopted by a rousing vote urging the judiciary committee at Albany to submit to a vote of the people a proposal to strike the word "male" from the state constitution. The hearing will occur to-day.[4] Miss Wald and the Nathans were on the platform and Graham Stokes and his very beautiful Yiddish wife.[5] It was wonderful!

It would not surprise me if I should find myself voting for John for President! I'm terribly afraid that you are not eligible!

Your loving Mother
F.K.

ALS, FKP, NN

1. FK apparently misremembered the day of the week and wrote the letter on Wednesday; the suffrage meeting took place on Tuesday, 27 March 1906.
2. In mid-Manhattan, Clinton Hall was a good meeting place for audiences that included both uptown and downtown participants.
3. James Graham Stokes (1872–1960), industrialist, socialist, and settlement house worker, stated that sweatshop conditions would be abolished if women had the vote (*NYT,* 28 March 1906, 2). Rose Schneiderman (1882–1972) emigrated with her family from Poland to New York City in 1890. She became active in the NWTUL in 1905 and in NAWSA around 1918.
4. Every year from 1906 until 1913, suffragists submitted a proposal to the New York legislature for an equal suffrage amendment to that state's constitution. Finally, in 1913, the legislature agreed to consider it (Harper, *History of Woman Suffrage,* 6:456–460).
5. Frederick Nathan (ca. 1842–1918), the stockbroker husband of Maud Nathan, strongly supported her suffrage work (Lagemann, *A Generation of Women,* 41, 54). Rose Pastor Stokes (1879–1933), socialist writer, emigrated from Russian Poland to the United States in 1890 and married James Graham Stokes in 1905. She wrote the resolution to the state judiciary committee (*NYT,* 28 March 1906, 2).

84. To Nicholas Kelley

163 South St. Pittsfield Mass.
July 11th [1906]

Darling Son,

It was the very best day of my life, that day twenty one years ago tomorrow, which brought you to us. For nothing but good has followed it. The only anxiety you ever caused me was thro' no fault of your own,—when you seemed to be getting smallpox at Miss Whitelaw's; and when you were ill with eyestrain in your Freshman year.

As for the good, it is more than can be said or written. If sons and daughters could only know their power of giving pleasure—and pain—how differently most of them would act!

The little token of affection and recognition which is all that I have for this wonderful day, I have asked Mr. [William] Nicholson to treat as yours, holding it subject to your order. I shall be glad if you can manage to keep it either for use in case of illness, or as part of some little investment.

Naturally, my mind turns towards your future, and I find myself wondering what changes you will form a part of. I have been making a little list of some of the more obvious ones which have come about during your brief span of life. It includes the partial freeing of Russia, the enfranchisement of women in four of our States, & Australia, New Zealand and Finland; the formation of the Australian Federation; and the rising of the tide of Socialism thro out the civilized world.[1]

When you were born, the emergence of the Orient seemed incalculably remote. It will fulfil itself during the span of life of your generation.

The modern transformation of agriculture by means of science and cooperation was a mere promise when you were born. To-day it is one of the most important factors in international evolution.

Life itself,—the human organism—registers some of the greatest gains. My childhood and youth were darkened by the horror of diphtheria. That is gone, forever, from human experience. And Dr. [George W.] Goler has shown how the lives of half the children now sacrificed can be saved by a single administrative measure.[2] Finally, if you reach the years of your grandfather, old age will have lost it terrors and cancer, one of its blackest shadows, will be under control.

As to your own share in these works of your day, I feel sure that it must be a noble one, fulfilling the promise of your childhood and youth.

I cannot help regretting the perplexities and insults which you have suffered during this year. But I do not believe that you are seriously hurt by them![3]

Whatever may befall, nothing can rob me of my pride and joy in the chapter of your life which closes to-day, or my proud and confident hope for the new chapter which opens tomorrow.

May every blessing be yours!

Your loving old mother
Florence Kelley

ALS, FKP, NN

1. The Russian Revolution of 1905 granted basic civil rights, including an expansion of voting rights. Wyoming (1890), Colorado (1893), Idaho (1896), and Utah (1896) allowed women to vote; Australia (1902), New Zealand (1893), and Finland (1906) granted the same privilege. The Australian Federation was established in 1901.
2. For George Goler's success in providing pasteurized milk to mothers and infants in Rochester, see Letter 77, FK to NK, 29 August 1905, above.
3. Referring to the end of his brief engagement with Dorothy Randolph earlier that year, NK wrote that "all my troubles have fallen from me. . . . It may be a shameful thing to feel, but I cannot help viewing Mrs. R. somewhat with feelings of gratitude. I do not think that if the D. R. thing had been right I should have had so unhappy and troubled a time with my own inner workings as I labored with throughout the past winter" (NK, Little Compton, R.I., to FK, 19 July 1906, KFP, NNC-RB; see also FK, New York, to NK, 17 January 1906 and 27 January 1906, FKP, NN).

85. To Lillian D. Wald

NATIONAL CONSUMERS' LEAGUE
OFFICE: 105 E. 22D ST.
NEW YORK CITY

11 Reed St., Pittsfield, Mass.
Aug. 15th 1906

Dear Sister Wald,

I'm not lost, altogether, just wandering a bit far from the fold.[1] Ko had to enter on his job in Cambridge yesterday, running Prospect Union. So I went to Sakonnet with him for a week, returning on Monday to Pittsfield when he went to Cambridge.

John is pegging daily at his Greek with mixed faithfulness and loathing. If he passes it, he can make Harvard this year. He is an enchanting companion, and if only modern society did not require a man to know anything, his future would be secure.

I've been pegging at reviews of Man, the Social Creator,[2] and at the beginning of a book with the inspiring title of Death, and its Social Causes.[3] I think Sister [Lavinia] Dock will like it. But I'm not sure of any other admirer. The men of death seem to be the landlords, milkmen, mothers and Employers. So far as I can see, only about 5 to the 1000 should die each year, instead of 18–22/1000 in New York city. The rest appears to be murder. Of course, cancer, eclampsia senility, heart disorders not due to infection, and some other rare causes of death would account for the 5/1000.

I'm frantic to know about Delancey Street![4]

Your loving old
F.K.

ALS, Wald Papers, NCC-RB

1. FK had come to Pittsfield for the month of August to monitor JK's studies and behavior (FK, Pittsfield, Mass., to NK, 1 August 1906, FKP, NN).
2. FK's review of Henry D. Lloyd's *Man: The Social Creator* (New York: Doubleday, Page and Company, 1906) appeared in *Charities and the Commons* 17 (1 December 1906): 466–467.
3. Although FK did not write a book or article titled "Death and Its Social Causes," her writings often mentioned disease and mortality. See, for example, *Some Ethical Gains through Legislation,* 213.
4. FK and Wald were campaigning against the Brooklyn Rapid Transit Company's attempt to construct an elevated train on Delancey Street. She later wrote NK that she thought the street had been saved (FK, Boston, to NK, ca. 10 March 1907, FKP, NN).

86. To Nicholas Kelley

NEW YORK,
254 HENRY STREET

Aug. 31st [1906]

Darling Son,

On my return from Phila., I find your dear letter. I never meant to have you go. For Grandma it was relief from suffering, that and that only.[1] I received my telegram on Monday about two in the afternoon. I arrived in New York at 8 p.m. and wired Billy [Kelley] at Chatta., Bert [Kelley]at Phila. and Polly [Marianne Kelley] at Pecon at White Plains. They were already in communication with Bert in Phila. This I learned by telephone. Billy proved to be at Atlantic City. He joined Bert on Tuesday and they went together to White Plains and took the casket to Phila. that night. On Wednesday the interment took place, at Ivy Hill, at twelve o'clock. They day was sombre, and we were sad beyond the power of words to express. It had been so long a life so full of pain and sorrow, so poor in joy and satisfaction. And Billy and I had much to regret. We had caused her grief and anxiety for many years, both of us.

That afternoon, Wednesday, I went with Billy to Long port where I spent yesterday coming to New York this morning.

I see now, when it is too late, that I have given you hours of needless waiting and expectation. But I hoped you might not even think of coming, since I had not asked you to come,—and you know from long experience that I send for you when in need.

Tomorrow, Sat. I go with Miss Wald to the Adirondacks for a week, returning Sept. 8th. It is the conference at the Martin's.[2]

I trust you may have been dilatory about depositing the little check. It turns out that, thro an error of Mary Sherman or of Josephine [Goldmark], my salary check was no[t] deposited on time, and yours, which I drew against it, would have fared ill if received promptly in N.Y. If you should have trouble with it, write me at once to the care of John Martin; Hurricane, Essex Co., N.Y. and I shall be able to make good.[3]

With warmest thanks for your good offers

Your loving Mother
F.K.

ALS, FKP, NN

1. CBK died on 27 August 1906.
2. John W. Martin (1864–1956) helped found the *American Fabian* in 1895, which his wife, Prestonia Mann Martin (b. 1861), edited from 1898 until its demise in 1900 (Martin, *Fabian Freeway,* 139–140, 142). FK stayed for a week in the Adirondacks at what she called the "Socialist Camp," where Lillian Wald, Graham Stokes, and others spent mornings in discussion and afternoons sleeping or walking (FK, the Adirondacks, New York, to NK, 8 September 1906, FKP, NN).
3. NK replied that he had "heard no bad news from the check yet" (NK, Cambridge, Mass., to FK, 5 September 1906, FKP, NN).

87. To Edith M. Howes[1]

NATIONAL CONSUMERS' LEAGUE
OFFICE: 105 E. 22D STREET
NEW YORK CITY

Sept. 10, 1906

Dear Miss Howes,

Unhappily, I have to be in Omaha on Oct. 8th and in Toledo, Ohio, on Oct. 3d.

I can, however, come to Boston for Oct. 1st. ~~3d inclusive~~ and shall be charmed to do so provided your cohorts will be assembled in numbers sufficient to make this seem to you worth while.

After that, I shall not be available until after the quarterly meeting on the 3d Friday in October.[2]

I felt sure that you would have balm for the trade union wound in the O'Sullivan case, and have mentioned it to no one else.[3]

To me, personally, the loss of Jessie Beale out of the constant intercourse is very grave. I love her for herself and because my Margaret dearly loved her.[4]

The Sidney Webbs block the way in England. Miss Black merely echoes Mrs. [Beatrice] Webb's arguments.[5] Moreover the cooperative movement, the trade unions and the Women's trade union League together, do really cover the ground there in some measure, which we cover here. But there is great need exactly in retail trade.

Yours faithfully
F. Kelley
I seem to have recovered entirely and to be entirely well, heart included!

ALS, "Goldmark, Josephine: Source Material," Box D1, NCL Records, DLC

1. Edith Howes (1855–1942) had taught at the Boston Trade School for Girls and had been elected in 1896 as the first president of the CL of Massachusetts. In 1907, she was serving on the Executive Committee of the CL of Massachusetts (NCL, Eighth Annual Report [1907], 74, Box A6, NCL Records, DLC).
2. FK attended the Executive Committee meeting of the CL of Massachusetts on 2 November (NCL, Eighth Annual Report [1907], 23, Box A6, NCL Records, DLC).
3. The alliance between consumers' leagues and trade unionists was sometimes strained; Mary Kenny O'Sullivan was more radical than many affiliated with the AFL and NWTUL.
4. Apparently Jessie Beale had recently left her position as corresponding secretary of the CL of Massachusetts (NCL, Seventh Annual Report [1906], 103, Box A5, NCL Records, DLC). MK had occasionally stayed with Jessie Beale in Boston.
5. Beatrice and Sidney Webb, who were at the height of their influence as Fabian socialists in 1905, wrote *The Co-operative Movement in Great Britain* (1899), *The Case for the Factory Acts* (1901), *Industrial Democracy* (1902), *Problems of Modern Industry* (1902), and *The History of Trade Unionism* (1902). Yet they trusted top-down politics more than grassroots activism. Beatrice Webb opposed woman suffrage (until February 1906), and after the landslide election of the Liberal Party in 1906, the Webbs remained loyal to outgoing Tory prime minister Arthur Balfour (MacKenzie and MacKenzie, *The Diary of Beatrice Webb,* 3:xiii, 439). Clementina Black (1854–1922), a co-founder of the British Women's Trade Union League, had a chapter in a 1902 revised edition of *The Case for the Factory Acts.* She later wrote *Sweated Industry and the Minimum Wage* (1907).

88. To Lillian D. Wald

Omaha, Nebraska, Oct. 9th [1906]

Beloved Lady

T'is a sad thing to have had no good-byes, but in about a week after you get this, I'll be calling you up over the telephone from the office.

T'would amuse you to see how great a prophet is this humble sister when thus far from her own country! Automobiles, dinners, interviews to burn; and at noon to-day the Governor of Nebraska will come from Lincoln to Omaha to preside (with the mayor at his right hand) at a luncheon where child labor laws will be expounded by yours truly![1] The wave of interest is really very remarkable, everywhere!

I start homeward, tomorrow, from Kearney, via Hull House Thursday, Warren Ohio Friday and Saturday, then Syracuse and home by the evening of Oct. 17th i.e. sleeping that night on Staten Island.[2]

The legislature here meets on Jan. 3d and it is the firm intent of the Juvenile Court contingent to place Nebraska at the head of the list of the States in the matter of child labor legislation. Since there are neither mines nor textile industries in the States, this should be easy.[3]

Your loving
F.K.

ALS, Wald Papers, NCC-RB

1. FK spoke to the Omaha Women's Club on 8 October 1906; she congratulated Nebraskans for their child labor law but criticized them for exploiting young boys in the telegraph messenger industry. She urged the state to enact a law requiring children to remain in school for forty weeks, as was the case in New York (*Omaha World Herald,* 9 October 1906, 2). The Social Service Club held a luncheon on 9 October in FK's honor that was attended by other Nebraska officials, including Governor John H. Mickey (Republican, 1903–1907) and Omaha mayor James C. Dahlman (Democrat, 1906–1918) (FK, Omaha, Neb., to NK, 9 October 1906, FKP, NN).
2. In Kearney, FK spoke at a meeting of the Nebraska State Federation of Women's Clubs on 10 October. The delegates voted to draft a bill for the Nebraska legislature requiring that unemployed children attend a full school year, that no child be employed until he or she had finished the fifth grade, and that no child under fourteen be permitted to work more than forty-eight hours a week (*Omaha World Herald,* 12 October 1906, 1).
3. On 29 March 1907, the Nebraska legislature approved a bill that had been introduced in its House of Representatives on 3 January to prohibit work in factories and stores by children under fourteen. It called for employment certificates for children between fourteen and sixteen stating that they had regularly attended school prior to employment (*House Journal of the Legislature of the State of Nebraska,* 96, 1117, 1180; *Laws, Joint Resolutions, Appropriations and Memorials,* 258–263).

89. To W. E. B. Du Bois

105 E. 22nd St.
New York City
Oct. 30th [1906?]

My dear Mr. DuBois,

I am asking the Macmillan Co. to send you a copy of my book, as a very small acknowledgement of the profound pleasure which your book has afforded me.[1]

Yours very truly
Florence Kelley

ALS, Du Bois Papers, MU

1. Sending a copy of her book *Some Ethical Gains through Legislation,* FK was responding to Du Bois's *The Souls of Black Folk: Essays and Sketches* (Chicago: A. C. McClurg, 1903).

90. To Caroline Bartlett Crane[1]

NATIONAL CONSUMERS' LEAGUE
OFFICE: 105 E. 22D STREET
NEW YORK CITY

Jan. 21st '07

My dear Mrs. Crane,

It was settled at the meeting of the Executive Committee, yesterday, that the annual meeting will be held in Chicago on the first Tuesday in March.[2]

I have handed your letter to the Secretary of the Committee on Food, and have written Mrs. Van Der Vaart suggesting that the subject be given prominence at the evening meeting.[3] I feel as sure as one reasonably can before receiving formal notice, that this will be done.

Personally, I think no task of greater importance is before the League than insisting that food inspection shall be bona fide.[4]

May I make one suggestion? In the popular mind Dr. Wiley is the Department of Agriculture. If, therefore, you refer to Mr. Wilson, it will be necessary to make the distinction absolutely clear.[5] If you refer to both gentlemen, this also should be made perfectly clear. From your letter I cannot tell.

Yours very truly
Florence Kelley

I ought to point out that the allotment of time to the subject of food will rest with the local committee which will have charge of the program; and the share of its time to be given to meat will rest with the Food Committee. I have, however, no doubt that both will consider your paper the most important one of the meeting.

F.K.

ALS, Crane Collection, MiKW

1. Caroline Bartlett Crane (1858–1935), a former Unitarian minister and a representative of the CL of Michigan, was instrumental in bringing about local meat inspection laws in Michigan. She also organized the Kalamazoo Women's Civic Improvement League.

2. The annual meeting of the NCL was held at Hull House on 5 March 1907 (NCL, Eighth Annual Report [1907], 11, Box A6, NCL Records, DLC).

3. The Pure Food and Drug Act went into effect on 1 January 1907, creating the first federal regulation of food and drugs and making illegal the production and shipment of "misbranded or adulterated" food via interstate commerce. The NCL monitored enforcement of the new law and frequently passed resolutions on that topic (NCL Annual Council Minutes, 1909–1920, Box A6, NCL Records, DLC). Harriet Van der Vaart was secretary of the CL of Illinois (*NYT,* 1 January 1907, 2; Sicherman, *Alice Hamilton,* 152).

4. On 11 February, the NCL Executive Committee met to organize protest against a U.S.

Senate amendment designed to emasculate the Pure Food and Drug Act (*NYT,* 12 February 1907, 16).

5. Harvey W. Wiley (1844–1903), a respected crusader for pure food laws, headed the Bureau of Chemistry in the Department of Agriculture, which administered the Pure Food and Drug Act. Agricultural and industrial interests were lobbying Secretary of Agriculture James Wilson (1835–1920) to prevent strict enforcement of the act.

91. To Jane Addams

Augusta, Maine
Jan. 23d '07

Beloved Lady

I read the Newer Ideals of Peace, all day yesterday, on the train coming hither. It is noble and wise and parts of it are very beautiful.[1]

It comes just at the fortunate moment, when the Fabians are turning their backs on democracy, and the orthodox socialists are neglecting the essential truths to preach race and class hatred.[2]

I'm coming to Chi. for the N.A.W. Suffrage meeting.[3] Of course, I'm coming to H.-H. But I'm well and hearty once more and have no possible excuse for occupying your room. So please let me have what we used to call the sleeping car on the third floor, or anything else that comes handy.

I'm longing to discuss the Ideals with you!

Your loving old
F.K.

ALS, JA Papers, PSC-P

1. FK was in Augusta to meet with the State Federation of Women's Clubs (NCL, Eighth Annual Report [1907], 36, Box A6, NCL Records, DLC). In her review of *Newer Ideals of Peace* (New York: Macmillan, 1907), FK wrote that JA's "prevailing thought is our need of self-government in a wide range of human interests, civic, educational and industrial; in city, state and nation; and, through these agencies, in international relations as well." FK noted JA's conviction that attention to the welfare of residents of crowded cities demonstrated that society was moving from "'a period of industrialism into a period of humanitarianism'" (undated clipping, *Jane Addams Papers,* Addendum, Reel 11, fr. 201; see also Sklar, "'Some of Us Who Deal with the Social Fabric,'" 80–96).

2. For the varieties of contemporary socialism in the United States, Britain, Europe, and Australia, see Walling, *Socialism As It Is.*

3. NAWSA's annual convention was held in Chicago on 14–19 February 1907.

92. To Lillian D. Wald

NATIONAL CONSUMERS' LEAGUE
OFFICE: 105 E. 22D STREET
NEW YORK CITY

Feb. 3d '07

Beloved Lady

Monsignor Lavelle blessed the Consumers' League all up hill and down dale, at the annual meeting, last Thursday. So it would be somewhat stultifying if they objected to my holding office after that.[1]

I have asked Macmillan Co. to send you two copies of my book (charged to me) in case it should seem to you discreet to get them into the hands of Governor Hughes and Mr. Parsons.[2] You see, the book had not been published when last I was an office Seeker!

Your loving
F.K.

ALS, Wald Papers, NN

1. At the sixteenth annual meeting of the CL of New York City, Monsignor Michael J. Lavelle (1856–1939), vicar general of New York, stated that he "would do as much as possible for the furtherance of its [the League's] aims" (*NYT,* 1 February 1907, 5). FK hoped to replace retiring P. Tecumseh Sherman as New York state commissioner of labor; she believed that Catholics would not oppose her appointment (FK, New York, to NK, 3 February 1907, FKP, NN).

2. Charles Evans Hughes (1862–1948) was Republican governor of New York from 1907 to 1910, U.S. Supreme Court justice from 1910 to 1916, and U.S. secretary of state from 1921 to 1925. Herbert Parsons (1869–1925; Republican congressman, 1905–1911) had been one of Hughes's campaign managers and was a close advisor. Hughes subsequently appointed John Williams as state labor commissioner (Wesser, *Charles Evans Hughes,* 65, 106, 311; see also see Letter 56, FK to Lillian Wald, 24 January 1899, note 2, above).

93. To Nicholas Kelley

[Cincinnati, Ohio]
Feb. 20th '07

Darling Son,

Bert has just telephoned that he is well and thriving and will call for me after my meeting to go out to his Suburb and spend the night with Patty and himself at Hotel Altamont.[1] Polly is in Radnor for a fortnight.

I have been to Cleveland again for two more lectures. Last night, Mayor [Tom] Johnson called for me and after spending an hour in the discussion of the limits of local self government, fetched me to the train in his automobile. We had spent Sunday afternoon discussing the same subject and he had surrendered as to the Beveridge bill.[2] It is going to be a long, hard fight to pass that bill. But sooner, or later, we shall reach the point which England reached in 1842!

We shall force recognition of the truth that the need, the claim, the human right of the child in Georgia is the same as that of a child in Ohio or Oregon; and that the claim is directed to the whole Republic, not merely to Georgia. This is Senator Beveridge's title to immortal fame,—that he is the first man to force this upon the mind and conscience of the nation.

It is an interesting and curious fact that the cry of States Rights arises always in connection with doing wrong! Enslaving people, overworking children, disfranchising negroes and women! Why do we never [see] the right asserted in connection with any novel and noble improvement? It is always connected with old established evil!

Your loving mother
F. Kelley

ALS, FKP, NN

1. In September 1906, AK had moved to yet another position selling insurance in what FK called "a wild cat scheme . . . alarmingly near the borderline even of the highest finance." He had not found a permanent home in Cincinnati for his wife Marianne, known as "Polly," and daughter Martha (1906–1998), known as "Patsy" (FK, New York, to NK, 20 September 1906, FKP, NN; AK, Cincinnati, Ohio, to FK, 11 September 1907, KFP, NCC-RB). FK was in Cincinnati to attend its consumers' league's annual meeting (NCL, Eighth Annual Report [1907], 36, Box A6, NCL Records, DLC).

2. Senator Albert J. Beveridge (1862–1927; Republican, Indiana, 1899–1911) introduced his bill (S. 6562) "to prevent the employment of children in factories and mines" on 5 December 1906. Shortly thereafter, Beveridge introduced another bill to regulate child labor in the District of Columbia. Neither house took action on these bills in the 1906–1907 congressional session (59th Cong., 2nd sess., *Cong. Rec.*, 5 December 1906 and 29 January 1907, 50, 1867). At the NCL annual meeting, FK analyzed the pros and cons of the bills and stated that Senator Beveridge intended to introduce the bills again in the 60th Congress (NCL, Eighth Annual Report [1907], 30–33, Box A6, NCL Records, DLC). The bill subsequently became the basis of the Keating-Owen Act, which Congress passed on 1 September 1916.

94. To Alice Stone Blackwell[1]

Cincinnati, Ohio
Feb. 21st '07

Dear Miss Blackwell,

Do you know the composition of the League of Women's National Organizations?

If not, will you publish in the Woman's Journal an enquiry from "a constant reader"? On the subject?[2]

Mrs. Schoff appears either to have really formed such an organization, or to be masquerading under the name.[3]

I have two ideas anent her. Can we show to the public the shadowy nature of her organization by asking for a file of her annual reports?

a. of the National Congress of Mothers;
b. of the League of Women's National Organizations?

And, a little later, can we show how Congress has "oblived" all other measures in which women are interested, but has stood by the Utah voters, women included in keeping their representative in the Senate?[4]

Gathering information as to a. and b. need not seem hostile. After we have all we can get, we shall know better what to do.

Yours sincerely
Florence Kelley

ALS, "General Correspondence, Kelley, Florence," Box 18, NAWSA Records, DLC

1. Alice Stone Blackwell (1857–1950), daughter of Lucy Stone and Henry Blackwell, edited the *Woman's Journal* from 1881 to 1917. She was also recording secretary of NAWSA for almost twenty years.
2. No letter from "A Constant Reader" appeared in the *Woman's Journal,* 26 February–9 March 1907.
3. Hannah Kent Schoff (1853–1940), president of the NCM (forerunner of the PTA) from 1902 to 1920, lived in Philadelphia and edited the NCM's journal, *Child Welfare.* FK viewed the NCM as a competitor because it promoted more conservative versions of child labor legislation than the NCL. Founded in 1897 by Alice Birney, wife of a Washington, D.C., lawyer, the NCM maintained a more elite membership than the NCL. While the NCL recruited trade union as well as elite members, the NCM relied on "women of position" to form local branches (National Congress of Mothers and Parent-Teacher Associations, *Triennial Hand-Book 1908–1911,* 20).
4. Representative Joseph Howell (1857–1918; Republican, 1903–1917).

95. To Alice Stone Blackwell

[Boston]
Mar. 17th '07

Dear Miss Blackwell,

Alas! On Friday afternoon and Saturday I was booked for Wellesley. To-day I am gobbled by my boy and to-morrow, after speaking to the Methodist ministers, at Wesleyan Hall, in the morning, I'm off for Lakeside, Conn.

However, before the ministers, I mean to come to 3 Park Street for a little while, trusting to luck for finding you.[1]

I'm too pleased for words over your skill in turning the symposium on the church to account to avoid an onslaught on the pulpit and turn the guns on the saloon allies of the antis. I envy you such dexterity![2]

Yours sincerely,
Florence Kelley

[inserted in margin: Confidential]
[inserted beneath the signature:]I had a fine opportunity to discredit a little our Congressional adversary Hon. John Jenkins of Wisconsin. I spoke three times in Milwaukee, twice in Osh Kosh, once in Green Bay, and twice in Madison. And every audience was visibly moved against him. He shall never be Speaker or Senator if I can help it.[3]

F.K.

ALS, "General Correspondence, Kelley Florence," Box 18, NAWSA Records, DLC

1. Offices of the *Woman's Journal* in Boston.
2. FK probably was referring to a conversation with Blackwell at NAWSA's annual convention, which was held in Chicago in 1907. Blackwell published FK's speech to the convention, in which she criticized the power of the House Judiciary Committee to keep certain measures, such as child labor laws and woman suffrage, from reaching the floor for debate and possible action (*Woman's Journal,* 16 March 1907, 1).
3. John J. Jenkins (1843–1911; Republican congressman, Wisconsin, 1895–1908) had presided over the woman suffrage hearing that FK attended as part of a delegation to the House Judiciary Committee in 1906 (see Letter 82, FK to NK, 18 February 1906, above). In campaigning against Jenkins, who was hostile to woman suffrage, FK joined an insurgent Republican Progressive coalition. Jenkins was defeated for the nomination by a La Follette Progressive (Harper, *History of Woman Suffrage,* 5:111; Griffith, "Prelude to Insurgency").

96. To Nicholas Kelley

[Minneapolis, Minn.]
July 1, 1907

Darling Son

Your special delivery letter reached me just at the church door yesterday, in Fargo, N. Dakota, as I was going to preach in the Methodist church. It was a joy and an inspiration and I preached the better for it!

I spent two days in the home of Judge Amidon of the Federal Circuit Court. His wife was away and he felt responsible for my being amused, so we talked about 8 hours in 24 each day.[1] They were about the most interesting days I ever spent!

He says the best opening for a young man to-day is Chicago; to get into a law firm which is easy for one with a good Harvard Law School record, and then secure a position as assistant prosecuting attorney.[2] There are many assistants and the numbers increase all the time. From that position everything is open in the law and in politics.

This seems to me to be sound, but I submit it along with all the other suggestions I can gather.

The rest of our conversations was about the senile fear which dominates the present Supreme Court of the United States whose average age is 74 years! It is the most aged court in the history of the nation! Its bogeyman is Socialism. Its chief occupation is denying power to the central government. But by means of the Lochner case (the New York Bakers' case) it has set all the state courts to work denying the powers of the states. ~~courts.~~[3] So, in general, its tendency is towards the production and promotion of Anarchy.

Meanwhile, the Heywood case goes its weary way, the papers are trying the defendants, the unions regard the men as <u>per</u>secuted not <u>pro</u>secuted;—and the telegraphers are having their two representatives in Congress draft bills for nationalizing all telegraph companies, as a step in <u>their</u> fight against the corporations.[4]

It certainly is the most interesting period in the history of the world! I am more thankful every day for the privilege of being alive and of having you!

Do use the letters of introduction! I hope and believe that you will be one of the makers of the new era; and knowing the right people is the greatest possible help along that road.

Your loving mother
Florence Kelley

I am so well that it seems as though I might live to be a hundred! We have had only one hot day and then I was in a cool place.

ALS, FKP, NN

1. Charles F. Amidon (1856–1937; U.S. District Judge of North Dakota, 1896–1928) and Beulah McHenry Amidon (b. 1866).
2. Upon graduating from Harvard in 1906, NK entered Harvard Law School. He was due to sail for Europe on 30 June 1907 for the summer. The trip was funded from his "patrimony" (FK, n.p., to NK, 22 May 1907, 1 June 1907, FKP, NN).
3. In April 1905, in *Lochner v. New York,* the U.S. Supreme Court overturned an 1896 New York law (the Bakeshop Act) that had established a 60-hour work week for bakers. Relying on the Fourteenth Amendment and precedents established in the 1873 *Slaughter-House Cases* to limit the power of states to regulate working conditions, the Court explicitly championed the unregulated workplace (see Woloch, *Muller v. Oregon,* 18–20).
4. The trial of William (Big Bill) Haywood began on 9 May 1907. Haywood, with Charles Moyer, was accused of authorizing a bomb that killed Idaho governor Frank Steunenberg in 1905 after the governor called out federal troops to put down a miners' strike. Haywood was acquitted on 28 July; Clarence Darrow defended him (Carlson, *Roughneck,* 111–135). During a nationwide strike of telegraphers, Samuel Small, president of the Commercial Telegraphers' Union, declared the union's intention to "start a movement in favor of Government ownership" (*NYT,* 24 June 1907, 2).

97. To Nicholas Kelley

[<u>Naskeag,</u>] Brooklin, Maine
care Mrs. Judge
July 6th 07

Darling Son,

Please use this address all summer. I shall be here until August 28th when I go to Pittsburgh, Pa., for a month of investigating the work of women there. I am here with five 5 teachers, spinsters named Balch. Two teach at St. Agnes' School in Albany, where Diane Gardner's sisters were pupils, and one at Wellesley. They have bought an abandoned farm, but I board in a wonderfully nice place next the farm.[1] It is astonishing how many teachers and nurses own little farms and small places in this land, and how easy it is to get good, comfortable ones.

I felt like an unnatural monster to be waking up in Fargo, N. D. and know that you had sailed at daybreak with no goodbyes. On Tuesday I passed through Montreal and had the same queer feeling all that day, as we came across northern Vermont and Southern New Hampshire on the way to Portland. If you think of it, do mention whether I asked you for my typewriter, or only meant to do so. I've arranged to have one sent from the office, but I hate to admit that I thought as many times as I did of that typewriter and never got around to speaking of it.

I hope to begin, tomorrow, to work on my book but Dieu dispose.[2]

Every beautiful day has been cause for rejoicing—for I knew you were having a prosperous voyage.

I know you will write as much as you can. I wonder whether you will have remembered, in Glasgow, that Jas Dalrymple the man in charge of the trams, is the same who so damaged the cause in Chicago.[3] And that Glasgow is trying to devise some scheme whereby suburban unearned increments can be secured for the municipality instead of the landsharks. I suspect the land system is one of the worst of the ills of Great Britain, and that we shall soon be having to use for our cities what she is working out for her whole territory.

Teddy has ordered a great squadron to San Francisco.[4] I hate to think of him using the big stick against both the Japanese and the unions. Our national life grows more complicated every day! The need for a leader through constructive measures in troublous times grows steadily more urgent.

Meantime in everything that relates to women we seem to move backward. Governor Hughes vetoed the teachers' "equal pay for equal work" bill in the same month when the court held that women are so far equal that they cannot be deprived of the right to work all night in factories![5] And in that same month Norway followed Finland in giving Parliamentary suffrage to women![6]

Do learn all you can for me, before I go next year!

Your loving Mother
F. Kelley

ALS, FKP, NN

1. FK later described her visit with the "middle-aged spinsters," who were "far worse together than when taken singly!" She and Emily Balch regularly escaped in Balch's rowboat, "eating our supper on some island and returning just in time for bed" (FK, Brookline, Mass., to NK, 28 August 1907, FKP, NN).
2. French; "God decides."
3. James Dalrymple (1860–1934) was manager of the Glasgow Corporation Tramways Department (Maver, "No Mean City").
4. The U.S. Navy announced on 4 July 1907 that eighteen to twenty battleships would sail in the winter to San Francisco (*NYT,* 5 July 1907, 1). In December, the fleet left Fort Monroe,

Virginia, for Japan, a move President Roosevelt characterized as a friendly gesture that would counter recent anti-Japanese sentiment in western states.

5. In vetoing the bill providing equal pay for women and men teachers in New York City on 29 May, Governor Charles Evans Hughes stated that although the women teachers' lower salaries were deplorable, any equal pay law should apply to all civil servants in New York (*NYT,* 30 May 1907, 2). In *People v. Williams,* the New York Court of Appeals voided a law prohibiting night work for women on 14 June, declaring that the law was "discriminative against female citizens in denying to them equal rights with men with respect to liberty of person, or of contract" (see Goldmark, *Impatient Crusader,* 147–149).

6. Women were granted suffrage in Norway on 14 June 1907.

98. To Nicholas Kelley

[Naskeag,] Brooklin, Hancock Co., Maine
August 25th '07

Darling Son

Your Görnergrat postal card, dated Aug. 4th, came yesterday—20 days in transit![1]

Hal [Lloyd] has forwarded you two instalments of cash, this month, first 125.00 and later $75.00. I trust it may have traveled more speedily!

I have paid $500.00 for an abandoned farm of such wonderful beauty that it bore comparison with the loveliest spots in Bar Harbor, Northeast and Seal, which I visited in process of visiting Miss Addams who was staying with the Bowens at Bar Harbor.[2] It is one of those rare spots on the Atlantic Coast which command the sunset over water![3] The house will be occupied by the former owner until June 1st. 1909 as part of the price, instead of $200.00 cash. This suited us both. It has beach, fir grove meadow, house and barn.

And there has not been one hot day this summer!

Its name is Seawest, Naskeag Point, (Brooklin) Hancock Co. Maine. But you won't have to write all that on your letters for two years yet! I think Brooklin need not be written.

Your letters have been a very great pleasure.[4] I trust that you are writing me fully today. For no one could guess, from our American papers, that there is a Socialist Conference in session.[5] There are columns of explanations of the meagre results of the Hague Conference.[6]

Yet, I cannot help feeling that this, too, is inching along towards the Federation of the World! The building of a Palace of Arbitration is a wonderful registering of the great desire of our time![7] I suppose the Socialist Congress draws to a close to day. I am very glad you have been there.

With deep regret that the end of the summer is here, I leave on Wednesday. I go to Waterville to see a factory. Thence, to Portland, Me. for a three days' meeting of the International Law Association to learn what I can,—thence to Pittsburgh, Pa., for a month at the bottom of the Pit, learning about working conditions of women and girls.

On Oct. 3d I lecture in Holyoke, Mass., on the 5th in New Haven. Between, I am coming to Cambridge to visit you. So keep the evening of Oct. 4th sacred to me!

Your loving mother
Florence Kelley
What day do you sail?[8]

ALS, FKP, NN

1. Although the postcard has not been recovered, NK wrote describing his hike up the Görnergrat, where he "rubbed noses" with the Briethorn, the Matterhorn, "and other beauties" (NK, Berne, to FK, 17 August 1907, KFP, NNC-RB).
2. Louise De Koven Bowen (1859–1953) was a Hull House benefactor and trustee and president of the Juvenile Protective Association. Her husband was Joseph T. Bowen.
3. In a memorandum dated 1 September 1907, FK described the property and terms of the sale: $500 to Allen H. Tainter immediately and another $500 on 1 January 1908 (FKP, NN).
4. NK had described attending parliamentary debates and visiting H. G. Wells in Folkstone (NK, London, to FK, 28 July 1907, KFP, NNC-RB).
5. The International Socialist Congress opened in Stuttgart on 18 August 1907. In an editorial on 20 August, the *New York Times* characterized Americans attending the congress as those "to whom their class is more than their country. . . . [A] man who attaches himself to what he thinks is his class, abjuring his allegiance to his country, is not and can not be a worthy American citizen" (*NYT*, 19 August 1907, 2 and 20 August 1907, 6).
6. The Hague Convention met from 15 June to 18 October with forty-four nations present but did not agree on a disarmament treaty.
7. The Permanent Court of Arbitration, established at the first Hague conference in 1899, was reaffirmed by the 1907 conference. The Hague Peace Palace was completed in 1913.
8. NK wrote that he would sail from Genoa on 14 September (NK, Paris, France, to FK, 17 August 1907, FKP, NN).

99. To Lillian D. Wald

NATIONAL CONSUMERS' LEAGUE
OFFICE: 105 E. 22D STREET
NEW YORK CITY

[Pittsburgh]
September 11th, 1907

Beloved Lady,

I write from Pittsburgh, whither I have come to take part in Paul Kellogg's investigation of industrial conditions here,—incidentally hoping to get some light for my Consumers' League. I saw Miss Waters on Labor Day,[1] and she urged me to follow up the question of the twelve or twenty-four hours shifts of the men in the blast furnaces, of which you heard when you were here;—or was it in rolling-mills?

Dr. John Commons of the University of Wisconsin is here. I spoke to him about this, but he flouted the idea of the possibility of men enduring the heat and strain of either kind of work for either twelve or twenty-four hours. So now my dander is up and I want to know more exactly about it. Whatever you tell me will be confidential. But I do ~~n~~ want to know where the works were, Alleghany, Pittsburgh, Braddock, or Homestead? What year you made the visit? What kind of works it was, rolling-mill, blast-furnace, pressed-steel-car works? Anything else, you can remember about it,—for instance how often the turn occurred which involved the long hours,—once a week, once a fortnight, once a month? How long the turn was,—12 hours, 24 hours? How many men it involved?[2]

Any clue will be valuable.

This place is so horrible, that Rivington street seems a fine lady compared with it,—and Henry street a Grande Dame—so aristocratic among communities as to be almost royalty!

Ko sails next Saturday from Naples for Boston. I hoped to read you his letters,—but I was reduced to reading them to Miss Waters and Miss Kittredge, instead. The letters to the Mc Donald's produced more joy than all the others together.[3]

John has gone to Arizona, where he has work on the same federal irrigation scheme upon which he was working in Montana.[4] He was so badly frost-bitten, last winter in Connecticut, that it would not be safe for him to try a Montana winter. But the summer seems to have made him strong and well, if he tells the truth in his cheerful letters.

This horrible job has three more weeks to run. Then I shall be coming back to civilization. If we can turn on the light strongly enough really to improve pretty much any little trifle, here, it will be like cooling off a part of the Inferno![5]

I bought a different farm—with a wonderful view of the sunset over the water, a grove, a long sea beach, a clam-flat (temporarily exhausted) a house (about to tumble down, I think), and thirty acres (more or less) of perfectly worthless farming land. It is considered the most desirable possession in the whole region because of its position. I paid five hundred dollars down, and am to pay five hundred more at New Year's! Heaven save the mark! I have hopes of paying for the whole out of current earnings. It is three hours sail by steamboat from Bar Harbor, four hours sail by steamboat from Rockland, and twenty-eight miles from a railway station. Its name is Seawest, Naskeag, Hancock Co. Maine. It is most beautiful! It is in the country of the pointed firs.[6] I hate to think of going to Europe next summer instead of going to Seawest! And I'm counting the weeks until I can have you come to me instead of going to Cap a l'Aigle!

It was an anxious story which Miss Waters told of your family! Do give my love and sympathy to Mrs. Barry![7] And keep for yourself all you can use thereof. It is a poor useless thing, but abundant!

Did you ever hear of anything so loony as Raymond Robins systematic attack upon Miss Addams because she did not resign from the Chicago school board when he was dropped from it?[8] Did you ever hear of a man resigning because a woman was dropped? And there was not a person on the board who had poorer practical judgment than he! I saw her at Bar Harbor (suffering from influenza, sciatica and an ulcerated tooth), and she seemed quite tranquil about the changes in the Board,—thought some of the new businessmen likely to do pretty well by the children. She was rather amused than annoyed at the attitude of the Robbins-es. But I think it is hateful.

Your loving
Florence Kelley

TLS, Wald Papers, NCC-RB

1. Paul Kellogg had recently organized the study of working and living conditions in Pittsburgh. The study's results, published from 1910 to 1914 in a series called the Pittsburgh Survey, brought new attention to the need for workmen's compensation and a shorter working day in the steel industry (see Kellogg, "The Pittsburgh Survey"). Yssabella Waters, one of the nurses at the Henry Street Settlement, was a close friend of Wald (Daniels, *Always a Sister,* 65).

2. Kelley was right and Commons wrong. The volume of the Pittsburgh Survey devoted to steel workers (Fitch, *The Steel Workers*), found that about 8,000 men were employed at the forty-four blast furnaces in Allegheny County, all of whom worked twelve-hour shifts seven days a week and 5,000 of whom worked a "long turn" of twenty-four hours on alternate Sundays and did not work on the other Sundays (170–177). Fitch found that "nearly four-fifths of the workmen [were] on a twelve-hour schedule, working longer hours from time to time" (171).

3. Mabel Kittredge (1867–1955), social worker and president of the Practical Housekeeping Centers in New York City. NK visited Ramsay MacDonald (1866–1937), then an MP and secretary of the Independent Labour Party, and his wife Margaret Gladstone MacDonald (1870–1911), a suffragist and member of the Women's Industrial Council. He described them as "perfect dears. . . . Mrs. M. particularly is great" (NK, London, to FK, 21 July 1907, KFP, NNC-RB).

4. While working for the United States Reclamation Service, an agency that oversaw management of water resources, in the spring of 1907, JK wrote that he was considering investing in a water-power scheme. He had recently taken a job as hotel night clerk in Phoenix (JK, Ft. Shaw, Mont., to FK, [spring 1907], and JK, Phoenix, Ariz., to FK [September? 1907], KFP, NNC-RB; FK, n.p., to NK, 29 March 1907, FK, [Brooklin, Me.], to NK, 20 July 1907, and FK, [Trinity Rectory?], to NK, 14 December 1907, both in FKP, NN).

5. In her article "Factory Inspection in Pittsburgh," FK criticized Pennsylvania's factory inspection department for keeping inadequate records of labor law violations. She described the long hours and hazardous conditions children suffered in Allegheny County's steel mills, glass and cigar factories, and drugstores. Her ten recommendations included shorter working hours for women and children and hiring inspectors under the civil service laws.

6. Sarah Orne Jewett (1849–1909) wrote of the Maine seacoast in *The Country of the Pointed Firs* (1896).

7. Probably Wald's sister, Julia, wife of Charles P. Barry.

8. JA was appointed to the Chicago School Board in 1905 along with other reformers, including lawyer Raymond Robins (1873–1954). In 1907, Chicago's new mayor asked many reformers on the school board, but not JA, to resign. Many expected JA to resign in protest (Davis, *American Heroine,* 131–134).

100. To Nicholas Kelley

105 E. 22nd St.
New York City
Oct. 19th 07

Darling Son

This is an enchanting October afternoon such as we always made it a point of conscience to spend in the woods, when I was in college. I am now in the office, making up arrears after a three days absence in Penna. where I visited my lifelong friend, Rachel Avery,[1] and lectured to the students at Swarthmore, the girls in a boarding school, and the women in a club. Sometimes I get so tired talking that it seems impossible to go on doing it. Then there always comes some gain so important that it seems even more impossible to stop. The present gain is the eight hours day for the children employed in manufacture in this state. It is working out exactly as it did in Illinois, four years ago.[2] The more valuable children are employed, as before, not dismissed. But new ones are not employed under 16 years of age, and the little ones are turned back into school. It is a fine, long step forward.

I am still at Miss Wald's. Shall come to Boston Saturday night late, or Sunday a week from tomorrow. Will let you know.

Your loving Mother
F. Kelley

ALS, FKP, NN

1. Rachel Foster Avery, who lived in Philadelphia, was serving as a first vice-president of NAWSA.
2. On 1 October 1907, the New York law limiting the workday of children under sixteen working in factories to eight hours went into effect (*NYT,* 1 October 1907, 11). The Illinois child labor law prohibiting children under sixteen from working more than eight hours a day or at night went into effect on 1 July 1903 (NCL, Fifth Annual Report [1904], 23, Box A5, NCL Records, DLC).

101. To Nicholas Kelley

GENERAL FEDERATION OF WOMEN'S CLUBS
1904–1906[1]

Detroit, Nov. 2nd '07

Darling Son,

Having an hour free, but my proper writing materials in my trunk at the station; I use this which is at hand.[2]

Do not fail to read Seth Low's article on National Control of Inter-State Railways Outlook Nov. 2.[3] It is as good, from the business man's point of view, as Judge [Charles] Amidon's paper from the Federal judge's point of view.[4] Railways and taxation will be the national problems of your early Manhood. And the years from now until 1915 will chiefly determine your usefulness, thereafter. By 1920 it will be clear to all that privately owned railways cannot be controlled. Perhaps they will then already be ancient history! We are moving very fast!

An excellent campaign is started in Massachusetts for the 8 hours day for children below 16 years. It will reach success within twelve months. A good campaign, here in Michigan, was started yesterday. But the legislature will not meet until Jan. 1909, so success, here, cannot be achieved for two years. The New Jersey campaign for the same end I am just starting, it may succeed this coming winter.[5]

There is a constitutional convention on, here, and my friends are asking for the vote for women. It will be the second effort in Michigan, and may prove successful.[6] All men except the repair gang have been dismissed from the night service of the New York City Telephone Company, and their places filled by girls at five dollars a week. This is due to the Court of Appeals decision [People v. Williams] that women's health is not hurt by working all night. But men cannot sweep streets more than eight hours by daylight.

Your loving Mother

ALS, FKP, NN

1. FK is listed on the GFWC letterhead as an officer of the Industrial Advisory Committee, which JA chaired.
2. FK was en route to the National Purity Congress in Battle Creek, where she spoke on "Wages, Votes, and Morals" (*Detroit News,* 1 November 1907, 19).
3. The text "Outlook, Nov. 2" is inserted above the line at the end of the sentence.
4. Seth Low (1850–1916) was president of Columbia University from 1890 to 1901 and mayor of New York City from 1901 to 1903.
5. The Michigan legislature passed a law in 1909 that required a minimum amount of schooling and made it illegal for children under fourteen to work. In 1910, New Jersey prohibited night work for children, and in 1911 the state enacted an eight-hour day for children under sixteen (Loughran, "The Historical Development of Child-Labor Legislation," 44, 55–56).
6. According to the *Detroit News,* delegates did not discuss the issue of woman suffrage at the Michigan constitutional convention, which met over several weeks in October and November 1907 (*Detroit News,* 6 November 1907, 6). Michigan women were not granted suffrage until 1918.

102. To Nicholas Kelley

CHARITIES AND THE COMMONS
105 EAST 22D STREET
NEW YORK

[Cleveland?] Nov. 7th '07

Darling Son,

T'is the best thing possible, that Mayor Johnson has nearly ten thousand majority in a city in which the normal Republican majority is nearly ten thousand.

He is pushing for three cent fares because that is nearer to gratis transportation than five cent fares.[1] He has done so much affirmative constructive work as has never been approached by any city of the size of Cleveland.

Moreover, it is wholesome notice to Mr. [Theodore] Roosevelt to keep out of city politics. I can hardly express my satisfaction over this election!

It was a very wonderful thing that Mr. Johnson did, when he left his campaign on the second day, and came down to Youngstown to speak at a Suffrage meeting![2]

We are having an exciting time in the matter of working hours. The laundry men of Oregon have appealed to the Supreme Court of the U.S. against an Oregon Supreme Court decision upholding the ten hours law for women. We, of course, are for the ten hours day by statute.[3]

So, now, we are trying to add a very powerful attorney (preferably Mr. Louis F. Brandeis of Boston) to the Atty. Gen'l of Oregon for the oral argument.[4] But nobody has any money. One offer of $30.00 is the largest yet!

Your loving Mother
Florence Kelley

ALS, FKP, NN

1. Democrat Tom L. Johnson, the reform mayor of Cleveland, was reelected to a fourth term by a plurality of 9,312 votes. For the importance of streetcar fares in urban American politics, see Bionaz, "'Streetcar City.'"
2. Johnson attended the Ohio Suffrage Association meeting on 11 October 1907 (FK, New York, to NK, 12 October 1907, FKP, NN).
3. This was the beginning of the NCL's work on the case that became *Muller v. Oregon*. For more on the case, see the introduction to Chapter 4 and Letter 104, FK to Nicholas Kelley, 20 January 1908, below.
4. For Goldmark's account of how FK connected the new *Muller* hours case with the *Ritchie* case of 1895, see *Impatient Crusader*, 143–144. A. M. Crawford was Oregon's attorney general. FK wrote NK that the case had been delayed until the second week in January. She added, "Fancy having to strive for the establishment of a law which has worked beneficently in England since 1844, in Germany since 1891 and in Mass. since 1876!" (FK, New York, to NK, 18 December 1907, FKP, NN).

103. To Nicholas Kelley

NATIONAL CONSUMERS' LEAGUE
OFFICE: 105 E. 22D STREET
NEW YORK CITY

Nov. 10th '07

Darling Son,

These are lively and painful days in the world of philanthropy. The Consumers' League of N. Y. City has $2000.00 tied up in the Knickerbocker bank.[1] The Nat'l League is more than usually penniless because we cannot send out our begging letters usually sent at this season, and most of our emergency guarantors have failed us.[2]

I have spent an irritating season at the Rand School of Social Science this morning, listening to Wm H. Kelly, formerly head of East Side House, denouncing Settlements, some and all, as bulwarks of Capitalism, deadly enemies of Socialism.[3] He doubtless knows what he made of his Settlement until he was dismissed for incompetence. But it is certainly bitter for a convinced Socialist to have to see such feather heads hindering progress! Doubtless, too, honest Xns feel so about their church.

Mr. Robert W. De Forest, Counsel for the Penna. coal roads (not the P.R.R.) has almost persuaded the Child Labor Committee to rescind its endorsement of the Beveridge child labor bill.[4] If he succeeds, my position will be an embarrassing one. I do not see how I can self respectingly remain in the committee and I hate to resign from it. Whatever its faults, the bill embodies the first attempt to deal justly with all the children and all the employers. And rescinding an endorsement of a federal bill, by a so-called National body is the most serious injury which can be inflicted upon a pending bill. Mr. De Forest plainly threatens that no Sage Foundation money will be forthcoming unless this quid pro quo is given him.[5]

Br'er [Lawrence] Veiller's head appears to have been completely turned by mere proximity to the Sage Found.[6] He is trying to anaconda every organization in sight,—myself included! The Metropolitan Parks Ass'n, the Tuberculosis Committee, the Congestion Investigation; he wishes to be the whole of each one of them. He appears singularly like T. Roosevelt.

I am to have half a morning of the festivity when the Charity Organization Society comes of age on Nov. 20th, to discuss the changes which have taken

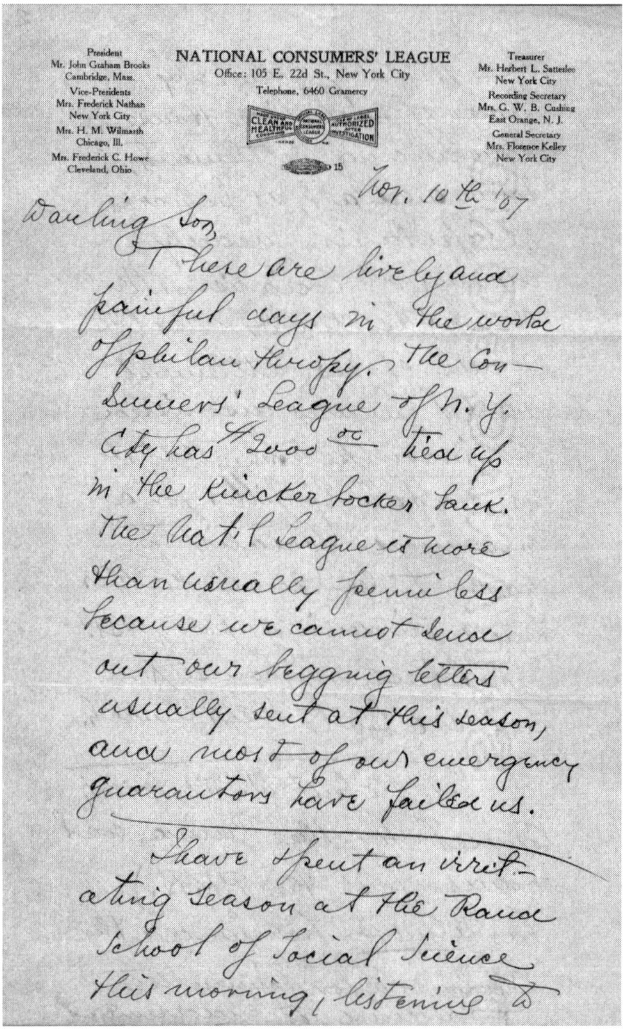

President
Mr. John Graham Brooks
Cambridge, Mass.
Vice-Presidents
Mrs. Frederick Nathan
New York City
Mrs. H. M. Wilmarth
Chicago, Ill.
Mrs. Frederick C. Howe
Cleveland, Ohio

NATIONAL CONSUMERS' LEAGUE
Office: 105 E. 22d St., New York City
Telephone, 6460 Gramercy

Treasurer
Mr. Herbert L. Satterlee
New York City
Recording Secretary
Mrs. G. W. B. Cushing
East Orange, N. J.
General Secretary
Mrs. Florence Kelley
New York City

Nov. 10th '07

Darling Son,

These are lively and painful days in the world of philanthropy. The Consumers' League of N.Y. City has $2000.00 tied up in the Knickerbocker bank. The Nat'l League is more than usually penniless because we cannot send out our begging letters usually sent at this season, and most of our emergency guarantors have failed us.

I have spent an irritating season at the Rand School of Social Science this morning, listening to

First page of Florence Kelley to Nicholas Kelley, 10 November 1907. Courtesy of the Florence Kelley Papers, Rare Books and Manuscripts Division, New York Public Library, Astor, Lenox and Tilden Foundations.

place during the period. Twenty five years seems to constitute the majority of societies.

My theme is the lost opportunity to deal with immigration as New Zealand has done, or in some constructive way. So I am deep in writing the paper.[7]

I am to be in Boston tomorrow night. I go by the 5 pm. Train on Wednesday I stay at the Essex, tear around all Thursday and return by the midnight train on Thursday.

If there is any chance of a glimpse of you, telephone me to the Essex Thursday morning. I'll keep 6:30 pm. Thursday on the chance of your being free to dine at the Essex with me. Pick me up there, and we'll go to the Parker House.

To-night I'm dining with Mrs. Burlingham.[8] I'll tell you, later, how it happened.

Your loving
Mother.

ALS, FKP, NN

1. The bank panic of 1907 led to the Federal Reserve Act of 1913. For the Knickerbocker Bank's role in the panic, see Fettig, "F. Augustus Heinze of Montana and the Panic of 1907".
2. At the end of 1907, the organization's cash on hand was $28.62 (Minutes of NCL Annual Meeting, 3 March 1908, Box A6, NCL Records, DLC).
3. In 1905, William H. Kelly's socialist perspective led him to denounce day nurseries: "I know of no confession of failure that society can make quite so ghastly as this—that nursing mothers must take their babes to day nurseries that they themselves may have opportunity to earn the money in the sweatshop or the tobacco factory that is needed to keep themselves and their children alive" (letter to *Charities and the Commons* 15 [14 October 1905]: 107).
4. Lawyer and philanthropist Robert W. De Forest (1848–1931) had been general counsel for Central Railroad of New Jersey, director of the New Jersey & New York Railroad Company and other businesses. In 1907, he became president of the Russell Sage Foundation. For FK's role in the creation of the NCLC in 1904, see Goldmark, *Impatient Crusader*, 87–92. For the Beveridge bill, see Letter 93, FK to NK, 20 February 1907, above.
5. The Russell Sage Foundation was established by Margaret Olivia Slocum Sage (1828–1918) in April 1907 with an endowment of $10 million to promote social science research that would aid in improving U.S. social conditions.
6. Much of the Russell Sage fortune, which was managed by his widow Olivia after his death in July 1906, came from his financing of railroad construction in the 1870s and 1880s (Crocker, *Mrs. Russell Sage*, 87–88, 222–224). Veiller had known De Forest, director of the foundation, from their work together on New York tenement legislation at the turn of the century. In 1910, with support from the Russell Sage Foundation, Veiller's power increased as the first director of the National Housing Association.
7. At the meeting, FK deplored the increased population densely packed into New York City's tenements. "We have lost the noblest opportunity of the quarter-century," she said, "which was to find a method of welcoming our immigrants, comprehensive enough to prevent congestion here at the port of entry and to enrich both the newcomers and the country which has through all this period has been hungry for men to come and occupy it." She urged her listeners to realize that "city, state and nation must be enlisted and brought into co-operation" to solve this growing problem (*Charities and the Commons* 19 [30 November 1907], 1124–1125).
8. Probably Louisa Lawrence Burlingham (d. 1937), mother of Charles Burlingham, a Harvard classmate of NK with whom he had traveled in Europe (FK, Brooklin, Me., to NK, 8 August [1907], FKP, NN).

Child Laborers at Danville, Virginia, Knitting Works, 1911. Courtesy of the Library of Congress, LC-DIG-nclc-04743.

4 1908 – 1916

"The Fight to Extend the Labor Law"

INTRODUCTION

To support Kelley's campaigns for "the child's right to leisure" and the right of wage-earning women to healthy working conditions and a living wage, local leagues quite distant from her New York City headquarters worked closely with her. The Oregon league was one of her most important allies, joining her in successfully defending Oregon's labor laws before the U.S. Supreme Court in 1908 and 1917, first establishing the constitutionality of state legislation limiting the hours of working women and then extending court approval to include laws limiting the hours of working men. In 1917 the NCL also worked with Oregon officials to defend the state's minimum wage law for women before the U.S. Supreme Court.[1]

By January 1908, Kelley's leadership of the NCL had reached a turning point. After nearly a decade of organization, consumers' leagues existed throughout the United States, their presence in cities such as Atlanta demonstrating the league's national strength. In almost every state, local consumers' leagues had participated in the passage of child labor laws, and leagues in many states had fostered the passage of laws that prohibited women as well as children from working longer than ten hours a day. Now Kelley brought the NCL's strength to bear on national legislation and policy.

Her first success came in April 1908 with the U.S. Supreme Court's ruling in *Muller v. Oregon,* which found state hours laws for women constitutional. She rejoiced in January when Louis Brandeis felt optimistic after he presented the NCL's path-breaking amicus brief in the case and celebrated her assistant's achievement in preparing that brief: "I am as proud of Josephine Goldmark as if she were my own!"[2]

Invited by the Oregon Consumers' League and coauthored under NCL auspices by Louis Brandeis and Josephine Goldmark, the brief's historic significance lay in its emphasis on nearly 100 pages of sociological evidence about the effects of long hours on women's health. Containing only a few pages of references to legal precedents, which were written by Louis Brandeis, most of the brief consisted of excerpts from a wide range of European and American publications collected by Josephine Goldmark, Brandeis's sister-in-law and Kelley's chief assistant. Later expanded in Goldmark's book *Fatigue and Efficiency* (1911), the brief drew on reports by state bureaus of labor statistics, factory inspectors, and physicians.

This sociological evidence was consistent with the Court's acknowledgment in its 1905 *Lochner* decision that states could regulate working hours if "there be some fair ground, reasonable in and of itself to say that there is material danger to the public health, or to the health of employees, if the hours of labor are not curtailed."[3] That "fair ground" became the fact that women were not as strong as men.

> Long hours of labor are dangerous for women primarily because of their special physical organization. In structure and function women are differentiated from men. Besides these anatomical and physiological differences, physicians are agreed that women are fundamentally weaker than men in all that makes for endurance: in muscular strength, in nervous energy, in the powers of persistent attention and application.[4]

The court agreed. Written by Associate Justice David Brewer, the *Muller* decision emphasized the thread in Goldmark's evidence about the effects of women's ill health on their children, changing the brief's physiological reasoning into an argument about motherhood. Insisting that its ruling in *Muller* did not question "in any respect the decision in *Lochner v. New York*," the decision found the Oregon law constitutional, not primarily because women were weaker than men but chiefly because "healthy mothers are essential to vigorous offspring" and "the well-being of the race" justified "legislation to protect her from the greed as well as the passion of man."[5]

The use of sociological evidence in the NCL brief (subsequently known as "the Brandeis brief") generated a long legacy that included the Supreme Court's historic ruling against school segregation in 1954. More immediately, the *Muller* decision prompted Kelley and the NCL to promote the passage of women's hours laws in states where such laws had not yet been enacted or, as in the case of Illinois, where they had been ruled unconstitutional.[6]

Kelley viewed labor legislation for women as a complement to the efforts of organized labor, and the NCL's post-*Muller* campaign for other state hours laws exemplified the link between social reformers and labor activists.[7] Trade union women championed hours legislation as a way to extend union gains of the eight-hour or ten-hour day throughout industries that employed women. In California, for example, the state legislature passed an eight-hour law for women in 1911, despite vigorous campaigns against the bill by employers, after women representing laundry workers, garment workers, and waitresses spoke effectively in its favor.[8]

With the constitutionality of women's hours laws resolved, Kelley turned her attention to an even more fundamental issue—women's low wages. From 1910 to 1915, she focused the NCL's attention on the enactment of the first minimum wage laws in the United States. Passed by states and applying only to women, these laws became the basis for federal legislation for men and women in 1938 that created a floor beneath which wages could not legally fall.

Kelley's correspondence with Katherine Edson illustrates her close work with women reformers in Massachusetts, Ohio, California, and Oregon during this minimum wage campaign. From 1912 to 1914, Kelley guided Edson to the latest writings on minimum wage laws in Britain and the United States and critiqued the inadequacies of the law in Massachusetts, the virtues of the law in Oregon, and the administration of minimum wage laws generally. Her letters urged Edson to extend the law to include canneries and to cover men as well as women.[9]

The field of Progressive reform grew more crowded in the years around 1910. Fortified by an invigorated woman suffrage movement, the NCL grew even more powerful and its links with women's networks more effective. And the phenomenal expansion of the social settlement movement fostered a crescendo of reform expertise among women college graduates in poor urban neighborhoods. Women, who had long been active in municipal and state politics, now emerged as major figures in national politics. In 1912, Jane Addams provided crucial support for Theodore Roosevelt's Progressive Party campaign for president. Nevertheless, women's reform activism remained rooted in their independent organizations, which now served as an effective base for women's independent influence in politics as well as in public life.

Florence Kelley's network of women reformers exemplified the interactive process of organizational autonomy and political clout. Particularly notable was the appointment of Julia Lathrop, Kelley's Hull House colleague, to head the U.S. Children's Bureau in 1912. Since 1909, Kelley and Lillian Wald had promoted the creation of a federal children's bureau as a means by which the national government could combat the high rates of infant and child mortality that made the United States one of the most dangerous nations for children in the western world. Endorsed and promoted by women's organizations, the U.S. Children's Bureau was staffed by women reformers despite the vigorous opposition of the National Public Health Association.[10]

No equivalent female-dominated national agency of government existed in contemporary England or Europe. British women such as Margaret Bondfield were shaping national policies about poverty and child welfare, but they did so through electoral politics, primarily by affiliating with the Liberal or Labour parties, and their gendered politics were much more firmly interwoven with male-dominated political culture than was true in the United States.[11] Tory women reformers also joined with men to affirm the "commons" and the common welfare.[12] In the United States, women's voices more often constituted a vanguard that led the way toward state-sponsored social responsibility in a political culture that valued the self-sufficient individual and small government.

As Kelley's power grew, she became the target of untrue accusations leveled by manufacturers who opposed the regulations that she promoted. As part of the coalition that obtained the passage of the Pure Food and Drug Act in 1906, she was attacked by the *American Food Journal* in "nasty" ways she considered libelous. Concerned about the effects of such attacks on the "reading public among club women," she understood their lethal potential. Yet she offered no effective response.[13]

Kelley's success placed her in the vanguard of an advancing wave of reform organizations, and she often lost patience with those she deemed less courageous. In 1908, she called the leaders of the National Child Labor Committee "moral cowards" because they appeased southern industry and failed to back the Beveridge federal child labor bill.[14] Her relationship with the NCLC remained stormy until 1930.

In 1915, she parted ways with the American Association for Labor Legislation, whose leaders had failed to back her minimum wage campaign because they thought American courts would never approve the constitutionality of wage legislation. Instead, they sought alternatives that would provide other benefits and in 1915 proposed a plan to fund health insurance for manual workers who earned less than $1200 a year by taxing wages as well as employers. This strategy she viewed as "fundamentally hostile toward wage legislation." She thought that "until we can have universal sickness insurance," a better way to promote wage-earners' health was through shorter hours and "a living wage by means of minimum wage legislation for both men and women; and to discourage in every possible way the wage-earning employment of mothers of young children."[15]

Kelley's wage campaign focused on the needs of single women, who constituted the great majority—about 75 percent—of wage-earning women in 1915. Her rationale accepted their permanence in the paid labor force and sought to raise their wages to a level that permitted them to support themselves independently and "in health." For that purpose state minimum wage legislation created wage boards that calculated the amount that single women needed to support themselves "in health." Because the legislation applied to "women," married women were also covered, but their presence weakened the logic of Kelley's legislative experiment because they did not live independently and their needs varied depending on the circumstances of their family economies. So, policies that encouraged married women to join the paid labor force undercut her arguments on behalf of wage legislation for (single) women and her effort to use single women as a wedge to establish wage legislation more generally.

The AALL's plan to provide childbirth health benefits to married wage-earning women clashed with Kelley's wage campaign and she attacked it relentlessly, living up to her Hull House reputation as a fighter for whom any weapon was a good weapon, "evidence, argument, irony or invective."[16] Women's groups were divided on the AALL's proposal, but her view prevailed.[17] A few years later she promoted maternal health through the Sheppard-Towner Act of 1921, which did not connect health benefits to the paid labor force.

In the long run Kelley's minimum wage strategy became the chief means by which American public policy sought to raise the income of poor working families. But in the short run, her vulnerability in the vanguard of that strategy alienated her from the potentially powerful ally of the AALL.

Although Kelley's place at the forefront of Progressive reform complicated her affiliation with some organizations, it awakened her to the untapped potential in other groups. A visit to Atlanta University in April 1908, where W. E. B. Du Bois was professor of history and sociology, brought her into his world.[18] She had written him earlier to express her admiration for his 1903 book, *Souls of Black Folk,* which passionately dissented from the hegemony of Booker T. Washington's policy of advancing the economic status of African Americans without advancing their civil rights.[19] She supported Du Bois's founding of the NAACP in New York City in 1909, and, as a member of its executive board from 1912 to 1932, was an important intermediary between Du Bois and his critics within the organization.[20]

Yet it was one thing to advocate the rights of African Americans and another to support the rights of Chinese immigrants. Although Kelley thought that her "record of twenty-one years of intimate contact with the immigrants should safeguard me against any charge of race or religious prejudice," she agreed with NCL president John Graham Brooks's advocacy of the selective exclusion of some immigrants, especially Chinese, writing. Nevertheless, she lived happily in a room in the Henry Street settlement on Manhattan's Lower East Side, where the population density was close to that of contemporary Calcutta and where Jews from Eastern Europe predominated. While visiting Oakland, she longed "to get back to my gentle Jews."[21]

Her pleasure in her New York residence intensified after Ko and his growing family moved to Manhattan in 1909. Soon after graduating from Harvard Law School that year, Ko married Augusta Maverick of San Antonio, and the couple settled on the Upper East Side. Kelley visited them frequently, often seeking Ko's advice about strategic choices she and the NCL confronted. Her visits to them soon included her grandchildren, Nicholas, born in 1910, Florence, born in 1912, and Augustus, born in 1914.[22]

In 1909 Kelley also began to spend summers in her Maine farmhouse on Penobscot Bay. Renovations opened one end of her house "into one big room with windows and glass doors on three sides and a fireplace on the fourth" and a view "south, west and north." In 1910 she warmly invited Augusta to spend the summer there with infant Nicky.[23] John Kelley was admitted to Harvard as a special student in 1908 but withdrew after two unsuccessful years to work in an Ontario mining camp.[24]

At the height of her success with minimum wage legislation, Kelley took time off during the summer of 1915 to promote the woman suffrage movement in Maine. "I have been doing difficult things for twenty years, but never anything to compare with this," she wrote Lucy Burns of the Congressional Union.[25] Compared to her well-oiled NCL machine and its wide base of support among women trade unionists and middle-class reformers, working in the suffrage movement was like herding cats, and she gladly passed that responsibility to others.

As war engulfed Europe, Kelley could dictate the terms by which she would participate in the American peace movement, but she could not halt the assaults on the values and institutions that had sustained her coalitions and achievements for more than twenty years. The nineteenth century was finally ending and the twentieth would pose enormous problems for her social rights agenda.

NOTES

1. For an overview of the context and consequence of much of this legal history, see Woloch, *Muller v. Oregon.*
2. See Letter 104, FK to NK, 20 January 1908, below.
3. *Lochner v. the People of State of New York,* 198 U.S. 45 (1905).
4. Brandeis and Goldmark, *Women in Industry,* 18.
5. Woloch, *Muller v. Oregon,* 149–150.
6. Goldmark, *Impatient Crusader,* 160–179.
7. See Letter 113, FK to William Kent, 4 August 1909, below.
8. Beyer, *History of Labor Legislation for Women in Three States,* 122–125.
9. FK to Katharine Philips Edson: Letter 119, 22 November 1912; Letter 122, 16 April 1914; and Letter 135, 16 July 1916 (all below).
10. Lindenmeyer, *The Right to Childhood,* 51, 55–56, 165–169.
11. See Bondfield, *A Life's Work*; and Graves, *Labour Women.*
12. See Pedersen, *Eleanor Rathbone and the Politics of Conscience.*
13. Letter 118, FK to NK, 4 August 1912, below.
14. See Letter 105, FK to NK, 6 April 1908, below. For the Beveridge child labor bill, see Letter 93, FK to NK, 20 February 1907, above.
15. Irene Osgood Andrews to Susan Kingsbury, 13 May 1912, AALL Records, NNCorI; Letter 131, FK to George E. Hooker, 17 December 1915, below.
16. Linn, *Jane Addams,*138–139.
17. Beatrix Hoffman, *The Wages of Sickness: The Politics of Health Insurance in Progressive America* (Durham: University of North Carolina Press, 2001), 135–162.
18. See Letter 106, FK to NK, 8 April 1908, below.
19. See Letter 89, FK to W. E. B. Du Bois, 30 October 1906, above; Wedin, *Inheritors of the Spirit,* 102. See also Lewis, *W.E.B. Du Bois,* 365–410.
20. See Letter 124, FK to Joel Spingarn, 27 July 1914, below.
21. Letter 112, FK to Augusta Maverick Kelley, 31 July 1909, below.
22. For NK's marriage in 1909, see Letter 112, FK to Augusta Maverick Kelley, 31 July 1909, note 1, below.
23. Letter 115, FK to NK, 9 July 1910, below.
24. Letter 116, FK to NK, 27 July 1911, below; Harvard University Archives Records; JK, Porcupine, Ontario, to FK, 28 June 1911, KFP, NNC-RB.
25. See Letter 127, FK to Lucy Burns, 6 September 1915, below.

104. To Nicholas Kelley

[New York City]
Jan. 20th '08

Darling Son

Have you told Will? You see, your letters are a bit indefinite, tho' they could not possibly be more interesting; and I have no tidings on that score since the letter from Lola, in which she said she was not free to do so. I trust that you have told him. For you see, you have become engaged to his sister-in-law under his roof.[1] Not to tell him must see to him at best inconsiderate. At worst, it might seem ignominious, even unmanly. Your relation to him is so unusual, he has been so more than brotherly, that I think the usual reasons for letting the lady in the case keep the secret as long as she prefers, do not hold here with regard to Will.

As soon as you tell me that Will knows, I will write with great pleasure to Augusta, Lola and Will. I wish I had had presence of mind to ask in replying to your first note. You see I was a bit "put about" as my English grandmother used to say. And my presence of mind was insufficient under the strain.[2]

I want to tell you the fine thing that Mr. Brandeis has done. He gave his services as counsel for the State of Oregon, sat waiting in Washington from Monday morning through Wednesday. The plea was heard on Wednesday afternoon (after being called for Monday) and he felt pretty cheerful about the result. In these days of muck raking and well grounded distrust of the profession, 'tis a delight to see a lawyer serving his country like that.

Josephine Goldmark, ca. 1927. Courtesy of Bryn Mawr College Library.

I am sending you a copy of the brief. It was made in November and December. It really needed a year's work. I am as proud of Josephine Goldmark as if she were my own![3]

The supreme court of Colorado has just pronounced unconstitutional a statute which forbade women to stand at their work more than eight hours in one day.

Good letter from John which I'll send on later.

Your Loving Mother
F. Kelley[4]

ALS, FKP, NN

1. In January 1908, NK told his mother about his engagement to Augusta Maverick of San Antonio, Texas. Will Lloyd was then a Chicago lawyer; in 1902 he had married Lola Maverick (1875–1944), later a prominent peace activist. Lola Maverick Lloyd was Augusta Maverick's sister. NK wrote, "Lola is the only person that knows, and you will not say anything to anybody will you? . . . And Mother dear, please write that you think it is just right. It would be dreadful if you were not to think well of Gus, since she has me in the hollow of her hand." (NK, Cambridge, to FK, 10 January 1908, KFP, NNC-RB).

2. Signing her letter "Your deeply sympathizing loving old mother," FK wrote NK giving her consent, but she worried whether he would have "the concentration you will need for your varied occupations, under this terrific strain!" (FK, New York, to NK, 10 January 1908, FKP, NN).

3. On 24 February in *Muller v. Oregon,* the U.S. Supreme Court unanimously upheld the constitutionality of Oregon's ten-hour-per-day legislation for women. Goldmark wrote all but the introductory portion of the brief that Louis Brandeis presented to the court's hearing on 15 January, compiling European and American sources that evaluated the effects of long working hours on women's health. The long-term importance of the Brandeis brief in American legal history lay in the Court's acceptance of the strategy that Kelley began in the 1895 *Ritchie* case of using sociological evidence instead of legal precedent. The court's acceptance of sociological evidence in 1908 created the basis for its approval in 1941 of the 1938 Fair Labor Standards Act, which regulated the working hours of and established a federal minimum wage for men and women. For more on the Brandeis brief and the Court's decision in *Muller v. Oregon,* see Goldmark, *Impatient Crusader*, 150–159; and Woloch, *Muller v. Oregon.*

4. NK responded that he had told Will of his engagement (NK, Cambridge, Mass., to FK, 21 January 1908, KFP, NNC-RB). Two days later, FK wrote Augusta expressing her happiness over the engagement. After the loss of her daughter, FK rejoiced that NK had chosen a wife "whom I know and love" (FK to Augusta Maverick, 23 January 1908, FKP, NN).

105. To Nicholas Kelley

Atlanta, Ga.,
April 6th [1908]

Darling Son,

The fourth annual meeting of the Nat'l Child Labor Committee closed yesterday afternoon.[1] It was an impressive rebuke to the policy of shunning the unpopular. The committee abandoned the Beveridge bill to please the South. In consequence the South, which naturally could not love us, now neither fears nor respects us. The one cheering thing in the situation is the fact that no Southern State is now without a child labor law, Nevada being the only state now left which has none. Moreover, there are now inspectors in Maryland, Kentucky, Tennessee, Alabama and Louisiana.

By 1910 we shall have a substantial harvest of gains for the children.

In Cincinnati, 18 months ago, we had Senator Beveridge and Miss Addams for our mass meeting. There were 3000 people, hot enthusiasm, and the best law in the country was passed in Ohio since then.[2]

Here, we had about 300 people, cold as ice. But I do not believe Dr. Adler and the rest of the moral cowards in the Committee see the point!

I have reserved berths on the Finland, sailing July 4th from New York.[3] I trust it may prove comfortable. The rooms seem very well placed, and we are not very far apart.

John writes that his job as rodman will come to an end in about three months and that, beginning next year, all men on the projects must be in the civil service which he scorns.[4]

Please return me the enclosed and, if you write him on the subject, do it as though you knew thru my letter not from his own.

I go northward on the midnight train to-night, reaching New York on April 8th '08

Your loving Mother
F. K.

ALS, FKP, NN

1. At the NCLC meeting on 4 April 1908, FK spoke about gathering statistics in New York state; at a session presided over by Felix Adler on 5 April, she spoke on "The Consumers' Responsibility for Child Labor" (*Atlanta Constitution:* 4 April 1908, 3, and 5 April 1908, C3).
2. Four thousand people attended the December 1906 NCLC meeting in Cincinnati, where they heard JA, Beveridge, and Adler ("The National Child Labor Meeting"). In 1908, Ohio passed a law limiting child labor to eight hours a day except in emergencies (Goldmark, *Child Labor Legislation*, 10).
3. In April, NK broached the subject of including Augusta Maverick in FK and NK's upcoming trip to Europe. FK responded favorably but was concerned about having to meet Augusta's expenses abroad (NK, Boston, to FK, 12 April 1908, KFP, NNC-RB; FK, New York, to NK, 13 April 1908, FKP, NN).
4. After losing his job at a Phoenix hotel because of violence toward an employer, JK found a new job working outdoors in Phoenix. He wrote his mother he would provide more details when "I find some paper" (FK, [New York], to NK, 16 February 1908 and FK, New York, 24 March 1908, both in FKP, NN; JK, Phoenix, Ariz., to FK, 7 April 1908, KFP, NNC-RB).

106. To Nicholas Kelley

105 E. 22nd St. [New York City]
April 8th 08

Darling Son,

It is a great pleasure to find, upon disembarking after two nights on a sleeping car, your cheerful and interesting letter of last Sunday.

By all means, accumulate all the good citizens you can for Chicago![1] The ruthlessness of Nature and of the population tend permanently to drive away everyone who is delicate in body, mind or spirit. It is robust virtue that you must acquire there in the citizenship. And I am certain that your plan will prove an admirable one provided you can manage a location reasonably accessible.

I had a strange and interesting experience in Atlanta. I went out to the Atlanta University to speak to the students. The President is Mr. Henry Ware, son of the man who founded the college, forty years ago next May. He is a person of the rarest, finest beauty and charm.[2] He seemed like Emerson come back to earth, the same tall stature and finely chiselled, strong, clear lines of brow, nose, chin, mouth. He and his wife, and her mother, live there as lonely as hermits. They train the black men and women 90 percent of whom in turn go out as teachers of other black people. It is a task which would call for noble consecration of spirit in any surroundings. In Atlanta it calls for heroes indeed. For everyone connected with the school is systematically boycotted.

We had a hearing before Governor Hughes on Wednesday, a week ago to-day and he conveys in some degree the same impression of being a person of great dignity firmness and fineness of character. But Mr. Ware is immeasurably more so. And the thought that the people of Atlanta deliberately cut themselves off from all contact like that!

When I finish this letter, my next will be to Mrs. Ware, telling her that it was worth the weary journey and the queer meetings to have the pleasure and the privilege of making their acquaintance and and seeing them hold the fort. It is a month, to-day since you all convoyed me to the South Station to go to Bridgeport. How much has happened meanwhile!

The South is in the most wonderful condition. Seething with the spirit of change, yet bound and tied with innumerable invisible hampering influences.

We'll talk about that on shipboard.[3]

Your loving mother
Florence Kelley

ALS, FKP, NN

1. NK had written about moving to Chicago after his graduation from law school, but he felt that "Chicago is all told pretty deficient in nice and interesting and cultivated people. . . . So I am buttonholing all the wise fellows here . . . and trying to lure 'em to Chicago" (NK, Cambridge, Mass., to FK, 5 April 1908, KFP, NNC-RB).

2. Edward T. Ware (1874–1927) was the third president (1907–1922) of Atlanta University, which was founded for African American students in 1865 by the American Missionary Foundation. He married Alice Holdship in 1905.

3. For FK and NK's European trip, see Letter 107, FK to NK, 19 June 1908, below.

107. To Nicholas Kelley

105 E. 22nd St. New York City
June 19th '08

Darling Son,

No record has been found of either first or second naturalization papers.[1]

I, therefore, suggest that you lay the following statement before Mr. Brandeis, (The whole [Felix] Adler tribe know the circumstances, so there is no bringing out of unsuspected skeletons in this case) following his advice.

Your father was and, so far as I can learn, still is a Russian subject.

I was married in Zurich, Switzerland, Oct. 17th 1884 and you were born there in 1885. We came to this country, arriving October 1886. In 1891 I left New York and went to Chicago. In March 1892 he brought habeas corpus proceedings to recover the custody of the three children. Judge Frank Baker awarded the custody to me.[2] In May proceedings were again brought to recover custody of yourself alone. You were again awarded to me.

Some years later (I am uncertain as to the date, but certainly before your 21st birthday) I obtained an absolute divorce and the court recorded my name and the names of all of you children as Kelley. [Inserted in margin: If the date of the divorce is important, wire Charles C. Arnold Winnetka, Ill. for date of decree. He was my counsel.]

Judge Baker has always insisted that I was never a Russian subject, that I could not forfeit my citizenship.[3]

If he is right, and if his decree made you (a minor) absolutely the ward of me a native citizen of America, did it place you where you would always have been if I had never been married at all? Does your status follow mine?

What is mine?

I have never been naturalized. I have taken the oath of allegiance to the Constitution three times (that I remember) when entering upon public office (always as a citizen). No one has ever raised the question of my being a citizen. I have voted in Chicago, as a citizen of Illinois, for a trustee of the university of Illinois, the only office for which women can vote there. No doubt ever arose in my mind as to my citizenship in that connection.[4]

Your loving mother
F.K.

ALS, FKP, NN

1. Because NK had been born in Germany, he was seeking proof of his naturalization as he prepared for his trip to Europe (see Letter 106, FK to NK, 8 April 1908, note 3, above). FK

and NK sailed from New York on 4 July. Augusta and her sister Lucy Maverick sailed on 30 May 1908 from Galveston for Bremen, where they met FK and NK (NK, Cambridge, Mass., to FK, 3 May 1908, FKP, NN).

2. Frank Baker (1840–1916) was judge of the circuit court of Cook County, Illinois, from 1887 to 1916.

3. No law protected or compromised FK's citizenship in connection with her 1884 marriage to a non-U.S. citizen, but a series of decisions by federal judges since 1800 had sustained the suspension of women's citizenship if they married non-citizens and lived abroad. This changed in 1907, when Congress passed the Expatriation Act, which voided the citizenship of all native-born American women living either in the United States or abroad if they married non-U.S. citizens. If FK had married a Russian citizen in 1908, she would have lost her citizenship. See Bredbenner, *A Nationality of Her Own*, 60–62; see also Montgomery, *"Gilded Prostitution,"* 249–253.

4. FK later wrote NK that she disliked raising questions about her citizenship and would not apply for a passport "unless you can produce some unusually good reason for opening up the painful subject" (FK, New York, to NK, ca. 25 June 1908, FKP, NN). Until 1915, passports were not needed for travel in Western Europe or for entry to or exit from the United States (Torpey, *The Invention of the Passport*, 117).

108. To Nicholas Kelley

Pension Dunand Rond Point du Plain Palais
Geneva [Switzerland] September 6th '08

Darling Son,

Your two letters gave me much pleasure, and the enclosed brings great relief to my mind.

You will, of course, never betray the fact that I have sent it to you.

The congress was interesting beyond all power of words to describe.[1] Women of eighteen nations agreed upon the Constitution and bye laws under which they will work. Before the meeting one wrote to the English secretary of the Hague Congress to enquire what precedents are available for international parliamentary law. He replied that there are none and that every contribution arrived at by the practically experimental work of any society is to be thank fully received.

There is urgent need of a short dictionary or vocabulary in twenty languages. Lucia Ames Mead, who was here, says it should be in 42 languages because there were so many countries represented at the Hague Conference.[2] She sent cordial regards to you.

I am filled with wonder how I could be cross to you once in Harzburg, once in Munich and once in Nürnberg. I remember each occasion with mortification; but it is almost worth while to suffer that for the sake of the fact that you have not, since you turned up in N.Y. on July 3d, said one word which I wish otherwise. That seems to me a sort of miracle!

The only thing I can think of by way of extenuation of my irascibility is that a person accustomed to work at high pressure for many years and suddenly subjected to complete idleness without—without muscular strength for great physical exertion to serve as an outlet for nervous energy—is under pretty heavy pressure.[3]

However, I think your summer has been enough glorified by Augusta's living and getting well,[4] to enable you to bear the memory of an occasional unjust onslaught from your loving

Mother

ALS, FKP, NN

1. FK attended the meeting of the ICW in Geneva on 1–5 September 1908. Founded in 1888 at a Washington, D.C., conference organized by Susan B. Anthony, Elizabeth Cady Stanton, and others to celebrate the fortieth anniversary of the Woman's Rights Convention at Seneca Falls, the ICW developed slowly, partly because its goal of bringing women together internationally was so general. However, at the 1904 meeting ICW delegates began to discuss woman suffrage, and the meeting that FK attended resolved to ask each national branch of the council "to draw up a report on existing unequal laws relating to the position of women, to be collated for submission to the various governments with a request for women's suffrage" (Lefaucheux, *Women in a Changing World,* 32). Delegates also discussed white slave traffic and double moral standards for men and women (*NYT:* 4 September 1908, 4; 6 September 1908, 3:3).

2. Lucia Ames Mead (1856–1936) was president of the Massachusetts Woman Suffrage Association from 1903 to 1909. She was a member of the Massachusetts consumers' league and was active in the American Peace Society. She wrote *Patriotism and the New Internationalism* (1906).

3. Details of FK's behavior abroad have not been recovered, but NK wrote his mother in September about his own propensity toward "irritating so much of the time the people I love best. . . . [W]hen it comes to really showing the spirit of lovingness I break down. And yet is not for want of loving the people" (NK, Mainz, Germany, to FK, 23 September 1908, KFP, NNC-RB).

4. Augusta's sister Lucy wrote NK on 27 June that Augusta was hospitalized in Bremer Haven, Germany, with typhoid fever. In September, Augusta wrote FK of her complete recovery: The doctor said "he would not have known me. I have gotten so thick" (Lucy Maverick to NK, 27 June 1908, FKP, NN; Augusta Maverick, Bremer Haven, to FK, 30 September 1908, FKP, NN).

109. To Nicholas Kelley

[Geneva, Switzerland]
Saturday noon, Sept. 26th '08

Darling Son

Your letters have come with delightful regularity but I observe with regret that, of the many which I have written, including a love letter to Augusta in Basel you seem to have received only a meager note sent to Strasburg.[1] This morning I forwarded in a yellow envelope addressed to the Kaiser Wilhelm II in care of the Lloyds in Bremen four letters which came together.

Marjorie Johnson,[2] Margaret's former roommate at Spring Green—Hillside School has come from London and is going to Lucern with me and thence to

Antwerp. So I shall be cherished almost as if it were you doing it. Is not this a lovely thing?

The conference has been one of extraordinary interest.[3] It has revealed social conditions more than all that I have read this summer. And it confirms my conviction that, although conditions are vastly better with us than they are here,—that is due to Nature and the wisdom of our ancestors. In our own Generation, we are squandering mercilessly the benefits which we have inherited. Never has this been so impressed upon me as now!

Do rest all that the conditions of the ship permit. The lifelong task that awaits you calls for steadiness and cool nerves. And don't blame yourself if your traveling sanitarium was not always a bed of roses for its factotum!

I am reaping now the benefit of the summer. This has been a hard pull. Long hours in bad air.

The amazing thing about the Conference is the diversity of people attending it. English, French, German, Italian, Spanish and Hungarian speakers besides ourselves the Swiss and one Russian have all been heard. Mr. Leroy Beaulieu (who is a transplanted Belgian whose mind seems to have run down in 1848); M. Raoul Jay and M. Le Comte d'Haussonville have been delightful.[4] They pay no attention whatever to the presiding officer but sit in their seats and talk to teach other across the audience. And what they say is so interesting that everyone listens breathless and votes as M. Raoul Jay wishes. The other two are old fogies and do not count.

A woman was here who has organized 6000 homeworkers in Germany!

Marjorie and are just starting to Les Coppet with the Conference. This evening there is a banquet and we take the ~~train~~ boat on Sunday morning at 6.00 for Montreux and thence the Bernese Oberland train for Lucern via Interlaken arriving in time for a conference tomorrow night.[5] If the weather is good (which it has been very little since you left) this should be one of the loveliest journeys possible. For Marjorie's sake, as well as my own, I hope it may be. I am indescribably touched by her coming in this way. She has sold her return ticket at a heavy loss in order to go with me on this jaunt to Lucern and Antwerp.

The nights have been so cold that I rejoiced to have my plaid, and the days are gray. So leaving Geneva is not so hard as it would have been a fortnight ago. With warmest love,

Your devoted old
F.K.

ALS, FKP, NN

1. NK's letters described a visit to a Basel picture gallery and a trip down the Rhine to Koblenz (NK, Strasbourg, Germany, to FK, 22 September 1908; NK, Koblenz, Germany, to FK, 24 September 1908, both in KFP, NNC-RB).

2. Marjorie Daw Johnson (ca. 1882–1975) was a resident at the Henry Street Settlement in the early 1900s and later a teacher of vocational education in Madison, Wisconsin (FK to Anne Geddes, [May 1927], Wald Papers, NNC-RB; Johnson, "Chickens to Moscow," 64).

3. The International Conference of Consumers' Leagues met in Geneva on 24–26 September 1908. Topics discussed were night work for women, homework, unions, labor law enforcement, an international label, and minimum wages. Maud Nathan, who also attended the conference, suggested there that minimum wage boards be established in the United States (NCL, Tenth Annual Report [1909], 32, Box A6, NCL Records, DLC; FK, "As Others See Us").

4. Anatole Beaulieu-Leroy (1842–1912) was a French publicist. Law professor Raoul Jay (1856–1921) was a founder in 1900 in Paris of the International Association for Labor Legislation. He was the author of *La protection légale des travailleurs* [Legal protection of workers] (1904) and *La limitation légale de la journée de travail en france. Rapport présenté à l'Association internationale pour la protection légale des travailleurs* [Legal limitations of the working day in France: Report presented to the International Association for Labor Legislation] (1906). Gabriel Paul Othenin de Cleron d'Haussonville (1843–1924) was a French legislator and writer.

5. FK was a delegate to the IALL meetings in Lucerne on 28–30 September. The conference planned to develop international standards for child labor and industrial workers' hours (Tenth Annual Report [1909], 35, Box A6, NCL Records, DLC; Commons, "The International Association for Labor Legislation"). In "As Others See Us," FK wrote about the development of sweatshop conditions in Europe produced by the demand in the United States for machine embroidery. She reported that European delegates to the meeting were skeptical about the ability of the United States to enforce its child labor laws (FK, "As Others See Us," 178–179).

110. To Nicholas Kelley

NATIONAL CONSUMERS' LEAGUE
OFFICE: 105 EAST 22D ST.
NEW YORK CITY

Nov. 7th 08

Darling Son,

Never was a windfall more welcome than the check in your letter of this morning![1] For I was embarrassed to borrow before I had repaid the summer loans. If my old League had only paid my October salary when due I need not have done it either! However, we are profiting, already, by returning prosperity.

Tomorrow I am to spend at Gaynes' Hill and shall ask pertinent questions about land etc. To-night I attend my first meeting of my local![2]

Governor Hughes has written to ask Miss Wald for suggestions for his legislative program![3] Miss [Lavinia] Dock and I are begging her to push for a recommendation of some extension of women suffrage. I think she will do it. But I do not know whether he will.

I do hope John stays much in the open. I think he should get his eyes fitted before he feels strain not after. It would be astonishing if he could do good academic work in the first week after his long time of living otherwise.[4]

I am feeling wonderfully spry despite arrears and the climate certainly wonderful.

Did you see the item from Denver? Judge Lindsey ran as an independent and had more votes than both his rivals. So many women scratched their ballots to vote for him that the presidential count was delayed and the Colorado returns could not be published until November 6th.[5] It was another indication of the significance of women's votes for the children!

Who will be President Eliot's successor?[6]

Your loving mother
F.K.

ALS, FKP, NN

1. NK had sent FK a check for $97.41 as the balance owed for his share of the expenses on the European trip and an earlier loan (NK to FK, 6 November 1908, KFP, NNC-RB).

2. FK was referring to the meeting of her socialist local. See Letter 111, FK to NK, 9 November 1908, below, for her reference to having joined "the party." The Socialist Party of America was founded in 1901 by Eugene V. Debs and others, who stressed the party's American identity in contrast to the Socialist Labor Party, which appealed primarily to immigrants. By 1908, the Socialist Party of America had "over 41,000 dues-paying members in over 3,000 locals" (Salvatore, *Eugene V. Debs,* 221).

3. Charles Evans Hughes was reelected governor on 2 November 1908, much to FK's satisfaction (FK to NK, [New York], 5 November 1908, FKP, NN).

4. JK had been admitted to Harvard in the fall of 1908 as a special student and was rooming with his brother. He did poorly his first semester and ultimately was placed on probation (NK, Cambridge, Mass., to FK, 17 October 1908; NK, Boston, Mass., to FK, 1 November 1908; JK, Cambridge, Mass., to FK, n.d., all in KFP, NNC-RB; Harvard University Archives Records).

5. As judge of the Juvenile and Family Court of Denver, Benjamin Lindsey (1869–1943) advocated reform of the juvenile penal system. In *Charities and the Commons* he recounted his successful election as juvenile court judge in 1904 "on account of the women voters" (Lindsey, "Judge Lindsey on Colorado Politics"). When he ran for governor of Colorado in 1908 as an independent, he came in third (*NYT,* 5 November 1908, 2). FK evidently was referring here to Lindsey's election in 1904.

6. Charles W. Eliot (1834–1926) was president of Harvard University from 1869 to 1909.

111. To Nicholas Kelley

105 E. 22nd St.
New York City
Nov. 9 '08

Darling Son,

That must be a wicked attempt at a merry test by C. Burlingham.[1] For no such rumor has reached my alert ear!

I spent yesterday afternoon with the Martins [John and Prestonia].[2] They "were not indignant["] at my joining the party—merely grieved in a friendly way. The Soc. vote here showed no gain since 1904. In Chicago it fell off about 20,000 as nearly as I can learn. No candidates here were elected.

I attended my first "local" meeting on Saturday night. Never have I seen forty such interesting men and women together without one dull face. Ernest Poole, and Charles Edward Russell, and Charlotte Teller represented the successful writers.[3] Only three foreign men and one woman,—all the rest three-generation Americans. It was very interesting. No one seemed at all cast down by the fact that the total gains in the whole country in four years seem to be only from 500 000 in 1904 to 600,000 in 1908.[4] More soon

Your loving Mother
F.K.

The enclosed came on Saturday and was answered instantly. No one knows how grateful I am to Augusta for getting so well.

ALS, FKP, NN

1. NK reported that his friend Charles Burlingham (1884–1979; B.A. Harvard 1906, L.L.B. Harvard 1908) had written that NK would be teaching in a girls' school the following year: "Is not that rather scandalous?" (NK, Boston, to FK, 8 November 1908, FKP, NN).
2. See Letter 86, FK to NK, 31 August 1906, above, for information about John and Prestonia Martin.
3. Ernest Poole (1880–1950) was a journalist and novelist; Charles Edward Russell (1860–1941) was an investigative journalist for the *Detroit Tribune* and the *New York World*; and Charlotte Teller (b. 1876) was a journalist, playwright, and suffragist who had written about German working women.
4. NK had inquired about the small Socialist vote: "Do you know the figures and the reason for them?" (NK, Boston, to FK, 8 November 1908, FKP, NN).

112. To Augusta Maverick Kelley

Oakland, Cal.
7-31-09

Dear Augusta

It was a very great pleasure to get your good letter this morning![1] There are so many amusing things happening here, all the time that it is impossible to begin to write them. And they are such farce comedy things. Never did I imagine that there were such queer folk in the world as crossed my vision in Washington. And Ko would have loved to be a fly on the door when I lectured to some hundred nuns in garb in the Catholic teachers' summer Institute, in the Christian Brothers' Business College, in Portland, with priests and Christian Brothers by scores—a regular co-educational occasion![2]

Tomorrow, I am to go to San Francisco for the first time since the earthquake.[3] I have an uncanny feeling about it tho' it is said to be far more substantial and beautiful than ever before.

Tell Ko that when I lectured in Hear[s]t Hall, Berkeley, last evening, his classmate Jack Lathrop came up and introduced himself and his wife.[4] They are a charming couple, and he is minister of the Unitarian church in Berkeley. I hope to meet him again on Sunday. Indeed, I am tempted to go to church for the purpose. But even without going to that extreme, they will probably be at a little tea that afternoon at the home of one of the professor's. I cannot express my thankfulness that you are not both settled here!

This is the Coast of the Cantankerous. Compared with the ferocity of the citizens of this coast towards each other and all Easterners, all the people I have ever known are gentle, friendly souls! I really long to get back to my gentle Jews.

It will be wonderfully fine to have you both within reach. Seven years without Ko was long slice out of a doting old mother's best years! However, having Ko and you, too, will soon make up for that!

I wonder whether Ko ever received a series of notes which I wrote him about a pleasant boarding place for the late summer, on Staten Isl—and at Fort Wadsworth.

Yours lovingly
F.K.

ALS, FKP, NN

1. Augusta Maverick and NK were married on 19 June 1909 in San Antonio. Although FK advised NK about who should be invited to the wedding and housing in New York, she did not attend the wedding (FK to NK, Cleveland, Ohio, 20 April 1909; FK, Warren, Ohio, to NK, 25 May 1909, both in FKP, NN). Four days before the wedding, FK wrote NK from Buffalo that she would be lecturing in New York on 18 June. "That evening you will, I suppose, be in San Antonio, bless you both!" She wrote again on the day before the wedding from New York, "I cannot help wishing that today John and I were with you, tho' I am quite sure that you are happy, this once, without us" (FK, Buffalo, N.Y., to NK, 15 June 1909; FK, New York, to NK, 18 June 1909, both in FKP, NN).

2. FK had been in the Northwest since 4 July, lecturing in Seattle and Portland. She spoke at the Catholic Institute on 22 July (NCL, Eleventh Annual Report [1910], 23, Box A6, NCL Records, DLC).

3. A major earthquake had devastated the city on 18 April 1906.

4. Hearst Hall was named for Phoebe Hearst, a major benefactor of the University of California who in 1897 became its first woman regent. Phoebe Hearst was the mother of newspaper magnate William Randolph Hearst. John Howland Lathrop (1880–1967; B.A. Harvard 1905), who had been influenced by FK when he was a Harvard undergraduate, became minister of the First Unitarian Church, Berkeley (1905–1911). As pastor of the First Unitarian Church in Brooklyn (1911–1957) he worked closely with FK. He married Lita Schlesinger in 1907.

113. To William Kent[1]

328 Grand Ave. Oakland, Cal.,[2]
8-4-09

My dear Mr. Kent

Thank you very much for the transportation, which I shall use with pleasure when it comes.[3] As a matter of current history, is it not true that bloodshed occurs chiefly in Russia, Turkey, Spain, South America and, in general, in those countries in which working people are not organized, as such, either in unions or in political parties? Are not the bloody outbreaks in our own country confined chiefly to the colonies of immigrants who have had,—at home and here,—little or no experience of either kind of organization? On the other hand, is it not conspicuously true that England and Germany, where both forms of organization have now reached the highest point known to history, are proverbially free from bloodshed? I put these statements as questions because I am honestly seeking light.

It seems to me that there is activity among social reformers far more in England and Germany than in countries where working people are unorganized. And surely Massachusetts, New York, Illinois, Ohio and Wisconsin have developed constructive reforms, and entered upon (sadly meagre) programs of industrial reform, just in proportion as the wage-earning voters have made their demands felt.

If more men of the educated class were taking the initiative as you are doing, the situation would be clearer. But you yourself are the strongest argument in favor of leaving the workers to their own devices and trying, in the future, to get things done by the beneficiaries of the present system towards changing it i.e. you, and Miss Addams and Mrs. [Olivia] Sage and the little band whose organ is the Survey.

But ten years' effort as secretary of the League is terribly discouraging. For there is a perfectly simple method of work, if only the moral zeal existed in middle class people. Trying to discover and organize that zeal is a task calculated to keep burning in the mind of anyone these questions for which your answers seem no more convincing than my own.

Yours sincerely
Florence Kelley

ALS, Kent Papers, CtY

1. FK probably knew William Kent (1864–1928) when he served on the Chicago City Council (1895–1897) and was active in civil service reform there. A political writer and U.S. congressman (Progressive Republican, California, 1911–1917), Kent was a leading conservationist and in 1907 donated to the federal government the tract that Theodore Roosevelt proclaimed Muir Woods National Monument one year later.

2. On 2 August 1909, FK met with the San Francisco Milk Commission. She later lectured in San Francisco and Oakland (NCL, Eleventh Annual Report [1910], 24, Box A6, NCL Records, DLC).

3. Railroad managers gave free passes to legislators and other politically prominent figures, who then passed them on to constituents. See Berge, *The Free Pass Bribery System.*

114. To Augusta Maverick Kelley

NATIONAL CONSUMERS' LEAGUE
OFFICE: 105 EAST 22D ST.
NEW YORK CITY

6-4-10

Dear Augusta

I hate to think of you as tired all the time, because I remember to this day how that felt after Ko came.

So I venture the following suggestions which you may take for what they are worth!

Nursing the boy[1] counts for about as much exertion—each time—as walking two miles when you are well, and entitles you to about as much rest on your back. This is what a Swiss gynaecologist told me, and I think it is a fair estimate. I mean that the drain on your vitality in supplying the milk is about like that$_x$

A well-fitted, soft, broad abdominal belt is the greatest possible comfort at the time and a great safeguard for the figure later on. If, when I was young, I had known what I know now, I should not be the shapeless old person you behold, and I should have escaped much suffering.

You cannot imagine what a joy it is for a hardworking old lady to acquire so dear a daughter and so charming a grandson.

Your loving old mother
F. Kelley

ALS, FKP, NN

1. Nicholas Kelley, Jr. ("Nicky") was born on 27 March 1910. He was FK's first grandchild.

115. To Nicholas Kelley

[Naskeag,] Brooklin, Hancock Co.,
Maine
7-9-10

Darling Son,

I have read the Promise[1] with very great interest and pleasure and with full agreement as to the main contention. There are, however, certain things which seem to be overlooked in all the consideration of international relations. Thus poverty is international. We are importing it by wholesale, but even if we were not doing that, our workers would be competing against it to their cost$_x$

Prostitution, too, is international and is inseparable from poverty$_x$ There are important treaties dealing ([vainly?]) with the white slave traffic. Most important of all, transportation and communication are international and finance has long been so with increasing completeness$_x$ Under these circumstances we are all obliged to think increasingly in terms of a federated world State. Otherwise the financiers will come de facto to represent in the life of the world the all-controlling, ungoverned element that they have long been in our own nation. Personally I believe that the coming struggle which may last throughout your lifetime and the baby's will be all hands against the financiers$_x$ They have won before our eyes in the case of the postal savings banks,[2] just as they have strangled the Russian revolution and are preparing the Enslavement of China. Keep your eye fixed on the international finances; and study our own State and national evolution always in its relation to that. In this one respect Mr. Croly's international idea seems to me inadequate$_x$ Nevertheless, I have not read so well thought out a book in many a long day.

I must go now and watch my neighbor chop out rotten plaster and wall-paper, with a view to throwing one end of my house into one big room with windows and glass doors on three sides and a fireplace on the fourth. It will look out south, west and north.

Your loving mother
F. Kelley

That was the outlook of the west room at Sakonnet$_x$
P.S. Tell Augusta, with my love, that she and my grandson are hereby invited for next summer from July 4th to any date in the Autumn to which she may care to stay. The farm is far lovelier than I remembered it$_x$ When next I go to Phila. I mean to add a codicil to my will specifically bequeathing the farm to little Nicholas.[3] At present I intend to occupy it for ninety years to come. But whenever I depart hence, it is to be his as a reward for coming so promptly among us and being so charming. Moreover the longer he has to wait for it, the better worth having it will become, both by reason of the growing trees and of the improved means of access.

Your loving Mother
F. K.

ALS, FKP, NN

1. Herbert David Croly (1869–1930) wrote *The Promise of American Life* (New York: Macmillan, 1909), an influential analysis of American political culture that called for a stronger central government as a means of preserving individual freedoms. Croly founded the *New Republic* in 1914, hoping to make it a voice for Progressive reform. In an earlier letter, FK argued that Croly "seems to me rather to miss the social need of the day, and greatly to underestimate the tempo at which we are moving politically. However, he may be more nearly right than I as to the latter point" (FK, Boston, to NK, ca. 1 July 1910, FKP, NN).

2. In June 1910, Congress passed legislation that enabled rural Americans to establish savings accounts at local post offices. Although the program had been promoted by agrarian interests for thirty-eight years, the bank lobby had opposed it. Postal savings accounts were limited to deposits of $500 and earned 2 percent interest (Schroedel and Snyder, "People's Banking,"

174, 192–193). NK agreed with FK that it was "the world against the financiers. My own small observation during the past year is that it is people with money who have power—more than governments, railroads or factories" (NK, New York, to FK, 13 July 1910, KFP, NNC-RB).

3. FK made her will on 6 June 1908, dividing her farm and savings equally between her sons. William R. Nicholson of Philadelphia, the Kelley family financial advisor, was named sole executor. NK replied, "What you say about Plans and the farm is very dear of you. I hope however [Nicky] will be your guest for many summers" (FK, New York, to NK, 6 June 1908, FKP, NN; NK to FK, 13 July 1910).

116. To Nicholas Kelley

Naskeag, [Brooklin,] Hancock Co., Maine
7-27-11

Darling Son,

Thank you very much for the reassurance as to the bad check. It is perfectly useless for me to make promises that I'll never do it again. I think I shall surely never again have the combination of a sick-and-absent clerk and John's wired demand. But who knows? [inserted in margin: I have sent a check to Miss Fleischmann[1] to be certified and forwarded to you.]

I fear you must suffer greatly from the heat! It is heavenly here. Nickie is as well and gay as can be, and Augusta looks more and more rested.[2] She is beautiful to see, and a joy to live with.

John has gained greatly. But he wakes us every night, talking in his sleep about the fire. He looks weary in the morning, has no power of sustained attention, and sleeps much of the day. However, he gains visibly.[3]

I am mulling over your conundrum about miscegenation and vice.[4] There is a fundament[al] consideration (under capitalism) which does not exist in the matter of miscegenation and does exist in the case of vice: i.e. the commercial gain from exploiting women derived by third parties, brothel keepers, physicians procurers, real estate owners and agents, brewers, distillers, saloon keepers etc.

This element in the evil has to be considered very seriously as forever stimulating wholesale, commercial vice. I cannot see that it comes in, at all, in the other case.

For the moment I have no further light upon your question.

Your grateful and loving old mother
F. Kelley

[They] are working on the L roof, Mr. Bradford[5] and Mr. Gott's brother, Prin Allen, Mr. Gott and the painter Henry Flye five in all. Work on my room is suspended pending the arrival of a particular kind of lumber. The chimney looks well, plastered.

ALS, FKP, NN

1. Marguerite C. Fleishman was FK's secretary for nine years (Fleishman, New York, to FK, 26 July 1918, FKP, NN; FK, Brooklin, Me., to NK, [July 1919?], FKP, NN).

2. Augusta and Nicky were still visiting on 6 August 1911 (FK, Naskeag, Me., to NK, 6 August 1911, FKP, NN.)

3. After two unsuccessful years at Harvard (1908–1910), JK worked at a gold mining camp in Porcupine, Ontario, from November 1910 until summer 1911. He wrote in June that his acquisition of one-third of two claims there "was a first class gamble." But even if he didn't succeed, he was "making a tremendously healthy living and that's more than I'd do in the city" (Harvard University Archives Records; JK, Porcupine, Ontario, to FK, 28 June 1911, KFP, NNC-RB). John had been greatly affected by the Great Porcupine Fire that killed 70 people and burned almost 500,000 acres of forest on 11 July 1911 ("Porcupine Fire").

4. NK had written: "What distinction do you make as to the wisdom of statutory suppression of miscegenation and of personal vice? If freedom and personal responsibility are the best, although perhaps imperfect, means of dealing with the undesirable tendency to miscegenation, why is not the same true in regard to personal vices?" (NK, Sea Gate, N.Y., to FK, 23 June 1911, FKP, NN). FK and NK were continuing a discussion begun in July 1910 of Croly's *The Promise of American Life* (see Letter 115, FK to NK, 9 July 1910, above). FK and NK would have known that Croly's mother was Jane Croly, author of *History of the Woman's Club Movement in America* (1898) and that Croly's father was David Goodman Croly, author of *Miscegenation: The Theory of the Blending of the Races* (1864), in which he called for racial amalgamation as the solution to the race problem in the United States, thereby challenging state laws that prohibited marriage between whites and African Americans. For the history of these laws, see Applebaum, "Miscegenation Statutes."

5. John C. Bradford, who lived nearby in Naskeag, was the caretaker for Seawest (Bradford, Naskeag, Me., to FK, 12 December 1911, FKP, NN).

117. To Jessica B. Peixotto[1]

COPY

[New York City]
April 15, 1912

Dr. Jessica B. Peixotto
Department of Economics
University of California
Berkeley, Cal.
Dear Miss Peixotto:—

The conditions you described exist in New York, Boston, Philadelphia, Cleveland, and Louisville, Kentucky,—five cities in which we have five of our best, most active and most useful Consumers' Leagues. In all these five cities, the Consumers' Leagues perform a function not performed by either the unions or the women's clubs. The Consumers' Leagues appeal continuously, year in and year out—twenty years in a stretch in the case of the older ones, to the purchasing public to do certain specific things.

A large part of that purchasing public is so violently opposed to the unions or, at best, so indifferent to them, that it would not respond to an appeal of the trade unions to do useful things which it promptly does when asked by the

Consumers' League. An example of this is the action of five thousand prosperous women in Philadelphia, who wrote personal letter two years in succession to the merchants of Philadelphia asking them to close their stores not later than 7 P.M. throughout the entire holiday season. In consequence of this personal effort, the shopping district of Philadelphia was dark and lonely after 7 P.M. throughout the Xmas season in both those years.[2]

The weakness of the activity of the unions in relation to the shopping public is the abiding hostility which they have called for, however unjustly, in the minds of tens of thousands shopping women. The weakness of the women's clubs, the whole country over, is their lack of continuity of effort.

An active Consumers' League can always co-operate with the unions in backing up a good law for the protection of working women and children. For instance, it would certainly be of value when next your legislature meets, if there were active Leagues all over the State ready to co-operate in promoting the creation of minimum wage boards, as the Consumers' League constituency in Massachusetts is doing this year.

The movement for minimum wage boards was first actively taken up by the Women's Trade Union League.[3] It seems likely to be carried to success in the near future chiefly by the efforts of a public commission and the Consumers' League constituency, the Women's Trade Union League being shaken to its foundation by inner dissension.[4]

CC, "General Correspondence: 'P,'" Box B20, NCL Records, DLC

1. Jessica Peixotto (1864–1941) received her Ph.D. from the University of California in 1900, the second doctorate that university gave to a woman. Founder and chair of the Heller Committee for Research in Social Economics, she primarily researched cost-of-living issues at the University of California at Berkeley. Peixotto was appointed to the California State Board of Charities and Corrections in 1912. She was on the CL of California's Board of Directors in 1911.

2. For example, Philadelphia department stores such as Wanamakers, Lit Brothers, and Snellenburgs closed at 6 P.M. during the Christmas season in 1910 (*Philadelphia Inquirer,* 15 December 1910, 5, 9, 16).

3. Minimum wage legislation was first proposed in the United States in 1908 by a network of women reformers in Boston affiliated with the Women's Educational and Industrial Union, the NWTUL, and the CL of Massachusetts. The NWTUL endorsed minimum wage legislation for women in 1909. Its initiative was modeled on that of the British WTUL, which, following the first minimum wage law enacted in 1896 for poorly paid workers in specific occupations in Victoria, Australia, endorsed minimum wage legislation for all poorly paid workers in British sweatshops (Robins, *Need of a National Training School for Women Organizers, the Minimum Wage, Industrial Education,* 3; see also Hart, *Bound by Our Constitution,* 24–28). Following up on Maud Nathan's recommendation at the Geneva conference in 1908 (see Letter 109, FK to NK, 26 September 1908, note 3, above), the NCL resolved that "the state and local leagues study the subject of wage boards with a view to a legislative campaign in 1910" (NCL, Tenth Annual Report [1909], 32, Box A6, NCL Records, DLC, 4).

4. In April 1912, the NWTUL split into two groups. One remained loyal to the AFL and craft unionism; another, including Mary Kenny O'Sullivan, supported industrial unionism and the striking women who joined the IWW during a prolonged textile strike in Lawrence, Massachusetts. See Dye, *As Equals and As Sisters,* 105.

118. To Nicholas Kelley

NATIONAL CONSUMERS' LEAGUE
OFFICE: 106 EAST 19TH ST.
NEW YORK CITY

Naskeag, [Brooklin,] Hancock Co., Me.
8-4-12

Darling Son

All the noble lawyers except Mr. [Louis] Brandeis, who have offered at various times to do legal work for us have shirked miserably on the rare occasions on which we have asked them to do any little thing, even to redrafting the form of our contract$_x$

The enclosed comes so close home—and is so nasty—that I do not wish to bother with any of them and I venture, therefore, to ask your opinion about it.[1]

The Amer. Food Jour. is a decent looking magazine subsidized by the glucose and borax interests, though I do not know exactly how we could prove this statement in Court.[2] It is a matter of common knowledge.

It opened fire on us two years ago last April, writing to all the Advisory Board to ask whether they had ever been asked to advise. A number answered that they had. Others approved of us and said they stood ready if asked.[3] Two fell down—Dr. Lederle[4] (who was incidentally revealed as bacteriologist to the rectifiers), and a Taft politician in Washington who proved to be in the pay of Borax. These traitors furnished to the enemy all the ammunition it has ever had. Both resigned from our Advisory Board and their resignations were accepted.

I have, of course, no idea of engaging in an editorial Contest in the Columns of Barrels and Bottles![5] It is the organ of the brewers who happen to wish for honest labeling and secured, with vigorous help from us, a decision favorable to the labeling of beer with all the constituents named in the label.

It seems to me, however, to be a case for a prayer to be delivered from our editorial friends.

The League is desperately poor.[6] My salary is in arrears. Only a screaming success could justify the expense involved in a libel suit.

The Amer. Food Journal has, hitherto, commanded a limited but decidedly influential reading public among club women. How far it can injure us with them no one can guess.

Polly [Marianna Parrish Kelley] has just arrived for a week. She is sleeping above stairs. Miss [Elizabeth H.] Houghton comes tomorrow night.

Your loving Mother
F.K.

ALS, FKP, NN

1. NK was practicing law at the firm of Cravath, Henderson and de Gersdorff in New York City.

2. The *American Food Journal,* published in Chicago, was edited by Herman B. Meyers. It had for many months attacked Harvey W. Wiley for his stringent enforcement of the Pure Food and Drug Act (see Letter 90, FK to Caroline B. Crane, 21 January 1907, above). In its 15 June 1912 issue, the *Journal* called the NCL a "fraudulent American organization, which represents no consumers" and had as its "principal occupation" the defense of Wiley ("The Parting Shot," 20; "Consumers' Leagues in Germany and America," 52).

3. The following month the *American Food Journal* reported on its correspondence with the NCL's "advisory board." According to the *Journal,* some members replied that they had been "asked to act as detectives and report suspicious foods." The article, which was wildly inaccurate in most of its assumptions and statements, was written to prove the proposition that the NCL was not a "genuine, *bona fide* organization" ("Whistling in the Dark," 73).

4. Chemist Ernst Joseph Lederle (1865–1921) was president and commissioner of the Department of Health of New York (1910–1914). The NCL's Council may be the organization that the *Journal* and FK referred to as the "advisory board." However, Lederle's name does not appear on any of the NCL committees in the organization's minutes; apparently he served for only a short time (NCL, Fourteenth Annual Report [1913], Box A6, NCL Records, DLC).

5. *Barrels and Bottles,* a monthly publication devoted to the interests of the retail liquor dealer, was published in Indianapolis.

6. At the end of 1911, the NCL had a balance of $412.08 (NCL, Thirteenth Annual Report [1912], 48, Box A6, NCL Records, DLC).

119. To Katherine Philips Edson[1]

NATIONAL CONSUMERS' LEAGUE
OFFICE: 106 EAST 19TH ST.
NEW YORK CITY

November 22, 1912

Mrs. Charles Farwell Edson
950 West 20th Street
Los Angeles, Cal.
Dear Mrs. Edson:—

Thank you for your inspiring volume! I am taking your questions in their order.

It is the best possible news that you are special agent in the Bureau of Labor Statistics. That rejoices my heart. Long may you stay!

The National Consumers' League is preparing a brief for use before the Supreme Court of the United States in support of the short working day in two cases arising, one in California and one in Ohio.[2] You doubtless know about the California case. Please keep us posted as to every item that you can learn about it.

It is our settled policy to recommend the extension of every law restricting working hours to the greatest possible number of industries. You cannot begin too soon to make the fight to extend the labor law to cover canneries, offices of all kinds, including telephone service, etc. Be sure we shall back you before the courts in every way possible.

Now as to minimum wage boards. I am sending you everything we have on the subject. The forthcoming issue of the Chicago University Journal of Political Economy will contain articles by Sidney Webb on minimum wage boards in England, and by myself on minimum wage board laws in the United States.[3] You may find these of service.

The Massachusetts law is bad in principle and self-stultifying in form.[4] It is restricted to women and children where it should apply to everybody, and it contains two ruinous clauses: one for the worst possible kind of court review, and one providing advertising so expensive as to be ruinous to the Commission at the outset.[5]

The Ohio constitutional amendment, on the other hand, applies to everybody and does everything which a state can do to assure to the law passed by the future legislature that the state courts shall not annul it.[6]

I will send you everything we can find on the subject, as fast as we find it. This is the reform which is nearest my heart this year, and I am delighted that you are working at it.[7]

Yours sincerely,
Florence Kelley

TLS, Edson Papers, CLU-SC

1. Katherine Edson was one of FK's most capable allies in what became one of her most successful campaigns—the enactment and enforcement of state minimum wage legislation.

2. These statues did not come before the Supreme Court. For the California law of 1911, see Beyer, *History of Labor Legislation for Women in Three States,* 122–125. For Ohio, see Brandeis, "Labor Legislation," 3:476.

3. In "The Economic Theory of a Legal Minimum Wage," Sidney Webb praised the success of minimum wage laws in all types of industry in Victoria, Canada, and argued for its establishment throughout Great Britain. "[T]o the economist," wrote Webb, "the enforcement of a Legal Minimum Wage appears but as the latest of the long series of Common Rules, which experience has proved to be (a) necessary to prevent national degradation; and (b) positively advantageous to industrial efficiency" (Webb "The Economic Theory of a Legal Minimum Wage," 989). In "Minimum-Wage Laws," FK stressed the need for minimum wage boards. For twenty years, the CL of New York City had tried "investigation, persuasion, and voluntary effort to the establishment of a living wage" before settling on the efficacy of these boards. They would "enlist in the difficult task of determining wages in certain subnormal industries the employers, the workers, and representatives of the consuming public; to bring to bear in each instance all the technical knowledge of the three sets of people richest in experience of the local details in that particular industry" (FK, "Minimum-Wage Laws," 1006–1007). See also Sklar, "Two Political Cultures in the Progressive Era."

4. FK's article criticized the recently enacted (4 June 1912) Massachusetts minimum wage law, which she feared would set a precedent for other states that was too weak. She argued that minimum wage laws should apply to both men and women because "the work and wages of men and women . . . interlock so closely that studies of the pay of women with the view to ascertaining what constitutes a living wage for them will entail turning the light upon men's

wage rates in the same industries." The Massachusetts law allowed an employer to protest to state courts that his business would be curtailed if he complied with the law; the court could then "revoke the decree" (FK, "Minimum-Wage Laws," 1003).

5. The Minimum Wage Commission of Massachusetts was required to publish all transgressions of the law in at least four newspapers in every Massachusetts county (FK, "Minimum-Wage Laws," 1001).

6. On 3 September 1912, voters approved a constitutional amendment in Ohio that gave the state legislature the power to pass laws "regulating the hours of labor, establishing a minimum wage, and providing for the comfort, health safety and general welfare of all employes." Kelley hoped that Ohio's enabling amendment would lead the way for wage laws for men and women because it included a clause that declared that "no other provision of the constitution shall impair or limit this power." She thought that any Ohio court that tried to void a minimum wage law "must find its basis of rejection in the constitution of the United States, not in the constitution of Ohio" (*NYT,* 4 September 1912, 1; FK, "Minimum-Wage Laws," 1004). But because the Ohio AFL opposed minimum wage laws for men, the enabling constitutional amendment did not lead to minimum wage legislation for either women or men until 1933, when the state legislature passed a minimum wage law for women and children (Brito, "Protective Legislation in Ohio," 174). The CL of Ohio did not sponsor a minimum wage bill until 1921 (Harrison, "The Consumers' League of Ohio," 41). The amendment to the Ohio Constitution is available at www.legislature.state.oh.us/constitution.

7. Edson developed a minimum wage bill for women that the California legislature enacted in 1913 (Braitman, "A California Stateswoman").

120. To John Graham Brooks

Permanent address including Sept. 20th
American Co., 11 rue Scribe, Paris
8-13-13[1]

Dear Mr. Brooks

May I try to express the keen and sustained pleasure which I found in reading your Syndicalism[2] from cover to cover in two days of travel from Portland Oregon to Corvallis (the Oregon State Agricultural College), and Eugene, the State University? It seems to me to be the one sane and useful publication on the subject in America!

Incidentally, the I.W.W. were behaving like Satan in Portland while I was there, July 12th to 19th. Two of their leaders were a Mr. Schwab, son of the Chicago Anarchist whose sentence was commuted by Governor Altgeld, and Dr. Equi a daughter of one of Garibaldi's thousand.[3] Anarchy has become hereditary from generation to generation among the immigrants and their children! I came home from the Pacific Coast and the Conference of Charities an active restrictionist! My only difficulty is this practical one:—It is obvious that every nation profits by welcoming the victims of religious persecution (Huguenots, Waldnesians, Pilgrims, Puritans, Quakers, even Mennonites, [Dakohortzi?] and Jews). But exactly how can we technically draw the line so as to admit the Russian Jews yet exclude the Catholic Slavs?

One thing we could surely do viz: provide that no girl under 21 years should come unless accompanied by older members of her family. Never in all history was any thing more cruel than what we do about young immigrant girls.

Surely our Yankee ingenuity ought to enable us to draw the difficult exclusion line above suggested. I am convinced that the Pacific Coast people are right about the Mongolians; and I am sure we are utter fools to endure the ruin of the Atlantic Coast by the invasion of Asia Minor and South Eastern Europe.

My record of twenty-one years of intimate contact with the immigrants should safeguard me against any charge of race or religious prejudice in this.

We are infinitely cruel to the immigrants themselves in Lawrence, Little Falls, Pittsburg, Chicago and the East Side, to say nothing of all the mines!

Your book confirmed my impression that we are all on the wrong track until we draw a sharp line between kinds of immigrants, actively enforcing our claim to select whom we will henceforth admit.

Do, please, publish a book on "Which brothers do we henceforth adopt into our family?"

Yours sincerely
Florence Kelley

ALS, Brooks Papers, MCR-S

1. FK sailed for Europe around 28 July 1913 to rest, write, and attend meetings of the IALL in Basel (9–10 September) and the International Conference of Consumers' Leagues in Antwerp (26–28 September) (NCL, *Fourteenth Annual Report* [1913], 17–19, Box A6, NCL Records, DLC).

2. Brooks's *American Syndicalism: The I. W. W.* (New York: Macmillan, 1913) examined the historical roots and future potential of the IWW. Founded in Chicago in 1905, it expanded from its work with western miners to a central role in the 1912 strike of textile workers in Lawrence, Massachusetts, when it claimed a national membership of 100,000. The IWW's threat to Progressive reform lay in its critique of the state as an instrument of oppression and its willingness to endorse violence as a means of establishing organized workers' control of the means of production. Christian socialists such as Brooks and reform socialists such as Kelley worried that the IWW's growing influence would undermine their incremental gains. As Brooks insisted, "If the wage earners are to get possession of the mills, as is the dream of the I.W.W., by no conceivable means will they get them except by decades of positive and coöperative work with those who now own and direct the invested capital which these mills represent. Never will they get them by the waste, the negations, and evil habits which sabotage begets" (157). Nevertheless, Brooks concluded that the IWW "should continue as one among other prodding annoyances that leave society without peace until it dedicates far more unselfish thought and strength to avoidable diseases like unmerited poverty, unemployment, grotesque inequalities in wealth possession, the forced prostitution of underpaid women, and our fatuous brutalities in dealing with crime" (214; italics in original).

3. Women struck at the Oregon Packing Company plant in Portland over low wages and unsanitary working conditions in June 1913. During testimony at the Portland City Hall, Dr. Marie Equi said she was "willing to shed her blood on the picket line." IWW agitators Dr. Equi and Rudolph Schwab were jailed, the latter for making threats against Portland's sheriff. By 18 July, the riots had subsided and most IWW members had been arrested (*Oregon Journal:* 12 July 1913, 2; 17 July 1913, 11; 18 July 1913, 1; and 19 July 1913, 1–2).

121. To Nicholas Kelley

Rheinfelden, [Switzerland]
9-13-13

Darling Son

Your letter and Gusta's came.[1] I am proud of my perspicacity in having inferred what happened as to the stamps.

The Berlin police have warned the Socialists that Van der [Tui]ssen and Huysmanns (both members of the Belgian Socialist party and Parliament) would be expelled if they attempted to address a small meeting of the heads of the German party which was to have been held yesterday, to go all over the procedure of the Belgians in preparation for their successful mass strike.[2]

The meeting was held but addressed by Germans instead of Belgians. It was in preparation for the Parteitag which opens tomorrow at Jena.[3]

The development within the Party in five years is most interesting. Besides all the political activities, there is now co-operative traveling, co-operative drama, and a deliberate attempt to outbid the Y.M.C.A. in the care of the young. Germans under 25 yrs do not vote and cannot attend political meetings until they are 18 years old.

I can hardly wait to get home to tell you about it,—it is all wonderful.

Women vote in all the ramifications of insurance administration. The Catholics use every endeavor to get their women out. They stultify, in the process, every possible opposition of their own to farther woman suffrage. Vorwärts is out now for the extension of the Reichstag suffrage to the Prussian Landtag.[4] This definitely throws the women overboard—Austria, Belgium and now Germany.[5] I suppose it is historically inevitable. But I'm mighty glad I live in America!

The experts of the various Countries meet next week, in Berne, to draft the International Treaty which will be signed by the ambassadors, in 1914, establishing the ten hours day for women throughout Europe—in factories only.[6]

Our Conference, last Tuesday and Wednesday, in Basel was most interesting. It was preparing for a treaty of 1916 on child labor. Millerand was there from France, and Herr Gaspar, head of the German Labor Department, and a former President of the Republic of Switzerland presided.[7]

The City of Basel gave us a fine banquet with the Burgomeister present, and toast by M. Millerand. Dr. Bauer says M. will be back in the Ministry inside of five years, and nothing will be done for Labor in France until then.

I carried a point against Herr Gaspar of which I am proud, especially as I was only an invited expert, and not a delegate! I'll tell you about it.

I'm afraid the return to town must have been trying for you!

Your loving Mother
F. Kelley

ALS, FKP, NN

1. One week later, NK wrote news of his family, who were vacationing at Little Compton, Rhode Island. He closed his letter with this tribute to FK: "There is nobody at all like you in the world. I am so proud of being your son I do not know what to do. But at the same time it makes me feel dreadfully second-rate. I am always hoping that I will speed up and improve, but I do not seem to do it" (NK, Little Compton, R.I., to FK, 20 August 1913, FKP, NN).

2. The German socialist national convention, or Parteitag, met in Jena to consider a general strike along the lines of a successful strike in Belgium in April 1913 (*NYT,* 15 September 1913, 4). Camille Huysmans (1871–1968) was a member of the Belgian House of Representatives (1910–1925) and secretary of the Second International (1905–1922).

3. The convention voted against a strike (*NYT,* 17 September 1913, 4).

4. *Vorwärts* was the official publication of the German Social Democratic Party.

5. Germany was a monarchy, or Kaiserreich, in which voting rights for the Reichtag were distinct from that of regional parliaments like the Prussian Landtag. Legally prohibited from holding public meetings until 1890, the SPD considered woman suffrage secondary to extending male voting rights in regional parliaments. Although women were prohibited from taking part in political meetings in Germany until 1908, their numbers and militancy within the SPD grew dramatically thereafter, and by 1913 they overflowed into unauthorized street demonstrations, which one frightened party leader said were "like a black snake" (Evans, *Comrades and Sisters,* 66–90).

6. From shipboard, FK wrote NK of her plan to "plant" in the mind of IALL secretary Dr. Stephen Bauer of Basel (1865–1934) certain "seed thoughts" before the ambassadors' meeting in Berne about the need to prohibit labor for all children under fourteen. Later she wrote how the United States had made a good "showing" at this meeting because thirty states limited women's workday to ten hours or less (FK to NK, 31 July 1913; FK, Rheinfelden, Switzerland, to NK, 7 September 1913, both in FKP, NN).

7. In an unsigned article, FK reported on the IALL meeting, beginning, "After all, America is not so far behind Europe in labor legislation." A major cause of lagging child labor laws in Europe was "the contract work of Italian children in Germany and France," which she thought resembled the difficulty of regulating child labor "among children of immigrants" in the United States. She thought the most challenging resolution for the United States was one that declared that "[i]nspection in respect to child labor should be strictly carried out and special statistics kept of contraventions of the law for the protection of children" ([FK], "International Commission on Child Labor Laws," 86). Alexandre Millerand (1859–1943), socialist member of the French Chamber of Deputies and minister of public works (1909–1910), minister of war (1912–1913, 1914–1915), and prime minister (1920), was president of France from 1920 to 1924.

122. To Katherine Philips Edson

NATIONAL CONSUMERS' LEAGUE
OFFICE: 106 EAST 19TH ST.
NEW YORK CITY

April 16, 1914

Mrs. Charles Farwell Edson
812 Higgins Building
Los Angeles, Cal.
Dear Mrs. Edson:-

The reason Miss Wald has been so slow to answer your question about the nursing is this: she does not wish to do anything to interfere with a shorter working day for the nurses, but she has had grave fears that their training in surgery and obstetrics would inevitably be hampered by the establishment of a fixed eight hours day.[1] What I am telling you now is the result of a conversation, and is not to be quoted until she gets to the point of writing you herself. I am saying this because I do not wish you to think her negligent, when she is only over-conscientious.

I am taking your other questions one by one.

It was, alas, not possible for me to read your paper because I was at the Alumnae Convention for only one session, from 8 to 9:30 last evening, returning to New York on the ten o'clock train, and getting to bed at two in the morning.[2] I have put your paper into the hands of Miss Vida Hunt Francis, and you will doubtless hear from her about it.[3]

About Miss [Lavinia] Dock. She is a literary person, in the sense that she writes admirably. She is, however, one of the most practical administrative persons in the whole history of nursing. She was for years the assistant head of the Johns Hopkins Training School for Nurses, and head of the Cook County Hospital Training School in Chicago. Her opinion should be received as authoritative, if that of anyone living is to be so received.

I wish I were competent to write you fully on the question whether apprentices should be paid less than the living wage. That is done under the wage boards of Australia and England, and is quite sure to be done in the earliest decisions in Massachusetts. The whole theory in Australia, England and Massachusetts is that the determinations must begin with industry as it is, with long warning that from year to year the standard will be screwed up. The Oregon view, as you doubtless know, is the opposite to this: that from the start a living for the employes must be a primary charge, and industries unable promptly to meet that charge must move elsewhere. They do not say this in so many words, but this is the net result of the decision.[4]

As to my health. I am still avoiding red meat and coffee. But the alarming symptoms, my puffy ankles, disappeared when I found a shoemaker who raised my broken arches, and enabled me to run about the surface of the earth as I have not run for two years. So far as I am able to judge, I am in better health now than I have been in nine years.

I wonder whether it is a shoemaker what you need! Nobody knows but you that I am the most systematic rester in the field of social work. I wish I could teach you that trick!

Yours sincerely and gratefully,
Florence Kelley

ALS, Edson Papers, CLU-SC

1. As a member of California's Industrial Welfare Commission, Edson was responsible for enforcing the state's new hours law. Edson's question about nursing was almost certainly related to her report on the recent (and controversial) decision of the U.S. Court of Appeals, which upheld the eight-hour law for student nurses in California (Edson, "Student Nurses and the Eight-Hour Law in California"). Nurses posed a special problem because they were required to work long hours to provide patients with consistent care, but the leading authority

on nurses' hours, nursing educator Mary Adelaide Nutting of Columbia Teachers College, had called for an eight-hour day as early as 1900.

2. The biennial convention of the Association of Collegiate Alumnae was held in Philadelphia in 1914 (*Journal of the Association of Collegiate Alumnae* 7 [1914]: 77).

3. Vida Hunt Francis (1870–1957) was a member of the executive board of the CL of Philadelphia and of the NCLC of Pennsylvania.

4. On 23 April 1914, in *Simpson v. O'Hara,* the Oregon Supreme Court upheld the state's minimum wage law for women in factories. When the decision was appealed to the U.S. Supreme Court in 1917, an evenly divided court allowed the law to continue. FK had analyzed recent minimum wage legislation in "The Case for the Minimum Wage."

123. To Alva Smith Vanderbilt Belmont[1]

Naskeag, [Brooklin,] Hancock Co. Me.
7-19-14

My dear Mrs. Belmont

Your very kind letter of July 15th reaches me to-day. It must have crossed one from me in which I tried to express a little of the pleasure I felt in having a share in the delightful meeting on July 8th.[2]

No one could fail to feel at the time that the audience was receptive and responsive. The editorials which have come to me from many parts of the country show the press to have been respectful and largely sympathetic.

You must surely feel great satisfaction in having helped, on a nationwide scale, in this summer when seven states are on the verge of definite action.

I am quite hopeless of expressing my appreciation of your thoughtful provision for the comfort of the speakers, and our continuing enjoyment of our visit to Newport.

In connection with the enclosed clipping, the Duchess of Marlborough[3] may be interested to know that forty of our forty eight states fix the age for beginning to work in mills at fourteen years. Four of the remaining eight have no mills,—Wyoming, Idaho, New Mexico and Nevada.

But the remaining four are great cotton manufacturing states in which children are employed, day and night, so cruelly young and so murderously long, that it is as if we were not a civilized nation.[4]

The most unwearied efforts, continued throughout many years, have thus far accomplished almost nothing for these particular children. I believe that international agitation is needed, and I have long advocated federal action, shutting the products of their labor out of interstate commerce.

The plight of our toiling children is the goad which spurs me on when suffrage work seems discouraging, because the old methods have so sadly failed to help the children.

Yours sincerely and gratefully
Florence Kelley

ALS, Group II: Box 191, NWP Records, DLC. Also available in Pardo, *National Woman's Party Papers, 1913–1974,* Reel 1.

1. Suffrage leader and socialite Alva Smith Vanderbilt Belmont (1853–1933) was the widow of Oliver H. P. Belmont and president of the Political Equality Association of New York. Born in Alabama to a family that backed the Confederacy, she was educated in France and moved with her mother and sister to New York City in the early 1870s, where they successfully sought acceptance in the social elite. In 1875, she married William Vanderbilt, grandson of railroad baron Cornelius Vanderbilt, whom she divorced in 1895 with a settlement that provided her with an income of $100,000 a year and a mansion in Newport, Rhode Island. In 1896 she married Oliver Belmont, son of a wealthy banker, and after his death in 1908 gave her attention and a considerable amount of her fortune to the suffrage movement (Geidel, "Alva E. Belmont").

2. On 8 July 1914, Belmont hosted a conference of women suffrage leaders from across the United States at her Newport mansion. She collected 500 prominent suffragists (including a few men) from all walks of life, including society women, women government officials, judges, educators, labor leaders, and reformers. The event was a media extravaganza, complete with a brass band; Belmont charged spectators $2 to enter the grounds, where they could hope for a glimpse of her daughter, the Duchess of Marlborough, or buy suffrage pencils, fans, and other paraphernalia. Women speakers, including a Chicago judge and a Colorado state senator, stressed the need for suffrage and the improvement of women's working conditions. Belmont gave a dinner for the conference speakers, including FK, on the evening of 7 July (*NYT*: 8 July 1914, 9; 9 July 1914, 7; Geidel, "Alva Belmont," 504–510).

3. Belmont's daughter, Consuelo Vanderbilt (1877–1964), married Charles Spencer-Churchill, ninth Duke of Marlborough, in 1895. The duchess, a featured speaker at the conference, spoke of her work in England to obtain better housing for working women and prisoners' families (*NYT*, 9 July 1914, 7). See also Stuart, *Consuelo and Alva Vanderbilt*, 343–346.

4. It was legal for children above the age of twelve to work in textile mills in the states of Mississippi, North Carolina, South Carolina, and Virginia (Sumner, *Child Labor Legislation in the United States*, 29–99).

124. To Joel Spingarn[1]

Naskeag, [Brooklin,] Hancock Co., Me.
7-27-14

Dear Mr. Spingarn

I do not know when the next board meeting will be.[2] I cannot be in N.Y. until after Labor Day. Whenever I can attend a meeting I hope to bring up the subject of juvenile Court work.

One of my Colleagues in the C. League, Jean Gordon, of New Orleans, has written frank reproaches for the Gainer Brown article, saying that the Women's Club of Memphis should have been appealed to.[3] But why? What have they ever done to deserve it?

Yours sincerely
Florence Kelley

ALS, Joel Spingarn Papers, DHU-MS

1. Joel Spingarn (1875–1939) and his brother Arthur (1878–1971) were independently wealthy from their father's tobacco interests. Descended from Austrian Jews who migrated to the United States in the 1840s, they viewed their lifelong involvement with the NAACP as con-

sistent with their identity as members of an ethnic minority. Joel joined the NAACP in November 1910 and immediately became one of its most active members, serving as chair of its Board of Directors from 1914 to 1919, as treasurer from 1919 to 1930, and as president from 1930 to 1939 (Ross, *J. E. Spingarn and the Rise of the NAACP*, 21, 69, 110; see also Carle, "Race, Class and Legal Ethics in the Early NAACP").

2. FK participated in the series of meetings that led to the founding of the NAACP in 1909. The initial call was issued on 12 February 1909 by Mary White Ovington and others. Ovington, the only white member of Niagara Movement through which W. E. B. Du Bois sought to establish an organizational alternative to Booker T. Washington's program of vocational education as a means of improving the lives of African Americans, was affiliated with the Greenwich House settlement. The 1909 meetings began with an informal reception at the Henry Street Settlement on 30 May. Over the next days they meet at the Charities Building. FK served on the NAACP's Board of Directors from its incorporation in 1912 until her death (Walling, "The Founding of the N.A.A.C.P.," 226; Ovington, *How the National Association for the Advancement of Colored People Began*; Lewis, *W. E. B. Du Bois*, 391–394).

3. Jean M. Gordon (1865–1932) was a factory inspector in New Orleans (1907–1911), a vice-president of the NCL (1909–1911), and NCL secretary for the southern states (1912–1913). She was also president of the Louisiana Woman Suffrage Association (1913–1920). Gordon was reacting to FK's June 1914 *Survey* article, "A Burglar Four Years Old in the Memphis Juvenile Court," which used the example of a four-year-old African American orphan named Gainer to criticize the segregated treatment of juvenile delinquents in Memphis. Photographs of the fine juvenile court building for white juveniles and the shabby structure for the black juveniles accompanied the article. FK praised the "strenuous effort of the Memphis colored women's clubs" to find a better site for the juvenile court for black children (319).

125. To Paul Kellogg

NATIONAL CONSUMERS' LEAGUE
OFFICE: 106 E. 19TH ST.
NEW YORK CITY

[Chicago]
10-18-14

Dear Mr. Kellogg

Until yesterday Peace has been farthest from my mind which has been harried by a deficit and a quarterly meeting. The deficit is decently reduced,[1] and the Quarterly meeting fortunately over. So on the train to Chicago yesterday I read your letter and the minutes of the meeting at 265 Henry Street.[2]

Today I am lunching with Mary Smith and Alice Hamilton and going over the text with them and will send the commented text to Miss Addams direct from here.

Personally I am for concentrating on Hamilton Holt's scheme and not publishing anything else.[3]

Yours Always
F. Kelley

ALS, Kellogg Papers, MnU-SW

Paul Kellogg, ca. 1925. Courtesy of the Paul Kellogg Papers, Social Welfare History Archives, University of Minnesota Libraries.

1. On 30 September 1914, the NCL had a balance of $245.68 (NCL, Annual Report for 1914–1916, 42–43, Box A6, NCL Records, DLC).

2. On 19 August, President Woodrow Wilson (1856–1924) issued a proclamation of U.S. neutrality after Germany declared war on Russia, France, and Great Britain. Twenty social activists, including JA, Emily Balch, FK, Paul Kellogg, and Lillian Wald, met at the Henry Street Settlement to consider a reaction to the European war, fearing the outbreak would threaten their social reform program. Historian C. Roland Marchand described this group's search for peace "as integrally connected with the advance of liberal or radical social and political programs at home" (Marchand, *The American Peace Movement and Social Reform,* 228; see also 225–232).

3. Hamilton Holt (1872–1951), who also attended the Henry Street meeting, was editor of the *Independent* (1913–1921) and in 1910 had founded the World Federation League. Holt proposed a world organization that advocated disarmament and sought to establish a set of international rules for all countries (*NYT,* 31 December 1914, 4).

126. To Paul Kellogg

6 W. 39th St., N.Y.
Lincoln's Birthday [February 12, 1915]

Dear Mr. Kellogg

I have read the enclosed and marked some trifling suggestions.[1]

But I cannot sign the appeal. It seems to me like the three Tailors of Tooley Street.[2]

During our own Civil War, if some English Quakers had addressed such an appeal to the American people we should all, both North and South, have hooted them, I think.

I cannot see that we have any mandate to speak for the neutral nations.[3] They may regard our so doing as an impertinence. On the other hand, What War has Done and is Doing seems to me extraordinarily fine.[4] If we could make that the basis of an appeal to the President to call a Conference of Neutral Nations; or an appeal to the Neutral Nations to form Hamilton Holt's League of Peace that would seem to me to have significance.[5]

I dislike the whole litany concept.[6] Certainly self-respecting people can address a litany only to the Almighty, not to millions of madmen butchering each other.

I cannot tell you how I hate not to be one of the signers. But I cannot expect to change everybody's opinion about the beseeching, and I cannot personally participate in the church services which beseech the Almighty.

Yours in much perplexity
F. Kelley[7]

Don't you think you ought to bring a libel suit against Pearson's? Their article seems to me to be clearly criminal libel.[8]
F.K.

ALS, Kellogg Papers, MnU-SW

1. Members of the group who met at Henry Street in September 1914 circulated a draft of "Towards the Peace That Shall Last," which outlined how war threatened social justice goals (Marchand, *The American Peace Movement and Social Reform*, 234–238). The manifesto was published in a special unpaginated section of *Survey* 33 (6 March 1915).
2. A traditional English rhyme referred to poor tailors of Tooley Street who grandiosely called themselves "We, the People of England."
3. The *Survey* insert asserted the rights of neutral nations to protest the war.
4. This section of the manifesto protested the blights, injuries, wrongs, and evils of war.
5. Holt continued to advocate a league of at least four major powers that would maintain peace; he also proposed that the league maintain an armed force greater than that of any country outside the league. His hope was that most nations would join the league so that the only force necessary would be an international police operation (*NYT*, 16 February 1915, 5).
6. FK was referring to the statement's repetitious use of "It has . . ." to describe the evils of war: for example, "IT HAS THREATENED the results of a hundred martyrdoms and revolutions and put in jeopardy those free governments which make possible still newer social conquests. IT HAS CRUSHED under iron heels the uprisings of civilization itself."
7. Ultimately, FK joined JA, Emily Balch, Holt, Kellogg, and others and signed the appeal, expressing "our duty to break silence and voice convictions" ("Towards the Peace That Shall Last").
8. In "How 'Tainted' Money Taints," George Creel had accused Kellogg and *Survey* of being tainted by Rockefeller Foundation money. Although *Survey* had been independent from the Charity Organization Society since 1912, before that date it and its antecedents—*Charities Review* (1891–1897), *Charities* (1897–1905), and *Charities and the Commons* (1905–1909)—were published by the Charity Organization Society, which did receive Rockefeller money. Creel's article fueled a dispute between Paul Kellogg and Frank P. Walsh, chair of the Federal Industrial Relations Commission, which began when Kellogg questioned the competence of the commission's work. Kellogg's position was conveyed in "Letting George Do It."

127. To Lucy Burns[1]

CONGRESSIONAL UNION FOR WOMAN SUFFRAGE
NATIONAL HEADQUARTERS, 1420 F STREET
WASHINGTON, D.C.[2]

[Naskeag, Brooklin, Maine]
~~8~~ 9-6-15

Dear Miss Burns

In another envelope I have sent photographs and an account, for the Suffragist, of the Conference or Convention in Portland.[3]

No mention is made of any election of officers for no one among the all-year-round residents was ripe for picking.

In the end, Mrs. Robert Treat Whitehouse will doubtless prove to be the proper state Chairman.[4] But she is not yet sufficiently confirmed in the faith of Congressional action to be just the right leader.

I hope you may find room for the editorial (unsigned) which I enclose herewith.[5]

Will you kindly send copies containing both (which I hope may be printed together) to the addresses given below? They will be read.

An excellent use for a part of the balance, which I turned over for the use of the Union in Maine, would be to send the Suffragist for three months to the women suggested for it hereinafter.

I hope I may see you before the details of the experience are blotted out by other activities. It is too sordid and mean to spend strength in writing.

But the effort is not wasted. The Whitehouses alone would be worth the trouble, and the Bangor group are most promising. The light is turned on the enemies within the Suffrage fold and they will shrivel in the end, but [not] in time for the present winter. Perhaps, in time for the short session in 1917.[6]

I think Mr. [Asher] Hines [Hinds] may die before the vote is taken.

Yours hopefully
Florence Kelley

For marked copies of the Convention number
Miss Helen. L. Bates Gt. Chebeague Island, Me.
Mrs. Louise Gilman Rounds, Lovitt Field., South Portland, Me
Mrs. Frederick P. Abbott Saco, Maine
Mrs. E. L. Hunt 150 State St., Bangor, Me.[7]
Mrs. R. T. Whitehouse, Squirrel Island, Me.,
Mrs. Beulah Bray, North Haven, Me.
Mrs. Julia A. Chatto East Surrey Me.
and the Maine delegation

For 3 mos. subscription free of the above list
Whitehouse
Chatto
Bray
Hunt
These people are honestly hoodooed by the national slanders, and seem to think it would be treason to subscribe to the Suffragist. But if they read it three months, they won't be able to live without it.

I think the account of the Convention should be unsigned.

I have been doing difficult things for twenty years, but never anything to compare with this. And I am glad to have had the vacation to give!

Yours Sincerely
F. Kelley

ALS, Group I: Box 31, NWP Records, DLC. Also available in Haggerty, *National Woman's Party Papers: The Suffrage Years, 1913–1920*, Reel 18.

1. Lucy Burns (1879–1966), then vice-president of the Congressional Union for Woman Suffrage and later vice-chairman of the NWP, edited *The Suffragist* from 1915 to 1916.
2. FK is listed on the letterhead as a member of the advisory council of the Congressional Union for Woman Suffrage.
3. Speaking at the Maine state convention of the Congressional Union for Woman Suffrage on 2 September 1915 in Portland, FK predicted that the suffrage movement had mustered enough votes to pass an equal suffrage amendment to the U.S. Constitution. In another speech in the evening, FK recounted her experiences as factory inspector and advocated working for a federal as well as a state equal suffrage amendment (*Portland Daily Eastern Argus,* 3 September 1915, 1). FK's article quoted verbatim the replies from the members of the 63rd Congress from Maine who were invited to attend, three of whom endorsed a U.S. constitutional amendment granting women suffrage (FK, "The Maine State Convention," 3, 8).
4. Mrs. Robert Treat Whitehouse, president of the Portland Junior Suffrage League, presided at the convention (*Portland Daily Eastern Argus,* 3 September 1915, 1).
5. FK's unsigned editorial, "The Maine Delegation," criticized U.S. senator Charles Fletcher Johnson (D., Me.) and U.S. representative Asher C. Hinds (1863–1919) (R., Me., 1911–1917) for their opposition to a U.S. constitutional amendment but concluded that there was "ground for hope" that in the forthcoming Congress, Maine delegates would "constitute a record more befitting so enlightened a state" (*The Suffragist,* 18 September 1915, 4).
6. Robert Treat Whitehouse was president of Maine's Equal Suffrage League. Maine voters defeated the federal suffrage amendment by a margin of two to one on 10 September 1917 (Harper, *History of Woman Suffrage,* 6:238, 241–244).
7. FK's article identified Helen N. Bates, president of the Maine State Woman Suffrage Association; Louise Gilman Rounds, vice-president of the Association; and Mrs. Frederick P. Abbott, president of the Maine State Federation of Women's Clubs (who was unable to attend). Augusta M. Hunt chaired Maine's Congressional Committee, a state-level division of NAWSA, in 1916 (FK, "The Maine State Convention," 3; Harper, *History of Woman Suffrage,* 6:238).

128. To Myrta Jones[1]

NATIONAL CONSUMERS' LEAGUE
GENERAL OFFICES: CRAFTSMAN BUILDING
6 EAST 39TH STREET, NEW YORK CITY

September 18, 1915

My dear Miss Jones:-

I have always thought it a misfortune that there has been, in our work, so little that appeals to men.

For this reason I hailed eagerly the opportunity to include prison labor, and the bill for safety at sea,[2] and the latter interested many valuable men.

Another field has gradually been created in which men can co-operate with us, and we have not yet availed ourselves of this opportunity. I refer to the public utilities subject to regulation by commissions, city councils and legislatures.

Subscribers for telephone service, users of gas and electric lighting, and passengers on cars and trains, are customers of these utilities, just as a woman buying gloves is a customer.

In most places, there is no limit to the hours of employment of workers hired by these corporations. Wherever there is a limit, it seems to apply only to motormen and conductors in the interests of passengers, and only exceptionally to women telephone operators.

At our annual meeting next November, in Cleveland, I shall recommend a resolution that we bring to the attention of the proper authorities the relation between overwork and unemployment, and ask our state and local leagues to take up this matter. If they do not respond, in particular cases, no harm will thereby be done. But a national organization must keep offering appropriate opportunities for co-operation for men and women living in many different parts of the country, under infinite varieties of conditions, to work with us.

Unemployment is uppermost in people's minds for a long time to come and if, in any city, groups of men can be enlisted in this attack upon unemployment by the method of re-distributing jobs by shortening the working day to eight hours in twenty-four, that will be clear gain.

I am writing this to forestall the objection that this will be a sudden extension of our activities. Notice is going to all the leagues so that they may consider the subject when they meet in the Fall, before the annual meeting.

The aim is 1. To give one more opportunity to men to co-operate.

2. To reduce unemployment by re-distributing both jobs and leisure to the extent of the 48 hours week, eight hours day, and one day's rest in seven for public utilities employes.[3]

Yours sincerely,
Florence Kelley

TLS, "General Correspondence: Kelley, Florence," Box B14, NCL Records, DLC

1. Myrta L. Jones (later Myrta Cannon) of Cleveland, formerly president of the CL of Ohio, had been vice-president of the NCL since 1911 (NCL, Twelfth Annual Report [1911], 1, Box A6, NCL Records, DLC).

2. FK wrote Senator Robert La Follette supporting his bill for safety at sea. At its 1914 annual meeting, the NCL endorsed that bill and the Booher-Hughes bill, which made all goods produced in prison subject to the laws of the states into which they were transported, included laws about sweated labor (FK, New York, to La Follette, 29 May 1914, La Follette Papers, DLC; NCL, Annual Report for 1914–1916, 57, Box A6, NCL Records, DLC; *NYT*, 30 May 1914, 10).

3. At its 1915 annual meeting, the NCL agreed to investigate "the study of wages and working conditions of employes of contractors for municipalities and public service corporations" (FK, "Twenty-Five Years of the Consumers' League Movement," 214).

129. To Myrta Jones

NATIONAL CONSUMERS' LEAGUE
GENERAL OFFICES: CRAFTSMAN BUILDING
6 EAST 39TH STREET, NEW YORK CITY

September 21, 1915

Dear Myrta:-

The idea of the public dinner appeals to me very much indeed. The only obstacle appears to be the lack of a speaker. Cleveland has had more than any city should be asked to bear of listening to me and, just off the bat, I do not know anyone who has thought even as much as I have done about the franchise corporations in their relation to the public as consumers and to the employes, as compared with employes who are employed directly by Uncle Sam, the state, the county, or the city, who get automatically the eight hours day in most cases.[1]

I have not made the kind of study of it which would enable me to say precisely what cities, or what state laws, assure their direct employes standardized hours and wages. But I do know the general triangular situation as between consumer, franchise corporations, and government in its various forms. I was astounded, for instance, to find that Professor Bemis was utterly blank on the subject; and that being the case, I do not know where to look for anyone likely to be more intelligent than he.[2]

I believe that the regulation of rates without consideration of hours and wages is virtually universal, and is one of the permanent vices of regulation as contrasted with public ownership. This very absence of knowledge on the subject on the part of ourselves and everybody else seems to me a strong argument for our occupying the field, staking the claim immediately, and starting the campaign of education.[3]

When we took up child labor, there appeared to be, for instance, only one man in Cleveland, Starr Cadwalader,[4] who knew that children under sixteen years old could not legally work in stores in Ohio after seven at night. When I stirred him ***Starr C.***[5] up to make that public, Mr. [Newton D.] Baker volunteered to prosecute all offenders, though he could perfectly well have remained passive and left that to the state officials, who never would have done anything. From my starting those two men, during a visit to the Goodrich House in 1901, arose the nationwide movement for early closing of work of children.

I believe that we are in a position to repeat the process with regard to short hours in relation to unemployment, if the idea should take root in Cleveland now, as the other idea took root there then. Cleveland is a wonderful center for spreading the infection of ideas in the East, just as Oregon has been on the Pacific Coast. If, however, we should attempt this, there would, I think, rest upon us a moral obligation to follow it up vigorously, forming a committee of men and going in for widespread inquiry. With Mr. Baker as president, that might readily prove to be a step of almost as great importance as the expansion of the work of the Legal Advisers.[6]

In all the recent study of unemployment, there appear to be two dominant tendencies:- one, to expand public exchanges, the other to get large employers to study their own labor turnover with the idea of reducing the hiring and firing i.e. the tendency toward keeping the same man in the same place longer than in the past. The redistribution of jobs by shortening hours I have nowhere seen discussed.

I am not sure whether I have said in any of my letters that I am not in favor of a church meeting for the first ~~meet~~***even***ing, under any circumstances. This is the case.

Yours sincerely,
F. Kelley

I have a nice letter to-day from Grace Drake,[7] written quite as tho she were well again. It cheers me greatly.

TLS, "General Correspondence: Kelley, Florence," Box B14, NCL Records, DLC

1. Franchise corporations were subcontractors for government entities.
2. Edward Bemis was rare among social scientists for choosing public service over academic security and prestige. With a Ph.D. from Johns Hopkins in 1885, he held a series of academic positions until his support for strikers led to his dismissal from the University of Chicago in 1895. He then served as an expert consultant on municipal ownership of public utilities, drawing on the authority of his writings, including *Municipal Ownership of Gas in the United States* (1891), and *Municipal Monopolies* (1899). In 1911 Cleveland mayor Tom Johnson praised Bemis as "an expert on the valuation of public service corporations, and the only such expert on the people's side" (Johnson, *My Story*, 132).
3. FK addressed this point in "Twenty-Five Years of the Consumers' League Movement," 214.
4. Starr Cadwallader (1869–1926) headed Goodrich House in Cleveland from 1896 to 1903 and later was a Cleveland school and city administrator.
5. The words "Starr C." are handwritten in the margin with a line indicating where they belong in the sentence.
6. The NCL's *Report for the Years 1914–1915–1916* contained a report by Pauline Goldmark, secretary of the NCL Committee on Public Utilities and Franchises, that reflected its concern

with the rights of employees of companies that subcontracted to the government (31–40, Box A6, NCL Records, DLC). Newton Baker succeeded John Graham Brooks as NCL president in 1915.

7. Grace B. Drake of Cleveland was a settlement worker and member of the executive committee of the CL of Ohio; in 1916 she served as president (NCL, *Report for the Years 1914–1915–1916,* 80, Box A6, NCL Records, DLC).

130. To Joel Spingarn

Room 43, 289 Fourth Ave.
N.Y. City
10-23-15

Confidential
My dear Mr. Spingarn

Dr. Cook and Dr. Jones met here, with me, this morning and we went carefully over the names of the present members, and of the possibilities for the Board of Directors.[1]

The feeling of the Committee was unanimous that new members should always be selected on grounds of substantive services to the Colored race—and preferably where possible to the N.A.A.C.P. already rendered,—and present members should be continued unless

a. They had expressed a desire to withdraw, or
b. had gone so far away to live as to be unavailable, or had
c. for reasons obvious to the Board, become useless or injurious.

The Committee was not agreed that this condition exists as to any member except Mrs. Morgenthau,[2] who falls under a., having expressed to me her conviction that her own place on the Board could be filled by a person who could better serve the N.A.A.C.P.

Mrs. Howe[3] is wholly unknown to both Dr. Cook and Dr. Morton Jones. I have known Mr. and Mrs. Howes for many years, but was unable to give chapter and verse for any active work in behalf of the N.A.A.C.P.

Professor Cook and Dr. Jones have known Mr. Sinclair many years, and thought the effect of failing to renominate him would be bad, because he had been beaten by the police in the riot over the Birth of a Nation,[4] and had, as I understand, also taken a valiant part as to Howard University (as to this item I am not well informed, and am not altogether clear as to Mr. Sinclair's activity in behalf of Howard[)]. The other two members were clear and firm in not wishing to vote for any substitute for him.

Mr. Hershaw[5] is directly in the service of Government, and in danger of suffering reprisals if he should take an active part in a protest against any policy of the Administration. It seemed unwise to nominate a man who ought not to be asked to do whatever may need to be done in Washington.

I am writing Dr. Du Bois why we took the present action.[6]

Yours sincerely
Florence Kelley

ALS, Joel Spingarn Papers, DHU-MS

1. NAACP board members FK; George William Cook (1855–1931), professor, dean, and acting president of Howard University; and Dr. Verina Morton-Jones (1865–1943) of Brooklyn were the members of the NAACP nominating committee. The selection of board members was especially important because the board was engaged in an ongoing struggle with W. E. B. Du Bois, the chief figure around which the NAACP had been founded in 1909, who was the editor of the NAACP's main publication, *The Crisis,* and the organization's director of publications and research. Du Bois wanted complete control of *The Crisis* and wanted to be free to pursue work outside the NAACP. In 1914, FK had written Spingarn that Du Bois's desire for "carte blanche" was "a bit staggering" (FK, New York, to Spingarn, 8 June 1914, Joel Spingarn Papers, DHU-MS; "Nominations for the Board of Directors," 86; "We Come of Age"; Kellogg, *NAACP,* 107–108; Lewis, *W. E. B. Du Bois,* 498).

2. Mrs. Max Morgenthau, Jr., of New York City, who had been on the board since 1913, withdrew (Kellogg, *NAACP,* 178).

3. Probably Marie Jenney Howe (ca. 1870–1934), Unitarian minister and wife of Frederic C. Howe, commissioner of immigration for the port of New York City (1914–1919). She did not become a member of the board.

4. Dr. William A. Sinclair of Philadelphia (b. 1858) had helped found the NAACP and served on its executive committee. The controversial film *Birth of a Nation,* which glorified the founding of the Ku Klux Klan and portrayed southern blacks in a racist manner, opened on 3 March 1915.

5. Lafayette M. Hershaw (1863–1945), former co-editor with Du Bois of *Horizon,* who was employed by the United States Land Office in 1915, did not serve on the board; Dr. Sinclair was renominated. Hershaw had recently written "Disfranchisement in the District of Columbia" (1915).

6. In the November 1915 issue of *The Crisis,* Du Bois published a statement that inaccurately claimed that the NAACP had assumed little financial responsibility for the journal. At a board meeting on 13 December, Du Bois refused to accept its proposal to limit his work for the NAACP to his editorship of *The Crisis.* Spingarn then threatened to resign, but Mary White Ovington and others persuaded him to remain as chair ("We Come of Age"; Kellogg, *NAACP,* 107–108; Lewis, *W. E. B. Du Bois,* 498–500). For the relationship between Du Bois and Spingarn, see 484–497 in Lewis, *W. E. B. Du Bois.*

131. To George E. Hooker

(COPY)

[New York City]
December 17, 1915.

Mr. George E. Hooker
Chicago City Club
Chicago, Ill.
Dear Mr. Hooker:-

We are actively opposed to the provisions of the draft bill of the Association for Labor Legislation[1] so far as regards women for the following reasons:

(1) We cannot see why the whole people should be taxed to pay for insurance against sickness of the wives of insured working men. If the farmers' wives, and all other wives, were also to be taken care of on grounds of the universal reduction of disease, there would be a logical basis for that; but while farmers' wives remain among the most overworked women in the world, we do not see why they, as a part of the general public, should share in the contribution which is to be made out of the taxes, to the expenses attending the illness of the wives of insured wage-earners.

(2) We do not see why unmarried, wage-earning women should have to pay, through their taxes, a share of the public contribution to this proposed care of the wives of insured married men.

(3) Grotesque is the proposal for a cash bonus to the married, insured, wage-earning woman at the time of the birth of her child. For this the self-respecting workingman, who maintains his wife in a home and pays for the birth of his children, must contribute to the cash premium paid his drunken neighbor. This proposal amounts to saying to the wage-earning husband: "Send your wife into a mill, factory or sweatshop, and the public will send you a present for your next baby." And the unmarried, wage-earning woman, employed at the next loom in a textile mill to that of the wife who gets this bonus, has to contribute (through her insurance payments) to the bonus, besides contributing (through the taxes) to the contribution of the public for the administration of the maternity benefit of the married, insured, wage-earning woman.

These are the only objections which we have yet clearly worked out. They are, however, sufficient to make it our obvious duty to oppose any measure which contains them.

From our point of view, until we can have universal sickness insurance, a better way to promote the health of wage-earners is to get a short working day and week, rest at night, and a living wage by means of minimum wage legislation for both men and women; and to discourage in every possible way the wage-earning employment of mothers of young children. The whole tendency of this bill appears to put the heaviest possible premium on employing them.

I am writing an article under the title, "Whose Wife Works for Wages and Why?"[2] I have been amazed to discover that the bill has been drawn in complete ignorance of this aspect of the matter. The last federal census appears not to have segregated married women in any way available for answering this question, though the schedules are believed to contain uncompiled material dealing with it. No city or state has any figures on the subject, so far as I have been able to learn. We are, therefore, reduced to using the facts of common knowledge, and they appear to sum up about as follows:

The men whose wives notoriously work for wages are—

(1) Alcoholics, men suffering from hookworm, tuberculosis, cancer, recognized insanity, epilepsy (at the institutional stage), and the disabling forms of venereal disease.
(2) The wives of Negroes. The whites generally charge that Negro husbands are lazy. The Negroes reply that the door of opportunity is closed to them. The fact remains that Negro wives are very largely employed as wage-earners.
(3) Finally, there is a considerable number of wage-earning wives of unskilled, unorganized aliens, particularly the non-English speaking ones.

From the point of view of eugenics, it appears undesirable to encourage by cash premiums, however slight, the multiplication of Class 1.

It is doubtful whether the great mass of white taxpayers will care to subsidize Class 2.

A cash bonus maternity benefit for Class 3 is an actual bribe to increased immigration of the most defenseless competitors in our industry.

These items of the proposed bill appear to be a slavish imitation of the bad English law.

Yours sincerely,
(Sd)Florence Kelley

CC, Box 17, Chicago City Club Records, ICHi

1. The social insurance committee of the AALL had prepared a bill on health insurance, which it included in its *Health Insurance* pamphlet, to introduce in state legislatures early in 1916 (Andrews, "Secretary's Report"). See the introduction to chapter 4, above, for FK's view of the AALL's bill.

2. Instead of publishing an article, FK prepared a "Memorandum on the Maternity Features of the Proposed Health Insurance Act," which she gave to Edward Devine for the Social Insurance Committee of the AALL to consider at their meeting in New York City on 22 December 1915. She also mailed a copy to George Hooker (FK, New York, to Hooker, 22 December 1915, Box 17, Chicago City Club Records, ICHi).

132. To Isaac M. Rubinow[1]

NATIONAL CONSUMERS' LEAGUE
289 FOURTH AVENUE, NEW YORK CITY

January 13, 1916
Dr. I. M. Rubinow
Ocean Accident and Guarantee Corporation
59 John Street, New York City
Dear Dr. Rubinow:

Thank you for your article, which I have read with care and interest![2]

It does not, however, meet my objections. When modern industry arose in England and Germany, it rested inevitably upon a basis of pauperized labor. When it arose in this country, it rested upon a basis of unmeasured free public land to be had for the taking. Although we have been lowering our standards of living and permitting our public land to be monopolized, the general American tradition still is that a man must maintain his wife and children; and the efforts of all my active life have been devoted to saving that standard as far as capitalism permits. Your whole article seems to me to be colored by the European tradition, and I hope that your views may not prevail in regard to the insurance of wage-earning married women.

To impose burdens on the unorganized, unskilled, or on women and children, with the idea that employers can be compelled to assume those burdens, is such an illusory, self-defeating undertaking, that only a lack of personal contact with wage-earners can explain your willingness to embark upon it, ***so far as I can see.***

With thanks for your friendly act in sending me the article, I am

Yours sincerely
Florence Kelley[3]

TLS, #5616, Rubinow Papers, NNCorI

1. Isaac M. Rubinow (1875–1936) immigrated to the United States from Russia at the age of eighteen. He earned an M.D. at New York University Medical School and a Ph.D. in economics at Columbia. His book *Social Insurance: With Special Reference to American Conditions* (1913) was the leading work on social security. Rubinow was a contributing editor to *Survey* and a member of the social insurance committee of the AALL that had drafted a health insurance bill (Rubinow, "Health Insurance: The Spread of the Movement," 407).

2. FK was probably referring to Rubinow's three-part article "Standards of Sickness Insurance" that appeared in the *Journal of Political Economy* (23 [March 1915]: 221–251; [April 1915]: 327–364; [May 1915]: 437–464). The articles analyzed health insurance policies in Scandinavia, Germany, Britain, and New Zealand.

3. Rubinow replied that "even if I do happen to live up town" his views were based on his "personal history" with "the wage working class." He also referred to "my personal relations, for the last twenty years or so, with the party movement." FK answered that she hoped he would "try again to convince this woman from Missouri" (Rubinow, New York, to FK, 19 January 1916, copy; FK, New York, to Rubinow, 24 January 1916, both in Rubinow Papers, NNCorI).

133. To Edith Abbott

Room 44, 289 Fourth Ave. N.Y.
1-30-16

Dear Edith Abbott

The National Consumers' League, as such,—is debarred from sending to the Senate any resolutions in favor of Mr. Brandeis because he is a brother-in-law of P. and J. Goldmark.[1]

So I have conceived the idea of writing you to ask whether you cannot get various Chicago people and organizations to work endorsing him. To have Mr. Brandeis and Mr. [Charles Evans] Hughes on the Supreme Bench would certainly give the U.S. Constitution a new lease of life, because they can be relied upon to restore to the States those powers which the State supreme courts have been annulling in the name of the U.S. ~~Supreme Court.~~ Constitution.

To illustrate:—When the Illinois Supreme Court annulled the Ill. 8 hours law for women in May 1895, it did so in the name of the U.S. Constitution and expressly said there could be no restriction because it was beyond the power of the state legislatures to enact such restrictions.

In his series of successful suits before the US S. Court, beginning with the Oregon decision in Jan. 1908, he has restored that power to Illinois, Ohio, Michigan, Oregon, New York and California in eight years, and has made it impossible for any State Court to deny it in future.

While others have talked loosely about States Rights and the Federal Constitution, he has restored and broadened essential rights of the States, and has removed from the U.S. Constitution the odium of being an obstacle to progress which State Courts had inflicted upon it, erroneously.

This service he rendered as a private citizen, generously giving his services as counsel, all these years, supervising the preparation of elaborate briefs, traveling hither and yonder at his own expense to make the oral arguments, and winning an unbroken series of cases before twelve courts.

This aspect of his work, his service in restoring essential rights and powers to the States, and in rehabilitating the U.S. Constitution, no one seems to recognize.

Can you get people to bring it to bear on the Senators from Illinois?[2]

Yours hopefully
F. Kelley

ALS, Abbott Papers, ICU

1. President Woodrow Wilson nominated Louis Brandeis to the U.S. Supreme Court on 28 January 1916. The Senate began confirmation hearings on 9 February.

2. FK's letter in *Survey* (36 [13 May 1916]: 191–193) praised Brandeis's accomplishments and addressed the controversy surrounding his nomination: "Never has there been kept at

work, month after month, to prevent a confirmation by the Senate a uniquely costly publicity bureau furnishing ex parte statements of alleged facts, for use as news and as raw material for editorials in every state in the Union." On 24 May, the Senate judiciary committee voted ten to eight in favor of Brandeis's nomination. The Senate followed suit on 1 June by a vote of forty-seven to twenty-two. Illinois senator James H. Lewis, Democrat, voted for Brandeis; Illinois senator Lawrence Y. Sherman, Republican, was absent (*NYT*, 2 June 1916, 1).

134. To Charles A. Prosser[1]

COPY

[New York City]
May 17, 1916

Mr. C. A. Prosser
The Wm. H. Dunwoody Industrial Institute
4th Avenue and 11th St. Minneapolis, Minn.
My dear Mr. Prosser:-

Thank you very much for your interesting letter of April 27![2] I have been away from New York so much of the time since then that I am still struggling with part of my April mail.

While I share your view in some respects, particularly in regard to the method of grants in aid, I am inclined to think that the word "education" should perhaps be broadened to include the creation of county centers for the education of mothers in the care of themselves and their very little children from birth to school age.

The mere abolition of illiteracy, on the other hand, seems to me to be taking care of itself, inasmuch as the Negroes in Georgia had reduced theirs from 90% to 30% by 1910, and are doubtless making the greatest reduction of all during the present decade, while Kentucky—which had long ranked excessively low—is wiping illiteracy bodily out of existence and proposes to be able to state truthfully in 1920 that it has within its borders no person of sound mind above the age of ten years unable to read and write.

While, therefore, I am strongly in favor of federal aid by the method of grants, I should want some thoroughly adequate guarantee that education was not to be construed merely as the reduction of illiteracy, and that the Negroes were to have a just share of the total.

I am taking the liberty of sending your letter with a copy of this to Dr. Dewey, for his consideration before the meeting of next Friday.[3]

Yours sincerely,
(signed) FLORENCE KELLEY

TL, "Obstetrical," Folder 4–15–5–1, Box 46, CB Records, RG102, MdCpNA

1. Charles A. Prosser (1871–1952) was assistant commissioner of education in Massachusetts (1910–1912) and director of the Dunwoody Industrial Institute in Minneapolis (1915–1945), whose mission was to provide industrial education regardless of race, creed, or religion.

2. Prosser had written FK about his support for federal grants to states for vocational education and recommended that the funds address "the removal of illiteracy" (Prosser, Minneapolis, to FK, 27 April 1916, copy, Folder 4–15–5–1, Box 46, CB Records, MdCpNA).

3. In May, FK wrote philosopher John Dewey (1859–1952), then teaching at Columbia University, that the plan for "county centers for the instruction of mothers and the reduction of mortality and morbidity of infants and young children" did not originate with her but with Julia Lathrop, who had been appointed by President William H. Taft in 1912 to head the newly established Children's Bureau. FK also wrote Lathrop enclosing copies of the Prosser correspondence and her letter to Dewey. She wrote that she hoped Lathrop could attend the 19 May meeting in New York City to discuss federal aid to education and "reclaim your kidnapped idea!" When Lathrop did not attend, FK urged her to emphasize to Dewey and others that "illiteracy should not occupy the center of the stage" in any federal program to aid education. Lathrop replied on that she tended to favor a bill focusing on illiteracy but might be "unpersuaded" (FK, New York, to John Dewey, 17 May 1916; FK, New York, to Lathrop, 17 May and 22 May 1916; Lathrop, Washington, D.C., to FK, 29 May 1916, copy, all in Folder 4–15–5–1, Box 46, CB Records, MdCpNA).

135. To Katherine Philips Edson

NATIONAL CONSUMERS' LEAGUE
GENERAL OFFICES, ~~CRAFTSMAN BUILDING~~
~~6 EAST 39TH ST., NEW YORK CITY~~

7-16-16
Naskeag, [Brooklin,] Hancock Co. Me.

Dear Mrs. Edson

I have no secretary here, either personal or official, and my arrears are pitiful to witness particularly if these weeks are viewed as vacation!

1. The rehearing in the Oregon minimum wage case is due to the following circumstances:—With Justices Lamar and Hughes on the Bench, the opinion was divided during 1915. Justice Lamar is dead and Justice Hughes is gone. The Court consists of only seven Justices in spite of the Confirmation of Justice Brandeis, for Justice Day who is friendly to our view has been ill for months and may never sit again.[1]

Justice Brandeis cannot sit in a case in which he appeared as counsel.

The only hope lies in the appointment of a modern man in the next few weeks before Congress adjourns.

For vacation appointments cannot be made to the Court. There is present talk of a New York City Tammany Catholic, altho there are now two Catholics,—Presiding Justice White and Justice McKenna. That will be disgraceful, but after appointing Baker and Brandeis there will perhaps be a revulsion towards the Reactionaries.[2]

2. The one thing which seems to strengthen all statutes and rulings is evidence of long, faithful and convincing investigation preceding action, published in clear and full official reports.

Our N.Y. State Court of Appeals reversed itself on women's work at night, making a point of the fact that, when it first decided (wrong) it had only an insufficient presentation of the case before it, and now in reversing itself and deciding right, it was acting in the light of the thorough investigation made by the N.Y. State Factories Investigating Committee.[3]

---

3. The method of selecting wage boards is most difficult. Of course you have the Bulletins and Second Annual Report of the Mass. Min. W. ~~B~~ Commission? That shows how all action in regard to the confectionery workers was stopped at the last moment on the ground that the original make-up of the Wage Board was defective.[4]

It is a horrid comment on our American wage earners that they cannot be democratically selected. But how can they, with no trade organization of their own?

I have been driven by conditions from advocating election of nomination by the workers, to advocating selection by the Commission except where the text of the statute commands election (if it ever does!).

---

4. If you have the recall of Commissions as a whole, and of individual Commissioners, on a basis such that the cost does not make it impossible ever to use it, I have no objection to Commissions. Ours, here, are pests. We have no Wage Commission. But the Labor members of the Industrial Commission are rotten through and through, traitors to the wage earners, and Lynch is personally dishonest beside.[5]

Reduplication and conflict of authority are self-defeating of course. But we have both, I greatly fear that this is too late to be of the slightest use to you.

Yours sincerely and hopefully
Florence Kelley

I do hope you will help put these anti-Suffrage Democrats out of office![6] But it won't do to print this wish because Newton D. Baker, Sec'y of War is President of my League!

ALS, Edson Papers, CLU-SC

1. As unpaid legal counsel for the NCL, Louis Brandeis had argued the case (*Simpson v. O'Hara*) in Oregon and again on 17 December 1914 when the decision was appealed to the U.S. Supreme Court (*Stettler v. O'Hara*), but no decision had yet been handed down (Goldmark, *Impatient Crusader*, 167–170; Urofsky and Levy, *Letters of Louis Brandeis*, 3:364). Joseph R.

Lamar (b. 1857), associate justice of the U.S. Supreme Court, had died on 2 January 1916, and Associate Justice Charles Evans Hughes had resigned to run for U.S. president on the Republican ticket. William R. Day (1849–1923) was associate justice from 1903 to 1922.

2. Edward D. White (1845–1921) was chief justice of the U.S. Supreme Court (1910–1921); Joseph McKenna (1843–1926) was associate justice (1898–1925). Besides the controversy over Brandeis's appointment, FK was referring to President Wilson's choice of NCL president Newton Baker, a member of the American League Against Militarism, as secretary of war.

3. On 26 March 1915, in *People v. Charles Schweinler Press,* the New York Court of Appeals upheld the prohibition on night work for women. After the Triangle Factory fire of March 1911, the New York legislature charged the state's Factory Investigating Commission with investigating sanitary and safety conditions in factories, wages, and other related issues such as living conditions of workers. FK was on the Advisory Board of this commission. Its final report in February 1915 concluded that the wages of many women and minors were too low to maintain a decent standard of living and recommended legislation to create a wage commission that would establish boards to determine the level of wages women and minor workers needed (Kerr, "The New York Factory Investigating Commission and the Minimum Wage Movement"; FK, New York, to Abram Elkus, 11 September 1914; Elkus, New York, to FK, 14 September 1914, copy, both in Factory Investigating Commission Correspondence, N-Ar.)

4. A suit filed by twenty-six candy manufacturers in the Massachusetts Supreme Court prevented the state's Minimum Wage Commission from establishing wages for candy workers ("Common Welfare," 36).

5. James M. Lynch (1867–1930), a member of the New York State Industrial Commission (1915–1921), advocated longer hours for women than those mandated in state regulations.

6. See Letter 136, FK to Norman Hapgood, 22 August 1916, below. In San Francisco, the NWP held an anti-Wilson rally on the eve of the election (*Los Angeles Times,* 5 November 1916, I:4). Edson and other California Progressives reluctantly supported Republican Charles Evans Hughes in the 1916 presidential campaign. Edson was one of fifteen representatives from the Women's National Republican Association to travel on Hughes's National Campaign Train to demonstrate women's support for the party (Braitman, "A California Stateswoman," 82–95).

136. To Norman Hapgood[1]

COPY

Naskeag, [Brooklin,] Hancock Co., Maine
August 22, 1916

Mr. Norman Hapgood
Woodrow Wilson Independent League
280 Madison Avenue, New York City
My dear Mr. Hapgood,

Your letter of August 17th reached me last evening, forwarded from the office.

In reply—since you ask the direct question—I am constrained to say that I hold it the duty of intelligent women to work actively for the defeat of President Wilson. To do otherwise would be to acquiesce in deferring our enfranchisement until after his second term.[2]

If twelve million or more men were placed as we are, would they consider any political issue as taking precedence over votes for themselves? To ask the question is to answer it. Never for a moment!

It is, however, not exclusively a matter of votes. The Party which impudently calls itself Democratic while denying votes to women and to Negro men, has made a recent record wholly bad so far as regards women as such.

The very modest program of Congressional legislation of the Consumers' League makes no progress. Senator Kenyon's little item of $6,000 for an enquiry into the cost of living of wage-earning families in the District of Columbia languishes on the Senate Calendar.[3]

The Women's Division in the Bureau of Labor Statistics, administratively created by Commissioner Charles P. Neill and admirably efficient under Marie Obenauer, has been completely wrecked.[4] She has resigned and no competent woman has been willing to become her successor, though several whom I know have been asked to do so. The work is stopped. Meanwhile the Casey bill for a Women's Division in the Department of Labor gets not even a Committee hearing in the House.[5]

The Supreme Court after delaying a decision in the case of the Oregon minimum wage law for women since December 17, 1914, has now ordered a rehearing after the election.

There is no bright spot.

On the other hand, it is Mr. Hughes who wrote the decision in the California eight hours case,—a decision broad enough to serve as foundation for the legislation of a generation in its own field.[6]

It is painful to part company with you, and Messrs. Kent, Price and Bruere.[7] But votes for millions of citizens are more important this fall than any other issue on which the President and Mr. Hughes differ.

Yours sincerely,
(signed) FLORENCE KELLEY[8]

TL, FKP, NN

1. Norman Hapgood (1868–1937) edited *Collier's Weekly* (1903–1912) and *Harper's Weekly* (1913–1916).

2. On 13 August 1916, the *New York Times* published a letter dated 7 August from President Wilson to the Jane Jefferson Club of Colorado that stated that the question of woman suffrage should be left to the states, in accordance with the Democratic Party platform (Link, *Papers of Woodrow Wilson,* 37:536–537). Therefore, as a member of Alice Paul's Congressional Union, Kelley endorsed the strategy of voting Wilson out of office.

3. Senator William S. Kenyon (1869–1933; Republican, Iowa, 1911–1922) had introduced his joint resolution seven months earlier, on 10 December 1915 (64th Cong., 1st sess., *Cong. Rec.,* 133).

4. Charles P. Neill (1865–1942) headed the U.S. Commission of Labor from 1905 to 1913. Marie Obenauer, co-author of *Effect of Minimum-Wage Determinations in Oregon* (1915), was later a columnist for *The Suffragist* (Lehrer, *Origins of Protective Labor Legislation for Women,* 106).

5. Congressman John J. Casey (1875–1929; Democrat, Pennsylvania, 1913–1917, 1919–1921, 1923–1925, 1927–1929) introduced two bills to establish a women's division in the Department of Labor (64th Cong., 1st sess., *Cong. Rec.*, 2 and 9 June 1916, 9192, 9426).

6. Writing for the U.S. Supreme Court's unanimous decision on 23 February 1915 upholding the California law (*Miller v. Wilson*), Justice Charles Evans Hughes stated that California's eight-hour law applied broadly to women in many types of occupations.

7. William Kent chaired the Woodrow Wilson Independent League, and New York City banker Henry Bruere (1882–1958) served as the league's treasurer. Mr. Price is possibly Joseph Morris Price (1870–1949), New York City industrialist and political reformer (Link, *Papers of Woodrow Wilson*, 37:432; 38:276; 40:215).

8. On 28 August, Hapgood wrote Wilson that the campaign had "found it desirable to put a good deal of time, recently, on the women situation." Hapgood suggested that Wilson court women's support by emphasizing his administration's work on "shorter hours for women, Children's Bureau, help to farm women, etc." (Link, *Papers of Woodrow Wilson*, 38:86–87). Wilson was narrowly reelected in November.

Members of the Women's Joint Congressional Committee, ca. 1921. *Front*: Mary Stewart, Mrs. Ellis Yost, Mrs. Maud Wood Park, Jeannette Rankin, Mrs. Florence Kelley, Lida Hafford. *Rear*: Mrs. La Rue Brown, Adah Bush, Betsy Edwards, Mrs. Raymond Morgan, Mrs. Arthur Watkins, Mrs. Milton P. Higgins, and Amy Maher. Courtesy of the Library of Congress, LC-USZ62-63740.

5 1917 – 1921

"The Work of the Nation"

INTRODUCTION

Florence Kelley was fifty-eight years old when the United States entered World War I on 6 April 1917. Her letters depict a reformer at the top of her game. Beginning in 1917, the NCL files preserved many more of Kelley's letters than was the case earlier; half of her recovered letters date from the last fifteen years of her life. Although probably due in part to better conservation techniques in the NCL office, this large number of letters also stemmed from Kelley's continued reliance on letter-writing as an organizing tool.

The realization of Kelley's vision of a guarantee to all the nation's children of the right to childhood and education seemed close at hand in 1917. The U.S. Children's Bureau, which she had helped establish five years earlier, remained the only national government bureau directed by women in the western world. Capably run by her friend Julia Lathrop, it now buttressed Kelley's achievements by aiding in the passage and enforcement of path-breaking federal laws, beginning with the Keating-Owen Child Labor Act in 1916. Another friend, Grace Abbott, moved to Washington to oversee the act's enforcement as head of the bureau's Child Labor Division.[1] These achievements were sustained by a constant barrage of letters that Kelley dispatched from the midst of her travels as well as from her desk in New York City. From Santa Monica, California, she wrote to Edith Abbott at the end of a long day, "I would re-write this, but it is the seventeenth and my arm aches!"[2]

Advances for women's right to leisure and a living wage were also accelerating in 1917, through state rather than federal laws. A decade after the NCL established the legality of the ten-hour day for working women, the league was promoting the eight-hour day as the national standard. By 1917, five states and the District of Columbia had eight-hour days for women, and the California eight-hour law, enforced by Kelley's ally, Katherine Edson, had been upheld by the Supreme Court.[3] Also in full swing in 1917 was Kelley's campaign for minimum wage laws for women, with laws already enacted in ten states.[4]

In the spring of 1917, she rejoiced over the Supreme Court's announcement of two decisions that made greater gains possible. One upheld the Oregon minimum wage law for women; the other upheld Oregon's ten-hour law for men. To Brandeis, who had helped with both cases, Kelley wrote, "Indeed, so far as our democratic evolution remains even partially orderly and peaceful, your contribution to that unspeakable blessing is an immeasurable one."[5]

The court's decision in *Bunting v. Oregon*, which upheld a ten-hour law for men and required employers who needed longer hours to pay overtime, exemplified the success of the NCL's strategy of using labor laws for women as an opening wedge for laws that protected all workers. The *Bunting* opinion did not mention the court's earlier rulings in *Lochner* or *Muller.* Instead, after quoting the Oregon Supreme Court's decision "that the custom in our industries does not sanction a longer service than ten hours per day," the national court tersely affirmed that judgment.[6] Thus rights that were established in custom became the legal standard. In *Bunting* as well as *Muller,* the NCL redefined what was permitted and forbidden in the industrial workplace by insisting that the court consider the realities of that workplace rather than abstract notions about the freedom of contract.

Yet the entry of the United States into the European war eclipsed Kelley's celebration of these court verdicts. War loomed as a catastrophic threat to the "radiant American future" that she and her allies had labored to create since the 1890s.[7] Writing a colleague in Oregon "not as a member of the Consumers' League, but as a human being and as a citizen of this Republic," she urged action against a bill that would create an American standing army.[8] She lamented the imprisonment of Eugene Debs and was "haunted by sorrow" that Randolph Bourne had not lived to interpret "the incomprehensible darkening of the mind and spirit of this whole nation."[9]

Nevertheless, the war also offered opportunities. President Wilson called upon NCL president Newton Baker to serve as secretary of war, and Baker appointed Kelley to the U.S. Board of Control of Labor Standards for army clothing.[10] In that capacity, she worked with Sidney Hillman to maintain union standards in garment shops that received military contracts and drew Grace Abbott into efforts to enforce state laws that prohibited women's night work.[11] Although she wrote Hillman that the army's garment-making policies were "heart-breaking," her committee was able to maintain standards in the quality of cloth used for military uniforms.[12] And Baker helped her repel an effort by meatpackers to discredit the NCL's regulatory efforts in that industry.[13]

At the height of American involvement in World War I, the U.S. Supreme Court invalidated the Keating-Owen Child Labor Act. The act drew on the commerce clause of the U.S. Constitution, which granted Congress the power to regulate interstate commerce. The act prohibited the interstate transportation of goods made at factories that employed children under the age of fourteen or children between the ages of fourteen and sixteen more than eight hours a day. In a five to four decision in 1918, the Supreme Court ruled that the act attempted an unconstitutional regulation of the production of goods. In 1919, Congress attempted to achieve the goals of Keating-Owen and meet the court's objections by imposing a tax on the employment of children. In 1922, the Court ruled this strategy unconstitutional as well.

As her horizons darkened, Kelley often grew impatient with allies such as Samuel Gompers and the National Child Labor Committee who were more willing to compromise on the details of child labor legislation, particularly if they could extend legislation to an otherwise reluctant South. Kelley was not willing to work with southerners at any price. New England textile manufacturers sought to evade labor legislation by moving their factories south, and it would take strong national laws to stem that flow. Kelley chose constancy over compromise and resigned from the National Child Labor Committee.[14]

The postwar world drew Kelley into international activism to a degree unmatched since her student days in Zurich in the 1880s. She described the founding meeting of the Women's International League for Peace and Freedom in 1919 as "unbelievably wonderful" and joined its effort to promote a lasting peace.[15] Back home, she joined the American branch of WILPF—after the departure of the "egocentrist" leadership of Anna Garlin Spencer—and promised "Beloved J.A." to work steadily in that group.[16] With Addams and Mary Smith and Alice Hamilton, she traveled to the WILPF conference in Vienna in 1921 with a renewed appreciation of "the Sacredness of human life everywhere, at all times."[17]

While Kelley maintained close ties with old friends associated with the social settlement movement, new friends emerged. Not surprisingly, her closest new friends helped with NCL fund-raising. Grace Drake, an anchor of the Consumers' League of Ohio, became a crucial member of the NCL's finance committee, and Kelley found it hard to plan the league's finances when Drake was absent in Europe.[18] Also serving on that committee were Mary Sanford and her life partner, Helen Stokes, both of whom Kelley knew from her work on the executive committee of the Intercollegiate Socialist Society.[19] Writing Sanford from Zurich in 1919, Kelley addressed her as "Sandy, love," and she responded with "My dear old Kelley."[20] They and other friends showered her with gifts when she sailed to Europe with Jane Addams and other old friends in June 1921.

Kelley sought to create new opportunities in the postwar world by adding industrial poisons to the NCL's agenda, but new initiatives were difficult to launch without additional funding and her Finance Committee was in disarray.[21] Her way forward came with the ratification of the woman suffrage amendment to the Constitution on 26 August 1920.[22] That historic event created powerful new opportunities for women's activism at the national level, and she quickly responded by aiding in the creation of two national organizations: the League of

Women Voters, and the Women's Joint Congressional Committee, both of which were founded in 1920 to promote the political and social agendas of the suffrage movement and women's organizations affiliated with the suffrage movement.[23] Although women had been voting in some states for decades (particularly in the West), these organizations focused their power as a national voting bloc.

Packed with potential for the advancement of her agenda, the WJCC became Kelley's second home. From that location, augmented by her close contact with Julia Lathrop at the Children's Bureau, she promoted one of the most significant achievements of her reform career, the passage in 1921 of the Sheppard-Towner Maternity and Infancy Protection Act, the first federal statute to allocate funding for human health. Her passionate efforts on behalf of that legislation began in 1920 when she vowed that women's votes would defeat congressmen who opposed it.[24] As the bill moved through Congress, she worked to preserve the Children's Bureau's control of its implementation and prevent encroachments by the U.S. Public Health Service.[25] Its successful passage in November 1921 marked a high point in the history of American women's political activism.[26]

Yet Kelley's celebration of that historic moment was obscured by the emergence of a profound and enduring threat to her legislative agenda—the National Women's Party's proposal of a constitutional amendment that "men and women shall have equal rights throughout the United States and in every place subject to its jurisdiction."[27] The NWP's proposed amendment imperiled Kelley's agenda of women's labor legislation as well as "the Sheppard-Towner bill, mothers' pensions, maternity insurance, etc.," as she pointed out to Roscoe Pound.[28] By 1921, Kelley's strategy of using gender difference to achieve social rights had become a familiar feature of progressive legal culture, and she readily recruited support to sustain it. Yet she could not so easily control court decisions and feared that courts would use the NWP's call for "identical treatment" as a reason to overturn social rights legislation. Henceforth much of her time and spirit was devoted to the defeat of the NWP's proposal. Consulting the legal opinion of Pound, she called "identical treatment" of women and men "insane" and feared that courts would reflect "the temper of the times" and yield to "the pressure of the madwomen."[29]

Kelley responded to this pressure by reorganizing the NCL's structure. She concentrated the organization's power in a newly created Board of Directors, to which she appointed lawyers Edward Costigan, Robert Szold, and Bernard Shientag.[30] She also added attorney Walter Wilbur to the NCL's Council and employed Dean Acheson as legal counsel.[31] This legion supplemented Newton Baker's legal expertise as NCL president and the ongoing support of Felix Frankfurter.

Kelley had worked with NWP members since 1915, when they were the Congressional Union,[32] and in 1921 she negotiated intensely with Alice Paul and other NWP leaders over the wording and potential impact of their planned amendment. "With every effort to give women complete political equality, I am of course in full sympathy," she wrote Paul. But believing the amendment's "sweeping provisions" would undercut "statutes affecting business or industrial relations of women," she resigned from the party's advisory committee.[33] She correctly predicted to a consumers' league colleague that "we shall have to oppose Alice Paul and her followers for years to come."[34]

Kelley prepared for the struggle by mobilizing five national organizations, "the National Consumers' League, The Women's Trade Union League, the League of Women Voters, the Y.W.C.A., and, presumably, the W.C.T.U."[35] United in the Women's Joint Congressional Committee, these groups constituted the centrist left of women's political culture as it had developed in the United States since the 1870s. They viewed women's interests as equal to but different from those of men, and their political activism, agenda, and power was based on that combination of equal but different. Seeking to promote women's interests as equal and similar to those of men, the National Woman's Party represented a small minority within the suffrage movement, but because they expressed an ideal that resonated with American individualism, it had the potential to grow. In the short run, NWP members fractured the women's movement and advanced an agenda of individual rights that Florence Kelley viewed as a grave threat to her agenda of social rights.

In this context Kelley's Maine farmhouse, Seawest, became a important refuge where she nurtured and was nurtured by family and friends. She needed it. In February 1919, her physician diagnosed "a tired heart," and she joked about being "a belated war casualty."[36] Seawest also located Kelley close to Jane Addams and Mary Smith's summer home in Hull's Cove, and Emily Balch's family home was just up the road in Brooklin.[37] Mary Dana Hicks Prang, mother of her beloved deceased friend Margaret Hicks, visited often at Seawest, as did Myrta Jones of the Consumers' League of Ohio.[38] John came and slept on his sailboat, *Diablesse,* which was often moored at his mother's dock. He still lacked steady work when he married Ann Valentine in 1920 and they piloted *Diablesse* across the Atlantic.[39]

Ko did not visit Seawest often, but she saw him at Little Compton, Rhode Island, where he and his family summered with the Lloyd family.[40] During the war Ko and his family moved to Washington, where for two years he worked in the U.S. Treasury on loans to foreign governments. So Kelley's frequent trips to the capital during these years included visits with Ko, Augusta, Nicholas, Florence, and Augustus.[41]

NOTES

1. Letter 142, FK to Newton Baker, 11 November 1918, below.
2. Letter 139, FK to Edith Abbott, 16 July 1917, below.
3. FK, *Women in Industry.*
4. Gordon, *The Development of Minimum-Wage Laws in the United States, 1912–1927,* 11.
5. Letter 137, FK to Brandeis, 9 April 1917, below.

6. Woloch, *Muller v. Oregon*, 151.
7. Letter 152, FK to Agnes de Lima, 1 January 1920, below.
8. Letter 138, FK to Katherine Trevitt, 25 June 1917, below. The United States entered World War I on 6 April 1917.
9. Letter 143, FK to Newton Baker, 7 February 1919; and Letter 152, FK to Agnes de Lima, 1 January 1920, both below.
10. Letter 140, FK to Newton Baker, 13 August 1917, below.
11. Letter 141, FK to Sidney Hillman, 17 August 1917, below.
12. Letter 140, FK to Baker, 13 August 1917.
13. Letter 149, FK to Newton Baker, 22 September 1919, below.
14. See Letter 151, FK to NK, 18 October 1919, note 5, below.
15. Letter 144, FK to Mary Rozet Smith, 22 May 1919, below.
16. Letter 155, FK to JA, 7 November 1920, below.
17. Letter 160, FK to NK, 5 June 1921, below.
18. For FK's relationship with Grace Drake, see Letter 129, FK to Myrta Jones, 21 September 1915, above; and Letter 145, FK to Mary R. Sanford, 14 June 1919; and Letter 150, FK to NK, 2 October 1919, below.
19. For more about the Intercollegiate Socialist Society, see Letter 151, FK to NK, 18 October 1919, below.
20. Letter 145, FK to Mary Sanford, 14 June 1919, below; Mary Sanford to FK, 17 June [1919], FKP, NN. Sanford provided a refuge for FK in her home in Bennington during the first weeks after Margaret's death (Letter 80, FK to NK, 29 October 1905, note 1, above). For Stokes and Sanford's membership on the NCL Finance Committee, see NCL, Tenth Annual Report [1909], List of Officers; and NCL Annual Council Minutes, 1917 and 1918, both in Box A6, NCL Records, DLC.
21. See Letter 148, FK to David Edsall, 9 September 1919; and Letter 150, FK to NK, 2 October 1919, both below.
22. For details about the passage and ratification of the Nineteenth Amendment, see Wilson, *The Women's Joint Congressional Committee and the Politics of Maternalism*, 9–12; and Lemons, *The Woman Citizen*, 12–14.
23. For the founding of the LWV, see Young, *In the Public Interest*, 45–53. For the founding of the WJCC, see Wilson, *The Women's Joint Congressional Committee and the Politics of Maternalism*, 9–26.
24. Letter 153, FK to Anna E. Rude, 13 June 1920, below.
25. Letter 157, FK to Julia Lathrop, 3 March 1921, below.
26. For the establishment of the Children's Bureau, see Lindenmeyer, *A Right to Childhood*, 9–29; Wilson, *The Women's Joint Congressional Committee and the Politics of Maternalism*, 29; and Goldmark, *Impatient Crusader*, 93–104.
27. 1923 ERA quoted in Hoff-Wilson, *Rights of Passage*, 121.
28. Letter 159, FK to Roscoe Pound, 3 June 1921, below.
29. Letter 159, FK to Pound, 3 June 1921.
30. "Annual Meeting of Members and of the Council," 17 November 1921, 10, Box A7, NCL Records.
31. Letter 165, FK to Felix Frankfurter, 28 November 1921, below.
32. Letter 127, FK to Lucy Burns, 6 September 1915, above.
33. Letter 163, FK to Alice Paul, 14 October 1921, below.
34. Letter 166, FK to A. Estelle Lauder, 30 November 1921, below.
35. Letter 166, FK to Lauder, 30 November 1921.
36. Letter 143, FK to Newton Baker, 7 February 1919, below.
37. For FK's summer relationship with JA, see Letter 201, FK to Grace Abbott, 11 August 1924; Letter 199, FK to Julia Lathrop, 28 July 1924; and Letter 235, FK to JA, 20 July 1927, all

below. The Balch siblings' summer residence is mentioned in Letter 64, FK to NK, 15 March 1902, above; Letter 97, FJK to NK, 6 July 1907, above; and Letter 236, FK to NK, 9 August 1927, below.

38. FK's long friendship with Mary Dana Hicks Prang is documented in Letter 69, FK to NK, 5 July 1903, above; and Letter 147, FK to NK, 25 July 1919; Letter 201, FK to Abbott, 11 August 1924; Letter 235, FK to JA, 20 July 1927; and Letter 272, FK to NK, 22 July 1931, below. Myrta Jones's frequent presence at Seawest is mentioned in Letter 147, FK to NK, 25 July 1919.

39. For JK's marriage to Ann Valentine, see Letter 160, FK to NK, 5 June 1921, note 3, below.

40. Letter 121, FK to NK, 13 September 1913, note 1, above.

41. Letter 150, FK to NK, 2 October 1919, below.

137. To Louis D. Brandeis

NATIONAL CONSUMERS' LEAGUE
289 FOURTH AVENUE
NEW YORK CITY

4-9-17

[D]ear Mr. Justice Brandeis

If I did not know from the inside the long story of genius, wisdom and hard work beginning nearly ten years ago,—in November 1907,—I should regard to-day's decisions as miracles nos. Fourteen and Fifteen![1]

As it is, they are triumphs instead of miracles.

There are no words wherewith to express the debt the wage earners of this Nation owe you for your labors in this field.

Indeed, so far as our democratic evolution remains even partially orderly and peaceful, your contribution to that unspeakable blessing is an immeasurable one.

Louis Brandeis, ca. 1910. Courtesy of the Library of Congress, LC-USZ62-92924.

This is no vain attempt to express the thanks due from others to you. It is a humble and reverent expression of appreciation of that which I have seen and know.[2]

Yours Sincerely
Florence Kelley

ALS, Brandeis Papers, KyLoU-L

1. In a tie vote (Brandeis not voting), the U.S. Supreme Court upheld the Oregon minimum wage law (*Stettler v. O'Hara*) on 9 April 1917. Because Brandeis had argued the *Stettler* case before the Oregon court in 1914, he recused himself from the decision. That same day, the court unanimously upheld Oregon's ten-hour working day for men (*Bunting v. Oregon*), a case Brandeis had worked on with Josephine Goldmark before his Supreme Court appointment (see Goldmark, *Impatient Crusader,* 167–172).
2. Brandeis replied, "It is a satisfaction to have lent some aid in your great work" (Brandeis, Washington, D.C., to FK, 12 April 1917, FKP, NN).

138. To Katherine Lucy Trevett

NATIONAL CONSUMERS' LEAGUE
289 FOURTH AVENUE, NEW YORK CITY

Personal Confidential
June 25, 1917

Dear Miss Trevett:-

Mr. [Newton] Baker did approve the resolution on grain saving, and it did go to the Senators and Representatives at the time of our meeting, and a surprising number of sympathetic replies followed.[1] As you know, the House passed the food bill on Saturday night by a vote of everybody against five, the five being three from Texas, one from Missouri, and one from New York! The bill is now before the Senate, and I trust that your letters to Senators Chamberlain and McNary may make them take an active interest.[2] The fight will be even fiercer than it has been in the House.

Not as a member of the Consumers' League, but as a human being and as a citizen of this Republic, I hope that you and all your friends are intimately acquainted with the bill introduced by Mr. Kahn of California, to create an enormous standing army, a year of compulsory service for all men, and twelve years in the reserve.[3] The ulterior object of such a measure cannot be anything but the oppression of labor at home, and a standing threat to Mexico and Japan. If we are not to have war after this war, the Kahn bill ought to be killed now, and almost no one seems to be aware of this.

The following is for your consideration and that of your friends in and out of your League, as far as you think it discreet to circulate it. It is not for publication.

You doubtless know that Congress has appropriated a million dollars for the use of Mr. Caminetti's Bureau in creating labor bureaus and distributing immigrants and American women and girls in industry. Mr. Caminetti is kept in office by the strength of trade unions of California, which are grateful to him for his exertions in behalf of the California eight hours day for women and other labor measures. Beside this, he has on his payroll Mrs. Eva Perry Moore, head of the National council of Women and former president of the General Federation of Women's Clubs.[4]

This complicated backing of Pacific Coast trade unionists and organized women ***from everywhere*** has hitherto made it impossible to do anything effective towards the removal of this atrociously incompetent, futile, wasteful federal officer. ~~He is unfortunately mentally unbalanced if not actively insane~~. Inasmuch as he has not provably committed burglary, arson, or murder, it has hitherto been impossible to dislodge him.

There are, however, certain things which can be done. If there is a placement bureau in your city, the Consumers' League can get into touch with it and ascertain how well, or ill, it is working. If there is one, it is of urgent importance that the League should know to what kind of places and on what terms women and girls are sent out by it.

If there is none, it is desirable to have a considerable number of letters written to Secretary W. B. Wilson (Department of Labor, Washington, D.C.) by women, not all on the same day but close together, on their own letterhead, not on League letterhead, enquiring what the prospect is for the creation of a placement office under Mr. Caminetti's Bureau in your city; and every such letter should ask for a complete list of the addresses of all the bureaus now at work in other cities and states.[5] [inserted in margin: ***This is what we can do.***]

The point is to bring to Secretary Wilson's attention the fact that there is widespread interest in the placement bureaus and in Mr. Caminetti, whose name should appear in every letter.

Long experience has taught me that there are only two ways of getting rid of worthless federal officers. One is to focus the attention of the whole country on the official ultimately responsible—in this case Secretary Wilson—and make it clear to him that his subordinate is persona non grata; the other is the method of unremitting conversation with exact facts for its basis. This is very slow and tiresome and for a long time appears to be useless: but in the end the official shrivels and disappears.

It is a monstrous thing that so great a sum for a purpose so important at this time should be either squandered outright, or used in ways injurious to the intended beneficiaries.

Yours sincerely,
Florence Kelley

TLS, "General Correspondence: 'T,'" Box B22, NCL Records, DLC

1. On 6 April 1917, the United States entered World War I by declaring war on Germany, Austria, and the Ottoman Empire. FK had prepared a resolution for the NCL Executive Committee that "urge[d] upon Congress the need of prohibiting the use of grain for beverages during the period of the war" (enclosure in FK to Richard Ely, 21 May 1917, Ely Papers, WHi).

2. On 23 June 1917, the House of Representatives passed the Lever Food and Fuel Control bill, the goal of which was to create a federal entity to manage the conservation and distribution of food and fuel resources during World War I. The bill was debated vigorously in the Senate for weeks but finally passed on 8 August. On 10 August, President Wilson issued an executive order that created the U.S. Food Administration and appointed Herbert Hoover as the administrator (65th Cong., 1st sess., *Cong. Rec.*, 4131, 4190, 5904–5927; *NYT:* 1 July 1917, II:2 and 11 August 1917, 1). The chief precedent for this wartime expansion of federal power was the enforcement of the 1906 Pure Food and Drug Act by federal inspectors under the direction of Dr. Harvey Wiley in the Bureau of Chemistry of the U.S. Department of Agriculture. In 1912, Wiley had resigned in protest when the secretary of agriculture overrode his efforts to prosecute grain dealers (Mullendore, *History of the United States Food Administration,* 53–57; Hilts, *Protecting America's Health,* 56–71; for more about Wiley, see Letter 90, FK to Caroline Bartlett Crane, 21 January 1907 and Letter 118, FK to NK, 4 August 1912, both above). Oregon's U.S. senators were George E. Chamberlain (1854–1928; Democrat, 1909–1921) and Charles L. McNary (1874–1944; Republican, 1917–1918, 1918–1944).

3. On 2 April 1917, Congressman Julius Kahn (1861–1924; Republican, California, 1899–1903, 1905–1924) introduced his bill "providing a system of national defense based upon universal liability to military training and service." Congress ultimately enacted the Selective Draft Act of 1917 (H.R. 3545). The new law "authorized the President to draft the maximum number of men necessary for prosecution of the war" (65th Cong., 1st sess., *Cong. Rec.*, 123, 2501; "Selective Draft Act of 1917," Act May 18, 1917, Ch. 15, 40 Stat. 76, U.S. Code).

4. Anthony Caminetti (1854–1923), a former U.S. congressman (Democrat, California, 1891–1895) and U.S. commissioner of immigration (1913–1921), sought to stiffen the Immigration Act of 1917 by strengthening measures to detect and imprison radicals. These measures were incorporated into the Immigration Act passed by Congress in 1918 (Preston, *Aliens and Dissenters,* 181–184). Eva Perry Moore (1852–1931) was president of the National Council of Women (1916–1925) and a member of the women's committee of the Council of National Defense (1917–1919).

5. Created in 1913, the U.S. Department of Labor evolved from the Bureau of Labor Statistics, established in 1884. William B. Wilson (1862–1934) was the first U.S. secretary of labor, serving from 1913 to 1921. When he was appointed, the Department of Labor had only 2,000 employees (1,700 of which worked for the Bureau of Immigration) and four bureaus—the Children's Bureau, the Bureau of Immigration, the Bureau of Naturalization, and the Bureau of Labor Statistics. In 1917, Wilson was in the process of building a national employment bureau service, which he was creating by using the eighty or so immigration offices across the United States as employment offices staffed by former employees of the Bureau of Immigration's information division. The national network found employment for almost 284,000 workers in 1917. Secretary Wilson's project had little support in Congress, but President Woodrow Wilson provided funds from the Office of the President in 1917 (MacLaury, *History of the Department of Labor*).

139. To Edith Abbott

Santa Monica, [California,] in Transit
7-16-17

Dear E. A.

I have to start homeward on July 19th!

Meanwhile I have this peaceful afternoon with John at work and no lecture on.[1]

So I'm propaganding for a new federal Constitution.

Sometime when you meet R. Pound[2] will you sow a seed thought about the electoral college and secret diplomacy etc.,—in his mind? I.e. that they are obsolete!

Also in the mind of one E. Freund?[3] The idea of a Twentieth Century Constitution is not new or peculiar. China, Portugal, Russia, Germany leading the way,—even such academic gents need not feel venture some!

I am not now suggesting the content of the instrument for their consideration,—merely the idea that we must have it soon.

It is heavenly here.

I hate to go to L.A. but I must start now, in order to change my ticket and get a berth not by the Canadian Pacific alas![4]

Yours affectionately

F. Kelley

I would re-write this, but it is the seventeenth and my arm aches!

Forgive that blot!

ALS, Abbott Papers, ICU

1. JK had written that he had found a job as an investment banker in Los Angeles at $20 a week and was determined to "plug along with the crowd," although he was not interested in industrial stocks and bonds. He wrote to FK: "I honestly believe it will be up to me to prove I can make good and then I can begin to be like Ko" (JK, Los Angeles, to FK, 18 June 1917, FKP, NN).
2. Roscoe Pound (1870–1964) was a professor of law (1910–1947) and dean (1916–1936) of Harvard University Law School. He was an honorary vice-president of the NCL.
3. Ernst Freund (1864–1932) was professor of law at the University of Chicago Law School (1902–1932).
4. FK spoke to the Los Angeles Chautauqua on 17 July 1917 (*Los Angeles Times,* 15 July 1917, II:11).

140. To Newton D. Baker

NATIONAL CONSUMERS' LEAGUE
289 FOURTH AVENUE, NEW YORK CITY

[Red Bank, N.J.]
August 13th, 1917

Hon. Newton D. Baker
Secretary of War
War Department
Washington, D.C.

IN RE ARMY UNIFORMS
PERSONAL, CONFIDENTIAL

My dear Mr. Secretary:-

An important element in the trouble in the needle trades is the habit of mind of the Quartermasters, from General Sharpe down.[1]

Their interest centers in quantity, quality and deliveries. No one of them seems to have imagination enough to recognize that deliveries depend upon conditions,—wages, hours, surroundings, methods of making labor bargains.

No change seems to have been made in form or substance of contracts since Miss [Josephine] Goldmark laid ugly facts before Mr. Lippmann in June, as to tenement house work involving diphtheria in the house with army overcoats.[2]

Nor is the enforcement of existing provisions improved since I brought similar evidence to Quartermaster General Sharpe's attention fifteen months ago. At that time I pointed out the New York State law and suggested that the facts could all be obtained continuously, and violation of contracts by sweating checked, through co-operation of the New York State Industrial Commission (by getting the use of its current records).

This co-operation General Sharpe did not seek. Only this July did he ask for the New York State data, and then in a form so unfortunate as to make compliance with his belated request improbable. The Quartermasters make excuses. One excuse is that the non-union manufacturers who now have virtually all the contracts have been getting contracts since the Civil War and "know how to file specifications." But the specifications are a disgrace to the Quartermasters, because they omit all safeguards for labor conditions. A workman is known by his tools. A quartermaster is known by the specifications he accepts.

Newton D. Baker, ca. 1918.
Courtesy of the Library of
Congress, LC-DIG-ggbain-21468.

The Quartermasters have learned nothing from our half century long American struggle against the sweating system, nor from England's heavy penalty for stupidity throughout her industry, which is at bottom identical with their stupidity in regard to army clothing.

Meanwhile the question which six weeks ago was asked in anxious whispers by friends, is now screamed in newspaper scareheads: "Are the drafted men to serve in scab uniforms?"

There is no more time to be lost. Hence this individual memorandum from me. The rut of usage is deep and the Quartermasters are all in it. You alone can get them out. We outsiders are valueless in their eyes. To them we are civilians, theorists without experience, Mr. Lippmann included and Captain Kruesi most of all, because he is new both to the army and the needle trades.[3]

Since the Quartermasters are impervious to enlightenment, they have to be commanded to change their line of action. No one but yourself can compel the prompt rewriting of the established contracts for army clothing so as to prescribe:-

a. the eight hours day:
b. a scale of wages agreed with the unions;
c. the number of present employes actually on the payroll and visible to the eyes of the army inspectors previous to the award of the contract;
d. the floor space and machines under control of the contractor before the award is made, with name and address of ever premises covered.

Without these items, and honest enforcement of them, sustained maximum deliveries are not to be had.

Dissatisfaction is, moreover, growing apace among manufacturers as well as wage-earners in the organized markets where the industry has been growing up for forty years.

The needle trades form the principal manufacturing industry of New York City. They are now in process of dispersal by the Quartermasters. To those who have shared in the long struggle for decent standards in this industry in New York, it is heart-breaking to see new scattered centers coming up with no standards whatever.

It is worse to know that this is blindly, stupidly, if not corruptly, fostered by the Quartermasters, as in the case of the city where I write this memorandum—Red Bank, New Jersey. This is a one man town. It belongs to Sigmund Eisner. He employed no union people if he knew it. He cut all wage scales, carried speeding to the uttermost, trained green hands when the trade was overcrowded with skill, and his enormous factory has for months been guarded by soldiers. To-day not a cutter's knife is moving. Production is at a standstill. Employes have been thrown into jail on trumped up pretexts. Bitterness centers upon the War Department with Mr. Eisner. For he has larger contracts than any union employer.[4]

This week a strike began in the factory of Sigel Bros. and Goodman in New York City, a non-union place with wretched facilities. Some of the cutters were assaulted, and an investigation asked by the employes. Police Commissioner Woods sent one of his own personal investigators with Hillman to the factory.[5] The investigator identified a gangster, who pointed out seven others hired by the concern to intimidate employes. While the strike is on[,] a fresh contract has been given this firm for 400,000 uniforms!

I fear this is only the beginning. There are strikes at Vineland, New Jersey, and in New York City. A very large one seems to be imminent in Brooklyn.

The Quartermasters are a very large root of the trouble, and there is no time to be lost. No one can act but yourself.

Is our Committee to be permanent? What exactly are its powers?[6]

Yours sincerely,
Florence Kelley

TLS, Baker Papers, DLC

1. In August 1917, Newton Baker appointed FK, Louis Kirstein (1867–1942, vice-president of Filene's department store and a Boston civic leader), and Captain Walter E. Kreusi (b. 1881, a reserve officer of the Quartermaster Corps) to a committee to investigate industrial conditions for the manufacture of uniforms (Baker, Washington, D.C., to FK, 13 August 1917, FKP, NN; *Christian Science Monitor,* 25 August 1917, 4; *NYT:* 8 October 1917, 11; Fraser, *Labor Will Rule,* 118). Major General Henry G. Sharpe (1858–1947) was army quartermaster general from 1916 to 1918.

2. When the United States entered the war, Walter Lippmann left the *New Republic* to work in the War Department.

3. Walter Kruesi had previously been director of the Milk and Baby Hygiene Association in Boston and superintendent of the Municipal Employment Bureau (*New York Times:* 30 July 1911, C10; 7 May 1916, E3).

4. Sigmund Eisner (1859–1925) was already manufacturing military uniforms for the Allied armies. Supplying uniforms for the U.S. military expanded his workforce to over 5,000 employees. Sidney Hillman (1887–1946), founder and president of the ACWA, reported that police in Red Bank had arrested ACWA officers and told them to leave the city immediately (Hillman, New York, to FK, 9 August 1917, copy, n.p., Box 4, ACWA Records, NNCorI).

5. FK wrote Lippmann that the ACWA's Hillman had "the most accurate and widereaching knowledge of the needle trades . . . of any man known to me" (FK, New York, to Lippman, 26 June 1917, Box 4, ACWA Records, NNCorI). Arthur Woods (1870–1942) was New York City police commissioner from 1914 to 1918.

6. Hillman wrote FK that he liked her recommendations and wanted her committee to have the power to supervise the production of uniforms (Hillman to FK, 9 August 1917). Baker approved the committee's report and appointed the committee to the Board of Control of Labor Standards in Army Clothing (Baker, Washington, D.C., to FK, 24 August 1917, FKP, NN; *NYT,* 25 August 1917, 4; Goldmark, *Impatient Crusader,* 130–131; see also Fraser, *Labor Will Rule,* 116–121).

141. To Sidney Hillman

NATIONAL CONSUMERS' LEAGUE
289 FOURTH AVENUE, NEW YORK CITY

August 17, 1917

Dear Mr. Hillman

Since I mailed a letter to you, I have had a long telephone message from Captain [Walter] Kruesi.

He says Mr. [Sigmund] Eisner insists that the War Department be represented next Monday at your conference with Mr. Eisner and Mr. Kenyon![1]

This seems to me very strange.

Capt. K. says General Smith wishes him, K., to be present. I told him Mr. Kerstein[2] thought no one should be there but E. & Kenyon and Hillman; that I certainly had no idea of being present, and that I thought it might spoil everything if either General Smith or Capt. K. were present. K.[ruesi] then said "If Eisner wishes it, and Gen'l Smith wishes it, do you think Hillman would object?" I said "No, of course not, but I think it may prevent a successful negotiation." He then said he would talk to Mr. Kerstein before deciding to come to New York.

I wrote Mr. Kerstein the substance of the conversation, but he may be out of town over Sunday, and I write this so that you may consult him over the telephone.

Captain Kruesi has no tact, and would be a terrible person to have present as a difficult negotiation!

Here's wishing you success![3]

Yours sincerely
Florence Kelley

ALS, Box 4, ACWA Records, NNCorl

1. Possibly C. C. Kenyon of Brooklyn, New York, a firm that Hillman had identified as one that did not observe labor standards (Hillman, n.p., to FK, 14 August 1917, Box 4, ACWA Records, NNCorI).
2. Louis E. Kirstein chaired the Board of Control of Labor Standards in Army Clothing.
3. Hillman announced on 25 August 1917 that the ACWA approved of the Board of Control of Labor Standards. Describing the "deplorable" conditions he had found in clothing factories that manufactured uniforms, he congratulated the NCL and other agencies for "stamping out the sweatshops and bringing about the employment of the skilled workers in the industry" (*NYT,* 26 August 1917, I:6). The Board of Control succeeded in establishing an eight-hour day and a 48-hour week for workers who produced army uniforms (Fraser, *Labor Will Rule,* 119).

142. To Newton D. Baker

NATIONAL CONSUMERS' LEAGUE
289 FOURTH AVENUE, NEW YORK CITY

November 11, 1918

Hon. Newton D. Baker
3017 N Street
Washington, D. C.
Dear Mr. President:-

Congratulations on the immeasurably great success of your efforts, and the cutting short of the war! The enclosed telegram speaks for itself. The occasion is yours!

Yours sincerely, and gratefully, and hopefully,
Florence Kelley

two enclosures
P.S. I am sending you the enclosed without waiting for the writer's permission.[1] Grace Abbott was the head of the Child Labor Division of the Children's Bureau, until the Supreme Court held the federal child labor law unconstitutional.[2] She is now with the War Labor Policies Board.[3] She shares my horror of nightwork for women, and my eager hope that no policy may be formally adopted overriding the state nightwork laws, so that violations such as are referred to in her letter may go down ***in*** history as the result of extraordinary, momentary war pressure, and not of a deliberate policy.[4]

TLS, Baker Papers, DLC

Enc: Grace Abbott, Washington, D.C., to FK, 7 November 1918

1. On the campaign to establish the Children's Bureau, see Goldmark, *Impatient Crusader,* 93–104. Grace Abbott's letter, which FK enclosed here, expressed hope that the War Department would "come out with a definite recommendation against night work without any exemptions whatever" (Baker Papers, DLC).

2. The Keating-Owen Act of 1916, passed to establish a national standard for child labor, relied on Article 1, Section 8 of the U.S. Constitution, which gave Congress the power to "regulate commerce with foreign nations, and among the several states." The U.S. Supreme Court invalidated the law in *Hammer v. Dagenhart* in 1918. The plaintiff in the case was a North Carolina father who opposed the power of Congress to regulate the labor of his two children in a cotton mill. The Court ruled in his favor, saying that if Congress had the power to regulate "matters entrusted to local authority by prohibition of the movement of commodities in interstate commerce, all freedom of commerce will be at an end, and the power of the states over local matters may be eliminated, and thus our system of government be practically destroyed" (*Hammer v. Dagenhart,* 247 U.S. 251 [1918]).

3. On Abbott's work with the War Labor Policies Board, see Costin, *Two Sisters for Social Justice,* 110–114.

4. Baker replied that he was gratified that the armistice meant that "the whole world is going to turn its attention to constructive and helpful things" (Baker, Washington, D.C., to FK, 14 November 1918, copy, Baker Papers, DLC).

143. To Newton D. Baker

Personal

[Atlantic City, N. J.]
2-7-1919

Dear Mr. Secretary

This is not a Consumers' League letter. It is a timely reminiscence of one of your old and faithful friends.

Nearly a quarter century ago, in the summer of 1894, I lived in Chicago when Mr. Cleveland sent the regular army thither, and Debs was sent to jail.[1]

Now Debs is in jail again, (or convicted by a federal judge and jury if still at large on bail[)].[2] In those days people feared the American Railway Union as they fear the I.W.W. to-day.

In 1896, 1900, 1904, 1908 the Democratic Party did not carry. Mr. Roosevelt's reckless egotism in 1912 split the Republican Party. Could Mr. Wilson have carried the election without that help?

Mr. Roosevelt is gone.[3]

Granting that the memory of the panic of 1892 lasted many years, the memory of the regular army in the service of capital by order of Mr. Cleveland lasted too, and that of the synchronous jailing of Debs.

It is an ominous coincidence now.

I am not a Republican. I did not cast my first vote, last November, for any Republican.[4] But I seem to see that this situation is as favorable for that party to-day as the summer of 1894 was, a quarter century ago.

Yours faithfully
Florence Kelley[5]

P.S. I'm marooned here by James Alexander Miller, for a few days, under the charge of "a tired heart." I suspect that I am a belated war casualty.[6]

ALS, Baker Papers, DLC

1. See Letter 39, FK to Henry D. Lloyd, 18 July 1894, above.
2. On 14 September 1918, Eugene Debs was sentenced to ten years in prison for violating the Espionage Act because of his criticism of the Wilson administration for its sedition prosecutions. The Espionage Act, passed by Congress on 15 June 1917, prohibited interfering with recruitment of armed forces, encouraging disloyalty among armed forces, and other behavior the government deemed to be disloyal.
3. Theodore Roosevelt ran as a third-party candidate on the Progressive, or "Bull Moose," ticket in 1912. He died on 6 January 1919.
4. New York enfranchised women through a referendum that adopted an amendment to the state constitution in 1917. This event provided impetus to the campaign for an amendment to the U.S. Constitution that would grant voting rights to all women (Harper, *History of Woman Suffrage,* 6:489; *NYT,* 7 November 1917, 1.)
5. In his reply, Baker called the parallel in FK's letter "impressive" but regretted that because of the demands of war-related work he had been unable to follow Debs's case. He promised

he would look into the matter (Baker, Washington, D.C., to FK, 10 February 1919, copy, Baker Papers, DLC). Debs's appeal was denied in March 1919.

6. James A. Miller (1874–1948) was professor of clinical medicine at College of Physicians and Surgeons of Columbia University (1913–1945).

144. To Mary Rozet Smith

NATIONAL CONSUMERS' LEAGUE
289 FOURTH AVENUE
NEW YORK CITY

Steamer Rotterdam
May 22nd 1919

Dear Mary

I left Zurich last Thursday, for Bern, Lausanne, Paris, Southampton Plymouth and this ship. As you doubtless know, my going was an act of faith, not of conviction. When anyone asked why I was going, I said "To black J. A.'s boots and lug her suitcases."[1] Of course, I was quite useless.

But next time I would go on my knees. It was unbelievably wonderful. There were twenty-five English women sitting with the Germans in front, and the Irish at one side, all alike engrossed in the common effort to do two things. First the English were obsessed with the passionate, overwhelming impulse to lift the blockade, modify the peace, and end the famine; second they wished greater power for women in the League of Nations, and many modifications in its provisions.[2]

There were fourteen nations represented by 126 delegates when I left, and no one of the nature of Rosika or of Frau Selenka among the number.[3] I think we had more than our share of weak sisters, with Mrs. Post, Mrs$_x$ [Lucia Ames] Mead, Katherine Fuller (!) Marion Cothren, Mrs. Ford and Miss Burritt.[4] But then, we were twenty-five all told, and no one was actively queer or obstructive.

The English leaders amazed everybody by emphasizing, at every opportunity, that they were all Socialists. This included Mrs. Pethick Lawrence, Crystal Macmillan, Mrs. Snowden[5] (of course), and all the lesser lights$_x$ Hitherto, I have found it hard to like Englishwomen, but this time I found myself their humble admirer.

In Paris we saw much of Mme. Duchesne who hopedd against hope for a passport until Wednesday, May 15th, when she finally wired that there was no hope.[6]

The solitary Italian, Rosa Genone, arrived on Tuesday, May 15th, and Mrs. Swannick that evening.[7]

The French women who took part, and the one Belgian, Mlle. La Fontaine,[8] were already in Switzerland, and needed no passports.

Never have I seen so generous a spirit in any group of human beings. Even Dr. Jacobs was amiable from the word 'Go!'[9]

Needless to say, J. A. presided to the satisfaction of everyone (but me! I thought she wasted one afternoon$_{x}$)$_{x}$ I heard people saying in the English delegation "What an excellent chairman, so fair, and not a moment a wasted." In the Austrian delegation a woman was saying "She is so willing to yield and say that she is wrong—"I'm sorry I made that blunder"—I shall always hear her saying that, and she makes so few blunders."

No one who was not there can ever conceive what it meant to the German and Austrian women. Poor things! Starved in body and soul. I cannot thing of them without tears. So noble and eager. The Bavarians feel that their great days have come and gone like a brief dream. Frau Baur a beautiful, loveable young woman was assistant Secretary of State and Frls. Augsburg and Heymann were members of the Bavarian Diet with seven other women, under Eisner. But after he was assassinated by Count Arco Valley, and much violence and bloodshed followed, the[y] resigned in protest.[10]

To-day for the first time in its history, Bavaria's army, railways and postoffice are controlled from Berlin. But women still have votes, and our friends are convinced that Democracy has come to stay, whatever vicissitudes may arise.

There was great difference of opinion among the members about the draft of the League of Nations. When I left, a Committee was at work on a report to go to Paris, and the whole Congress on a long series of resolutions to go back to the National branches for study and for actions in their own Countries.[11]

The public meetings were in the Aula[12] of the University of Zurich where I was a student five and thirty years ago. The audiences were tremendous, many men being present,—and sympathetic in an extraordinary degree.

J. A. was at her very best. She loved the whole undertaking, tho I think the widespread horror of the League of Nations, and especially of the Peace terms among the members was a surprise and a disappointment.

The day before I left, May 15th, word came that she is to go into Germany. So she will not sail on the Noordam on May /June[13] 23d.[14]

With dear love Yours always
Florence Kelley

ALS, JA Papers, PSC-P. Also published and annotated in Sklar, Schüler, and Strasser, *Social Justice Feminists*, 240–242 (hereafter *Social Justice Feminists* in annotations to this letter).

1. FK sailed on 9 April 1919 as part of the American delegation to the second Women's International Congress for Permanent Peace, held 15–19 May 1919. JA headed the delegation (FK, New York, to NK, 9 April 1919, FKP, NN). For a report on the conference, see WILPF, *Report of the International Congress of Women: Zurich, May 12 to 17, 1919*.

2. The congress's first resolution advocated an end to the Allied blockade of food supplies to Germany and urged the peace negotiators meeting at Versailles near Paris "to develop the inter-allied organizations formed for purposes of war into an international organiza-

tion for purposes of peace, so that the resources of the world—food, raw materials, finance, transport—shall be made available for the relief of the peoples of all countries from famine and pestilence." Although the congress passed no resolution either for or against the proposed League of Nations, the group sent "careful suggestions" to the Paris negotiators (JA, *Peace and Bread,* 160–161, 164). The congress also passed a resolution denouncing the prospective terms of the German peace treaty: "By guaranteeing the fruits of secret treaties to the conquerors the terms of peace have tacitly sanctioned secret diplomacy, denied the principle of self-determination, recognized the rights of the victors to the spoils. . . . By demanding disarmament from one set of belligerents only the principle of justice is violated and the rule of force is continued" (*NYT,* 16 May 1919, 13).

3. Rosika Schwimmer (1877–1948) founded the Hungarian Feminist Association and co-founded the Women's Peace Party during World War I; German journalist Margarethe Salenka (1860–1923) founded the Committee for Rallies for the Peace Conference in 1898–1899 (*Social Justice Feminists,* 204, 230).

4. Alice Thatcher Post (1853–1947) was vice-president of the Anti-Imperialist League (*Social Justice Feminists,* 232). Catherine Eastman Fuller was a New York City editor; Marion Benedict Cothren (1880–1949) was a New York City lawyer and suffragist; Clara Bryant Ford (1866–1950) was the wife of Henry Ford; and Marion T. Burritt was active in the Peace Society of New York (*NYT,* 7 March 1914, 13).

5. Suffragist Emmeline Pethick-Lawrence (1867–1954) had attended the 1915 ICW; Chrystal Macmillan (1882–1937) was secretary of the International Women Suffrage Alliance (1913–1920) and secretary of the ICW in 1915; Ethel Annakin Snowden (1880–1951) was a British socialist and suffragist (*Social Justice Feminists,* 230, 204).

6. Gabrielle Laforcade Duchène (1878–1954) was a French journalist who worked on child welfare and anti-sweatshop issues (*Social Justice Feminists,* 209).

7. Rosa Genoni was an Italian fashion designer and suffragist; Helena Swanwick (1864–1939) was a British suffragist and organizer of the 1915 ICW at The Hague (*Social Justice Feminists,* 208, 241).

8. Leonie La Fontaine (1859–1949) was president of the Belgian National Women's Council from 1913 to 1919 (*Social Justice Feminists,* 232).

9. Dutch physician Aletta Jacobs (1854–1929) had helped organize the ICW meeting in 1915 (*Social Justice Feminists,* 191).

10. Gertrud Baer (1890–1981) was a German journalist and teacher. Anita Augspurg (1857–1943) and Lida Gustava Heymann (1868–1943) were leaders in the radical wing of the German women's movement (*Social Justice Feminists,* 341, 346). Kurt Eisner (1867–1919), a leader of the Independent Socialist Party, headed the Bavarian government during a brief revolution in 1919. He was killed by Count Anton Graf Arco-Valley, a Jewish German army officer, on 21 February 1919 (Hardin, *Dictionary of Literary Biography,* 100–105).

11. Genoni, Duchène, Macmillan, and JA were part of the delegation that carried the resolutions of the Zurich congress that protested the terms of the Versailles treaty to the Paris negotiators. Authorities in Paris informed them that women's views would be considered in the various national plebiscites and that a woman might become a member of the Commission on International Labor Legislation (*NYT:* 20 May 1919, 5, and 8 June 1919, 10).

12. German: "auditorium."

13. "/June" is inserted above the line after "May."

14. After delivering the congress's resolutions to Colonel Edward M. House and others in Paris, JA and Alice Hamilton toured Germany before returning to the United States in August. For their tour, see Sklar and Amidon, "How Did Women Activists Promote Peace in Their 1915 Tour of Warring European Capitals?"

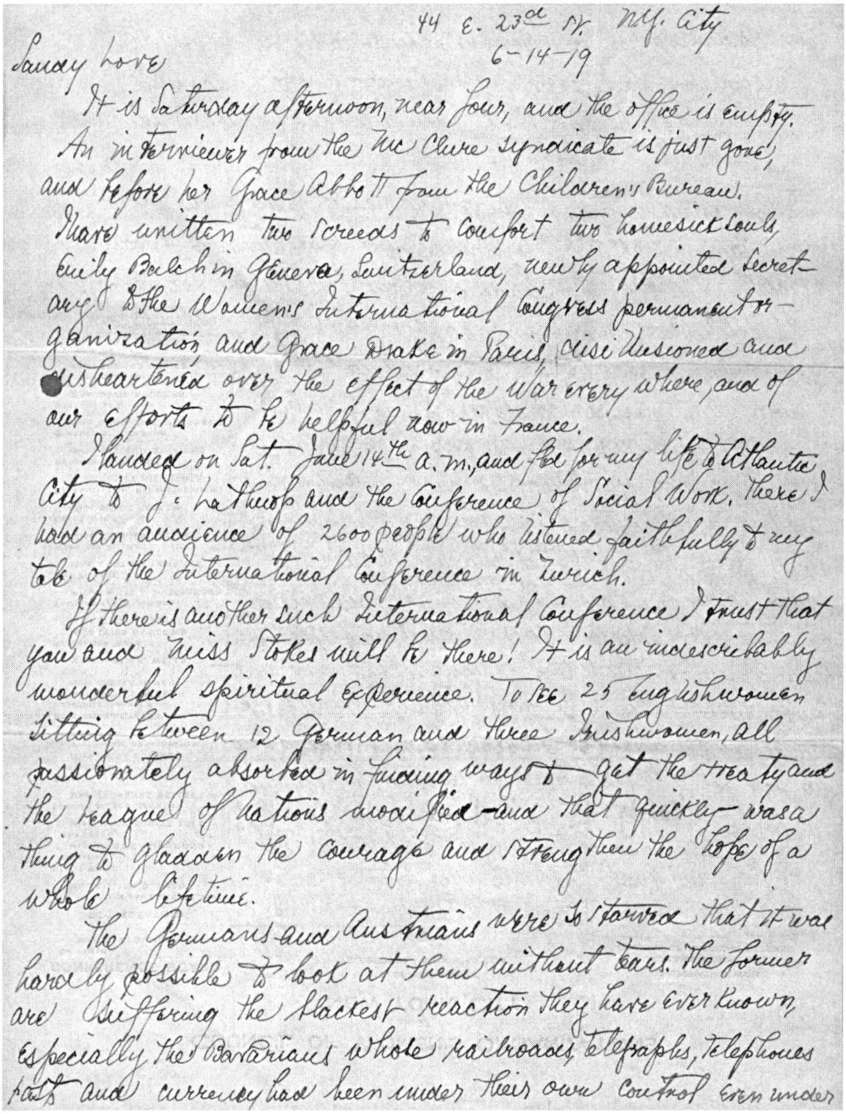
44 E. 23d St. N.Y. City
6-14-19

Sandy Love

It is Saturday afternoon, near four, and the office is empty. An interviewer from the McClure syndicate is just gone, and before her Grace Abbott from the Children's Bureau.

I have written two screeds to comfort two homesick souls, Emily Balch in Geneva, Switzerland, newly appointed Secretary of the Women's International Congress permanent organization and Grace Drake in Paris, disillusioned and disheartened over the effect of the war everywhere, and of our efforts to be helpful now in France.

I landed on Sat. June 14th a.m., and fled for my life to Atlantic City to J. Lathrop and the Conference of Social Work. There I had an audience of 2600 people who listened faithfully to my tale of the International Conference in Zurich.

If there is another such International Conference I trust that you and Miss Stokes will be there! It is an indescribably wonderful spiritual experience. To see 25 Englishwomen sitting between 12 German and three Irishwomen, all passionately absorbed in finding ways to get the treaty and the League of Nations modified—and that quickly—was a thing to gladden the courage and strengthen the hope of a whole lifetime.

The Germans and Austrians were so starved that it was hardly possible to look at them without tears. The former are suffering the blackest reaction they have ever known, especially the Bavarians whose railroads, telegraphs, telephones, posts and currency had been under their own control even under

First page of Florence Kelley to Mary R. Sanford, 14 June 1919. Courtesy of the Florence Kelley Papers, Rare Books and Manuscripts Division, New York Public Library, Astor, Lenox and Tilden Foundations.

145. To Mary R. Sanford

44 E. 23d St. N.Y. City
6-14-19

Sandy Love

It is Saturday afternoon, near four, and the office is empty. An interviewer from the Mc Clure syndicate is just gone, and before her Grace Abbott from the Children's Bureau. I have written two screeds to comfort two homesick souls, Emily Balch in Geneva, Switzerland, newly appointed Secretary to the Women's International Congress permanent organization,[1] and Grace Drake in Paris, disillusioned and disheartened over the effect of the War every where, and of our efforts to be helpful now in France.

I landed on Sat. June 14th a.m., and fled for my life to Atlantic City to J. Lathrop and the Conference of Social Work. There I had an audience of 2600 people who listened faithfully to my tale of the International Conference in Zurich.[2]

If there is another such International Conference I trust that you and Miss Stokes will be there![3] It is an indescribably wonderful spiritual experience. To see 25 Englishwomen sitting between 12 German and three Irishwomen, all passionately absorbed in finding ways to get the treaty and the League of Nations modified—and that quickly—was a thing to gladden the courage and strengthen the hope of a whole lifetime.

The Germans and Austrians were so starved that it was hardly possible to look at them without tears. The former are suffering the blackest reaction they have ever known, especially the Bavarians whose railroads, telegraphs, telephones posts and currency had been under their own control even under the Hohenzollern, are now wholly beneath the heel of the Prussians. Yet even those women have undaunted faith in the future that men and women are to create soon!

In Vienna a very fine young journalist, Frau Scheu-Riesz is chairman of the Commission for rewriting the school books.[4] She has the leading geographers, historians, teachers of literature and language, as heads of committee working with her. They are eliminating everything that could cause contempt or hatred in the minds of the pupils. Another Vienna woman is head of a school for teaching girls agriculture and horticulture. They have been socialized since the revolution and are required to have~~r~~ ready on May 15th to June 1st one million plants to be sold at cost to working people for their gardens. The school is municipal and must contribute to the city food supply. Frau Hertzka said her girls were at work at 6 a.m. daily, singing for joy at their task of feeding the starving city.[5] It was all unbelievably wonderful!

Dear Sandy! We must keep young and gay for the good time coming!

Your loving old
Kelley

ALS, FKP, NN

1. That permanent organization, WILPF, grew out of the 1915 International Women's Peace Conference at the Hague. It met for the first time in 1919. Emily Balch had been dismissed from her position as economics professor at Wellesley because of her opposition to the war and her absence from campus to attend that conference.

2. Actually, FK returned to New York on 31 May 1919 (FK, Atlantic City, N.J., to NK, 1 June 1919, FKP, NN). On 6 June, FK told the National Conference of Social Work that by agreeing to the embargo that kept food from reaching defeated countries, the United States was complicit in the starvation of Europe's people and that the news of this suffering was not getting through to the American public (*NYT,* 6 June 1919, 5).

3. Helen Phelps Stokes, sister of James Graham Stokes, served on the NCL Finance Committee as early as 1908 and in 1917 and 1918 (NCL, Tenth Annual Report [1909], List of Officers; and NCL Annual Council Minutes, 1917 and 1918, both in Box A6, NCL Records, DLC.). Born into a wealthy philanthropic family in New York City, she was a central figure in the Intercollegiate Socialist Society in 1910 and in 1918 helped found what became the American Civil Liberties Union (*NYT:* 14 December 1908, 8, and 30 December 1910, 7; Helen Phelps Stokes, Ridgefield, Conn., to FK, 10 August 1918 and 2 September 1918, FKP, NN).

4. Helene Scheu-Riesz was the author of *Der Revolutionär: Eine Lebensgeschichte* (The Revolutionary: A Life's History) (1918) and *Books as Tools in War and Peace* (1940s).

5. Possibly peace advocate Yella Hertzka (*NYT,* 2 October 1920, 8).

146. To Newton D. Baker

NATIONAL CONSUMERS' LEAGUE
~~289 FOURTH AVENUE~~ ***44 EAST 23RD ST.,*** NEW YORK CITY

June 19, 1919

Hon. Newton D. Baker
3017 N Street, N.W.
Washington, D. C.
Dear Mr. Baker:-

I have read Frontiers of Freedom with the keenest interest.[1] Many noble passages in it encourage me to venture to write you this letter, which has nothing to do with the Consumers' League.

I am assuming that the Germans will sign the treaty at once, and the President will return home and will enter upon his speaking tour quickly thereafter.[2] I am assuming, too, that you have influence with him as of old. Is it too much to hope that he may proclaim to our disturbed country that peace has indeed come to America, by taking the following measures <u>before</u> starting on his tour;-

1. Exercising executive clemency to the uttermost limit, releasing prisoners, both civil and military, who are not proven guilty of actual crimes of violence?

2. Publishing an urgent recommendation for the immediate repeal of the espionage law? and
3. Appointing your least beloved colleague in the Cabinet ambassador to Timbuctu or Boorioboolaga?[3]

It is my rooted conviction that every day while these three measures are delayed is time for acres of seed-sowing for the I. W. W., the anarchists and the bomb throwers; and that nothing could so palsy the tongues and pens of critics of the President, his whole policy during the last six months, and his League of Nations, as this threefold gift of peace on earth, goodwill to men—at home!

Yours sincerely,
Florence Kelley[4]

TLS, Baker Papers, DLC

1. Newton D. Baker, *Frontiers of Freedom* (New York: George H. Doran, 1918).
2. The Germans signed the Treaty of Versailles on 28 June 1919. President Wilson returned to the United States on 8 July and presented the treaty to the Senate for ratification on 10 July. To muster popular support for the treaty, he planned to tour the United States beginning in September.
3. FK probably was referring to William G. McAdoo (1863–1941), secretary of the treasury, who had opposed Baker on several issues (Beaver, *Newton D. Baker and the American War Effort*, 104–105).
4. Baker responded to all three points of FK's letter, writing that executive clemency "is really being exercised steadily by both the Department of Justice and the War Department on a scale quite beyond what one would imagine from the newspaper description of it." He told her that the Espionage Act was being revoked on the day he wrote. As for the "colleague to whom you refer," Baker wrote that he "has some admitted blind spots, but some very robust virtues" (Baker, Washington, D.C., to FK, 21 June 1919, copy, Baker Papers, DLC).

147. To Nicholas Kelley

Naskeag, Hancock Co., Me.
7-25-19

Darling Son

This is one of three Northwest days that come in a summer, and the schooner sailed away about ten in the morning with ten persons aboard and supplies of lobster, biscuits and candy for a long day.[1] They were to sail first to Blue Hill and then, if everything favored, to Bar Harbor and back. There were John and his sailor and cook (!) Mr. Bradford and Myrta Jones from Cleveland (here for the fourth time), John's two Richmond friends, Anne Valentine and Emma Sampson, my life saving cook Clemmy, and little Rose whom I brought again for the summer. I could not go because Mrs. [Mary Dana Hicks] Prang had written that she would be here between July 20th and Aug. 1st, and would let me know in advance. But letters from her sometimes come after she has arrived, and I could not risk finding her sitting on the porch, hungry and tired on our return.

So I am giving myself this pleasure instead of the sailing party.

It has been a delight to have John and his young folks here. He is like a different person since the Armistice, and, in his present rôle, he is almost unrecognizable.[2]

I am wanted as a character witness in the Lusk-Rand School case which begins next Monday. So I suppose I must go to N.Y. on the night train some night next week. The days here are so grey and cool, or so radiant with strong breezes and varying skies that I hate the change. But I should be a shirk if I let that charter go by the board without a protest![3]

Yesterday we sent off 15000 words to the Jour. of Industrial Hygiene, on the textiles. Now for the Senate Document.[4] I think I have at last a program for the League for the third ten years.[5]

The celebration comes in November.[6] I hope to propose a campaign against poisons in industry such as lead which is increasing enormously, chlorine in bleaching etc. etc.

This will be added to the old tasks,—getting wages and hours improved. It is a very far reaching undertaking upon which at present no one appears to have embarked.

We can get the facts from Alice Hamilton, and furnish the publicity. Our motto, henceforth, should, I think, be "Keep the light turned on." We have never had a motto. But we need one now.

Don't trouble to answer this. Just send a postal once in a while, to let me know that you are not melted.

Augusta [Kelley] held out a hope that I might meet you in Sakonnet after next month. That is half the joy of this wonderful summer!

Your loving
Mother

ALS, FKP, NN

1. FK sailed with JK in his schooner from New York as far as Plymouth, Mass; she reached her summer home on 8 July 1919 (FK, Brooklin, Me., to NK, 12 July 1919, FKP, NN).
2. Recently JK had worked at several odd jobs, among them surveyor and farmer. When the United States entered the war, he wrote FK that he would not enlist: "It is too cruel to go out systematically to mangle and maim other people. I am not a particle more irritated with the Hohenzollern than with the Wilson, and neither of them seem to me to be worth fighting for" (JK, Los Angeles, to FK, 18 June 1917, FKP, NN).
3. State senator Clayton R. Lusk of New York (1872–1959; Republican, 1919–1924) had formed a committee to investigate the Rand School of Social Science and the American Socialist Society, which ran the school. Following this investigation, New York's attorney general tried unsuccessfully to revoke the school's charter on the grounds that it had distributed and sold radical literature (*NYT,* 11 July 1919, 10, 24; Pfannestiel, *Rethinking the Red Scare,* 75–96).
4. FK told NK that her forthcoming article "Wage Earning Women in War Time: Textiles" would be an abridgment of the NCL's YWCA report. She noted that Senator Robert M. La Follette had offered the franking privilege of his office and that the Senate would print and distribute 100,000 copies of the report (FK, New York, to NK, 21 June 1919, FKP, NN). The

YWCA report might have been Eleanor L. Lattimore and Ray S. Trent, *Legal Recognition of Industrial Women* (New York: Industrial Committee, War Work Council of the National Board Young Women's Christian Associations, 1919), a pamphlet in FK's library at Seawest, Maine, given to K. K. Sklar by the M. S. Lane family, who now own the house. On the campaign against poisons in industry, see Letter 148, FK to David Edsall, 9 September 1919, below.

5. The NCL's ten-year program can be found in "Resolutions Passed at 20th Annual Meeting of the National Consumer's League" ("Leaflets, Historical," Box 2, NCL Records, DLC).

6. For the twentieth annual meeting, see NCL Council Minutes, 21 November 1919, 1–5 (Box A7, NCL Records, DLC).

148. To David L. Edsall[1]

COPY

[New York City]
September 9, 1919

Dr. David L. Edsall
80 Marlboro Street
Boston, Mass.
Dear Dr. Edsall:-

The next annual meeting of the National Consumers' League will be the twentieth anniversary of its foundation. On the corresponding occasion ten years ago, we adopted a ten-years program consisting of three parts:—minimum wage commissions for the states and the District of Columbia, the short working day for women and minors, and prolonged education. The war has so expedited the two latter undertakings, that we can no longer claim them as our own. They have become largely the work of the nation. Obviously, we must keep on with them, but with additions.

On Thursday last, I had a long conversation with Secretary Baker on the relation of the Consumers' League to industrial poisons, and I made to him the proposal which sums up briefly and crudely as follows:

a) We should again adopt a ten-years program which must, of course, be within strictly industrial limits;
b) We could appropriately add to our former planks a plank, of which the enclosed memorandum expresses the gist,—the form being the crudest possible tentative draft, lacking at present all provision for enforcement.[2]

At first thought, Secretary Baker's objections to the proposal were two:

a) That it was too narrow,—that it should, if we went into the subject of health, reach very far indeed; and
b) That an amendment to the Constitution should not be a legislative provision, but a statement of general principles, conferring upon Congress power to embody those principles.[3]

Later, however, he agreed with me that the National Consumers' League must confine itself closely to the area of industry, and that in a future paragraph specifying the manner of enforcement power could be conferred upon Congress.

Drafting that paragraph would be the legal task of our adviser, Mr. Frankfurter.[4] He, therefore, referred me for conference to you and to Mr. Frankfurter, saying that he considered legislation—including, if necessary, a constitutional amendment—within the legitimate field of the League, and thought it timely that we should adopt in November a ten-years program of which that should be the principal new element.

Having been at work since 1882 in the field of labor legislation, I am convinced by disheartening experience of the futility of diffused education of public opinion, and of state and congressional legislation under the Constitution as it stands today. The progress which might reasonably have been expected in thirty-seven years of effort by orderly constitutional methods, has been effectively and uniformly blocked by the interpretations which the courts placed upon our Ancient Instrument.

On the other hand, American legislation has offered not the faintest stimulus to our famous, characteristic, American gift of ingenuity to discover harmless materials and healthful processes. I am convinced that a serious, nationwide educational campaign carried on for ten years—as the child labor campaign has been carried on during the last ten years—would have as its by-product a revolution in the technique of industry, whatever Congress might do in the way of delay of the proposed amendment.

Yours sincerely,
(signed) FLORENCE KELLEY

P.S. I appreciate that it is asking a great deal, when I venture to beg you to send me your opinion as to the suitability of such a proposal for discussion and possible action at our twentieth annual meeting on November 20th and 21st next. If the subject is to come up, notice has to be sent to the various Leagues sixty days in advance, and my understanding is that before Secretary Baker discusses the matter any further, he desires an expression of opinion from you and from Mr. Frankfurter.[5]

CC, "NCL Correspondence 1915–1922," Box 157, Frankfurter Papers, DLC

1. Dr. David L. Edsall (1869–1945) was dean of Harvard Medical School (1918–1935). He was instrumental in getting Alice Hamilton appointed at Harvard as assistant professor of industrial medicine in January 1919 (Sicherman, *Alice Hamilton,* 209–210, 217).
2. FK had sent Newton Baker a memorandum proposing as a twentieth amendment to the Constitution a "Lifesaving Amendment" that prohibited the use of poisons in industry (FK, Brooklin, Me., to Baker, 18 August 1919, Baker Papers, DLC).
3. Baker had told FK in August that he thought it "better to draw the amendment in the form of declaring that the health of the people of the United States is a matter of national concern and that Congress shall have the power to conserve the public health by the regula-

tion or prohibition of dangerous or noxious occupations" (Baker, [Washington, D.C.], to FK, 25 August 1919, Baker Papers).

4. Felix Frankfurter became the NCL's legal advisor after Brandeis was appointed to the U.S. Supreme Court in 1916 (NCL, *Report for the Years 1914–1915–1916,* 24–25, Box A6, NCL Papers, DLC).

5. Edsall declined to render an opinion on a constitutional amendment but wrote, "I can not see that there is anything but justice in strict legislation concerning industrial poisoning. It is purely a thing imposed upon mankind by the indifference or greed of people who cause the poisoning" (David L. Edsall, Boston, to FK, 11 September 1919, copy, "NCL Correspondence 1915–1922," Box 157, Frankfurter Papers). Frankfurter wrote, "Are we not getting a little into conflict in assuming that we have to choose either the constitutional amendment or legislative help in case the Supreme Court sustains the new child labor law?" (Frankfurter, Cambridge, Mass., to FK, 6 October 1919, copy, "NCL Correspondence 1915–1922," Box 157, Frankfurter Papers). He was referring to the Child Labor Tax Law enacted by Congress in February 1919, which imposed an excise tax of 10 percent on the annual net profits of manufacturers who employed children in violation of specified age and hours standards.

The resolution on industrial poisons was point seven of the ten-year plan the NCL Council passed at its annual meeting in Louisville on 21 November (NCL Council Minutes, 21 November 1919, 7, Box A7, NCL Records, DLC). It emphasized the enormous increase of "poisonous processes and materials" during the war.

149. To Newton D. Baker

NATIONAL CONSUMERS' LEAGUE
44 EAST TWENTY-THIRD STREET, NEW YORK CITY

September 22, 1919

Hon. Newton D. Baker
3017 N Street
Washington, D. C.
Dear Mr. Baker:

Herewith I return Dr. McCracken's letter. Our friend, Mr. Weld of Swift and Company, has disappeared from the surface, and no longer publicly interests himself in the activities of the National Consumers' League. In his place, however, Mr. Louis F. Swift appears to have addressed to each [of] our vice-presidents a letter of enquiry or reproach, or both, in regard to our attitude towards the packers.[1]

I enclose also a copy of the resolution adopted at the June meeting of the League, at which you presided, under which Miss Haver and I have been acting. I have appeared before the Senate Committee, and she has worked with Mrs. [Mabel Cory] Costigan, with Miss Rigby of the Christian Science Monitor, and other agencies of approach to a wider public than our too limited membership.[2]

The enclosed correspondence between Mr. Swift and President Burton of the University of Minnesota[3] appears to be a link in this interesting chain of propaganda by the packers. In the light of the Burton letter and Mr. Weld's letter to you, I can only suggest an enquiry from you to President McCracken as to the nature of the recent work of the Consumers' League which has awakened his anxiety!

Yours sincerely,
Florence Kelley

five enclosures

TLS, Baker Papers, DLC

1. In April 1919, FK launched an attack on the domination of the food industry by five major meatpacking manufacturers. Arguing that this lowered the wages of meatpacking employees and increased the cost of food products, she also endorsed a recent investigation of the meatpacking industry by the Federal Trade Commission (FK, "The Consumer and the Near Future"). FK's article resulted in two public exchanges of letters between FK and Lewis D. H. Weld (b. 1882), manager of the Commercial Research Department of Swift and Co., in which Weld attacked FK's article and the trade commission and FK defended the commission's investigation (*Survey* 42: "Communications" [28 June 1919]: 503–504; and "Communications" [9 August 1919]: 712–713). Louis F. Swift (1861–1937) succeeded his father as head of Swift & Co. in 1903. Henry N. MacCracken (1880–1970), president of Vassar College (1915–1946) and an honorary NCL vice-president, had apparently expressed concern to Baker about the NCL's policy toward the meatpackers, and Baker had asked FK for advice before responding to him (Baker, Washington, D.C., to FK, 18 September 1919, copy, Baker Papers, DLC). For more about the exchange between McCracken and Baker, see Letter 151, FK to NK, 18 October 1919, below.

2. In June, the NCL Executive Committee resolved to cooperate with the government's investigations into the meatpacking industry (NCL Executive Committee Minutes, 12 June 1919, 4, Box A7, NCL Records, DLC; the resolution is preserved with FK's letter of 22 September in the Baker Papers). Suffragist and writer Jesse R. Haver (later Butler; 1886–1989) was secretary of the CL of the District of Columbia and chaired its legislative committee in 1919.

FK testified at the Senate's hearings on five large meatpacking corporations that had been accused of profiteering during and after the war. In response to these accusations, the meatpackers ran full-page advertisements in Washington, D.C., newspapers that denied the charges and invited the public to consult them for "facts and figures" that would prove their innocence (display ad in *The Washington Post,* 19 August 1919, 5). According to FK, *The Christian Science Monitor* was the only significant daily newspaper that did not advertise meatpackers' products ("The Consumer and the Near Future," 6). With other members of the CL of the District of Columbia, Haver monitored the hearings and sought a woman reporter at the *Monitor* to break the story of the meatpackers' hearings, which Washington newspapers that ran the meatpackers' ads had not covered (*Christian Science Monitor,* 1 June 1919, E3; *Washington Post,* 20 July 1919, 17). She later recalled that the meatpackers were very surprised when FK appeared to testify: "And of course that upset them terribly. They knew who Florence Kelley was, don't worry!" (Gluck, "Interview with Jesse Haver Butler").

3. Marion LeRoy Burton (1874–1925) was president of the University of Minnesota (1917–1920), president of the University of Michigan (1920–1925), and an honorary vice-president of the NCL.

150. To Nicholas Kelley

NATIONAL CONSUMERS' LEAGUE
~~289 FOURTH AVENUE~~44 E. 23 ST. NEW YORK CITY

10-2-19

Beloved Son

It looks as though I should have to come down for a hearing on Oct 8th. Will Augusta and the children be there? Otherwise I can go, again, to the Ontario and J. Lathrop. You did not mention the house number in de Sales Street, or how to reach it from the Union Station.[1]

This has been a vortex hard to keep from drowning in. No funds, Grace Drake in Europe and the whole Finance Committee scattered,[2] Miss [Marguerite] Fleishman married ten days ago, and an admirable new secretary here but not acquainted with her duties.

Fortunately I seem to have profited immensely by my spring and summer.

On the first and last Sundays John took me for September cruises on the Sound,—enchanting experiences which keyed me aright for the week following each one. In the middle, Miss Wald asked me one Sunday to Saugatuck Conn., her weekend country home.

From my 11th story window, I see Madison Square and Fifth avenue crowds from a flattering distance. All these things have kept me cheerful through these depressing weeks of revelations of our share in the European murder so wholesale and so mean![3]

W.W.'s career is short measured by the long life of Europe.[4] And next year our turn will come.[5]

Dear love to you
F.K.

ALS, FKP, NN

1. Since July 1918, NK had been working in the U.S. Treasury Department in charge of loans to foreign governments. He was promoted to assistant secretary in June 1920 (FK, New York, to NK, 10 June 1920, FKP, NN). In addition to Nicky, Nicholas and Augusta Kelley's children now included Florence ("Florrie"), age seven, and Augustus, age five.

2. FK later wrote Newton Baker that Grace Drake and Helen Stokes had been "our financial props" during this period (FK to Baker, 14 February 1920, Baker Papers, DLC).

3. FK had brought back from her European trip photographs of starving children (e.g., a ten-year-old Viennese girl who weighed thirty-six pounds). These were published in her *Survey* article "The Condition of Europe." Throughout the fall, newspapers carried headlines about war-ravaged Europe.

4. NK replied, "I fear that W. W. is an ill man" (NK, Washington, D.C., to FK, 3 October 1919, FKP, NN). Despite President Wilson's fervent lobbying, the Senate voted not to ratify the Treaty of Versailles on 19 November 1919.

5. On 4 June 1919, Congress had approved the Nineteenth Amendment allowing women to vote; sixteen states had ratified it by October (see FK, "A Challenge to Social Workers"). The amendment was ratified on 26 August 1920, and women voted in the 1920 presidential election.

151. To Nicholas Kelley

Hotel Ten Eyck Albany N.Y.
Sat A.M. 10-18-19

Beloved Son

In this year of shame and sorrow for our international crimes and our home atrocities against Negroes and wage earners, this has been a week of cheering experiences for me.[1] So I snatch an hour before train time to share with you.

On Monday, in Attleboro, Mass., I spoke to a Community Brotherhood in an admirable school house, in an auditorium which seats 1200 and was half full of people from 16 to 80 years old. It is the old lyceum modernized. There was an interesting flaw however.

Attleboro has 18000 people. Its industry is cheap jewelry. There was recently a strike. Therefore the Universalist preacher who runs the Brotherhood was afraid of questions from the floor. But he was also afraid to have no questions. So he announced that all who wished to ask any, could come forward at 10 pm! Six faithful souls 5 American and 1 Austrian argued for forty minutes beginning at ten p.m.! Thereafter I caught a 12:30 midnight for N.Y. at Providence and was driven out at 5.30 a.m. (by the foul air) in N.Y. Took a room at the Belmont, slept until 10 a.m. then went to the Women's Joint Legislative Committee to defeat Speaker Sweet,[2] and caught a one o'clock for Vassar.

The Packers had scared Pres. McCracken about the "widened activities" of the C. League. So N. D. B. wrote him that he (N. D. B.) had asked me to confer with him (McC.) as I was about to go to Vassar.[3] (In fact, I as Pres. of the I.S.S., was to speak to the Vassar branch of the I.S.S.!)[4] So there was a cordial letter from McC. to both of us, and a fine conference with him and the Economics and Sociology Faculty, who are unusually good folks,—and a cordial time all round. The students are my especial joy and Prof. Mills is a trump.[5] I talked Socialism straight to the ISS branch for an hour.

I slept 12 hours, and acquired a small group of friends in the Senior class, and reached the office on Wed. at eleven or thereabouts for a mountain of mail. Slept in my own bed Wed. night and came here Thursday arriving in drenching rain with a heavy suitcase. Student girls from the St. College for Teachers met, fed and sheltered me, and convoyed me to the meeting of the Convocation where the Head Shirk in the Educational system of N.Y. State was presiding. This Convocation gave Hon. R. Lansing an L.L.D. last evening. But on Wed. eve. it was a Conference of the T.U. leaders and the Commrs. of Education, Health and Labor intended to get the brakes firmly down on the Child Labor Comms., the C. Leagues and all other people who object to having the children of this state handed over bodily to Labor and Capital.[6]

More soon! (The Head Shirk is John Finley)[7]

Love to you all.

I have to go to my train
I hope to spend the night on the Yacht.

Your run-around Granny

ALS, FKP, NN

1. The vengeful blockade of Germany lasted from the end of hostilities in October 1918 to the Treaty of Versailles in June 1919, causing high rates of starvation and death, especially among children (Hamilton and Addams, "After the Lean Years"). A race riot in Chicago from 27 July to 8 August 1919 left twenty-three African Americans and fifteen whites dead and 537 wounded (Tuttle, *Race Riot,* 64). In October 1919, the nation was in the midst of a wave of postwar strikes, including a strike by steel workers from 22 September to 8 January 1920 (Filippelli, *Labor Conflict in the United States,* 498–502).

2. Thaddeus C. Sweet (1872–1928) was speaker of the New York State Assembly (1914–1920) and U.S. congressman (Republican, New York, 1923–1928). FK began attacking Sweet in April 1919 for his failure to support a minimum wage bill with enforcement powers. Shortly thereafter, the WJLC was formed in New York to promote progressive legislation for women and it mounted a campaign to defeat Sweet. In 1921, Sweet retired from the state legislature. After failing in his ambition to become governor of or a senator from New York, he won election to the U.S. House of Representatives in 1923 (FK, "Minimum Wage Protest," 83; Mackenzie, "The Challenge to Autocracy," 853). On the WJLC, see FK, New York, to Minnie F. Cunningham, 21 June 1920, "Wages and Hours: Correspondence, 1919–1929," Box C49, NCL Records, DLC; and McGuire, "'A Catalyst for Reform,'" 1, 87, 96–117.

3. Newton Baker told FK that his correspondence with Henry MacCracken had prompted his desire for a closer relationship with Vassar's Department of Economics, "both because I think it would give young women in colleges some real clinical experience, and also because I think it would bring them more readily into active association with us after their graduation" (Baker, Washington, D.C., to FK, 1 October 1919, copy, Baker Papers, DLC).

4. Founded in 1905, the Intercollegiate Socialist Society, which had chapters at many colleges and universities, aimed to acquaint students with the dangers of capitalism and the advantages of a society based on socialist principles. In 1921, it was reorganized into the LID.

5. Herbert E. Mills (1861–1946) taught economics at Vassar (1890–1931).

6. The joint conference of New York University and the state industrial commission on child welfare was held in Albany on 17–18 October. At the evening convocation of the regents of New York University, Robert Lansing (1864–1928), U.S. Secretary of State (1915–1920), urged support for the League of Nations. The conference closed with a recommendation that a commission examine and consider for revision all child welfare legislation in New York State (*Albany Evening Journal:* 17 October 1919, 3, and 18 October 1919, 1). In this context, the NCLC adopted an agenda that placed "Federal Aid to Elementary Education" and "Health" before a "Federal Child Labor Law." FK responded by resigning from the NCLC, denouncing its decision "to spread the work of the Committee thin over an immeasurable area instead of continuing to strive to achieve the abolition of child labor ("Fifteenth Annual Report of the General Secretary of the National Child Labor Committee," 30 September 1919; National Child Labor Committee, "Eleventh Annual Meeting of Corporation," [18 November 1919], both in NCLC Records, DLC; FK quote in Trattner, *Crusade for the Children,* 158).

7. John H. Finley (1863–1940), president of City College of New York (1903–1913), was New York State commissioner of education from 1913 to 1921. During World War I, he resolutely repressed political dissent and ruled against all the cases in which New York teachers argued for their right to free speech (Gettleman, *An Elusive Presence,* 244–245). As commissioner of education, he was present at the Wednesday evening meeting FK described here.

152. To Agnes de Lima[1]

[Atlantic City, N.J.]
1-1-20

Dear Agnes

I spent last night reading the Untimely Papers,[2] and all to-day I have been haunted by sorrow that he [Randolph Bourne] is not now interpreting the incomprehensible darkening of the mind and spirit of this whole nation.

Walter Lippman's current lament that we did not tie up afresh, at the armistice, with the British Empire brings fresh evidence of the loss we have suffered in Randolph Bourne's going.[3] For Walter Lippman will be taken seriously as spokesman for the new generation.

The Papers show how far we have traveled in the mournful year when we said Peace Peace! and there was no peace.

And the poignant words alas!—that gift no one inherits! "towards a more radiant American future"!

"The war will leave the country spiritually impoverished, because of the draining away of sentiment into the channels of war$_x$"

"Perhaps literature that can be paled by war will not be missed."

"If America has lost its political isolation, it is all the more obligated to maintain its spiritual integrity."[4]

Grief for the loss of that flaming torch lies deeper after a year, because our intel[le]ctual poverty and need are better plumbed, and the meagreness of our thinking is naked under the sun.

Thank you, dear Agnes, for the book. There is comfort in knowing that others are to come. We must see to it that they never get out of print.

May this be, at least, a better year!

Yours affectionately
F.K.

ALS, Bourne Papers, NCC-RB

1. Journalist Agnes de Lima (1887–1974) was a close friend of public intellectual, writer, and social critic Randolph Bourne (1886–1918) (Sandeen, *Letters of Randolph Bourne,* 400). De Lima worked in the NCL office in 1919 (FK, Brooklin, Me., to Molly Dewson, 18 July 1919, Dewson Papers, MCR-S) and the NCL published her report on women's night work in New Jersey in 1920 (*Night-Working Mothers in Textile Industries*).

2. Bourne's posthumous work, *Untimely Papers* (New York: B. W. Huebsch, 1919), was one of the earliest and most scathing critiques of intellectuals who supported World War I in the United States and elsewhere. FK knew Bourne as a fellow member of the Intercollegiate Socialist Society.

3. In a review of Harold Stearns's *Liberalism in America,* Lippman wrote that in the war's aftermath "a golden opportunity was lost to make a great advance in human relations." Because Woodrow Wilson did not ally the United States with Britain, he "cut himself off from

the nation in which liberalism is mature and powerful" (*New Republic* 21 [31 December 1919]: 151).

4. FK was quoting from pages 107, 109, and 110 of Bourne's work. Her tribute, "Randolph Bourne," was published in *The Intercollegiate Socialist* (February 1919): 8.

153. To Anna E. Rude[1]

NATIONAL CONSUMERS' LEAGUE
44 EAST 23RD STREET, NEW YORK CITY

6-13-20

Dear Dr. Rude

I am filled with new hope by the unheard of success of the post office employes. On May 15th they seemed to have not a ghost of a chance of increased salaries. I saw Mr. Mondell about it.[2]

On June 7, President Wilson signed a bill giving them $33,000,000 in the fiscal year beginning July 1st 1920, rising to $43,000,000 four years hence.

They did it by publicity in three weeks. We have more than five months. We ought to carry our bill before Xmas![3]

Their case was meritorious but they won by their organization and by their

1. publicity. They are all voting adults,
2. they are every where, they have put
3. powerful enemies out of public life;
4. because they hold civil service positions, virtually life jobs, it is well known to politicians that they are lasting friends or foes.

Contrast the babies! Unlike the postal employes

They have no votes,
They have no organization,
They contribute to no campaign funds,
They cherish no rancor,
They write no letters,
They command no votes   Let them die!

Unlike the cotton raisers,
the hog raisers, the cattle raisers
the lobster fishers,
Babies

Produce no wealth, on the contrary they cost money
Join no political parties,
Hold no patriots responsible for untimely death or lifelong suffering,
Punish no political enemies,

Maintain no lobby,
Buttonhole no lawgivers   Let them die!

Can you give me the names of the committees to whom the bill went in 1918 and 1919, in House and Senate?[4]

This year, 1920 to what Committee did it go in the House?

I wish to work out a list of men who had it before them at three sessions, two sessions and (if there were any such) at this last session only.[5]

Some specialists can then help me to find which of them can be converted or spurred to action, and which ought to be eliminated (on their general record) in November. This is a grand year for elimination.

Yours with fresh hope
Florence Kelley

ALS, "Prot of Maternity and Infancy," Folder 10,406, Box 120, CB Records, RG102, MdCpNA

1. Dr. Anna E. Rude, director of the Division of Hygiene of the U.S. Children's Bureau, had written FK about the legislative status of the Sheppard-Towner bill (Rude, Washington, D.C., to FK, 27 May 1920, "Prot of Maternity and Infancy," Box 120, CB Records, MdCpNA). Rude hoped for action before Congress adjourned. The bill allocated federal funds to states that provided matching funds for preventive health education for mothers of infants. It mandated states to create boards of maternity and infant hygiene that included health care providers (Lindenmeyer, *A Right to Childhood,* 78–79).

2. Franklin W. Mondell (1860–1939), U.S. congressman (Republican, Wyoming, 1899–1923). The post office employees' bill (H.R. 14338), which gave employees "compensation on an equitable basis," passed the Senate and House on 5 June 1920 (66th Cong., 2nd sess., *Cong. Rec.,* 8620, 8662).

3. Senator Morris Sheppard (1875–1941; Democrat, Texas, 1911–1941), introduced S. 3259 on 20 October 1919, a bill "for the public protection of maternity and infancy." It was reported out of the Senate Committee on Public Health and National Quarantine on 2 June 1920. Representative Horace M. Towner (1855–1937; Republican, Iowa, 1911–1923) introduced the parallel bill, H.R. 10925, on 5 December 1919; it was referred to the House Committee on Interstate and Foreign Commerce (66th Cong., 1st sess., *Cong. Rec.,* 7157; 66th Cong. 2nd sess., *Cong. Rec.,* 214, 8161). The 66th Congress took no further action on either bill, but President Harding signed the bill into law on 24 November 1921.

4. FK needed this information as part of her mobilization of support for the WJCC, which was founded five months later.

5. Rude's assistant, Caroline Fleming, sent FK a list of the members of congressional committees that she sought. She referred to the new group that "is in the process of formation" and felt that the Sheppard-Towner bill had "a fair chance" of being enacted (Fleming, n.p., to FK, 17 June 1920, Folder 10,406, Box 120, CB Records, MdCpNA). In the *Survey* on June 19, FK implored readers to write their congressmen and senators, asking "Will you vote this year to pass the Sheppard-Towner bill to save mothers and babies?" (FK, "Why Let Children Die?" 401).

154. To Nicholas Kelley

Columbus, Ohio
10-1-20

Darling Son

I hope Augusta and the bairns are with you, and that your weather is as perfect as this day.

Yesterday I was in Marion, listening to Senator Harding's promises to the new voters.[1] The promises were evidently written for him by highly intelligent, well-informed women. We were presented to him by Mrs. Raymond Robbins![2]

He was on the Senate Committee on U.S. Public Health,—Senator France chairman,[3]—which favorably reported the Sheppard-Towner bill for Public Protection to Maternity and Infancy. But he committed himself to the whole subject, yesterday, in a manner very surprising to Mrs. Robbins, Mrs. Gifford Pinchot, and myself.[4] He will have no rest until the bill is passed! I was thinking while he was speaking what a strange path we have traveled since the Roosevelt campaign in 1912. Then we had no Children's Bureau, no poor-old dotard discrediting the idea of a federal Department of Labor, no women voters.[5]

But the candidate, exactly like this one, acted as funnel for the ideas of a few so called radical social workers to pour their ideas through!

This year we are all women. No man seems to have one single constructive idea. And the whole war horror has happened!

It was all badly managed yesterday except a glorious luncheon and dinner for all the pilgrims by the Commercial Club,—all men!

The local Committee marched us a mile over horrible brick pavements,—very bad—to the Front Porch where several men and the leading women sat while the rest of us stood jammed, on sharp pebbles, for more than an hour! Then came handshaking! They should have had a hall!

Tomorrow I go to Dayton to see Mr. Cox by appointment on Monday.[6] Today I am recovering very successfully and pleasantly from the aching fatigue of yesterday.

I have a large double room, with a huge double bed, in the Columbus Y.W.C.A., looking out upon the Ohio State House and its grounds with dying elms. There is standing room only in every hotel!

I keep wondering what Florence will be going to see presidential candidates about when she is my age, a little over a half century hence?

Will there be a President then? I do not believe so. The task is too terrible. I think there may be a Council, à la Swisse electing its own presiding officer.

Altho Mr. Harding was talking about Social Justice he never referred to the Packers or to the Honest Cloth bill. He seems to know nothing in the world but Article X and Article V. of the Covenant.[7]

I am going home on Monday night.

On Thursday, just as I was starting, I received your letter of September 5th, and one from Florence and from Lewis Maverick, all forwarded from Naskeag![8]

Yours was a fine long volume!

Thank you for it!

Please ask Florence whether she ever received a gift which Miss [Grace] Drake sent her by mail via Little Compton?

Miss Drake is afraid it has been lost in the mail.

Your loving Mother
F.K.

ALS, FKP, NN

1. Warren G. Harding (1865–1923), Ohio senator and 1920 Republican nominee for president, advocated expansion of the Children's Bureau and "better prevention of the abuses of child labor" in his speech on "Social Justice," an event his campaign organized for women voters. Harding "urged an eight-hour day for women everywhere . . . and better prevention of abuses of child labor." He also advocated "extension of the Children's Bureau." Yet he said "I could not even consider a policy of social justice which is conceived, as so many visionaries conceive it, as a right of mankind. I will only consider it as an obligation of mankind" (*Christian Science Monitor,* 2 October 1920, 4; see also Lemons, *The Woman Citizen,* 87–89).

2. Margaret Dreier Robins (1868–1945), NWTUL president (1907–1922) and social reformer, married Raymond Robins in 1905.

3. Joseph I. France (1873–1939) was a Republican senator from Maryland from 1917 to 1923.

4. Cornelia Bryce Pinchot (1881–1960), social activist and Republican Party worker, married Gifford Pinchot in 1914.

5. The U.S. Department of Labor was established in 1913 after fifty years of pressure from labor activists. The campaign was finally successful when Progressives gained political power (McLaury, *History of the Department of Labor*).

6. On 4 October 1920, FK led a delegation representing the NCL and the newly formed LWV to meet with Ohio governor James M. Cox (1870–1957), the Democratic nominee for president. The group queried Cox on his stand on child welfare, equal citizenship for married women, and honesty in cloth manufacturing (*NYT,* 5 October 1919, 2).

7. For background on the honest cloth bill, see Letter 156, FK to Robert La Follette, 18 December 1920, below. For more about corruption among the meatpackers, see Letter 149, FK to Newton Baker, 22 September 1919, and Letter 151, FK to NK, 18 October 1919, both above. In his meeting with the women, Harding devoted considerable time to explaining his opposition to Article 10 of the League of Nations covenant, which called for member nations to defend the political independence of all other members. Harding stated that women of the United States "did not wish to give their sons and husbands for sacrifice at the call of an extra-constitutional body" (*NYT,* 2 October 1920, 2). Article 5 of the covenant required unanimous consent of all members to league decisions.

8. Lewis Maverick (b. ca. 1877) was a former Rough Rider in the Spanish-American War and the brother of Augusta Kelley (*NYT,* 20 June 1926, 12).

155. To Jane Addams

265 Henry St. [New York City]
Sunday morning 11-7-20

Beloved J. A.

Since the incubus of Mrs. Spencer's egocentrist presiding at the meetings was removed,[1] and you persuaded Mabel Kittredge to serve as President,[2] I've enlisted as a private in the ranks of the Section for the U.S., promising to work steadily as long as she keeps the helm.

She is doing an immediate practical stroke in submitting to the membership vote a proposed selection from the Zurich resolutions, to be submitted to the President elect with as much publicity as possible in connection with his approaching conference on the whole subject.[3]

[Inserted in the margin: We had a lively meeting Thursday!]

Also, she has a fine scheme for a series of luncheons, beginning in January, at the various clubs, City, Civic, Cosmopolitan, Women's University, etc. with crack speakers on Mexico, Japan etc. and inviting the club members to join at the close of the meeting. A similar series is already underway in Boston.

Having survived Crystal Eastman, Margaret Johnson Lane, Mrs. Spencer et al, I do really believe that the Section will go ahead, sad as it is to have lost Mrs. Karsten.[4]

I write this because I was doubtful when you recommended M. K.

Yours devotedly
F. K.

Dear love to M[ary]. R[ozet]. S[mith].

ALS, JA Papers, PSC-P

1. Minister, lecturer, and philanthropist Anna Garlin Spencer (1851–1931) was author of *Women's Share in Social Culture* (1913), which argued that women should advance ethical perspectives in public policy based on their identities as mothers. In 1919, she became a founder and in 1920 served briefly as president of the U.S. branch of WILPF.

2. Mabel Hyde Kittredge, a close friend of Alice Hamilton, had traveled with Hamilton and JA to attend the ICW in 1915. She was the superintendent of the Association of Practical Housekeeping Centers, which had a network of model apartments in New York City where neighborhood residents could learn practical housekeeping skills (Sicherman, *Alice Hamilton,* 186, 189; Woods and Kennedy, *Handbook of Settlements,* 191–192).

3. An article in *Survey* described the "scores of resolutions slowly discussed, translated, passed or rejected by the women" at Zurich, including "resolutions on education, on freedom of press and speech, on self-determination for small nationalities, on labor and feminist programs to be worked out by the permanent bureau which the conference voted to establish at Geneva" (Chamberlain, "The Women at Zurich," 428). For the Zurich resolutions, see WILPF, *Report of the International Congress of Women: Zurich, May 12 to 17, 1919*. For FK's account of the Zurich conference, see Letter 144, FK to Mary Rozet Smith, 22 May 1919, above. While President-elect Warren Harding stated that the United States would not join the League of

Nations, he said he would work for "reconstructing the plan for an association of nations" (*NYT*, 5 November 1920, 1, 7).

4. Lawyer, social reformer, and pacifist Crystal Eastman (1881–1928) was active in the New York State branch of the Woman's Peace Party. Because of her reputation for not following up with tasks she agreed to do, many WILPF members were not displeased when Eastman was refused a passport in 1919 and could not attend the Zurich conference (Foster, *The Women and the Warriors*, 41). Eleanor Daggett Karsten (d. 1946) was secretary to JA. After an unstable start, the U.S. branch of WILPF became a strong organization (41–44.) In 1921, FK presided over a WILPF meeting hosted by the U.S. section of the league that asked President Harding to convene a conference of Great Britain, Japan, and the United States to discuss naval disarmament (*NYT*, 10 April 1921, 20).

156. To Robert W. La Follette[1]

NATIONAL CONSUMERS' LEAGUE
44 EAST 23RD STREET, NEW YORK CITY

December 18, 1920.

Honorable Robert W. La Follette,
Senate Office Building,
Washington, D. C.
Dear Sir:

Herewith I have the honor to transmit the results of an enquiry made in 1918, 1919 and 1920, as to the standards obtaining in certain of the textile industries. The facts gathered in the earlier years led, in November 1919, to the inclusion in the Ten Years' Program of the National Consumers' League, of a resolution that it support an "Honest Cloth" bill. On the basis of farther observations made in 1920 the League endorsed the Rogers bill, H.R. 13136, "to protect the public against fraud by prohibiting the manufacture, sale, or transportation in interstate commerce of misbranded, misrepresented, or falsely described articles, to regulate the traffic therein, and for other purposes."[2]

During the war the United States government in assigning contracts for soldiers' uniforms, overcoats and blankets, not only insisted upon a prescribed quality of cloth to contain a specified maximum amount of reworked wool, but enforced certain standards as to labor conditions under which these goods were manufactured.

Civilians, however, have always been and still are unable to enforce for their own benefit standards of either kind. It is our hope that the Rogers bill may facilitate the establishment of workable commercial standards.

Yours sincerely,
Florence Kelley

General Secretary, National Consumers' League.

TLS, "Survey—'An Honest Cloth Law,'" Box D3, NCL Records, DLC

Enc: "An Honest Cloth Law: Commercial and Social Standards in the Textile Industries," edited by FK

1. Senator Robert M. La Follette (1855–1925, Republican, Wisconsin, 1906–1925), responding to the election of Harding and the attacks on civil liberties of Progressives like himself, invited FK to attend a 17 December 1920 meeting in Washington to set up a Bureau of Research and Publicity that would monitor members of Congress and "compile the material required by Senators and Representatives in opposing reactionary legislation and advancing progressive measures" (La Follette to FK, Washington, D.C., 15 December 1920, FKP, NN; Murphy, *World War I and the Origin of Civil Liberties in the United States*).

2. The resolution was adopted at the NCL Council Meeting in Philadelphia (NCL Council Minutes, 18 November 1920, 3, Box A7, NCL Records, DLC). John Jacob Rogers (1881–1925; Republican, Massachusetts, 1913–1925) introduced his bill on 18 March 1920, but the 66th Congress took no action on it (66th Cong., 2nd sess., *Cong. Rec.*, 4564).

157. To Julia C. Lathrop

NATIONAL CONSUMERS' LEAGUE
44 EAST 23RD STREET, NEW YORK CITY

March 3rd, 1921.

Miss Julia Lathrop,
Children's Bureau,
Washington, D.C.
Dear J. Lathrop,

The enclosed explains itself. Our bill is, of course, dead and the threat seems obvious that an effort will be made to give the enforcement of the future bill to the Public Health Service, or incorporate the whole idea in some public welfare department, —or some other deviltry![1]

In reviewing the winter I am quite clear on two points. First, that the League of Women Voters fell down flat on publicity, and made the hideous and fatal mistake of leaving its executive officer to support herself by lecturing while she toiled as legislative agent.[2] Only the most utter inexperience can explain, and nothing can excuse, such cruel paltriness. I am not discussing our own sins of omission. They shriek to Heaven and need no comment.

Beside all this, however, there is one criticism which I have heard many times and have never been able to meet satisfactorily to myself. It is that the states which derive the least benefit from the present efforts to save mothers and babies would, under the law, continue to receive the least benefit. I refer to the states with the greatest area and the smallest population. It is, I think, not an accident that among the men on the Steering and Rules Committees who killed the bill are Rodenberg, Egypt, Ill; Philip Campbell, Kansas; Schall, Minn.; Mr. Snell, the least populated Congressional District in New York State; I am not certain that Mr. Pou, North Carolina, remained hostile; Royal C. Johnson, South Dakota; Garrett, Tenn.; Dale, Vermont; Mendell [Franklin W. Mondell], Wyoming.[3]

Julia Lathrop, ca. 1921. Courtesy of the Library of Congress, LC-USZ62-111462.

Is there any way in which this difficulty can be met? No one of these men is a lame duck. Every one of them will have great weight in the coming Congress. The mere insertion by the Senate of the provision that the work shall be done chiefly in the remote areas does not help. The share of the constituents of each of these enemies remains almost microscopic compared with the share of New York State, and the fact that New York State has both rural mountain areas and, also slums filled with aliens needing this help, fails to convince these men.

If you were in the Committee Room throughout the first Hearing (Monday and Tuesday) before the Committee on Interstate and Foreign Commerce, you must have heard the member from Texas, Mr. Rayburn, complain more than once that his State would contribute heavily to the taxes which would be spent in the rich and populous Northern states.[4]

I have been racking my brain without inventing any cracker for this tough-shelled nut. Have you ever considered the possibility of an alternative basis of distribution?[5]

At Albany we are in the deepest depths of reaction, not only winning nothing, but by way of losing measures unanimously upheld by our reactionary Court of Appeals.[6] What could go further than that?

Yours devotedly,
Florence Kelley

FK/DM

TLS, "General (Sheppard-Towner Bill)," Folder 10–6–0, Box 232, CB Records, RG102, MdCpNA

1. Throughout the winter, in correspondence with Anna Rude and Lathrop's office, FK had closely followed the prospects for passage of the Sheppard-Towner bill. After lengthy debate, the Senate passed the bill on 18 December 1920; it was then referred to the House Committee on Interstate and Foreign Commerce on 20 December. The bill was reported on 28 January 1921 but was not brought to a House vote before the 66th Congress ended on 4 March (66th Cong., 3rd sess., *Cong. Rec.*, 498–512, 581, 2179).

2. Minnie Fisher Cunningham (1882–1964), who had been active in the woman suffrage campaign, became executive secretary of the LWV in 1920.

3. Congressmen William A. Rodenberg (1865–1937; Republican, Illinois, 1899–1901, 1903–1913, 1915–1923), Philip P. Campbell (1862–1941; Republican, Kansas, 1903–1923), Thomas D. Schall (1878–1935; Republican, Minnesota, 1915–1925; U.S. Senator, 1925–1935), Bertrand H. Snell (1870–1958; Republican, New York, 1915–1939), Edward W. Pou (1863–1934; Democrat, North Carolina, 1901–1934), Royal C. Johnson (1882–1939; Republican, South Dakota, 1915–1933), Finis J. Garrett (1875–1956; Democrat, Tennessee, 1905–1929), Porter H. Dale (1867–1933; Republican, Vermont, 1915–1923; U.S. Senator, 1923–1933), Charles E. Winter (1870–1948; Republican, New York, 1923–1929).

4. Congressman Samuel T. Rayburn (1882–1961; Democrat, Texas, 1913–1961, Speaker of the House, 1940–1961). For FK's testimony in December 1920, see Lemons, *The Woman Citizen*, 155–156.

5. Lathrop responded that she had "never been able to work out an alternative method of distribution" and doubted that Congress would take up the issue (Lathrop to Kelley, Washington, D.C., 5 March 1921, copy, Folder 10–6–0, Box 232, CB Records, MdCpNA).

In her article "Congress and the Babies," FK deplored the congressional delay of the bill that had been introduced in 1918. "Since then, she wrote, "approximately 625,000 babies have died from causes (chiefly preventable) prenatal or connected with childbirth and early infancy." She saw as hopeful the fact that six states had already appropriated funds in the expectation that the Sheppard-Towner bill would pass (FK, "Congress and the Babies," 200).

On 11 April 1921, Horace Towner reintroduced the maternity and infancy protection bill in the House, and on 20 May, the Senate reported Morris Sheppard's version (S. 1039) out of committee (67th Cong., 1st sess., *Cong. Rec.*, 98, 1561).

6. Kelley feared the New York legislature would pass the Betts bill to grant women equal rights with men in industry, which would jeopardize the 1915 New York Court of Appeals decision upholding New York's night work law. With Mary Van Kleeck of the Russell Sage Foundation and representatives of New York State's League of Women Voters, the state's Federation of Labor, and the Federated Council of Churches, FK testified against the bill on 23 March; it did not become law (*NYT*, 24 March 1921, 19; McGuire, "'A Catalyst for Reform,'" 1–137).

158. To Elsie Hill[1]

NATIONAL CONSUMERS' LEAGUE
44 EAST 23RD STREET, NEW YORK CITY

March 21st, 1921.

Miss Elsie Hill,
National Woman's Party,
421 Bond Building,
Washington D. C.

Dear Elsie Hill,

Please accept my congratulations on your office of Chairman of the Executive Committee of the National Woman's Party.

I have your invitation to continue a member of the Advisory Committee and to take part in a deputation to Mr. Harding in behalf of a bill to remove all discriminations against women.[2]

I shall be glad to remain a member of the Advisory Committee until I can assure myself how the new Party interprets the words "discrimination and disabilities." The madwomen who gather under the banner of Nora Blatch,[3] calling themselves the League of Equal Opportunity, construe the words "sex discrimination" to include the eight hours day, the night work law, the law for minimum wage commissions, mothers' pensions, widows' pensions, endowment of motherhood and all those measures for the protection, particularly the industrial protection, of women for which I have been working for thirty years.

There was so much applause on February 17th for Nora Blatch's presentation of their catch words (their invented statistics and general misrepresentation of the industrial situation) on the part of the younger members of the audience that I have been ever since rather anxious minded about them.[4]

Everything will, of course, depend upon the interpretation that the courts and the law makers place upon the words "sex disability." If they interpret these words to mean merely exclusion from jury duty, from equal guardianship of children, from divorce on equal conditions, from a fair share in the family property during marriage and at the death of the husband, I am, of course, for all those changes.

To say Equality, Equality when there is no Equality, when Nature herself has created permanent physical inequality, can, however, be as stupid and as deadly as to cry Peace, Peace, when there is no peace.[5] And I shall, if necessary, spend the rest of my life fighting every attempt to compel American wage earning women to wait for the short working day and week. For rest at night and wage commissions, until our reactionary Labor leaders are converted to getting those things for men also, by law, which women have already got for themselves even without votes in a large number of states.

Because of my doubt as to the ultimate position of the Women's Party in this supremely important matter I can't definitely say today that I can join the deputation. I shall be delighted if you can give me convincing facts to show that my apprehensions are without foundation.[6] In any case, I am always

Yours affectionately,
Florence Kelley

TLS, Group II: Box 10, NWP Records, DLC

1. Suffrage leader Elsie Hill (1883–1970) retained her maiden name after her marriage to Albert Levitt in 1921 (*NYT*, 27 January 1922, 8).

2. The newly formed NWP sought a constitutional amendment stating that "neither political nor common law disabilities on account of sex or marriage shall exist within the several states, the United States, or any place subject to the jurisdiction of the United States" (quoted in Felix Frankfurter, "Memorandum on the Proposed Amendment to the United States Constitution presented by the National Woman's Party," 21 July 1921, Group I: Box 4, NWP Records, DLC).

3. Nora Blatch Barney (1883–1971), a civil engineer and architect, was the granddaughter of Elizabeth Cady Stanton.

4. The NWP's convention in Washington, D.C. on 17–18 February 1921 featured a number of speakers, including FK. The *New York Times* reported that Barney's speech raised the "battle cry of 'absolute equality for women,' which it was explained meant the abolition of their special privileges as well as of the discriminations against them." Barney asked, "'Are women, when they demand legal equality, willing to assume responsibilities that go with that equality?' 'Absolute equality,' came the answer, amid cheering" (*NYT*, 17 February 1921, 11).

FK anticipated the division within the women's movement in a *Survey* article in March 1921. The NWP, which was primarily business and professional women, strove to have women treated legally the same as men, disregarding the benefits of hours and wage legislation passed for wage-earning women. Kelley wrote, "How cruel, therefore, is the pretension of certain organizations of professional and business women to decide for the wage-earners, without consulting them, what statutory safeguards they are henceforth to do without!" Would the NWP, FK wondered, "failing to discriminate between the needs of the professional group and those of the wage-earning multitude—become the effective tool of exploiting employers who maintain and seek to prolong these industrial evils?" (FK, "The New Woman's Party," 827). For background to the ERA issue, see Sklar, "Why Were Most Politically Active Women Opposed to the ERA in the 1920s?" 25–35; and Sklar with Procita and Segal, "Who Won the Debate over the Equal Rights Amendment in the 1920s?"

5. Kelley was quoting the words of the prophet Jeremiah in the Bible: "For they have healed the hurt of the daughter of my people slightly, saying, Peace, peace; when there is no peace." Jeremiah 8:11.

6. Hill replied that the NWP council would never agree to an "attempt to overthrow the progress in laws for women which you care so much about, and have helped to make the country care" (Hill, Washington, D.C., to FK, 21 March 1921, Group II: Box 10, NWP Records, DLC). She also hoped FK would join the deputation to President Harding on 6 April, but FK declined, saying, "Blanket measures in the hands of the courts are as dangerous as anything can possibly be" (FK, New York, to Hill, 23 March 1921, Group II: Box 10, NWP Records, DLC).

159. To Roscoe Pound

[New York City]
June 3rd, 1921.

Mr. Roscoe Pound,
Harvard Law School,
Cambridge, Mass.
Dear Mr. Pound,

I am sailing tomorrow for Rotterdam on my way to attend the conference of the Women's International League for Peace and Freedom. Today I have received a visit from Alice Paul, following many visits from Miss Younger and Miss [Elsie]

Hill in Washington, on the subject of the enclosed drafts of proposed amendments to the Constitution of the United States.[1] These are, on the surface, less alarming than three or four earlier drafts which they showed me. In confidence I happen to know, though I should not, that this has been criticized by Justice Holmes.[2] I never feel certain, however, that I know exactly ***what happened*** when these ladies wrote a person whom I did not hear make the statement.

Miss Paul said that she would write you about it. As I do not know precisely how my words will sound when she quotes them I am taking the precaution to tell you my opinion of these drafts.

There is at this moment an insanity prevalent among women where one would least expect it. This insanity expresses itself in eager demands for identical treatment with that accorded to men. The slogans of the insane are, "A fair field and no favor,—Equal rights for women, nothing more,—We ask no privileges now that we have the vote."

It is idle to explain to them that, if these ideas prevail, not only will the statutory working day and legal wage, the provisions for seats when at work, for rest rooms, and all other special items which are more necessary for women than for men, (however much men may need them), will all be swept away,———to say nothing of maternity hospitals under the Sheppard-Towner bill, mothers' pensions, maternity insurance, etc. etc.

My fear is that the drafts submitted do, in spite of all the criticism that they have undergone, still involve danger of the same nature that we have been encountering in connection with "due process."

Another fear, related to that, is that the temper of the times cannot fail to dispose the courts, especially the lower courts, to yield more or less under the pressure of the madwomen.

I cannot reread and revise this letter as I would gladly do if I were not obliged to write also to Mr. [Newton] Baker and Mr. [Felix] Frankfurter, to whom Miss Paul is sending the draft for their criticism.

I told her that, of course, whenever you and they agreed that the draft was safe as far as any legal authority can tell in advance of the court's decision, I should of course make no objection to it, assuming that that draft then became the final one.[3]

Assuring you that I should not be trespassing on your interest in the peaceful development of industry under the law, if there were not in plain sight an immediate campaign that will be carried on until an amendment of this general nature is adopted, or the leaders of the Woman's Party all die of old age, I am,

Yours gratefully,

FK/IM
Dictated 6/3/21
Signed in Mrs. Kelley's absence.

CC, "Equal Rights Amendment: Correspondence: General: 1921–1931," Box C4, NCL Records, DLC

1. See Letter 158, FK to Elsie Hill, 21 March 1921, above. Suffragist and social reformer Maud Younger (1870–1936) had worked on the successful passage of woman suffrage in California through an amendment to the state constitution in 1911. She was one of the few reformers who had previously worked with the NWTUL and NCL yet chose to work with Alice Paul and the NWP after 1920. Hill had sent FK a draft of the amendment with the hope that "it is satisfactory to you from the point of welfare legislation" (Hill, [Washington, D.C.], to FK, 27 May 1921, copy, Group II: Box 12, NWP Records, DLC).

2. Oliver Wendell Holmes, Jr. (1841–1935), was an associate justice of the U.S. Supreme Court from 1902 to 1932.

3. FK wrote Hill that she still could not endorse the recent draft. She told her that she needed to discuss it with her legal advisors and then submit it to the NCL annual meeting in November (FK, New York, to Hill, 3 June 1921, Group II: Box 12, NWP Records). Despite her reservations, FK was named to the NWP's national advisory council on 19 June 1921 (*NYT*, 20 June 1921, 2).

160. To Nicholas Kelley

S.S. New Amsterdam
June 5th, 1921

Beloved Son

I am overwhelmed by the magnificence of your gifts and by a third one from Augusta,—a vast box of Cornwell's chocolates. The roses decorate our table, the cherries are shared with pleasure by Miss Addams and Mary Smith, and delight me with their beauty and refreshing quality.[1]

I am suddenly flooded with books and other gifts, from a dozen friends, and find it unexpectedly pleasant.

We are a party often, much more congenial and more influential than two years ago. Miss Addams, Miss Smith, Dr. [Alice] Hamilton and Dorothy North,—one of my roommates,—came from H.H.; Miss Rose Nichols, a landscape architect from Boston, is engineering a bevy of four Japanese and one Chinese students,—on the basis that they are picked young people who will influence their countries in the near future. They come by a later ship. I forgot another H.-H. delegate, Mrs. Kohn who is of the general nature of J. Goldmark, gentle, lovable and highly intelligent.[2]

The ship is very good. The state room, different from any that I have ever had, is unexpectedly comfortable. It is shaped thus,—

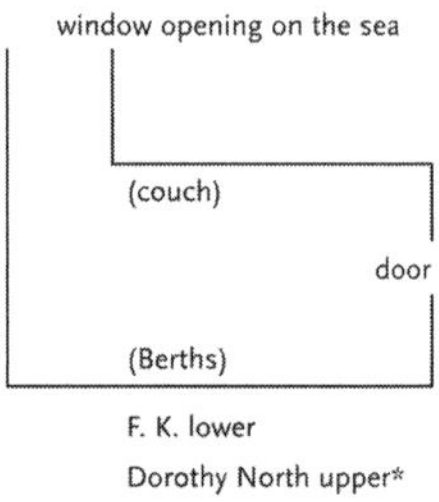

So we have daylight and direct ventilation which we did not expect. The table is excellent and not greasy.

I'm writing my first letter with my new safety waterman.

In case Mrs. Louise Carey Rosett or Mrs. Spiering, should communicate with you about Naskeag, will you please write a line to Mr. John C. Bradford, accrediting either or both as worthy to have the key and to move in to Seawest?

I took the liberty of asking them to apply to you for such a letter, because there would not be time to get an answer to a letter to me, after they learn when they can get away for their vacations, if they ever can. I am writing Mr. Bradford all the details. I had no time to communicate with any of them after a conversation about a week before sailing. It is the husband's vacation which is variable and may never materialize. Both couples are very nice[.]

My second roommate is a young Quaker who is shepherding Wm and Mary Bancroft of Wilmington, Del., to England to a Conference of Friends. William is 86 and Mary and Mary is about 80. She contributed $200 to the fund for feeding the students at our summer school. I like the Quakers, more and more and am glad that my grandfather [Isaac Pugh] was a birthright Quaker.

The boat is fairly comfortable if we ignore the extortionate charge of $130.00 plus war tax with three in a room, on the deck four flights down, from the Library where I write at this moment.

Yesterday (and two nights) all portholes were closed and the fog, wind and waves made my heart ache over Ann's prospect of thirty days on Diablesse beginning, perhaps, with two or three like that.[3]

Sunday and to-day have been glorious.

With renewed thanks,
Your loving Mother

Thursday June 9th 1921

Miss Addams hopes to be well enough, tomorrow, for a conference of our ten members to form a skeleton draft of our collective ideas for the program for Vienna.[4] I'm hoping that we (Americans) may be a unit for disarmament and abolition of capital punishment; and that we may submit an acceptable plan for a celebration, five years hence of the Declaration of Independence (150 years after 1876) and of the Semi-centennial of Wyoming's enfranchisement of women. The latter will be six years belated by the war. But the Chicago Exposition was not hurt by being belated. My idea is that Women's contribution to permanent Peace can best be made by concerted worldwide emphasis upon the Sacredness of human life everywhere, at all times.

So I'll be bringing home with me, I hope, the beginnings of plans for a practical step away from the world of war to the New World of goodwill and Leisure.

Do not trouble to answer this. And, dear Son, don't be spent and don't miss a fourth vacation.[5]

Your loving mother
FK

ALS, FKP, NN

1. FK was traveling to Vienna, where meetings of WILPF were to be held on 10 to 16 July 1921 ("Women of the World," 75).

2. Dorothy North, later Haskins (1886–1962), had previously worked with the American Friends Service Committee in Austria. Rose Nichols (1872–1960) was a founder of WILPF. Esther Loeb Kohn (1875–1965,) a Hull House resident since 1909, often managed Hull House in JA's absence (Hyman and Moore, *Jewish Women in America,* 747–749).

3. Ann Valentine married JK in 1920, and NK congratulated FK in "getting so fine a daughter-in-law" (NK, [Washington, D.C.], to FK, 1 August 1920, FKP, NN). John and Ann Kelley were sailing from New York to England on his yacht.

4. On JA's agenda were the continuing famine in Europe, a reduction in militaristic education, and women's work in maintaining peace (see JA, *Peace and Bread,* 225–226).

5. In her next letter, FK reiterated her concern for NK: "The fear haunts me, day and night, that after an August without a vacation, I may find you one of the spent men. That possibility I face with anguish" (FK, aboard the *New Amsterdam,* to NK, 12 [June] 1921, FKP, NN). In April 1921, NK resigned as assistant secretary of the treasury in the Wilson administration and returned to practicing law in New York City as a member of the firm of Larkin, Rathbone and Perry.

161. To Nicholas Kelley

Heidelberg, [Germany]
July 1st 1921

Darling Son

I am spending an entirely restful and most beautiful week, here where I ended my wedding journey in October 1884, full of hope and confidence in myself and all the world. Until to-day when it is raining hard, the weather has been all that travelers could wish, and this place, on a hill above the ruined castle, looking up the valley of the Neckar and down across a great plain to Mannheim, is superlatively lovely. How I wish you were here!
[inserted in margin: Miss Conklin is an excellent traveling companion.]

However, when you are my age and need to get away farther than Sakonnet, Heidelberg will still be here as it has been since the 13th century when the university was founded.

So far as I can yet judge, my coming was a mistake so far as J.A. and the Conference are concerned. But for me personally the first four weeks, which end tomorrow, have been very valuable indeed.

No books, letters, articles, newspapers or European ~~articles~~ travelers in America could give any idea of the situation comparable to this slow journey from Rotterdam to Vienna. Holland is bursting with prosperity. The Holsteins are typical of the country. There are uncounted thousands of them. They stand motionless, looking across an almost invisible ditch at an area of new mown grass. They lie down and look at it! They are so fat that they can hardly waddle.

Rotterdam and Amsterdam are building vast new dry docks. Amsterdam is building a whole new city quarter of working men's homes through the Catholic Co-operative Society, and a public exhibit of competitive designs for farther similar undertakings indicates that this is regarded as the first [of] many.

The scale of the plans offered in the competition puts utterly to shame the exhibit that you and I visited with George Hooker, in 1908, in Munich. In Amsterdam there was provision for baths, and for book shelves built into the walls of the living rooms; and there were no such tiny rooms; tho these are urban and those were rural.

We have had no inconveniences of travel except one custom-house about like that on going from Belgium into Germany in 1908. But the officials are all servile now instead of the old insolence. That is about as painful as the old manners.

It was dreadful to see the Oriental and the black soldiers—conscripts of France, along the Rhine.[1] The effect is indescribable. In part it is the suggestion of what the Future may have in store for Nicky's generation, if the Europeans develop the practice of fighting by the use of colored conscript armies!

We have seen no signs of malnutrition as serious as the rickety legs of the children that impressed you in Bremer haven in 1908. The children have good legs.

In the papers we read that in Duisburg [Germany], a great mfg. center, the Belgian officers requisitioned the Quakers' cooking utensils and dishes, with which they had been feeding school children, giving as excuse the needs of the soldiers. Hitherto they have ignored the Quakers' polite requests to have their things restored.

This first ten days in G. is a continuous pleasant surprise. There are no signs of poverty. We have been in Cologne, Coblenz, Mainz and now Heidelberg. Naturally we have observed the children. Their legs are sturdy and well nourished. And there are fewer pasty-faced children than we see every day in Henry Street. In the open air markets, in the working class districts, fruit and vegetables are offered for sale, and myriads of flowers.

The day of the insufficient fats is gone. Ham, bacon, sausage in many varieties are everywhere. The missing evidences of prosperity are smoking chimneys, motor cars, and men in the fields where the harvest seems meagre compared with the heavily fertilized lavishly cultivated Holland agriculture.

The bright colored skirts and neckerchiefs of the women in the Vineyards are very beautiful in the mild sunshine of these June days, and if we did not read such things as the announcement in the Frankfurter Zeitung that people 70 years old can obtain cards for daily milk, and people 74 yrs. old can get cards for white bread, it would be hard to believe the stories of mass poverty.

True we do not see many cattle. But the horses are all well fed and not aged, worn out hacks. We are assured, however, that the hundreds of long barges towed Southward up the Rhein are carrying coal out of the country, to points convenient for shipment to France.

Everywhere breakfast is poor. The only good one was at the YWCA hostess house in Coblenz where we had excellent coffee, American white-flour rolls, honey and eggs. But everywhere else the remaining meals are excellent tho frugal.

Travel is painfully cheap and I am far within my limit.

I dare not think of John and Ann in mid ocean.[2] Indeed, I am almost as afraid to think of you! Tho' I trust that you're off, to-day, to Sakonnet.

Your loving Mother
F. K.

Permanent address to and including Aug. 15th
Vienna Hofburg 1 Micehaelethof

ALS, FKP, NN

1. The Treaty of Versailles called for French troops to occupy both banks of the Rhine in Germany for five to fifteen years. During the winter and spring of 1921 a controversy arose over the presence of North African troops in the French occupational army. Hoping to stir up anti-French sentiment, Germans and German-Americans accused these troops of raping and molesting white women and children (see, e.g., *NYT,* 11 February 1921, 3, and 26 May 1921, 12; *The Nation,* 12 [9 March 1921]: 365; "Horror on the Rhine," *Jane Addams Papers,* Reel 32, frames 847–1001).

2. FK wrote from Innsbruck that the *Diablesse,* piloted by JK and Ann Valentine Kelley, had reached Cowes, England, on 18 July 1921. FK planned to meet the couple on 17 August before sailing from Southampton on 27 August (FK, Innsbruck, Austria, to NK, 14 August 1921, FKP, NN). Writing soon after their arrival in England, JK urged FK not to worry about him: "I seem forced to do things calculated to disturb people who love me and people whom I love.—but God knows I don't do them for that reason. My curse or blessing is that I am fascinated by the seemingly impossible" (JK, [Cowes, England], to FK, 30 July 1921, FKP, NN; see also "New York Yachtsman Crosses Atlantic Again in Small Craft," *New York World,* 11 August 1922, 3).

162. To Molly Dewson

NATIONAL CONSUMERS' LEAGUE
44 EAST 23RD STREET, NEW YORK CITY

[Vienna, Austria]
July 7th 1921

Dear Sister Dewson

I have just received the first letters from the office, and learn with regret and anxiety that Miss Faulkner has taken another job.[1] I know that this concerns your own personal contentment with your job very closely, and I am all the more sorry!

The same batch contains a letter from J. Lathrop with Congratulations on winning the case in the D.C. Court of Appeals.[2] That really outweighs every discouraging thing that has happened in the States, in your especial field, in this last year of reaction! For it is a Federal Court, and it is set on a hill, and with Justice [Edward D.] White gone from the Supreme Court of the U.S., there is reason to expect, with confidence, that we can now get a final favorable decision. White was an evil inheritance from Grover Cleveland, and Mr. Harding seems hardly likely to appoint a lay Jesuit from Louisiana to succeed him![3]

Molly Dewson, ca. 1929. Courtesy of the Schlesinger Library, Radcliffe Institute, Harvard University.

It was White who left the previous decision four to four! He voted against, and Mr. Brandeis could not vote for.[4]

I don't know how to congratulate you enough upon having a concrete result of such national importance to satisfy your mind. That is a satisfaction that I never get, and I'm moved to envy, along with my gratitude for your very hard and very effective work in our common cause.

The week's work of the Executive Committee of the International Conference is at an end, and the Conference itself opens this morning. There are women here from Poland, Hungary, Transylvania, the U Kraine, Ireland, to say nothing of Germany, France, Italy. They are as unified as though they were all from Castine!

The one exception—Rosika Schwimmer—is medically recognized as not mentally responsible, and is not a delegate. But everyone is endlessly patient with her because of her services years ago to the Suffrage cause. Otherwise peace reigns as completely as it did two years ago at Zurich.

There will be women from China and Japan, California and the State of Washington, and two colored women.[5]

I sit and admire my polyglot sisters until I almost burst!

Yours affectionately Florence Kelley

over

I hope Janon's reply to your letter was satisfactory![6] I had a long conversation with him, but he did not show me his letter to you or mention its contents,—if he wrote!

I am trying to get the Conference to consider coming to America in 1926 when the Declaration of Independence will be 150 years old. It will meet once before that, but it needs long notice in advance of so long a journey.

The time is not yet ripe for reviving the International Conferences of the Consumers' League. The soldiers will have to be gone from the Rhein first!

F.K.[7]

ALS, Dewson Papers, MCR-S

1. Dewson replied that she was "exceedingly sorry about Miss Faulkner. She brought to the N.C.L. a quality that increased its efficiency a great deal" (Dewson, Castine, Me., to FK, 3 August 1921, FKP, NN).

2. On 6 June 1921, the District of Columbia Court of Appeals denied the appeal from the Children's Hospital (*Adkins v. Children's Hospital*). The court rejected the hospital's suit, which sought to prevent the D.C. minimum wage board from requiring a wage of at least $16.50 a week for all its women employees, and ruled that Congress could justifiably make laws "for the promotion of health, safety, morals and welfare of those subject to its jurisdiction" (*NYT*, 7 June 1921, 27). As research secretary for the NCL, Dewson had worked with Frankfurter on the brief for the case (Goldmark, *Impatient Crusader*, 172–173). On the U.S. Supreme Court decision on *Adkins v. Children's Hospital*, see Letter 179, FK to Julia Lathrop, 21 April 1923, below. For more on Dewson's employment, see FK, New York, to Dewson, 16, 17 June and FK, Brooklin, Me., to Dewson, 18 July 1919, all in Dewson Papers, MCR-S.

3. Justice Edward D. White had attended Mount St. Mary's College in Emmitsburg, Maryland.

4. See Letter 137, FK to Louis Brandeis, 9 April 1917, above.

5. In an article in the September 1921 issue of *Survey*, FK praised the accomplishments and goals of the WILPF conference. She noted that woman suffrage in many countries had given delegates from twenty-eight countries hope for reforms in education and for economic equality. FK reported that WILPF intended to work with the League of Nations to change the postwar treaties and that it wholeheartedly supported President Warren Harding's forthcoming disarmament conference (FK, "The Women's Congress at Vienna"; see also JA, *Peace and Bread*, 223–246).

6. FK may have been referring to Janon Fisher, whose wife was a Maryland delegate to the NCL Council in 1921 (NCL Council Minutes, 17 November 1921, 1, Box A7, NCL Records, DLC).

7. Dewson replied, "It was great to win in Washington and this rehearing is in the words of F. F. 'to make mockery of courts and law'" (Dewson to FK, 3 August 1921).

163. To Alice Paul

NATIONAL CONSUMERS' LEAGUE
44 EAST 23RD STREET, NEW YORK CITY

October 14th, 1921.

Miss Alice Paul,
Headquarters Woman's Party,
Washington, D. C.

My dear Miss Paul,

Senator Curtis tells me that he has promised to introduce a blanket measure intended to remove the political disabilities of women.[1] With every effort to give women complete political equality, I am of course in full sympathy.

Any attempt, however, to combine with that sweeping provisions, either by amendment to the Constitution or by statutes affecting business or industrial relations of women, is contrary to the settled policy of this organization for the past twenty-two years, for the present, and for the immediate future.

Under existing conditions I must, therefore, ask to have my name removed from the list of members of the Advisory Committee of the National Woman's Party.[2]

Yours sincerely,
Florence Kelley

FK/DM

TLS, Group II: Box 10, NWP Records, DLC

1. Charles R. Curtis had informed FK on 28 September 1921 that he would introduce an ERA whenever Paul had prepared a final version. As of 29 October, the draft read: "No political, civil, or legal disabilities or inequalities on account of sex, or on account of marriage unless applying alike to both sexes, shall exist within the United States or any place subject to their jurisdiction" (FK to Millie R. Trumbull, 14 October 1921; FK, draft of letter to Charles Curtis (D., Kansas), 29 October 1921, both in "Equal Rights Amendment: Correspondence: General: 1921," Box C4, NCL Records, DLC).
2. In the fall of 1921, FK wrote to CL members and other activists to rally opposition to the ERA (see, e.g., FK to Katherine P. Edson, 19 October 1921, "Equal Rights Amendment: Correspondence: General: 1921," Box C4, NCL Records, DLC).

164. To Maud Younger

NATIONAL CONSUMERS' LEAGUE
44 EAST 23RD STREET, NEW YORK CITY

October 19th, 1921.

Miss Maud Younger,
National Woman's Party,
25 First Street, N. E.,
Washington, D. C.
Dear Miss Younger,

Thank you for your courteous and friendly letter of October 15th. It is indeed painful to me ever to be obliged to oppose you. Your present activities, however, run counter to my continuous efforts of more than five and thirty years, and I cannot stand idly by. As to the political equality of women, I am committed to it in every phase. As a lawyer and an executive of this organization, I am opposed both on principle and in the light of long experience to blanket measures, ***and vague words in bills and constitutional amendments.***

With regard to your letter of October 15th, the obvious reason that no one has submitted a draft "which would make it clear that our amendment touched upon the political, and civil, and legal discriminations and did not touch the field of industrial legislation" is, that such a draft is unthinkable.[1] The courts alone could make such a decision. If your measures should unhappily be enacted there would, it is greatly to be feared, follow another fifteen years of effort necessary to a final agreement by the courts as to the meaning of your ambiguous phraseology.[2]

The first duty of the bill drafters is to make a bill so simple, clear, and precise that no extraneous comment is necessary to tell the court or the people what it is intended to do. That would be no responsible authority on constitutional law who should sign his name to such a draft as you have been requesting. They are prudent advisers who inform you that, "so far as one can predict, your amendment will not be interpreted as touching protective legislation for women."[3] For no one can safely predict! It would, indeed, be selling goods under false pretenses to give any assurance that your measures will not prove ruinous to protective legislation for wage earning women.

Has any authority on constitutional interpretation defined for you the constitutional significance of the phrases "civil disabilities", "civil inequalities", and "privileges and immunities"?

Whatever the ultimate effect of this adventure in the field of legislation may be, it is a sad waste of energy that agitation, instead of being directed to getting measures passed on which thinking women agree, is confused by the over ambitious character of the undertaking. I begrudge, for instance, every hour of the thousands that I shall have to spend in adverse criticism of these measures. There is so much constructive work waiting to be done, to which those hours could be given!

Yours sincerely,
Florence Kelley

FK/IM

TLS, Group II: Box 15, NWP Records, DLC

1. Younger had written that the NWP had consulted several lawyers FK had suggested for a possible draft but that none had thus far supplied a draft (Younger, Washington, D.C., to FK, 15 October 1921, "Equal Rights Amendment: Correspondence: General: 1921," Box C4, NCL Records, DLC).

2. See Letter 163, FK to Alice Paul, 14 October 1921, above.

3. In her 15 October letter, Younger wrote: "Other legal authorities, however, some of whom we understand are among the most eminent in the United States, have given us most valuable help in drawing up the measure."

Felix Frankfurter, 1918. Courtesy of the Library of Congress, LC-USZ62-36966.

165. To Felix Frankfurter

NATIONAL CONSUMERS' LEAGUE
44 EAST 23RD STREET, NEW YORK CITY

November 28th, 1921.

Mr. Felix Frankfurter,
Harvard Law School,
Cambridge, Mass.
Dear Mr. Frankfurter,

At the annual meeting in Washington the Council voted as follows:-

> Whereas a movement has been publicly launched for an amendment to the Constitution of the United States, the effect of which while pending before Congress cannot be clearly foreseen, but may affect the work for the protection of women in industry of Consumers' Leagues both state and National, and
>
> Whereas the League is fortunate in enjoying the services of counsel most generously bestowed, therefore
>
> Resolved that we ask counsel to prepare a statement for the guidance of the Leagues in regard to this amendment.

This was done because we are still without a definitely formulated policy voted by either the Council or the Executive Committee concerning Alice Paul's pestiferous proposed blanket amendment to the federal Constitution.[1]

Nevertheless, I ventured to announce Dean Acheson's subject on our final program as, "Why We Oppose the Woman's Party Amendment." This was taken up by the press all over the country and, of course, especially in Washington. Miss Paul's contingent were, therefore, eagerly awaiting me on the 15th, demanding that we permit them to announce Mr. Frank Walsh for the luncheon in reply to Dean Acheson.[2] ***We did not!***

A Miss Spruance of Wilmington, Delaware, belonging to both the Woman's Party and our League, demanded to know who "WE" were in my announcement. I explained that "WE" were yourself as general counsel, Dean Acheson, Mr. Wilbur, Mr. [Edward P.] Costigan, Robert Szold, Mr. Shientag, and of course, Mr. [Newton D.] Baker, all of counsel.[3]

This unworthy evasion was for the purpose of avoiding a vote at that meeting in Washington, where members of the Woman's Party could have made unpleasant scenes.

I write now to ask whether, under these circumstances, you will write a statement more formal than your letter to Miss Smith?[4] Or whether you wish me to take over your letter to her and use it as our basic statement throughout the present phase of the campaign for the amendment? I think you could make one stronger than that.

Second, I forget whether I wrote you that the Woman's Party has already passed, in Wisconsin, a so-called model blanket bill, and sent two agitators to Louisiana and Alabama to try to pass the Wisconsin bill there.[5] In Louisiana that failed.[6] I do not yet know about Alabama.

I understand that the federal amendment is not yet introduced,—though both Senator Curtis and Mr. Fess regard themselves as in honor bound to introduce it in December.[7] It has made an incredible amount of confusion even before being introduced. What will it do when it is before Congress!

The First Board meeting will be held on Saturday next, December 3rd, when we shall hope to elect Mrs. Borden Harriman, the new President of the District of Columbia League, chairman.[8]

Yours hopefully,
Florence Kelley

FK/DM

TLS, "NCL Correspondence 1915–1922," Box 157, Frankfurter Papers, DLC

1. The resolution was adopted at the NCL Council meeting in Washington, D.C., in November 1921 (NCL Council Minutes, 17 November 1921, 2, Box A7, NCL Records, DLC).
2. Dean Acheson (1893–1971), later U.S. secretary of state under Harry Truman, clerked for Louis Brandeis from 1919 to 1921. Acheson, an NCL Council member, spoke at the NCL

luncheon on 16 November. Attorney Frank P. Walsh (1864–1939) headed the U.S. Commission on Industrial Relations (1913–1915) and offered legal advice to Paul about the ERA. But in November, he told Ethel Smith that he opposed the amendment (Frank Walsh, Washington, D.C., to Alice Paul, 10 November 1921, copy, Group II: Box 16, NWP Records, DLC). For more about Walsh, see Letter 126, FK to Paul Kellogg, 12 February 1915, above.

3. Edith Spruance, an NWP member, was a member of the CL of Delaware (Edith Spruance to Alice Paul, 13 December 1921, Group II: Box 17, NWP Records). New York attorney Robert Szold (1889–1977) represented the child labor legislation position in *Hammer v. Dagenhart* (1918) (*NYT*, 12 December 1921, 17; Urofsky and Levy, *Letters of Louis D. Brandeis*, 4:375; *NYT*, 13 November 1977, 44). Walter Wilbur, chair of the child welfare council of South Carolina, was elected to the NCL Council on Frankfurter's recommendation (NCL Council Minutes, 17 November 1921, 6, Box A7). Bernard Shientag (1887–1952) was chief counsel to the New York Industrial Commission (1919–1921) and later a New York City Court justice (1924–1930). Shientag and Szold were members of the NCL's Board of Directors.

4. In September, Frankfurter had written to Ethel Smith to denounce the ERA, calling it a "crude and ruthless constitutional amendment." He wrote that the ERA would write into the U.S. Constitution "a dangerous law-suit, jeopardizing the effort of the nation and the states to deal justly with its women workers" (Frankfurter, Hadlyme, Conn., to Ethel Smith, 8 September 1921, copy, "Equal Rights Amendment: Correspondence: General: 1921," Box C4, NCL Records, DLC). Smith (1877–1951), suffragist and member of the National Federation of Federal Employees Union, led the NWTUL's Legislative Department in Washington (Butler, *Two Paths to Equality*, 72–89).

5. The Wisconsin equal rights law, enacted in June 1921, ordered state officials to interpret state laws as including women "unless such construction will deny to females the special protection and privileges they now enjoy for the general welfare" (Lemons, *The Woman Citizen*, 187).

6. Apparently the state law strategy worked in Louisiana; in December, NWP leaders celebrated the Louisiana legislature's new law removing nine legal and political discriminations against women. The legislature also struck out of the state's civil code the statement that there are "essential differences between men and women because of sex." But the new law left women vulnerable in the areas of property rights, child custody, and jury service (*NYT*, 3 December 1921, 23).

7. FK had drafted a letter to Senator Charles Curtis setting forth the legal problems the ERA would produce, including threats to protective legislation for women wage earners (FK to Curtis, 21 October 1921, "Equal Rights Amendment: Correspondence: General: 1921," Box C4, NCL Records, DLC). Congressman Simeon D. Fess (1861–1936; Republican, Ohio, 1913–1923) was later U.S. senator (1923–1935).

8. Florence Harriman was elected as chair of the NCL's new Board of Directors at the board's 3 December 1921 meeting. She held the position until November 1932 (NCL Board of Directors Minutes, 3 December 1921, 1, and 10 November 1932, 4, Box A2, NCL Records, DLC). For the reorganization of the NCL's executive body, see Letter 166, FK to A. Estelle Lauder, 30 November 1921, note 3, below.

Newton Baker, who did not attend the annual meeting, wrote FK that the new organization of the NCL would put it "on a business basis and supply us with a group about the general offices in New York who can be relied upon for counsel and will not leave you and your immediate staff so wholly dependent upon your own resources" (Baker, Cleveland, Ohio, to FK, 16 December 1921, "General Correspondence: Baker, Newton D.," Box B11, NCL Records, DLC).

166. To A. Estelle Lauder[1]

[New York City]
[November 30th, 1921]

Miss A. Estelle Lauder, Executive Secretary
Consumers' League of Eastern Pennsylvania
814 Otis Building, Philadelphia, Pa.
Dear Miss Lauder,

At last the five national organizations which will have to work together, if anything effective is to be done to check Alice Paul's amendment, are nearly ready to fire. They are, of course, the National Consumers' League, The Women's Trade Union League, the League of Women Voters, the Y.W.C.A., and, presumably, the W.C.T.U.

I have today acquired inside knowledge that Shippen Lewis' partner is being effectively worked upon by a dear friend in one of these organizations.[2] It is impossible for us to call upon Felix Frankfurter to waste his time and strength, (which we so urgently need for other legitimate uses) in enlightening or debating with other counsel outside of the court room. Six months of the kind of thing which has been happening to Mr. Frankfurter in the way of imposition on his generosity would be very likely to make him decide to turn his professional efforts in directions which involve him in less waste of time in footless correspondence.

I am writing in this blunt way because every day at least one mail brings me either notice that some one has been writing to him, or the request that I write to him, about matters which he has never undertaken to deal with in our service.

I hope that a week from today we may be able to announce a definite policy with regard to the amendment, which the state and local Leagues can adopt or reject.[3] We shall have to oppose Alice Paul and her followers for years to come. Let us not begin by sacrificing our most precious asset,—the services of lawyers whom we can never replace if we lose them.

Yours still hopefully,

FK/D

CC, "Equal Rights Amendment: Correspondence: General: 1921," Box C4, NCL Records, DLC

1. A. Estelle Lauder (fl. 1936) immigrated to the United States from Germany in 1909. She had attended annual NCL Council meetings as a delegate from the CL of Eastern Pennsylvania since 1917. She was the author of *Trailing Behind; or, How Pennsylvania Compares with Other States in Protective Legislation for Working Women and Children* (Philadelphia: Joint Labor Legislative Committee, 1922). She had written FK about her distress over the fact that attorney Shippen Lewis (1887–1952), who provided legal counsel to her league, was col-

laborating with Paul in the drafting of the ERA and offering "an opinion . . . contrary to that of Felix Frankfurter and those associated with him." Concerned that Lewis's actions would "cause us considerable difficulty here in Pennsylvania," she asked if Frankfurter could open a conversation with Lewis (Estelle Lauder, Philadelphia, Pa., to FK, 28 November 1921, "Equal Rights Amendment: Correspondence: General: 1921," Box C4, NCL Records, DLC; *NYT,* 18 May 1952, 92).

2. The partner FK mentions was likely one of the members of Lewis's Philadelphia law firm, W. Logan MacCoy, Harold Evans, or Arthur Emlen Hutchinson (Shippen Lewis, Philadelphia, Pa., to Alice Paul, 28 November 1921, Group II: Box 17, NWP Records, DLC).

The NWTUL, the LWV, and other organizations that supported protective legislation waged a fierce battle in 1921 to convince Paul's attorneys that the proposed ERA would harm women workers. Members of the NWTUL were especially active in this endeavor with some degree of success. For example, William Draper Lewis, dean of the law school of the University of Pennsylvania, perhaps the most powerful of Paul's team of attorneys, refused to support the ERA unless a clause safeguarding protective labor legislation was added. He wrote the secretary of the NWTUL that "if no such clause is inserted, then the amendment should be opposed, and I should be glad to co-operate with you in any movement to that end" (William Draper Lewis, n.p., to Frieda S. Miller, [ca. December 1921], copy, Group II: Box 17, NWP Records, DLC).

3. FK sought the adoption of an anti-ERA resolution at the annual NCL Council meeting in Washington on 16 and 17 November, but a number of delegates supported the ERA and she was not successful (see Letter 165, FK to Felix Frankfurter, 28 November 1921, above). Here she refers to the first meeting of the new Board of Directors on 3 December 1921, which passed a resolution authorizing FK to inform ERA supporters that unless the wording of the ERA was changed to "safeguard the validity of the legislation for women, such as the National Consumers' League has advocated throughout its existence," the league would actively oppose the amendment (NCL Board of Directors Minutes, 3 December 1921, 1–2, Box A7, NCL Records). FK's ability to stack the new Board of Directors with opponents of the amendment prompted Edith Spruance to report to Alice Paul that "Mrs Kelley now considers herself regularly authorized to oppose the amendment in the name of the National Consumers' League" (Edith Spruance, Wilmington, Del., to Alice Paul, 13 December 1921, Group II: Box 17, NWP Records, DLC). As late as December 1921, the NWP was predicting that the ERA would not threaten protective labor legislation for women (*NYT,* 12 December 1921, 17).

167. To Clara Southwick

[New York City]
December 17th, 1921.

Miss Clara Southwick, Executive Secretary,
The Ford Building, 10th and Market Streets,
Wilmington, Delaware.
My Dear Miss Southwick,

On Sunday evening, December 4th, Mrs. [Maud Wood] Park; Mrs. Richard Edwards of Peru, Indiana, chairman of the Legislative Committee of the League of Women Voters; Miss Hafford, Congressional Legislative Agent of the Federation of Women's Clubs; Miss Ethel Smith, the Executive Secretary of the Women's Trade Union League; Mrs. Yost, the Congressional Agent of the

Women's Christian Temperance Union, and I spent two hours,—from 8 o'clock until 10,—with Miss Alice Paul, Mrs. Lawrence Lewis and Miss Maud Younger, at the Hotel Continental in Washington, discussing the possibility of an amendment to their amendment, to protect the existing labor statutes for women.[1]

On the following day, Mr. Dean Acheson, at the urgent solicitation of Mrs. [Alice] Brandeis, called on Miss Paul to offer one more last amendment to her amendment.[2] Mr. Acheson understood that Miss Paul flatly refused it, and so reported on Monday, December 5th, to the Committee on Industry of the Women's Joint Congressional Committee, which was meeting at the headquarters of the Women's Trade Union League.[3]

We have, therefore, carried out the vote of the Board of Directors of the Consumers' League at its first meeting, when I was instructed to communicate with Miss Paul as to the possibility of a safeguarding amendment in her amendment,—and I have also carried it out in the spirit of the letter received from Miss McKay[4] as to the form of our resolution.

In parting at the end of the evening I said to Miss Paul,—"I have still not given up hope." And Miss Paul said,—"We have not taken the last irrevocable step. Our amendment is not yet introduced."

Representative Fess went to Ohio on Wednesday, December 14th, carrying with him a copy of the proposed amendment, unchanged from the form in which we discussed it at the meeting of the Board of Directors on December 3rd. I therefore sent him last night the original of which the enclosed is a copy.[5]

Will you and Miss McKay go over this and will you ask her then to send me her opinion as to the usefulness of a multigraphed or printed leaflet containing the substance of this with, perhaps, some slight additions or improvements,—to go to key members of our local Leagues as soon as Senator [Charles] Curtis actually does write me that he has introduced his joint resolution?

Yours sincerely,

General Secretary.

CC, "Equal Rights Amendment: Correspondence: General: 1921," Box C4, NCL Records, DLC

1. Marie Stuart Edwards was first vice-president of the LWV. Lida Hafford was director of the GFWC's national headquarters in Washington, D.C., from 1920 to 1925 (Laws, *History of the Ohio Federation of Women's Clubs,* 41–45). Lenna Lowe Yost (1878–1972), former president of the West Virginia State WCTU and president of the West Virginia Equal Suffrage League (1916–1919), chaired West Virginia's state ratification committee in 1920 (Harper, *History of Woman Suffrage,* 6:687, 697; West Virginia State Archives, "Lenna Lowe Yost"). Dora Lewis (1896–1978) was national treasurer and member of the National Executive Committee of the NWP in 1921 (Mrs. Lawrence Lewis, "Letter to the Editor," *The Nation,* 26 March 1921, document 19 in Sklar and Dias, "How Did the NWP Address the Enfranchisement of Black Women, 1919–1924?").

FK told Maud Wood Park that she wanted "one final interview with Alice Paul," preferably at a neutral site, before Congress opened. She wrote and telegraphed Paul on 2 December to invite her to the meeting on 4 December, the day after the NCL's new Board of Directors met for the first time (FK, New York, to Park, 30 November 1921, "Equal Rights Amendment: Correspondence: General: 1921," Box C4, NCL Records, DLC; FK to Paul, Group II: Box 17, NWP Records, DLC).

2. Acheson told FK that he was still trying to get the NWP to revise the language in its amendment, which stated that protective legislation for women "shall not be held to impose a disability or inequality within the meaning of this Amendment" (Dean Acheson, Washington, D.C., to FK, 7 December 1921, "Equal Rights Amendment: Correspondence: General: 1921," Box C4, NCL Records).

3. The WJCC, which was formed on 22 November 1920 and continued until 1970, became the single most effective channel for women's legislative activism after 1920. It was launched by ten national organizations, including the LWV, the NWTUL, the NCL, the GFWC, and the WCTU, and at the height of its power in the early 1920s it drew on the political clout of 12 million women to promote a political agenda that FK did much to shape. The WJCC's objective was to serve as a clearinghouse for organizations that promoted legislation pertaining to women, and it was responsible for the passage of a wide range of reform legislation (Constitutional By-Laws of the Women's Joint Congressional Committee, Minutes of the WJCC, December 30, 1921, WJCC Records, DLC; Lemons, *Woman Citizen,* 56–57; Wilson, *The Women's Joint Congressional Committee*).

4. See Letter 166, FK to A. Estelle Lauder, 30 November 1921, above. Margaret E. McKay was president of the CL of Delaware and an NCL board member.

5. In her letter to Congressman Simeon D. Fess, FK raised twenty questions on marriage, sex, wage-earning women, and police powers that needed to be "carefully considered" before an ERA was adopted (FK, n.p., to Simeon D. Fess, 16 December 1921, copy, "Equal Rights Amendment: Correspondence: General: 1921," Box C4, NCL Records, DLC).

Adkins decision cartoon, published in *New York World*, 1923. Courtesy of the Library of Congress, LC-MS-29660–2 C-Mss div.

6 1922 – 1924

"Necessary Protection for Women"

INTRODUCTION

Florence Kelley's letters in the early 1920s reveal a powerful politician at work in a national arena where opponents were steadily gaining ground. In the best of times success generated more, not less, work, but now the new power of her adversaries made every step forward more arduous.

Much of her work remained incomplete and all of it was complicated by court proceedings. She had to find alternatives to the federal child labor laws that had been declared unconstitutional by the Supreme Court in June 1918 and May 1922. Her success with the Sheppard-Tower Act created a vast agenda at the state level because the act allocated federal money only to states that provided matching funds, requiring separate campaigns in each state. And her legislative successes had to be defended in state as well as federal courts. Court approval of the Sheppard-Towner Act was still pending in January 1922, and a new case involving the minimum wage law of the District of Columbia was moving toward the Supreme Court.

An ominous sea change seemed underway in American political culture. Elite magazines such as the *Atlantic Monthly* grossly misrepresented child labor laws. The U.S. Department of War authored, printed, and distributed a libelous flyer that attacked Kelley and her allies, claiming she advocated "the gradual abolition of property privileges."[1] Old friends like Newton Baker lost courage. New friends like Felix Frankfurter and Walter Lippmann seemed only semi-reliable.

Her extensive achievements now required aggressive defenses. She energetically repelled attacks on social rights by consulting intensively with her closest allies, meeting judiciously with those who were now former allies, and writing passionately for the wider public. She organized meetings, promoted constitutional amendments, lobbied state legislatures, and, above all, kept the NCL in fighting trim.

First she moved to meet the challenge posed by the National Woman's Party. Its proposed constitutional amendment threatened to erode her base, and she countered it directly and quickly. Her main tactic was a pamphlet, *Twenty Questions,* that denounced and sought to expose the inadequacy of the NWP's plan to provide "equal rights" for women without recognizing women's different needs. Published by the NCL in 1922, the pamphlet asked a series of questions related to "Marriage," "Sex," "Wage Earning Women," and "The Police Powers." "Will husbands need to continue to support their wives?" "What will become of . . . penalties for rape?" "What safeguards will wage-earning women have to compensate the disadvantages which they everywhere tend to suffer in competing with men—i.e., longer hours and lower wages?" "Will the National Woman's Party publicly answer the question,—'Do you believe that the states should have the constitutional power to pass protective legislation affecting women if and when, in their judgment, it becomes advisable?' Yes? or No?"[2]

This last question reflected Kelley's conviction that NWP members were "'Little Sisters' of the United States Chamber of Commerce, the National Manufacturers' Associations" and other groups whose lawyers tried to defeat labor legislation in Albany. She explained to fellow socialist and member of Congress Victor Berger that "whenever the Eight Hours Bill, Minimum Wage Bill, or any other bill intended to make industry more advantageous for women, is up for consideration Doris Stevens appears for the Woman's Party against the bill *and on the same side as those lawyers.*"[3]

Another crucial front was the struggle for state appropriations for the Sheppard-Towner Act. Seeking positive publicity for that effort in New York, she wrote Walter Lippmann at a late hour from her office "on the way to the midnight train to Washington." Women's organizations were well organized, she said: "The United Organizations for the Sheppard-Towner bill (27 in number) are working as harmoniously for the N.Y. appropriation as the fourteen national organizations did in Washington for the Federal bill." She explained that the act would be administered by New York's "excellent Bureau of Child Hygiene in the State Health Department," which she defended against the governor's misrepresentation, and promised to fight his effort to create an alternative maternal health bureau that he would control.[4]

Moving smoothly from the interstices of Albany politics to coalitions supporting a federal child labor amendment, Kelley's letters often followed her frequently traveled route between New York City and Washington, D.C. One written to Julia Lathrop from Washington in February 1923 summarized the multiple national fronts of that political moment. A lower court had just ruled positively on Sheppard-Towner. The Senate Judiciary Committee was soon expected to report favorably on the Child Labor Amendment, votes for which were being recruited by an Illinois Republican Senator. Felix Frankfurter would soon "argue the case for the D.C. minimum wage board," for which the NCL had "filed an enormous brief" paid for by Dorothy Whitney Straight. The real purpose of the letter (written with Grace Abbott) was to urge Lathrop to lead "the campaign for keeping the Children's Bureau intact" and oppose the Harding administration's plan to separate child labor and child welfare. "Of course we all know what that means for the working children!" Kelley declared, pointing out that "Labor" would probably agree to Harding's plan. She hoped Lathrop could begin to work on this issue in a couple of weeks.[5]

Kelley's expectations for her network were ambitious and her standards for legislation were high. When she and her supporters decided to campaign for an amendment to the U.S. Constitution, the amendment's wording reflected her standards: "Congress shall have power to limit, regulate, and prohibit the labor of persons under 18 years of age." Calling for the regulation of "labor" rather than "employment," the amendment included children who worked in tenements in family groups and were not actually employed as individuals. But this wording also allowed her opponents to mischaracterize the amendment as preventing children from helping on the family farm or with the dinner dishes. And the age limit of eighteen rather than sixteen undercut support she might otherwise have gained from working-class constituencies. Soon after Congress sent the amendment to the states in 1924, it was defeated in the key states of Massachusetts and Ohio.[6]

In mid-February 1923, Kelley wrote Julia Lathrop of the pending Supreme Court ruling on the District of Columbia minimum wage law, "Heaven help us if the decision is wrong!"[7] In a jarring setback to her agenda, the court ruled in early April that the wage law violated the right of employers to due process. The statute called for wages "sufficient to supply the necessary cost of living for a woman worker and maintain her in good health and protect her morals," but the court rejected that gendered premise as well as the law's view of employer responsibility.[8]

The decision argued that laws for women could no longer serve as a possible opening wedge for all workers because changes in "the contractual, political, and civil status of women, culminating in the Nineteenth Amendment," have brought "the ancient inequality of the sexes. . . . almost, if not quite, to the vanishing point." If it were taken seriously, this belief that equality had been achieved between the sexes would have undercut the NWP's call for a constitutional amendment as well as Florence Kelley's campaigns for gender-specific legislation, but the Court's sentiments about the end of that "ancient inequality" did not have much impact.[9] Indeed, most of the *Adkins* ruling focused on the ethics of wage legislation rather than the politics of gender, declaring that "the ethical right of every worker, man or woman, to a living wage may be conceded" but "the fallacy of the proposed method of attaining it is that it assumes that every employer is bound at all events to furnish it."[10]

The decision defended employers who paid less than a living wage: "The employer, by paying a fair equivalent for the service rendered, though not sufficient to support the employee, has neither caused nor contributed to her poverty. On the contrary, to the extent of what he pays, he has relieved it." Employers might be required "to pay with fair relation to the extent of the benefit obtained from the service. . . . But a statute which prescribes payment. . . solely with relation to circumstances apart from the contract of employment, . . . is so clearly the product of a naked, arbitrary exercise of power that it cannot be allowed to stand under the Constitution of the United States."[11] Thus, working people had the right to a living wage but not to a law that required employers to pay it.

Kelley called the ruling "chapter three of the Dred Scott decision," seeing it in a lineage of rights denied to free blacks in 1857, to wage-earning children in 1918 and 1922, and to wage-earning women in 1923. She placed her faith in a future in which women would serve on all federal courts and "several competent, learned women" would be added to the Supreme Court; she supported a bill requiring that at least seven U.S. Supreme Court justices concur in any decision that declared a congressional law unconstitutional; and she sought to restrict the Court's use of the due process clause of the Fourteenth Amendment to aid employers. In the long term, she hoped for "a modern Constitution and a modern minded Supreme Court."[12]

But short term solutions to "the present crisis" remained elusive.[13] She emphatically disagreed with Frankfurter on the wording of a new minimum wage bill for the District of Columbia, feeling that "fair wages" was too vague and that her term—"the health of the workers"—was "the only solid foundation of wage determinations."[14] She also disagreed with Gompers's strategy of a constitutional amendment that would establish an omnibus list of labor rights. Always her own person and still the head of the minimum wage movement, she turned away from Frankfurter and Gompers and sought support among women, but she was unable to persuade Ethel Smith and others in the Women's Trade Union League to support a separate minimum wage amendment.[15] She hoped NCL leaders would endorse a gender-neutral amendment that would "forbid the employment of any person at wages less than sufficient for maintenance in health" but "sorrowfully" abandoned it after a gathering of "the clans" did not endorse it.[16] She moved forward in October with her board's endorsement of a federal bill "providing that the court shall not declare a state law unconstitutional unless at least seven of its members concur in favor of such decision, and that they shall not declare an act of Congress unconstitutional unless the court is unanimous."[17]

In her work with the NAACP, Kelley encountered complications similar to those created by the NWP's break with the mainstream suffrage movement. She wrote an article for *The Crisis* that warned against a group of women recently admitted to membership in the WJCC who, countering the goals of the NAACP, were "red hot" for a bill that championed the right of states to control federal money allocated to school funding. By contrast, Kelley strongly supported the extension of federal power in the Dyer anti-lynching bill, and the NCL board unanimously resolved to support the bill.[18]

Influenced by her understanding of the power of racial prejudice within American political culture, Kelley pursued its trail within the National Woman's Party. Lavinia Egan obliged by writing her that the Woman's Party sought "to give the women of each group equality of rights with the men of the same group ... professional women with professional men: women in industry with men in industry: business women with business men: Japanese women citizens with Japanese men citizens of the United States: Negro women with Negro men." Kelley triumphantly wrote NWP supporter and former resident of the Henry Street settlement Lavinia Dock, "That looks to me like caste, not equality."[19] She asked Victor Berger, "What do you think the Negroes think of this kind of South Carolina equality?"[20]

As she met these challenges, the organizational vitality of the National Consumers' League remained a fundamental priority. Troubled by Newton Baker's alliance with the Cleveland Chamber of Commerce, she accepted his resignation as president of the NCL and organized the appointment of John R. Commons to replace him. Commons brought many talents to the league, including his standing as a leading public intellectual with expertise on labor issues. Most important, Commons shared Kelley's desire to curb the power of the Supreme Court.[21] Kelley greatly valued gifted assistants such as Molly Dewson and found it hard to accept their departure.[22] The NCL's membership remained stable at 8,000, but Kelley's constant search for funds was mostly unrewarded.[23] She could not find funding for an initiative about industrial toxins, but John Commons helped the NCL cooperate with the League of Women Voters in educating their members about workmen's unemployment insurance.[24]

Kelley and the NCL needed to be strong to survive the vicious attacks on their patriotism that reached a crescendo in 1924 with the publication of a flyer by the U.S. Department of War that characterized Kelley as advocating "the gradual abolition of property privileges."[25] The flyer's inflammatory title, "The Socialist-Pacifist Movement in America is an Absolutely Fundamental and Integral Part of International Socialism," was a quote from the 1920 report on seditious activities compiled by the Lusk Committee of the New York State Legislature.

The flyer used lines to depict links between fourteen major women's organizations and two other groups: the WJCC, which coordinated the women's movement's post-1920 legislative agenda; and the National Council for the Prevention of War, a liberal group that opposed war and supported the League of Nations. These links supposedly demonstrated the connections between the women's movement and "the Socialist-Pacifist Movement." The chart was published in the *Dearborn Independent* with an article, "Are Women's Clubs Used by Bolshevists?"[26] Kelley viewed this attack as gravely serious, writing Herbert Swope, editor of the *New York World,* "It is this League which suffers from this use of the ammunition thus supplied by the War Department to our enemies."[27] Noticeably absent from the chart was the National Woman's Party, who, as critics of labor legislation, had made friends among anti-socialists.

When the WJCC investigated the source of the chart, it discovered that Lucia Maxwell, assistant to General Amos A. Fries of the Chemical Warfare Bureau of the Department of War, had compiled it. Maud Wood Park, head of the WJCC, protested to Secretary of War John Weeks that the chart was full of errors and that the intention was to vilify the WJCC. He replied that "all the charts complained of in the possession of the Chemical Warfare Service have been ordered destroyed."[28]

But the damage had been done. Scurrilous articles were reprinted and distributed by WJCC opponents, including the manufacturer's association in Louisville, Kentucky, a city with a strong consumers' league. In a published protest about the ongoing use of the chart, Carrie Chapman Catt asked what the manufacturers feared, "Is it the abolition of child labor, education or peace?" She concluded, "Women of America, don't get frightened; think. Don't be intimidated; act."[29]

Florence Kelley was part of the postwar strength of the women's international peace movement that put women's organizations on a collision course with supporters of the expansion of American military. Near her farmhouse in Maine in August 1924, she attended a protest meeting against Secretary of War Weeks's plan for "Defense Day," and the wife of a D.C. judge alerted her to the song, "I Did Not Raise My Son To Be A Slacker," a World War I anti-pacifist song set to music composed by Mrs. Amos Fries.[30]

This collision between women's organizations and the Department of War was itself part of a larger antagonism between the mainstream women's movement, which supported child labor and other social legislation, and the growing strength of right-wing groups, including groups of women, that opposed such legislation. That antagonism was evident by 1919 in the pages of *The Woman Patriot,* which then called itself *The Woman Patriot: For Home and National Defense Against Woman Suffrage, Feminism and Socialism.*[31] In 1924, as *The Woman Patriot: Dedicated to the Defense of The Family and The State AGAINST Feminism and Socialism,* the periodical attacked Kelley as the most subversive woman reformer; two years later it launched a sustained attack on her in a petition against the Sheppard-Towner act, which was published over seven months and read into the *Congressional Record.*[32]

Writers for *The Woman Patriot* were closely allied with men anti-suffragists, such as J. S. Eichelberger, who opposed the social agenda of the women's movement even more than they opposed votes for women. In a 1924 letter to Julia Lathrop, Kelley referred to Eichelberger as a defender of Weeks's attack on the women's movement. She probably also knew him as the head of public relations for The National Association Opposed to Woman Suffrage, a women's group, as well as field secretary of the Men's National Anti-Suffrage Association when it was reconstituted as the American Constitutional League in 1917. In 1919 he served as "business manager" of *The Woman Patriot* and in 1922 joined other anti-suffragist men in creating the Sentinels of the Republic.[33] Vigorously opposing the social agenda of the women's movement, the Sentinels served as a "clearinghouse for all who felt it was time to look sharp to the rights of States and individuals, and resist steadfastly all inroads on the guarantees provided in the United States Constitution."[34]

In this new alignment of women along the political spectrum from right to left, the momentum from the woman suffrage movement carried many women forward in a centrist mainstream that supported social justice legislation. Florence Kelley used her networks and influence to defend that mainstream. She denounced the misrepresentations of social legislation that appeared in *The Atlantic Monthly*, called on Jane Addams to promote a positive view of the child labor amendment in publications that "reach the rural and the small town mind," and urged Frances Perkins to mobilize Herbert Bayard Swope and Walter Lippmann, two opinion-shapers on the centrist left.[35] Meanwhile, she prepared to influence the Senate when its members considered new nominees to the Supreme Court, found comfort in the company of old friends such as Mabel and Edward Costigan, and applauded the support women were giving Senator Robert La Follette's campaign for the presidency.[36] Although she planned to work for La Follette and did not support Coolidge, she hoped for the defeat of the Democratic candidate, who was allied with J. P. Morgan and had objected to having "this brief Brandeised" when the Keating-Owen child labor law came before the Supreme Court.[37]

Kelley rejoiced in the proximity of her grandchildren in Manhattan. Florence, ten years old in 1922, happily accompanied "Granny" on visits to friends, including a visit to Mary Hill Swope, where "no one talked politics," but politics was almost certainly in the air.[38] Ko's family lived near Gramercy Park and the 15th Street Friends Meeting House, not far from where "Granny" lived at the Henry Street Settlement in lower Manhattan, so visiting them was relatively easy.[39]

Her "cubicle" at Henry Street comfortably accommodated "four mahogany pieces"—"bookcase, bed, dressing table and chair"—but as Kelley aged, the inconveniences of Henry Street began to grate.[40] She welcomed the opportunity to stay in John and Ann's apartment in June and July of 1922: "It will be a great comfort to be free from stairs, fire-engines, the playground, and the hot, noisy, confused dining room." But she acknowledged that "by fall, I suppose I shall be glad to be back in Henry Street."[41] In the summer, her farmhouse in Maine continued to serve as a retreat where she welcomed family and friends; Jane Addams and Emily Balch stayed overnight in August 1924.

NOTES

1. For more about the spider web chart and its impact on women's culture, see Cott, *The Grounding of Modern Feminism*, 249–260; and Sklar and Baker, "How Did Women Peace Activists Respond to 'Red Scare' Attacks during the 1920s?"

2. FK, *Twenty Questions about the Federal Amendment Proposed by the National Woman's Party*.

3. Letter 188, FK to Victor Berger, 19 December 1923, below. Emphasis in original.

4. Letter 171, FK to Walter Lippmann, 17 February 1922, below.
5. Letter 177, FK to Julia Lathrop, 18 February 1923, below.
6. For more on the child labor amendment in these years, see Letter 176, FK to Alice Hamilton, 13 October 1922; Letter 177, FK to Julia Lathrop, 18 February 1923; Letter 190, FK to Molly Dewson, 17 February 1924; Letter 192, FK to Molly Dewson, 26 March 1924; Letter 191, FK to Annette Mann, 15 March 1924; Letter 193, FK to Ellery Sedgwick, 1 April 1924; Letter 195, FK to Herbert Bayard Swope, 27 May 1924; Letter 202, FK to Jane Addams, 11 October 1924; and Letter 203, FK to Frances Perkins, 4 December 1924, all below.
7. Letter 177, FK to Julia Lathrop, 18 February 1923, below.
8. *Adkins v. Children's Hospital of the District of Columbia,* 262 U.S. 525 (1923).
9. *Adkins v. Children's Hospital.* See also Hart, *Bound by Our Constitution,* 122–129.
10. *Adkins v. Children's Hospital.*
11. *Adkins v. Children's Hospital.*
12. Letter 179, FK to Lathrop, 21 April 1923; and Letter 180, FK to James Haight, 19 May 1923, both below.
13. Letter 182, FK to Edward Costigan, 31 May 1923, below.
14. Letter 181, FK to Felix Frankfurter, 26 May 1923, below.
15. Letter 182, FK to Costigan, 31 May 1923, below. See also Letter 183, FK to Edward Costigan, 2 October 1923, below.
16. FK, New York, to Lathrop, [before 28 May 1923], Lathrop Papers; and Letter 183, FK to Costigan, 2 October 1923, below.
17. Charles Amidon, Fargo, N.D., to FK, 3 October 1923, copy, "Correspondence (Florence Kelley): Amidon, Charles F., 1922–1925," Box C4, NCL Records, DLC.
18. Letter 184, FK to W. E. B. Du Bois, 18 October 1923; Letter 186, FK to James Weldon Johnson, 13 November 1923; and Letter 189, FK to Joseph Deal, 18 January 1924, all below.
19. Letter 187, FK to Lavinia Dock, 24 November 1923, below.
20. Letter 188, FK to Victor Berger, 19 December 1923, below.
21. Letter 172, FK to Newton Baker, 3 June 1922; Letter 185, FK to Charles Amidon, 26 October 1923; and Letter 197, FK to Edward Costigan, 7 July 1924, all below.
22. Letter 190, FK to Molly Dewson, 17 February 1924; and Letter 192, FK to Dewson, 26 March 1924, both below.
23. Letter 192, FK to Dewson, 26 March 1924; and Letter 194, FK to Roger Baldwin, 6 May 1924.
24. Letter 200, FK to John Commons, after 2 August 1924, below.
25. For the *Woman Patriot*'s attacks on FK, see Wilson, *The Women's Joint Congressional Committee and the Politics of Maternalism,* 61–62, 136, 151. For the National Council for the Prevention of War, see DeBenedetti, *The Peace Reform in American History,* 109, 113, 114, 130, and 132. See also Lucia Maxwell, "Spider Web Chart: The Socialist-Pacifist Movement in America Is an Absolutely Fundamental and Integral Part of International Socialism," *Dearborn Independent* 24 (22 March 1924), reprinted in Sklar and Baker, "How Did Women Peace Activists respond to 'Red Scare' Attacks during the 1920s?"

In addition to the NCL, the spider web chart named the League of Women Voters, the General Federation of Women's Clubs, the Woman's Christian Temperance Union, the National Congress of Mothers and Parent-Teacher Association, the National Women's Trade Union [League], the American Home Economics Association, the American Association of University Women, the National Council of Jewish Women, the Girls Friendly Society, the Young Women's Christian Association, the National Association of Business and Professional Women, the Women's International League for Peace and Freedom, and the Women's Committee for World Disarmament. See Maxwell, "Spider Web Chart."
26. "Are Women's Clubs 'Used' by Bolshevists?" *Dearborn Independent* 24 (15 March 1924), 2.

27. Letter 195, FK to Herbert Bayard Swope, 27 May 1924, below.
28. Catt, "Poison Propaganda," 14, 32–33, which reprints a letter from Maud Wood Park to John W. Weeks, Washington, D.C., 2 April 1924 (pp. 14, 32); and John W. Weeks to Maud Wood Park, Washington, D.C., 16 April 1924 (p. 32).
29. Catt, "Poison Propaganda," 33.
30. Letter 201, FK to Grace Abbott, 11 August 1924, below.
31. This was the masthead the *Woman Patriot* used until 1 November 1919.
32. "Congress Proves Amendment Means What It Says," Woman Patriot 8 (15 July 1924): 2. See "A Petition to the United States Senate," Parts 1–7, *Woman Patriot* (15 May 1926 to 15 August 1926).
33. "Statement of the Ownership, Management, Circulation, etc. . . . of the Woman Patriot," *The Woman Patriot: For Home and National Defense Against Woman Suffrage, Feminism and Socialism* 3 (11 October 1919): 5.
34. Jablonsky, *The Home, Heaven, and Mother Party,* 114; Marshall, *Splintered Sisterhood,* 78, 203; Neilson, *Un-American Womanhood,* 54–72.
35. Letter 193, FK to Ellery Sedgwick, 1 April 1924; Letter 202, FK to JA, 11 October 1924; and Letter 203, FK to Frances Perkins, 4 December 1924, all below.
36. Letter 201, FK to Grace Abbott, 11 August 1924, below.
37. Letter 201, FK to Abbott, 11 August 1924.
38. Letter 170, FK to NK, ca. 23 January 1922, below.
39. Today the Kelley House is part of the Friends Seminary, a K–12 school.
40. Letter 236, FK to NK, 9 August 1927, below.
41. Letter 170, FK to NK, ca. 23 January 1922.

168. To Grace Abbott[1]

[New York City]
Monday Jan. 8th 1921 [1922]
Dear Grace

The morning is as lovely as New Year's morning. But instead of the loveliness of Rock Creek Park, there is the din of boys in the playground under my window! How different Alas!

Criticisms of Twenty Questions have begun to come in. One is that Age of Consent Laws should be completed in two ways.[2] A. They should be made uniform in all the States at the 21st birthday. B. Penalties for debauching boys are just as much needed, and should apply to women as to men.

Obviously this means no federal amendment. But it has raised the question, in my mind, whether perhaps, you may have an up-to-date chart, or a graded list, of the age of consent laws in the States, from which, for instance, the L.W.V. could make its own chart?[3]

Certainly, if we are all going to oppose the program of the "Shortcut" ladies, we shall have to tackle intellingently, at retail, that which they are attempting at wholesale.

By we I do not mean the Consumers, but the appropriate contingent of organized women.

You have doubtless seen how charmingly Governor Miller has "passed the "buck" to the N.Y. legislature![4]

Yours affectionately
Florence Kelley

ALS, "Sexual Crimes," Folder 10–5–5, Box 232, CB Records, RG102, MdCpNA

1. After strong support from FK and many women's organizations, President Harding appointed Abbott chief of the Children's Bureau on 19 August 1921, succeeding Julia Lathrop (*NYT,* 20 August 1921, 8; see also Costin, *Two Sisters for Social Justice,* 120–124).

2. One question in FK, *Twenty Questions about the Federal Amendment Proposed by the National Women's Party* was "Will all of the age of consent laws be wiped out?" (5). For more on laws that governed the age of girls and women with whom men could legally have sexual relations, see Doak, Park, and Lee, "How Did Gender and Class Shape the Age of Consent Campaign within the Social Purity Movement, 1886–1914?"

3. Abbott enclosed a list of state laws regarding the age of consent in her reply. She was against any standard for states until laws were enacted to apply to young men as well. In thanking Abbott, FK concluded that "no blanket law will improve them. Only a long process of educating the public, and who will do that?" (Abbott, Washington, D.C., to FK, 14 January 1922, copy; FK, New York, to Abbott, 23 February 1922, both in Folder 10–5–5, Box 232, CB Records, MdCpNA).

4. In a press conference in early January, Nathan L. Miller (1868–1953), Republican governor of New York (1921–1923), criticized the Sheppard-Towner Maternity and Infancy Protection Act, which Congress had passed in November 1921. The legislation authorized $7.5 million

to states, to be administered by the U.S. Children's Bureau. The amount designated to each state depended upon that state's population and the matching funds it would provide. Miller stated that "the public will get to expect to be nursed from the cradle to the grave, and I do not think that is a good thing" (*NYT,* 5 January 1922, 4).

169. To Edward P. Costigan

[New York City]
January 12th, 1922.

Mr. Edward P. Costigan,
The Brighton,
Washington, D. C.
Dear Mr. Costigan,

Thank you very much for your letter of January seventh. I was authorized by the Board to appear before the Interstate Commerce Commission and shall follow your suggestions, for which I am indeed grateful.[1]

Unhappily at the first meeting of the Board in December, it laid down the rule that it would not act on any bill which the members had not had an opportunity to examine in advance, and as your letter reached me on January 9th, the morning of the day of the second meeting, the bill went over.[2] I am now getting a copy for each member of the Board, except yourself, and there will be no excuse for delay next time.

I don't know how to thank you enough for your letter to Mr. Maxwell Reed.[3] He has become the devil's advocate of the Board,—most amiable and eager to help. At the meeting it developed that his wife is a member of the Woman's Party and he a convert to their federal amendment, which he defended with the same arguments that Mrs. Costigan will remember the Delaware lady producing at

Edward P. Costigan, 1925. Courtesy of the Library of Congress, LC-USZ62-105093.

the annual meeting. The effect was to crystallize the Board solidly against the amendment, as to which there had been luke-warmness at the first meeting,[4] and ardently for our Ten Years' Program. He is inevitably going to be useful because his intentions are good and he is active and he serves as irritant and stimulant. It was one of the few truly delightful and cheering Board meetings!

Yours sincerely and as always gratefully,

P.S. I know you will show this to Mrs. Costigan and I will, therefore, not write her separately but merely enclose this copy of Mrs. Harriman's letter.[5]

F.K.

CC, "General Correspondence: Costigan, Mr. and Mrs. Edward P.," Box B12, NCL Records, DLC

1. Costigan served on the U.S. Tariff Commission from 1917 to 1928. He advised FK that lowered railroad rates would result in "increased business" and should therefore bring about "wages to workers which will sustain proper living standards" (Edward P. Costigan, Washington, D.C., to FK, 7 January 1922, "General Correspondence: Costigan, Mr. and Mrs. Edward P.," Box B12, NCL Records, DLC).

2. Costigan had sent FK a copy of the Capper-Volstead bill. He said that he and Mabel Costigan hoped the NCL would endorse the bill. Costigan's solution to a postwar agricultural crisis that threatened small producers entailed cooperative marketing that connected farmers with urban consumers. The Capper-Volstead bill, which passed in 1922, legalized producer cooperatives and exempted them from antitrust legislation. The opposing strategy of price supports that relied on public funding, embodied in the McNary-Haugen bill, did not pass (Nordin, *From Prairie Farmer to Entrepreneur,* 58–59). FK had previously written Mabel Costigan about creating a federal food commission, an agency she hoped would be housed in the Department of Commerce (Costigan, Washington, D.C., to FK, 7 January 1922; FK, New York, to Mabel Costigan, 16 March 1921, both in "General Correspondence: Costigan, Mr. and Mrs. Edward P.," Box B12, NCL Records, DLC).

3. Costigan enclosed his letter to NCL board member William Maxwell Reed (1871–1962), a writer of scientific books for children. In it, Costigan countered Reed's claim that the NCL's financial difficulties would weaken its clout with legislatures. He wrote that the NCL "is a present-day illustration of the truth that progress is generally achieved by minorities working too often with a restricted budget. . . . Certainly in the Congressional hearings in this city, Mrs. Florence Kelley, unassisted, speaking in the name of the consumers of the country, is more than equal to an army with banners" (Edward P. Costigan, Washington, D.C., to Reed, 7 January 1922, "General Correspondence: Costigan, Mr. and Mrs. Edward P.," Box B12, NCL Records, DLC). At the board meeting, Reed was named chair of the Finance Committee, a position he held for only a few months. In April, he resigned as a director because of his "approval of the blanket legislative program of the National Woman's Party" and his belief that "unanimity of the Board on this question was desirable" (NCL Board of Directors Minutes, 9 January 1922, 3, and 10 April 1922, 4, both in Box A2, NCL Records, DLC).

4. Reed was the only director to oppose the NCL's resolution against the ERA (NCL Board of Directors Minutes, 9 January 1922, 3, Box A2, NCL Records, DLC).

5. FK's letter to Florence Harriman expressed regret that Harriman's illness prevented her from enjoying "the lively discussion of our policy with regard to the federal amendment" (FK, New York, to Florence Harriman, 12 January 1922, "General Correspondence: 'H,'" Box B13, NCL Records, DLC).

170. To Nicholas Kelley

Jan. [ca. 23] 1922
R. 1102 44 E. 23
[New York City]

Beloved Son

What I thought was going to be a good vacation seems to be dragging out into an exile. From my European journeys, I know how long the weeks are before deferred sailings.[1]

So, now, when it is probably too late to do any good, I'm becoming motherly, and sent you two Atlantics the other day, and now this, after some weeklies.

Just after you left the Sheppard-Towner bill passed, and the President Harding signed it on Thanksgiving Eve. Now Governor Miller is talking against it. On Saturday, in an address to the Bar Association, he denounced it.[2] So that long struggle is not yet ended. For the State has to co-operate.[3]

Meanwhile, I think the enclosed may amuse you. Paragraph 20 is Felix Frankfurters. 15 and 16 come from Bernard Shientag. The original suggestion that we needed something of the nature of 1–10 incl. came from a worried uplifter. I fear we may have the confusion with us for a long time.[4]

I was sick with tonsilitis, in December, and felt very much below par for a month. But now I'm spry and chipper again. I seem to be rather improved by the departure of Mr. Shillady, tho' that is thankless, because he really did gather in about $30 000.00 a year when every other organization had to take in sail, and we had a few thousand more than ever, and ended the year without a deficit.[5] He was dissatisfied with having to spend his whole time on money raising. He went on Jan. 15th.

The weather has been wonderful! The children have just finished a whole week of skating in Gramercy Park! This morning is so cold that I think they may be having another coming. They are simply delightful. I took Florence to call on Mary Hill Swope.[6] P. Goldmark was there and a Mrs. Webster. Everybody talked about Schoolboys, the Swopes having four. On the way home F. said "Granny! I like your friends so much! How do you get such nice ones? My last one was very nice and then, all at once, she cheated in Examination! They were so interesting this afternoon. No one talked politics or any of that silly stuff!" Instead of growing less charming, she is more so all the time.

The Disarmament Conference is dying an inglorious, slow death. Nothing definite about Shantung. Fresh evasions about Siberia and Corea. Great irritation spreading against France and Japan.[7]

Now a fresh Presidential Conference about Agriculture. The general tone of the press now toward our farmers is that applied to the Reds of all descriptions in 1920.[8] [Eugene V.] Debs was released on Xmas day but there is no real amnesty.[9] Only the real friends of the prisoners do anything about them. There is no popular movement for amnesty.

The rage against the Agricultural bloc (in the press) is amazing.[10]

John and Ann are sailing next month, and I'm taking their apartment until July 1st. It will be a great comfort to be free from stairs, fire-engines, the playground, and the hot, noisy, confused dining room. By fall, I suppose I shall be glad to be back in Henry Street. They expect to sail the boat home and enter her in the race around Long Island in August. That means going East on a Liner in February and West in Diablesse in June and July.

I hope you are finding some good recreation in your lengthy sojourn!

I miss you horribly!

Your loving
Ma

ALS, FKP, NN

1. NK was reappointed as assistant secretary of the treasury in March 1921 (*NYT,* 11 March 1921, 3). Since November 1921, he had been in Peru on behalf of American banking interests. He returned to the United States in February 1922.

2. Governor Nathan Miller spoke to the New York State Bar Association on 21 January. He told his audience that the Constitution provided for "'the common defense and general welfare'" and that this did not include "the practice of medicine or midwifery." Thus, the Sheppard-Towner Act was "a violation of the United States Constitution" (*NYT,* 22 January 1922, 19).

3. For more on the outcome of FK's effort to push the states of New York and Maine to accept Sheppard-Towner funds, see Letter 171, FK to Walter Lippman, 17 February 1922; and Letter 174, FK to Percival Baxter, 30 July 1922, both below.

4. FK apparently enclosed a draft of *Twenty Questions* that the NCL had considered at its January meeting. Frankfurter telegraphed replacements for questions thirteen and twenty (NCL Board of Directors Minutes, 9 January 1922, 3, Box A2, NCL Records, DLC).

5. Social worker John R. Shillady (b. 1875), the former secretary of the NAACP, was executive director of the NCL from 1920 to 1922. He was hired to direct the NCL's ten-year program (*Christian Science Monitor,* 20 August 1920, 6). At the March Board of Directors meeting, the treasurer reported a deficit of $3,791.40 (NCL Council Minutes, 1920–1922; NCL Board of Directors Minutes, 13 March 1922, 1, both in Box A2, NCL Records, DLC). See Letter 190, FK to Molly Dewson, 17 February 1924, below, for further details on the NCL's finances.

6. Mary Hill Swope (ca. 1871–1955), a Hull House resident, was the daughter of Thomas Hill, president of Harvard University (1862–1868). She had studied with John Dewey at the University of Chicago. When Hill married Gerard Swope in 1901, JA presided at their wedding. Gerard Swope arrived at Hull House in 1897, two years before FK's departure. In 1922, he became president of General Electric Company (Loth, *Swope of G.E.,* 43, 106–108).

7. The Washington Naval Conference began on 11 November 1921. The Five-Power Naval Limitation Treaty signed at the conference's conclusion on 6 February 1922 scrapped a considerable number of warships, but it did not apply to every warship that Britain, Japan, France, Italy, and the United States owned. Japan agreed to leave Siberia and cede some of its authority in the Shantung Peninsula back to China. For more on naval disarmament, see LoCasto and Sklar, "Pacifism vs. Patriotism in Women's Organizations in the 1920s: How Was the Debate Shaped by the Expansion of the American Military?"

8. In the winter of 1922, Secretary of Agriculture Henry C. Wallace called a National Agricultural Conference in Washington that discussed ways to permit farmers to act together in marketing associations. However, the conference decided against federal guarantees of mini-

mum prices for farm goods (*NYT,* 27 January 1922, 1). In an editorial condemning price-fixing, the *New York Times* stated that "it is vain for the farmers to protest that they ought not to be expected to sell below the cost of production. Others have had to do it. Nor can the farmers demand supplies below the price asked by manufacturers" (*NYT,* 30 January 1922, 10).

9. President Harding commuted the sentences of Debs and twenty-three other political prisoners on 23 December 1921 (Salvatore, *Eugene V. Debs,* 327).

10. In the early 1920s the "farm bloc" emerged as a bipartisan congressional group that exercised a new form of interest-group politics by controlling legislative committees. An example of its success in 1921 was the Packers and Stockyards Act (Bradley, "The Farm Bloc").

171. To Walter Lippmann

NATIONAL CONSUMERS' LEAGUE
44 EAST 23RD STREET
NEW YORK CITY

2-17-22

Dear Mr. Lippmann

At last I can report that Senator Duell has introduced an enabling act for the acceptance of the Sheppard-Towner law by New York State.

It is Senate 708 and referred to the Comm. on Public Health. He will push it in the Senate and then in the ~~House~~ Assembly as Senate bill No. ___. The Appropriation bill will not go in until after hearings on this first of the twin measures.

Meanwhile the Tribune announces that the HARDING MILLER ADMINISTRATION will, within a fortnight, introduce a measure for a State Bureau of Maternity and Infancy ignoring the Sheppard-Towner Law. It will be administered exclusively for N.Y. State by the State Health Department.[1]

Either the ~~Harding~~ Miller Administration does not know that we have already an excellent Bureau of Child Hygiene in the State Health Department under Dr. Florence McKay,[2] or it is trying to fool the people!

Also it cannot have read the Sheppard-Towner law, for this expressly designates the Children's Bureau in the State Health Department as the agency to administer the joint Federal and State Fund, in every state in which such a Bureau exists.

Can it be that the Miller Administration really means to duplicate the present Bureau of Child Hygiene?

Finally does Governor Miller think it is economy to refuse the ten thousand dollars which Uncle Sam offers each State as a gift?

And the $75000 a year for five years to be had by matching it, dollar for dollar?

The United Organizations for the Sheppard-Towner bill (27 in number) are working as harmoniously for the N.Y. appropriation as the fourteen national organizations did in Washington for the Federal bill, with Mrs. Montgomery Hare in charge of publicity.[3]

If the Miller administration really does introduce any thing separate from Senator Duell's bill it will get a run for its money![4]

Yours hopefully
Florence Kelley

The eccentricity of this epistle is due to the late hour. I am writing in the office, on the way to the midnight train to Washington.

ALS, Lippmann Papers, CtY

1. The New York State legislature passed a bill authorizing $100,000 for a state bureau instead of Holland S. Duell's bill for the Sheppard-Towner Act (*NYT,* 20 February 1922, 10; 18 March 1922, 2).

2. McKay headed the Bureau of Child Hygiene from 1921 to 1926 (*NYT,* 7 March 1926, II:6).

3. Constance Parsons Hare (1873–1962) was a New York City civic leader and the wife of prominent Democrat Montgomery Hare (*NYT,* 19 June 1962, 35). The "United Organizations" refers to the WJCC. For more on its promotion of Sheppard-Towner legislation, see Wilson, *The Women's Joint Congressional Committee,* 27–49.

4. Nineteen women's organizations united to lobby for the implementation of maternity services under the Sheppard-Towner Act in New York State. FK wrote Marion Parkhurst, congressional secretary of the LWV, that the state legislature had before it "two bills,—one appropriating money nominally in the interest of maternity and infancy, but really specifically required by the statute to be applied to many other groups of children and minors,—and one without money paving the way for the Sheppard-Towner cooperation next year. God forgive us,—it was the best we could do!" (FK, New York, to Marion Parkhurst, 10 March 1922, Box 25, LWV Papers, DLC). On 17 March the New York legislature approved appropriations for an independent state bureau, thus rejecting funds provided by the Sheppard-Towner Act. In April the legislature and Governor Nathan Miller approved a sum of $130,000 (supplemented by a $30,000 allocation from the state Health Department) for the protection of mothers and infants of the state. FK feared that the $160,000 would "be spread thin over the training of public health nurses, the supervision of mid-wives, the care of poliomyelitis and other cripples, the blind, and surveys of the diseases and defects of children. All this is, of course, in spite of the urgent criticism and objections from the United Organizations for the Sheppard-Towner bill" (*NYT:* 20 February 1922, 10, 18 March 1922, 2, and 4 April 1922, 21; FK, New York, to Maud Wood Park, 20 March 1922, Box 25, LWV Papers, DLC).

172. To Newton D. Baker

[New York City]
June 3rd, 1922.

Hon. Newton D. Baker,
Union National Bank Building,
Cleveland, Ohio.
My dear Mr. Baker,

The leaflets which you gave me I have been circulating among the members of the Board, beginning with Mr. [Robert] Szold and Mr. [Edward P.] Costigan. I understood you to say that that publication stated your present position.[1]

Every intelligent member of the League, like every other intelligent citizen is, of course, deeply troubled by the fight led by the Chambers of Commerce against all unions indiscriminately.

Unless I hear from you to the contrary, I should be very glad to hand this letter from you to me about among the members of the meeting on June 15th, for their information.[2] There is, I think, no present question of the National Consumers' League taking action or even defining its position with regard to the fight against the unions. Every ray of light, however, that any of us can get or contribute seems specially valuable at this moment.

Referring to your note of May 25th, in which you spoke of Mr. Costigan's proposed rough draft for a federal amendment,—everything has moved with bewildering speed. As you have seen from the papers, Mr. Gompers arranged for a hearing before the House Committee on the Judiciary for last Thursday, and in the afternoon at his office, pursuant to a previous call, there was held a conference of people invited by him from different organizations, for the purpose of forming a permanent body to work for the abolition of child labor in this country.[3]

A committee of ten was created, consisting of Mr. Gompers, Chairman of the whole undertaking,—myself as First Vice-Chairman, a representative of the Women's Trade Union League as Secretary, Mr. Lovejoy, Maud Wood Park, Mrs. Glenn Swiggett, representing the National Council of Women, and Mrs. Alice Winter of the General Federation of Women's Clubs.[4]

This committee was instructed to draft a federal amendment and a bill, presumably related to the amendment as the Volstead law is related to the prohibition amendment,[5]—and report at the meeting the last week of June. Everything went so fast that there was no time to telegraph for approval, and it seemed dangerous to leave the Federation of Labor in possession,—especially it seemed dangerous to let the public get the idea that the Federation has patented or copyrighted this national movement.[6]

I acted, therefore, in full confidence that the Board would approve my serving as First Vice-Chairman and will give serious consideration on June 15th to the subject of a federal amendment.

Yours always sincerely,

FK/DM

CC, "General Correspondence: Baker, Newton D.," Box B11, NCL Records, DLC

1. Baker and FK had exchanged letters regarding a public letter that Baker, as president of the Cleveland Chamber of Commerce, had written indicating that he opposed the closed shop policy of the local painters' union. Baker explained that while he supported unions and collective bargaining, he believed "that the present tendency of labor unions to create air-tight monopolies in their several trades and combine with corresponding monopolies of employers to exploit the public is wrong and destructive of all the just and sound purposes for which labor unions can be formed" (Baker, Cleveland, Ohio, to FK, 12 May 1922, "General Correspondence: Baker, Newton D.," Box B11, NCL Records, DLC).

2. In his letter of 31 May 1922, Baker restated his views about unions, adding that because of his recent exchanges with the Painters' Union of Cleveland and the Cleveland Chamber of Commerce, "it is now possible for me to advocate with members of the Chamber that they give up policies of professed exclusive non-unionism." However, in this exchange, which the chamber published as a pamphlet, his support for the closed union shop was equivocal (Baker, Cleveland, Ohio, to FK, 31 May 1922, "General Correspondence: Baker, Newton D.," Box B11, NCL Records, DLC; see [Cleveland Chamber of Commerce], *Correspondence between the Painters' Union and Mr. Baker,* [10 May 1922], in the same folder). At its 15 June meeting, the Board of Directors passed a resolution stating that Baker's letter to the Painters' Union did not represent its own position (NCL Board of Directors Minutes, 6, Box A2, NCL Records, DLC).

3. In 1919, responding to the Supreme Court decision in *Hammer v. Dagenhart,* Congress enacted legislation that taxed employers of children. This action relied on its power "to lay and collect taxes" as provided for in Article 1, Section 8 of the U.S. Constitution. For the Child Labor Tax Law, see Letter 148, FK to David Edsall, 9 September 1919, note 5, above. On 15 May 1922, in *Bailey v. Drexel Furniture Co.,* the U.S. Supreme Court ruled that law unconstitutional, declaring as they had in *Hammer v. Dagenhart* that "to regulate the hours of labor of children in factories and mines within the states [was] a purely state authority" and that the effort to regulate child labor through taxation must be "equally futile."

The committee FK was referring to became the Permanent Conference for the Abolition of Child Labor. It consisted of organizations connected with the WJCC, including the NCL, the NWTUL, the LWV, the WCTU, the YWCA, the National Federation of Business and Professional Women's Clubs, and the NCLC. The AFL's Amendment Drafting Committee also participated. Absent from this coalition were educators from organizations such as the National Education Association (Felt, *Hostages of Fortune,* 196–197; Wilson, *The Women's Joint Congressional Committee,* 70–74, 77, 116; FK, New York, to Maud Wood Park, 18 June 1922, Box 25, LWV Papers, DLC; Reed, "Child-Labor Legislation," 282).

Although Gompers initiated the first meetings of the group that became the Permanent Conference, FK was aware that he disliked the need for a child labor amendment but saw it as inevitable and was not a strong leader of the push for the amendment. "To my mind, the net result of Thursday and Friday is that the working children, like the mothers and babies, will have to be saved by the Fourteen Organizations under the ostensible presidency of Mr. Gompers, but in truth by Mrs. Park's generalship," she wrote (FK to Grace Abbott, 5 June 1922, "General Correspondence: Abbott, Grace," Box B10, NCL Records, DLC).

4. Committee members included Owen R. Lovejoy (1866–1941), general secretary of the NCLC; Matilde Lindsay, representing the NWTUL (*NYT,* 2 June 1922, 19;); and Emma Bain Swiggett was active in the Pan-American International Women's Committee (*NYT,* 2 September 1923, 10). Maud Wood Park (1871–1955) had led NAWSA in lobbying Congress for the woman's suffrage amendment from 1917 to 1920. She became the first president of the LWV (1920–1924) and in 1920 helped organize the WJCC. The National Council of Women, formed in 1888, attempted to bring representatives from all women's organizations in the United States into one umbrella group to promote social change to benefit women. Because its membership was so varied, its agenda was diffuse and cultural issues predominated. The council did not endorse woman suffrage until 1910 (Harper, *History of Woman Suffrage,* 6:793–794; Breckinridge, *Women in the Twentieth Century,* 84–85). Alice Ames Winter (1865–1944), daughter of FK's friend Charles W. Ames and president of the GFWC (1920–1924), also helped establish the WJCC in 1920.

5. The Volstead Act of 1919 provided for enforcement of the Eighteenth Amendment to the Constitution, which prohibited the sale of liquor in the United States.

6. After the 15 May 1922 Supreme Court decision in *Bailey v. Drexel,* the NCL took the lead in drafting a constitutional amendment to give Congress the power to regulate child labor.

Grace Abbott asked Edward P. Costigan, a member of the NCL Board of Directors, to draft the amendment, which he then took to the NCL board meeting of 15 June. At that meeting, the board discussed the best legal strategy for obtaining that power for Congress and approved a resolution authorizing FK to take Costigan's draft to the Permanent Conference for the Abolition of Child Labor. At its meeting in Washington in July, the Permanent Conference adopted the NCL draft over one proposed by the AFL. The AFL draft sought to ban specific forms of child labor rather than give Congress power to regulate child labor (NCL Board of Directors Minutes, 2–6, Box A2, NCL Records, DLC; Edward P. Costigan, Washington, D.C., to FK, 22 July 1922, copy, KFP, NCC-RB).

173. To Sophonisba Breckinridge[1]

[New York City]
Naskeag, Brooklin, Maine (Over Labor Day)[2]
July 5th, 1922.

Miss S. P. Breckinridge,
Green Hall,
University of Chicago,
Chicago, Ill.
Dear Miss Breckinridge,

Grace Abbott made me very happy yesterday by spending the 4th with me.[3] Naturally we talked of you. She held out the hope that you might be able to give me some clues, up to date within a year or two, in connection with an inquiry that I am making in my vacation.

I do not, of course, wish to ask you to make any inquiries or spend any appreciable amount of time in looking through back reports. But if, by any good

Sophonisba P. Breckinridge, ca. 1917. Courtesy of the Special Collections Research Center, University of Chicago.

luck, you have any reasonably current light on the following points, I should indeed be grateful.

Felix Frankfurter insists that we must do some constructive work in the field of equality legislation and not content ourselves with our former minimum wage and eight hours bills.

On the other hand, we have letters of incorporation which put jury service, sex offenses, illegitimacy etc., wholly outside our bailiwick.

What seems practicable is to collect and print replies to the following questions:-

Is it your understanding that the phrase equal guardianship, as generally used, includes the following four points?

1. Guardianship of the child's person?
2. " " " " estate?
3. The right to control the child's earnings?
4. The right to sue for loss of child's services through its death or disability caused by a third party?

Have you any available material as to the following:-

Industrial Rights of the Wife

1. In New York State, a wife may own a laundry, or a bakery, and all profits thereof as though she were unmarried.
2. She may work in a laundry or bakery as a wage earner, and own and dispose of her earnings as though she were unmarried.
3. But if she takes in washing, or bakes pies for sale, or nurses a patient under the husband's roof, he can collect her earnings under a surviving common law disability of the wife.

It is our conviction that the final way to dispose of the blanket bills is to get excellent laws quickly in the various fields covered.[4]

Yours hopefully,

FK/DM

CC, "Equal Rights Amendment: Correspondence: 1922," Box C4, NLC Records, DLC

1. Sophonisba Breckinridge (1866–1948; Ph.D. University of Chicago 1901) lived at Hull House from 1907 to 1920 and was part of the circle of women reformers in Chicago. In 1908 she headed the research department at the Chicago School of Civics and Philanthropy, which became the Graduate School of Social Service Administration at the University of Chicago in 1920.

2. FK was soon to leave New York for Maine and included her summer address.

3. Abbott had visited FK to discuss different drafts of the child labor amendment and strategies for disengaging from Samuel Gompers's Permanent Conference for the Abolition of Child Labor. Abbott urged that the WJCC "get out from under [Gompers's] leadership and go it alone. He won't really help and his name is a hindrance to both reactionaries and liberals"

(Abbott, Washington, D.C., to FK, [2] July 1922, "Child Labor: Amendment: Ratification: General File, 1922–1930," Box C1, NCL Records, DLC). At its September meeting, the NCL Board of Directors decided not "to attend further meetings of the [Permanent] Conference" (NCL Board of Directors Minutes, 15 September 1922, 3, Box A2, NCL Records, DLC).

4. FK's questions were probably prompted by the fact that the NWP's legal staff was researching New York laws that discriminated against women in cases of guardianship and women's paid work at home (*NYT,* 18 September 1922, 15). Breckinridge replied that the matter of mothers' rights had been recently "merged in the question of the child's rights, and the creation of these new state guardianships under probate courts and juvenile courts has made the law very confused and difficult for studying." She had told Abbott that she would try to create "a suggested scheme for study in that field" (Breckinridge, Chicago, to FK, 3 August 1922, "Equal Rights Amendment: Correspondence: General: 1921–31," Box C4, NCL Records, DLC).

174. To Percival B. Baxter[1]

NATIONAL CONSUMERS' LEAGUE
44 EAST 23RD STREET
NEW YORK CITY

Brooklin, Hancock Co., Maine
July 30th, 1922

Hon. Percival P. Baxter
Governor of Maine,
Augusta Maine,
Dear Sir,

Because you may be in a position to veto the acceptance of the Sheppard-Towner law by the legislature next January, I am venturing, as a taxpayer and homeowner in Maine, to record my respectful protest against your recent decision not accept that law and the money appropriated by Congress for the immediate benefit of babies and their mothers.

I submit for your consideration some facts to which no reference is made in the statement of reasons for the decision. I assume that they have not hitherto been brought to your attention. They relate to the amount of money, state and federal, now available, for the use of which plans for the benefit of mothers and babies could now be made if you had accepted the law.

The decision raises anew the question so often heard in Washington while the Sheppard-Towner bill was pending in Congress: "Why does New England let babies die?" It raises, also, the new question "Why does Maine show a higher infant mortality rate than four other New England states?"

For Maine ranks Number 22, among 24 states which compose the birth registration area.[2] Only Maryland (Number 23) and South Carolina (Number 24), stand lower. Maine loses, before their first birthday 102 in each thousand babies born alive, while Maryland loses 104 and South Carolina 116.

If Maine, instead of Oregon led all the states, with only 62 deaths before the first birthday, in each 1000 babies born alive, the decision might be more readily understood. Or if Maine instead of New Hampshire, stood at the head of the five New England states that are in the birth registration area, rather than at the foot of this list, with 40 more babies lost in their first year in each 1000 born alive than Oregon, and 14 more lost in each 1000 than New Hampshire,—the decision would be more comprehensible

The birth registration area consists of the 24 states which register over 90% of their births. All the New England states except Rhode Island are in this group. Rhode Island does not register 90% of the births within her borders and is, therefore, excluded by the U. S. Census from the birth registration area.

The 24 states in the birth registration area contain according to the U.S. Bureau of Vital Statistics (figures for 1920, the latest obtainable), 59.8% of the population of this country, or 63,659,441 people.

For the purpose of convenient comparison, these 24 states are divided into five groups:

DEATHS UNDER 1 YEAR
In Each Thousand Babies Born Alive

GROUP I
Less than 70 in 1000

Oregon	62
Nebraska	64
Minnesota	66
Washington	66

GROUP II
Less Than 80 in 1000

Utah	71
Kansas	73
Kentucky	73
California	74
Wisconsin	77

GROUP III
Less Than 90 in 1000

Indiana	82
Ohio	83
Virginia	84
North Carolina	85
New York	86
New Hampshire	88

GROUP IV
Less Than 100 in 1000

District Columbia	91
Massachusetts	91
Connecticut	92
Michigan	92
Vermont	96
Pennsylvania	97

GROUP V
MORE than 100 in 1000

Maine	102
Maryland	104
South Carolina	116

In Group I. where less than 70 babies in 1000 die before the first birthday, no new New England state appears,

In Group II., where less than 80 babies in 1000 die, no New England state appears.

In Group III where 80 to 90 babies in 1000 dies, New Hampshire ~~Haven~~ appears.

In Group IV where 90 to 100 babies die, three New England states appear, Massachusetts with 91 deaths, Connecticut with 92, and Vermont with 96 deaths in 1000 babies born alive.

In Group V, where more than 100 babies die in 1000 born alive, Maine appears with Maryland and South Carolina.

These current, detailed, authoritative figures explain in part the wide discussion ***of the*** question[3] "Why does New England let babies die?"

Citizens of Maine, women especially, are eager to know "How long will Maine let babies die?"

There are other reasons for the widespread interest. One is the sad fact that Massachusetts and Rhode Island have refused the federal money offered for 1922 and 1923, but have not, like New York, made an appropriation from State taxes equal to all that the babies and their mothers would have had if the Sheppard-Towner law had been accepted. This was done when the legislature appropriated $160,000.00 for the State, outside of New York City which pays nearly a million dollars annually for mothers and babies out of local taxation.

The statement ***in the decision*** that $5000.00 from the contingent fund now in the hand of the State Health Commissioner are "a sum equal that offered by the federal government" seems to rest upon a misapprehension.

In a letter dated July 24, the Chairman of the Federal Board of Maternal and Child Hygiene writes from Washington, in reply to my enquiry,[4] "if the state was not already expending any money for maternity and infancy, the $5,000.00 which Governor Baxter is setting aside for this work could have been at once increased to $20,000.00 if he had accepted the Act, by the federal government as follows ["as follows" moved from after "Act"]:

$ 5,000.00 for 1922, unmatched by the state

$ 5,000.00 for 1923, unmatched by the state

$ 5,000.00 if matched by the state.

Besides these sums, whatever the Maine Child Welfare Division is doing could have been set up to match $5,179.77 to which Maine is entitled in 1923."

The years mentioned begin, of course on July 1st.

I am not challenging the legality of the decision. The question raised is whether it is either humane or necessary; and whether the new voters, when they know all the facts, will approve it.[5]

The threat of Massachusetts to deprive, if possible, mothers and babies in every state of the benefits of the Sheppard-Towner maternity and infancy act, and in any case to delay these benefits, is not to be taken too seriously.[6] A state which attacks the validity of a congressional statute, must first obtain from the Supreme Court of the United States, leave to proceed. Massachusetts had not taken this step before the adjournment of the United States Supreme Court for the summer, although the Attorney General of Massachusetts had had ample time to do so.

In view, also of the numerous decisions of the Supreme Court upholding statutes which involve co-operation between the states and the federal government, there seems to be little probability that the Supreme Court will reverse its well established position in regard to legislation of this character.

Respectfully requesting a reply to the question whether it is your intention to co-operate with the legislature if it accepts the Sheppard-Towner act, I am

Yours very truly
Florence Kelley[7]

Formerly Chairman of the Subcommittee on the Sheppard-Towner Act, in the Women's Joint Congressional Committee

TDft + AN, "Sheppard-Towner Act: Correspondence, 1922–1931," Box C43, NCL Papers, DLC

1. Baxter (1876–1969), a Republican, was governor of Maine (1921–1925).
2. Much of FK's information in this letter came from correspondence with Grace Abbott. FK thanked Abbott for the "good ammunition about the S T. law and Maine. . . . Gov. Baxter is a peg to hang some education on!" (FK, Brooklin, Me., to Abbott, 28 July 1922, Abbott Papers, ICU; see also FK, Brooklin, Me., to Abbott, 19 July 1922, Abbott Papers, ICU; FK, Brooklin, Me., to Abbott, 22 July 1922 and 23 July 1922, "Central File," Folder 11-23-2, Box 248, CB Records, RG102, MdCpNA; and Abbott, Washington, D.C., to FK, 27 July 1922, "Child Labor Amendment Ratification, 1922–1930: General File," Box C1, NCL Records, DLC.)
3. Before FK's editing, this line read: "figures explain in part why the question is widely discussed."
4. Although the letter from which FK quoted was not recovered and although Children's Bureau publications do not identify the chair of the board, it was likely Grace Abbott. For the legislation that established the Federal Board of Maternity and Infant Hygiene to approve state plans for federally appropriated Sheppard-Towner funds, see U.S. Children's Bureau, *The Promotion of the Welfare and Hygiene of Maternity and Infancy*, 135.
5. FK moved this paragraph, which originally followed the paragraph ending "out of local taxation."
6. Massachusetts not only refused to accept the Sheppard-Towner law; it also sued the U.S. Supreme Court on the grounds that the act encroached on the rights of local police and the property rights of Massachusetts citizens (Costin, *Two Sisters for Social Justice*, 139).
7. The *Daily Kennebec Journal* published the final version of FK's letter to Baxter, along with an editorial questioning FK's use of statistics for only one year. It stated that Maine could take better care of its babies without the "paltry sum" offered by the Sheppard-Towner act: "Would [FK] have the people of Maine conclude that an inspector sent from Washington would regulate our affairs better than Maine people?" (*Daily Kennebec Journal*, 16 August 1922, 6).

175. To Julia C. Lathrop

NATIONAL CONSUMERS' LEAGUE
44 EAST 23RD STREET
NEW YORK CITY

September 27, 1922

Miss Julia Lathrop,
1204 National Avenue,
Rockford, Ill.
Dear Sister Lathrop:

The Woman's Party will hold a Conference in Washington, beginning November 11th, at which it will make public its decision with regard to a Blanket Amendment and the blanketing of state laws. The Consumers' League dare not let that meeting occur without holding immediately before it one to affirm the co-operation of a multitude of other organizations in favor of labor[x] [inserted in margin: ***and other protective***] legislation for women. We are, therefore, calling a Conference on What Women Want, to be held in Washington on November 9th, two days after the Election and two days before the Woman's Party Conference. I wired Miss Addams and yourself to-day begging you both to hold the evening of November 9th free for this Conference. You will be by far the most important speakers both of you.

Our plan is to have, if possible, the great hall in the Natural History Museum filled with Trade Union men and women, and all those organizations like the League of Women Voters, General Federation of Women's Clubs, Business and Professional Women's League, etc., which co-operate with us. And, finally, the charity workers who depend upon special legislation for compelling deserting husbands to maintain their families, etc. etc.

Do come! Success depends upon you two.[1]

Your
F.K.

FK:A

TLS, Lathrop Papers, IRoC

1. At its conference, the NWP pledged to carry the campaign for an ERA into forty-two states. The group voted to delay any introduction of the ERA in Congress until the final wording was determined (*NYT,* 13 November 1922, 14). Lathrop presided at the NCL's "What Women Want" conference, held in Washington, D.C., on 10 November 1922 in conjunction with the league's annual meeting (*Washington Post,* 11 November 1922, 5). FK wrote Newton Baker that the NCL's annual meeting, held on 9–10 November with twelve national organizations in attendance, "developed into a demonstration (entirely free from personalities)" to protest the NWP's agenda (FK, New York, to Baker, 14 November 1922, "Equal Rights Amendment: Correspondence: General, 1921–1931," Box C4, NCL Records, DLC). She informed Baker that she was sending out a message under her name that praised the sacrifice of Susan B. Anthony and deplored the NWP's sponsorship of the ERA, "the purpose of which is to deprive American women, for all time, of the right to differ, and to place upon them forever the yoke of uniformity with the achievements of men." On 18 November, the NCL announced that it would not work with the NWP to abolish legislation that discriminated against women because the NWP was opposed to protective legislation for women workers (*NYT:* 30 October 1922, 17 November 1922, 14; *Washington Post,* 11 November 1922, 5; FK, New York, to Baker, 14 November 1922, Box C4, "Equal Rights Amendment: Correspondence: General, 1921–1931," NCL Records, DLC; *NYT,* 19 November 1922, 23).

176. To Alice Hamilton

[New York City]
October 13, 1922

Miss Alice Hamilton,
c/o INDUSTRIAL HYGIENE
Harvard Medical School,
Cambridge, Mass.
Dear Alice Hamilton:

I wish I could agree with you as to Felix. I should be much more hopeful of the quick passage of our amendment if I could. There is no proposal to relax effort in the states, though [he?] insisted at the Directors' meeting, to which he kindly came, that such relaxation would be inevitable.[1]

The enclosed copy of the McCormick resolution for the amendment is correct.[2] The wording is, unhappily, clumsy, but none of us could frame it better. Perhaps the Committee on the Judiciary may make some valuable improvement in it. I hope so. The effort is to express three points:

1. To confer a new power upon Congress;
2. To retain for the states all the powers they now have;
3. To avoid taking any power away from Congress in the process of giving it a new one.

Nothing could be more explicit than Felix' refusal to help draft or improve the amendment or to promote its passage.

What especially endears to me Mrs. [Maud Wood] Park's Women's Joint Legislative Committee is its effective espousal of the principle that there must be cooperation between Congress and the states; that progress without is hopping on one leg instead of walking on two.

Alice Hamilton, 1919. Courtesy of Schlesinger Library, Radcliffe Institute, Harvard University.

The experience of Grace Abbott is conclusive that during the short period of the life of the first federal child labor law, both the state administrations and the people in the states were stimulated to greater activity than ever before, this activity being inevitably paralyzed by the two Supreme Court decisions in turn.

If I believed that federal legislation inevitably superceded state laws I should share Felix' view, but the evidence with regard to roads, schools (including universities) soldiers (though that is always and everywhere a foul spot) is against him. His argument was perfectly academic and without any proof whatever throughout our Directors' meeting—a reiteration of the assertion that every increase in the area of the power of Congress must inevitably weaken the states. Where would all the great state universities be today if that were true? Every one of them is based on the theory of cooperation between the federal and state governments and lives from year to year by the practice thereof.

Yours gratefully and affectionately, though stubbornly,

FK:A

CC, "Child Labor: Amendment: Congressional, 1922–1924," Box C1, NCL Records, DLC

1. Hamilton wrote that she believed that Felix Frankfurter was not opposed to a child labor amendment, "only that he thinks more children will be kept out of factories by a strong local feeling against child labor than by a law passed in Washington." Frankfurter wrote that although FK would find him "heterodox" on the child labor amendment draft, he was "eager to be of what help I can" (Hamilton, Boston, to FK, 6 October 1922, "Child Labor: Amendment: Congressional, 1922–1924," Box C1, NCL Records, DLC; Frankfurter, Cambridge, Mass., to FK, 16 June 1922, both in "Minimum Wages: NCLC, 1922–1931," Box C40, NCL Records, DLC.) At the NCL board's June 1922 meeting, Frankfurter stated his opposition to the amendment but said that if the board voted to support it, he favored some changes in the wording of the draft the board was considering. Frankfurter objected to a federal amendment because he anticipated that it would be difficult for the federal government to enforce it adequately (NCL Board of Directors Minutes, 15 June 1922, 3–4, Box A2, NCL Records, DLC).

2. Senator J. Medill McCormick (1877–1925; Republican, Illinois, 1919–1925) joined the Progressive Party in 1912, rejoining the Republican Party in 1916. He introduced a joint resolution for a child labor amendment on 26 July 1922. Two other similar joint resolutions were introduced in the Senate and twelve in the House in this session. All were referred to their respective judiciary committees (67th Cong. 2nd session, *Cong. Rec.*, 26 July 1922, 10642 and passim.).

177. To Julia C. Lathrop

NATIONAL CONSUMERS' LEAGUE
44 EAST 23RD STREET
NEW YORK CITY

[Washington, D.C.]
2-18-23

Dearest J. Lathrop

Grace Abbott and I are writing in your and her apartment this cold Sunday morning in the midst of agitations

a. the lowest court, Judge McCoy has upheld the Sheppard Towner law, expressly stating, however, that the Constitutional question will be dealt with by the U.S. Supreme Court;[1]

b. The Senate Committee on the Judiciary is to report tomorrow on the Children's Amendment favorably.[2] The point is to get the Committee to vote on these laws in these last exciting days. The report has been read to Mr. [Samuel] Gompers! The drive is on to-day for votes with Br'er Medill McCormick[3] running around to get promises!

c. The Supreme Court (U.S.) will hear Felix Frankfurter on Feb. 26, or 27, or 28, argue the case for the D.C. minimum wage board. We have filed an enormous brief again, for which Mrs. Straight is paying.[4] Heaven help us if the decision is wrong!

d. And finally the real subject of this letter. The plan for the reorganization has been made public, and you doubtless have the scheme that G. A. sent you recently.[5]

We think you will have to [author?] the campaign for keeping the Children's Bureau intact. As you know the proposed reorganization leaves child labor in the Labor Department and puts everything else in the new Welfare Department. Of course we all know what that means for the working children!

The mischief of the situation is that Labor will doubtless think this all logical and right. But any dismemberment is bad and this is about the worst possible.

What are your suggestions? Assuming that until after March Fourth nothing can be actually begin?[6]

I forgot to say that we hope for a favorable report from the House Judiciary Committee before Congress dies.[7]

Love from us both
F.K.

ALS, Lathrop Papers, IRoC

1. Walter I. McCoy (1859–1933) was associate justice of the District of Columbia Supreme Court from 1914 to 1918 and U.S. Supreme Court justice from 1918 to 1929. He issued his decision on 16 February 1923. The lawsuit, which was brought by Woman Patriot member Harriet Frothingham of Massachusetts to test the Sheppard-Towner Act, had sued the government to prevent maternity law funds from being distributed on the grounds that the act usurped the power of local self-government. The case was appealed to the U.S. Supreme Court, which upheld the law (*NYT*: 17 February 1923, 9, and 5 June 1923, 11).

2. The Senate Judiciary Committee sent to the Senate its preferred version of its amendment: "The Congress shall have power, concurrent with that of the several States, to limit or prohibit the labor of persons under the age of 18 years" (67th Cong., 4th sess., *Cong. Rec.*, 24 February 1923, 4459–4460, 4467).

3. For Senator McCormick's role in introducing the child labor amendment, see Letter 176, FK to Alice Hamilton, 13 October 1922, above.
4. Dorothy Whitney Straight, later Elmhirst (1887–1968), heir to the William C. Whitney public utilities fortune and a founder of the *New Republic,* donated $5,000 (FK, New York, to Richard T. Ely, 5 March 1923, Ely Papers, WHi; Rauchway, "A Gentleman's Club in a Woman's Sphere").
5. The plan to reorganize several government departments included a new Department of Education and Public Welfare (*NYT,* 14 February 1923, 8). For background on the threats to the jurisdiction of the Children's Bureau, see Costin, *Two Sisters for Social Justice,* 145–147.
6. The reorganization plan was suspended indefinitely (*NYT,* 2 March 1923, 9).
7. The House Judiciary Committee reported the child labor amendment on 23 February (67th Cong., 4th sess., *Cong. Rec.,* 23 February 1923, 4445).

178. To Harry W. Laidler[1]

[New York City]
March 22, 1923

Mr. Harry W. Laidler,
League for Industrial Democracy,
70 Fifth Avenue,
New York City
Dear Mr. Laidler:

Thank you very much for your friendly and cheering letter of March 15th.[2]

There are two reasons for my decision with regard to the League for Industrial Democracy. One is the necessity of devoting all my waking hours to building up the Consumers' League, and the other is the growing conviction that I am not clear enough as to what the League for Industrial Democracy does and says and thinks. When we were working to promote the study of socialism in the colleges, I seemed to myself to know what I was doing.

I prefer now to concentrate upon such concrete things as the enactment of a federal child labor amendment, the defense of the minimum wage law in the federal courts, a share in reducing the usurped powers of the Supreme Court of the United States within my own lifetime; opposition to the blanket equality legislation of the Woman's Party; and promoting the transformation of food production, e.g. especially control of the packing industry. All these large undertakings fall within the letters of incorporation of the National Consumers' League.

Because this laborious spade-work never captivates the imagination of young people, I think it is better for the old and experienced to concentrate closely upon it.

I shall always want to read every word that you write, and hope you will let me know of your publications.

Yours sincerely,

CC, "General Correspondence: 'L,'" Box B14, NCL Records, DLC

1. Laidler (1884–1970), executive director of the LID (1921–1957), was editor of the *Intercollegiate Socialist* and the *Socialist Review* (1913–1921). FK had been president (1918–1920) and vice-president (1912–1918; 1921–1923) of the LID (Martin, *Fabian Freeway,* 499).

2. In his letter from a stop on a speaking tour, Laidler expressed regret that FK would no longer be vice-president of the LID. He wrote: "I cannot tell you what your cooperation has meant to all of us, and particularly to myself in the old days of the I.S.S. and in the newer days of the League [for Industrial Democracy]. It was you who kept the I.S.S. going in the days of the war when you stepped into the breach and assumed the presidency of the organization" (Laidler, Grinnell, Iowa, to FK, 16 March 1923, "General Correspondence: 'L,'" Box B14, NCL Records).

179. To Julia C. Lathrop

NATIONAL CONSUMERS' LEAGUE
ROOM 1102, EAST 23RD STREET
NEW YORK CITY

4-21-23

Dearest J. Lathrop

Thank you very much for the check! I found my tickets waiting at the La Salle Street Station!

The enclosed milk and water declaration will amuse you. Felix obviously cannot both practise before the Supreme Court, and also blaspheme it in public.[1] Hence our gentle courtesy!

In fact the decision is chapter three of the Dred Scott decision thus:—

Dred Scott	Taney	C.J.
Fed Child Labor I B	White	C.J. }
" " " II		}
D.C. minimum wage	Taft	C.J.[2]

I am more than ever firmly convinced that we must have women in all federal courts; and

Borah's 7–2 requirement;[3] and an effective restriction upon the due process clause which no one has hitherto succeeded in framing.[4]

However, this half century having already given us Suffrage and prohibition can safely be counted upon to give us further blessings! Chief among 'em a modern Constitution and a modern minded Supreme Court.

Great is my faith.

After May 1st, our address will be 156 Fifth Ave. ~~Cor.~~ Room 1126[5]

Your devoted and grateful
F.K.

ALS, Lathrop Papers, IRoC

1. On 9 April 1923, in *Adkins v. Children's Hospital,* a five-to-three decision written by Justice George Sutherland (1862–1942; Associate Justice, 1922–1938), the U.S. Supreme Court invali-

dated the 1921 minimum wage law for District of Columbia women workers (for the 1921 law, see Letter 162, FK to Molly Dewson, 7 July 1921, note 1, above; for the NCL's successful work to get the District of Columbia law passed, see Gluck, "Interview with Jessie Haver Butler.") Louis Brandeis recused himself because of his previous argument before the court in *Muller v. Oregon*. Felix Frankfurter wired his opinion that the "most ominous part of opinion is suggestion that Muller doctrine has been supplanted by nineteenth amendment." Despite the *Adkins* ruling against laws for women only, he suggested "vigorous pronouncement by League and aggressive campaign as to importance of dealing with peculiar position of women in industry" (Frankfurter, Cambridge, Mass., to FK, 10 April 1923, copy, "NCL Correspondence, 1923," Box 157, Frankfurter Papers, DLC.)

2. Roger B. Taney (1777–1864) was chief justice of the U.S. Supreme Court from 1836 to 1854; Edward Douglass White was chief justice from 19 December 1910 to 19 May 1921; and William Howard Taft was chief justice from 11 July 1921 to 3 February 1930. In the Dred Scott decision of 1857 (*Scott v. Sanford*), written by Chief Justice Taney, the court ruled that enslaved people did not become free when they traveled to free states, setting in motion the legal pursuit of slaves in free territories and thereby expanding the reach of slave codes throughout the United States. Kelley passionately compared the Adkins and Dred Scott decisions in a speech given to the National Conference of Social Work on 18 May 1923: "Following [the Adkins decision], wages of the most ill-paid women in the District of Columbia have been cut. Under the pressure of competition in American industry at this time, it establishes in the practical experience of the unorganized, the unskilled, the illiterate, the alien, and the industrially sub-normal women wage-earners, the constitutional right to starve. This is a new 'Dred Scott' decision" (FK, "Progress of Labor Legislation for Women," 114; *NYT*, 19 May 1923, 3).

White was chief justice when the Court ruled that Congress had no power to regulate the hours of labor for child workers in *Hammer v. Dagenhart* (1918). FK erred in identifying White as chief justice in the child labor case of *Bailey v. Drexel Furniture Co.* (1922). Taft was chief justice of the U.S. Supreme Court from 1921 to 1930 and was one of the three dissenters in the *Adkins* case.

3. On 5 February 1923, Senator William Borah (1865–1940; Republican, Idaho, 1907–1940) introduced a bill requiring that at least seven U.S. Supreme Court justices concur in declaring a congressional law unconstitutional. It was referred to the Judiciary Committee (67th Cong., 4th sess., *Cong. Rec.*, 5 February 1923, 3004; *NYT*, 6 February 1923, 4).

4. Beginning with *The Slaughterhouse Cases* in 1873, the Supreme Court had interpreted the due process clause of the Fourteenth Amendment as applicable to corporations, thereby giving businesses "rights" that took precedence over state regulations.

5. The NCL was leasing its previous office space (Molly Dewson, New York, to FK, 27 March 1923, "General Correspondence: Dewson, Mary," Box B12, NCL Records, DLC).

180. To James A. Haight[1]

[New York City]
May 19, 1923

Dear Jim:

I agree with you, of course, entirely as to interpreting the Fourteenth and Fifth Amendments.[2] The question that confronts this organization at the present moment is, how can we compel the Supreme Court to do this? We are considering several constructive proposals:

1. As Roscoe Pound of the Harvard Law School points out in His delightful volume "The Spirit of the Common Law",[3] the Court is numerically far too small.

It started with five judges in 1789. I do not know when the number was increased to seven, but we all know the scandal connected with its increase to nine persons in order to revise the decision which upheld the first income tax law.[4] An illustration of the quantitative insufficiency of the Court is afforded by our experience with it in 1917, when the minimum wage law and the Oregon ten hours law were before it. At that time the Court pondered the subject twenty-eight months and, having forgotten the first argument (by Mr. Brandeis) called for a reargument which was made by Mr. Felix Frankfurter, Mr. Brandeis having been advanced to the Supreme Court he was debarred, of course, from sitting in a case in which he had appeared as counsel. The Court thereupon divided, four to four, allowing the decision of the Oregon Supreme Court to stand.[5]

This was a feeble precedent when the recent case reached the Supreme Court from an adverse decision of the Court of Appeals of the District of Columbia. This time Mr. Taft, newly returned from a trip to Europe to see the judicial process in action in England, insisted upon a prompt decision. The resultant green gooseberry decision you have seen.

2. The Court should be strengthened by the addition of several competent, learned women. Monopoly of making and unmaking, teaching, interpreting, applying, administering and enforcing the law by either sex has hitherto been eminently unsuccessful. In the past three years the United States Supreme Court has three times served notice that women and children are not to expect Justice or Mercy under the present Constitution as interpreted by the present Court.

3. Among the considerations which weigh heavily in selecting judges at present are geography, religion and party affiliations. This should be far more discussed. Almost nobody knows these facts. It is very significant that quickly following the death of Justice White, we have the Catholic Pierce Butler appointed,[6] while more than one hundred years elapsed after the Court was created before a Jew was appointed to it. Throughout 134 years the Court has been predominantly Protestant. These considerations should, of course, be non-existent.

There has, on the other hand, been much criticism of the appointment of two Justices from the single State of Massachusetts [Oliver Wendell Holmes, Jr., and Brandeis], admirable as both have been. Since these considerations are now of great weight, the addition of women to the Court looms up by analogy as inevitable. Although the number of available candidates is small, Judge Florence Allen of the Supreme Court of Ohio would be an admirable choice,[7] and there are other women practicing.

It is singular that judicial experience is not a requirement enforced for this high office.

What do you think of Senator La Follette's proposal that if the Supreme Court has held a measure unconstitutional it should nevertheless become a law if Congress passes it either twice or by a two-thirds majority?[8]

Our boy Nicky is to go off to Phillips Exeter next September at the age of thirteen and a half. I sincerely hope there may be no hazing there. I congratulate you on your grandsons.[9] I had so little imagination in my youth that I never conceived the delight they afford until mine were actually affording it.

With love to all the Haights, and the hope that you may give serious consideration to my questions about the Supreme Court, I am always

Yours affectionately,

CC, "Plans to Curb Supreme Court, Jan. 1, 1924–Aug. 1924," Box C41, NCL Records, DLC

1. James A. Haight, B.A. Cornell 1879, a college friend of FK's from Oshkosh, Wisconsin, was a prominent Seattle attorney (Hewett, *Cornell University,* 4:266; FK, *Notes of Sixty Years,* 52; and Division of Rare and Manuscript Collections, Cornell University Library).

2. Haight had written that the Fourteenth and Fifteenth Amendments were not "a specific limitation on government" but rather "a general guaranty of individual rights, a statement of a fundamental principle of free government. . . . [They] should therefore receive a construction not narrow or specific but broad and general" (Haight, Seattle, Wash., to FK, 9 May 1923, "Plans to Curb Supreme Court, Jan. 1, 1924–Aug. 1924," Box C41, NCL Records, DLC).

3. Roscoe Pound, *The Spirit of the Common Law* (Boston: Marshall Jones Co., 1921).

4. In 1862, Congress added a tenth justice to the U.S. Supreme Court, then in 1866 it reduced the number to seven. In 1869, Congress increased the number of justices to nine. The first income tax law was upheld in 1881 in *Springer v. United States,* but in 1895, in *Pollock v. Farmers' Loan & Trust Co.,* the Supreme Court ruled that an 1894 income tax law was unconstitutional (Hall, *Oxford Companion to the Supreme Court,* 425–426).

5. For the 1917 court rulings in the Oregon minimum wage case (*Stettler v. O'Hara*) and men's hours case (*Bunting v. Oregon*), see Letter 137, FK to Louis D. Brandeis, 9 April 1917, above.

6. Pierce Butler (1866–1939) was a U.S Supreme Court justice from 1923 to 1939.

7. Florence Allen (1884–1966) received her law degree from NYU in 1913 and had lived at the Henry Street Settlement. She was elected as an Ohio Supreme Court judge in 1922.

8. At the AFL's 1922 meeting in Cincinnati (which FK attended), Robert La Follette had announced his proposal for a constitutional amendment: "'That no inferior Federal Judge shall set aside a law of Congress on the ground that it is unconstitutional. That if the Supreme Court assumes to decide any law of Congress unconstitutional, or by interpretation undertakes to assert a public policy at variance with the statutory declaration of Congress, which alone under our system is authorized to determine the public policies of Government, the Congress may, by repassing the law, nullify the action of the court'" (*NYT,* 15 June 1922, 1).

9. Haight had described his two grandsons, each about one year old: "They are not quite ready for Phillips Exeter or St. Paul's" (Haight to FK, 9 May 1923).

181. To Felix Frankfurter

NATIONAL CONSUMERS' LEAGUE
~~44 EAST 23RD STREET~~*156 FIFTH AVENUE, NEW YORK*

May 26, 1923

Mr. Felix Frankfurter,
Harvard Law School,
Cambridge, Mass.
Dear Mr. Frankfurter:

Thank you very much for your letters of May 23rd and 25th. The next session of Congress is six months off, and I shall doubtless learn a lot meanwhile.[1]

Taking the first letter first, I have not seen the bill for a D.C. law in final form.[2] I am not, however merely skeptical about any provision as to "fair wages" and regard for the financial state of the industry. I am convinced that they are wrong in principle and that, if we advocate them, we shall be creating lasting trouble for our own future.[3]

The words fair wages are as incapable of standard definition as due process. Compulsory reference to the financial state of the industry undermines the only solid foundation of wage determinations, which is the health of the workers. An industry incapable of maintaining its "adult workers of ordinary average ability" in health is a liability for any community, not an asset. Why should it be prolonged as a parasite upon the most defenseless workers and their families?

As to my impatience with further tinkering with legislation,—what have I done but tinker for forty-one years? My tragic error was failing to do both at once. I should have pushed a far-reaching Amendment from 1895 on, while promoting statutes and decisions. Far from being mutually exclusive both are necessary, now as then.

Thus far in reply to your argument of the 23rd; next the main point in that of the 25th.

Why do you fancy that I think an Amendment can be quickly obtained? My father seconded Mr. Sargent's[4] Joint Resolution for a Suffrage Amendment in 1875 and continued to introduce it after Mr. Sargent went to the Senate until my father's death in 1889. My grandfather's aunt attended the first meeting (Seneca Falls 1848) at which votes for women were proposed in this country.[5] I have no illusions as to the speed for either a D.C. law or an Amendment.

The people at large have only the faintest interest in the D.C. and its laws. The permanent impossibility of getting decent District schools shows this. The nationwide interest in the Sutherland decision roots not at all in the District law but in two fears,—that it[x*] [inserted in margin: [x*]***the decision***] may destroy the thirteen State minimum wage laws and that it certainly weakens, and may destroy by undermining, the State laws regulating hours.

It follows that according to your program there must be agreement among ourselves, and in the States, as to the content of the D.C. law; that it must be passed and then upheld. In the light of our experience could the testing in the Courts be expected to cost less than three years?

I see, of course, that as far as it goes your program calls for fighting. With regard to a federal Amendment it is, however, clearly a policy of waiting. I am at a loss to understand wherein there is conflict between your proposals,—which the League will, of course, push to the limit of its ability, as soon as agreement is reached as to the form and content of the D.C. bill,—and the proposal for a simultaneous introduction of an amendment. There is no logical conflict. The federal Suffrage Amendment and the agitation for State laws were pushed simultaneously for many years, and each agitation helped the other. It seems to be a case where "This ought ye to have done and not to have left the other undone".[6]

Yours sincerely,
Florence Kelley[7]

FK:A

TLS, "NCL Correspondence, 1923," Box 157, Frankfurter Papers, DLC

1. Although Frankfurter's letters of 23 and 25 May 1923 have not been recovered, he wrote FK on 4 May that he regarded as "essential" a new minimum wage act for the District of Columbia "which shall stand the test of challenge in the courts." He reported that he was working on such a bill. He opposed a campaign for a constitutional amendment on the minimum wage, viewing it as "a programme of the remotest possibilities" (Frankfurter, n.p., to FK, 4 May 1923, copy, "NCL Correspondence, 1923," Box 157, Frankfurter Papers, DLC).
2. For further discussion of the District of Columbia law, see Letter 182, FK to Edward Costigan, 31 May 1923, below.
3. Frankfurter's use of the term "fair" deferred to Justice Sutherland's opinion in *Adkins* that held acceptable "a statute requiring an employer to pay . . . the value of the service rendered, even to pay with fair relation to the extent of the benefit obtained." The *Adkins* decision rejected as a violation of due process to employers the D.C. statute's call for wages "sufficient to supply the necessary cost of living for a woman workers and maintain her in good health and protect her morals" (*Adkins v. Children's Hospital,* 555, 559). Frankfurter's draft empowered the minimum wage board to investigate occupations in which "a substantial number of women or minors . . . are not receiving fair, reasonable and adequate compensation for the service rendered, but are receiving as wages less than the fair minimum value of the service rendered" ("Extracts from Bill to Create Board of Industrial Welfare and Standards in the District of Columbia which Professor Frankfurter Proposes for Introduction in Congress in December," "Minimum Wage Conference, 1923," Box C50, NCL Records, DLC).
4. Aaron Augustus Sargent (1827–1887) was a Republican from California who served in the U.S. House of Representatives (1861–1863, 1869–1873) and in the U.S. Senate (1873–1879).
5. Sarah Pugh (1800–1884), actually FK's maternal grandfather's sister, did not attend the 1848 Seneca Falls convention, although she did participate in other women's rights conventions (see Letter 75, FK to NK, 15 July 1905, note 1, above). Often regarded as the beginning of the woman suffrage movement, the convention was held 19–20 July 1848 at Seneca Falls, New York. The ninth resolution the convention endorsed declared women's "sacred right to

the elective franchise" (Gordon, *The Selected Papers of Elizabeth Cady Stanton and Susan B. Anthony*, 1:77).

6. Matthew 23:23.

7. Frankfurter replied on 31 May that he was concerned that valuable time and effort would be lost if FK and Molly Dewson concentrated on preparing a constitutional amendment to mandate a minimum wage (Frankfurter, n.p., to FK, 31 May 1923, copy, "NCL Correspondence, 1923," Box 157, Frankfurter Papers, DLC). For more on FK's uneasy alliance with Frankfurter, see Hart, *Bound by Our Constitution*, 138–143.

182. To Edward P. Costigan

156 Fifth Avenue, New York City
May 31, 1923

Mr. E.P. Costigan,
U.S. Tariff Commission,
Washington, D.C.
Dear Mr. Costigan:

As usual this is an appeal for wisdom from you and Mrs. [Mabel] Costigan.

Mr. Gompers is repeating in re the minimum wage decision his procedure of last year with regard to the child labor decision, with one difference. He is operating thru Ethel Smith and the Women's Trade Union League who either do not see what is happening to them, or else are afraid to stand up for themselves.[1]

At the close of the Women's Trade Union League Conference in Washington, a Committee of three was appointed, Ethel Smith, Matthew Voll and myself, to arrange another aggregation, like Mr. Gompers' Child Labor Conference, to push the Federation's huge, vague Labor Amendment. After a long conversation with Ethel Smith in which the above plan became unmistakably clear, I explained that I have no mandate to carry the League into any cooperative action in regard to the minimum wage decision.[2] This is, however, only the first of three difficult elements in the present crisis.

The Brotherhoods are having a comprehensive Amendment prepared,[3] and Mr. Frankfurter has drafted a D.C. minimum wage bill which he desires to have supersede and exclude for some years all efforts by our League for an Amendment. In this bill he has incorporated Justice Sutherland's idea of a fair wage; fair reasonable compensation.[4]

This is alarming because the words are as vague as due process, and because the idea is an innovation alien to all experience with minimum wage laws, in the English speaking world.

Mr. J. J. Mallon who, with Tawney, is the leading English authority on minimum wage laws said, when I asked his opinion of this experiment:—"Nothing could be more un-English." This seems to me to carry weight because the English are the people who have succeeded with minimum wage legislation, and there are 3,000,000 wage earners in England now getting the benefit of it, besides all those in Australia, New Zealand, Tasmania and Canada.[5] Unhappily, Mr. Mallon sailed for England yesterday.

In the hope of using the summer to get some clarified, united opinion within our own membership, before the annual meeting, we have invited about 75 people for June 12th. We shall be fortunate to have 25 of them. I am, therefore, sending to the 75 these three enclosures asking for comments in writing from all who cannot come.[6]

Yours sincerely,

FK:A

CC, "Plans to Curb Supreme Court: 1922–1923," Box C40, NCL Records, DLC

1. FK and Molly Dewson attended the conference in Washington in May 1923 that the NWTUL had organized to discuss the ramifications of the *Adkins* decision on state minimum wage laws. At the conference Samuel Gompers advocated a constitutional amendment authorizing Congress to override Supreme Court decisions (*NYT*, 16 May 1923, 21).
2. After the conference FK declined further cooperation with Gompers and others because of previous "unsatisfactory experience" on the child labor amendment ("Report of Secretary," NCL Board of Directors Minutes, 25 October 1923, 1, Box A2; FK to Ethel Smith, 24 May 1923, "Wages and Hours: Correspondence, 1919–1931," Box C49, both in NCL Records, DLC). Matthew Woll (1880–1956) was an AFL vice-president and a close ally of Gompers.
3. The AFL's proposed amendment was discussed in a session chair by Samuel Gompers at a Conference on Women's Wages and the Supreme Court Decision, held in Washington on 15–16 May at the NWTUL headquarters. It called for an "Amendment of the Federal Constitution for the broad purpose of insuring protection of social legislation and the rights of labor" (Matthew Woll, Ethel M. Smith, and John A. Ryan to Samuel Gompers, 26 June 1923, WTUL Papers).
4. For Frankfurter's proposed bill, see Letter 181, FK to Felix Frankfurter, 26 May 1923, note 3, above.
5. Economic historian Richard Henry Tawney (1880–1962) was the author of *The Establishment of Minimum Rates in the Chain-Making Industry under The Trade Boards Act of 1909* (1914), *The Establishment of Minimum Rates in the Tailoring Industry under The Trade Boards Act of 1909* (1915) and "The Minimum Wage in Great Britain" (*New Republic*, 28 June 1922). In his study of the Elizabethan wage regulation act of 1563, Tawney noted that the state regulation of wages had ended relatively recently in the 1820s (Tawney, "The Assessment of Wages in England by the Justices of the Peace"). James Joseph Mallon (1875–1961) was warden of Toynbee Hall in London and former secretary of Britain's National League to Establish a Minimum Wage. At a meeting with the NCL in early May, Mallon criticized the *Adkins* decision and described the success of Britain's minimum wage policy (*NYT*, 13 May 1923, II:8).
6. The conference, which was held at the NCL offices, was attended by twenty-eight people. As FK reported to Lathrop, some members concluded they could not back Frankfurter's bill for a "fair minimum wage," but they did not want to work with the AFL on a constitutional amendment either. The group was also not enthusiastic about FK's plan for a constitutional amendment to "forbid the employment of any person at wages less than sufficient for maintenance in health" (FK, New York, to Lathrop, [before 28 May 1923], Lathrop Papers, IRoC; FK, New York, to Lathrop, 14 June 1923, "General Correspondence: Lathrop, Julia C.," Box B15, NCL Records, DLC).

183. To Edward P. Costigan

[New York City]
October 2, 1923

Mr. E.P. Costigan,
2123 California Street,
Washington, D.C.
Dear Mr. Costigan:

The clans have been gathering and I have been talking to the members and officers as they have come along. I myself have been taught by the pressure of painful circumstance, so that I am at last sorrowfully ready to abandon the idea of a minimum wage amendment. I still think it would be the best thing if we could get it, but I am convinced that we cannot get it, among the reasons being the following:

1. On May 18th, at the close of the Industrial session of the Conference of Social Work, I was talking with Ethel Smith about the condition created by the decision of the United States Supreme Court, and the lack of unity among the different organizations, and even among the members of the same organization. She said in a perfectly amicable tone, with friendly looks, in substance and I think almost exactly in these words: "You wouldn't expect, would you, to have the Labor Women go out for an amendment for minimum wage legislation alone? You know the A.F. of L. would not do that, and you would not expect the women to attempt to act independently of the A.F. of L. about any amendment."

After long cogitation I am convinced that that is the situation that the Labor women will take whatever the Labor men will help them get, and will not try for anything else.

As you know, Ethel Smith has been running in connection with an amendment (minimum wage plus plus) more or less the same kind of committee that we have been struggling with anent a child labor amendment.[1] Hers is smaller and more made up of women. Some time ago she sent me a synopsis to date of their activities. Mrs. Costigan may perhaps have received a duplicate of that. If not I can send you a copy.

Yesterday I had a long talk with Mrs. Jackson, a very active member of the Board of Directors, and Clara Beyer, Secretary of the Consumers' League of New York, on the subject of the coming Labor amendment.[2] Confidentially Clara said that Ethel would efficiently oppose any such all-comprehending basketful of items as are jumbled in the draft that is still under discussion by the Brotherhoods. I saw a proof of it some months ago, but under such bonds of confidence that I was not free to make a copy.[3] It contained provisions for the farmers, etc., and all known things ever discussed by advocates of labor legislation. I am not sanguine about Ethel Smith's power to modify Mr. Gompers, if in the near future (i.e. by the time of his return to Washington late in November) he should have any A.F. of L. draft ready to submit.

The net result of yesterday's survey of the situation was an agreement that I should write you this letter begging you to make, as promptly as you find it possible, the more comprehensive draft of which you have often spoken to me as preferable to a mere minimum wage draft; this to be multigraphed here and submitted immediately to the Law Committee, with a view to having ready for the annual meeting something which we can propose to Ethel Smith as an expression of our preference in the matter, so that she can urge her committee to endorse this.[4]

We all appreciate that this is a great deal to ask, but we know that you are deeply interested in getting an amendment that will really amend in the direction of rational labor legislation; and that you recognize the strategic value of our coming as quickly as possible to an agreement which we can submit to the larger group as that which we favor.[5]

Yours hopefully,
FK:A

CC, "Plans to Curb Supreme Court: 1922–1923," Box C40, NCL Records, DLC

1. On 29 June 1923, Smith had asked FK to serve on a committee called Women's Wage Problems and Supreme Court Decisions to consider proposals to deal with the minimum wage problem. Apparently FK did not join this committee, whose membership included Mabel Costigan, Samuel Gompers, and Maud Wood Park (Smith et al., Washington, D.C., to FK, "Plans to Curb Supreme Court: 1922–1923," Box C40, NCL Records, DLC).
2. Alice Day Jackson (1872–1926) had been recording secretary of the CL of New York City and had served on the NCL Board of Directors since 1917. Clara Mortensen Beyer (1892–1990) had previously worked for Felix Frankfurter on the War Labor Policies Board and had served as secretary of the Minimum Wage Board for the District of Columbia (see Beyer, "What Is Equality?").
3. Frankfurter had sent FK a copy of the AFL's proposed amendment, asking that she not circulate it (Frankfurter, Cambridge, Mass., to FK, 31 May 1923, copy, "NCL Correspondence, 1923," Box 157, Felix Frankfurter Papers, DLC).
4. In her answer to FK's letter of 30 October (unrecovered), Smith invited FK to "participate actively in the discussions" of her Conference Committee on Women's Wage Problems and Supreme Court Decisions (Smith, Washington, D.C., to FK, 3 November 1923, "Plans to Curb Supreme Court: 1922–1923," Box C40, NCL Records, DLC).
5. Costigan could not attend the November meeting. At that meeting, the NCL Council did not discuss a minimum wage bill or a constitutional amendment (Costigan, Washington, D.C., to FK, 19 October 1923, "Plans to Curb Supreme Court, 1922–1923," Box C40; NCL Council Minutes, 8–9 November 1923, both in Box A7, NCL Records, DLC).

184. To W. E. B. Du Bois

NATIONAL CONSUMERS' LEAGUE
156 FIFTH AVENUE
NEW YORK CITY

October 18, 1923

Dr. W.E. DuBois,
69 Fifth Avenue,
New York City
My dear Dr. DuBois:

I know that there was some slight change in my article, but I am entirely content with the form in which it appeared.[1]

You will, I feel sure, be gratified to know that the National Federation of Teachers has filed objections to the bill on precisely the same grounds as our own. This is eminently necessary because a second organization calling itself the National Committee for a Department of Education has been admitted to the Women's Joint Congressional Committee, with Marian Parkhurst its legislative agent.[2] She is an experienced and highly skillful lobbyist, having been closely identified with the three bills passed since Thanksgiving 1921 when President Harding signed the Sheppard-Towner bill. The others are the Cable Independent Citizenship law affecting the international situations of wives; and the Reclassification Law signed by President Harding last Spring, which might, in my opinion, not have been passed for two or three years yet without the pressure of the 16 national organizations which make up the Women's Joint Congressional Committee.[3]

In the active body of this W.J.C.C. there are now four persons—two favorable to the Sterling bill in its present form, and two, (Miss Borchardt of the National Federation of Teachers and myself) who oppose it.[4] As the General Federation of Women's Clubs is red hot for this measure, the N.A.A.C.P. will have to work with might and main, if the bill is to be rewritten in the interest both of safeguarding federal funds, and rescuing the interests of the Colored people.[5] A word to the wise is sufficient.[6]

Yours sincerely,
Florence Kelley
FK:A

TLS, Du Bois Papers, MU

1. FK and Du Bois opposed the Sterling bill because it left too much power to the states. Du Bois had asked FK's permission to print her article, "The Sterling Discrimination Bill," in *The Crisis*. In early 1922, *The Crisis* had denounced Senator Thomas Sterling's bill to create a department of education, which he had introduced by in April 1921 (Du Bois, New York,

to FK, 23 July 1923, Du Bois Papers, MU; 67th Cong., 1st sess., *Cong. Rec.*, 27 April 1921, 691; "Vicious Provisions of a Great Bill," *The Crisis* 23 [February 1922]: 152–153.) As FK pointed out in her article, the bill would give states the ultimate authority in dispensing funds for public schools. She warned *Crisis* readers not to support this bill because it would allow southern states to continue segregation in public schools. She wrote, "For colored people, American, Japanese, Chinese or Indian, the interest of the National Educational Association in the Sterling bill is a menace" (*The Crisis* 26 [October 1923]: 252–253). Earlier FK had written Minnie Fisher Cunningham regarding the LWV's role in protesting the bill: "[T]he more the public understands how the bill should be rewritten the better" (FK, Brooklin, Me., to Cunningham, 26 August 1923, Box 25, LWV Papers, DLC).

2. Marion I. Parkhurst, one of the first women members of the Republican National Committee and a LWV member, was a delegate to the party's national convention in 1924 (*NYT*, 18 May 1924, 13 and 29 November 1925, IX:8).

3. The Married Women's Independent Citizenship Act, sponsored by Congressman John L. Cable (1884–1971; Republican, Ohio, 1921–1925) and enacted by Congress on 8 September 1922, permitted U.S. women to retain their citizenship when married to foreigners and immigrant women to be naturalized in procedures equal to those of men (See Lemons, *Woman Citizen*, 65–67, 80–112; Bredbenner, *A Nationality of Her Own*, 117, 149). The Classification Act of 1923, also known as the Sterling-Lehlbach Act, sponsored by Congressman Frederick R. Lehlbach (1876–1937; Republican, New Jersey, 1915–1937), created a federal board to oversee uniform salaries and conditions for promotion of federal employees regardless of sex (67th Cong., 4th sess., *Cong. Rec.*, 3 March 1923, 5531–5532; "Reclassification Endangered," 20).

4. Selma Borchardt (1895–1968) was legislative representative and vice-president of the American Federation of Teachers from 1921 to 1935 (American Federation of Teachers Collection Guide, Walter P. Reuther Library, Wayne State University).

5. In 1923, the GFWC had 2 million members. Its support for rural education was defined in Chase, "The Social Program of the General Federation of Women's Clubs," 465, 468.

6. The 68th Congress considered several bills that proposed a U.S. Department of Education but approved none. The U.S. Department of Education was finally created in 1979.

185. To Charles Amidon

[New York City]
October 26, 1923

Judge Charles F. Amidon
742 Stepney Place
Inglewood, California
My dear Judge Amidon:

At the approaching annual meeting, November 8th and 9th, we shall elect Professor John R. Commons President of the League, to succeed former Secretary Baker who will remain as an honorary Vice-President.[1]

In deep confidence I handed to Professor Commons an extract from your letter to me on the subject of the Supreme Court.[2] This so stimulated him that he has now sent me the enclosed tentative draft of a proposition in regard to the Judges, with the request that I submit to you and Mr. [Felix] Frankfurter for criticism and suggestion.

Meantime, at our Directors' meeting last night, we adopted the following motion made by Commissioner [Bernard] Shientag of the New York State Labor Department, an active member of our Board:-

> "That we recommend to the annual meeting that the League introduce and crusade for a bill to require seven Justices of the United States Supreme Court to concur in pronouncing federal and state legislation unconstitutional."[3]

Your letter to me of October 3rd is, I believe, a most significant turning point in the history of this League. Before it came, no one, so far as I know, in our ranks was even considering the possibility that had been suggested by Alice Stone Blackwell that we could initiate this action.[4] Now it finds virtually no opposition among us, although there is widespread belief that the Court will nullify the law as soon as it is passed. Our members agree, however, that such nullification would greatly expedite the federal amendment, going very far in the direction of restraint upon the usurpations of the court.

Please accept my heartfelt, personal thanks for the great benefit that you have conferred upon us. And please believe that I have not abused your confidence in writing me so frankly.[5]

Yours gratefully and sincerely
(Signed) FLORENCE KELLEY

FK:VC

CC, "Correspondence (Florence Kelley): Amidon, Charles F., 1922–1925," Box C40, NCL Records, DLC

1. Baker's conflict with FK and the NCL over the issue of open shops in Cleveland was what FK described to Commons as "the climax of a rapidly progressing change in his relation to the industrial question" that forced the Nominating Committee to ask him to vacate his office as president (FK, New York, to Commons, 28 May 1923, "Minimum Wages: Supreme Court, Plans to Curb: 1922–1923," Box C40, NCL Records; see also Letter 172, FK to Newton Baker, 3 June 1922, above). She wrote several gracious letters to Baker offering him the opportunity to submit his resignation, noting that the "catastrophe" of the *Adkins* decision and the divided political climate in its wake required more "close intimate participation" of the NCL's officers than he could give. Baker's response was equally gracious and acknowledged "opportunities for service which I missed." He wrote that he continued to look forward to future opportunities to serve the NCL (FK, New York, to Baker, 11 June 1923 and 29 August 1923; Baker, Cleveland, Ohio, to FK, 7 December 1923, "General Correspondence: Baker, Newton D.," Box B11, NCL Records, DLC). Baker became an NCL honorary vice-president.

2. Amidon had just seen the NCL's proposed amendment to curb the power of the Supreme Court and had written an enthusiastic and supportive critique. Amidon wrote, "The Supreme Court devotes most of its time now to passing on constitutional questions. They ought to be expert in applying the constitution to the Nation's life. On the contrary, the fact is they have become pedantic and refined, and reverse laws upon petty considerations." The recent *Adkins* decision was one example. He suggested that Congress pass a law "providing that the court shall not declare a state law unconstitutional unless at least seven of its members concur in favor of such decision, and that they shall not declare an act of Congress unconstitutional unless the court is unanimous" (Amidon, Fargo, N.D., to FK, 3 October 1923, copy, "Correspondence (Florence Kelley): Amidon, Charles F., 1922–1925," Box C4, NCL Records).

3. NCL Board of Directors Minutes, 25 October 1923, 2, Box A2, NCL Records, DLC. FK wrote Maud Wood Park that the board's action was "an inexpressible relief . . . after a thousand opinions, for six months, have prevented any effective move!" (FK, New York, to Park, [26 October 1923], Box 25, LWV Papers, DLC).

4. Blackwell wrote two editorials for the *Woman Citizen* suggesting that Article III of the U.S. Constitution allowed Congress "to take away from the jurisdiction of the Supreme Court any cases other than those specifically mentioned, whenever Congress shall choose to do so." ("The Children and the Courts," *Woman Citizen* 7 [15 July 1922]: 12; "Congress Could—But Didn't," *Woman Citizen* 7 [9 September 1922]: 15.)

5. Amidon replied to FK on 2 November, commenting in detail on aspects of John Commons's draft. He reiterated his point that "[t]here ought to be a difference between the power to declare a state law unconstitutional and a federal law. . . . All other countries that have written constitutions make this difference" (Amidon, Fargo, N.D., to FK, 2 November 1923, copy, "Correspondence (Florence Kelley): Amidon, Charles F., 1922–1925," Box C40, NCL Papers, DLC). At its annual meeting the NCL council approved a resolution authorizing President Commons to appoint a committee to consider the question of limiting the power of federal courts (NCL Council Minutes, 9 November 1923, 3–4, Box A7, NCL Papers, DLC).

186. To James Weldon Johnson [1]

NATIONAL CONSUMERS' LEAGUE
~~ROOM 1102, 44 EAST 23RD STREET~~*156 5TH AVE.*
NEW YORK CITY

11-13-23

My dear Mr. Johnson

It gives me great pleasure to notify you that the enclosed resolution was unanimously adopted last Friday, Nov. 9th, by the National Consumers' League at its 24th annual meeting.[2]

I am doing what I can to get publicity for it.

Especially I wish to do all that we can to carry out the intent of the closing paragraph. As to the Washington end of the campaign, I wish to be at your command, and to take no step without your approval.

I have no assignment which seems to me more important and only one which I consider <u>as</u> important as this.

Yours hopefully,
Florence Kelley[3]

ALS, Group 1, Part Three, Series A, Box C-196, NAACP Papers, DLC

1. Johnson (1871–1938), a writer and former U.S. consul to Venezuela and Nicaragua, was the NAACP's executive secretary from 1920 to 1930.

2. Congressman Leonidas C. Dyer (1871–1957; Republican, Missouri, 1911–1914, 1915–1933) had introduced an anti-lynching bill in 1922. The House approved it, but southern senators filibustered against it and no action was taken in the next Congress. Seeking broad support for the measure, FK had earlier written Marion Parkhurst urging the LWV's endorsement of the bill. She hoped that Parkhurst could soon "report that your organization has taken action in behalf of this eminently humane and life-saving measure" (FK, New York, to Parkhurst, 10 November 1922, Box 25, LWV Papers, DLC). The NCL's resolution noted the growth of

the Ku Klux Klan and endorsed Dyer's bill, "a life saving measure for the prevention of mob violence" and requested that FK "work for its passage" (NCL Council Minutes, 9 November 1923, 5–6, 11, Box A7, NCL Records, DLC). Marion Parkhurst responded that "the National League at its convention in Baltimore did not take up any action on the anti-lynching and I do not think the matter was brought up" (LWV Congressional Secretary to FK, 15 November 1922, Box 25, LWV Records, DLC).

3. In Johnson's absence, Walter F. White (1893–1955), NAACP assistant secretary in 1923, acknowledged FK's letter with its "splendid resolution" and informed her that it was being released to the "the white and colored newspapers of the country" (White, n.p., to FK, 15 November 1923, copy, Group 1, Part Three, Series A, Box C-196, NAACP Papers).

187. To Lavinia L. Dock

NATIONAL CONSUMERS' LEAGUE
156 FIFTH AVENUE, NEW YORK CITY

November 24th, 1923.

Miss L. L. Dock
Fayetteville
Adams Co., Penn.
Dear Sister Dock:

Thank you for your letter. I sometimes think it is easier to clear up debatable questions in writing than in any way,—especially when both sides are by nature gifted with eloquence.[1]

So here goes an attempt to answer your questions! As to the first: I have thought ever since the constituting meeting of the new Woman's Party in Washington, that according to the interpretation there set forth of its aims, the Sheppard-Towner law would go down in the crash, if a blanket equality amendment were adopted, and the Supreme Court interpreted it. This opinion was confirmed when Miss [Alice] Paul told me that a member of the Party had gone to the Capitol to oppose the S.-T. law. It was further confirmed at a hearing at which well-known members of the Party appeared. It is further confirmed by the reasoning of Senator [George] Sutherland in the decision against the District of Columbia Minimum Wage Law, in which he minimizes the claim of the health of women as an important consideration. My opinion is therefore neither new nor hysterical. There can be no final definition of the significance of the word "equal" except by the Supreme Court of the United States; until it speaks your interpretation, ***and*** mine, are alike speculative. Miss Lavinia Egan states the definition of the Woman's Party as follows:

> "It is to give the women of each group equality of rights with the men of the same group that the Woman's Party is working: professional women with professional men: women in industry with men in industry: business women with business men: Japanese women citizens with Japanese men citizens of the United States: Negro women with Negro men." ***That looks to me like caste, not equality.***[2]

The ***Supreme Court*** definitions of "equal rights" in the so-called "Negro" Amendments, the fourteenth and fifteenth, have been continuously injurious, first, to the Negroes, and afterward to White women and children. I see no reason for expecting the Court to interpret fresh attempts to put political and social equality into the Constitution ~~to be~~ more favorabl***y*** to women than they have ***done*** in the past. I am, in principle, averse to giving the Court any fresh opportunities to interpret ambiguous terms, and the present wording of the blanket amendment is no less ambiguous than its predecessor.

Second: the whole attempt to cover the needs of women by means of a federal amendment is, I am convinced, misdirected effort. Everything,—that it is hoped could be done by the amendment—can in fact be done more quickly and safely by statutes, and by modernising the Supreme Court, and the lower courts. I say this in reply to your statement, "I can simply never believe that it must be either disabilities with life, or equal rights with death,—and I wonder very much if you really believe it yourself." as the Woman's Party ***opposes*** (perversely, I think) a***ll*** special provision***s*** for the health of women in industry, the whole subject is muddled.

One thing Life has clearly taught me,—women in industry must have special laws, they cannot live in health without them. ***T***hese laws must remain special until the men in the American labor movement so far overtake the English and Continental workingmen in their intelligence, as to insist upon protection for themselves. It is not part of the duty of women to attempt to force this upon them; and it is utterly inhumane to delay necessary protection for women for the sake of an equality,—as to the meaning of which hardly any two persons seem to agree. I am, for instance, entitled to interpret "equality" as "identical" just as you are entitled to interpret it otherwise; and in the end, the Court may adopt a third interpretation wholly divergent from both.

Meantime the Sheppard-Towner law, the Cable independent citizenship law for alien wives, and new Lehlbach law applying civil service reform principles to women in Government employ show that, without waiting for an Amendment we can get statutes adapted to the special changes we desire. Here are three important ones signed in three years.[3]

And the root of the trouble all the time is the Courts. We must have women on them,—50-50.

Nov. 30th. Word has just come that Mrs. Wald died this morning at eight o'clock and I am off to 265.[4]

Anyhow we are only differing about the extent of our demands for women. I want everything that men have and lot more to compensate for the {burdens} of motherhood.[5]

Yours devotedly
F. Kelley

TLS + AN, "Equal Rights Amendment: Correspondence: General: 1921–1931," Box C4, NCL Records, DLC

1. Although Dock's letter is unrecovered, she had publicly questioned some of the arguments against the ERA, including those of FK, in a letter to *Survey.* Dock wrote, "When all those inequalities are banished from statutory law, as they must and will be, women's entire legal and social position will be quite as much stronger than it is at present" (Dock, "The Right to Differ," 530).

2. Lavinia Egan (1863–1945) was a Louisiana writer and member of the National Council of the NWP. FK was quoting from Egan's letter of 16 September to her (Washington, D.C., "Equal Rights Amendment: Correspondence: General: 1921–31," Box C4, NCL Records, DLC).

3. FK was referring here to the Classification Act of 1923; for more, see Letter 184, FK to W. E. B. Du Bois, 18 October 1923, note 3, above.

4. Minnie Schwarz Wald was Lillian Wald's mother.

5. In a printed "Letter to Nurses," supporting the ERA, Dock argued that the NWP did not "attempt to say what method for controlling conditions of labor is best," only that "conditions should be made better for all workers without regard to sex. . . . The young of both sexes should be protected even much more amply than at present, but to link women and children together in labor laws, as has been done in the past, is a serious error" (Dock, "Letter to Nurses," written 22 December 1923, Fayetteville, Pa., "Equal Rights Amendment: Correspondence: General: 1921–31," Box C4, NCL Records, DLC).

188. To Victor L. Berger[1]

NATIONAL CONSUMERS' LEAGUE
156 FIFTH AVENUE, NEW YORK CITY

December 19, 1923

Hon. Victor L. Berger,
House Office Building,
Washington, D.C.

Personal-Confidential

Dear Comrade Berger:

Herewith I acknowledge receipt of your letter of December 17th, in reply to mine enclosing our Twenty Questions about the proposed Equal Rights Amendment to the Constitution of the United States.

I am going to express myself to you quite bluntly as one Socialist to another.

Of all the shams that I have encountered in my 64 years of human experience this I, as a Socialist, consider the meanest. The women who pretend to be making heroic exertions to get "equal rights" for all women are, in practice, the Little Sisters of the United States Chamber of Commerce, the National Manufacturers' Associations, the National Conference Board (the great national purveyors of fake industrial statistics), and the Associated Industries. This last organization is a New York State combination of the Mercantile and Manufacturing Interests of this State. Its lawyers appear at Albany at hearings on all labor bills, and whenever the Eight Hours Bill, Minimum Wage Bill, or any other bill intended to make industry more advantageous for women, is up for consideration Doris

Stevens appears for the Woman's Party against the bill ***and on the same side as those lawyers.***[2]

Her position is that, now that women have votes they must have no protection that does not apply in identical words to men in industry. During the last three years they have created sufficient confusion in the Legislature to prevent the passage of the bills for the Eight Hours Day and Minimum Wage legislation. The Woman's Party boasts in its organ of the cooperation of the Chamber of Commerce of Rochester and the Chamber of Commerce of Denver, Colorado, two of the most reactionary chambers of commerce in the United States. The Rochester one bore the brunt of the Seneca Falls meeting of the Woman's Party, furnishing automobiles to carry crowds from Rochester to Seneca Falls. The Denver Chamber of Commerce did the same thing for the later meeting at the Garden of the Gods in Colorado.[3]

I hope you will take our Twenty Questions seriously. None of the great organizations of Capital against Labor could by direct effort accomplish what these Little Sisters accomplish in protecting the Interests against even the smallest regulations in behalf of wage-earning women.

It is notorious in Washington that members of the Woman's Party cultivated the friendship of the Counsel against the District of Columbia Minimum Wage law so effectively that Justice [George] Sutherland put some of the actual words furnished by these women into his decision. Indeed his decision rests in part on their contention that women who have votes do not need to have health where health has to be promoted by labor legislation.

You have, most unhappily, been away from Washington during the years in which the Woman's Party has changed from good to exceedingly bad and dangerous. I was a member of the Party when it was expediting Suffrage, and until it held the meeting at which it gave out the following as its principle of action:—

> "It is to give the women of each group equality of rights with the men of the same group that the Woman's Party is working: professional women with professional men: women in industry with men in industry: business women with business men: Japanese women citizens with Japanese men citizens of the United States: Negro women with Negro men."

What do you think the Negroes think of this kind of South Carolina equality? I prefer the Wisconsin brand myself.

This letter is not for publication. But if you agree with me, I can write a letter about it that would not risk a libel suit as this would!

Yours sincerely
Florence Kelley

TLS + AN, Box 14, Berger Papers, WHi

1. Victor L. Berger (1860–1929) was a Socialist from Wisconsin who served in U.S. House of Representatives from 1911 to 1913 and 1923 to 1929.

2. Doris Stevens (1892–1963) had been active in the NWP's suffrage campaign and was on its Executive Committee. The NWP sided with manufacturing interests to oppose the eight-hour and minimum wage bills. At hearings before the New York legislature on 27 February 1923, Stevens justified this stance, stating that "we rather consider ourselves as experts, as to how the conditions of men and women in industry should be bettered" (*NYT,* 28 February 1923, 6). For more on Doris Stevens, see Butler, *Two Paths to Equality,* 90–113.

3. At the seventy-fifth anniversary of the Seneca Falls Woman's Rights Convention, the NWP formally committed itself to the ERA and Alice Paul announced that she would initiate the ERA campaign in Colorado on 1 August (*NYT:* 21 July 1923, 8; 22 July 1923, 1).

189. To Joseph T. Deal[1]

NATIONAL CONSUMERS' LEAGUE
156 FIFTH AVENUE, NEW YORK CITY

January 18, 1924.

Hon. Joseph T. Deal,
House Office Building,
Washington, D. C.
Dear Sir:—

The Dyer Anti-Lynching bill having been favorably reported by the House Committee on the Judiciary, this organization respectfully requests that this life-saving measure be brought to a vote of the House at the earliest suitable moment in order to remove the possibility of a repetition of last years' failure to pass it.

Enclosed is a copy of the resolution adopted by the 24th Annual Meeting of the National Consumers' League.[2]

Yours respectfully,
Florence Kelley

General Secretary[3]
FK:A

TLS, "General Correspondence: Kelley, Florence," Box B14, NCL Records, DLC

1. Joseph T. Deal (1860–1942), a Virginia Democrat, served in Congress from 1921 to 1929.

2. See Letter 186, FK to James Weldon Johnson, 13 November 1923, above.

3. Replying at the bottom of the page of FK's letter, Deal stated that he would "do all in my power to defeat your bill—It is not only uncalled for but vicious & finally unconstitutional." On 19 January 1924, the bill was placed on the House calendar. In a speech before the House on 4 June, Dyer challenged those who said his bill had no chance of passage because any consideration of it "would bring on a Democratic filibuster" and thus tie up all pending legislation. He stated, "[T]he prevalence in many States of the spirit which tolerates lynching, accompanied too often with inhuman cruelty, and the inability or unwillingness of the public authorities to punish the persons who are guilty of this crime, threaten very seriously the future peace of the Nation" (68th Cong., 1st sess., *Cong. Rec.,* 19 January 1924, 10538, 1180). Nevertheless, the House took no action on Dyer's bill.

190. To Molly Dewson

NATIONAL CONSUMERS' LEAGUE
156 FIFTH AVENUE, NEW YORK CITY

2-17-24

Dear Sister Dewson

As you see, I have slept on your letter not one night but four. And I cannot pretend that it comes as a surprise, you have not concealed your boredom. But it was bound to be a blow at any time.

The League has never offered any worldly rewards. Drudgery and delay—spade work with or without a following harvest—are inherent in it. And I see no prospect of change in that.

But over against your view of the outlook I set my view.

In 1925, forty-two legislatures will be in session. If we do not make a nation-wide drive for the 8 hours day in 1925, who will? Already Premier MacDonald is agitating for putting the 1919 international convention for the 8 hours day (for all ages and both sexes?) into effect.[1] This should be an effective stimulus for this laggard Republic.

The idea that a publicity agent could take your place is piffle! If an honest, useful publicity agent should appear, we could take her on for a while, when needed, and you could run her.

The time is over-ripe for a long step forward there, i.e. towards the 8 hours day.

Josephine [Goldmark] will never come back. After Mr. [Louis] Brandeis' appointment, her interest was never the same. The choice of your successor would be neither Josephine nor a publicity agent. It would be among persons now unknown to me.

While I continue able to work, I shall strive to modernize the Court and the Constitution. My debates with the Woman's Party are one percent against an Amendment which will never be adopted, and 99% for women judges and a responsible Court. The Children's Amendment will be out of the way this year, and the decks clear for modernizing action.

We have 8000 subscribers. We had, in 1923 without either Mr. [John] Shillady or Daisy's [Florence Harriman's] Committee, more money than ever before, tho the whole year came after the D.C. Supreme Court's adverse decision; and 8 months (Apr. 11th to New Years) came after the Sutherland decision.[2] The League is not dying, and I believe its program was never so useful.

So unless you have already a definite engagement in view, I hope that instead of seeking one, you will propose the changes that you think desirable for the League and for yourself, and stay on.[3]

Yours affectionately
F. Kelley

ALS, Dewson Papers, MCR-S

1. Although elected in 1924 as Britain's first prime minister from the Labour Party, Ramsay MacDonald headed a coalition government that relied on Liberal Party votes and could advance only a narrow range of social legislation, primarily related to housing and education. For his failure to enact the ILO's 1919 convention on hours, see Cole, *A Short History of the British Working-Class Movement,* 172.

2. FK's optimistic summary omitted outstanding bills that brought the annual reckoning to a deficit of $3,107.34 for 1923 (NCL Council Minutes, 8 November 1923, 3, 12, Box A7, NCL Records, DLC). Even though annual income increased steadily during the early 1920s, the NCL had greater expenses associated with their legal defense of labor legislation. Dues from members in the state leagues accounted for most of its income, but this was not enough to cover the increased expenses. FK and other office staff often had to wait months to be paid, and FK at times loaned the league money to cover shortfalls. Several times during this decade, wealthy supporters gave large sums. For example, Dorothy Straight gave $21,000 during the period 1920 to 1923 (NCL Council Minutes, 1920, Accountant's Statement, 3; NCL Board of Directors Minutes, 9 January 1922, 1; NCL Council Minutes, 1923, 3; NCL Council Minutes, 1924, Auditor's Report, 1; all in Box A7, NCL Records, DLC. See also Letter 177, FK to Julia Lathrop, 18 February 1923, above). In 1924, Hannah Heyman left a bequest of $10,000 to the league (NCL Board of Directors Minutes, 23 October 1924, 2, Box A2, NCL Records). The Milbank Memorial Fund gave a grant of $7,000 in 1927 (NCL Council Minutes, 1928, 3, Box A8, NCL Records). Although these injections of cash were welcome and much needed, they did not solve the structural problem that the increased workload of defending labor legislation for women required more income than the league could easily raise.

3. Dewson left her post at the NCL in 1924 to concentrate on lobbying for women's protective legislation in New York State. At the May meeting of the Board of Directors, her resignation was accepted "with great regret and keen appreciation" for her contributions to the NCL's work (NCL Board of Directors Minutes, 22 May 1924, 4, Box A2, NCL Records, DLC). Dewson served as president of the CL of New York City from 1925 to 1931 and remained active in both the NCL and the WJLC.

191. To Annette Mann[1]

[New York City]
March 15, 1924

Miss Annette Mann,
Consumers' League of Cincinnati,
25 East 9th Street,
Cincinnati, Ohio
Dear Miss Mann:

There is a crisis in the fate of the federal child labor amendment, centered in Ohio. Mr. Longworth can get it out of the Judiciary Committee.[2] If he cannot do this he should resign and let a more competent man take his exceedingly important place.[3]

The title of the Amendment is H.J.R. 184 introduced by I. M. Foster of Ohio.[4] No one could have done better for it than he has done. But the Chairman of the Committee on the Judiciary, Mr. Graham of Philadelphia, is pursuing a policy of delay, and Mr. Longworth is letting him do this, while making promises to the friends of the measure which are broken as soon as made.[5]

It is up to the citizens of Ohio to cheer up Mr. Foster, who needs backing in his own state, and to poke up Mr. Longworth so that it will hurt him enough to make him get the Amendment out of the House Judiciary Committee.

I am sending Mr. Dearness a special delivery letter containing the above facts, and urging him to get a dozen telegrams to Mr. Longworth from the most influential people possible immediately on receiving my letter. I hope you will communicate with him, and divide the field so that the largest number of communications possible by your joint effort may reach Mr. Longworth from his own constituency.[6]

Enclosed is the final text of the Amendment.[7]

Yours sincerely,

FK:A

CC, "Child Labor: Amendment: Congressional, 1922–1924," Box C1, NCL Records, DLC

1. Annette Mann was executive secretary of the CL of Cincinnati and author of *Women in Factories: A Study of Working Conditions in 275 Industrial Establishments in Cincinnati* (1918).
2. Nicholas Longworth (1869–1931; Republican, Ohio, 1903–1913, 1915–1931) of Cincinnati was House floor leader.
3. Since June 1922, FK, Grace Abbott, Mabel Costigan, and others had been working on a suitable text for the child labor amendment and were closely following its fate in Congress (see Letter 172, FK to Newton Baker, 3 June 1922, note 6, above).
4. On 13 February 1924, Congressman Israel M. Foster (1873–1950; Republican, Ohio, 1919–1925) introduced the amendment in the House, which was referred to the House Judiciary Committee (68th Cong., 1st sess., *Cong. Rec.*, 13 February 1924, 2411).
5. George S. Graham (1850–1931) was a Pennsylvania Republican who served in Congress from 1913 to 1931.
6. FK wrote Mabel Costigan in March that she was "flooding Ohio with appeals to our friends to get after Mr. Longworth." Apparently Mann acted quickly, for FK wrote her one week later to thank her for her help. Foster placed H.J.R. 184 on the House calendar later that month (68th Cong., 1st sess., *Cong. Rec.*, 28 March 1924, 5194). FK wrote Longworth to thank him on behalf of the NCL for "his recent activity as Floor Leader" and urged him to keep pressing for a favorable vote on the amendment (FK, [New York], to Mabel Costigan, 15 March 1924; FK, [New York], to Annette Mann, 21 March 1924; FK, [New York], to Nicholas Longworth, 29 March 1924, all letters in "Child Labor: Amendment: Congressional, 1922–1924," Box C1, NCL Records, DLC).
7. The amendment read: "Section 1. The Congress shall have power to limit, regulate, and prohibit the labor of persons under 18 years of age. Section 2. The power of the several States is unimpaired by this article except that the operation of State laws shall be suspended to the extent necessary to give effect to legislation enacted by Congress" (68th Cong., 1st sess., *Cong. Rec.*, 25 April 1924, 7166).

192. To Molly Dewson

NATIONAL CONSUMERS' LEAGUE
156 FIFTH AVENUE
NEW YORK CITY

March 26, 1924

Dear Miss Dewson:

I know you will be enchanted to get the enclosed which Mr. Goldsmith presented to me personally as a token of affection and appreciation for this office and everybody in it! His exuberance was beautiful! He said the case was won by the brief that we let him have—that the oral argument was entirely subordinate to the brief.[1] In fact, however, Mr. Brandeis told Josephine [Goldmark] that his modest method of presentation made an excellent impression upon the Court.

Mr. Goldsmith pointed out that the Court makes no reference either to Bunting or to Adamson, but sticks tight to Muller. I was much interested when he pointed this out, but on reading the whole decision I think our dear friend Goldsmith is revealed as not knowing that Holden vs. Hardy 169 U.S. 366,395 is a case affecting solely men working underground in mines or smelters.[2]

Be that as it may, however, the decision appears in the minds of all the lawyers I know who have seen it, to settle forevermore the question of the right of the states to restrict the working hours of women. This means a volte face on the part of [George] Sutherland. Mr. Goldsmith generously expressed the opinion that he was learning. Other people, less kindly, say that he was scared! There is one wicked paragraph in the Radice decision. Referring to Adkins vs. The Children's Hospital, Sutherland says: "But that case presented a question entirely different from that now being considered. The statute in the Adkins case was a wage-fixing law pure and simple. It had nothing to do with the hours and conditions of labor, etc." That is bad medicine. Otherwise the decision is priceless and precious.

Nothing is further from my intention than any idea of ceasing to be ready at every hour of the day and night to defend the constitutionality of every labor law dealing with hours, wages, men, women, minors or children. The last economy I propose to enter upon is going without your successor. I wish you might in the end decide to be your own, but one we will certainly have. Tomorrow night's Directors' meeting will consider something new, e.g. asking the Garland Fund for $15,000 to investigate poisons.[3] Alice Hamilton is coming on from Boston to argue the case, and Josephine Goldmark will probably come up from Washington where she is visiting her sick sister, Mrs. [Alice] Brandeis.

This is for the sake of having something new and different to offer people who have gone stale on hours and wages. It is a field which no one else has ever entered in this country, and interlocks with workmen's compensation for disease. I will write you later what is decided.

Since I began this letter a telegram has come from Grace Abbott saying that the House Committee on the Judiciary had reported the federal child labor Amendment, and that Mr. [Israel] Foster applied instantly for a rule to get it on the calendar, having been put in charge of getting the vote on the Floor by our enemy George Graham of Philadelphia, Chairman of the Committee, much against Mr. Graham's will.

Miss Bogue sent the $1,000 ten days ago. If you will tell me about how and where to pay the debt you contracted in advance of your trip, I will pay it without waiting for your return.

Any advance news of the time of your coming will be useful at this end, besides being pleasant.

Yours faithfully,
Florence Kelley

FK:A

TLS, "Wages and Hours: Correspondence, 1919–1931," Box C49, NCL Records, DLC

1. On 10 March 1924, the U.S. Supreme Court in *Radice v. People of New York* unanimously upheld New York's law preventing women from working from 10 P.M. to 6 A.M. Irving I. Goldsmith (1881–1951), deputy attorney general for New York State, argued the case before the court in January. In her report to the NCL Board of Directors, FK stated that the brief Goldsmith used was based on Josephine Goldmark's updated version of arguments that had been used before the New York Court of Appeals in 1914 (*NYT,* 4 June 1951, 27; "Secretary's Report," NCL Board of Directors Minutes, 27 March 1924, 1, Box A2, NCL Records, DLC). Goldmark's research findings were published as Brandeis and Goldmark, *The People of the State of New York, against Charles Schweinler Press, a Corporation, Defendant. A Summary of "Facts of Knowledge" Submitted on Behalf of the People in Support of Its Brief on the Law* (1914).

2. For the *Bunting* decision, see Letter 137, FK to Louis Brandeis, 9 April 1917, above; for the *Muller* decision, see Letter 104, FK to NK, 20 January 1908, above. The Adamson Act, passed in 1916, limited the work day of railroad workers engaged in interstate commerce to eight hours. The Supreme Court narrowly upheld the law in 1917 in *Wilson v. N.Y.* In *Holden v. Hardy* (1898), the Court had upheld Utah's eight-hour law for miners.

3. The NCL board authorized FK "to reorganize the committee on dangerous fumes and dust, and to plan a scheme of work and see whether facts can be collected" (NCL Board of Directors Minutes, 27 March 1924, 5, Box A2, NCL Records, DLC). For the Garland Fund, see FK to Roger Baldwin, 6 May 1924, note 2, below.

193. To Ellery Sedgwick[1]

[New York City]
April 1, 1924

Mr. Ellery Sedgwick,
8 Arlington Street,
Boston 17, Mass.

My dear Mr. Sedgwick:

Since reading your note I am at a loss to know what amends Mr. Warren and the Atlantic can make to the children injured by his cruel caricatures of the Sheppard-Towner Act and the federal child labor Amendment. The enclosed clipping shows what Representative Graham of Philadelphia has already done with the nonsense about blueberries and college students.[2] Every state has had power to perpetuate such idiocy, but which one ever tried it? And why should Congress have less sense than the states?

Fortunately the House Judiciary Committee was not impressed by the minority report and voted Mr. Graham down 14 to 6, a second of the six being a Tammany Democrat, Mr. Royal Weller. The other four adverse votes came from Southern Democrats.

It cannot, I think, be a proud experience for the Atlantic whose readers have in the Past looked to it with confidence, to be printing multiple misrepresentation as ammunition against the children, and to such a Congressman. Mr. Graham, though Chairman of an important Committee of the House, is flouted by his fellow Committee members. He is treated as the mouthpiece of Pennsylvania manufacturers who for a half century have notoriously worked to perpetuate tariff protection for themselves. As a native Philadelphian I know how they have opposed all this time measures intended to safeguard the life, health and welfare of their employees, down to the youngest wage-earners and their most helplessly dependent relations i.e., down to the littlest mill children and to their baby brothers and sisters (too early dead), and to their mothers needlessly endangered by childbirth and its consequences. From such new company will not the Atlantic free itself?[3]

Yours sincerely,
FK:A

CC, "Press and Periodicals: *Atlantic Monthly*, 1923–1925," Box B20, NCL Records, DLC

1. Sedgwick (1872–1960) edited the *Atlantic Monthly* from 1909 to 1938.
2. The *Atlantic Monthly* had published an article by Boston attorney Bentley W. Warren (1864–1947) that decried the recent expansion of the federal government. Warren specifically attacked the U.S. Children's Bureau, the Sheppard-Towner Act, and the proposed child labor amendment. He wrote that because of the child labor amendment, "the New England farmer's boy could not pick blueberries on the hills; the city schoolboy could not sell papers after school; the country boy, white or black, could not work in the cotton, wheat, or hay fields of the South or West; the college student even, if under eighteen, could not work to pay his way through college" (Warren, "Destroying Our 'Indestructible States,'" 375). FK's enclosure apparently described George Graham's minority report from the House Judiciary Committee in which Graham used Warren's language word for word without attribution (*NYT*, 31 March 1924, 2).
3. In April, FK wrote Sedgwick canceling her *Atlantic* subscription. Sedgwick replied that FK's response "illustrates the essential difficulty which besets all reform": because FK had disagreed "with a single article . . . you part company with us on all issues." FK responded that it was not the magazine's differing opinion that prompted her subscription cancellation

but its "printing misrepresentations of important legislation, at a critical moment, and failing to make amends though the facts are readily ascertainable" (FK, New York, to Sedgwick, 15 April 1924; Sedgwick, Boston, to FK, 16 May 1924; FK, New York, to Sedgwick, 26 May 1924, all letters in "*Atlantic Monthly,* 1923–1925," Box B20, NCL Records, DLC).

On 17 April, FK sent out a form letter asking recipients to write or telegraph members of Congress immediately to urge them to support the child labor amendment so it could be sent to the forty-four legislatures in session in 1925 for ratification. On 26 April, the House passed the amendment. It came before the Senate on 28 April and FK sent out another form letter requesting that letters be sent to Senate whip Charles Curtis. On 2 June, the Senate approved H.J.R. 184 (FK to "Dear Friend," 17 April 1924, CLM Records, MCR-S; FK to "Dear Friend," 2 May 1924, Lathrop Papers, IRoC; 68th Cong., 1st sess., *Cong. Rec.*, 2 June 1924, 7295, 7337, 10142).

194. To Roger Baldwin[1]

COPY

[New York City]
May 6, 1924

Mr. Roger Baldwin,
American Fund for Public Service,[2]
70 Fifth Avenue,
New York City
Dear Mr. Baldwin:

Following our conversation at the Civic Club, I send this memorandum.[3]

We appeal to the American Fund for Public Service for $15,000 a year for three years for the following purpose to be attained by the following means:-

Under the scientific guidance of Dr. Alice Hamilton of the Harvard Faculty, who is also our most active Vice-President, we propose to use the machinery and trained constituency of the Consumers' League to stop the injurious use in industry of the following substances:-

1. Granite for tombstones. Granite tombstones are both deadly and unnecessary. Tuberculosis accompanies their production because of a machine which makes 3000 blows a minute and corresponding volumes of peculiarly irritating and deadly dust. Silica dust cuts the workers' lung tissue. Other (non-injurious) materials are abundantly available.

2. Lead in potteries used in injurious ways. England has fifteen times less lead poisoning than we in potteries producing the same qualities of goods. The present tariff is prohibitive as to all non-poisonous English pottery ware. Only the very rich can afford to buy it. A large constituency in the United States would buy this English ware as a matter of conscience if they could afford to do so. It is made with leadless glaze, which can be produced in this country instead of our lead glaze.

3. Benzol where young girls are employed, and everywhere without the utmost precautions to avoid injury to all employees. This is an ultra dangerous

poison, rapidly spreading because it is the quickest and cheapest solvent on the market.

Our proposed means include:-

(a) As to potteries, making known the superiority (from the point of view of the health of the workers) of the English ware, and the immediately practicable steps toward manufacturing our American product equally safely;

(b) Introducing bills in several legislatures in the hope of obtaining some first steps towards prompt improvement, and of arousing sustained public opinion such as has made the permanent changes achieved by these methods in England. Propaganda for these bills can begin immediately.

In none of these industries is there danger of duplication of effort. The potteries are largely non-union, and such unions as exist do not welcome women or unskilled men. Only the painters are now looked after, and there are no women painters.

In reply to your suggestion as to a budget, I have made a draft and am waiting for the comments of Alice Hamilton and Mary Dewson before sending it out. (The former is momentarily out of reach). I am anxious to have it substantially workable for the whole time for which we are asking for money. We suggested gifts in three consecutive years because it is not worth our while to undertake the proposed educational and legislative work for less than three years, and we should have no justification for undertaking it and having to stop in the middle because a one year's or two years' guarantee ended.

We have no basis for hoping that any of the Foundations with which we are now acquainted will change their attitude toward us in 1925 or 1926. We have twice received $50 from a little trust created as a memorial known as the Grant-Sherburne Fund. We have been turned down twice by the Laura Spelman Fund, twice by the Milbank Memorial Fund (through the efforts of Mr. Shillady the Milbank Fund gave us money two successive years, before it adopted its present policy of doing its work itself through its own direct agents), twice by the Harkness Fund, twice by the Sage Foundation, and we know of no other refusals that we can decently go a-courting.[4]

Yours sincerely,
(Signed) Florence Kelley.[5]

FK:A

CC, "General Correspondence: 'B,'" Box B10, NCL Records, DLC

1. Roger N. Baldwin (1884–1981), a civil rights activist, was executive director of the ACLU (1920–1950) and a member of the LID Board of Directors.

2. The American Fund for Public Service, also known as the Garland Fund, was established in 1921 by a millionaire socialist, Charles Garland, to "promote experiments for the public welfare" (*NYT,* 14 January 1924, 7). The Garland Fund was well known for its support of socialist and leftist organizations and projects, including the Rand School of Social Science, the League for Industrial Democracy, and the socialist New York newspaper *The Call* (*NYT,* 13 April 1923, 1).

3. FK had met with Baldwin, Alice Hamilton, and LID co-director Norman Thomas on 28 April 1924 to discuss funding prospects from the American Fund for Public Service (also known as the Garland Fund) so the NCL could publicize industrial poisoning more widely (FK, New York, to Harry F. Ward, 18 April 1924, "General Correspondence: Hamilton, Alice," Box B13, NCL Records, DLC; Magat, *Unlikely Partners*, 17–18).

4. By "Harkness Fund," FK presumably meant the Commonwealth Fund, created by Anna Harkness, widow of Stephen Harkness, one of the original investors in Standard Oil. The Commonwealth Fund supported health care projects (*New York Times*, 17 July 1921, 72). For the Sage Foundation, see Letter 103, FK to NK, 10 November 1907, note 6, above.

5. FK followed up her request with an itemized budget and emphasized that Hamilton would donate her time and expertise. Hamilton wrote FK that she hoped that limiting the goals of the program to items one and two (lead poisoning in pottery and tuberculosis in granite-cutting) would induce the Garland Fund to provide $10,000 (FK, New York, to Baldwin, 16 May 1924, copy, "General Correspondence: 'B,'" Box B10; Hamilton, Chicago, to FK, 20 and 28 May 1924, "General Correspondence: Hamilton, Alice," Box B13, both in NCL Records, DLC). In October, FK reported that officials at the Garland Fund had rejected the NCL's funding request, saying that they thought the NCL could raise the money elsewhere (NCL Board of Directors Minutes, 23 October 1924, 2, Box A2, NCL Records, DLC).

195. To Herbert Bayard Swope[1]

[New York City]
May 27, 1924

Mr. Herbert Bayard Swope,
Executive Editor,
The World,
63 Park Row, New York
My dear Mr. Swope:

The admirable publicity given by the World to the Senate investigations[2] has suggested to our Board of Directors that you may be interested in some evidence in our possession of continuing persecution of and propaganda against this League by the War Department.[3] It is directed against us as one of a number of organizations united in pushing the federal child labor amendment, and some other measures now before Congress.[4] Most virulently of all the propaganda is directed personally against Miss Jane Addams of Hull House.

Mr. and Mrs. [Mary Hill] Gerard Swope will vouch to you for this being a responsible organization.[5] They have known us more than a quarter century and are among our regular contributors.

For these reasons I am venturing to ask you to give me a few moments to-morrow if possible, to explain a current phase which I do not wish to telephone or write.

We have in our possession a chart known in Washington as the Spider Web Chart of the Chemical Warfare Division of the War Department.[6] It was prepared under direction of General A. Fries, Chief of that Division and secretly circulated with his knowledge, until Secretary Weeks was compelled to write a formal apology for its existence.[7]

Secretary Weeks stated that he had instructed General Fries to cease to distribute the chart, to destroy all copies then remaining in the War Department, and to recall so far as possible all copies which General Fries or his subordinates had caused to be circulated.[8] We have, however, no means of knowing to what extent this instruction has been obeyed. Secretary Weeks' letter of apology for the chart was made public at the meeting of the League of Women Voters Convention on Thursday, April 24th, and was given to the press on that date. If I recollect aright, the World carried it as news.[9] Since that time General Fries has continued to repeat, on public occasions, scurrilous and libelous statements which he had previously circulated through the chart.

The scurrilous material from the Spider Web Chart has been published in two issues of the Dearborn Independent, and more recently reprinted for broadcasting circulation by the Manufacturers' Association of Kentucky, and most recently by the Associated Industries of this state, by whom it is at present circulated.[10]

It is this League which suffers from this use of the ammunition thus supplied by the War Department to our enemies.[11]

Yours sincerely,

FK:A

CC, "Press and Periodicals: *New York World,* 1924–1930," Box B20, NCL Records, DLC

1. Herbert Bayard Swope (1882–1958) was the brother of Gerard Swope and executive editor of the *New York World* from 1920 to 1928.

2. In the early months of Calvin Coolidge's presidency, Congress began a series of investigations into corruption in the Harding administration. A major scandal emerged when Congress learned that Secretary of the Interior Albert Fall had leased reserve lands in Teapot Dome, Wyoming, to oil producers. The *New York World* had recently run an editorial that was highly critical of former attorney general Harry Daugherty, whom President Coolidge had dismissed for corrupt dealings. It indicted the Republican Party in a full-page editorial, "The Cycle of Corruption" (*New York World:* 26 April 1924, 8 and 6 June 1924, 12).

3. For more about the attacks on Progressive women, see Lemons, *Woman Citizen,* 209–225; Cott, *The Grounding of Modern Feminism,* 242, 249–250, 259.

4. In 1922–1923, War Department librarian Lucia Maxwell had drawn a chart that had three columns of boxes. Boxes in the central column listed fourteen national women's organizations. Maxwell drew lines on the chart that linked these groups with boxes at the top of the chart for the WJCC and the National Council for the Prevention of War. Those boxes and boxes in the left and right columns named prominent women in these organizations and accused them of supporting socialist beliefs (for more on the chart, see Letter 238, FK to AK, 17 September 1927, below; the chart is reproduced in Document 3 in Sklar and Baker, "How Did Women Peace Activists Respond to 'Red Scare' Attacks during the 1920s?")

5. After their departure from Hull House, Mary Hill Swope and Gerard Swope remained active in social reform circles. His policies as president of General Electric launched American welfare capitalism (Perrin, "Swope of Hull-House"; Loth, *Swope of G.E.,* 201–240).

6. In March 1924, journalist and playwright Sidney Howard had sent FK a copy of Maxwell's War Department document, asking for her response to its characterization of her. To the charge that she fostered the "gradual abolition of property privileges," FK replied that although

she had been "for forty years in favor of public ownership of such property" as mines, forests, and city playgrounds, she was not a Communist. "The words [Socialist and Communist] are mutually exclusive they are antagonistic opposites, as every intelligent person knows" (Howard, New York, to FK, 19 March 1924; FK, New York, to Howard, 5 April 1924, copy, both in FKP, NN).

7. Because the chart was fundamentally an attack on the WJCC, that organization led the response to it with a hand-delivered letter demanding that U.S. Secretary of War Weeks (1860–1926; served 1921–1925) order all copies of the charts destroyed. The letter declared, "Twelve million women voters do not propose to bear this scurrilous and contemptible attack by a . . . government department without redress." Two weeks later, Weeks replied that the charts had been "ordered destroyed" (Maud Wood Park et al., Washington, D.C., to John W. Weeks, 2 April 1924, quoted in Minutes of the Meeting of the Women's Joint Congressional Committee, 7 April 1924, 3–5; Weeks, Washington, D.C., to Park, 16 April 1924, quoted in Report of the "Special Committee" of the Women's Joint Congressional Committee, 12 May 1924, 4, both in WJCC Records, DLC).

8. Brigadier General Amos A. Fries (1873–1963) was chief of the chemical warfare service in the War Department (1920–1929).

9. The *New York World* quoted the 10 April letter from Secretary Weeks, in which he expressed regret that "the charts were circulated by any branch of the War Department." Maud Wood Park read Weeks's letter at the LWV convention in Buffalo (*New York World,* 26 April 1924, 9). The *New York Times* also carried the story (*NYT,* 26 April 1924, 8).

10. The *Dearborn Independent* published "Are Women's Clubs 'Used' by Bolsheviks?" on 15 March 1924 (p. 2) and "Spider Web Chart: The Socialist-Pacifist Movement in America Is an Absolutely Fundamental and Integral Part of International Socialism" on 22 March 1924 (p. 11).

11. On 8 June, the *New York World* carried an extensive analysis of the issue of the spider web chart written by Leonard Cline (1893–1929), a journalist at the *New York World* and *New Republic,* who called it "the most important in the history of the privy campaign of the United States Army against the women of the country." In an editorial the following day, the *New York World* claimed sarcastically that "all members of these societies should be deported to Russia. Perhaps all feminine organizations and agitation should be forbidden by statute" (*New York World:* 8 June 1924, 1S, 10–11S, and 9 June 1924, 10). FK sent Swope a letter admiring "the skill with which Mr. Cline used every item of available evidence of this outrage, and fastened the responsibility upon the guilty individuals" (FK, New York, to Swope, 11 June 1924, "Press and Periodicals: *New York World,* 1924–1930," Box B20, NCL Records, DLC). For FK's recollection of Cline's reportage about the spider web chart, see Letter 238, FK to AK, 17 September 1927, below.

196. To Newton D. Baker

[New York City]
June 24, 1924

Hon. Newton D. Baker,
Cox Headquarters,
Hotel Waldorf-Astoria,
New York City
Dear Mr. Baker:

I write to beg you to come to a conference dinner, small and informal, on Tuesday July 1st, at 6:30 P.M. at the Women's City Club, 22 Park Avenue, northwest corner of 35th Street and Park Avenue.[1] It is to discuss a draft for a tentative, proposed amendment to the Constitution, dealing with the powers of the courts to veto social and industrial legislation, state and federal. ***A similar*** ~~***disc***~~ ***discussion was held at the time of the annual meeting last November and a still earlier meeting in May 1923 following the Sutherland decision.***[2]

For two years, 14 national organizations of women have been cooperating to restore to the children of the country the equal protection of the federal child labor law held unconstitutional by the Supreme Court in 1922. Congress having now passed a joint resolution and sent it to the states, at least one year—probably two—will elapse in the process of ratification. A third year, at least, will be needed for getting a third federal child labor law. Thus, upon the most sanguine calculations, the children will have lost five years of protection. Literally millions of women will have been striving during that time to undo the destructive work of the Supreme Court.

For 14 months, since April 1923, every state minimum wage law has been enfeebled by the Sutherland decision. Three have been undergoing a test in the state courts.[3] No one can guess how long a dozen other, similar, necessary measures will be half paralyzed before the Supreme Court either upholds, as a state measure, what it forbids as a federal law, or decides that the women of this Republic cannot (through either the Congress or the legislatures) enjoy the protection which English-speaking women have had increasingly since 1910, except the few who live in New Brunswick and Nova Scotia!

Since last November we have been collecting opinions, chiefly from members of the faculties of law schools, on the question: "Should the powers of the courts of last resort be restricted? And if so, by what changes in the Constitution?"

~~It will, I know, be a sort of miracle if you can give us the evening of July 1st. I have no words to say how eagerly I hope this may be possible.~~

I sent you an invitation yesterday, to the Cox headquarters not then knowing that you were at the Belmont.[4]

Hoping that you may be with us I am

Yours sincerely,

FK:A

TDft + AN, "Plans to Curb Supreme Court, Jan. 1, 1924–Aug. 1924," Box C41, NCL Records, DLC

1. John R. Commons had informed NCL board members that he wanted to meet with the members of the (House) Committee on the Judiciary in early July (NCL Board of Directors Minutes, 22 May 1924, 2, Box A2, NCL Records, DLC). In response, FK issued invitations to the 1 July 1924 conference to Dean Acheson, John G. Brooks, Edward Costigan, Felix Frankfurter, Ernst Freund, and Roscoe Pound, among many others (all letters in "Plans to Curb Supreme Court: Jan.-Aug. 1924," Box C41, NCL Records, DLC).
2. FK probably was referring to the Conference on Women's Wages and the Supreme Court Decision ("Report of Secretary," NCL Board of Directors Minutes, 25 October 1923, 1, Box A2,

NCL Records, DLC; see also NCL Board of Directors Minutes, 16 April 1923, 2). For more on this conference, see Letter 182, FK to Edward Costigan, 31 May 1923, note 3, above.

3. FK and other reformers feared that the Sutherland decision in *Adkins v. Children's Hospital* would reverse the decades of work behind the establishment of minimum wage laws in fifteen states and the District of Columbia and Puerto Rico from 1912 to 1919. Although the repercussions of the decision rippled through state minimum wage boards over the next few years, minimum wage laws in two-thirds of states with minimum wage laws withstood the storm. After 1924, courts in four states and Puerto Rico declared minimum wage laws unconstitutional: Wisconsin (*Folding Furniture Company v. Industrial Commission*, 300 Fed. 991 [1924]), Puerto Rico (*People v. Laurnaga & Co.*, 32 Puerto Rico 766 [1924]), Arizona (*Murphy v. Sardell*, 269 U.S. 530 [1925]), Kansas (*Topeka Laundry Company v. Court of Industrial Relations*, 119 Kansas 12 [1925]), and Minnesota (*Stevenson v. St. Clair*, 161 Minn. 444 [1925]). A challenge to the California law ended when the case was dismissed (*Gainer v. A. B. C. Dohrman et al.*; see Letter 205, FK to John Commons, 26 February 1925, note 2, below), and the high court in Massachusetts upheld a non-mandatory law (*Commonwealth v. Boston Transcript Co.*, 249 Mass. 477 [1924]) (Brandeis, "Minimum Wage Legislation," 504–505n14).

4. Baker was planning to nominate James M. Cox for president at the Democrat National Convention in New York City, but Cox's candidacy received little support and eventually the Democrats nominated John W. Davis (1873–1955), a former congressman and ambassador to Great Britain (*NYT*, 26 June 1924, 3). Although Baker was unable to attend, he replied that he believed he would have been in the minority at the discussion: "[L]egislative and constitutional restraints upon the courts seem to me approaching the problem from the wrong end" (Baker, Cleveland, Ohio, to FK, 14 July 1924, "Plans to Curb Supreme Court: Jan.-Aug. 1924," Box C41, NCL Records).

197. To Edward P. Costigan

COPY

Naskeag, Brooklin,
Hancock County, Maine
July 7, 1924

Mr. Edward Costigan,
U.S. Tariff Commission,
Washington, D.C.
Dear Mr. Costigan:

It was really worse to have you absent from our conference of July 1st than from any previous conference or meeting that we have ever had. Dr. Commons appeared with the green gooseberry draft for a federal amendment, of which I think a copy went to you with one or more of the notices.[1] If by any misadventure you have not received a copy, please let me know and I will send you one.

Dr. Commons has simplified our whole terribly difficult problem down to this: Does the United States need to have the final decision rest with the judiciary or with Congress? And he is for having it rest with Congress under two provisos:

1. That Congress shall re-enact the invalidated Congressional statute within three years of action by the Court, and
2. That there shall be a two-thirds majority vote of the Congress.

So far I know no one else among the persons present was willing to abandon the referendum to the states as a part of the process of amending the Constitution. What disturbed everybody present was the increasing frequency with which the court amends the Constitution by interpretation, with*out* further ceremony, and the deadly consequence of this when every little crossroads justice assumes the power to pronounce state laws contrary to the federal Constitution.

Dr. Commons brought word that he had had a long talk with Senator La Follette, who is at last at work upon a draft for his amendment with the aid of Donald Richberg, a practising lawyer in Chicago. Mr. Richberg's draft was the worst muddle conceivable.[2]

Do please beg Mrs. Costigan to write me, when she comes back, everything that she possibly can about the Cleveland convention.[3] We get no Metropolitan daily news as yet, and the weeklies go wrong in the mails half the time. I am pining to know what the Woman's Party did, and what the Communists did, and what the prospect seems to be, and how a poor exile from town can help between now and Labor Day, and anything more that Mrs. Costigan feels moved to tell me.

Yours sincerely,
Florence Kelley

CC, "Plans to Curb Supreme Court: W. G. Rice Material 1924," Box C41, NCL Records, DLC

1. John Commons's draft read, "Whenever any provision of any Federal Treaty or statute, or of any state constitution or statute has been held by the Supreme Court of the United States to violate the Federal Constitution, Congress shall have power to reverse the decision of the Supreme Court on the issue of constitutionality by a statute passed within three years from the entry of judgment by the Supreme Court. Congress shall have power to carry out the provisions of this amendment by appropriate legislation" ("Proposed Amendment to the U.S. Constitution," "Plans to Curb Supreme Court: W. G. Rice Material 1924," Box C41, NCL Records, DLC).

2. For Robert La Follette's proposal, see Letter 180, FK to James Haight, 19 May 1923, note 8, above. Donald R. Richberg (1881–1960) had been counsel for the Illinois Progressive Party in 1912 and was a lawyer for several railroad unions in the 1920s. In summing up the 1 July conference, FK wrote Commons that no one favored La Follette's proposal and that Richberg's was "too new for any of us to have an opinion" (FK, Brooklin, Me., to John R. Commons, 9 July 1924, copy, "Plans to Curb Supreme Court: W. G. Rice Material," Box C41, NCL Records, DLC).

3. The Progressive Party, which met in Cleveland on 4–5 July 1924, nominated Robert La Follette for president. Mabel Costigan spoke at the convention on 4 July (*NYT:* 5 July 1924, 5 and 6 July 1924, 5).

198. To Laurence Todd[1]

Naskeag, Brooklin, Hancock Co., Maine
July 22, 1924

Confidential. Neither my name nor that of the Consumers' League to be used

Mr. Laurence Todd,
1410 "H" St., N.W.
Washington, D.C.
Dear Mr. Todd:

Your letter of July 17th came to me last night in this remote village. Although I do not personally know Senator Neely, and have not his child labor record here, which might be a slight guide, I am inclined to believe that he is acting usefully in an excellent cause.[2] It looks as though he might be trying his case in the papers, knowing that without nationwide help from the press he has no chance in West Virginia courts.

The Consumers' League ceased to be active in the field of prison labor when we lost, I think in 1913, the man who had been the invaluable chairman of the committee on that subject. I cannot remember his name but can give you two clues to his identity. He worked several years in the congressional library under Herbert Putnam; and his name in appears in Edmond Kelly's "Twentieth Century Socialism" as the person who did all the reference work in checking quotations and citations for Mr. Kelly for that volume.[3] The latter died in 1907 or 1908, and the book appeared in the spring following his death in the fall. This man knows, I believe, more disinterestedly the developments in relation to prison manufacture then and since, than any other person.

In case you cannot locate him promptly, I remember that, even then, before the war, Milton F. Goodman was notorious in Chicago and elsewhere (as the Quaker Letchworth, for whom Letchworth Village in New York is now gloriously named had been before him) as the expert combination of advertised patriot and philanthropist, and terrible exploiter of prisoners.[4] If he is still living, there is no reason to suppose that he is in any respect changed in character or activities.

The West Virginia State penitentiary at Moundsville has always been the worst exploited penitentiary outside of the states where the stockade, whiplash and shallow grave are regular accompaniments of prison labor as a state institution. The Reliance Manufacturing Company was then, as it is now, the most widely ramified exploiter known to me in this field. Before the war, Joseph P. Beyer, always a state official and a terrible hypocrite, was a Siamese twin of the exploiting prison manufacturers. If he has ceased to be one, a miracle must have accompanied his conversion.

If, as I assume, Senator Neely was elected by Labor in West Virginia or hopes to be re-elected by Labor, it is of course to the A. F. of L. that he looks. However much Mr. [Samuel] Gompers may have been defeated in the fight against prison labor, at least he has never sat down on the job.

It is possible that Ethel Smith, legislative agent of the National Women's Trade Union League, may be able to give you further facts or clues. Indeed, one of the horrors of this whole exploitation has been the use of male prisoners to keep down wages of free women wage-earners by forced competition of men in prison held in industries from which their destructive competition has not yet been banished by the legislative or the boycotting activities of men as customers.

This policy serves to keep prisoners slaves after they finish their terms and leave prison walls. Because they can then get no other work but serve, in some cases, the same exploiters in factories run in communities in which there are prisons, men made for many years petticoats for women in the Moundsville Penitentiary and also under the shadow of that penitentiary, in concerns belonging to prison exploiters, where men remained again for years, the slaves of their poverty and their past record used unscrupulously against them.

Yours sincerely,

CC, FKP, NN

1. Laurence Todd (1882–1957), former secretary to Socialist Congressman Meyer London, was correspondent for the Federated Press from 1919 to 1933.

2. Matthew M. Neely (1874–1958) was a Virginia Democrat who served in the U.S. Senate from 1923 and 1929 and 1931 to 1941. Todd had apparently sent FK a flyer Neely wrote that described his suit against authorities responsible for contracts on prison labor between the Moundsville, West Virginia, prison and contractors in several states (FK, Brooklin, Me., to Leonard Cline, 24 July 1924, FKP, NN).

3. FK may have been referring either to Julian Leavitt (1878–1939), who had written on prison labor and chaired a special NCL committee on prison contract labor in 1912–1913, or to J. Lebovitz of the Library of Congress. Social reformer and sociologist Edmond Kelly (1851–1909) acknowledged Lebovitz in his preface to *Twentieth Century Socialism* (New York: Longmans, Green, and Co., 1910) for help with statistics. Rufus W. Weeks acknowledged FK for her editorial assistance in his introduction to Kelly's work (xiv-xv). George Herbert Putnam (1861–1955) was librarian of Congress from 1899 to 1939.

In her NCL report for 1912, FK had described how prison labor in the Moundsville prison undercut the prices for clothing manufactured with the NCL label, stating that the public was generally unaware of the "extent and sinister importance of the products thrown upon the market by public prisons and private places of incarceration supported wholly or partly by public funds" ("Report of the General Secretary," NCL, Thirteenth Annual Report [1912], 15–17, Box A7, NCL Records, DLC).

4. In 1900, Milton Frank Goodman (1872–1930) began the Reliance Manufacturing Company of Illinois, which made men's work clothing. In 1920 he served in the Chicago district of the ordnance department of the U.S. Army and in 1926 was identified as part of a "prison trust" that was smuggling prison-made garments to Canada (*NYT,* 21 October 1930, 25; Marquis, *Who's Who in Chicago,* 345; *Chicago Tribune:* 26 May 1920, 10; and 18 February 1926, 11). William P. Letchworth (1823–1910), who was appointed to the New York State Board of Charities in 1873, helped establish a state-supported colony near Rochester in 1892 for dependent disabled people, especially epileptics, who had previously been incarcerated in state prisons.

199. To Julia C. Lathrop

NATIONAL CONSUMERS' LEAGUE
156 FIFTH AVENUE
NEW YORK CITY

Naskeag, Brooklin,
Hancock Co., Maine
July 28, 1924

Dearest J. Lathrop:

It would be entertaining to see you look like a slacker, as you suggest in your letter of July 19th, received at last in this remote Maine village! Of course, the death of young Calvin Coolidge changes the aspect of everything in regard to delegations to his father, and I do not care to press the point at this time.[1]

You have doubtless seen Mr. Leonard Cline's reply to Mr. Eichelberger in the New Republic for July 23. If only the New Republic had a larger reading circle*!* So far Secretary [John] Weeks and Generals [Amos] Fries and Bo*w*ley have come into their own only in the columns of the New York World and the New Republic.[2] Mr. Cline writes me that he is preparing articles for some other periodicals. I do not know what they are. But none of that is enough. Yet I know no more than you do what can be done to Generals Fries and Bo*w*ley. It is horrifying to think of the latter being made a major general next year.

As to Mr. Chafee's inside information about Judge Rugg of the Supreme Court of Massachusetts,[3] all we can do is consider steps to be taken at the time, when we learn who compose the new third of the Senate.[4] My point is that we lost out in the case of Justices [Pierce] Butler and [George] Sutherland because we had not been thinking, and were not ready to oppose them in the Senate before the nominations actually took place and as soon as they were made public. I do not imagine that even our friends among the senators, for instance Shipstead, Brookhart, Magnus, etc. know the name of Rugg.[5]

Enough senators voted in 1918 for the District of Columbia minimum wage law to defeat the ratification of Judge Rugg, on the ground that his reactionary decision on the Massachusetts minimum wage law is a sufficient sample of what he would do on the Supreme bench to make him impossible (though they might not specify this reason for a vote against him*!*). But we do not know how many of those men will be elected this fall or are now holdovers. So we can only take the advice of Henry Muzy's little boy when he said "Now, Dad, think hard and guess quick."

I saw J.A. a fortnight ago when she had already been at Hull's Cove a full week, and I did not like her looks. She was weariness incarnate.

Yours devotedly
Florence Kelley

TLS, Lathrop Papers, IRoC

1. In her letter to FK, Lathrop had reflected on the recent LWV board meeting, where members had discussed the possibility of an interview with President Coolidge. She hoped that she "did not look at this distance like a slacker," but she "came away from the . . . meeting of the League of Women Voters Board in much doubt as to how to proceed regarding a delegation to the President," adding that no one at the LWV had heard from NWTUL member Ethel Smith yet about the topic (Lathrop, n.p., to FK, 19 July 1924, copy, Lathrop Papers, IRoC). Calvin Coolidge, Jr., had died of blood poisoning on 7 July 1924 (*NYT*, 8 July 1924, 1).

2. Leonard Cline wrote a two-part article, "The War on the Peace Seekers," for the *New Republic* (39 [2 and 9 July 1924]: 149–150, 184–185) in which he criticized the War Department's tactics in creating the spider web chart and raising false alarms of a Bolshevik threat from the women listed in it. In the *New Republic*'s 30 July 1924 issue (39:273–274), J. S. Eichelberger of Washington, D.C., editor of the *Woman Patriot*, accused Cline of inaccuracies in his articles, claims Cline refuted in his reply. In his 2 July article, Cline described Brigadier General Albert J. Bowley's (1875–1945) speech to the Columbus, Ohio, Chamber of Commerce on 7 March 1924. Bowley (who forbade press coverage of his speech) reportedly declared that the YWCA and various colleges were indoctrinating American youth with communism and called JA "the reddest of the reds" (Cline, "The War on the Peace Seekers," 150).

3. Zechariah Chafee, Jr. (1885–1957), civil libertarian and professor at Harvard Law School (1916–1956), wrote that if reelected, Coolidge would appoint Arthur P. Rugg (1862–1938) to the first vacancy on the Supreme Court. Rugg had just "pronounced the dubious decision against an important clause of the Mass. Minimum Wage Law," wrote Chafee (Zechariah Chafee, Jr., Sorrento, Me., to FK, 29 June [1924], "Plans to Curb Supreme Court: 1924," Box C41, NCL Records, DLC). Although Coolidge was reelected, Rugg was not appointed to the U.S. Supreme Court; he served as chief justice of the Massachusetts Supreme Court from 1911 to 1938.

4. 1924 was an election year for the U.S. Senate; Republicans increased their majority by four.

5. Minnesota Senator Henrik Shipstead (1881–1960) served in Congress as a member of the Farmer-Labor Party from 1923 to 1940 and as a Republican from 1940 to 1947. Iowa Senator Smith W. Brookhart (1869–1944) served as a Progressive Republican from 1922 to 1926 and as a Republican from 1927 to 1933. Minnesota Senator Magnus Johnson (1871–1936) served as a member of the Farmer-Labor Party from 1923 to 1925.

200. To John R. Commons

Naskeag, Brooklin,
Hancock Co., Maine
[after 2 August 1924]

Dear Dr. Commons:

Thank you very much for your letter of August 2nd.

The Women in Industry committee of the League of Women Voters, of which Dr. Mary R. Carroll of the Economics Department of Goucher College is chairman, resolved at its annual convention in Buffalo, in April, to cooperate with us in circulating a pamphlet on workmen's unemployment insurance, according to the Wisconsin idea, to be illustrated by a popular statement of the provisions of the Huber Bill.[1] Dr. Carroll is now in Europe.

The Committee was about to vote the proposal down when I said that I

John R. Commons, 1919.
Courtesy of the Wisconsin
Historical Society.

would ask you to prepare it. They wish to begin to circulate it in September. At our annual meeting in Washington in 1922 we discussed at the dinner the underlying principle of the Huber Bill. This leaflet is supposed to be a b c enlightenment for inquiring but uninstructed members of both leagues.

My conscience was bad about asking you to take on an extra job. So I gathered some printed matter for use in my vacation, and have written a few paragraphs of raw material which I send herewith for you to use, or change, or reject, as you see fit. I may have emphasized the wrong things.

I feel certain that the rank and file of our membership think of unemployment in terms primarily of unemployables and secondarily (the more instructed members), of placement and labor turnover. The twin ideas of mass unemployment as an incident of competitive industry, and the feasibility of placing the whole financial responsibility for it upon employers as a class will, I am sure, be as new to the majority of us as though they had never been discussed anywhere.

Mrs. McCarthy[2] of the Madison Legislative Reference Library sent me a valuable analysis so well popularized that I think, if it went in bodily, even our uninformed Eastern readers could not fail to understand it. But they would doubtless be more likely to read the pamphlet if the substance were in literary form instead of being quite so baldly in analysis form.

*Enclosed is a letter from Mr. Richard of the Amalgamated.[3] In another envelope I am sending some pamphlets with which you have doubtless long been acquainted. He sent them in reply to my request for the very latest word. They need not be returned.

In the same envelope is a model pamphlet of the League of Women Voters, sent by them as a guide for size and form of their share of the whole edition.[4] We can print any cover that we like.

When you are ready to go to press, please send one copy of the finished text and a draft for a cover-title-page for the Consumers' League to our office.

Yours sincerely and gratefully

As I have unfortunately spilled a bottle of ink over it, I am not sending it. Florence Kelley

CC, "Unemployment Compensation: Wisconsin Act, 1931," Box C49, NCL Records, DLC

Note: Handwritten additions not in FK's hand.

1. Among the problems the LWV considered at its annual convention in April 1924 was "improvement of conditions of women in industry" (*NYT*, 25 April 1924, 20). Mollie Ray Carroll (b. 1890) wrote *Labor and Politics: The Attitude of the American Federation of Labor towards Legislation and Politics* (1923). In May, the NCL Board of Directors authorized FK to work with the LWV in distributing a "condensed analysis" of the Huber unemployment insurance bill, which Commons had prepared in 1921 for the Wisconsin legislature's consideration. Commons agreed in his letter of 2 August to prepare such a pamphlet (Madison, Wisconsin, 2 August 1924, "Unemployment Compensation: Wisconsin Act, 1931, Box C49; NCL Board of Directors Minutes, 22 May 1924, 2–3, both in Box A2, NCL Records, DLC). The Huber bill called for unemployment payments of $1 a day for up to thirteen weeks to non-farm, non-public employees (See John R. Commons, "Prevention of Unemployment and the Huber Bill," paper read at the annual meeting of the National Civic Federation, January 21, 1922, and Allen B. Forsberg, "A Digest of the 1923 Huber Unemployment Insurance Bill," both in "Unemployment Compensation: Wisconsin Act, 1931," Box C49, NCL Records, DLC).
2. The Legislative Reference Library, where Lucile McCarthy worked, was part of the Wisconsin Free Library Commission (McCarthy to FK, 7 October 1924, "Unemployment Compensation: General File, 1924–1932," Box C48, NCL Records, DLC).
3. D. J. Richard was a member of the Amalgamated Clothing Workers in New York City (FK, Naskeag, Brooklin, Me., to D. J. Richard, 31 July 1924, "Plans to Curb Supreme Court: W. G. Rice Material, 1924," Box C41, NCL Records, DLC).
4. Throughout the fall, FK corresponded with Commons, Carroll, and Allen Forsberg of the University of Chicago regarding details of the pamphlet's publication. The revisions FK suggested in the final draft were incorporated in John R. Commons and Allen B. Forsberg, *Unemployment Compensation and Prevention* (Washington, D.C.: Distributed by the Committee on Women in Industry, National League of Women Voters, September 1924). The pamphlet credited the origin of unemployment compensation to the "Protocols of Peace" agreement forged by the Amalgamated in New York City that ended the garment industry strike of 1909–1910 (Unemployment Compensation: General File, 1924–1932", Box C48, NCL Records, DLC).

201. To Grace Abbott

Naskeag, Brooklin,
Hancock Co., Maine
August 11, 1924

Dear Grace:

Your letter of August 6th reached me Saturday night, and I was glad indeed to get it. The best news in it, of course, is of Mrs. Abbott's recovery.[1]

As to Justice [Arthur] Rugg, my point is that we ought to get his record, which I think we can very readily do through Felix [Frankfurter], and have it fresh in the minds of all our trusty friends in the Senate when the time comes.

The road to Coolidge inspires me with no more hope than yourself. What I fear is that the division in the Republican ranks may throw the election to Mr. Davis, and remembering his perfunctory argument in favor of the first child labor bill and his refusal to "have this brief Brandeised", I certainly do not feel reconciled to having the Morgan firm in the White House.[2]

It is all a horrid situation except the new participation of women in behalf of Senator La Follette. That is something new under the sun, and Mrs. Costigan's call to women seems to me to have her clear style and Mr. [Edward] Costigan's backing.[3] When I get too discouraged, I remember the Costigans.

I have authorized the use of my name as an elector for La Follette. Since, however, I cannot go to New York City to vote in the primaries this month, it may turn out that I am ineligible. I hope not. I have also promised Mrs. Costigan to work on her committee on womens' activities, but the only thing I have been able actually to do is to speak once in a church here to about thirty persons, with the result that the wife of Judge McCoy of the District of Columbia, who voted right in the District of Columbia Court on the D.C. minimum wage bill, is very much stirred up and has sent me with her visiting card a copy of a ditty "I Did Not Raise My Son To Be A Slacker", set to music composed by Mrs. Amos Fries![4]

Also I went with Mrs. [Mary Dana Hicks] Prang and my household yesterday to a very fine community church twenty-five miles away, where a protest meeting was held and a memorandum signed addressed to Secretary [John W.] Weeks, strongly recommending him to abandon Mobilization Day.[5] It was very good for the souls of the people present, whatever effect it may in the end have on Secretary Weeks.

If you have any suggestions,—Mrs. Costigan has hitherto sent me none,—for activities possible to one marooned in Maine in this critical month, please send them along forthwith. I have a stenographer on half time and am bursting with zeal, but have no ideas.

I am leaving here on August 29th, so do not waste any letters on the Maine post-office towards the end of the month.

Miss Addams and Emily Balch spent the night here Friday. J.A. looks haggard and worn, but has no bad symptoms and is full of energy, and has raised almost the last dollar necessary for paying for the W. I. L. convention and summer school. That seems to me a miracle.[6]

Yours devotedly,

CC, "General Correspondence: Abbott, Grace," Box B10, NCL Records, DLC

1. Abbott had written that her mother, Elizabeth Griffin Abbott (b. 1845), was gradually beginning to walk again (Grace Abbott, Washington, D.C., to FK, 6 August 1924, FKP, NN; see also Costin, *Two Sisters for Social Justice,* 4, 246).

2. Coolidge would probably be reelected, Abbott had written, but "with a Congress that will not support him" (Abbott to FK, 6 August 1924). Democrat presidential nominee John W. Davis, who since 1921 had served as counsel to J. P. Morgan and Company, had argued the case for the Keating-Owen Child Labor Act in *Hammer v. Dagenhart* in 1917. During the presidential campaign, Davis refused to take a stand on the child labor amendment (Harbaugh, *Lawyer's Lawyer,* 116–117, 208).

3. Mabel Costigan was named secretary of the Robert La Follette Presidential Campaign Committee on 25 July 1924 (*NYT,* 26 July 1924, 1, FKP). Abbott wrote that "Mrs. Costigan is busy all the time she can spare on [La Follette's] campaign and is enjoying it enormously" (Grace Abbott to FK, 6 August 1924, FKP, NN).

4. Kate Philbrick married Walter I. McCoy in October 1888. Elizabeth Wait married Amos A. Fries in 1899. "I Didn't Raise My Boy to Be a Slacker" was a song written by Gerald G. Lively in 1917 that responded to the pacifist popular song "I Didn't Raise My Boy to Be a Soldier."

5. Mobilization Day, a celebration of U.S. military preparedness, evoked considerable controversy, especially from peace advocates. It was carried out as planned on 12 September (*NYT:* 4 August 1924, 15; 1 September 1924, 12; and 13 September 1924, 1).

6.WILPF's fourth international congress was held in Washington, D.C., in May 1924. JA raised money to pay the travel expenses of delegates from war-torn Europe. See Sklar, Schüler, and Strasser, *Social Justice Feminists,* 287–300.

202. To Jane Addams

NATIONAL CONSUMERS' LEAGUE
156 FIFTH AVENUE
NEW YORK CITY

10-11-24

Dear J.A.

Evidently the flu which came when you left destroyed my last remaining wits. Certainly I never meant to give you that useless work! I <u>think</u> the enclosed is correct, and I know the money is in the bank.

The periodicals are promising cheeringly. Delineator and Designer, Pictorial and Good Housekeeping are definite.* [<u>inserted in margin:</u> *Their own people are doing their articles.] Also Today's Housewife, a queer sheet. Hopeful but not final are Farm and Fireside and McCall's and Ladies' Home Journal.[1] There is this vicious circle in the way. The periodical wishes to see the article. Also the writer wishes to know for <u>what</u> periodical. So it is hard to start the contributors.

The point to be covered is as follows:—Since the Amendment was sent to the States, the misrepresentations of the purpose and content of the amendment have increased in virulence and in circulation in the rural regions unbelievably.

They are circulated chiefly in magazines published here to sell goods to the farmers, such as Farm and Fireside, the Rural New Yorker etc.[2]

They sing Ellery Sedgwick's song about the girl who need never again wash dishes, when her mother asks her to help; the boy who cannot drive the cows to pasture until he is 18; and the ensuing ruin to their characters.[3]

The Rural New Yorker says we wish to nationalize the children à la Russe. Almost all agree that Congress will use all the power it gets thru the Amendment all the time. Otherwise why give it power to prohibit labor to the 18th birthday?

Of course, Congress believed, always, that it had all this new power, all the time. But it never attempted to do all these fool things with the power it turned out not to have.

Why this Fear of Congress?

Can it be because Congress had those [Teapot Dome] investigations?[4] And passed bills over the President's veto? Because it was independent and unafraid in a Congressional year?[5]

But you know far better than I do how to reach the rural and the small town mind. That is what this particular crusade is aimed at;—to reassure the legislators and their constituents that the Amendment is not a Law, and that Congress consists of men like themselves elected every two years, who can be kept at home if they pass a bad law; while the law is amended or repealed if it is found unfit. The Amendment is a means to the end of letting Congress help the children in backward states.

The evil thing is leaving the children without the equal protection of the law which they so urgently need![6]

Yours always
F.K.

ALS, JA Papers, PSC-P

1. FK was following up on her earlier request that JA write a 2,000-word article for one of the women's monthlies urging ratification of the child labor amendment (FK, New York, to JA, 27 September 1924, PSC-P). Besides *Good Housekeeping* (founded in 1885) and *Ladies Home Journal* (founded in 1883), FK refers to other women's journals: *The Delineator* (1873–1937) and its sister publication *Designer, Pictorial Review* (1899–1939), and *McCall's* (1873). All were very popular in the 1920s. *Farm and Fireside* (1877), published out of Springfield, Ohio, was a national agricultural journal (Mott, *A History of American Magazines,* 3:481, 4:337, 362, 536, 580; 5:125). FK had already written articles on behalf of the child labor amendment for *Woman's Home Companion* in January 1923 and *Good Housekeeping* in February 1923.

2. Legislatures in Georgia and Louisiana had already rejected the amendment. The *Rural New Yorker* was a popular nationally distributed agricultural journal (Mott, *A History of American Magazines,* 2:89; 3:152).

3. See Letter 193, FK to Ellery Sedgwick, 1 April 1924, above.

4. See Letter 195, FK to Herbert Bayard Swope, 27 May 1924, above.

5. Although the Republicans had majorities in both the Senate and the House, each body had enough Progressives to tilt the balance of power. The 68th Congress passed two bills over President Coolidge's veto: a bill to increase the salaries of postal workers and a bill to provide bonuses to World War I veterans. It also rejected Coolidge's nominee to the position of at-

torney general, Charles B. Warren, because it judged that he was too close to the sugar trust. This was the first time Congress had rejected a presidential nominee to a cabinet position in sixty years (Rogers, "First and Second Sessions of the Sixty-Eighth Congress," 761–762).

6. FK sent further terms for JA's proposed article for *McCall's* (FK, New York, to JA, 16 October 1924 and 17 October 1924, PSC-P), but JA never wrote the article (FK, New York, to Thomas J. Walsh, 31 December 1924, copy, "Child Labor Amendment: Ratification, 1922–1930, General File," Box C1, NCL Records, DLC).

203. To Frances Perkins[1]

[New York City]
December 4, 1924

Dear Frances:

Is there any living Democrat in this state, beside the Governor and the State Department of Labor, who is right on the Children's Amendment, and might be able to influence Herbert Bayard Swope and Walter Lippmann, or either of them?

The World has not yet adapted an editorial policy with regard to the amendment. At the end of a long interview with Walter yesterday he said that they would not adopt it without first having a conference with me. Walter, I feel certain, is a lost soul on this subject and will definitely have to be re-educated from A. to Z. Mr. Swope is so ill-informed that he told me night before last he did not see why a federal amendment was needed when the number of children, 10 to 13 inclusive, was shown in the 1920 census to be so trivial.

If the World, owned and edited by "liberal" Jews, stands with Cardinal O'Connell against the children it will make quick ratification in New York State

Frances Perkins, 1918. Courtesy of the Library of Congress, LC-USZ62-123275.

no easy task, and will have a horrible effect throughout the Southern textile states and in New England.[2] Cannot Mr. [Bernard] Shientag in some way bring the Governor to bear on Mr. Swope? Of course no one must know that I am inciting these activities. I have written Nelle, but I am leaving Mr. Shientag and the Governor to you.[3]

R.S.V.P. P.D.Q.![4]

Yours sincerely,

CC, "Child Labor Amendment: Ratification, 1922–1930, General File," Box C1, NCL Records, DLC

1. Governor Alfred E. Smith (1873–1944; governor of New York, 1918–1921, 1923–1928) appointed Perkins to the New York State Industrial Commission in 1919.

2. William Henry O'Connell (1859–1944), archbishop of Boston (1907–1944), was named a cardinal in 1911. He opposed the child labor amendment in part because he feared that compulsory education laws would lead to federal control over parents' choice of schools for their children (Abell, *American Catholicism and Social Action,* 225).

3. In her letter to Nelle Swartz (ca. 1882–1952), director of the New York State Bureau of Women in Industry (1919–1929), FK stated that she feared that the *New York World* would "go wrong editorially" about the federal child labor amendment unless Swartz and others wrote to Lippmann (*NYT,* 6 March 1952, 31; FK, New York, to Swartz, 4 December 1924, "Child Labor: Amendment: Ratification: General File, 1922–1930," Box C1, NCL Records, DLC).

4. In a lengthy editorial, the *New York World* cited improvements in laws restricting child labor on the state level and concluded that "it is not necessary and may be highly undesirable" to solve child labor violations by turning to "Congress and to the Federal Administration" (8 December 1924, 10). Perkins replied to FK that she had asked Governor Smith to pressure Swope and Lippmann without success: "[T]he editorial was out before we knew it. Ridiculous position, isn't it" (Perkins, New York, to FK, 11 December 1924, "Press and Periodicals: *New York World,* 1924–1930," Box B20, NCL Records, DLC).

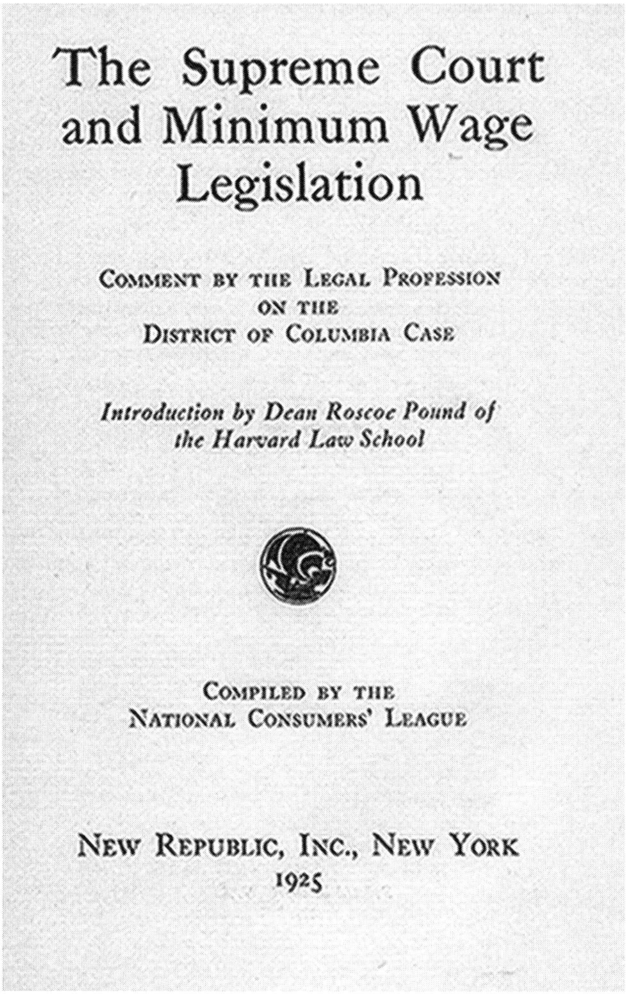
The Supreme Court and Minimum Wage Legislation

COMMENT BY THE LEGAL PROFESSION
ON THE
DISTRICT OF COLUMBIA CASE

Introduction by Dean Roscoe Pound of the Harvard Law School

COMPILED BY THE
NATIONAL CONSUMERS' LEAGUE

NEW REPUBLIC, INC., NEW YORK
1925

Cover of *The Supreme Court and Minimum Wage Legislation.* Courtesy of the New Republic.

7 1925 – 1927

"No Good Decision Seems Secure from Reversal"

INTRODUCTION

Florence Kelley's letters from the mid-1920s reflect the long-term perspective she gained by writing a series of five autobiographical articles for *Survey.* Weaving together exhortations about the present with recollections of the past, her memoir was initially undertaken to defend her patriotic identity against right-wing attacks. Her editor at *Survey* called it "waving the flag from the family tree!"[1] It proved a salutary exercise, giving her a deeply meaningful perspective on her long-term achievements that energized her for current struggles.

Many letters from this period have a retrospective tone. To John Fitch in 1925 she apologized for her behavior at their first meeting in 1907. "I was myself such a raging furnace, so consumed with burning indignation against everything that I saw, and smelt, and breathed, and loathed, that I had no appreciation whatever of the merit of your power of insight and passionless statement of undistorted facts."[2] Fitch responded sympathetically. "I did a great deal of raging at that time. . . whenever I got into conversation with smug and comfortable people who were quite satisfied that steel workers should work twelve hours a day and be discharged if they tried to join unions."[3]

Her historical perspective spurred her to judge some allies harshly. Ever since Gompers allied with businessmen in the National Civic Federation in 1900, she had known that she could not rely on him to advance her agenda, but now she vented her resentment. To Fitch she wondered whether "in the interest of the truth of history" someone ought to point out the failures of "the unfortunate policy of Mr. Gompers and his colleagues through nearly half a century in relation to women, non-English speaking immigrants, and Negroes." Wage earners in these groups were all injured by his policies, and the "proportion of scabs" was increased, while "militant unionism was prevented from reaching the dimensions which were needed," and "industrial unrest was prolonged and enlarged."[4]

Kelley's three legislative priorities in the mid-1920s—the child labor amendment, state laws to compensate industrial injuries suffered by child workers, and a minimum wage amendment—expressed her lifelong commitment to the unskilled wage earners the AFL tended to ignore. The child labor amendment and the minimum wage amendment were strategies that responded to the Supreme Court's rulings against congressional legislation. Children's compensation laws offered a new way to make employers responsible for the hidden costs of child labor.

Kelley's letters on behalf of the child labor amendment peppered politicians, state officials, journalists, and colleagues with vivid particulars about the actions she urged each of them to take in their own professional contexts.[5] To Lippmann (who needed educating on the issue) she presented the long history of the struggle against child labor since 1895.[6] To Charlotte Carr of the New York Department of Labor she denied that the amendment was dead, insisting that, like the suffragists, she was "prepared to fight 70 years" if necessary.[7] She devoted NCL resources to a petition drive in New York State, imitating Carrie Chapman Catt's strategy with the suffrage movement in that state. Kelley pointed out that "in a suffrage referendum in 1915, New York lost by a large majority; in 1917 suffrage was ratified by a large majority," adding that Catt attributed the rapid turnaround to her petition to the legislature with the signatures of over 1 million women in 1917.[8] Yet her fear of right-wing attacks meant that she did not announce the petition drive publicly.[9] She sought "100,000 good signatures and 1,000 sponsors, before we seek any publicity."[10] But by 1927, two years into the campaign, the petition drive had collected only 5,495 signatures, and her closest allies as well as the NCL board questioned her unshakable commitment to it.[11] When Grace Abbott asked her to give up the petitions and pay more attention to the urgent needs of the Children's Bureau, Kelley asked, "What alternative method of interesting any leading eastern state has anyone proposed?" Abbott replied, "I have to admit that no one has proposed any alternative method, and I have none."[12]

Kelley moved forward, but she found herself more and more alone in the vanguard of the movement against child labor. She urged Lillian Wald to follow her example and resign from the NCLC. She denounced their "mildewing observations" about the amendment and "our petition" and published criticisms of the Massachusetts Child Labor Committee's "obsolete" program, which had been "suitable in the first quarter of this century, but not now."[13]

Kelley blazed a trail by using the new workmen's compensation laws to collect statistics on injuries suffered by minors.[14] This gave her new ammunition to combat claims by the National Association of Manufacturers that the child labor problem was solved. In the spring of 1927, she explained to John Commons, "When we entered this field, ten months ago, my aim was to show, from the available public records, that the employment of minors below the age of 18 years is still very large, very widespread and very dangerous to them." But she was finding it difficult to locate data, and she asked if he had any students who could help her locate statistics about the number of child laborers injured in Wisconsin since its law changed in 1917 from double to triple compensation for children who were illegally employed. She thought that "[t]he effort to get facts and advertise them can act as a stimulus to State officials," who could publicize the extent of child labor and support the enactment of better laws.[15]

In the years following the *Adkins* decision, the NCL struggled to find an effective response. Minimum wage advocates watched two state minimum wage laws fall in 1925.[16] The topic of a federal minimum wage amendment came up once again, with NCL members from states with minimum wage boards advocating the strategy. One of the strongest such states was California, where Katherine Philips Edson ensured the effectiveness of her state's Industrial Welfare Commission, which the NCL had helped establish.[17] When Edson wired a telegram with a resolution that the NCL pursue a minimum wage amendment, the council voted not to support the measure despite Kelley's strong endorsement, preferring instead to endorse the Massachusetts-type minimum wage law, the weakest of all such statutes.[18] She accepted this decision partly because local advocates maintained state minimum wage laws despite the Adkins decision, John Commons's support of the revised Wisconsin law being an example.[19]

Also clamoring for her attention were ongoing issues related to Sheppard-Towner, the NWP, the NAACP, the Children's Bureau, and libelous right-wing attacks. Such attacks on women's organizations had changed the terms of debate. "The prestige of the women's organizations is badly shattered," Kelley wrote the editor of the *Woman Citizen,* "and this damage expresses itself hideously in the refusal of the U.S. Senate to appropriate funds . . . for the Sheppard-Towner act." Yet, ever optimistic, she hoped this vote could be reversed if "enough spade work" was done in the states and "the Progressives do enough smashing of the reactionaries in the election."[20]

Meanwhile, the NWP was scoring new victories. At a conference called by the Women's Bureau in January 1926, "[t]he Women's Party came like a pirate band attempting to sink a peaceful canal boat crew of Quakers."[21] They disrupted the proceedings and forced a motion that the bureau should compile and publish a comprehensive study on how protective labor legislation affected women workers. The motion specified that the bureau's head, Mary Anderson, should appoint an advisory board for the study that included a balance of advocates and opponents of protective labor legislation. Kelley's first reaction to this development was negative. She wrote her friend Katherine Edson of her sympathy for Anderson's position: "You can see what Hell on Earth that honest Swede is destined to experience in the next three years."[22] But after seeing a prepublication version of the study a year later, Kelley's opinion changed. She told Anderson enthusiastically that the study "may prove an epoch-maker!" It would "so illuminate the defects in our official records, both federal and state, concerning women in industry" that it might lead her and her colleagues to "bless the name of the justly accursed Woman's Party."[23]

Kelley looked for ways to build coalitions with the NAACP. She wrote Grace Abbott that she felt that the combination of the "Negro press" and "friendly white press" plus "the rest of our organizations and membership lists" could work together to defeat senators who had voted against the Dyer anti-lynching bill in upcoming elections. She asked Abbott to "send me a list of our villains, I will compare it with the N.A.A.C.P. list of their villains."[24] She also consolidated the coalition between the NCL and the NAACP by exposing the NWP's poor record on the voting rights of black women.[25] She deferred to the leadership of NAACP officers, asking them for pre-publication comments and suggestions on her race-related writings.[26]

Right-wing attacks became more aggressive in the summer of 1926. She wrote Paul Kellogg that "the fight against the Sheppard-Towner Act is vicious to the last degree." She told him that Delaware senator Thomas Bayard had read into the *Congressional Record* "thirty-five pages of the Woman Patriot's abusive misrepresentations, with me as the chief Villain Acting for Moscow!"[27] For advice about whether she should sue the *Woman Patriot* for libel, she turned to her friend, John Ryan, a valued ally in the minimum wage campaign of the 1910s, who by the 1920s was a professor and Catholic University and a leading social justice voice in the Catholic church in the United States. The suit would be in her name and the NCL's; it would be funded by the NCL. Yet even as she considered this strategy, she realized its futility, since "the Woman Patriot is merely a mask for the National Manufacturers' Association. . . . [The] Association would immediately create another agency to continue its vile work."[28]

Although she decided that the "foul nest" of the Woman Patriot was "too insane to be worth tackling," she nevertheless sought new advice about suing a year later when the Daughters of the American Revolution circulated what Kelley called their "slander-pamphlet,"[29] *The Common Enemy,* which accused pacifists, advocates of social justice, members of labor unions, and members of the women's movement of "boring from within" to abolish the U.S. government.[30] She wrote Jane Addams that "the time has come when there must be a libel suit to stop this endless and even more wide-spread sewage."[31] Yet the suit would have been located in Massachusetts, where the DAR had its headquarters, and the "reactionary" temper of the Massachusetts courts deterred her.[32]

Kelley was a perfect target for these attacks because she was a socialist. And indeed her understanding of her work—and the enemies it attracted—was shaped by the socialist critique of industrial capitalism that she had mastered in the 1880s. Without that analysis she would not have come so far and accomplished so much. When Carrie Chapman Catt asked her about her socialist beliefs, she did not deny them.[33] But also foundational to her achievements and her place in American politics were what she emphasized in her memoir—Quaker meetings, "the golden rule," and "Grandaunt Sarah."[34] Her privileged Philadelphia girlhood and her distinguished family heritage was crucial to her authority among her contemporaries, and right-wing attacks on her sought to dislodge that identity by calling her Mrs. Wischnewetzky. No wonder she fought back. And no wonder that her memoir of that Philadelphia girlhood was her best weapon.

Other retrospection in her letters of these years included a brief history of the consumers' label, an account to brother Albert of the "Spider Web" chart, and, inspired by the pending execution of Sacco and Vanzetti in 1927, her thoughts about the hanging of Chicago anarchists in 1887.[35] When Lillian Wald asked her to list the social achievements of the past forty years, she placed "votes for women" first and "the unparalleled and astounding progress of the Negro race" second. As outstanding failures she listed the Supreme Court vetoes of child labor and minimum wage laws, the delay of the federal child labor amendment, the absence of women in the U.S. Senate, and "the pitifully small number of women who are full professors in state universities and in colleges of the first rank."[36]

Responding to Wald about her hopes for the future, she listed the child labor amendment first, and second, "expansion of the settlement movement, each group being a center of hospitality for people and for ideas."[37] In other letters, she anticipated the future in her support for old age pensions and for the International Labour Organization and other forms of international cooperation.[38]

Although Kelley moved out of the Henry Street Settlement and into a small apartment in 1927, her relationship with Lillian Wald remained very close. That year she thanked Wald for the seasonal gifts of cherries, pears, Christmas tree, and "nighties."[39] She also remained close to Julia Lathrop, as did Ko, who had known her as a boy at Hull House. Mother and son decided to "divide" the photograph of Lathrop that she sent with a Christmas card; Kelley let Ko have it "part of the winter" and she took it to Maine in the summer. She admonished Lathrop, "You never act as if you knew how fond he and I are of you."[40]

When she took time to evaluate her own circumstances, Kelley's fundamental optimism always emerged. In the spring of 1927, she told her brother Albert, "After all, here I am at the helm of a powerful organization, enjoying life and planning a happy summer in Maine."[41] The press of work that summer prompted her to hire two secretaries at Seawest in Maine, "one compiling the next pamphlet of the League on legal deaths and mutilations of wage-earning children, and one on my everlasting reminiscences."[42] She worked with them on her porch, "watching the occasional small sloops and cats tilting their way in a heavy breeze."[43]

NOTES

1. Paul Kellogg to FK, 28 August 1926, FKP, NN
2. Letter 208, FK to John Fitch, 26 March 1925, below.
3. Fitch to FK, 28 March 1925, "General Correspondence: Fitch, John A.," Box B12, NCL Records, DLC.
4. Letter 208, FK to Fitch, 26 March 1925.
5. Letter 204, FK to Royal Copeland, 19 January 1925; and Letter 206, FK to Walter Lipp-

mann, 14 March 1925, both below. See also Letter 207, FK to Julia Lathrop, 20 March 1925; Letter 209, FK to Charlotte Carr, 28 April 1925; Letter 213, FK to James Hamilton, 24 May 1926; Letter 215, FK to Edward Keating, 22 July 1926; Letter 216, FK to Virginia Roderick, 24 July 1926; Letter 232, FK to Pauline Goldmark, 27 May 1927; Letter 237, FK to Robert La Follette, Jr., 20 August 1927; and Letter 239, FK to Walter Lippmann, 16 November 1927, all below.

6. Letter 239, FK to Lippmann, 16 November 1927.

7. Letter 209, FK to Carr, 28 April 1925.

8. "Minutes of the Board of Directors," 15 October 1925, 2, Box A2, NCL Records.

9.Letter 216, FK to Roderick, 24 July 1926, note 2; Letter 229, FK to Lillian Wald, 4 April 1927, note 3, both below.

10. Letter 232, FK to Goldmark, 27 May 1927.

11. NCL Board of Directors Minutes, 5 May 1927, 2, Box A2, NCL Records, DLC; Letter 232, FK to Goldmark, 27 May 1927; Letter 244, FK to Mabel Costigan, 30 June 1928, below.

12. Letter 232, FK to Goldmark, 27 May 1927.

13. Letter 229, FK to Wald, 4 April 1927.

14. Letter 209, FK to Carr, 28 April 1925; Letter 213, FK to James Hamilton, 24 May 1926, below.

15. Letter 228, FK to John Commons, 26 March 1927, below.

16. The Kansas supreme court overturned that state's law in *Topeka Laundry Co. v. Court of Industrial Relations,* and the U.S. Supreme Court overturned Arizona's law in *Murphy v. Sardell.*

17. "Minutes of the Morning Session of the Annual Meeting of the National Consumers' League, 20 November 1925," 8–10, Box A2, NCL Records.

18. Edson's telegram said "Please get endorsement of federal amendment. Have asked Pillsbury and other minimum wage friends to draft amendment which Senator Johnson will introduce and fight for. We in California hope for other help but if withheld we shall make the fight alone." Kelley told the council that she did not think that the resolution to support the Massachusetts-type law "would have been considered at all if the telegram had come before that meeting instead of after." "Minutes of the Morning Session of the Annual Meeting," 38–38; 9–10; Letter 210, FK to Katherine Philips Edson, 2 December 1925, below.

19. Letter 205, FK to John Commons, 26 February 1925, below.

20. Letter 216, FK to Roderick, 24 July 1926, below. See note 4 of this letter for the extension of Sheppard-Towner funding in 1926.

21. Letter 211, FK to Katherine Philips Edson, 28 January 1926, below.

22. Letter 211, FK to Edson, 28 January 1926.

23. Letter 219, FK to Mary Anderson, 10 December 1926, below.

24. Letter 223, FK to Grace Abbott, 21 January 1927, below.

25. Letter 226, FK to Arthur Spingarn, 8 February 1927, below.

26. Letter 226, FK to Spingarn, 8 February 1927.

27. Letter 217, FK to Paul Kellogg, 17 August 1926, below.

28. Letter 218, FK to John Ryan, 20 August 1926, below.

29. Letter 235, FK to JA, 20 July 1927, below.

30. [Key Men of America,] *The Common Enemy,* 3, 7–11; see also *NYT:* 1 April 1928, 3:1–2; and 1 July 1927, 24.

31. Letter 235, FK to JA, 20 July 1927. Pacifist JA had been a particular target of the DAR's attack; see *NYT,* 1 April 1928, 3:2.

32. Letter 237, FK to La Follette, 20 August 1927. This was probably a wise decision. In 1928, Mrs. Helen Brumley Baldwin, a DAR member from Boonton, New Jersey, sued Methodist minister Rev. William H. Bridge for libel when he wrote a letter to the editor of the local newspaper accusing her of "lying imputations" and "playing the communist game." The

minister, who was defended by an ACLU attorney, countersued. The judge ruled that there was no finding of libel in either case (*NYT*, 11 October 1928, 19).

33. See Letter 233, FK to Carrie Chapman Catt, 4 June 1927, below.

34. FK, *Notes of Sixty Years*, 24.

35. Letter 212, FK to Seward Simons, 20 March 1926; Letter 238, FK to AK, 17 September 1927; Letter 227, FK to Julia Lathrop, 22 March 1927, all below.

36. Letter 224, FK to Lillian Wald, 21 January 1927, below.

37. Letter 224, FK to Wald, 21 January 1927.

38. Letter 220, FK to JA, 1 January 1927; Letter 234, FK to Myrta Jones, 14 July 1927, both below.

39. Letter 224, FK to Lillian Wald, 21 January 1927.

40. Letter 227, FK to Julia Lathrop, 22 March 1927.

41. Letter 231, FK to AK, 24 May 1927, below.

42. Letter 235, FK to JA, 20 July 1927.

43. Letter 234, FK to Myrta Jones, 14 July 1927.

204. To Royal S. Copeland[1]

[New York City]
January 19, 1925

Hon. Royal S. Copeland,
Senate Office Building,
Washington, D.C.
My dear Senator Copeland:

Because the almost unanimous vote of the New York State Delegation in Congress for prompt reference of the federal child labor amendment to the legislatures for ratification is constantly overlooked in the public discussions here, I am venturing to write you about our disastrous New York State situation. I need not describe it to you.[2] I have no doubt that you know more about it in some respects than we do.

I am convinced that you can, at this moment, do more than any other citizen of the State to prevent further disaster on a national scale.

Is it not possible for you to make at an early date a speech which, when widely distributed throughout the country, may keep other states from following the misleading example of Governor Smith and Senator Wadsworth in attempting to use an extralegal referendum as a means of delay?[3]

There is widespread paralyzing fear among convinced advocates of the value of the referendum in general that (in opposing its application in Mr. Clayton's bill for a referendum of opinion on the child labor amendment),[4] they may be misinterpreted as opposing the principle.

You will be recognized as one who speaks with authority and without prejudice as [a] Senator from a state in which the referendum works well because it is wisely safeguarded by the State Constitution.

Herewith I send samples of leaflets that we are distributing in large quantities. You know, of course, the latest one,—"Truths and Half Truths about the Amendment".[5]

When we point with pride to the vote of the New York Delegation, we are told "But that was before the Massachusetts vote."[6] This is an important reason for an early speech from you to countervail this baleful Smith-Wadsworth co-operation.

Yours sincerely,

CC, "Child Labor Amendment: Ratification: General File, 1922–1930," Box C1, NCL Records, DLC

1. Royal Samuel Copeland (1868–1938) was a Democrat from New York who served in the U.S. Senate from 1923 to 1928; he was also a physician.

2. Opposition to the child labor amendment in New York came from businessmen, farmers, and the Catholic church. Opponents charged that the amendment was a communist plot, an infringement on state's rights, and an attempt to "nationalize America's children" by preventing them from performing housework for their parents (Felt, *Hostages of Fortune,* 198–205). Alfred E. Smith and U.S. senator James W. Wadsworth, Jr. (1877–1952; Republican, New York, 1915–1927) favored a popular referendum on the amendment because they believed the referendum would not pass.

Seeking support for the child labor amendment primarily from senators and representatives from agricultural states, FK turned to Senator Copeland reluctantly. In a letter to Grace Abbott, FK wrote: "I have no idea what would happen if Copeland came out for ratification. That is a personal fight between Copeland and Smith, and I have no confidence in either. I expect harm for the children from everything that either of them does" (FK to Grace Abbott, 15 January 1925, "General Correspondence: Abbott, Grace," Box B10, NCL Records, DLC).

3. Calling Wadsworth the "leader of all the reactionaries in the United States," FK opposed any delay to ratification because "whoever has the most money to buy the most space on the front page of the newspapers, and the most time on the most expensive radio stations, wins the referendum" (FK to Ada M. Schull, 7 January 1925, and FK to Mrs. Rouse, 7 January 1925, both in "Child Labor Amendment: Ratification: General File, 1922–1930," Box C1, NCL Records).

4. Probably New York Republican Walter F. Clayton (b. 1865), who served in the State Assembly from 1921 to 1925.

5. *Truths and Half-Truths about Child Labor* (Washington, D.C.: Organizations Associated for Ratification of the Child Labor Amendment, 1925).

6. Massachusetts voters had soundly defeated the child labor amendment in a referendum in November 1924 (Felt, *Hostages of Fortune,* 208).

205. To John R. Commons

[New York City]
February 26, 1925

Dear Dr. Commons:

I learn with deepest regret of Dean [Roscoe] Pound's final refusal to accep[t] the Presidency of the University of Wisconsin; then with comfort of the decision to delay the appeal of the Wisconsin minimum wage case to the Supreme Court at Washington, until there should be new legislation in Wisconsin.[1] I assume that this means some approximation to the Massachusetts law. While that law is very inferior to the District of Columbia and California statutes, it is so much better than nothing that I feel confident the Wisconsin decision is a wise one.

The news from California is,-

(a) That the minimum wage statute is restored to usefulness by the action of the State Supreme Court in throwing out Senator T. C. West's fraudulent case; but that

(b) He proceeded immediately, with the utmost impudence, to introduce a bill for the total repeal of the California statute. It seems unthinkable that he should be able to make any headway with this proposal,.and there has been no publicity about it since the first announcement about three weeks ago on the introduction of his bill.[2]

There seems to be little hope of our escaping a referendum in November (which would decide nothing, being extra-legal procedure) but would be held in all the confusion of the fight on Mayor Hylan, and could hardly be expected to do anything but complicate an already too-mixed situation.[3]

There was a superb hearing on Tuesday before the Joint Committee of both Houses of the legislature.[4] Such demonstrations, however, seem to have no effect whatever on our Wet Catholic Governor, and our Wet Protestant Senator Wadsworth, who together constitute the machine in this machine-ridden state.

I will send you more news as soon as we have any.[5]

Yours sincerely,

CC, "Correspondence: Commons, John R., 1924–1929," Box C40, NCL Records, DLC

1. The Wisconsin minimum wage law was struck down in federal court in January 1925 (NCL Board of Directors Minutes, 5 February 1925, 5, Box A2, NCL Records, DLC). Instead of appealing, John Commons and his students redrafted the law. The amended law included language about women's wages that Commons felt made it consistent with the *Adkins* decision (Commons to FK, Madison, 3 March 1925, "Minimum Wages: Correspondence [Florence Kelley]: Commons, John R., 1924–29," Box C40, NCL Records, DLC). Instead of the D.C. statute's reference to "the necessary cost of living to . . . women workers to maintain them in good health and to protect their morals," the Wisconsin law prohibited "oppressive wages," stating: "No wage paid or agreed to be paid by any employer to any adult female employee shall be oppressive. Any wage lower than a reasonable and adequate compensation for the services rendered shall be deemed oppressive and is hereby prohibited." Despite this change in the law's language, the Wisconsin Industrial Commission continued to regulate wages on a cost-of-living basis. This law prevailed until Congress passed the Fair Labor Standards Act in 1938 (Schmidt, "History of Labor Legislation in Wisconsin," 248, 251, 253–255, 1925 Wisconsin law quoted on page 248; Haferbecker, *Wisconsin Labor Laws*, 103).

2. Shortly after the *Adkins* decision, a suit was filed against the California Industrial Welfare Commission under the name of Miss Helen Gainer. The suit claimed that the state minimum wage for women ($16/week) deprived her of the opportunity of being hired for a job as a "learner" in a candy factory at $6/week. Gainer later said that she had no knowledge of this case or its facts and had signed a document she had not read that was prepared by

State senator T. C. West, who wanted to initiate a suit against the industrial commission. Although the case was based on West's deception of Gainer, it entered the California court system as a post-*Adkins* test of the constitutionality of the minimum wage law for 150,000 women workers. The NCL mobilized Frankfurter, Dewson, and Commons to write a strong defense of the California law, *State Minimum Wage Laws in Practice.* In January 1925, when West refused to drop the suit at Gainer's request, she changed attorneys and wrote to the chief justice of the supreme court of California repudiating the case (*Los Angeles Times:* 5 January 1925, 4 and 7 January 1925, 7; Judge W. A. Beasley to Roscoe Pound, 13 February 1925, "Wages and Hours: California Minimum Wage Case, 1924–25," Box C49, NCL Records, DLC). The California supreme court dismissed the case on 27 January 1925 (NCL Board of Directors Minutes, 5 February 1925, 5, Box A2, NCL Records, DLC).

3. Democrat John Francis Hylan (1868–1936) was the mayor of New York City from 1918 to 1925. Governor Al Smith and Tammany Hall, the machine of the Democratic Party, did not support Hylan for reelection in 1925.

4. FK was referring to the hearing on the child labor amendment at New York's Senate and Assembly judiciary committees on 24 February 1925, at which the president of the state federation of labor declared, "I can readily understand why the members of the State Chamber of Commerce are opposed to this amendment. The reason is that so many employers have become rich from child labor." Representatives of the Brooklyn Women's Club, the New York City Board of Trade, the New York State Chamber of Commerce, and the Roman Catholic Church spoke against the amendment at the hearing (*New York Herald Tribune,* 25 February 1925, 5; *NYT,* 25 February 1925, 2).

5. In March, the New York senate approved an autumn referendum on the child labor amendment, but Governor Smith postponed the measure for the rest of the 1925 session (Felt, *Hostages of Fortune,* 210). By 30 April 1925, only four states had approved the child labor amendment and sixteen states had voted it down (NCL Board of Directors Minutes, 30 April 1925, 1, Box A2, NCL Records, DLC).

206. To Walter Lippmann

[New York City]
March 14, 1925

Mr. Walter Lippmann,
50 Washington Mews,
New York City
PERSONAL
My dear Mr. Lippmann:

Why select poor old Sister Shumway for editorial scourging?[1] Are her lies more poisonous than those of Cardinal [William Henry] O'Connell and Mr. Louis Coolidge?[2] Or of Senators Reed and King?[3] She must, of course, be an annoying comrade in arms in the Battalion of Death, being so grotesque and fantastic! It would ***naturally*** be pleasanter for them if she were more discreetly silent and mildewing in her methods, like Cardinal Hayes let us say.[4]

After all, a Battalion cannot standardize manners within its ranks. That's not what it's there for. And besides she is too old to reform. If a whipping boy is needed, why not use Ralph Easly?[5]

And now comes this editorial.[6] Remembering the glittering brilliancy of your youth,[7] I ask myself, "Why trust the young workers to 48 ***more*** ~~***or more***~~ ~~***less***~~ obscure legislatures with all their repudiations of party pledges, in preference to one Congress with the eyes of the nation upon it, and the United States Supreme Court sitting under the same roof?"

Yours sincerely,

CC + AN, "Press and Periodicals: *New York World*, 1924–1940," Box B20, NCL Records, DLC

1. Representing the Brooklyn Women's Club at the joint hearing of New York's House and Senate judiciary committees on the child labor amendment on 24 February 1925, Florence Shumway had charged, "This amendment was known of in Soviet Russia before it ever was heard of in the United States. It is nothing but a move to nationalize the children of America" (*NYT*, 26 February 1925). On 26 February, an editorial in the *New York World* exposed the inaccuracy of Shumway's claim, explaining that the first sponsors of the child labor bill in 1906 were "not unwashed Bolsheviks but the conservative Theodore Roosevelt and the fastidious [Republican senator] Henry Cabot Lodge." The Keating-Owens bill had passed in 1916, "while Nicholas II still ruled Russia." Even though the *New York World* opposed a federal amendment because it believed that "the objects it seeks can better be achieved by the States," Lippman wrote that "it dislikes to see persons who sponsor it misrepresented as agents of Moscow" (*New York World*, 26 February 1925, 12).

2. Louis Coolidge (1861–1925), a Republican political publicist and former treasurer of United Shoe Manufacturing Company (1909–1924), belonged to the conservative group Sentinels of the Republic, which was founded in 1922 to oppose progressive reform efforts, including the child labor amendment (*NYT*, 20 August 1922).

3. Senators James A. Reed (1861–1944; Democrat, Missouri, 1911–1928) and William H. King (1863–1949; Democrat, Utah, 1917–1940) led the opposition in Congress to the amendment. In a letter to Robert Prentice of the National Republican Club on 7 January 1925, FK called Senator Reed "unbelievably abusive of the advocates of the federal amendment" on the Senate floor and charged that he had "made . . . many statements contrary to the facts of [the advocates'] personal history and intent" (FK to Robert Kelly Prentice, 7 January 1925, "Child Labor Amendment: Ratification: General File, 1922–1930," Box C1, NCL Records, DLC).

4. New York Catholics, including Patrick Joseph Hayes (1867–1938), archbishop of New York (1919–1938), opposed the child labor amendment.

5. Ralph M. Easley (1856–1939) organized the National Civic Federation, based in New York City, in 1900 to bring together businessmen and conservative labor leaders such as Samuel Gompers. Easley opposed the minimum wage, old age pensions, and unemployment insurance.

6. On 13 March, the *New York World* had published an editorial in favor of the New York legislature's decision to postpone a ratification vote (*New York World*, 13 March 1925, 8).

7. FK had known Lippmann since his days at Harvard, where he organized a chapter of the Intercollegiate Socialist Society in 1908. FK and Lippmann shared a podium at the second annual convention of the Intercollegiate Socialist Society in 1910 (Steel, *Walter Lippmann and the American Century*, 24–25; *NYT*, 30 December 1910, 7).

207. To Julia C. Lathrop

COPY

[New York City]
March 20, 1925

Dearest J. Lathrop:

Thanks for your cheering tidings about Messrs. Rosenwald, Hoover, etc. I shan't feel safe until the next appropriation bill is out of the way, lest our two Bureaus be beheaded before it comes up, or starved out after.[1]

I don't understand the President's mind well enough to comment on your interesting idea of having a delegation in behalf of all of the scientific work. The Bureau of Standards would, I suppose, loom large among the bureaus. I shall get all the light on Amherst that I can.[2]

You know, of course, that we are to have no action at Albany this year. This gives us nine months in which to work until the next meeting of the legislature.[3] Of course Governor [Alfred E.] Smith, however long he may remain in office, can always create distraction by recommending a preliminary reference to the people.

For New York and New Jersey, I think there is not a minute to lose before beginning work on a copy of Mrs. Catt's old petition.[4] It took two years and was laid before the legislature with 1,030,000 signatures, arranged according to townships up-State, voting precincts in the big cities, assembly and senatorial districts everywhere. Although the petition observed the forms of a plea, it was in reality an appalling warning to the legislature, even though women signers in those days were not yet voters.

It was voted today by the New York State Ratification Committee to defer the final form of working plan until we know the working plan of the O.A.R. This morning I advocated reorganization of the O.A.R. and removal to this town, with a change of name, and the adoption of a plan based on the bitter experiences of the last 90 days.[5] I had to leave the meeting and do not know exactly what was done in the end.

People cannot believe that there is nothing constructive to be had from the O.A.R. I myself had to go to Washington really to find that there is nobody there from whom any constructive suggestion for the states can be extracted. I have not yet recovered form the shock of Grace Abbott's telling me, a fortnight ago, that there was nothing to do but for all the states to grub along, every one on its own!

We cannot raise any money here, at the moment, for a comprehensive plan because every possible giver starts out with saying,—"What's the use of winning in New York if all the other states are going to continue to fail? What is the plan of the National Committee, or the Central Committee?" or whatever in their ignorance they call it.

CC, "General Correspondence: Lathrop, Julia C.," Box B15, NCL Records, DLC

1. Julius Rosenwald (1862–1932), a philanthropist who was a founding partner of Sears, Roebuck and Co., sponsored a program to build public schools, shops, and teachers' homes in areas of fifteen southern states with large populations of African Americans. In a letter written three days earlier, Lathrop had reassured FK that Rosenwald had repeatedly met with Secretary of Commerce Herbert Hoover (1874–1964) and that the success of his visits had convinced her that "the Childrens Bureau and the Womens Bureau will be saved" (Lathrop, Rockford, Ill., to FK, 17 March 1927, "General Correspondence: Lathrop, Julia C.," Box B15, NCL Records, DLC).

2. Lathrop had asked FK's advice about sending a delegation to President Coolidge to assure White House support for continued funding and to defend the "purely scientific standard of management" developed by the Children's Bureau, the Women's Bureau, and the Bureau of Labor Statistics. She asked FK for recommendations for a "safe & sound professor" who could help, perhaps someone at Amherst (Lathrop to FK, 17 March 1827).

3. The New York State Legislature ended its 1925 session on 27 March; the 1926 session began on 4 January (*New York Times:* 28 March 1925, 1; and 5 January 1926, 3).

4. FK was referring to her plan for a drive to secure signatures on a petition in support of ratifying the child labor amendment in New York State. With this strategy, she moved to the front of the campaign against child labor but also left her constituency behind. Her plan imitated Carrie Chapman Catt's well-publicized petition drive before the 1917 referendum that granted women the vote in New York State. Her goal was to get 1 million signatures to present to the state legislature, as Catt had done eight years earlier (Harper, *History of Woman Suffrage,* 6:465–468; Goldmark, *Impatient Crusader,* 118). For more about the petition campaign, see Letter 214, FK to John Lapp, 16 June 1926; Letter 229, FK to Lillian Wald, 4 April 1927; Letter 232, FK to Pauline Goldmark, 27 May 1927; and Letter 244, FK to Mabel Costigan, 30 June 1928, all below.)

5. The child labor amendment, which Congress passed in June 1924, went to forty-four state legislatures for ratification in January 1925. By 31 January 1925, three states had ratified (Arkansas, Arizona, and California) and eight states had rejected ratification (Massachusetts, Georgia, Louisiana, North Carolina, South Carolina, Kansas, Texas, and Oklahoma). Julia Lathrop remained optimistic: "A state once ratifying, ratifies for all time, but a state refusing to ratify may at any time reconsider" (*NYT,* 31 January 1925, 5).

The Organizations Associated for Ratification of the Child Labor Amendment included delegates from the PTA, the LWV, the NCL, the NWTUL, the AALL, and the NCLC (Lemons, *The Woman Citizen,* 146). FK was concerned about the leadership of the group and wrote Grace Abbott, "So far as people are concerned who live in New York the contribution of the O.A.R has been nil" (FK, New York, to Abbott, 27 March 1925, "General Correspondence: Abbott, Grace," Box B10, NCL Records, DLC). Ethel Smith wrote FK that although the staff of Organizations United worked "literally night and day" to prepare, print, and distribute literature to member organizations, they were not financially able to work for ratification in the states (Smith, Washington, D.C., to FK, 31 March 1925, "General Correspondence: Smith, Ethel," Box B21, NCL Records, DLC).

208. To John A. Fitch[1]

[New York City]
March 26, 1925

Mr. John A. Fitch,
New York School of Social Work,
105 East 22nd Street,
New York City
Dear Mr. Fitch:

I had the pleasure of two three-hour periods of reading your book without interruption, on the way to Wilmington and back this week. It was indeed an unusual pleasure.[2]

I remember well how impatient I used to be 18 long years ago, in Pittsburgh, because at that time your mind used to seem to me as clear and cool as a great French glass window.[3] I was myself such a raging furnace, so consumed with burning indignation against everything that I saw, and smelt, and breathed, and loathed, that I had no appreciation whatever of the merit of your power of insight and passionless statement of undistorted facts. Your book seems to me, in the light of all that has gone between 1907 and 1925, a priceless contribution in this difficult time.

Especially was I impressed by your candid statement that if the unions used spies their ethical standards would not be violated by so doing. And I was moved to wonder mildly whether we ought not sometime to have a statement, from the point of view of the public well-being, as to the unfortunate policy of Mr. Gompers and his colleagues through nearly half a century in relation to women, non-English speaking immigrants, and Negroes.[4] They were all injured by it. The proportion of scabs in our labor world was increased by it. The total volume of militant unionism was prevented from reaching the dimensions which were needed, and a persistent corroding cause of industrial unrest was prolonged and enlarged.

I can, of course, see excellent reasons for your not playing up this aspect of the labor movement, but sometime, in the interest of the truth of history it ought to be done. Don't you agree with me as to this?[5]

Yours sincerely,

CC, "General Correspondence: Fitch, John A.," Box B12, NCL Records, DLC

1. John A. Fitch (1881–1959) had been taught political science at the University of Wisconsin by John R. Commons. From 1917 to 1946, he taught labor relations at the New York School of Social Work.
2. John A. Fitch, *The Causes of Industrial Unrest* (New York: Harper and Bros., 1924).
3. In 1907, FK and John Fitch were both working on the Pittsburgh Survey. Fitch's publication for the survey was titled *The Steel Workers* (New York: Charities Publication Committee,

1910). For FK's participation, see Letter 97, FK to NK, 6 July 1907; Letter 98, FK to NK, 25 August 1907; and Letter 99, FK to Lillian Wald, 11 September 1907; all above.

4. As leader of the AFL, Samuel Gompers "usually ignored unskilled workers to guarantee continued benefits for craft unionists," opposed the industrial unionism promoted by Eugene Debs, often opposed protective labor laws for women, and allowed Jim Crow unionism to continue (Fink, *Biographical Dictionary of American Labor Leaders,* 129–130).

5. Fitch agreed with FK that a "thorough examination should be made of [Gompers's] policies by a friendly and truthful reporter." But Fitch objected to her memory of him as cool in 1907, insisting that "I did a great deal of raging at that time, in fact, I came very near to developing a permanent stutter on account of the jam of words that rushed to the surface whenever I got into conversation with smug and comfortable people who were quite satisfied that steel workers should work twelve hours a day and be discharged if they tried to join unions" (Fitch, New York, to FK, 28 March 1925, "General Correspondence: Fitch, John A.," Box B12, NCL Records, DLC).

209. To Charlotte E. Carr[1]

[New York City]
April 28, 1925

Miss Charlotte E. Carr,
New York State Department of Labor,
124 East 28th Street,
New York City
My dear Miss Carr:

Thank you very much for your enlightening letter. I did not realize that Miss [Nelle] Swartz had already sailed or I should have written to you direct.

I do not know that I made it clear in my letter why we consider this enquiry so exceedingly important at this time.[2] The National Consumers' League does not for a moment consider that the federal child labor amendment is dead. On the contrary, we are prepared to fight 70 years, so to speak, as the suffragists did for the validity of that indispensably necessary amendment.

The need for fresh information throughout the fight will increase as victory approaches, because the Manufacturers Association is now taking these interesting steps:[3] it announces that,-

(1) The Amendment is dead;

(2) The Association has removed the need for it by admirable state laws which it has had passed where needed;

(3) There is no considerable number of children now working for their living;

(4) The Association has provided for the enactment of any future child labor laws that may be needed;

(5) The census figures for 1920 are obsolete because of the good work carried through since then by the Manufacturers Association in its state legislative campaigns.

Silly as all this is, there are unhappily voting citizens only too eager to swallow it whole. Under the circumstances the studies of your Bureau as to the compensated children, and the more recent one as to the effects of industry on children, are worth their weight in diamonds.

I am constantly in my correspondence suggesting to the officers of other states that similar studies should be made, especially a compensation study wherever there is a compensation law. It is by such careful presentation of facts that, in the end, the National Manufacturers Association—the modern Herod[4]—will be defeated. I know of no other source of hope so promising as this.[5]

Yours sincerely,

CC, "Compensation for Injuries: General File, 1922–1933," Box C2, NCL Records, DLC

1. Charlotte E. Carr (1890–1956) was then the acting director of the Bureau of Women in Industry in New York's Department of Labor. Later in 1925, she was appointed chief of the new Bureau of Women and Children in Pennsylvania's Department of Labor and Industry. She directed Hull House from 1937 to 1943.

2. Earlier in April, Carr had written to tell FK that the New York State Department of Labor was developing a study to examine the effects of the state's double compensation law for children under eighteen employed in industry. The state was planning to visit each injured child worker who was receiving double compensation to determine if child laborers lacked incentive to return to work when compensation payments exceeded their earnings as workers. New York State was considering handling double compensation cases like lump sum payments with a board that would decide the merits of each case and "whether or not the money shall be given out weekly or retained for the claimant's use at a later date" (Carr, Albany, N.Y., to FK, 21 April [1925], "Compensation for Injuries: General File, 1922–1933," Box C2, NCL Records, DLC). By 1925, forty-three of the forty-eight states had workmen's compensation laws, but only three states—New York, New Jersey, and Wisconsin—had double compensation laws that required employers to pay children injured at work double the rate of workmen's compensation. New York State's double compensation law was passed in 1923 (*NYT:* 29 October 1928, 8, and 14 June 1927, 26).

3. In April 1925, the National Committee for the Rejection of the Twentieth Amendment published the pamphlet *Why the Child Labor Amendment Failed* (Washington, D.C.), by James Emery (Box 13, Papers of the National Association of Manufacturers, Hagley Library, cited in Wilson, *The Women's Joint Congressional Committee,* 209n73).

4. Searching for the newborn Jesus, King Herod of Judea "slew all the children that were in Bethlehem . . . from two years old and under"; Matthew 2:1–23.

5. In June, Carr reported to FK that no statistical evidence was available on the effect of the double compensation law (Carr, Albany, N.Y., to FK, 5 June 1925, "Compensation for Injuries: General File, 1922–1933," Box C2, NCL Records, DLC).

210. To Katherine Philips Edson

NATIONAL CONSUMERS' LEAGUE
156 FIFTH AVENUE, ROOM 1129
NEW YORK CITY

December 2, 1925

Mrs. Katherine Philips Edson,
Industrial Welfare Commission,
620 State Building,
San Francisco, California
Dear Mrs. Edson:

I write in deep dismay from which I have not been able to recover since our annual meeting. Your telegram was read, but not one vote or voice could be found for approving an amendment the text of which was not before the meeting.[1]

The meeting was strongly and actively opposed to a federal minimum wage amendment, believing that:

(a) It would make no progress at this time, certainly east of the Mississippi, and probably nowhere except in the four states which have ratified the child labor amendment;

(b) The introduction of a minimum wage amendment now would hinder ratification of the child labor amendment and give considerable strength to the infamous Wadsworth-Garrett measure.[2]

For these reasons they adopted the enclosed resolution.[3]

The bad form of the resolution suggests the long struggle to prevent its being even worse.[4] The presiding officer was determined that we should be actively opposed to any amendment, and motions to that effect were introduced. ***Professor John R. Commons, President of the League, was most unhappily not presiding, but a man from Rhode Island,[5] where they have never had a minimum wage law!***

Personally, I have been publicly and privately in favor of a federal minimum wage amendment since April 10, 1923; but the experiences of the past year with the child labor amendment have left me in a minority which has constantly shrunk.

The enclosed letter from Estelle Lauder, Secretary of the Consumers' League of Eastern Pennsylvania, states correctly the action that was taken ***at our annual meeting.***

Yours sincerely, a***nd in deep mourning over Justice Holmes surrender to tradition***[6]
Florence Kelley

TLS, Edson Papers, CLU-SC

Enc: A. Estelle Lauder to FK, 30 November 1925, Philadelphia

1. At the NCL annual meeting on 19 November 1925 in Boston, FK read a telegram from Edson that requested NCL endorsement for a possible constitutional amendment on a minimum wage to be introduced by Senator Hiram Johnson (Republican, California, 1917–1946). The NCL Council passed a resolution to refer the matter to the Board of Directors for consideration (NCL Council Minutes, 19 November 1925, 3, Box A2, NCL Records, DLC).

2. On 8 December, Senator James Wadsworth and Representative Finis James Garrett (1875–1956; Democrat, Tennessee, 1905–1928) introduced a joint resolution that attempted

to redefine how amendments were made to the U.S. Constitution. Directed at stopping the child labor amendment, the Wadsworth-Garrett amendment would have allowed proposed amendments to be "forever killed" if 25 percent of state legislatures rejected it. It specified that legislatures could reject an amendment at any time, but in order to ratify an amendment a state legislature would have to wait until a new legislature was installed in the next state election (69th Cong., 1st session, *Cong. Rec.*, 8 December 1925, 455, 486, 7203). FK encouraged members of the Board of Directors to write to members of the House Judiciary Committee to protest the proposed amendment and provided a list of their names for distribution ("Secretary's Report," NCL Directors Minutes, 18 February 1926, 3, Box A2, NCL Records, DLC). Congress did not pass the Wadsworth-Garrett measure.

3. FK enclosed a letter from Estelle Lauder, research secretary of the CL of Eastern Pennsylvania, that described Lauder's unsuccessful effort to gain council support for Edson's plea for an amendment (Lauder to FK, 30 November 1925, enc.).

4. The resolution stated, "Whereas, There is increasing evidence that women's wages in many occupations are too low to maintain them in health, and Whereas, Minimum wage legislation has proved to be most efficacious in meeting the problem, Be it Resolved, That the National Consumers' League continue to work in behalf of minimum wage legislation." This resolution pleased FK because it avoided supporting the voluntary Massachusetts model of minimum wage legislation, which the Board of Directors had endorsed in October (NCL Board of Directors Minutes, 15 October 1925, 4, Box A2, NCL Records, DLC).

5. Theodore Pierce, president of the CL of Rhode Island, chaired the meeting (NCL Council Minutes, 19 November 1925, Box A2, NCL Records, DLC).

6. The dissenting opinions of Oliver Wendell Holmes, Jr., which often supported FK's agenda, included those in *Lochner v. New York* (1904) and *Adkins v. Children's Hospital* (1923). His *Adkins* dissent, which supported the constitutionality of minimum wage legislation for women, concluded, "When so many intelligent persons, who have studied the matter more than any of us can, have thought that the means are effective and are worth the price, it seems to me impossible to deny that the belief reasonably may be held by reasonable men" (Lief, *The Dissenting Opinions of Mr. Justice Holmes,* 4, 21). However, on 19 October, in *Murphy v. Sardell,* Holmes joined the majority in upholding a lower court's decision nullifying the Arizona minimum wage law. He asked that the decision include his statement that his "concurrence is solely upon the ground that he regards himself bound by the decision in *Adkins v. Children's Hospital*" (*NYT,* 20 October 1925, 16; and White, *Justice Oliver Wendell Holmes,* 396–397, 570).

211. To Katherine Philips Edson

NATIONAL CONSUMERS' LEAGUE
156 FIFTH AVENUE, ROOM 1129
NEW YORK CITY

January 28, 1926

Dear Mrs. Edson:

We were all heartbroken over your absence from Washington which we understand was because of illness. I hope you have made a quick and complete recovery.[1]

It would be much better if that Conference had never been held, but since it was held we needed you badly.[2] The Women's Party came like a pirate band

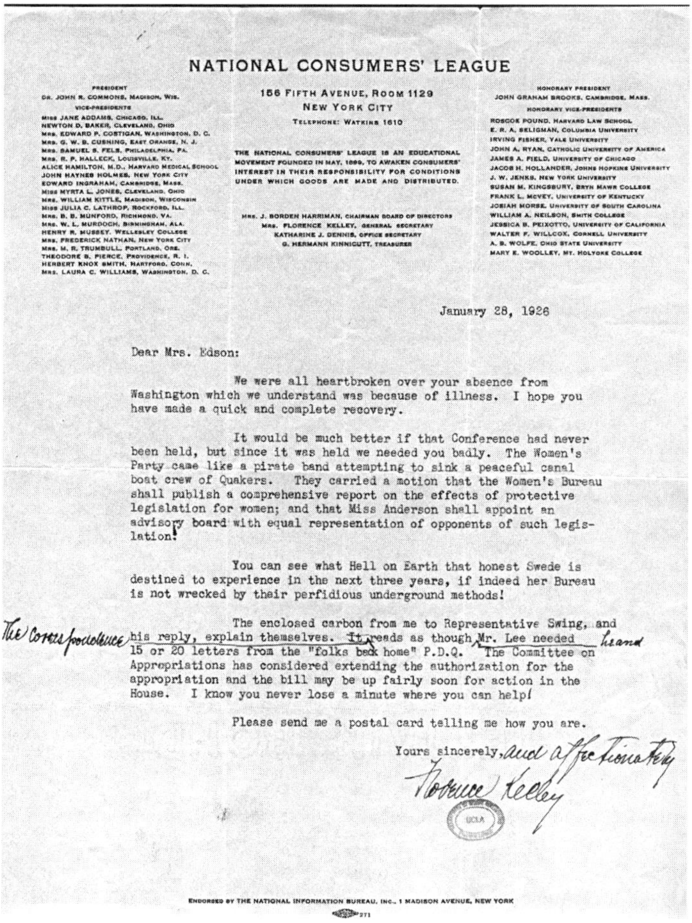

NATIONAL CONSUMERS' LEAGUE

PRESIDENT
DR. JOHN R. COMMONS, MADISON, WIS.
VICE-PRESIDENTS
MISS JANE ADDAMS, CHICAGO, ILL.
NEWTON D. BAKER, CLEVELAND, OHIO
MRS. EDWARD P. COSTIGAN, WASHINGTON, D. C.
MRS. G. W. B. CUSHING, EAST ORANGE, N. J.
MRS. SAMUEL S. FELS, PHILADELPHIA, PA.
MRS. R. P. HALLECK, LOUISVILLE, KY.
ALICE HAMILTON, M.D., HARVARD MEDICAL SCHOOL
JOHN HAYNES HOLMES, NEW YORK CITY
EDWARD INGRAHAM, CAMBRIDGE, MASS.
MISS MYRTA L. JONES, CLEVELAND, OHIO
MRS. WILLIAM KITTLE, MADISON, WISCONSIN
MISS JULIA C. LATHROP, ROCKFORD, ILL.
MRS. B. B. MUNFORD, RICHMOND, VA.
MRS. W. L. MURDOCH, BIRMINGHAM, ALA.
HENRY R. MUSSEY, WELLESLEY COLLEGE
MRS. FREDERICK NATHAN, NEW YORK CITY
MRS. M. R. TRUMBULL, PORTLAND, ORE.
THEODORE B. PIERCE, PROVIDENCE, R. I.
HERBERT KNOX SMITH, HARTFORD, CONN.
MRS. LAURA C. WILLIAMS, WASHINGTON, D. C.

156 FIFTH AVENUE, ROOM 1129
NEW YORK CITY
TELEPHONE: WATKINS 1610

THE NATIONAL CONSUMERS' LEAGUE IS AN EDUCATIONAL MOVEMENT FOUNDED IN MAY, 1899, TO AWAKEN CONSUMERS' INTEREST IN THEIR RESPONSIBILITY FOR CONDITIONS UNDER WHICH GOODS ARE MADE AND DISTRIBUTED.

MRS. J. BORDEN HARRIMAN, CHAIRMAN BOARD OF DIRECTORS
MRS. FLORENCE KELLEY, GENERAL SECRETARY
KATHARINE J. DENNIS, OFFICE SECRETARY
G. HERMANN KINNICUTT, TREASURER

HONORARY PRESIDENT
JOHN GRAHAM BROOKS, CAMBRIDGE, MASS.
HONORARY VICE-PRESIDENTS
ROSCOE POUND, HARVARD LAW SCHOOL
E. R. A. SELIGMAN, COLUMBIA UNIVERSITY
IRVING FISHER, YALE UNIVERSITY
JOHN A. RYAN, CATHOLIC UNIVERSITY OF AMERICA
JAMES A. FIELD, UNIVERSITY OF CHICAGO
JACOB H. HOLLANDER, JOHNS HOPKINS UNIVERSITY
J. W. JENKS, NEW YORK UNIVERSITY
SUSAN M. KINGSBURY, BRYN MAWR COLLEGE
FRANK L. MCVEY, UNIVERSITY OF KENTUCKY
JOSIAH MORSE, UNIVERSITY OF SOUTH CAROLINA
WILLIAM A. NEILSON, SMITH COLLEGE
JESSICA B. PEIXOTTO, UNIVERSITY OF CALIFORNIA
WALTER F. WILLCOX, CORNELL UNIVERSITY
A. B. WOLFE, OHIO STATE UNIVERSITY
MARY E. WOOLLEY, MT. HOLYOKE COLLEGE

January 28, 1926

Dear Mrs. Edson:

We were all heartbroken over your absence from Washington which we understand was because of illness. I hope you have made a quick and complete recovery.

It would be much better if that Conference had never been held, but since it was held we needed you badly. The Women's Party came like a pirate band attempting to sink a peaceful canal boat crew of Quakers. They carried a motion that the Women's Bureau shall publish a comprehensive report on the effects of protective legislation for women; and that Miss Anderson shall appoint an advisory board with equal representation of opponents of such legislation!

You can see what Hell on Earth that honest Swede is destined to experience in the next three years, if indeed her Bureau is not wrecked by their perfidious underground methods!

The enclosed carbon from me to Representative Swing, and his reply, explain themselves. ~~It~~ The Correspondence reads as though he and Mr. Lee needed 15 or 20 letters from the "folks back home" P.D.Q. The Committee on Appropriations has considered extending the authorization for the appropriation and the bill may be up fairly soon for action in the House. I know you never lose a minute where you can help!

Please send me a postal card telling me how you are.

Yours sincerely, and affectionately
Florence Kelley

ENDORSED BY THE NATIONAL INFORMATION BUREAU, INC., 1 MADISON AVENUE, NEW YORK
271

Florence Kelley to Katherine Philips Edson, 28 January 1926. Courtesy of the Katherine Philips Edson Papers, 1870–1933, Department of Special Collections, UCLA Library.

attempting to sink a peaceful canal boat crew of Quakers. They carried a motion that the Women's Bureau shall publish a comprehensive report on the effects of protective legislation for women; and that Miss Anderson shall appoint an advisory board with equal representation of opponents of such legislation![3]

You can see what Hell on Earth that honest Swede is destined to experience in the next three years, if indeed her Bureau is not wrecked by their perfidious underground methods![4]

The enclosed carbon from me to Representative Swing, and his reply, explain themselves. ~~It~~ ***The correspondence*** reads as though ***he and*** Mr. Lee needed 15 or 20 letters from the "folks back home" P.D.Q.[5] The Committee on Appropriations has considered extending the authorization for the appropriation and the bill may be up fairly soon for action in the House. I know you never lose a minute where you can help***!***

Please send me a postal card telling me how you are.

Yours sincerely, ***and affectionately***
Florence Kelley

TLS, Edson Papers, CLU-SC

1. For the events that transpired at the NCL annual meeting that Edson was not able to attend, see Letter 210, FK to Katherine Philips Edson, 2 December 1925, above.

2. On 18–22 January 1926, women representing 107 national organizations attended the Second Women's Industrial Conference sponsored by the Women's Bureau in Washington, D.C. Delegates discussed industrial and trade union relations, working conditions and health problems, and the actions of state and federal governments to help women wage earners ("The Second Women's Industrial Conference and the Assaults upon It," Document 28 in Sklar with Procita and Segal, "Who Won the Debate over the Equal Rights Amendment in the 1920s?").

3. Mary Anderson (1872–1964), a native of Sweden, had previously worked as an organizer for the NWTUL (1911–1920). From 1920 to 1944, she directed the Women's Bureau. Anderson deliberately omitted a discussion of minimum wage legislation from the program to avoid attacks on the policy (Anderson, [Washington, D.C.], to FK, 21 November 1925, copy, WTUL Papers, MCR-S). Delegates from the NWP disrupted the first session of the conference and demanded with a "chaos of voices, cheers, and hisses" that the issue of "Equal Rights in industry" be placed on the program (*NYT*, 20 January 1926, 27). After an extra session was added, a compromise resolution was passed requiring the Women's Bureau to conduct an extensive study to determine the effects of protective legislation on women and to establish an advisory committee with "equal representation of both sides of the controversy over special legislation for women" (Black, "Equal Rights at the Industrial Conference").

4. Members of the advisory committee, which included three proponents of protective labor legislation, three members of the NWP, and a three-member Technical Consulting Committee consisting of the director of industrial studies of a well-known philanthropy, a former U.S. commissioner of labor, and an engineer, could not agree how to study the effects of labor legislation on women workers. The three opponents of protective labor legislation wanted to hold hearings and call witnesses, while the three proponents wanted to use standard scientific methods the Women's Bureau had been using for its publications. Members of the Technical Consulting Committee pointed out that at hearings previously held in New York and Illinois, employers had paid the expenses of women workers to testify against protective legislation. The conflict over methods could not be resolved, and Anderson disbanded the committee, noting that it was a "purely unofficial body" and had "fulfilled its function of advising on the scope of the study." The study proceeded with "accepted methods of scientific investigation" and was published as Winslow, *Effects of Labor Legislation on the Employment Opportunities of Women* ("The General Welfare"; Lemons, *The Woman Citizen,* 192–195). Anderson later wrote that this report used "almost the entire staff and nearly the whole appropriation of the Women's Bureau for about two years" (Anderson, *Woman at Work,* 170). She later told FK that she regretted that they "had considerable difficulty getting evidence of the extent and type of opposition to the various laws," which made it "seem as though the enactment of special legislation had been achieved without very great opposition" (Anderson, Washington, D.C., to FK, 17 December 1926, "General Correspondence, Anderson, Mary," Box B10, NCL Records, DLC).

5. In January, FK sent a letter to every U.S. senator and representative to solicit their support for renewed Sheppard-Towner appropriations. By 27 January, FK had received thirty-eight responses. FK forwarded the responses of uncooperative members of Congress to personal friends from their home states to encourage them to pressure them to support the bill (FK to Mabel Costigan, 27 January 1926, "Sheppard-Towner Act: Correspondence, 1922–1931," Box C43, NCL Records, DLC). FK was hoping that Edson could influence Congressman Philip D. Swing (1884–1963; Republican, California, 1921–1932). Gordon Lee (1859–1927; U.S. congressman, Democrat, Georgia, 1905–1927) was a member of the House Appropriations Committee (69th Cong., 1st sess., *Cong Rec.*, 391).

212. To Seward C. Simons

[New York City]
March 20, 1926

Mr. Seward C. Simons,
Los Angeles Chamber of Commerce,
1151 South Broadway,
Los Angeles, California
My dear Mr. Simons:

I am glad to tell you our relation to labels.[1]

We have been an incorporated organization with headquarters here in New York since 1899. Our first activity was the creation of a label to be used by manufacturers of stitched white cotton underwear for women. This industry was selected because of the sweatshop conditions under which it was very largely conducted, the starvation wages and slavishly excessive hours of labor under which women and very young girls were employed by thousands.

Our label never guaranteed anything. We set up four standards and said that the employers listed by us and authorized by us to use our label, so far as we were able to learn, more nearly than any other employers approached complete maintenance of these standards in their factories:-

1. All work was done on the premises and no goods were sent out for any process;
2. The working day did not exceed 10 hours, and there was no nightwork;
3. Children below the age of 16 years were not employed;
4. The labor laws of the state were obeyed.

We could never go into the matter of wages, for lack of minimum wage legislation, and because state bureaus of labor statistics either did not exist or had no adequate equipment for giving comprehensive, trustworthy information concerning wages.

We announced to the trade unions that we had no intention of competing with any label that they might desire to establish, but would withdraw from the field whenever they could afford convincing evidence of organization in the needle trades capable of backing a trustworthy label.

This condition arose during the war and we abandoned our label. For several years there was no label in the needle industries producing garments for women. In 1925, however, the Ladies International Garment Workers Union put on the market a label which is immeasurably stronger than ours ever was or could have hoped to be. The Prosanis Label we are endorsing unqualifiedly.[2] It has as its foundation the Joint Board of Sanitary Control of a vast and powerful trade union, embracing ***virtually*** all the employers in ***this branch of***[3] the industry in this great centre of production, and every branch of employees, united by the Joint Board which safeguards the health of purchasers.

It is our belief that the creation of this label is the longest step forward in the needle trades taken in this or any other country, at this or any other time.

The bulletins of the various state and local Leagues recommend this label, our speakers advocate it, we take part in expositions at which it is exhibited, we buy the products that carry it, and are open to suggestions as to other possible methods of effective help.

I have answered your letter with the utmost candor. In return I shall be glad of a frank and comprehensive statement of the attitude of the Los Angeles Chamber of Commerce with regard to the use of Labels by trade unions, and ***other*** organizations.[4]

Yours very truly,

CC, "Consumers Label and Labeling: Prosanis Label," Box C4, NCL Records, DLC

Note: Handwritten additions not in FK's hand.

1. Simons, manager of the Domestic Trade Department of the Los Angeles Chamber of Commerce and son of a Cornell friend of FK, had requested information about the NCL's experience with garment labels (Seward C. Simons, Los Angeles, to FK, 5 March 1926, "Consumers Label and Labeling: Prosanis Label," Box C4, NCL Records, DLC).

2. Organized in 1910, New York State's Joint Board of Sanitary Control inspected and rated the sanitation of places that produced women's clothing. Only those establishments that received the Joint Board's A or B grade could use the Prosanis label in women's garments. First appearing on women's cloaks, skirts, and dresses in 1925, the label also signified that the clothing was produced in union shops with good wage agreements with its workers, not in sweatshops (NCL Council Minutes, 20 November 1925, 7–9, Box A7, NCL Records, DLC).

3. The words "virtually" and "in this branch of" were inserted above the line by hand after the letter was typed.

4. Simons replied that the labels were unnecessary in California because of strict state laws regarding the eight-hour workday, sanitary conditions, and child labor. He opposed the NCL's promotion of a union label because it would discriminate against California manufacturers with open shops. Simons argued that if the NCL urged the adoption of the Prosanis label in California, it "would be a step in retrogression and against the interest of both the manufacturers here and the consumers" (Simons, Los Angeles, to FK, 30 March 1926, "Consumers Label and Labeling: Prosanis Label," Box C4, NCL Records, DLC).

213. To James A. Hamilton[1]

[New York City]
May 24, 1926

Hon. James A. Hamilton,
Commissioner, New York State Department of Labor,
124 East 28th Street,
New York City
My dear Mr. Hamilton:

I have just re-read, in connection with an article that I am writing for our members, your speech of May 21st last year, at the meeting of Associated Industries, at Syracuse. It is so very valuable that I am taking the liberty of asking for some farther facts of the same kind, a year having intervened.

My article deals with the terrible revelations of minors killed and injured in industry recently published by the Federal Children's Bureau, and by the State of Wisconsin, and by the Consumers' League of Eastern Pennsylvania.[2]

In connection with these revelations I am calling attention to the Lorain Steel Company, at Moxham, Pa., as described by the Pennsylvania Labor and Industry Bulletin for February 1926. It appears to have gone 115 days with 1800 employes and no lost-time accident, ending December 21, 1925. The pattern department record is 765 days without a lost-time accident; and the electrical foundry comes next with 520 such days.

This League wishes to start a modest, and for the present confidential, list of manufacturing establishments which have very low accident rates.[3] We do not need necessarily to show that they have arrived at these low rates quickly or recently. We do not know how long the Lorain Company may have been striving for its present fine standing in this regard.

We wish to head our list,—"What Has Been Done Can Be Done". Naturally we want only authentic examples, and not confined to the metal trades. This is not an advertising scheme either for the Consumers' League or for the places listed. It is intended solely to impress members and friends of the League, and such other enlightened folk (sadly few at present) as can be induced to show some interest in the subject.

Personally I have been stimulated to ask the advice of competent people about the possibility of such a list by two recent events. First, the recent publication of Nelle Swartz, Grace Abbott, the Wisconsin Industrial Commission, and my colleague in Pennsylvania, Estelle Lauder with her recent pamphlet "Accidents to Working Children in Pennsylvania, in 1923".[4] Second, the ominous threat of the approaching appointment of the New York State Legislature's enquiry Committee on the subject of our Labor Law and Labor Department, with especial reference to the cost of Workmen's Compensation.[5]

CC, "Safety Honor List," Box C43, NCL Records, DLC

1. James A. Hamilton (1876–1950) was New York City correction commissioner under Mayor John F. Hylan (1918–1922) and New York State industrial commissioner from 1924 to 1929. He administered the state's Bureau of Compensation (*NYT,* 25 June 1928, 23).

2. FK, "Children's Compensation for Industrial Accidents," *Survey* 56 (1 June 1926): 323–325.

3. In confidential letters, FK solicited the names of large manufacturers who had lowered the number of industrial injuries for the NCL's Safety Honor List (FK to Mrs. [H. Otto] Wittpenn, 23 May 1926, copy; and L. W. Hatch, New York, to FK, 29 May 1926, both in "Safety Honor List," Box C43, NCL Records, DLC).

4. Nelle Swartz published frequently in New York State's *Industrial Bulletin.* For Grace Abbott's writings on child labor, see Costin, *Two Sisters for Social Justice,* 294–295. The Wisconsin Industrial Commission published a monthly periodical, *Wisconsin Labor Statistics.* Estelle Lauder had recently been deeply involved in the writing and publication of Consumers' League of Eastern Pennsylvania, *Accidents to Working Children in Pennsylvania in 1923* (Philadelphia: Consumers' League of Eastern Pennsylvania, 1925).

5. Frances Perkins advised the NCL against creating a separate NCL Safety Honor List because of the great potential for error and because the state's Merit Rating Board of the Workmen's Compensation Service Bureau now had the power to impose penalties on employers when employees were injured at work (Frances Perkins, New York, to FK, 27 May 1926, "Safety Honor List," Box C43, NCL Records, DLC).

214. To John A. Lapp

NATIONAL CONSUMERS' LEAGUE
156 FIFTH AVENUE, ROOM 1129
NEW YORK CITY

June 16, 1926

My dear Dr. Lapp

Before entering on the business of this letter, I must tell you that by far the most inspiriting and strengthening experience of my attendance at the Cleveland Conference was hearing your clear cut statement at the close of Miss Addams' address on Tuesday night.[1] It gave me fresh respect for our rather feeble-minded Conference.

I write to call your attention to the shameful treatment by the hotels of colored members of the Conference at Cleveland. The Statler Hotel was expecially brutal to Miss Hunter, head of Phyllis Wheatley House in Cleveland. The Park Manor Hotel refused to have any colored people sleep under its roof. And one hotel,—I have forgotten which,—changed its policy after making a definite promise with regard to the colored members, saying that it was one of a chain and was compelled to conform to the rule of the other hotels in the chain.

My colleagues on the Board of the National Association for the Advancement of Colored People tell me that all Statler Hotels banish all Negroes, allowing neither employees nor guests on the premises. They tell me, also, that one deciding argument against the Conference going to Tennessee was the certainty that Negroes would be badly treated there, whereas presumably there will be no serious discrimination in Des Moines.

In view of the perfidy of the chain hotels referred to above, do you not think the officers of the Conference should communicate with the local Des Moines committee thus early in the year, before any notices go out to intending visitors to the Conference. I think there should be a written pledge from every hotel that there will be no race discrimination. Certainly I should not dream of staying in any hotel which refused to my fellow members either bed or board. I am sure that a considerable number of members of the Conference feel as I do about this.

You will, I know be interested to learn that we are to hold our first conference of signers of our enrollment petition in behalf of the federal child labor amendment next Friday afternoon, June 18th, for the purpose of pooling our wisdom as to methods of getting the largest number of signers between now and October.[2]

Yours sincerely,

CC, FKP, NN

1. The National Conference of Social Work held its 1926 meeting in Cleveland. It elected John A. Lapp (b. ca. 1880), a prominent layman in the Catholic church, as its president for 1927. He strongly endorsed the child labor amendment (*Cleveland Plain Dealer*, 2 June 1926, 3; Smith, "Behemoth Walks Again," 360).

JA spoke at the conference about how in the 1890s social workers had challenged the structure of society, but in the 1920s social work had become divorced from social theory. Lapp followed her speech with "a ringing statement of his own faith in social action by legislation" and in "social justice" (Smith, "Behemoth Walks Again," 360).

2. Jeanie V. Minor of the NCLC was among those FK invited to the petition conference. In June 1926, FK had 1,500 signatures and had put 2,500 blank petitions in the hands of "trusted friends" (FK to [Jeanie V.] Minor, 12 June 1926, NYCLC Records, N). For more on the petition drive, see Letter 207, FK to Julia Lathrop, 20 March 1925, above, and Letter 232, FK to Pauline Goldmark, 27 May 1927; Letter 229, FK to Lillian Wald, 4 April 1927; and Letter 244, FK to Mabel Costigan, 30 June 1928, all below.

215. To Edward P. Keating[1]

NATIONAL CONSUMERS' LEAGUE
156 FIFTH AVENUE
NEW YORK CITY

[Naskeag, Brooklin, Maine]
July 22, 1926.

Dear Mr. Keating:

Thank you for your notice of my Survey article about workmen's compensation for children[2] and, of course, always for your untiring interest in the maternity and infancy act.

This letter is to inquire whether it would be possible for you to keep the subject up, of the reports of labor officials in the States on children's compensation. It is certainly surprising that the famous workmen's compensation administrators in Ohio have kept their records so unintelligently that they will have no information about the children that can be printed separately, and therefore intelligently, before next year. It is almost more than I can believe that this is true, but it is! Only the State officials possess the data. Without it reformers cannot deal intelligently with the great evil of death and mutilation of children due to industry.

Even with the stimulus of the report of the Federal Children's Bureau, and of the Women's and Children's Bureau of the New York Labor Department, and the example of Wisconsin's consolidated report of last January and February,—wholly devoted to child labor, and chiefly to children's compensation—Pennsylvania and Ohio seem to be the only States that are getting ready to improve their ways.

I feel confident that the organ of the Brotherhoods must be very powerful in influencing these laggard States' administrative bodies,—miserable politicians most of them,—too unintelligent to know the evil results of their omissions to furnish necessary figures.

Please do not think that this merely hot weather sputtering! The information about children's compensation is the best ammunition known to me in behalf of the federal children's amendment, and we must all work together to force the States to furnish this ammunition in abundance.

Hoping this summer may deal leniently with you in Washington, I am

Yours still hopefully,
Florence Kelley[3]

TLS, Rubinow Papers, NNCorl

1. Democrat Edward P. Keating (1875–1965) sponsored the Keating-Owen Child Labor Act in 1916 while serving as a representative from Colorado (1913–1919). After losing the 1918 election, Keating edited and managed *Labor,* the official weekly newspaper of the associated railroad labor organizations.
2. FK, "Children's Compensation for Industrial Accidents," *Survey* 56 (1 June 1926): 323–325.
3. Keating replied that *Labor* "would be glad to continue the discussion" of children's compensation (Keating, n.p., to FK, 27 July 1926, Kheel Center Archives). However, no editorials or articles on the issue appeared in *Labor* from July through October 1926.

216. To Virginia Roderick[1]

[Naskeag, Brooklin, Maine]
July 24th, 1926.

Dear Miss Roderick:

Thank you very much for your interesting letter of July 22nd. I am glad you like my Survey article.[2] I live in hope that by some heaven-sent miracle the election may turn out so unmistakably against Senator [James] Wadsworth and Governor [Alfred] Smith that we can make public our enrollment work in behalf of ratification by the New York legislature.

Please never send out such "fear-thought" as the phrase "failure of the child labor amendment." It has not failed; it is merely delayed.[3]

The effect of the delay is, however, exceedingly bad. It enables the National Manufacturers' Association and the trumpeter thereof, the National Industrial Conference Board, to proclaim failure with a paralyzing effect. The only measure passed since June 22nd, 1924, aside from ratification by Arkansas, Arizona, California and Wisconsin, is a rather feeble minimum statute with inadequate provision for enforcement in Georgia. The prestige of the women's organizations is badly shattered, and this damage expresses itself hideously in the refusal of the U.S. Senate to appropriate funds at the session recently closed for the two years period beginning July 1st, 1927, for the Sheppard-Towner act.

The Senate's action, or inaction, is not fatal, provided enough spade work is done in the States between now and December, and provided the Progressives do enough smashing of the reactionaries in the election. Nothing less can, in my opinion, save the day for the children.

On the chance that you may wish to comment on the present situation, I enclose the list of twenty-seven Senators who failed to vote for or against the bill on June 15th. Some of them are known to be friends who were honestly compelled to be absent. But even they should not be allowed to forget who expect them to be present and voting next time.[4]

It is sad, indeed, to see [William] Borah among the Yeas along with Bayard, Butler, [William H.] King, Pepper and [James A.] Reed of Missouri. What company![5]

A letter to Grace Abbott asking for a copy of the action taken by the Women's Committee on the Sheppard-Towner Act will bring you, if not the record itself, a trust-worthy suggestion as to the way to get it.[6] Work is so largely suspended in Washington after Congress adjourns that I do not know where to tell you to write, but the Children's Bureau will know. It would be well to say on the envelope, If absent, Office please open.

Sincerely yours,

CC, FKP, NN

1. Virginia Roderick edited the *Woman Citizen* from 1921 to 1931.
2. FK, "Children's Compensation for Industrial Accidents," *Survey* 56 (1 June 1926): 323–325.
3. FK was apparently referring to language in Roderick's unrecovered letter of 22 July 1926.
4. In August 1926, Roderick ran an editorial in *Woman Citizen* criticizing the Senate for failing to pass the Sheppard-Towner extension and alerting readers that senators needed to act "early in the December session. This is one of the most important issues for women to think about in the coming election of Senators" ("An Election Issue—Mothers," 25).
5. The House approved a two-year extension of the Sheppard-Towner Act (H.R. 7555) on

5 April. In the Senate, however, it faced a concerted attack led by Senator William H. King, and the Senate voted only to consider the bill. (For King's opposition to the child labor amendment, see Letter 206, FK to Walter Lippman, 14 March 1925, note 3, above.) FK names senators who voted against (not for) this motion, including Thomas F. Bayard, Jr. (1868–1942; Democrat, Delaware, 1921–1929); William M. Butler (1861–1937; Republican, Massachusetts, 1923–1926); and George W. Pepper (1867–1961; Republican, Pennsylvania, 1922–1927) (69th Cong. 1st sess., *Cong. Rec.*, 5 April 1926 and 15 June 1926, 6925–6926, 11270).

6. FK was referring to the Women's Joint Congressional Committee.

217. To Paul Kellogg

Naskeag, Brooklin, Me.
August 17th, 1926.
Dear Paul:

Herewith I am sending ten pages of manuscript which should, I think, follow the chronological schedule. As usual, I shall have to rely largely upon you for ordering the material in these two articles—as I hope they may prove to be.[1]

My reason for pressing hard for October first, is the imminent election of one third of the Senate.[2] The fight against the Sheppard-Towner Act is vicious to the last degree. It goes so far that Senator Bayard, of Delaware, read into the Congressional Record, in July, thirty-five pages of the Woman Patriot's abusive misrepresentations, with me as the chief Villain Acting for Moscow![3]

Furthermore, action by the Senate in December is necessary to enable the biennial legislatures to match with State funds what Congress appropriates.[4]

It would seem to me treason or blasphemy (or both) to lose the opportunity to bring home to the people who have this one last chance to save and make permanent the Sheppard-Towner work,—what it means to mothers who will be wantonly bereft of their children if Smoot and [William H.] King of Utah, Phipps of Colorado, Moses[5] and [James] Wadsworth and Bayard et Al, using the Woman Patriot, carry the day!

If my own poor mother's melancholy thirty years should stir again some of those friends of the Act who have been too easily lulled to rest,—I should feel compensated for the labor of the whole book.[6]

CC, FKP, NN

1. Writing FK about publishing her memoirs in installments in *Survey,* Kellogg stated that he "was gun-shy of starting a series until we have several installments in hand" and expressed doubt that he could print the first article in the October issue. He assured her, however, that the series had "a great, big human relation to the whole situation around us" (Kellogg to FK, 11 August 1926, FKP, NN).

2. In "My Philadelphia," FK attributed the deaths of her five sisters to the "prevailing ignorance of the hygiene of infancy." She devoted several pages to the merits of the Sheppard-Towner Act, concluding, "I should be false to the memory of a tender and grief-stricken mother if these pages were printed without reference to the need of action by Congress at the December Session" ("My Philadelphia," 61). FK's autobiographical *Survey* articles are reprinted in FK, *Notes of Sixty Years.*

3. On 3 July 1926, Senator Thomas Bayard read into the *Congressional Record* a "memorial" from the *Woman Patriot* (Lemons, *The Woman Citizen,* 14; 69th Cong. 1st sess., *Cong. Rec.,* 3 July 1926, 12918–12952). This protest against the extension of the Sheppard-Towner Act, printed in the *Woman Patriot* from 15 May to 15 August 1926, contained extensive and repetitive accusations that FK was masterminding "revolution by legislation." Characterizing FK as "Engels's American lieutenant," the *Woman Patriot* examined her career in detail with selective quotations from her writings and testimony at congressional hearings (12931–12936). Although the memorial also targeted Grace Abbott, JA, and Julia Lathrop, FK was the center of its attack, which named her as part of a Bolshevik plan to "subvert and corrupt the minds of children" (12941). The memorial declared, "For 40 years modern revolutionary communism, under the original, direct instructions of Friederich Engels and Karl Marx, its founders, has had in the United States a thoroughly trained, educated, and experienced leader, who is perhaps the ablest legislative general communism has produced—Mrs. Florence Kelley" (12931). FK subsequently wrote Kellogg that the *Woman Patriot* memorial seemed "to surpass any infamy, even the Spider-Web chart" (FK to Kellogg, 20 August 1926, copy, FKP, NN).

4. In this era, many state legislatures met only every other year.

5. Senator Reed Smoot (1862–1941), a Republican from Utah, served from 1903 to 1933. Senator Lawrence C. Phipps (1862–1958), a Republican from Colorado, served from 1919 to 1931. Senator George H. Moses (1869–1944), a Republican from New Hampshire, served from 1918 to 1933.

6. Kellogg wrote FK that he viewed it as not only as "the story of a girlhood spent in the city of our national independence (waving the flag from the family tree!), but, second an interpretation of the springs of the impulses which *inspirited* your life work (and so of genuine interest not only to those who know you, but to those on the fringe to whom we can thus dramatize your story.)" He also felt the article was a "smashing blow for the Shepherd-Towner bill" (Kellogg, Magog, Quebec, to FK, 28 August 1926, FKP, NN).

218. To John A. Ryan[1]

Naskeag, Brooklin, Maine.
August 20th, 1926.

Dear Dr. Ryan:

Thank you very much for Senator Bayard's Encyclopedia of Errors.[2] My manners and my disposition alike have suffered severely from a critical rereading thereof.

I write now to consult you as one of our most widely experienced Vice Presidents as to steps to be taken with reference to this latest atrocity of the Woman Patriot.[3] Your reply will, of course, be strictly confidential unless you authorize me to show it to my son, an experienced lawyer, and to Robert Szold, the most active member of our legal committee of the board of directors.

Do you think, knowing the District of Columbia courts as you do, that anything could be gained by our bringing a libel suit against Mary Kilbreth[4] and the Woman Patriot? Such a suit would, of course, have to be brought in my name and that of the National Consumers League. It would have to be financed by the League, but I think that might not be very difficult.

To lose such a suit would be an incalculably great disaster. To win it would merely silence the persons named in the libel bill.

If I am correct in my supposition that the Woman Patriot is merely a mask for the National Manufacturers' Association, which could not conveniently crusade against babies, but profits undoubtedly by every attack on the W.J.C.C. and its individual members[5]—little would be gained even by a successful suit for heavy damages, because the Manufacturers' Association would immediately create another agency to continue its vile work.

On the other hand, silence does appear to give consent.

Although Congress knows the Patriot and [J. S.] Eichelberger, Kilbreth and company, the country at large does not know them for what they are, and I fear they may do great harm to the Sheppard-Towner bill this winter.[6]

In case the libel suit does not commend itself to you, what would you think of the National Consumers League printing Twenty Questions about the Woman Patriot? This would, of course, be a feeble substitute for a successful suit.[7]

Hoping this unusually hot summer has not injured your health, I am

Yours sincerely and gratefully,

CC, FKP, NN

1. John A. Ryan (1869–1945) was professor of moral theology and industrial ethics at Catholic University (1915–1937). His Ph.D. dissertation, published as *A Living Wage: Its Ethical and Economic Aspects* (1906), provided arguments for a minimum wage that drew on Catholic teachings. In 1910, he spoke to the NCL annual meeting about the minimum wage (Sklar, "Two Political Cultures in the Progressive Era," 58).

2. See Letter 217, FK to Paul Kellogg, 17 August 1926, above.

3. John Ryan had been an honorary vice-president of the NCL since 1917 (NCL, *Report for the Years 1914–1915–1916,* frontispiece, Box A6, NCL Records, DLC).

4. Mary Kilbreth (1869–1957), whom historian Thomas J. Jablonsky calls "obsessed with visions of secret plots and hidden motives," was closely aligned with the Sentinels of the Republic and was the former president of the National Association Opposed to Woman Suffrage and president of its successor, the Woman Patriot Publishing Company. She swore that the information in the *Woman Patriot* petition was accurate (Jablonsky, *The Home, Heaven, and Mother Party,* 113–114; 69th Cong., 1st sess., *Cong. Rec.,* 3 July 1926, 12952).

5. The *Woman Patriot* petition called the WJCC "a device for misrepresenting the masses of organized women without consulting them, and for tricking the United States Congress by pretended mass support by women of the Kelley program" (69th Cong., 1st sess., *Cong. Rec.,* 3 July 1926, 12933).

6. For information on J. S. Eichelberger, see the introduction to chapter 6 and Letter 199, FK to Julia Lathrop, 28 July 1924, note 2, above.

7. Although no reply from Ryan has been recovered, several of FK's correspondents advised her against suing for libel. Grace Abbott wrote, "Unless one is prepared to spend a good deal of money, I think a libel suit makes one ridiculous" (Grace Abbott, Lake Tahoe, Calif., to FK, 2 September [1926], "General Correspondence: Abbott, Grace," Box B10, NCL Records, DLC). Katherine Lenroot wrote that Senator Morris Sheppard believed that a suit "would only increase the publicity given the material" (Lenroot, Washington, D.C., to FK, 27 September 1926, "Children's Bureau: General File, 1925–1962," Box C3, NCL Records, DLC).

On 11 December, Senator Sheppard inserted in the *Congressional Record* a letter from Children's Bureau chief Grace Abbott of 23 November 1926 that refuted (with examples) many of the charges in the *Woman Patriot* memorial. Abbott concluded, "Whether a measure is not socialist or communist becomes for the Woman Patriot a matter of definition by the Woman Patriot. It obviously regards as communistic or socialistic anything which it opposes" (69th Cong., 2nd sess., *Cong. Rec.*, 11 December 1926, 290–292). In January, Senator Bayard read into the record portions of Mary Kilbreth's 13 December 1926 letter to him denying that the Woman Patriot had "made any misstatements, misquotations unfair partial quotations, or material statistical errors, as charged by Miss Abbott" and noted that Abbott had not addressed "all the indisputable and undisputed facts regarding Mrs. Florence's Kelley 40-year campaign for socialist legislation" (69th Cong., 2nd sess., *Cong. Rec.*, 8 and 10 January 1927, 1285, 1345).

219. To Mary Anderson

[New York City]
December 10, 1926

Dear Miss Anderson:

I read at one sitting night before last the tentative draft statement concerning statutes enacted in New York State applying to the employment of wage-earning women.[1] As a chronology of the enactment of statutes I find it correct so far as I know, and valuable because it is so compact.

I suggest, however, that any such baldly chronological skeleton would, if published as it stands, be misleading. The influence upon the long, slow process of enactment of judicial decisions of the Supreme Court of the United States is so decisive that some reference is necessary to the nightwork decision of 1908 in the Oregon case, and the recent decision in the Radice case upholding the amendment to the nightwork law as it affects waitresses in restaurants.[2]

From the time in 1907 when the New York Court of Appeals held the nightwork provision, applying to women over 21 in manufacture, unconstitutional, until in 1914 the same Court reversed itself following the United States Supreme Court decision of 1908 upholding the Oregon 10-hours law for women, the demoralised enforcement of the law applying to women under the age of 21 years was complete and inevitable, and all the effort made to save that provision on the statute books was in fact lost, because of the incurable facility for evading it.[3]

The decision in the Radice case is important, first because in this period of reaction when no good decision seems secure from reversal, the Supreme Court was unanimous in reaffirming the power of New York State to ***protect*** a specific group of employees.

Every chronology of the enactment of protective legislation gives an unduly favorable impression of progress unless the interruptions by the Court are stated and their disastrous effects interpreted. Even though it may be a part of the plan to deal with the Courts [in a] separate chapter as one of the influences affecting progress in this field, the present skeleton would be open to hostile criticism if these points were disregarded.

May I suggest, also, that in the parenthesis on the title page the word "Labor" seems necessary at the end of the first line, to read thus—"First Draft of one Section of the History of Labor Legislation Affecting Women["]?

I am wondering where, if at all, the figures are to be found which alone can show the steady growth of employment of women, both minors and adults, under legislation and without legislation between 1884 and 1926. The only sources that come to my mind are the federal enquiries of 1899 and 1908; the U.S. census figures of 1890, 1900, 1910 and 1920—so sadly defective; and the publications of the Department of Commerce. This study of yours may prove an epoch-maker! It will so illuminate the defects in our official records, both federal and state, concerning women in industry, that it will be easy in future to compel an entirely different treatment of the whole subject.[4] In that case we may yet bless the name of the justly accursed Woman's Party which instigated this whole invaluable inquiry! Who can foretell!

With congratulations on this most promising beginning, and admiration for the thoroughgoing documentation of every point, I am

Yours sincerely,

CC, "General Correspondence: Anderson, Mary," Box B10, NCL Records, DLC

1. On 6 December 1926, Anderson had sent FK a draft of the New York section of the Women's Bureau study of labor legislation for women in New York, Massachusetts, and California, later published as Clara M. Beyer, *History of Labor Legislation for Women in Three States* (1929) ("General Correspondence: Anderson, Mary," Box B10, NCL Records, DLC).

2. For *Muller v. Oregon*, see Letter 104, FK to NK, 20 January 1908, above; for *Radice v. New York*, see Letter 192, FK to Mary Dewson, 26 March 1924, above.

3. For *People v. Williams*, see Letter 97, FK to NK, 6 July 1907, above; for *People v. Chas. Schweinler Press*, see Letter 135, FK to Katherine Edson, 16 July 1916, above.

4. Anderson thanked FK for her careful criticisms and said that they were "just what we hoped to get" when she and her staff sent the report to individuals who were knowledgeable about the New York legislature's activities over the past decades (Anderson, Washington, D.C., to FK, 17 December 1926, "General Correspondence, Anderson, Mary," Box B10, NCL Records, DLC).

220. To Jane Addams

52 Gramercy Park [New York City]
New Year's Day 1926 [1927]

Dearest J.A.

Here's my very best New Year's greeting, and hopes for a better year than '26!

Please don't think that what follows is irony! It's dead earnest. I've told a man named A. Epstein,—at present the salaried secretary of the Penna. State Commission on old age pensions,—that he may use my name and I will beg you to let him use yours, to promote a National Association for Old Age Pensions.[1] It is really true that our names have value!

The Penna. Court has held their state law unconstitutional. But that does not prove that it is.[2]

Meanwhile Mr. Epstein's salary and office, and his appointment run to May 1st. We think he can build up enough membership to run itself thereafter, between now and May 1st.

We don't ask anything "off" your dear self but your name as an honorary V.P.

That is worth diamonds and pearls for a national undertaking.

Isn't it hideous that we had over 700 suicides in this town last year? Many, many of them lonely old people! In the midst of all this wealth!

Herewith I'm sending a copy of our latest little publication.[3] It is fine to have Illinois publishing current facts in monthly bulletins. Do you know who started the Labor Commissioner to doing that? No other one does that. I'm referring now to children's compensation for injuries in industry, about which it is so exceedingly difficult to get any current facts.

Will you please tell me in what year you graduated from Rockford Female Seminary? In my Notes of Sixty Years I'm referring to you, J.[ulia] C. L.[athrop], Anna Howard Shaw,[4] and Mrs. [Carrie Chapman] Catt as being students while I was, 1876–1886. Not all that time, but in that decade.

Isn't it fine to see England forced to yield to China?[5]

I've just finished the biography of the Fourth Earl of Clarendon who died in 1870.[6] It was amazing to read his terrified prophecy of the present descent of England to the rank of a second class power. But he expected it even earlier!

I hope you're not overdoing! I'm so restive on this chaise longue, I do not know how much longer I can hold out.[7] No one knows how I've admired your long patience!

Your devoted old
F.K.

ALS, JA Papers, PSC-P

1. Abraham Epstein (1892–1942) headed the Pennsylvania Commission on Old Age Pensions from 1918 to 1927, when the state of Pennsylvania disbanded the commission. Epstein believed that pension programs should be operated by the government with an end to redistributing wealth. JA replied that she was "delighted to join forces with you in an effort toward old age pensions" (JA, Chicago, to FK, 10 January 1927, FKP, NN).
2. The Pennsylvania Pension Act was declared unconstitutional in 1924.
3. Presumably *Children's Compensation for Industrial Accidents: How the States Love Their Children,* NCL Pamphlet no. 1 (New York: National Consumers' League, 1926).
4. Anna Howard Shaw (1847–1919) was president of NAWSA from 1904 to 1915.
5. On 25 December 1926, the British Foreign Office issued a statement that renounced British treaty rights in China, marking the end of the gunboat power by which Britain had ruled parts of China and the onset of the success of the nationalist revolution (1923–1928) (*NYT:* 26 December 1926, 1; Bickers, *Britain in China,* 5).

6. Herbert E. Maxwell wrote *Life and Letters of George William Frederick Villiers, Fourth Earl of Clarendon* (London: E. Arnold, 1913). Clarendon (1800–1870) was British foreign secretary during the Crimean War and in the 1860s.

7. Since June 1926, suffering from varicose veins and phlebitis, FK had been more or less "chained to the chaise-longue" with only brief forays such as a trip to Cleveland for the NCL's annual council meeting in November (FK to Ethel Small, 29 April 1927, FKP, NN; FK to Alice Hamilton, 4 December 1926, "General Correspondence: Hamilton, Alice," Box B13, NCL Records, DLC).

221. To Consumers' League Branches

NIGHTLETTER

[New York City]
January 4, 1927

WOMENS JOINT CONGRESSIONAL COMMITTEE VOTED YESTERDAY TO REQUEST MEMBER ORGANIZATIONS TO WIRE THEIR BRANCHES TO WIRE THEIR SENATORS TO URGE SUPPORT OF MOTION TO BRING UP PARKER-PHIPPS BILL AND TO SUPPORT TWO YEARS EXTENSION OF SHEPPARD-TOWNER ACT[1] PLEASE WIRE YOUR SENATORS AND REQUEST YOUR MEMBERS TO DO LIKEWISE

FLORENCE KELLEY

Chge National Consumers' League

TEL, "Sheppard Towner Act: Correspondence, 1922–1931," Box C43, NCL Records, DLC

1. The Parker-Phipps bill was another version of H.R. 7555, the bill to extend the Sheppard-Towner Act. FK wrote Grace Abbott that she was following the WJCC's request to wire consumers' league branches but was concentrating only on "the hopeful ones," since the branches met infrequently. She thought her editorial in *Survey* asking readers to "use the mails, the press, the pulpit and platform and telephone . . . to demand of their senators face to face an early favorable vote upon this life-saving measure" was more effective (FK to Abbott, 4 January 1927, copy, "General Correspondence: Abbott, Grace," Box B10, NCL Records, DLC; Untitled editorial, *Survey* 57 [1 January 1927]: 467).

222. To James Couzens[1]

[New York City]
January 19, 1927

My dear Senator Couzens:

The Maternity and Infancy measure even in its unsatisfactory form is immeasurably better than having the whole organization wiped out next June.[2] In behalf of the National Consumers' League I thank you very much for the help that you gave; and I beg to explain that the filibuster and the final vote were as completely blanketed in the New York papers as anything I have ever known that was pending in Congress.

Miss Lillian D. Wald, who has been profoundly interested in both the Children's Bureau and the Maternity Act since the earliest discussion of both, telephoned me Monday night to ask whether an item that she had just read in a metropolitan paper of Monday, January 17th, was correct in reporting that the measure had passed Congress, without stating the date of its passage. The metropolitan press is an amazing phenomena! She and I and our secretaries have been watching for the past fortnight, day by day, for current news!

Yours sincerely,

CC, "Sheppard-Towner Act: Correspondence, 1922–1931," Box C43, NCL Records, DLC

1. James Couzens (1872–1936; U.S. senator, Republican, Michigan, 1922–1936) wrote FK that the Senate had approved the Sheppard-Towner extension on the night of 13 January (Couzens, Washington, D.C., to FK, 15 January 1927, "Sheppard-Towner Act: Correspondence, 1922–1931," Box C43, NCL Records, DLC).

2. In the Senate, after strenuous objection against the Sheppard-Towner extension from James Reed, William H. King, and others, Morris Sheppard offered an amendment to the bill on 13 January that set the expiration date of the act as 30 June 1929. The Senate thus agreed to allow Sheppard-Towner to continue for only two more years; the House had already approved the extension in the first session of Congress (69th Cong., 2nd sess., *Cong. Rec.*, 19 January 1927, 371, 1572–1585, 1940).

Grace Abbott wrote FK that she knew she would be disappointed, but "we have done very well to get [the extension]" (Abbott, Washington, D.C., to FK, [14 January 1927], "General Correspondence: Abbott, Grace," Box B10, NCL Records, DLC). FK replied that in the next two years "it must surely be possible to invent some device to save [senators'] faces and still continue the work. Anyhow, the accursed Woman Patriot has not dished the Bureau and the W.J.C.C. to any such extent as they set out to do. I find mean consolation in that" (FK to Abbott, 19 January 1927, "General Correspondence: Abbott, Grace," Box B10, NCL Records, DLC). In an unsigned editorial on the compromise measure, FK named William King, James Reed, Thomas Bayard, Hiram Bingham, Edwin Broussard, and James Wadsworth as senators who were trying to kill the extension (*Survey* 57 [15 February 1927]: 623).

223. To Grace Abbott

[New York City]
January 21, 1927

Dear Grace:

I don't know how far the villains, Bingham and company, are identical with those who killed the Dyer Anti-Lynching bill last winter by a filibuster.[1] If you will send me a list of our villains, I will compare it with the N.A.A.C.P. list of their villains. The League of Women Voters, of course, knows who ours are.[2]

It occurs to me that if all,—acting with an appearance of independence,—

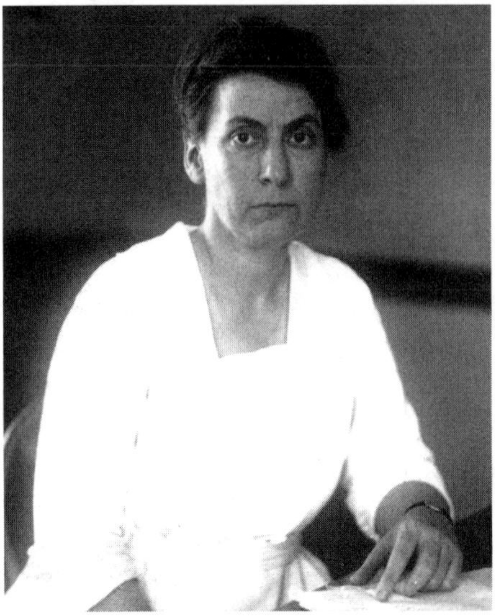

Grace Abbott, 1929. Courtesy of the Library of Congress, LC-USZ62-111723.

the N.A.A.C.P. using the Negro press and the friendly white press, and the rest of us our organizations and membership lists,—undertook a continuing publication of the bad record of these gentlemen as they make it—we ought to be able to contribute a good deal toward putting them out of the Senate, those coming up for re-election in 1929 and 1931 having been systematically followed up meantime.

Naturally the Negroes can do more in Delaware, Maryland and some western states, (perhaps even a few votes being available against Bingham in Connecticut) than elsewhere, the rest of us working wherever we are stronger.

If [James A.] Reed of Missouri should change his mind as our dear, good Norris did,[3] and decide to stay in the Senate, the Negroes could be very helpful, provided they were well drilled in advance as to his relation to the filibuster against the Dyer bill. I am sure you get my point.[4]

But who can defeat [William H.] King of Utah, or Broussard?[5]

Yours hopefully,

CC, "General Correspondence: Abbott, Grace," Box B10, NCL Records, DLC

1. Representative Leonidas Dyer led congressional efforts to pass federal laws criminalizing lynching beginning in 1918 and continuing through the 1920s. When Dyer's first bill was defeated in 1919, the NAACP campaigned to defeat the congressional opponents of the bill. In 1925, Dyer amended his bill to include violence against African Americans as well as deaths from lynching. He was confident that the bill would pass with this amendment, but the bill never got out of the judiciary committees of the House and Senate of the 69th Congress (69th Cong., 1st sess., *Cong. Rec.*, 7 and 8 December 1925, 447, 475; *Washington Post*, 5 December 1925, 2; Hixson, "Moorfield Storey and the Defense of the Dyer Anti-Lynching Bill"). For FK's first encounter with the Dyer anti-lynching bill, see Letter 186, FK to James

Weldon Johnson, 13 November 1923, above. Hiram Bingham (1875–1956), a Republican from Connecticut, was U.S. senator from 1924 to 1933.

2. FK's reliance on the LWV for "a list of our villains" arose from her knowledge of its "stability, its reasoned courage, its list of achievements big and little and all permanent" (FK to Mabel Costigan, 11 May 1928, copy, "General Correspondence: Costigan, Mr. and Mrs. Edward P.," Box B12, NCL Records, DLC).

3. George W. Norris (1861–1944) a Republican from Nebraska, was U.S. senator from 1913 to 1943.

4. After Governor Aiken of South Carolina failed to take actions that would punish the lynchers of three African American men in October 1926 (after he had repeatedly promised to do so), Walter White urged all members of the NAACP to work for the passage of the Dyer Anti-Lynching bill, which was before Congress in January 1927 (*NYT*, 3 January 1927, 3). The number of lynchings in 1926 was almost double that of the previous year (*The Nation*, 19 January 1927, 52). *The Crisis* stated in its February issue that lynchings increased in 1926 because "[t]he fear of the Dyer Bill has been removed from the minds of the murderers. This is but a louder call for Federal legislation. There is no civilized country on earth which would allow in one year thirty-four mob murders to occur without even investigation in most cases and in no case with adequate attempt at punishment" (*The Crisis* 33 [February 1927]: 180–181). Lynching finally became a federal crime with the 1965 Civil Rights Act. On 13 June 2005, the U.S. Senate passed a resolution that apologized for failing to pass anti-lynching legislation in the 1920s and 1930s when mob violence against blacks was common (*NYT*, 14 June 2005, 15).

5. Edwin S. Broussard (1874–1934), a Democrat from Louisiana, was a U.S. senator from 1921 to 1933.

224. To Lillian D. Wald

NATIONAL CONSUMERS' LEAGUE
156 FIFTH AVENUE
NEW YORK CITY

January 21, 1921[7]

Beloved Lady:

In reply to your omnibus questions, I respectfully submit the enclosed.[1]

Please tell me what you want these ideas for? And if any of these are not clear please be so kind as to telephone or write. I am very curious about this.

I never told you how I feasted on the cherries and pears, and loved the Christmas tree, and still luxuriate in the nighties!

Yours devotedly,
F. K.

[Enc:]

SOCIAL ACHIEVEMENTS OF FORTY YEARS

1. Votes for women. Although itself political, this underlies social gains and makes them easier to achieve, and to hold;
2. The unparalleled and astounding progress of the Negro race;
3. The creation of the nursing profession. There were nurses at work fifty

years ago, but only a handful, and so far as I know only one training school, and that here in New York City. As to these details you know better than I. The creation of the profession as a great and important part of the educational movement in this country, and of the life-saving movement also, falls well within the time since 1886.

4. Settlements, as
   (a) Centers of hospitality to people and to ideas;
   (b) Sources of discovery of social needs previously undiscovered;
   (c) Interpreters of the unknown poor to their blind and deaf fellow-citizens;
   (d) Improvers of their physical surroundings (streets, schools, and federal, state and municipal care in general for the most defenceless);
5. The Children's Bureau;
6. Rural good roads;

FAILURES

1. The U.S. Supreme Court's vetoes of the federal child labor laws, and the minimum wage law;
2. The legislatures' delay of the federal child labor amendment; and the timorous attitude of the National and State Child Labor Committees in response thereto.
3. The absence of women from the United States Senate;
4. The pitifully small number of women who are full professors in state universities and in colleges of the first rank;
5. The collapse of the tuberculosis crusade;
6. The community chest movement. This has become an engine of repression of social thought and action, both in its communities and as to the work of great and beneficent national organizations.

THE FUTURE

Urgent immediate needs:

1. Ratification of the federal child labor amendment;
2. Expansion of the settlement movement, each group being a center of hospitality for people and for ideas;
3. Universal acceptance of the principle that the intelligence which created mass production can, and must, make industry safe;
4. The opening wide of all tax supported and tax exempt universities, colleges and hospitals to women, as students, as interns in hospitals, and as full professors;
5. The Cabinet made responsible to Congress for interrogation at all times, not merely for investigation after the event;

6. Nominees for the Cabinet should be ratified by the vote of the Congressional District in which they live, as is done in England. This would prevent a Cabinet made up of lame ducks.

TLS, Wald Papers, NN

1. Wald wrote FK, "I miss you terribly when people ask for statements of achievements, and visions of the future. Will you not be a darling and dictate . . . what in your judgment have been the social achievements and failures in the past forty years, and what you would want of the future" (Wald to FK, 19 January 1927, FKP, NN).

225. To Edith Valet Cook[1]

[New York City]
January 24, 1927

Dear Mrs. Cook:

The enclosed slip will doubtless interest you, though it has nothing directly to do either with the work of the National Consumers' League on the compensation question or with the field of the League of Women Voters. It is on a subject in which I have been deeply interested for a number of years, because it is so exceedingly difficult to get even enlightened people to realize the sinister effect on the fate of Negro women of these laws wherever they exist.

In states where, as in New York, intermarriage between the races is not prohibited, the ever present possibility that a man who betrays or assaults a Negro girl may be compelled to marry her is a permanent element of protection for Negro women and girls. This element of protection is obliterated, of course, as soon as a prohibition of intermarriage is enacted.

In nearly every Southern state Negro girls may be seduced or assaulted with impunity by white men, and such offenses are common beyond the imagination of Northern women.

Since the migration of Negroes from the South an epidemic of these bills in legislatures in the last few years has become almost nationwide. I am sure you will wish to throw your weight against the bill mentioned in the clipping.[2]

Yours sincerely,

CC, "General Correspondence: Kelley, Florence," Box B14, NCL Records, DLC

1. Edith Valet Cook (b. 1892) was secretary of the Connecticut Child Welfare Association and in 1927 a member of the Connecticut House of Representatives (Cook to FK, 7 January 1927, "Child Labor: Compensation for Injuries: Kiennell Case," Box C2, NCL Records, DLC). She was active in the LWV of Connecticut.

2. Cook thanked FK for bringing to her attention "the marriage bill which has been brought to the Conn. Legislature" and said she would write to the NAACP for more information about its position (Cook to FK, 6 February 1927, "General Correspondence: Kelley, Florence," Box B14, NCL Records, DLC). *The Crisis* carried an editorial refuting the charge that the NAACP advocated marriage between whites and blacks. The NAACP, stated *The Crisis,*

"simply declares that if white folk will have sexual commerce with blacks, this must take place under legal restrictions; that prohibition of such legal marriage is a direct bid for bastards and prostitutes and removes all civilized protection from colored girls and women; and finally that if two grown, sane, healthy persons wish to marry that that is their business" (*The Crisis* 33 [January 1927]: 128–129).

226. To Arthur B. Spingarn[1]

[New York City]
February 8, 1927

Dear Mr. Spingarn:

Can you spare a few minutes to read these pages,[2] and tell me whether publishing them in the Nation can in your opinion

(a) Hurt the feelings of any Colored people?
(b) Make the Negroes appear ludicrously negligible as voters?
(c) Write myself down as a person whose sense of proportion is lost?

My own overwhelming impulse is to throw this apple of discord into the ranks of the enemy, unless there is substantial danger of hoisting ourselves with my own petard!

I know you will answer as frankly as I ask.

Incidentally, will you please tell me who is the Treasurer of the Civic Club?

Yours sincerely,

CC, FKP, NN

1. Arthur B. Spingarn, a New York City lawyer, was vice-president of the NAACP from 1911 to 1940.
2. FK's letter to the editor of *The Nation* dated 8 February 1927 returned to the deficiencies of the ERA, which she described as an amendment "whose slumber has been annually disturbed by a hearing." Her letter asked, "Where do advocates of the Equality Amendment stand on the White Primary in Texas, which excludes Negro voters, men and women alike?" She said that the NWP needed to "define equality at the polls, as thoroughly as it has defined . . . equality in the factory and the legislature" ("What Kind of Equality for Women?" 237).

227. To Julia C. Lathrop

[New York City]
March 22, 1927

Dearest J. Lathrop:

Enclosed is Mr. Sigmund Zeisler's terrible account of the Anarchists trial. The public compunction about the Sacco-Vanzetti case seems to indicate that there is a wider diffusion of public conscience to which appeal can be made against such violations of justice in time of great excitement, than there was

40 years ago.[1] This is the only ray of comfort—and a poor dim ray—that I have been able to discover since reading this account of the Anarchist trial.

Your friendly loan of the paper served an unforeseen and valuable purpose. I had been exhausting the resources of the Public Library information department in search of the number of Illinois judges who were sitting in 1895 and held our Illinois 8-hours law unconstitutional. On the very first page Mr. Zeisler states that the judges in 1888 were seven.

Never, never again will I be befooled by any loving friend into thinking that she is positively absolutely leaving this town when she says she is. If I had only had sense enough not to take you literally that Saturday night, what a pleasant lunch Grace Drake and I might have enjoyed enticing you hither! But I am a poor gullible fool!

Grace Abbott is to be here tomorrow, speaking in the evening and having a luncheon Wednesday noon at which I am to be allowed to make a few broken remarks. I believe it is of very great importance that we should keep up a continuous series of demonstrations of public approval of her and her work, all kinds of organizations of men and women being gradually put on record before the time comes for the new Sheppard-Towner appropriation, in some disguising form to be introduced and pushed early next winter.

As I understand it, the great sin of omission of the women's organizations really occurred in March 1926, when we failed to concentrate all our efforts on the Senate immediately after the House had, in February, authorized the prolongation of the Act and adequate appropriations for two years. If we had made a sufficient demonstration of power and zeal before the end of the long session, I do not believe the Senate would have dared to act as brutally as it did from July 1926 on. It is always hard to make up afterwards for a neglected demonstration of strength. I think this what we have to lay ourselves out to do, to render impossible all three lines of attack which we well know the enemy have in mind. First to dismember the Bureau and distribute the parts; second to let it die outright on June 30, 1929; and third to kill it if these methods fail, by getting rid of Grace and putting in her place somebody of the general nature of the present woman on the Civil Service Commission.

My only excuse for falling down last year is that I really was ill, much more seriously than I knew at the time, and was unfit and unable to fight when the fighting was good.[2]

I am chagrined that I did not thank you for your photograph. It was the most precious Christmas card that I received. Ko was here when it came, and we agreed to divide its presence, letting him have it part of the winter, when I dine with them every week, and taking it to Maine myself in the summer. You never act as if you knew how fond he and I are of you.

Are you going to Des Moines? And if so, at what hotel will you be? I cannot get any answer from Jane [Addams] or Mary [Rozet Smith].

Yours devotedly,

CC, "General Correspondence: Lathrop, Julia C.," Box B15, NCL Records, DLC

1. Sigmund Zeisler (1860–1931) had been an associate defender of the Chicago anarchists in 1884. His article on that case in November 1926 concluded that the defendants had been convicted and hanged not from the evidence that they had been murderers but because of their anarchism (see Zeisler, "Reminiscences of the Anarchist Case"). In 1921, Italian immigrants Nicola Sacco (b. 1891) and Bartolomeo Vanzetti (b. 1888), acknowledged anarchists, were convicted of murdering two shoe company employees in South Braintree, Massachusetts. Their death sentences were appealed to the Massachusetts Supreme Court. For more about this case, see Letter 236, FK to NK, 9 August 1927, below.

2. Lathrop replied that she felt "encouraged about the future" of the Children's Bureau. She did not agree that ground had been lost during the last congressional session: "[T]he triumph of our cause was remarkable and leaves us a breathing space and a spark of life." But she implored FK not to be "ill again for any Cause's sake" (Lathrop, Rockford, Ill., to FK, 27 [March] 1927, FKP, NN).

228. To John R. Commons

[New York City]
March 26, 1927

Dear Dr. Commons:

Enclosed herewith please find a copy of the revised edition of our first pamphlet on Children's Compensation for Industrial Injuries.[1]

We now have in the printers' hands a second pamphlet. It is a condensed statement of the inequalities and insufficiencies of these laws in the 48 states.[2]

When we entered this field, ten months ago, my aim was to show, from the available public records, that the employment of minors below the age of 18 years is still very large, very widespread and very dangerous to them. The accessible information proves, however, to be meager, and usually old before it is printed.

That interest is now strengthened by another. The effort to get facts and advertise them can act as a stimulus to State officials. We are now trying to learn what the injured minors really get in the four states which prescribe double or treble compensation for children illegally employed. The four are Missouri (since the November election last year) New Jersey, New York and Wisconsin.[3]

This letter is to ask whether there is not some student or group of students whom you could lead to dig out the records the number of injured minors who have received awards since Wisconsin changed, in 1917, from excluding from compensation minors illegally employed to prescribing double or triple compensation for them. And what awards the injured minors actually received?

This is, of course, more difficult where the law is administered by the Courts, than where it is centralized. But if it can be shown for instance, for Milwaukee and for a small, single-industry-town, that would be very valuable.[4]

We understand that the occupations forbidden to minors as hazardous, are divided into two groups viz: those designated in the statute, and those specified by the Industrial Welfare Commission.

CC, "General Correspondence: Commons, John R.," Box B11, NCL Records, DLC

1. The NCL published *Children's Compensation for Industrial Accidents: How the States Love Their Children* on 23 January 1927. FK believed that "injuries" was a more accurate word than "accidents." This first pamphlet in a four-part series used the word "accidents" in its title; others in the series used the word "injuries."

2. *Children's Compensation for Industrial Injuries: What Price Children?* NCL Pamphlet no. 2 (New York: National Consumers' League, 1927).

3. For FK's previous effort to obtain statistics about compensation for children injured at work, see Letter 209, FK to Charlotte Carr, 28 April 1925, above.

4. Commons replied that he could not hire any students right away but hoped that the following year he could arrange to have several students receive academic credit for the research (Commons to FK, Madison, Wisc., 8 April 1927, "General Correspondence: Commons, John R.," Box B11, NCL Records, DLC). FK thanked him and stressed again the need to present evidence that workmen's compensation for children "has been of substantial value." She closed by stating, "I am probably the most unwearied hoper in the United States" (FK to Commons, 13 April 1927, copy, both in "General Correspondence: Commons, John R.," Box B11, NCL Records, DLC).

229. To Lillian D. Wald

[New York City]
April 4, 1927

Beloved Lady:

How long are you going to continue to give the weight of your honored name to the National Child Labor Committee, which is incessantly occupied in spreading the idea in its printed matter, and in other ways, that the time is not ripe for our petition? Sometimes their mildewing observations relate to the amendment itself as a whole, and sometimes specifically to our petition.[1]

Am I right in thinking that both J. Lathrop and J. Addams have resigned from the Board? If you don't feel moved to do so, do you not feel under any moral obligation to use your influence with the Board to get them to abandon this policy of obstruction? I don't want to get into an open fight with them, but if they keep on doing this I shall in a very short time be driven to denounce them as obstructionists, and question the validity of their claim that they represent the interest of working children in this country in this quarter century.

The Survey Midmonthly will contain a signed criticism by me of the Massachusetts Child Labor Committee on the basis that its program is largely obsolete; that it was suitable in the first quarter of this century, but not now.[2]

This is the line I shall take with regard to the National Child Labor Committee unless there is some effective protest inside the Board.

The samples of signatures copied from Mrs. LaBoutillier's blank show how very valuable are the names she was gathering when she was stopped.[3]

Yours devotedly,

CC, FKP, NN

1. FK explained her dispute with Wald and the NCLC in a letter to Grace Abbott three days later: "I am having a strenuous time with Miss Wald." She thought it "very wrong" that Wald did not put pressure on the NCLC board to support the child labor amendment. FK felt that the executive board of the NCLC was confusing potential supporters of the child labor amendment by publishing statements questioning its "validity and desirability." In 1929, Wald was still a member of the NCLC (FK to Abbott, 7 April 1927, "General Correspondence: Abbott, Grace," Box B10, NCL Records, DLC; Trattner, *Crusade for the Children,* 288n66).

2. In her letter to *The Survey,* FK contended that new machines and industrial poisons presented increasing dangers to child laborers. "How can Massachusetts," she asked, "be regarded as an 'advanced state' while she still cuts her list of prohibited hazards at the 16th birthday? And while she does not yet, like Illinois, print in her Monthly Labor Bulletin the deaths, dismemberments, mutilations and lesser injuries suffered by wage-earning minors in the preceding month?" ("Child Labor in Massachusetts," 119).

3. FK continued to vigorously support the petition drive in New York in support of ratification of the child labor amendment ("Secretary's Report," NCL Board of Directors Minutes, 11 January 1927, 2, and 5 May 1927, 3–4, both in Box A2, NCL Records, DLC).

230. To Warren Gibbs[1]

NATIONAL CONSUMERS' LEAGUE
156 FIFTH AVENUE
NEW YORK CITY

April 7, 1927

My dear Mr. Gibbs:

Your letter came duly, but illness has delayed my reply. Before committing myself to a subscription for William and Mary College, I need to know what the prospect is for Negro men and women students.

For many years I have been a member of the Board of the National Association for the Advancement of Colored People. In view of the gross discrimination against Negro education, both public and in regard to privately endowed colleges and universities, I should be utterly inconsistent if I should subscribe to a college exclusively for white people. The small amount that I am able to give for educational purposes I consider mortgaged to the promotion of Negro education in the South.[2]

Yours sincerely,

CC, FKP, NN

1. Warren Gibbs taught accounting and business at the College of William and Mary from 1926 to 1960 (information from John D. Haskell, Jr., Director of Manuscripts and Rare Books, Earl Gregg Swem Library, College of William and Mary).

2. In March 1927, FK rejected a request from the Phi Beta Kappa Sesquicentennial Endowment Fund on the same grounds (FK to Phi Beta Kappa Foundation, [22?] March 1927, FKP, NN).

231. To Albert B. Kelley

[New York City]
5-24-27

Beloved Brother

Your dear letters have been three to my one since I flitted two weeks ago to-day.[1] But I am so reinforced by the experience of making without damage so considerable and so "old timey" a journey, that I can safely promise you to do better henceforth.[2]

A delightfully exuberant note from Patsy was here when I came last evening. And this evening Augusta telephoned that Pat has landed a summer job on the Nation. I have a shamelessly brazen hunch that my old comrade-in-arms, Ozzy, may have thought none the worse of the superlatively attractive niece because this old Aunty lurks in the background.[3] And dear Brother don't, I beseech you, take it too hard! It will be a jazz episode for Pat to smile over all the rest of her life. And her head won't be turned. She must turn out stuff, and take her turn waiting for it to see the light. And tho' he is well padded and lined as sole owners of weeklies go, Ozzy is a thrifty one!

I'm writing her a note of congratulation, & I hope you may succeed in conquering your aversion enough to be cordial to Pat about this maiden effort in journalism. For no later triumph can ever excel this first thrill. I know because (when I was three years her senior) I underwent a weekly recurrent ecstasy, as I wrote of my green-gooseberry observations in England and Switzerland for the organ of the Grand Army of the Republic in 1883 and 1884![4]

I long so deeply to see you succeed in keeping the in constant touch with these exceedingly gifted young Kelleys, that there is hardly a conceivable concession that I would not gladly see you make of taste, prepossession, preference (anything but deeply rooted, reasoned conviction), for the sake of their feeling your warm, unbroken, sympathy with their experiences of youthful life and effort.

You will be sorry to hear that John is in bed the third day fighting off pneumonia. It started last week as influenza, and seems to be broken to-day, after a series of half delirious nights of fever. Ann has pulled him through![5]

Keep on with your doctors! They have been more wisely chosen than some of my assortment. But after all, here I am at the helm of a powerful organization, enjoying life and planning a happy summer in Maine. And from each one I have learned some valuable item.

I foresee that a strenuous test of your discretion will come with good golf weather, of which there seems to have been almost none hereabouts.

Good-night! It has struck ten, and this is my Sunday letter going into the chute on Tuesday night. This Sunday I was on the train from noon on, and Indiana was one vast park filled with the tender green of wheat and oats, and whitened with the candles of thousands of horse chestnut trees! An immeasurable area of loveliness under thin grey clouds!

Stand fast, dear brother! And don't fear to express all the love you feel for those young hearts!

F.K.

ALS, FKP, NN

Env: Mr. A. B. Kelley, Penn Athletic Club, Phila. Pa.

1. After visiting in Chicago at Hull House, FK traveled to Des Moines for the National Conference of Social Work, 11–18 May 1927 (FK, Des Moines, Iowa, to NK, 14 May 1927, FKP, NN).
2. AK had written most recently of his happiness in courting Esther King (AK, Philadelphia, Pa., to FK, 10 May 1927, FKP, NN).
3. AK's daughter Martha ("Patsy") was a student at Radcliffe. Progressive Oswald Garrison Villard (1872–1949) was a writer and editor at *The Nation* from 1918 to 1940 and co-founder of the NAACP.
4. For her articles in the *Washington National Tribune,* see Letter 6, FK to William D. Kelley, 2 January 1884, above.
5. Shortly after this writing, Ann and JK divorced in Paris; she married pacifist newspaper cartoonist Oscar Cesare in December (*NYT:* 5 June 1927, II:1, and 16 December 1927, 28). In an undated letter, JK wrote, "I seem to be the only feminist I know who really believes that a woman is not immoral if she follows her heart from one man to another" (JK [New York], to FK, [summer 1927], FKP, NN).

232. To Pauline Goldmark

[New York City]
May 27, 1927

Dear Pauline:

The long delay in acknowledging your letter of May 12th is due to two things.[1] First, it reached me in Des Moines, and second I have waited before answering it to talk with as many as possible of the people in closest touch with the Children's Bureau, viz. Grace Abbott, Edith Abbott, Miss [Sophonisba] Breckinridge, Miss Addams, and Mrs. Esther Kohn (at Hull House). I had hoped to see Julia Lathrop on her landing, but our trains passed each other between here and Chicago, and I have, therefore, missed what would probably have been very conservative advice.

I have, naturally, been continuously posted about the war on the Children's Bureau since the days of President Taft, and I have at no time been light-hearted about the danger to the Bureau involved in work for the Amendment. With Senator [James W.] Wadsworth defeated and [James A.] Reed of Missouri up for election in '28, however, our enemies seem to me weaker rather than stronger than they have been on several occasions.[2]

On one point I am, I confess, much clearer than I was on May 5th, the day of our meeting. I am convinced that work underground for the amendment in this state must continue, so far as our initiative can control, until we have at least 100,000 good signatures and 1,000 sponsors, before we seek any publicity.[3]

I had a comprehensive talk with Grace Abbott at Des Moines. She considers that the most useful thing for the amendment is perennial pointing out of the failure of the states. We are, of course, making the most substantive contribution to that process that is being made by any organization, through our continuing study of the astounding cruelties of the states towards children injured in industry.

Grace has never been enthusiastic about the petition method. She is, however, always contemptuous of New York in regard to forward movements. It did surprise me to have her say that, in her opinion, if New York were the next state to ratify the effect on the rest of the country would be hardly appreciable. I pointed out to her that there are more voters in this state than in the whole five that have ratified, together with the next three that are likely to ratify, e.g. Nebraska, Nevada, and some other agricultural state, perhaps North Dakota.[4]

To my question—"What alternative method of interesting any leading eastern state has anyone proposed?" she said "I have to admit that no one has proposed any alternative method, and I have none."

Please tell me for my enlightenment who are "the many sources" from whom you gather that "this is a critical time for the Children's Bureau"? Did you talk with Mrs. [Maud Wood] Park about it? If not, from whom did you get the impression that she believes that "the time has come to try and stem the tide"? I quote because your letter being hand-written I assume that you have no copy of it. Do you refer to the memorandum of the committee of the Women's Joint Congressional Committee, sent to its member organizations for their opinion as to the wisdom of adopting a policy of continuous rebuttal of attacks upon the Committee and its various activities?

If I do not know exactly about the sources of your anxiety, I naturally cannot fully share the anxiety scarcely at all, except as to the fact that you are alarmed without knowing the basis of your alarm. Personally, I have never been anything but alarmed about the Bureau. It seems to me amazing that it has been able to crusade as it has done without suffering far more effective onslaughts.

All the criticisms of members of the Board have been followed literally, except Robert Szold's suggestion that the observation "If this [is] the cream what must the skim milk be?" should come out.

With many additional changes I mailed the draft to Grace Abbott last evening, and as soon as it comes back I will send it to you as modified, for further suggestions.[5]

You know how highly I have always rated the value of your criticisms. I have no doubt that whenever we can sit down together with the Twenty Questions and a half day free, we can make them much more valuable and reduce any possible danger that may lurk in them. If this is not possible, can you come next Thursday afternoon at the close of your day and take dinner with me, and go over the draft returned by Grace?

Yours sincerely,

CC, "Children's Bureau: Publicity and Resolutions, 1930–1931," Box C3, NCL Records, DLC

1. Goldmark had written that she and her sister Josephine believed that the campaign to ratify the child labor amendment was draining strength and energy needed to save the Children's Bureau: "[A]ctive propaganda for the amendment here in the East adds fuel to this fire that is threatening the Children's Bureau, and for that reason I seriously question the wisdom of the work in New York" (Goldmark, n.p., to FK, 12 May 1927, copy, "Children's Bureau: Publicity and Resolutions, 1930–1931," Box C3, NCL Records, DLC).

2. Republican James W. Wadsworth was defeated in the 1926 election. Mary Garrett Hay, a leader of the state's Republican Party who was active in the LWV and the GFWC, said that women had defeated him because "Wadsworth never did anything for man, woman, or child while holding public office." Democrat Robert F. Wagner defeated him (*NYT*, 9 November 1926, 3).

3. Two years into the NCL's petition campaign, it had collected only 5,495 signatures. The Board of Directors discussed a policy of "retrenchment" in light of the NCL's budget constraints at its May meeting, which Goldmark attended. FK argued against abandoning either of the league's chief activities, ratification of the child labor amendment and study of children's compensation (NCL Board of Directors Minutes, 5 May 1927, 2, Box A2, NCL Records, DLC).

4. Arkansas had ratified the child labor amendment in 1924; Arizona, California, and Wisconsin in 1925; and Montana in 1927. In 1929, Nebraska's Senate voted to ratify the amendment, but the House vetoed it. North Dakota ratified in 1933, Nevada in 1937.

5. FK sent a draft titled "~~Twenty~~ Answers to ~~Twenty~~ Questions: The Pending Child Labor Amendment" to Frances Perkins for her comment. FK wrote that it would be "handed out to signers and circulators." The draft of "Answers to Questions" assured the skeptical that children working on farms and in households would not be affected and that federal inspectors would not be sent into parents' homes. It listed the weaknesses in various state laws regarding workmen's compensation for children (FK, New York, to Frances Perkins, 27 May 1927, Perkins Papers, NCC-RB). For FK's New York petition drive and Grace Abbott's stand on the amendment, see Goldmark, *Impatient Crusader*, 118–119; and Costin, *Two Sisters for Social Justice*, 156–158.

233. To Carrie Chapman Catt

NATIONAL CONSUMERS' LEAGUE
156 FIFTH AVENUE, ROOM 1129
NEW YORK CITY

Personal
June 4, 1927

Dear Mrs. Catt:

Your letter of June 3rd has just come. It is persuasive and convince~~inges~~ ***me*** and herewith I am complying, stipulating however, certain changes in the paragraphs which you have enclosed, and asking to see them again when you have revised them.[1]

1. If Dr. W____________ is no longer living, I am unaware of that fact. Certainly I cannot authorize the statement that he died, and I ask that it be cut out as I have indicated on page 8.

2. You say: "She is not and never was a revolutionist and never advocated it." This statement, thus unqualified, is absolutely untrue. The Socialist Party, when I joined it in Switzerland in 1884, was a revolutionary party, and I made no mental reservations in joining it. The line following what I have quoted naturally goes down with it. If I should authorize the publication of those two lines, I should join in the company of Liars. Having avoided that company until now, when I am nearly 68 years old, I do not intend to be exposed to the charge that I belong to it.

For the two lines which I ask to have obliterated I suggest the following substitute which is perfectly true:-

> She is not, and she never was, a Bolshevist or a Communist. The charge that she is or ever was either a Bolshevist or a Communist is absolutely without foundation, and is utterly and wilfully untrue.

[Frederick] Engels' book which I translated, and published, and paid for,[2] ~~was a~~ ***closed with a*** prophecy of revolution in England in the near future. The introduction which Engels wrote in 1886 for the American edition of my translation, was a careful consideration of the prospects of Socialism, far-from-Fabianism, in this country. The still existing copies, chiefly in libraries public and private, where they may survive for a century, carry my names, both Kelley and W____________ (though in this country there has been no second edition printed). Mr. Engels died in London in 1895. I repeat, to safeguard us both from certain contradiction, when your article is published, that I can no more repudiate having been a revolutionary Socialist than Al Smith can repudiate the Catholic church.

In reply to your first sheet of questions I submit the following:

The originator of the Children's Bureau is Lillian D. Wald, founder and head of the Henry Street Settlement and the Henry Street Visiting Nurses, in New York City. The initiat~~ive~~***or*** in promoting the establishment of the Children's Bureau,—the Act creating which was signed by President Taft in 1912,—was the National Child Labor Committee. At that time its Chairman was Dr. Felix Adler, and Mr. Paul Warburg and Mr. Isaac Seligman,[3] well-known bankers in New York City, were active members of the Board of Trustees, of which ***Miss Wald and*** I also w~~as a~~***ere*** member***s***.

I should be proud to be the originator of the idea of the child labor amendment, and the chief driving force in getting it submitted. I cannot truthfully claim to have been either one, nor can the amendment be attributed to the National Child Labor Committee. It was written by a group of Senators, and passed through Congress by the united efforts of 41 different states and national organizations.

I am proud to have been the first Chairman of the subcommittee of the Women's Joint Congressional Committee, appointed at the first meeting of that Committee on December 6th (if I remember the day of the month correctly) in 1920, for the purpose of promoting the bill for the Hygiene and Welfare of Maternity and Infancy. I did not suggest the bill.

I am opposed to the creation of a federal Department of Education. Before the Great War I favored the idea.

This covers, so far as I can do it, all the questions you have asked, and the two important errors of fact to be eliminated.

Please believe, dear Mrs. Catt, that I appreciate both your motive and what you are doing. Neither you nor your secretary gave me any information about the occasion i.e. the D.A.R. activities, for your present publication, and I was, therefore, at a complete disadvantage and unable to answer you intelligently.[4]

With sincere regret for the delay, and hoping that you may achieve your end, I am

Yours sincerely and devotedly,
Florence Kelley

P.S. I have no attacks upon me except the Congressional Record which you cite and the enclosed pages from a Maine paper. Please return them They are [sole?] copies and cannot be replaced.

TLS, "General Correspondence: Kelley, Florence," Box 18, NAWSA Records, DLC

Enc: Questions

1. Catt had written FK in late May that she was preparing an open letter to the DAR that concentrated on FK and JA because they were "the two persons most cruelly persecuted in the literature of the anti-Reds in circulation" (For the 1926 attack on FK, JA, and others, see Letter 217, FK to Paul Kellogg, 17 August 1926, above). In early June, Catt followed up with a set of questions for FK to confirm: Was FK a "Revolutionary Communist"? Had she translated Frederick Engels's works? Did she originate the idea of the Woman's Bureau, the Sheppard-Towner Act, and/or the child labor amendment? If not FK, who was the "driving force" behind these developments? Catt concluded that she had never "been so riled over anything as I have the treatment you and Jane Addams have received. I have not minded my own share in it because my feelings are copper plated, but I have cared about you two" (Catt to FK, 27 May 1927; Catt to FK, 3 June 1927, both in "General Correspondence: 'C,'" Box B11, NCL Records, DLC).

2. See Letters 11, 12, and 13, FK to Engels, 10 January 1886, 9 June 1886, and 6 June 1887, above.

3. New York banker Paul Moritz Warburg (1868–1932), a German immigrant, was appointed to the first Federal Reserve Board in 1914. Isaac N. Seligman (b. 1855) headed the New York

City banking firm of J. & W. Seligman from 1894 until his death in 1917 and was one of the founders of the National Child Labor Association.

4. Catt thanked FK for her "cooperation." She hoped "to stir the liberals inside of the D.A.R. to take some action" and warned her that the *Woman Patriot* attack of 1926 was not "old stuff" but was "being actively circulated by the DAR, and probably others, all over the country" (Catt, New York, to FK, 11 June 1927, "General Correspondence: 'C,'" Box B11, NCL Records, DLC). Thanking Catt for her forthcoming article, FK stated that she felt "embarrassed to be participating in the preparation of an article in which you so super-kindly call me a 'very great woman',—even tho this will, of course, be taken as meant to counterbalance the portrait of an abandoned vil[l]ain in which I have learned to recognize my character in caricature" (FK to Catt, 23 June 1927, Catt Papers, DLC).

Catt, a contributing editor to the *Woman Citizen*, published two articles there. In "Lies-At-Large" (12 [June 1j927]: 10–11, 41), she charged that "self-styled patriots have wandered far away from facts and truth. . . . Whoever says they [the accused] are red, lies." One month later, *Woman Citizen* published Catt's "An Open Letter to the D.A.R.," which specifically refuted accusations against JA, FK, and Rose Schneiderman (*Woman Citizen* 12 [July 1927]:10–12, 41). Describing the attacks on FK as "the most atrocious treatment that any women in the United States" had ever experienced, Catt's defense of FK used almost verbatim the language of FK's letter except for the paragraph on Engels, which she omitted. She stated, "Florence Kelley is a very great woman, and thousands of honorable, patriotic, non-Socialistic Americans would take oath that no D.A.R. possesses truer patriotism or nobler loyalty to this government than does she" (41).

Catt's "Open Letter" received national attention and praise from several *Woman Citizen* readers, including Eleanor Roosevelt ("Editorially Speaking," *Woman Citizen* 12 [August 1927]: 20; "With Our Readers," *Woman Citizen* 12 [September 1927]: 41). A *New York Times* editorial criticized the DAR and praised Catt's "overwhelming refutation" of the charges against JA and FK, pointing out that "damaging assertions" that could not possibly be true had caused the public to lose faith "in anything which the authors may say" (*NYT*, 24 July 1927, II:8). For more about public reaction to the DAR's attacks, see Lemons, *The Woman Citizen*, 223–224.

234. To Myrta Jones

Naskeag [Brooklin] Maine over Labor Day
July 14th, 1927

Dear Myrta:

It is a fine sailing day and we are working on the west porch watching the occasional small sloops and cats tilting their way in a heavy breeze, which has shifted from northwest to southwest since 9.00 A.M., when we began.

I have at last a stenographer-secretary, and this morning we have tackled the fifth chapter of my reminiscences. This deals with the current sequel to the old struggle for the 8-hours day. That struggle dates, so far as leisure by law for women is concerned, from 1893, my first year at Hull House, which is described in the June Survey.[1]

Here's hoping you take the Survey and have seen the June issue.

Do you see the American Labor Legislation Review? Its June issue chronicles what I believe to be one of the most important international news items since the War. France has ratified the 8-hours day convention, adopted in Washington in 1919 by the International Labor Conference, delayed until now chiefly by our own selves.[2]

I am convinced that France'[s] present action opens the way for our Consumers' League to retake the lead that we lost during the War and have never resumed. Please do not be frightened and think that the northwest wind and Pierce's coffee are making me see visions and dream dreams.

This situation is external and full of promise. Here is our opportunity to begin again to work at Washington as we were doing until 1913 when, after Congress adjourned, I went to Berne instead of coming here, and attended what proved to be ***I believe*** the last International Convention of the Association for Labor Legislation[3] until the Washington International Labor Convention in 1919 adopted the draft convention for a world 8-hours day for men, women and children in industry.

It is this which France has now ratified. You doubtless remember that when Czecho-Slovakia adopted her new constitution becoming a republic, she put the 8-hours day firmly into both.[4]

The United States, being a federation, ~~has to~~ ***must*** choose one of two methods: either all our states can approve this Convention and authorize the President and Senate to sign a treaty of ratification, or the President and the Senate can go ahead and do it of their own volition, as they did in the case of migratory birds.[5] But who can conceive of Mr. Wilson, Mr. Harding or Mr. Coolidge going ahead in such a case?

Obviously the coming President, whoever he may be, and the coming Senate, whatever we may elect, will have to be pushed, and that will be the task of women for a considerable number of years to come.

I write you all this by way of giving an account to you, the Vice-President, most deeply, directly and personally interested in the manner of my use of this vacation.[6] More soon.

Yours devotedly,

FK: MF

CC, FKP, NN

1. FK, "I Go to Work," *Survey Graphic* 58 (1 June 1927): 271–274, 301; reprinted in FK, *Notes of Sixty Years,* 77–89. This fifth portion was published two years later as "Thirty Years of the Consumers' League."

2. The International Labor Conference, sponsored by the League of Nations (which established the ILO), was held in Washington, D.C., from 29 October to 29 November 1919. The conference proposed international standards of labor legislation that included the eight-hour day and limitation of night work for women and children ("Conventions of the International Labor Conference," II:288). In 1919, the ILO adopted conventions limiting the work day to eight hours (Hours of Work [Industry] Convention, convention 1) and preventing women from working at night (Night Work [Women] Convention, convention 4) and sent them to countries for ratification.

The *American Labor Legislation Review* devoted a section of its June 1927 issue to international standards of labor protection. Professor Herbert Heaton of Queen's University in Canada wrote that "the wind is blowing in the direction of an economic United States of Europe. If that comes, the pressure of competition of labor standards will be relieved" (Heaton, "'Social Justice' Motive in Creating International Labor Standards," 166). Mary Van Kleeck, director of industrial studies at the Russell Sage Foundation, argued that the United States should join the ILO. She wrote that the ILO studies had shown "the desirability of studying the problem of labor standards industry by industry, going beyond national boundaries and striking deeper into the economic forces which in the last analysis determine labor standards" (Van Kleeck, "How the United States Can Aid the International Labor Organization through Research," 170). On 2 February, France announced its plan to ratify the eight-hour day as proposed by the ILO's Hours of Work (Industry) Convention (1919) (*NYT*, 3 February 1927, 35). It did so on 26 February.

3. See Letter 121, FK to NK, 13 September 1913, above.

4. On 27 July, FK had written to John B. Andrews, president of the American Association for Labor Legislation and editor of the *American Labor Legislation Review*, to ask him which countries had ratified the convention. He replied that Greece (1920); Roumania, India, and Czechoslovakia (1921); Bulgaria (1923); Chile and Italy (1925); Belgium (1926); and France (1927) had ratified (Andrews, New York, to FK, 27 July 1927, FKP, NN). FK incorporated these facts and several of the themes of this letter in her article "Leisure by Law for Women."

5. Columbia University law professor J. P. Chamberlain felt that the United States should join the ILO, citing the 1918 Migratory Bird Treaty between United States and Canada as an example of a treaty that overrode state legislation (Chamberlain, "The United States and the International Labor Organization").

6. Jones replied, "I am pleased with the mental picture of you and our secretary working on the West Porch." She had learned through friends of the improvement in FK's leg: "Has the new treatment performed a miracle?" Jones enclosed a check for $200 as an installment toward FK's summer secretary's salary (Jones, Cleveland, to FK, 20 July [1927], FKP, NN).

235. To Jane Addams

MRS. FLORENCE KELLEY
NASKEAG, BROOKLIN
MAINE

July 20, 1927

Dearest J. A.:

The Balch's bring the tidings, which give me the usual summer joy, that you are actually at Hull's Cove.

I missed a call yesterday afternoon from them because I was taking John's mother-in-law, Martha McNeill, to Ellsworth on her way home.[1] So I do not know how serious the consequences may be of a rumored tumble since you arrived. Here's hoping they may not have been serious at all.

Have you seen the D.A.R. slander-pamphlet, The Common Enemy? Mrs. Catt published a fierce, but evidently not fierce enough, attack upon it in the current Woman Citizen which has been feeble-mindedly answered by Mrs. Grace Brosseau, President General of the D.A.R.[2] I think the time has come when there must be a libel suit to stop this endless and even more wide-spread sewage.

Have you read Professional Patriots?[3]

I am impressed by the fact that Fred Marvin has been broken and the New York Commercial killed by a lawsuit brought against the latter jointly with the Security League by Norman Thomas, Arthur Garfield Hays, McAlister Coleman and a Mrs. Frank whom I do not know.[4]

McAlister Coleman tells me that they sued for $25,000 each, carefully selecting their judge in the New York court; that the suit cost them almost nothing, being entered by friends in the legal profession; that they had no intention of letting it come to trial, but are carefully keeping it hanging; that Fred Marvin came to Norman Thomas and begged on his knees that they withdraw it, but Norman summoned courage to tell him that they needed money for the cause and that $100,000 would not begin to pay them for his lies and insults.

The New York Commercial was an old and, of late years, feeble journal, and the scandal of this suit put an end to it.

I am asking Mary Dreier if she and Mrs. Robbins will back Rose Schneiderman in such a suit.[5] Rose, I feel confident, would be delighted to bring it, if she had the Woman's Trade Union League behind her, which would be impossible without Mary Dreier and perhaps Mrs. Robbins.

Ko would, of course, see me through, though I think the costs would be trifling.

We should, I suppose, each have her own counsel, and the suit would have to be entered where the offense was committed. This geographical item I have not yet obtained. I have always assumed that the D.A.R. headquarters were in Washington with their building.

How do you feel about this? Do you take literally the Quaker injunction to keep out of the courts? Hollingsworth Wood is, of course, a lawyer and a Quaker of the most faithful.[6]

Ko has recently united with the Society of Friends but continues his work at 20 Broadway being, I gather, neither more nor less conscientious in his practice than he has always been.

I have asked the office to get me a dozen copies of The Common Enemy, and will send you one as soon as they come.

Rose Schneiderman and I could, at a pinch, go ahead without you so far as we ourselves are concerned, but I am not at all clear what the effect on public opinion would be of our doing so. The suit is ***considered*** ~~brought~~, of course, not in the hope of extracting pelf from the D.A.R. but of closing its insolent and mendacious hydra-headed collection of mouths, to say nothing of its ink bottles and typewriters.

Until I learned of the eminently successful outcome of the Norman Thomas suit, I had been unwilling even to consider Mr. Chenery's urgent entreaties that I sue the Woman Patriot.[7] That foul nest seemed~~, however,~~ too insane to be worth tackling under any circumstances.

The D.A.R. is another and entirely different story. Please write me what you think.

I cannot come to Hull's Cove this summer because I am working with two secretaries, one compiling the next pamphlet of the League on legal deaths and mutilation*s* of wage-earning children, and one on my everlasting reminiscences.

Mrs. [Mary Dana Hicks] Prang is not here, being apparently fatally ill in the New England Sanitarium at Melrose. Blind, alas, and palsied, though with her incredible, gallant spirit she managed to spend the winter in Arizona, going thither immediately after her ninetieth-birthday dinner and returning a few weeks ago for medical care in the sanitarium.

Dear love to Mary [Rozet Smith]. I am assuming that her coming to the land of rain and fogs means that the asthma is conquered.

What are the chances of your ***both***[8] coming over for ***next*** Sunday dinner? Then we could talk over the possibilities of the D.A.R. lawsuit with or without your participation.[9]

Yours ***always devotedly***
F.K.

TLS, Addams Collection, IRoC

1. Ann Kelley's mother, Martha Chamberlayne Valentine McNeill of Richmond, Virginia, frequently visited FK at Seawest, and their friendship continued after JK and Ann's divorce (Martha McNeill, Richmond, Va., to FK, 24 July 1927, FKP, NN).

2. See Letter 233, FK to Carrie Chapman Catt, 4 June 1927, above. *The Common Enemy,* written by the Key Men of America for the DAR, named ninety organizations, including the YMCA, the YWCA, the NAACP, and the U.S. Department of Labor, that were tainted with radicalism. The national DAR prohibited local branches from inviting speakers from these organizations (Lemons, *The Woman Citizen,* 223). Grace Lincoln Hall Brosseau (b. 1872), president of the DAR, opposed the extension of the Sheppard-Towner Act in a letter that Thomas Bayard inserted in the *Congressional Record* (69th Cong., 2nd sess., 8 January 1927, 1280–1281). Brosseau answered Catt's "An Open Letter to the D.A.R." by stating that Catt "is either strangely misinformed or willfully unobserving if she fails to recognize the evidences of communism in America. Furthermore she has not in the slightest degree impressed us with our guilt; nor will she deter us in our efforts along any lines of endeavor we may have chosen" (*NYT,* 14 July 1927, 14).

3. Norman Hapgood, ed., *Professional Patriots: An Exposure of the Personalities, Methods and Objectives in the Organized Effort to Exploit Patriotic Impulses in These United States During and After the Late War* (New York: Boni, 1927).

4. The *New York Commercial,* which had a circulation of about 10,000, was purchased by Ridder Brothers on 31 December 1926 (*NYT,* 1 January 1927, 24). Fred Marvin (1868–1939) had edited the *Commercial* since 1925. FK told Marian Parkhurst that she believed that Marvin had supplied information to the DAR for publication in *The Common Enemy* (FK to Parkhurst, 13 August 1927, copy, FKP, NN). Norman M. Thomas (1884–1968) helped establish in 1917 what later became the ACLU. As head of the Socialist Party after the death of Eugene Debs in 1926, Thomas ran for a number of offices on the Socialist ticket, including U.S. president. He served as co-director of the LID from 1922 to 1937. Arthur Garfield Hays (1881–1954) helped found and served as counsel to the ACLU. Journalist and author McAlister Coleman (b. 1889) later wrote a biography of Debs.

5. Mary Dreier (1875–1963), labor and peace activist, served as chair of the WJLC (New York) from 1918 to 1924 and in 1926. Her older sister Margaret Dreier Robins had been named

in the spider web chart (see Letter 195, FK to Herbert Bayard Swope, 27 May 1924, above). Rose Schneiderman had been attacked as the "Red Rose of Anarchy" at the DAR's national conference in 1927 (Lemons, *The Woman Citizen*, 223).

6. Quaker Hollingsworth Wood (1873–1956) was president of the National Urban League and an ACLU activist.

7. William L. Chenery (1884–1974), a former Hull House resident, was editor and publisher of *Collier's Weekly*. For the *Woman Patriot*'s attacks on FK and others, see Letter 217, FK to Paul Kellogg, 17 August 1926, above.

8. The word "both" is inserted above the line after "your."

9. JA replied, "I don't believe that I could go in for a libel suit. It is not exactly my Quakerishness—it's the whole situation" (JA, Hull's Cove, Me., to FK, 25 July 1927, FKP, NN). Julia Lathrop also advised against a suit, "Of course you have a good case. But I dread to see you, who have been so patient and so generous to a thousand good causes, rewarded by the privilege of instituting a libel suit" (Lathrop, Rockford, Ill., to FK, 25 July [1927], FKP, NN). JA and FK met for dinner on 17 August (FK to AK, 28 August 1927, FKP, NN.) FK's letter and JA's reply are reprinted in Sklar and Baker, "How Did Women Peace Activists Respond to 'Red Scare' Attacks during the 1920s?"

236. To Nicholas Kelley

[Brooklin, Maine]
Over Labor Day
August 9, 1927

Beloved Son

Enclosed is a draft copy of my article for the Social Service Review, edited by Miss [Sophonisba] Breckinridge and Miss [Edith] Abbott for the U. of Chicago Graduate School of Social Service Administration. It is to appear in the December issue, and we shall have reprints for use with Congress if, and when, the Woman's Party attempts to carry out its threatend "drive" for its Equality Amendment so-called.[1]

For accuracy of facts concerning L.[ouis] D. B.[randeis], F.[elix] F.[rankfurter], and J.[udge] G.[oldsmith], I have sent a copy to F. F. who is always very generous about revising details. Unhappily it must have reached him at a moment of intense anxiety about Governor Fuller's then approaching decision.[2]

By now poor F. F. must be whirling like a Dervish in an effort to get, today, reprieve enough to enable him to get habeas corpus or certiorari to the U.S.S.C. via Mr. Justice Holmes at his summer home on the North Shore. In any case, he can be in no mood for going back to 1908 and making sure that I have not been guilty, in this paper, of any thing equivalent to my recently mailing to 20 Broadway a letter intended for you at 80 Broadway!

Parenthetically we were trying on Sunday, Mrs. Laura Williams, Bessie [Balch] and Emily Balch and I, to remember the name of the third defendant in the Moyer-Heyward and ? case in Idaho 20 years ago this summer. We read greedily, all summer long, every issue of the "Age of Reason" or whatever the paper was, about Borah's prosecution. That was the beginning of his career! And now we cannot even remember who was the third defendant![3]

The moral of that is clear as applied to those romantic revolutionists who believe that anything is gained for the cause of progress by these murderous travesties of justice. How far have the Chicago anarchists' executions contributed to clarify American public opinion? The Moyer-Hayward trial is largely fog and cloud in the memories even of those as keenly interested at the time as Emily and I. How long will this world-clamor hold on, whether the victims are hanged or reprieved?[4]

If I ever have an instant needed to be confirmed in my conviction that the only hope for peaceful progress is eternal pegging away at the slow process of improving the laws, this latest atrocity would seal that conviction for life. May I never live to see another trial like this!

All of this is by way of explaining my asking you to read the kind of article you loathe, and criticize it.

It has to be back in Chicago by August 31st.

Yours always gratefully,

P.S. As to the Pennington,—I do wish to engage the room.[5] Will they let me have my own furniture, and can it be crammed into the room you describe? I mean the four mahogany pieces which were comfortably stowed in my cubicle at Miss [Lillian] Wald's, i.e., bookcase, bed, dressing table and chair.

If you think they will go in, pl~~ace~~***ease*** sign on for October 1st. My lease at 54 runs until then.

I do not know exactly what to do about Patsy. I am leaving here on Labor Day, and I hate more than I can say to tell her; because that means that she will have to move to the Emersons', or would Augusta and Margaret be back as early as September 6th, and would Augusta want to gather Pat in until time for her to go back to Radcliffe?[6] My understanding is that she still has one term before her degree.

This is the kind of easterly storm that we do not expect until September but often get in August.

Your grateful and loving
Ma

TLS, FKP, NN

1. In "Leisure by Law for Woman," FK criticized the NWP, writing that the organization had "unquestionably contributed toward slackening the progress of urgently needed, new safeguarding laws in the states" (31–32).

2. The decision of whether to execute Nicola Sacco and Bartolomeo Vanzetti was referred to Governor Alvan T. Fuller (1878–1958), Republican governor of Massachusetts (1925–1929), who formed a committee to advise him. On 3 August 1927, Fuller declared that the trial proceedings had been in order. Frankfurter and other lawyers were working for the commutation of the sentence, but Supreme Court Justice Oliver Wendell Holmes, Jr., denied their *certiorari* (a writ calling into question a lower court's decision) on 20 August (*NYT,* 21 August 1927, 1). NK wrote, "I am not as certain as I should like to be that there was no mistake in the trial of Sacco and Vanzetti, nor that they are guilty. But I am not certain at all that they are innocent"

(FK to Breckinridge, 6 August 1927, copy; and NK, New York, to FK, 13 August 1928, both in FKP, NN). Sacco and Vanzetti were executed on 23 August.

3. Laura C. Williams of Washington, D.C., was an NCL vice-president from 1926 to 1928; she was also an officer in the Washington, D.C., branch of the LWV in 1922 (*Washington Post,* 26 March 1922, 6). On the Heywood trial, see Letter 96, FK to NK, 1 July 1907, above. William E. Borah was special prosecutor in the Haywood trial. The third defendant was George A. Pettibone.

4. As in the Sacco and Venzetti case, the trial of Bill Haywood, Charles Moyer, and George Pettibone in Boise, Idaho, in 1907 involved questionable police methods and collusion among police, judges, prosecutors, and employers (Dubofsky, *We Shall Be All,* 98–105).

5. FK had written NK earlier that she could save money and be closer to his family by taking a room at the Pennington Friends House, a residential community founded by Quakers that was near the 15th Street Meeting House of the Religious Society of Friends. She wanted to be sure that the hotel was "free from any aroma of charity" and had an elevator. After visiting the hotel, NK expressed concern about the number of stairs FK would have to climb. He wrote his mother that he had rented the room for her, "although with some misgivings." He found the room "rather pleasant," but he was not sure "how it would strike you as a place for entertaining guests" (FK to NK, 15 July 1927; NK, New York, to FK, 5 August and 13 August 1927, all in FKP, NN).

6. During the summer, Patsy Kelley had been staying in FK's rooms at 52 Gramercy Park while working for *The Nation* (FK to AK, 29 June 1927, FKP, NN; see Letter 231, FK to AK, 24 May 1927, above). "Margaret" was probably a servant in the Nicholas Kelley household (NK to FK, 5 October 1931, FKP, NN).

237. To Robert M. La Follette, Jr.[1]

MRS. FLORENCE KELLEY
NASKEAG, BROOKLIN
MAINE

8-20-27

My dear Senator La Follette

I have just had the pleasure ~~and the pleasure,~~ and the honor, of a week's visit from Mrs. Laura Williams of Washington.

In the course of it, she said that she understood, that you were considering introducing a bill to deal with the present misuses of the Congressional Record.

Like every other powerful agent, the Record when misused can do great harm. Senator Bayard's printing in it, in July last year, Miss Mary Kilbreth's perjured affidavit attesting the truth of the Woman's~~s~~ Patriot's libels concerning Grace Abbott and me undoubtedly injured the Children's Bureau and the Consumers League, and continues even yet to do so.[2]

That tissue of lies is now circulated in Massachusetts, in a reprint, by and of the Woman's Patriot group, Mrs. Robinson, sister inlaw of Professor James Harvey Robinson and wife of his brother, a professor at Harvard.[3] The fact that the libels appear in the Record makes them not only unpunishable but respectable in the eyes of Massachusetts reactionaries. Fourteen months after those libels were made public at the expense of the taxpayers, the Government Printing Office is publishing reprints paid for from unknown sources. They carry its imprint.[4]

However desirable it may be (and it is often of immense use), to have reprints available for private circulation, it is utterly intolerable that such poisonous libels as these should be kept in circulation as privileged matter because of Senator Bayard's first outrage last year, in getting them into the Record and thus obtaining the franking privilege for them.

I am seriously thinking of testing the degree of privilege that attaches to reprints, made a year after the publication of libels that were never even incorporated in a speech!

They were in the form of a petition from the Woman Patriot to Congress not to prolong the appropriation for the ~~W~~ Maternity and Infancy Act.

I understand that the D.A.R. is now allowing the circulation of these reprints at its meetings.

The only thing that gives me pause is the reactionary character of the Massachusetts Courts, and the temper of the Massachusetts ruling class.

I am taking advantage of my vacation in the country to write you thus in detail because this perverted misuse of the Record is a much more serious evil than appears upon the surface.

The delay ~~ede~~ in ratification of the children's amendment ~~is~~ was greatly aided by libelous attacks upon its ~~the~~ friends ~~of the Amendment~~ by Senators King of Utah and Bayard repeated on the floor of the Senate while the Amendment was pending, and circulated in reprints and in the press after it was submitted to the States.[5]

With warmest regards for yourself and your family, and hoping for Mrs. La Follette's complete and speedy recovery,[6] I am

ALDft, FKP, NN

1. Robert M. La Follette, Jr. (1895–1953), U.S. senator from Wisconsin for the Republican-Progressive Party (1925–1947), continued his father's pursuit of social justice agendas.

2. See Letter 217, FK to Paul Kellogg, 17 August 1926, and Letter 218, FK to John Ryan, 20 August 1926, both above.

3. In 1887, Margaret Casson married Benjamin Lincoln Robinson (1864–1935), head of Harvard University's Gray Herbarium. Her brother-in-law, historian James Harvey Robinson (1863–1936), was a founder of the New School for Social Research in New York City.

4. FK wrote Carrie Chapman Catt about the libel suit she was considering: "I have no reason to believe that circulating the Congressional Record itself is libel, but circulating a reprint from it at public meeting of the D.A.R. by members of the D.A.R. would, I believe, clearly constitute libel" (FK to Catt, 12 August 1927, copy, FKP, NN).

5. Thomas Bayard spoke at length in the Senate against the child labor amendment on 31 May 1924. William H. King interrupted Bayard to ask if the latter knew that FK was "a follower of Karl Marx in communism" (68th Cong., 1st sess., *Cong. Rec.*, 31 May 1924, 10007).

6. Belle Case La Follette (1859–1931), like her husband and son, was an active social reformer. By August, FK had nearly abandoned her plan to sue the DAR, writing Marian Parkhurst, "My chance of a successful law suits seems Alas! To be dwindling" (FK to Parkhurst, 30 August 1928, copy, FKP, NN).

238. To Albert B. Kelley

52 Gramercy Park N. [New York City]
Saturday afternoon
9-17-27

Beloved Brother

You made this week a doubly happy one, by your demonstration of returning vigor,—so wonderful compared with last Christmas and last spring,—and then by your delightful letter.

This is one of the loveliest days of the year. The grass in the little park is still emerald. Some congenial friends of many years are pausing, near-by, en route from a New England vacation to Louisville, where they co-operate with our efforts through thick and thin. This is an annually recurring pleasure and reinforcement of morale.

I'm wondering whether Young Martha Mott has brought it about that you and I read the Nation on the same day of the week? Never until last night did I feel confident that I knew the inner significance of the word macabre![1] At this point I pause to cut out her review and paste it on the inside back cover of this year's account book, where seeing it daily, I shall get it impressed upon my unstable memory.

That is now done. In the process I made a pathetic discovery. Poor Cline, the author of her book, has just escaped first the noose, and now, life imprisonment! He is to spend a year in Tolland County jail (Connecticut) and pay a fine instead. He has long been a periodical drinker. He is one of the most skillful and conscientious reporters I have ever known. He did me and several of my friends an important service two years ago$_x$ And now, when he has been in horrible trouble since the Sunday, last spring when you and John [Kelley] lunched with me, and I gave him a small check for Cline's wife's immediate use, along comes Pat and gives Cline's book an original and unusual lift![2]

You may be interested to know what he did for us. Bayard Swope, Executive Editor of the World, sent him to me (a total stranger) to get, at my request, a true statement about Secretary of War [John W.] Weeks' famous Spider Web Chart.[3]

This was a huge wall-chart showing three columns, a middle one as wide as both the side ones. In the middle was a list of the names of about 70 organizations of women (nearly all more or less confused as to names or spelling, or both).

The side columns contained a weird collections of names of alleged officers and members, inaccurate in every way.

Above and below was a loathsome mess of denunciation of us all indiscriminately. Responsible for it all was, directly, Brigadier General Amos R. Fries, chief of the Chemical Warfare division of the War Department. The names of the individuals attacked were connected with the organizations by criss crossing fine lines intended to indicate secret, perhaps conspiratory co-operative activities.

Cline wrote three very powerful analytical articles which appeared on three consecutive days, one being a Sunday feature article, besides procuring a powerful editorial.

Secretary Weeks apologized in person and in writing to the organizations, and ordered the chart withdrawn.

At this point the bore arrived, en route from Maine to Washington. She stayed from 4 to 8 p.m.! Then I had to go to bed.

It is now 3 a.m. Sunday, and I am using the mail shute and special stamps, being surely too late for your club messenger's visit to the post-office.

Before I was able to learn about the suitability of Alpine rays for my queer skin, the question has arisen whether the milder infra-red rays are not better adapted to an elderly person. So I am seeking light, this week, on both.

Good-bye for this morning, dear companion of this bad year! Now that the birthdays are cheerfully past, may the new cycle be as much better as it promises![4]

Your loving sister
F.K.

ALS, FKP, NN

1. See Letter 231, FK to AK, 24 May 1927, above. Signing her brief review "Martha Mott," Patsy Kelley characterized *The Dark Chamber* by Leonard Cline as "Credible Macabre" (*The Nation* 125 [21 September 1927]: 290).
2. On 23 May 1927, Leonard Cline was arraigned on murder charges for shooting his house-guest Wilfred Pryor Irwin on 16 May. Just before he was to be tried on 14 September, he pled guilty to manslaughter and was sentenced to a one-year prison term and fined $1,000. His wife was Katharine Cline (*NYT*: 24 May 1927, 27 and 15 September 1927, 31).
3. For Cline's previous work and the spider web chart, see Letter 195, FK to Herbert Bayard Swope, 27 May 1924, and Letter 199, FK to Julia Lathrop, 28 July 1924, both above.
4. AK wrote that his health was "steadily improving" and that he expected his divorce from Marianna Kelley to be final on 7 October (AK, Philadelphia, Pa., to FK, 5 October 1927, FKP, NN).

239. To Walter Lippmann

NATIONAL CONSUMERS' LEAGUE
156 FIFTH AVENUE, ROOM 1129
NEW YORK CITY

November 16, 1927

Dear Mr. Lippmann

The essential evil of the Manufacturers' Child Labor Program is the sinister fact that it constitutes the latest link in an unbroken chain of resistance to enlightened child labor legislation.[1]

If this Program were a beginning following a past of protracted innocence, there would be no such urgent need for all hands on deck. From the 8 hours day law in Illinois in 1895 "for female employees" from the 14th birthday on to the 8 hours bill in New York last Winter, which included girls from 16 years of age up,[2] no such health measure has been allowed to escape effective opposition before the legislature, or before the state courts, or before some federal court.

Full notice has been served upon the American public that the National Association of Manufacturers means business now, as it has done in all this long history. But you and the New Republic are, so far as I know, unique in your editorial appreciation of the nature of this leopard.[3] The press has, almost unanimously, gullibly assumed that the leopard is changing its spots. The significance of the threat for the children of this Republic is being glossed over by F. Ernest Johnson, Chairman of the Executive Committee of the National Child Labor Committee, and Executive also of the Federation of Church of Christ in America.[4] You know the good record of that organization in getting the 8 hours day for men in the steel industry! What are we to think when it faces with equanimity the threat to lengthen the working day for children 14 years old, in mines and factories, to nine P.M. starting at seven and making an enforceable 8 hours day administratively impossible?

Whose claim on my heart is prior—that of the children for whom I have striven forty years, or that of the most brilliant defender to whom they could turn on Manhattan Island?

Yours hopefully—and confidently
Florence Kelley

I hope you have the printed matter sent with my letter last night.[5]

TLS, Lippmann Papers, CtY

1. The NAM had recently issued a bulletin establishing standards it believed necessary for the "further legal protection of children 14 and 15 years of age." Included were provisions that children had to complete the sixth grade, that children in factories and mining could not work more than forty-eight hours a week, and that children in factories and mining could not work before 7 A.M. or after 9 P.M. (*NYT*, 25 November 1927, 38). FK analyzed these provisions in "The Manufacturers' Plan for Child Labor," alerting readers to the dangers of the new program. "What means has the average, well-informed citizen of knowing how retrograde is the proposal to set up, as a nationwide standard, the fourteenth birthday and the sixth school grade? Even well-read, sympathetic people without contact with factories cannot conceive the multiple risks that lurk in manufacture awaiting adolescent children" (71).

2. Despite Republican opposition, the New York legislature approved a forty-eight hour work week (with some exceptions) for women in March 1927 (*NYT*, 23 March 1927, 10).

3. Responding to a *New Republic* editorial praising the NAM program, FK argued that the program set lower standards for child labor than were already established in many states, a point she had also made in her *Survey* article ("The Week," *Survey* 52 [19 October 1927]: 221–222). She wrote, "Under pretense of abolishing night work, the eight-hour day is made possible, by reëstablishing the abandoned closing hour of 9 P.M. Today Idaho alone has this closing hour. Texas and California alone have a later one, 10 P.M. . . . What quality of 'protection of children fourteen and fifteen years of age' is this, depriving them of the most

important safeguard of their health—a long night's rest, a long break between one day's work and the next?" (FK, "Can the Leopard Change Its Spots?" 289).

4. Reverend F. Ernest Johnson was executive secretary of the Department of Research and Education of Federal Council of Churches of Christ in America from 1918 to 1950 (Survey Associates records, MnU-SW). He wrote "Facing Industrial Facts in the Churches."

5. FK invited Lippmann to speak at the NCL's annual meeting, but he postponed accepting, writing that "I hate particularly to talk when I have to talk off the top of my mind, and have no feeling of any depth of understanding or background." However, he continued, "The idea of dressing down the authors of this program does appeal to me somewhat" (FK to Lippmann, 15 November 1927; Lippmann, New York, to FK, 15 November 1927, copy, both in Lippmann Papers, CtY). The *New York World* published an editorial on 30 November deploring the "decline in interest in the subject [of the child labor amendment]. . . . But it is only a question of time when the backward States must conform to more advanced standards." It lauded the "public-spirited men and women who are keeping up the good fight for the right of children to their childhood" and called for support of their cause ("Child-Labor Legislation Lags," *New York World*, 30 November 1927, 12). FK thanked Lippmann for the editorial, and he replied, "We want to help you as much as we can in this fight. Our feeling is that having opposed the federal amendment, we have a very special moral obligation to help state action" (FK to Lippmann, 2 December 1927, Lippmann Papers; Lippmann, New York, to FK, 5 December 1927, "Press and Periodicals: *New York World*, 1924–1930," Box B20, NCL Records, DLC).

At its annual meeting on 28–29 November (at which Lippmann did not speak), the NCL resolved to make the public aware of the "significance and probable results" of the NAM program and to work with NCL members in states where the legislature was meeting "to initiate and support measures tending to raise further existing educational and labor standards" ("Resolutions," NCL Annual Meeting Minutes, 1927, 1, Box A8, NCL Records, DLC).

New York City Candy Worker, 1928. Source: Consumers' League of New York City, *Behind the Scenes in Candy Factories* (New York: Consumers' League of New York, 1928), image courtesy of Kheel Center for Labor-Management Documentation and Archives, School of Industrial and Labor Relations, Cornell University.

8 1928 – 1931

"How to Keep the Interest of the Careless Public Alive"

INTRODUCTION

Florence Kelley's letters in the late 1920s and early 1930s depict her forceful defense of her achievements of the past forty years and her pursuit of new initiatives. Though still laced with crisis, her correspondence shows that her enemies had grown more familiar and she had recovered some allies. Signalling the health of her agenda, she moved it forward into the South, where child labor was most embedded and wage-earners most embattled.

In the fall of 1929, the NCL celebrated the 30th anniversary of its founding with a program featuring "Industrial Transition in the South." Writing Roscoe Pound about that event, Kelley described the league's forward momentum. "Following the long paralysis of effort after the Sutherland [Adkins] decision, there is at last a strong, widespread stirring of interest in social legislation, enormously accentuated by the recent experience of working mothers and children in North Carolina and Tennessee."[1]

Kelley was responding swiftly to the violent repression of unions in the southern textile industry. Led by women workers protesting low wages and the "stretch out," which increased the number of looms or spindles maintained by each worker, textile workers struck in the spring of 1929 in Elizabethton, Tennessee, and Gastonia, North Carolina, and struggled to form local branches of the United Textile Workers of America. With the aid of hundreds of national guardsmen, employers successfully crushed the nascent union. Unions were not firmly established in the southern textile industry until the 1936 Wagner Act protected the organizing efforts of the Congress of Industrial Organizations and the 1938 Fair Labor Standards Act created national hours and wages standards.[2] By the fall of 1929, the failure of the union effort was clear and Florence Kelley offered an alternative—state labor legislation backed by public monitoring of its enforcement.[3]

Kelley viewed the exploitative southern textile industry as part of the larger history in which "American industry has never paid its social costs."[4] Instead, industry was subsidized by the public and private resources that cared for those it injured or exhausted. Child labor was the best example of high social costs American industry shirked. In the child labor amendment she continued to seek national standards that would stop the "sacrifice of minors and children to machines."[5] She urged the New York Child Labor Committee to endorse the national standards being pursued in England.[6]

The National Association of Manufacturers' new strategy of offering their own child labor policies enormously complicated her landscape. "The Association never rests," she wrote the head of the Consumers' League of Ohio, and she had no doubt that its program "is, definitely and continuously, intended to bring down the standards of progressive states."[7] The NAM's expansion into many surrogates and state branches meant that "child labor is no longer a problem. It is a vast and growing evil."[8] She denounced the NAM's recommendations that children be permitted to leave school at their fourteenth birthday and called the NCLC cowards for supporting the NAM plan. "I have long considered the Committee an obstacle to progress and wish it would disband in the interest of the children," she wrote a member of the NCLC board in 1929.[9]

Until May 1928, Kelley's best hope in her battle against child labor was her not-yet-publicized petition campaign for the child labor amendment. Yet her closest friends on the NCL board thought that her petition quest was unproductive and was wasting NCL resources. Probably after they had failed to convince her to abandon it, they staged a palace coup at the NCL board meeting, seized control of NCL finances, and dismissed the staff who were working on the petition drive. Outraged, Kelley consulted Ko, who promised to support her and her work for the amendment if she decided to resign as executive secretary of the NCL.[10] By September 1930, Kelley had stepped away from the still-elusive child labor amendment and begun to hope that uniform state laws could achieve the same result.[11]

She continued to assemble data on state compensation for injured children, and the NCL remained the most complete repository of information on that topic and on recent child labor laws. In June 1931, she reported to Frances Perkins that "the harvest of gains for the children" from forty-four legislatures in session was "shockingly meager," with Pennsylvania's new double compensation law and North Carolina's law forbidding girls under eighteen to work between 9 P.M. and 6 A.M. being "the only important gains in the whole country."[12]

Other urgent ongoing issues were the related struggles to preserve the Children's Bureau and extend the funding of the Sheppard-Towner Act. A March 1930 meeting of the WJCC subcommittee on Sheppard-Towner attracted "all eighteen persons representing eighteen organizations, a full roll call."[13] After the meeting Kelley hastened to urge Elizabeth Magee to apply political pressure on Ohio congressman John Cooper, whose support she deemed essential.[14] More than a year later, the Children's Bureau was safe, but funding was never restored to the Sheppard-Towner Act.[15]

Blocked on many fronts and threatened with erosion, her agenda was nevertheless too well established for her opponents to overturn it altogether. She referred to hours laws as the "old established safeguards," and newspapers began to view them as part of "the American standard of living."[16] Hours laws were defended by trade unions, she noted with gratification, and "a phalanx of organizations whose members are permanently interested as a matter of health and public welfare in the short working day and week and absence of work at night for men, women, youth and children."[17]

Part of the success of her agenda was due to the fact that men benefited from legislation that regulated women's hours. As Kelley explained to the editor of the *Portland (Maine) Evening News,* "courts are slow to uphold restrictions on the working hours of men but . . . men benefit largely by the shortening of the hours of all the people whose work interlocks with their own."[18] Yet she admitted that sustained attacks on her gendered strategy made it difficult to move forward on that front. "[T]he efforts of the Associated Industries and their willing tool the Womans Party" made the "waitresses law" enacted in 1917 "the object of almost continuous assault," along with the coverage of clerical workers by hours laws.[19]

The "waitresses law" enacted in New York in 1917 and upheld by the U.S. Supreme Court that year was a good example of how gendered laws developed their own logic and momentum. Kelley and her allies supported restrictions on women's night work (usually from midnight to 6 A.M.) because without such laws limitations on women's hours proved too difficult to enforce; when employees came and went, night and day, laws providing for an eight- or ten-hour day were easily evaded.[20] Most women workers, even waitresses, supported restrictions on women's night work because they did not want to be required to work during those hours or because they wanted night jobs to go to the men in their families.[21] But just as no single hours policy could benefit all men, no single hours policy could fit the circumstances of all women, and the employment of some women, especially professional women, was negatively affected by gendered hours laws. Kelley's gendered strategy could not afford to recognize these exceptions. For her, much more was involved than gender; the entire edifice of workplace regulation was at stake.

Kelley carried her struggle against the NWP into women's organizations, where she spoke against the blanket amendment and on behalf of laws that advanced women's rights on an issue-by-issue basis. She reported to Elizabeth Magee in June 1929, "It is evident that the Zonta's, like the Business and Professional Woman's Clubs are split on the progress of the Woman's Party and a lively fight is going on inside both national organizations." Other women's organizations, especially those affiliated with social reform, were less divided. "Representatives of the Y.W.C.A., and of the Children's Court, and a group of dietitians were all opposed to the whole equality platform."[22]

One clear gain in these years was the NCL's decision to advance minimum wages by reviving the white list, this time for candy manufacturers. The early NCL strategy of white lists had used the power of purchasers to improve working conditions in garment-making in the 1890s.[23] Now focusing on wages paid in the candy industry, which primarily employed women and children, the NCL promoted a national standard in a chronically underpaid occupation. Kelley thought that was "the only way now open to us to affect wages since the Sutherland decision destroyed the minimum wage laws."[24] When some state leagues urged that local candy manufacturers be added to the white list even if they paid lower wages than the metropolitan manufacturers, Kelley firmly denied their request. In a letter to all local leagues she declared, "It is my earnest hope that the state leagues will urge the local candy manufacturers to comply with the standards set up for the combined White List of New York State and Cleveland, Ohio; and that this list may ultimately cover a large part of industrial America." She insisted that "the National Consumers' League could not approve of any lower beginning wage than $14.00 a week anywhere for any purpose."[25]

The NCL's investigation of the occupational effects of radium was another new initiative. In 1924, the health commissioner of Orange, New Jersey, asked the secretary of the Consumers' League of New Jersey "to inquire into the nature of the industrial disease which was disabling, and even killing, men and women employed in making luminous watch and clock faces."[26] The NCL Council then voted to ask its Committee on Industrial Poisons "to promote the establishment of industrial hygiene bureaus in the Labor Department. And also to work for legislation making all occupational diseases compensable."[27] This venture reunited Kelley with her Hull House companion, Dr. Alice Hamilton, now a professor of occupational medicine at Harvard Medical School, and Josephine Goldmark, who had been working with the Russell Sage Foundation and other agencies since 1917. Their efforts were rewarded by sensationalist press coverage of the gruesome effects of radium on those who worked with it.[28]

Like others of her generation, particularly those who promoted industrial regulation, Kelley was attracted in these years to the Taylor Society, a group that promoted the application of scientific management principles to industrial work. Kelley hoped the society could promote less exploitative industrial standards. She was heartened by the society's influence in the southern textile industry, which led employers to support bills "prohibiting employment of any girl below the age of eighteen years at night in a cotton mill."[29]

No black children (or adults) were employed in the textile industry, but issues pertaining to state and federal legislation also entered into Kelley's work with the NAACP. Those issues centered on federal funding for education and, beginning in 1929, Kelley urged the NAACP to create "a standing Committee against Discrimination in Education."[30] That year she and Du Bois wrote the secretary of the interior to complain about the discriminatory allocation of federal funds for education.[31] She also complained to a regional planning association in New York City about discriminatory housing practices.[32] Ever the politician, she called the annual meeting of the NAACP in 1930 "by far the best yet" because the convention adopted "my resolution that the women of the auxiliaries to the branches be urged to make a house to house canvass, to assure the registration of Negro men and women in every district." She thought this "promises a lesson to Mr. Hoover in November wherever the Negro vote forms the balance of power."[33]

American politics began to change decisively after the collapse of the stock market in October 1929. Since that collapse made congressional action seem patriotic rather than communistic, attacks on socialists diminished rapidly. In the spring of 1931 Kelley attended a conference in Washington, D.C., that included Robert La Follette, Jr., her old friend Edward Costigan, and others that the *New York Times* called "progressive or left-wing members of both major political parties." They advocated congressional legislation "to prevent economic chaos and starvation."[34] But Kelley did not live to see the cascade of legislation called the New Deal.

The rapid decline in Florence Kelley's health can be traced in her last summer letters from Maine. In 1928 she was happy to be in "Fog Land" for "seventy days of quiet here on my granite farm."[35] And in 1930 she referred to "working on the porch" there. But in December 1930 she mentioned "dictating in bed," and when she wrote from Maine in 1931, she said, "I arrived here so tired that I was not really rested for two full weeks."[36]

In the fall of 1931, Kelley was hospitalized for colon cancer in a room not too far from where as a girl she had visited her grandparents in Germantown, Pennsylvania. Tributes poured in from friends and colleagues. She especially noted a "glorious floral exhibit" from her "dear friends of the N.A.A.C.P."[37] Unable to attend the NCL annual dinner in November 1931, she doubtless learned of the tribute to her there by Edward Costigan, who mentioned "the matchless individuality, the life-long public vision, the amazing humanitarian devotion and the wealth and splendor of mind and heart of the National Secretary of the Consumers' League"[38]

A younger generation carried Kelley's agenda forward after her death in February 1932. Typified by Eleanor Roosevelt, who acknowledged Kelley as "a very remarkable person" at an NCL dinner in November 1928, and Frances Perkins, who was appointed industrial commissioner of New York by the new governor in 1929 and secretary of labor of the United States in 1933, this generation did much to establish the social rights of citizenship after Franklin Delano Roosevelt became president in 1932.

Florence Kelley left the National Consumers' League in robust condition for her successor, Lucy Mason. Having celebrated its 30th anniversary in 1929, the league moved forward into a new era, continuing the model that Kelley had established of achieving nationwide change through careful attention to local politics.

NOTES

1. Letter 252, FK to Roscoe Pound, 15 October 1929, below.

2. Hall, Leloudis, Korstad, Murphy, Jones, and Daly, *Like a Family*, 212–236, 254; and Hall, "Disorderly Women," 354–382.

3. After Kelley's death in 1932, the campaign for the rights of southern textile workers moved to the center of the NCL's agenda, energized by Kelley's successor, Lucy Mason. Storrs, *Civilizing Capitalism*, 64–67, 88, and passim.

4. *NYT*, 17 November 1929, 19; "Mrs. Kelley Looks Ahead," 326.

5. See Letter 270, FK to Frances Perkins, 12 June 1931, note 2, below; and "The Child and the Machine," in *Proceedings of the Twenty-Sixth Annual Conference of the National Child Labor Committee*, "National Child Labor Committee, 1922–31," Box C40, NCL Records, DLC.

6. Letter 254, FK to George Alger, 18 December 1929, below.

7. Letter 260, FK to Elizabeth Magee, 24 April 1930, below.

8. Letter 260, FK to Magee, 24 April 1930.

9. Letter 255, FK to Joseph Swan, 18 December 1929, below.

10. Letter 244, FK to Mabel Costigan, 30 June 1928, below.

11. Letter 262, FK to Mabel Costigan, 23 September 1930, below.

12. Letter 270, FK to Frances Perkins, 12 June 1931, below.

13. Letter 257, FK to Elizabeth S. Magee, 5 March 1930, below.

14. Letter 257, FK to Magee, 5 March 1930.

15. Letter 268, FK to Elizabeth Magee, 5 May 1931, below.

16. Editorial, *Portland (Maine) Evening News*, 30 March 1928, 6.

17. Letter 240, FK to Ernest Gruening, 29 March 1928, below.

18. Letter 240, FK to Gruening, 29 March 1928.

19. Letter 240, FK to Gruening, 29 March 1928.

20. McGuire, "Making the Case for Night Work Legislation in Progressive Era New York," 47–70. New York's 1917 law was upheld in 1923 in *Radice v. New York*; for more about that decision, see Letter 192, FK to Mary Dewson, 26 March 1924, above.

21. See Cobble, *Dishing It Out*, 162–165.

22. Letter 250, FK to Elizabeth Magee, 3 and 7 June 1929, below.

23. Letter 247, FK to Presidents of State Consumers' Leagues, 10 January 1929, below.

24. Letter 250, FK to Magee, 3 June 1929, below.

25. Letter 247, FK to Presidents of State Consumers' Leagues, 10 January 1929, below.

26. Letter 242, FK to *New York World*, 11 June 1928, note 2, below.

27. NCL Council Minutes, 20 November 1925, 37, Box A7, NCL Records, DLC.

28. See Letter 243, FK to Alice Hamilton, 20 June 1928, below.

29. Letter 271, FK to Millie Trumbull, 10 July 1931, below. See also Storrs, *Civilizing Capitalism*, 72–76.

30. Letter 248, FK to Walter White, 14 January 1929, note 1, below.

31. Letter 251, FK and W. E. B. Du Bois to Ray Wilbur, 9 July 1929, below.

32. Letter 259, FK to George McAneny, 29 March 1930, below.

33. Letter 261, FK to NK, 5 July 1930, below.

34. *NYT*, 12 March 1931, 1, 21, 57.

35. Letter 244, FK to Mabel Costigan, 30 June 1928, below.

36. Letter 264, FK to Grace Drake, 6 December 1930; and Letter 272, FK to NK, 22 July 1931, both below.

37. Letter 274, FK to Albert and Esther Kelley, 21 October 1931, below.

38. NCL, "Thirty-Second Annual Luncheon Meeting," 24 November 1931, 3, 21, Box A8, NCL Records, DLC.

240. To Ernest Gruening[1]

[New York City]
March 29, 1928

Mr. Ernest Gruening, Editor
Portland Evening News
Portland, Maine
My dear Mr. Gruening

It gives me great pleasure to send you the enclosed tidings, which you may see before my letter reaches you.

There has been an evil widespread effort this year to destroy old established safeguards for the health and wellbeing of women workers. It has taken hard work both in Massachusetts and in New York to frustrate this movement. As you see by the enclosed slip the vote was closer than is satisfactory which finally disposed in Massachusetts of the effort to allow women and girls over 16 to work in cotton mills until ten o'clock at night.[2]

There seems to have been a second bill, or a second provision in this bill, intended to add 78 hours a year to the present limit of work in other industries as well of women and girls over 16. I am not clear whether that also has been voted down. I have not the text of the defeated bill before me as I write.

Here in New York the effort to lower standards was twofold. The waitresses law, enacted in 1917, has been the object of almost continuous assault since it was signed and took effect. Through the exertions of the Associated Industries of New York,[3] our branch of the National Manufacturers' Association, the waitresses law was carried to the Supreme Court of the United States by Judge Irving Goldsmith before his elevation to the Supreme Court of New York. It was unanimously upheld by the Supreme Court of the United States.

Undiscouraged by that defeat, however, the Associated Industries almost carried a measure this year to exempt all waitresses at all ages from all safeguarding restrictions upon their working hours. ***This was killed by a vote on the floor, three days before adjournment.***[4]

The second object of attack in New York State was the restriction of hours of clerical workers. As late as March first this bill was introduced under the following insidiously misleading title, "An Act to amend the labor law in relation to definitions".[5]

The workers who were to be deprived of their safeguards were doing clerical work including bookkeeping, stenography, multigraphing, mechanical addressing, or other mechanical or clerical operations incidental thereto in a factory or a factory building or elsewhere.

In the same way in another paragraph women and girls in mercantile establishments were to be left without limit to their working hours by the following amending words—"except offices where clerical work including bookkeeping, stenography, multigraphing, mechanical addressing, or other mechanical or clerical operations incidental thereto is carried on". ***This evil measure died in the Committee on rules.***[6]

New York and Massachusetts are exceptional among the forty-eight states in having, beside the regular trade unions, a phalanx of organizations whose members are permanently interested as a matter of health and public welfare in the short working day and week and absence of work at night for men, women, youth and children. They have all learned in the school of experience that the courts are slow to uphold restrictions on the working hours of men but that men benefit largely by the shortening of the hours of all the people whose work interlocks with their own, and this is one of the reasons for unceasing effort in these states to widen the area of statutory short hours for working women, youth and children; ***and to frustrate the efforts of the Associated Industries and their willing tool the Womans Party.***[7]

Yours hopefully

CC, "Wages and Hours: Correspondence, 1919–1929," Box C49, NCL Records, DLC

Note: Handwritten additions are not in FK's hand.

1. Ernest Gruening (1887–1974), general manager of *The Nation* (1920–1923) and a founder of the *Portland Evening News* in 1927, used his newspaper to expose utilities monopolies in Maine. Concerned about the relaxation of labor legislation in Massachusetts regarding women's work in textile manufacturing, he had written FK to ask for material for an editorial (Gruening, Portland, Maine, to FK, 21 March 1928, "Wages and Hours: Correspondence, 1919–1929," Box C49, NCL Records, DLC).

2. The Massachusetts law of 1919 put a 48-hour work week into effect, establishing a nine-hour day and half a day on Saturday for women workers. This legislation, which was strongly backed by the United Textile Workers of America, made the 48-hour week standard for men as well as women workers. Each year thereafter, Massachusetts textile manufacturers petitioned the state legislature to increase the work week to fifty-four hours and the maximum daily hours to ten, threatening that otherwise the textile industry would move to the South. For example, in 1928, the manufacturers claimed that the hours laws were "an absolute discrimination against the textile industry." Their efforts were not successful. See Beyer, *History of Labor Legislation for Women in Three States,* 38–42; and *NYT:* 9 January 1928, 16, and 15 January 1928, 14.

3. The Associated Industries, organized in 1914, was a group of 1,500 major employers in New York (Felt, *Hostages of Fortune,* 81).

4. For an overview of support for hours legislation by waitress's unions in the 1920s, see Cobble, *Dishing It Out,* 116, 284–285; and "Wages and Hours of Union Hotel and Restaurant Employees."

5. The New York State Legislature was scheduled to end its 1928 session on 22 March (*NYT,* 8 March 1928, 3).

6. The House Rules Committee dismissed the proposed amendments to the state's 40-hour work-week law on 13 March (*NYT,* 14 March 1928, 20). For the hours of clerical workers, see Strom, *Beyond the Typewriter,* 205; and Erickson, *The Employment of Women in Offices.*

7. Gruening thanked FK for her information and enclosed the *Portland Evening News*'s editorial of 30 March, which declared as a "victory for the American standard of living" the Massachusetts legislature's recent rejection of a bill allowing women in the textile industry to work at night (Gruening to FK, 30 March 1928, "Wages and Hours: Correspondence, 1919–1931," Box C49, NCL Records, DLC).

241. To Harold Gifford[1]

[New York City]
June 11, 1928

Dr. H. Gifford
1620 Medical Arts Building
Omaha, Nebraska
Dear Dr. Gifford

It is pleasant to get your friendly letter of the 6th.

It is too bad about the Socialists and Communists. They have been fighting each other for seventy years, or thereabouts, to the disadvantage of everybody concerned. I see no prospect, however, of any cessation of their warfare.[2]

The Daily Worker has, I fear, contributed far less to the spread of truth, peace, and reconstruction, than to confusion and misrepresentation. Not one sincere tear could I weep if it should quit, quite the reverse.[3] I wish I could write a more positively appreciative and laudatory opinion of the Worker but candor is what you want, I am sure.

What we dreadfully need is constructive, transitional work. When we try to do it some court, state or federal, surely stops us. So that a great mass of energetic, conscientious, people are now either paralyzed by discouragement or embittered by repression and an infinite amount of necessary transitional work remains undone.

A sad example of this is the long delay in ratifying the federal children's amendment. I sometimes think seriously of abandoning the Consumers' League to devote all my remaining years and energies to promoting that amendment, so convinced am I that Congress and the states must cooperate as they have been doing under the Sheppard-Towner Act, and would be able to do under the federal amendment, if only we could get it ratified.

Yours still hopefully

CC, FKP, NN

1. Harold Gifford (1858–1929, Cornell class of 1879) was a surgeon in Omaha (Hewett, *Cornell University,* 4: 248; www.whonamedit.com/doctor.cfm/1830.html, accessed 29 March 2005).
2. Gifford had expressed concern about the "row between the socialists and the communists. . . . When they are both working for the same end it seems strange that there is no way of bringing them together" (Harold Gifford, Omaha, Neb., to FK, 6 June 1928, FKP, NN).
3. Four years earlier, FK had written the communist publication *The Daily Worker* asking that it not be sent to her: "I have been actively opposed to Communism for nearly 40 years" (FK, [New York], to Daily Worker, 8 September 1924, copy, FKP, NN). FK's commitment to parliamentary rather than revolutionary socialism began before her move to Hull House in 1891. See Sklar, *Florence Kelley and the Nation's Work,* 215–216.

242. To the *New York World*

[New York City]
June 11, 1928

To the New York World
Gentlemen

It is a pleasure to express the keen appreciation of this League for the powerful backing so effectively afforded by the World to the afflicted workers of the U.S. Radium Corporation. At its latest meeting the Board of Directors unanimously voted to send this letter following the invaluable services that you have rendered.[1]

For three years this increasing industrial danger has been the source of deep concern; since the Consumers' League of New Jersey at the request of the Orange Board of Health first looked in 1925 into the illness of those employes, the World's articles and editorials are the first enlightening nation-wide publicity bestowed upon this unimaginable danger.[2]

Although this pitiful story has now entered upon a less sensational phase, there remain several questions from which the attention of the public can not safely be diverted for months to come.

First, as to the victims and the settlements regarding their pensions. Who guarantees the continued solvency of the U.S. Radium Corporation, in case the lives of the sufferers are prolonged?

Second, the amount of the corporation's indebtedness appears to have been made dependent upon three physicians continuing to be of the unanimous opinion that the patients do suffer from radium.

Third, must these physicians agree annually or is their first agreement permanently binding upon the corporation?

Fourth, what would happen if the corporation should go into bankruptcy?

The guarantor of good faith appears to be anonymous, an unusual arrangement certainly in the settlement of a damage suit. Who guarantees the guarantor? Or is the corporation bonded for a term of years? Or only annually? Is it bonded at all?

Greater and darker mysteries concern the public. Does anyone yet know where and by whom the fatal material used by the corporation is produced? Or how many concerns are now making and selling it?

The facts recently divulged concerning Waterbury[3] and the existence of a headquarters of the U.S. Radium Corporation under the eaves of the New York City Department of Health suggest unknown further developments, and call for widespread searching intelligent inquiry.

The authoritative medical statements in English to date, those of Drs. Cecil and Katherine Drinker, of Drs. Harrison S. Martland, Goetler, Canlon, and Kneff, and the courageous warning of Dr. Robert E. Humphries of the Orange

Orthopedic Hospital to physicians everywhere have been largely lost to sight in the excitement of the trial.[4]

Greatest of the services of the World in the end will probably have been the notice it has served upon purchasers everywhere to be on their guard against the ever increasing array of industrial poisons. Who knows now what may be going on in the pockets of the bearers of luminous watch faces? What does anyone really know of this mysterious substance?

Already there have been violent excitements over circumstances attending the production of ethyl-gasoline and more widespread though less noisy apprehensions as to the effect of bensole upon women and girls in an ever widening range of occupations. Surely this is a strange time for denunciation of the school system in behalf of release of children 14 and 15 years old to enter the field of mass production with speed and poison awaiting their young inexperience.[5]

CC, "Press and Periodicals: *New York World,* 1924–1930," Box B20, NCL Records, DLC

1. On 5 June 1928, the *New York World* carried a front-page article on the settlement of $10,000 outright and $600 a year thereafter from the U.S. Radium Corporation of Orange, New Jersey, to five of its women employees who had radium poisoning as a result of their work. The *World's* editorial viewed the settlement as "welcome news. . . . The plaintiffs, the defendant corporation and the public which has been so deeply concerned in this pitiful story may all be congratulated upon this amicable settlement. The corporation might have fared much worse before a jury" (*New York World,* 5 June 1928, 1, 4, 12). For more about the NCL's investigation of the poisonings at the U.S. Radium Corporation, see Letter 243, FK to Alice Hamilton, 20 June 1928, and Letter 244, FK to Mabel Costigan, 30 June 1928, both below; Goldmark, *Impatient Crusader,* 189–204; and Neuzil, *Mass Media & Environmental Conflict,* 33–52.

2. In 1924, the CL of New Jersey began investigating cases of radium necrosis after the deaths of four women employed in watch factories using radium paint for the luminous dials. At its 1925 meeting, the NCL Council voted to ask the league's Committee on Industrial Poisons "to promote the establishment of industrial hygiene bureaus in the Labor Department. And also to work for legislation making all occupational diseases compensable" (NCL Council Minutes, 20 November 1925, 37, Box A7, NCL Records, DLC). In 1926, FK had asked Ethelbert Stewart (1857–1936), U.S. commissioner of labor statistics (1920–1932), to identify the manufacturers who sold the radium material associated with the deaths, but he replied that the bureau kept these records confidential (FK, New York, to Ethelbert Stewart, 14 April 1926, copy; Ethelbert Stewart, [New York], to FK, 16 April 1926, both in "Radium Poisoning: Correspondence: 1924–1928," Box C42, NCL Records, DLC). By 1928, thirteen women employees of U.S. Radium Corporation had died (*New York World,* 5 June 1928, 1).

3. Two radium dial painters employed at the Waterbury Clock Company in Connecticut had died by July 1928 (*New York World,* 16 July 1928, 10).

4. Cecil K. Drinker (1887–1956), professor of applied physiology at Harvard, helped found the *Journal of Industrial Hygiene.* He and his wife Katherine Rotan Drinker (1889–1956), also a physician, co-authored "Necrosis in the Jaw in Radium Workers," *Journal of Industrial Hygiene* (August 1925): 373–384. Harrison S. Martland (1883–1954) was a pathologist for the city of Newark from 1909 to 1953. Philip Conlon and Joseph P. Knef co-authored "Some Unrecognized Dangers in the Use and Handling of Radioactive Substances" (*Journal of American Medicine* [5 December 1925]). Alexander O. Gettler (1883–1968) was a New York City toxicologist (*The Scientist* 11 [17 March 1997]: 23).

5. No letter from FK appeared in the *New York World* in the days after 11 June.

243. To Alice Hamilton

[New York City]
June 20, 1928

Dear Alice

As you know from Pauline [Goldmark]'s letter of last evening, Miss [Marguerite] Marsh[1] and I had a fairly long talk with Walter Lippmann yesterday at three—he being in shirt sleeves, quite immaculate, and very slightly apologetic for them.[2]

He is much interested in going on with the radium subject, but says that our material is insufficient from the point of view of the World, and he hopes that we shall have more readable stuff, which has not already been printed all over the country for him to keep the subject open.[3]

He can not begin before July 5th, but starting on that day, the sooner and the more, the better from the journalist's point of view. He was very frank about Dr. Lewinski-Corwin.[4] He said it was, of course, for us to decide whose initiative this should be. He could not remember whether the World or the doctors had taken the initiative in regard to tetra-ethyl, but he is definitely of the opinion that for purposes of pressure, it is better for the doctors to fall in after the World.

I am a little worried about Dr. Lewinski-Corwin's waiting long enough. He was eager, both when J[osephine Goldmark] and I talked to him, and again yesterday when I talked to him over the wire, about getting his letter off, though I understood him to say clearly both times—though reluctantly—that he would do nothing except with your approval as to the mailing. He is instructed to write in the name of the Academy, and he is very happy about this immediate action on the day on which the subject was first presented to it.

We have dug out the following items:—

a) At this late date Mr. Berry tells me that he assumed all along that we knew that radio-light products, so far as this country is concerned, originated on the battle field in Europe.[5]
b) During the war the Orange plant was a government plant with huge production for the army, and he thought the navy also.

Meantime, my son John had learned from the Pioneer Instrument Company in Brooklyn yesterday that they sell large quantities of radio light nautical equipment for ships and boats and yachts, particularly speed boats, as to which they are now specializing.

We showed W. L. Ethelbert Stewart's report, and he was much impressed by the one item, 119 purchasers.

Mr. Berry has found a U. of Pa. doctor, who may do but this is still too uncertain for anybody but you to know it. I am not very hopeful about it.

Clark, the capitalist of the Radium Corporation, was a classmate in the

Harvard Law School of Walter Lippmann. He regards C. as a very fine fellow and a Romantic.[6]

Miss Marsh has dug out the enclosed list. I am sending a copy of it to Commissioner Harris.[7]

The following question has arisen:—

On what paper should the letter from you to the different physicians go out?

I am confident that it is not wise for me to sign that letter. You are the proper person to do it and it can only create confusion to have a layman butting in, especially as I shall be in Maine after next Saturday. If any layman were going to sign it J. Goldmark would be the most appropriate one because of her wide acquaintance with physicians from her nursing study, with which a fairly large number identified themselves in different ways.

I think, however, that she also is leaving town before long.

Yours devotedly

CC, "Radium Poisoning: Correspondence: 1928," Box C42, NCL Records, DLC

1. Marguerite Marsh, research secretary at the NCL, was co-author (with Dorothy Myers and FK) of *Children's Compensation for Industrial Accidents* (1926) and (with FK) *Labor Legislation for Women and Its Effects on Earnings and Conditions of Labor* (1929).
2. Saying "all experts of standing are with us," Hamilton asked FK to recruit Lippmann to urge U.S. surgeon general Hugh S. Cumming (1869–1948; in office 1920–1936) to call a conference on radium poisoning immediately. Recent cases in Connecticut had shown "danger widespread," she said (Hamilton, Chicago, to FK, 28 May 1928, "Radium Poisoning: Correspondence: 1928," Box C42, NCL Records, DLC).
3. FK had written to Laura Williams about her alliance with government officials and journalists in a campaign against radium: "We have been working very hard, Alice Hamilton, Josephine Goldmark, Miss Marsh, the research secretary, and myself to get the U.S. Surgeon-General, Dr. Hugh Cumming, to make the kind of survey of radium production that he made three years ago of tetra-ethyl gasoline." She continued, "We have some grounds of hope, but not so firm as we could wish, because we have to depend in large measure upon the N.Y. World, and no one knows which way that cat will jump at the critical moment" (FK to Williams, [Brooklin/Naskeag, Me.], [12 July 1928], copy, "General Correspondence: 'W,'" Box B25, NCL Records, DLC).
4. Edward H. Lewinski-Corwin (b. 1885) was secretary of the National Academy of Medicine.
5. Raymond Berry was the attorney for the radium victims (Goldmark, *Impatient Crusader*, 195; see also Neuzil, *Mass Media & Environmental Conflict*, 42–44).
6. U.S. District Court judge for New Jersey William Clark (1891–1957), a stockholder in U.S. Radium Corporation, had acted as a mediator in the suit the radium victims brought. The *World* praised Clark for his "humane accomplishment" (*New York World*, 5 June 1928, 1, 12).
7. Probably the enclosure listed the names of potential signers of the letter to Cumming. FK followed her letter to Hamilton with another, also on 20 June, describing a conversation with Louis Harris (1882–1939), New York City health commissioner (1926–1928), who felt that a previous investigation of the U.S. Radium Corporation was incomplete and expressed interest in cooperating with the project (FK, New York, to Hamilton, 20 June 1928, "Radium Poisoning: Correspondence: 1928," Box C42, NCL Records, DLC).

Mabel Cory Costigan, ca. 1918. Courtesy of the Carrie Chapman Catt Collection, Bryn Mawr College Library.

244. To Mabel Cory Costigan

[Naskeag, Brooklin, Maine]
June 30, 1928

Mrs. E. D. Costigan.
Detroit St.
Denver, Colorado.
Dear Mrs. Costigan:

As you see from the letter-head, I have arrived in Fog Land and am to have, all told, seventy days of quiet here on my granite farm.

It seems years since you left Washington, and Grace Abbott had already gone.[1]

The Women's Joint Congressional Committee, without you, appears to have flattened out completely.[2]

With a better Congress than many that have gone before, Clara Beyer's District of Columbia child labor law seems to be the only monument to the year 1928, unless some miracle should be wrought during December.[3]

The activity of our League in these late months, has been, at least, exciting. The enclosed candy white list sums up the work of the New York State League for the whole year. It has achieved astonishing success. The starting wage for inexperienced workers is $14.00 instead of $7, 8, 9, 10, or 11,—not because it is a satisfactory figure, but because it is all that could be obtained in a first negotiation. The question is the same old question that always loomed up in the days of the New York City department store white list—how to keep the interest of the careless public alive enough to stir the pride of the retail merchants when the novelty wears off.[4]

The excitement in the national office has been twofold.

Just as we arrived at the 20,000 signature to our child labor petition, four of my best friends, Mary Dewson, Pauline Goldmark, Grace Drake, annexing a newcomer on the board, Mrs. Francis Pollak, formed an informal committee to finance the League the rest of the fiscal year until October 30th. They had the May quarterly meeting give them power to act for the reduction of expense, the reduction of the staff, the redistribution of work in the office and all the League's activities. They dismissed the petition secretary and her stenographer with a second stenographer and a half-time typist, thus saving $500.00 a month, although we had no deficit and all the bills were paid to date.[5]

I was so alarmed, so filled with dread, that all the time, effort, and money spent on the petition might be abandoned, that I seriously consulted my son, Nicholas, as to what I should do if this committee were reappointed at the annual meeting, and its powers continued.

He very simply offered, if nothing better could be managed, and I resigned, to stake me, as long as I continue active, to the extent of $5,000 a year toward for the amendment in any way that might seem, from time to time, most promising.

The idea of the League following in the footsteps of the National Child Labor Committee and Wiley Swift[6] seemed utterly unbearable to both of us, so I accepted the offer contingently, and with this moral and financial backing assured, found myself able to consider ways and means of altering the situation during the coming five months, so as to avoid a crisis and continue work for the amendment within the Consumers' League, even though it might be on a somewhat reduced scale.

Julia Lathrop came to New York a day or so before I left and we had a very long luncheon and conference, after which I felt still further confidence as to the future and the amendment.

As you doubtless know both from Washington and Grace Abbott, Nebraska is continuing uninterrupted work for ratification.[7]

The changed attitude of people in general in New York is astonishing. There is, no longer any fear of signing. The time of ridicule and the fear thereof, is past.[8]

When she was summarily dismissed, my colleague, Hortense Reed, was working out a plan for sharing booths in eight county fairs with the W.C.T.U. women, and it is possible that I may do this next year in the northern part of the state if the League insists upon having, as at present, a quasi-assistant for me, part of whose time will be devoted to research in the field of children's compensation, instead of a petition secretary <u>and</u> a research secretary, as we had had for fifteen months up to the recent convulsion.

I know the situation in Colorado well enough to imagine how far away ratification must seem to you in that once progressive state!

In New York, however, with the arch-enemy of ratification, our once progressive governor either [in?] the White House or restored to the business world, it will not be, by any means, utterly sad to consider seriously presenting the petition in 1929 or 1930.[9]

The other excitement promises to be intense and short-lived henceforward.

It dates back originally to May 1925 in the little city of Orange, New Jersey. The health commissioner of Orange asked our New Jersey secretary, Miss Wylie, to inquire into the nature of the industrial disease which was disabling, and even killing, men and women employed in making luminous watch and clock faces.[10]

She has been at work at this ever since and a damage case has just been settled out of court, which started fifteen months ago with the demand for a million and a half dollars for the five victims who united in bringing a suit against the U.S. Radium Corporation.

The developments in the course of the suit were so monstrous, that we have taken the initiative in urging upon our old friend, Dr. Hugh Cumming of the U.S. Public Health Service, the duty of making such a nation-wide survey as he made a few years ago of the production of tetra-ethyl gasoline. In consequence of that survey the Standard Oil Company no longer produces or sells tetra-ethyl gasoline.

It is not definitely shown whether the production of luminous objects can ever be made safe for the workers under the U.S. Constitution, as interpreted by the U.S. Supreme Court.

The demand for luminous objects, meanwhile, increases and multiplies with bewildering speed to meet the increase in aeroplane and speedboat production, ***Two new fields.***[11]

CC, "General Correspondence: Costigan, Mr. and Mrs. Edward P.," Box B12, NCL Records, DLC

Note: Handwritten corrections not in FK's hand.

1. Abbott was recuperating in Colorado from tuberculosis and had taken a leave of absence as chief of the Children's Bureau. She returned to the bureau in October 1928 (Costin, *Two Sisters for Social Justice,* 164–166).

2. In March 1928, Edward Costigan had resigned from his position on the U.S. Tariff Commission and the Costigans had returned to Denver, Colorado. That year, the national president of the LWV commissioned Mabel Cory Costigan to establish a chapter of the LWV in Denver ("Inventory of the League of Women Voters of the Pikes Peak Region Records").

3. On 29 May 1928, the House and Senate agreed on the law restricting conditions of employment for children under eighteen in the District of Columbia (70th Cong., 1st sess., *Cong. Rec.,* 3646, 10555).

4. Fifty-five of New York's 191 candy manufacturers were placed on the NYCL's White List. Because list standards included compliance with state hours and overtime laws and "a beginning wage of $14 a week," the strategy served as an alternative to minimum wage legislation (*NYT:* 3 June 1928, 20:8). For more about the Candy White List, see Letter 247,

FK to Presidents of State Consumers' Leagues, 10 January 1929; Letter 250, FK to Elizabeth Magee, 3 and 7 June 1929; Letter 253, FK to Eleanor Roosevelt, 16 December 1929; and Letter 266, FK to Anthony Dirksen, 11 February 1931, all below.

5. Inez Pollak (ca. 1872–1956) was active in New York City school reform and opposed the NAM's program for employing school-age children. She joined the board in November 1927, having become FK's valued assistant that year in publicity about child labor (FK, New York, to Pollak, 22 December 1927, "Child Labor: Manufacturers' Program, 1927–1930," Box C2, NCL Records, DLC; Pollak, Keene Valley, N.Y., to FK, 29 July 1928, FKP, N). The NCL Board of Directors voted to empower a committee "to revise the work and staff of the League, with least possible injury to its activities, in order to avoid a possible deficit." The treasurer's report indicated that thanks to a gift of $7,000 from the Milbank Foundation (probably for the NCL's campaign against radium-induced occupational illness), the NCL had no deficit and all bills had been paid.

In May, the new committee, which also included Josephine Goldmark, met with FK. The committee ended FK's extensive financial commitment to the child labor petition drive, which had included $500 a month for four staff members (*NYT,* 25 February 1956, 19; NCL Board of Directors Minutes, 10 November 1927, 2; NCL Board of Directors Minutes, 25 May 1928, 3; Meeting of Program Committee, 31 May 1928, 1–3, all three in Box A2, NCL Records, DLC; NCL Annual Meeting Minutes, 15 November 1928, 2–4, Box A8, NCL Records, DLC; Goldmark, *Impatient Crusader,* 118–120).

6. With the appointment of Wiley H. Swift (b. 1875) as acting secretary of the NCLC in February 1926 (upon the retirement of Owen Lovejoy), the NCLC's leadership in child labor reform ended and it had become a clearinghouse of information. Born and educated in the South, Swift did not support the federal child labor amendment and instead advocated co-operation with the NAM's child labor proposals (Swift, "The Child Labor Position," 72–73). FK had denounced the NAM's program in her recent article "The Manufacturers' Program Won't Do." See also Letter 229, FK to Lillian Wald, 4 April 1927, above; and Trattner, *Crusade for the Children,* 180–181.

7. Nebraska did not ratify the child labor amendment before the passage of the Fair Labor Standards Act in 1938.

8. The NCL's petition secretary issued a report late in 1927 that listed 120 New York State groups that were "actively cooperating" with FK's petition campaign. The list included many men's and women's labor unions, churches, women's organizations, and settlement houses. African American and Jewish labor, civic, and religious organizations figured prominently on the list ("Report of the Petition Secretary, February 7, 1927 to October 31, 1927," attachment to NCL Board of Directors Minutes, 10 November 1927, Box A2, NCL Records, DLC).

9. Alfred E. Smith, governor of New York and the Democratic nominee for president in 1928, was influenced by the NAM's plan to defeat the child labor amendment by calling for state referendums. See note 2 in Letter 204, FK to Royal Copeland, 19 January 1925, above.

10. Katherine G. T. Wiley was executive secretary of the CL of New Jersey.

11. Mabel Costigan replied that she was "more than interested" in all the news FK had sent and reported that when Edward Costigan read the letter he had said "'That is the best letter Mrs. Kelley has ever sent us.'" Mabel concluded "Bless your dear Nicholas!" (Mabel Costigan, Denver, Colo., to FK, 7 July 1928, FKP, N).

245. To Bruce Bliven[1]

[New York City]
September 13, 1928

Mr. Bruce Bliven
The New Republic
421 West 21st Street
New York City
Dear Mr. Bliven

In reply to your letter of the 11th, asking for what Presidential candidate I will vote, I have to make this disgraceful reply,—disgraceful both to Uncle Sam and to the American public, but I venture to hope not altogether disgraceful to me.

On May first, next year, I shall have been thirty years Secretary of this unpopular organization. During that long period the League has uniformly granted me an extraordinary degree of freedom in the expression of my personal opinion and the use of my name as an officer of other equally unpopular bodies. At the present moment, however, we have pending before the Treasury, a suit for restoration of exemption from the Federal Income Tax of contributions to our branch Leagues. We have to prove to the satisfaction of the Treasury that we are an organization educational and philanthropic. The confidence of the Treasury in the validity of our arguments would, undoubtedly, be shaken if the executive officer of the League should announce the intention of voting for Norman Thomas and James Maurer.[2] Please, therefore, keep this statement for your private information.

I am seizing every possible opportunity to talk for these candidates within the range of my acquaintance and I wonder, impatiently, how many more years I must wear this annual muzzle.

Yours sincerely

FK:HH

CC, FKP, NN

1. Bliven (1889–1977) was editor at the *New Republic* (1923–1955).
2. On 13 April 1928, the Socialist Party nominated Thomas and Maurer (1864–1944), a labor official and former member of the Pennsylvania house of representatives, for U.S. president and vice-president, respectively.

246. To Alice Hamilton

[New York City]
November 22, 1928

Dr. Alice Hamilton
Harvard Medical School
Cambridge, Mass
Dear Alice

I have just had the good news from Mabel Kittredge that you are expected to land tomorrow, Friday the 23rd.[1] I hope your voyage has been as painless as possible and that you are coming back to a satisfactory winter.

We had the dinner on November 15th with Mrs. Franklin Roosevelt[2] as Toastmaster and dear old John Commons making the first glitteringly brilliant speech ever credited to him. It was a minute and forty seconds long. Surgeon-General Cumming neither came nor sent Dr. Thompson but did send Dr. James P. Leake, who spoke with the most painful degree of non-committal caution, except as to the all important point.[3] He did say flatly that Dr. Cumming expected to call, in the near future, a conference such as he had called in connection with tetra-ethyl. Dr. Norris made a very solid contribution, very impressive and not too long and President Neilson of Smith, who to our great surprise and delight came to the dinner because he was in town about other things and spending the week at the Astor, achieved a masterpiece.[4]

It is now up to you to let Dr. Cumming know that you are back and expecting him to act.[5] As always

Yours devotedly

CC, "Radium Poisoning: Surgeon-General Conference, 1928," Box C43, NCL Records, DLC

1. Hamilton had sailed for Europe on 12 October 1928 to attend a conference in Geneva (Hamilton, Bass River, Mass., to FK, 9 October 1928, "Radium Poisoning: Surgeon-General Conference, 1928," Box C43, NCL Records, DLC).

2. Introducing FK at the NCL dinner at the Hotel Astor, toastmistress Eleanor Roosevelt (1884–1962) said that the NCL "has done very remarkable things and it has done them under the leadership of a very remarkable person" (NCL Annual Meeting Minutes, 15 November 1928, 162, Box A8, NCL Records, DLC). During the years when Molly Dewson worked closely with FK (1919–1924), she drew Roosevelt into FK's network; Roosevelt had served as vice-president of the Women's City Club, a prominent reform organization, when Dewson was its civic secretary (McGuire, "'A Catalyst for Reform,'" 282–286). Roosevelt's ties to the NCL grew stronger in 1932, when as First Lady she formed a close friendship with FK's successor Lucy Mason (Beasley, Shulman, and Beasley, *The Eleanor Roosevelt Encyclopedia,* 132, 330, 363–365).

3. FK had hoped to persuade U.S. surgeon general Hugh S. Cumming or his deputy Lewis R. Thompson (1883–1954) to attend. At the annual meeting, Dr. James P. Leake (1881–1973) of the U.S. Public Health Service stated that many manufacturers should have been more

aware of the dangers of radium poisoning and were therefore responsible for it (NCL Annual Meeting Minutes, 15 November 1928, 152–153, Box A8, NCL Records, DLC).

4. Charles Norris, chief medical examiner for New York City, showed photographs that illustrated the ravages of radium on the bodies of the New Jersey women. William Allen Neilson (1869–1946), president of Smith College (1917–1939) and a member of the board of the NAACP, concluded the evening with a plea that in a time of record prosperity, "let us pay if necessary a little dearer for what we buy; let us distribute a little more in wages and let us give a little longer breathing space to the children of whom we have heard such heartrending details in order that the world at large may not point to us as the country that not only hogs the wealth of the world, but hogs it for a class." The NCL passed a resolution asking for an investigation into the causes of radium poisoning (NCL Annual Meeting Minutes, 15 November 1928, 161–162, Box A8, NCL Records, DLC; *NYT,* 17 November 1928, 9.)

5. Hamilton replied that a conference on radium poisoning would be held very soon and that the league's effort would be "crowned with success." The following month, Cumming invited FK to the conference in Washington, and FK happily accepted (Alice Hamilton, Boston, to FK, 27 November 1928; Hugh Cumming, Washington, D.C., to FK, 10 December 1929, copy; FK to Cumming, 13 December; all letters in "Radium Poisoning: Surgeon-General Conference, 1928," Box C43, NCL Records, DLC). At the conference, about seventy-five experts passed a resolution asking Cumming to appoint two commissions to determine the best means of protecting workers from radium poisoning (*NYT,* 21 December 1928, 14; see also Sicherman, *Alice Hamilton,* 312–313; and Hamilton, *Exploring the Dangerous Trades,* 416–417).

247. To Presidents of State Consumers' Leagues

NATIONAL CONSUMERS' LEAGUE
156 FIFTH AVENUE, ROOM 1129
NEW YORK CITY

January 10, 1929

On January 8th, 1929 at a luncheon of the Board of the New York State Consumers' League, Mrs. R. P. Halleck,[1] President of the Consumers' League of Kentucky, who was present as a guest, brought up a difficulty that had arisen in Kentucky regarding the desirability of adopting $14.00 as a beginning wage, as a standard for the candy White List.[2]

Hoping to forestall similar questions from other Leagues, I am sending to all state presidents, my reply to Mrs. Halleck.

The original White List, started in the winter of 1888 and 1889, applied only to stores in New York City because there was only a local city league, and at that time no other.

When the National Consumers' League came into existence, its first activity was agreeing upon a standard to be presented to all manufacturers throughout the country, in the special branch in which the National League and all the state and local leagues were then interested.[3]

The National League has been in active sympathy with the New York Candy White List work in every aspect, the investigation, the methods, the cooperation with local public authorities, and the standards for the White List.

All the accumulated experience of those earlier years shows that it would be fatal to introduce varying local standards in a nationally advertised branch of production.

It is my earnest hope that the state leagues will urge the local candy manufacturers to comply with the standards set up for the combined White List of New York State and Cleveland, Ohio; and that this list may ultimately cover a large part of industrial America, and that no local White Lists may be issued with lower standards.[4] Certainly the National Consumers' League could not approve of any lower beginning wage than $14.00 a week anywhere for any purpose.

Hoping that you, too, are keenly interested in this new work by means of the White List, I am,

Yours Sincerely
Florence Kelley

TLS, "Scrapbooks, 1924–58: Form Letters and Publications 1924–1929," Box F1, NCL Records, DLC

1. Louisville native Annie Ainslie Halleck (b. 1867; B.A. Vassar) was an influential figure in the reform circles of the South and a stalwart NCL member; she had served as a vice-president of the national league in 1916 (NCL Annual Council Minutes and Proceedings, 1916, 72, Box A6, NCL Records, DLC). The Kentucky consumers' league she founded in 1901 and led as president was "one of the oldest and most solidly female branches." Women in the CL of Kentucky successfully lobbied for a child labor law in 1902 and a ten-hour law for women in 1912. Their efforts to pass a minimum wage law in the state were not successful, however (Storrs, *Civilizing Capitalism,* 144, 159–160, 266).

2. Molly Dewson began investigating candy manufacturing establishments in New York State in 1928 in preparation for the construction of a Candy White List for the NYCL (see *NYT,* 18 March 1928, 162). At the NCL Board of Directors meeting on 31 January 1929, she reported that the investigation had been a great success. New York manufacturers wanted the investigation to expand to other states, and manufacturers in Ohio, New Jersey, Rhode Island, and Pennsylvania wanted to be added to the list. Dewson wanted to construct a national White List as soon as possible, and the directors immediately began strategizing about how to stretch the budget to include the new work (NCL Board of Directors Minutes, 31 January 1929, 2, Box A2, NCL Records, DLC). For more about the NCL's work with the Candy White Lists, see Letter 244, FK to Mabel Costigan, 30 June 1928, above; and Letter 250, FK to Elizabeth Magee, 3 and 7 June 1929; Letter 253, FK to Eleanor Roosevelt, 16 December 1929; and Letter 266, FK to Anthony Dirksen, 11 February 1931, all below.

3. For more on the promotion of white lists by the CL of New York in the 1890s and the NCL at its founding, see Nathan, *Story of an Epoch-Making Movement,* 234–236; and Sklar, *Florence Kelley and the Nation's Work,* 308–311.

4. Dewson was certain that the White List would raise wages for candy workers across the country. She hoped that this work would serve to "bring [smaller] leagues back to life" and establish new leagues and reported that candy manufacturers "are with us, doing everything we wanted." At the April meeting, the directors appointed a committee of five that included Frances Perkins and Josephine Goldmark to draft a national standard (NCL Board of Directors Minutes, 23 April 1929, 2–3, Box A2, NCL Records, DLC).

248. To Walter White

NATIONAL CONSUMERS' LEAGUE
156 FIFTH AVENUE
NEW YORK CITY

January 14, 1929

Dear Mr. White

The enclosed memorandum seems to embrace the main points of our conversation of last Friday, leaving the definite proposal to start in Atlanta to come up separately, as a continuance of what has once been successfully done there.[1]

I am writing Mr. Charles S. Johnson at Fisk, a long series of questions as to Mississippi,[2] but am not taking up the matter of Dr. Du Bois' articles which should appear as a book. He under took at my request to cover that part of the subject.

It will, I think, be wiser to let the whole plan come to the Board as a suggestion or recommendation from several of us, rather than from me alone, though I hereby present myself as a candidate for membership on the Committee if one is created.[3]

Yours sincerely
Florence Kelley

TLS, Du Bois Papers, MU

Enc: Memorandum for the Board of the N.A.A.C.P. Concerning Discrimination in Public Education

1. FK's memo noted the NAACP's "immensely effective permanent work" in combating school segregation but said it could do even more by creating "a standing Committee against Discrimination in Education." She suggested that the committee focus first on Mississippi with a plan that "would illuminate and warn against the level of discrimination in public education which will surround Northern industry on going South" (undated draft of enclosed memo, Du Bois Papers, MU). At its 11 February board meeting, the NAACP formed a Committee on the Unequal Expenditure of Public School Funds with Du Bois as chairman and FK as vice-chairman ("Minutes of the Meeting of the Board of Directors, February 11, 1929," 3, NAACP Board Minutes, NBiSU). In 1917, Atlanta had been the first southern city to establish a chapter of the NAACP (Werum, "Elite Control in State and Nation," 154).

2. Charles Spurgeon Johnson (1893–1956), editor of *Opportunity,* the journal of the Urban League, was head of the social sciences department at Fisk University in 1928. He thanked FK for her letter and sent her a list of Mississippi residents who should receive copies of FK's article "A Skeleton in Industry's Closet," which used statistics about increased industrial accidents to minors to attack the NAM's program, which Johnson said had generated "more and younger, ignorant, inexperienced" workers (Johnson, Nashville, Tenn., to FK, 22 January 1929, Du Bois Papers, MU).

3. White replied that FK's memo "in its entirety" would be presented to the NAACP board on 11 February 1929 (White, [New York], to FK, 15 January 1929, Du Bois Papers, MU). The April 1929 issue of *The Crisis* carried an article by Du Bois which stated that the "next step"

in the NAACP's agenda was "a forward movement all along the line to secure justice for Negro children in the schools of the nation. . . . [H]alf the black children of school age in the South today have no chance to receive a thorough education through the grammar grades, and . . . not one tenth have a high education open to them" ([Du Bois], "Education," 132). In July, the NAACP annual meeting adopted a statement about "the crying shame of denial of common school training to Negro children" that was "a matter calling for investigation and remedy" ([Du Bois], "Message to the American People," 265).

249. To Frances Perkins

[New York City]
January 17, 1929

Dear Frances

It is a lasting grief that I did not know when and where you were to be inducted into office![1] In the same way I did not know until three weeks after the death of Mary Richmond and the funeral services held so nearby.[2]

However, the main thing is that you are already at work and there will be less death, misery and poverty because you are at the helm. Don't let it wear upon you any more than you can help.

Not only your beneficiaries will need you but I can see Mr. Roosevelt depending upon your wisdom more and more as his army of villains settle down to the business of bedevilling him.[3]

Your proud and happy old friend
FK

CC, "General Correspondence: Perkins, Frances, 1929–1938," Box B20, NCL Records, DLC

1. Governor Franklin Roosevelt (1882–1945) had appointed Perkins industrial commissioner for New York; she was inducted on 15 January 1929. Earlier he had replied to FK's recommendation that he appoint Perkins, writing "I have taken the same view of this situation as you do" (Franklin Roosevelt, New York, to FK, 26 December 1928, FKP, NN).
2. Mary Richmond (b. 1861), social worker and director of the Charity Organization Department of the Russell Sage Foundation, died on 12 September 1928.
3. In her reply, Perkins expressed regret that FK had not been there: "I would have given a good deal to have you here for I regard you as the head of the family in this enterprise which binds us all together" (Perkins, New York, to FK, 30 January 1929, "General Correspondence: Perkins, Frances, 1929–1938," Box B20, NCL Records, DLC).

250. To Elizabeth S. Magee[1]

NATIONAL CONSUMERS' LEAGUE
156 FIFTH AVENUE, ROOM 1129
NEW YORK CITY

June 3, 1929 [and June 7]

Dear Miss Magee

Thank you very much for your letter of June 1st and your experience with the Zonta Club.[2] I am speaking to a Zonta Club tonight in Jersey City who seem to be sending delegates to the Erie Zonta meeting and to the annual or biennial meeting of the Business and Professional Women's Club.[3]

I do not know who is to speak for the Woman's Party tonight. I, am of course, speaking for legislation and against the Party.

June 7, 1929

I was dreadfully fatigued by the Zonta meeting and the hea***t*** and am only today feeling like myself, and hasten to write you. It is evident that the Zonta's, like the Business and Professional Woman's Clubs are split on the progress of the Woman's Party and a lively fight is going on inside both national organizations.

The meeting which I addressed was split. Representatives of the Y.W.C.A., and of the Children's Court, and a group of dietitians were all opposed to the whole equality platform. The subject matter of the evening was a resolution in which the word equal did not appear. The resolution read "Men and women shall be free in business, the professions, and industry. All laws regulating or prohibiting the employment of women shall be based upon the nature of the occupation and not upon sex." It is much more insidious in this form than in the old form with equality in it.

I hope Miss [Myrta] Jones has shown you my letter to her in which I stated my conviction that the National must participate in the work for the candy white list, on the basis that it is the only way now open to us to affect wages since the Sutherland decision destroyed the minimum wage laws.[4]

I am recurring to the subject of the dropped requirement of an examination of food handlers, when employed and also after a year. At the close of the Board meeting at which the recommendations were adopted to be sent out, Judge [Bernard] Shientag said that he would like to have it made clear that he is convinced of the value of that provision, and agreed to abandon it solely for the sake of harmony with the Ohio League. Miss Pauline Goldmark said that she also knew from experience the importance of that requirement, having seen for ~~six~~ ***several***[5] years its effects on employes of the American Telephone and Telegraph Company.[6]

The rule that there must be periodical examinations automatically excludes people who are aware that they are out of health. They do not apply for employment. ***A***nd the whole staff, from the bus boys in the company restaurants up, avoid much loss of time because of this requirement. In the case of food handlers it is more obviously valuable to the public.

Miss Goldmark agreed with Judge Shientag that this should not be a requirement. ***F***or places in which future whi***t***e lists may be started, it was the opinion of Miss [Molly] Dewson, Miss [Estelle] Lauder and myself, when we went over the notes of the Board meeting of May 27th, that this element of cleanliness could be mentioned as recommended though not required, in contrast to other recommendations.[7]

Miss Lauder is to report on her addition to the joint list, as soon as she has anything final.[8]

Yours sincerely
Florence Kelley

TLS, "General Correspondence: Magee, Elizabeth," Box B16, NCL Records, DLC

1. Elizabeth S. Magee (1889–1972) was the executive secretary of the Cleveland-based CL of Ohio and a member of the NCL Board of Directors. She later became the NCL's general secretary (Oberlin College archives; "General Correspondence: Magee, Elizabeth," Box B16, NCL Records, DLC).

2. Zonta was founded in 1919 by journalist Marian de Forest, who conceived of the organization as a community service organization of women experts. Only those who worked at least 50 percent of their time in executive positions were eligible for membership, and each club could have only one representative from each business classification. De Forest's idea was that each club could then apply a broad range of expertise to community problems (Zonta Web site at http://www.zonta.org).

3. Zonta held its national convention in Erie, Pennsylvania in 1929 (*The Zonta Club Manual*, 61).

4. For the centrality of wages in the white list strategy, see Letter 247, FK to Presidents of States Consumers' Leagues, 10 January 1929, above.

5. The word "several" is handwritten above the crossed-out word "six."

6. Goldmark had advised American Telephone and Telegraph regarding health issues of its women employees since 1921.

7. Despite the effort of the Permanent Candy Committee to create national standards, the CL of Ohio objected to a standard in the proposed White List that required all food handlers in White List establishments to have a medical examination when they were hired and annually thereafter, and the committee decided to drop that standard as a requirement "in the interest of establishing . . . standards on which all Leagues could agree." But the committee stood firm on a beginning minimum weekly wage of $14 for a work week of forty-four or more hours. ([Robert Szold], untitled report of the Permanent Candy Committee, 14 April 1929; and n.a., "Resolutions of the Permanent Candy Committee," 27 September 1929, 1–2, both in "Candy White List: Permanent Candy Committee," Box C1, NCL Records, DLC; NCL Board of Directors Minutes, 10 October 1929, 2, Box A2, NCL Records, DLC.) For more about the NCL's work with Candy White Lists, see Letter 244, FK to Mabel Costigan, 30 June 1928, and Letter 247, FK to Presidents of State Consumers' Leagues, 10 January 1929, both above; and Letter 253, FK to Eleanor Roosevelt, 16 December 1929, and Letter 266, FK to Anthony Dirksen, 11 February 1931, both below.

8. At the NCL Annual Council meeting in November, Lauder, a member of the Board of Directors, reported that the CL of Eastern Pennsylvania still had no white list because low wages made Philadelphia candy makers ineligible. Her league was using the strategy of recommending that settlement houses and church groups buy their bulk candy at Christmas from manufacturers on the New York White List with success (NCL Board of Directors Minutes, 27 May 1929, 3, Box A2, NCL Records, DLC; NCL Council Minutes, 14 November 1929, 43–45, Box A8, NCL Records, DLC).

251. To Ray L. Wilbur

[Naskeag, Brooklin, Maine]
[9 July 1929]

Education ***omit***[1]
To ***The Honorable*** R. L. Wilbur, Secretary of the Interior:
Sir:

You are asking an Advisory Committee of Education to study the present relations of the Federal Government to education, and recommend a future program.[2] One group will consider the educational activities of the United States Government, their administration and future. A second group, will consider United States aid to colleges, and a third group, United States aid to primary and secondary education. Of the 45 persons appointed, not a single Negro appears, although in justice to ~~our~~ ***their*** number and educational needs, at least 4 colored men ~~or~~ ***and*** women ought to sit. The white South is liberally over-represented by at least 12 members~~.~~ ***of the Advisory Committee.***

It is, Sir, well-known that the American Negro is openly, frankly and ~~impudently~~ ***ruthlessly?*** discriminated against today***:***

1. In the distribution of Land Grant Funds,
2. In the distribution of the Smith-Lever and Smith-Hughes funds,[3]
3. In all other ***federal*** government appropriations for education.
4. In ~~all~~? state appropriations for public schools.

In the name, therefore, of 12 million Americans, may we ask you to require ***induce*** your Committee~~s~~:

1. To ascertain the exact figures as to the distribution of ***federal*** government funds among white and black children?
2. To ascertain the exact distribution of state educational funds among black and white children.
3. To make recommendations for further just distribution of United States Government funds to those states only who ***accept methods of recording disbursements adapted to reveal the allotments to children of the races respectively*** ~~will tell the truth about present conditions~~, and *thus* permit the United States government ***and the whole body of citizens who pay federal taxes*** to know (in the future) where its educational money ***in fact*** goes.

We beg, Sir, that in such inquiries colored people be consulted and their advice followed.

In behalf of the Education Committee of the Board of Directors of the National Association for the Advancement of Colored People.

W. E. B. Du Bois Chairman
Florence Kelley ***Kelley***[4]

TDft + AN, Du Bois Papers, MU

1. This letter to Wilbur was drafted by Du Bois and sent to FK for her review (see Du Bois, [New York], to FK, 25 June 1929, copy, Du Bois Papers, MU). FK's revisions are indicated by her deletions and her (italicized) additions. Mid-sentence question marks are FK's queries to Du Bois. In her cover letter to Du Bois, FK wrote that she hoped that her delay had not "frustrated the intention of the Board in appointing us to do its work in the field of educating" and explained that he could "approve and accept my suggested modifications as I accept your original draft" (FK, [Brooklin, Me.], to Du Bois, 9 July 1929, Du Bois Papers, MU).

2. The announcement of the commission appointed by Ray L. Wilbur (1875–1949), president of Stanford University (1916–1943) and U.S. secretary of the interior (1929–1933), appeared in *Survey* (62 [15 August 1929]: 532).

3. The Smith-Lever Act of 1914 funded agricultural extension education in land-grant colleges. The Smith-Hughes Act of 1917 provided federal funds for agricultural and vocational education in secondary schools.

4. FK followed this draft with a letter to Du Bois that stated her hope that their memo would generate widespread and lasting publicity (FK, n.p., to Du Bois, 10 July 1929, copy, Du Bois Papers, MU). *The Crisis* printed the text of FK and Du Bois's joint letter, which included many of FK's revisions. In a postscript to the letter that reported on the interior secretary's response, Du Bois commented that the recent addition of three African Americans to the commission was "excellent so far as it goes but puts unfair burdens on three public officials who cannot always say what they think and it does not promise a thorough threshing out of the race discrimination in public educational funds" ("Money for Education," 317).

252. To Roscoe Pound

NATIONAL CONSUMERS' LEAGUE
156 FIFTH AVENUE, ROOM 1129
NEW YORK CITY

October 15, 1929

Dean Roscoe Pound
Law Enforcement Commission[1]
Washington, D.C.
My dear Mr. Pound

We are celebrating on November 14th, 15th and 16th, by a three days meeting, the 30th anniversary of the founding of this League.[2]

With great pleasure I am sending you this unanimous invitation of the Board to address our luncheon at the Hotel Astor on Saturday, November 16th at one o'clock.

Following the long paralysis of effort after the Sutherland decision, there is at last a strong, widespread stirring of interest in social legislation, enormously accentuated by the recent experience of working mothers and children in North Carolina and Tennessee.[3]

Once more it is demonstrated to all the world that social legislation for women and children in the Southern industrial states must be established. The acute suffering now attending the effort of the North Carolina workers to protect by unions alone, life, health, safety and wages is worse than the experience of workers in the same industries in England in the Forty's,—so infinitely greater are the resources of the employers in our Southern states, and so appalling is the strain of modern speeding combined with the twelve-hours day, nightwork and starvation wages, aggravated by child labor.

We are centering this anniversary occasion upon "Industrial Transition in the South".

Our constructive proposal is cooperative effort to be carried out over a long period with kindred organizations in behalf of minimum wage laws for minors in industry. Their mass is now so great that, covering boys and girls alike, the effect of substantial improvement for them would inevitably tend to raise the rates of women and of the unskilled next above the mass of minors. Our confidence as to this is based upon the brief experience of the states which had minimum wage laws prior to 1923; and also upon the experience of California where this beneficent tendency of minimum wage legislation is conspicuous. The workers next above those who are protected by wage rules are enabled to improve their own wages.

The question of constitutionality seems excluded in the case of minors. So far as the Southern textile strikes arise from starvation wages of women and minors, crime incident thereto roots obviously in the Sutherland decision.

We ask you to address us on this occasion because no one else covers the ground with such authority as yourself. In re-entering a field akin to that in which our efforts have once been frustrated we shall greatly need the weight of your helpful words.[4]

Yours hopefully

CC, Abbott Papers, ICU

1. Pound was secretary of President Hoover's National Commission on Law Observance and Enforcement, also known as the Wickersham Commission. Hoover formed the commission, which was comprised mostly of lawyers, judges, and academics, to enforce the Volstead Act and remedy "failures of law enforcement and judicial procedure" (*NYT,* 21 May 1929, 1).

2. FK enclosed a copy of her letter to Pound in a note to Grace Abbott, asking her to try to persuade Pound to accept the invitation (FK to Abbott, 15 October 1929, Abbott Papers, ICU).

3. In April 1929, women in textile factories in Elizabethton, North Carolina, had struck over low wages; the governor responded by summoning the National Guard. This strike and another in Tennessee textile mills generated national attention about poor working conditions and women's low pay in the textile industry. In *Survey,* FK described Senator Burton K. Wheeler's call for an investigation of labor conditions in southern textile plants. She wrote

that since the 1923 *Adkins* minimum wage decision, "the trade union with its clumsy and uncertain apparatus of strikes is [the women's] only alternative, their sole effective safeguard against the starvation standards of the southern mills" (FK, "Our Newest South," 344).

4. Pound declined the NCL invitation, and Senator Wheeler telegraphed regrets at the last minute (NCL Board of Directors Minutes, 14 November 1929, 1, Box A2, NCL Records, DLC; Wheeler to FK, 16 November 1929, Washington, D.C., FKP, NN). The NCL annual meeting devoted much of its program to analysis of southern industries and testimony from two of the women strikers. It adopted resolutions that called for a shorter work week and a minimum wage for minors (*NYT*, 17 November 1929, 19). At the 30th anniversary luncheon, FK spoke of the need for Americans to realize "that American industry . . . has never paid its social costs. . . . This war in the South is lowering northern standards" ("Mrs. Kelley Looks Ahead," 326).

253. To Eleanor Roosevelt[1]

NATIONAL CONSUMERS' LEAGUE
156 FIFTH AVENUE
NEW YORK CITY

December 16, 1929

Dear Mrs. Roosevelt

From Philadelphia I hear that our friends there are hoping you may address the Consumers' League of Eastern Pennsylvania.

I know that you are not "New York state minded"; yet I venture to point out that I am certain, that nothing else could so further all our efforts in behalf of the White List as you can by helping the Pennsylvanians to prove that our list is becoming truly a national one.[2]

Last year the list contained only New York concerns. This year Eastern Pennsylvania and Ohio are both included.

With warmest good wishes,

Yours sincerely,
Florence Kelley

TLS, Box 7, "Consumers' League," Correspondence 1928–1932, Papers of Eleanor Roosevelt, NHyF

1. The only recovered letter from Roosevelt to FK is a request for a copy of a NAM pamphlet containing supportive excerpts from "President Harding's statements" across the top of each page (Eleanor Roosevelt, New York, to FK, 20 June 1928, FKP, NN).

2. Eleanor Roosevelt would have been well informed about the CLNY's 1928 white list campaign through her friendship with Molly Dewson, CLNY president and leader of the campaign (Ware, *Partner and I*, 153–154). For more about the NCL's work with Candy White Lists, see Letter 244, FK to Mabel Costigan, 30 June 1928; Letter 247, FK to Presidents of State Consumers' Leagues, 10 January 1929; Letter 250, FK to Elizabeth Magee, 3 June 1929, all above; and Letter 266, FK to Anthony Dirksen, 11 February 1931, below.

254. To George W. Alger[1]

[New York City]
December 18, 1929

Dear Mr. Alger

It was a pleasure to see even your back the other night at the Phi Beta Kappa dinner.

This morning I have the enclosed from Mr. Swan.[2] Meanwhile I had what seemed to be a promising letter from Paul Douglas of the University of Chicago whom I have known from his youth. He was considering accepti***ng*** the position as successor to Mr. Wiley Swift but has since decided adversely.[3]

Enclosed is a copy of my reply to Mr. Swan of which I am not proud but I may never again have such an opening for telling the truth to that organization.

Now as to troubles nearer home. You doubtless heard or saw what Grace Abbot had to say about New York in relation to child labor,[4] and I hope you may have seen from the arguments advanced in the course of the discussion of the English proposal to raise the school-leaving age for all children to the 15th birthday. Among others they include the following:

1. The measure would be in the interest of the children
2. Of the country promising future higher intelligence in the working class?
3. Of the unemployed men who would in some measure take the place of the children i.e. of those not replaced by new machinery.
4. It would require more teachers in this time of unemployment, they being chiefly men
5. It would call for school seats for approximately half a million children thereby furnishing work for the building trades in the best possible investment of public funds.

I submit that every argument except the size of the demand for school buildings applies to New York and should be acted upon by the New York Child Labor Committee immediately. I have been nagging Miss Minor in vain about this for years.[5] Henceforth, I mean to nag the whole Committee.

This letter is therefore, to inquire whether you agree that we should have a called meeting of the Board not later than January 10th to act on the proposal that we commit ourselves to the effort to enact the simple proposal that from and after January 1st next, we abolish the present permission to leave school at the age of 14 years applying as it now does to children 14 to 15 years of age, if they have passed the 8th grade. This would involve some appropriate change in relation to the children who can now leave at the 15th birthday and the 6th grade, but that is a detail.

With the best of wishes for the holidays, I am,

As always, yours sincerely and annoyingly[6]

CC, "General Correspondence: 'S,'" Box B21, NCL Records, DLC

Note: We have silently completed words that were truncated where the right margin was torn.

1. Alger (1872–1967), a New York lawyer active in child labor reform, had helped found the NYCLC in 1903 (Felt, *Hostages of Fortune,* 217).
2. Joseph R. Swan (1878–1965), a New York banker and president of Guaranty Company, was a member of the board and treasurer of the NCLC (Minute Book, 28 October 1926, Records of the NCLC, DLC). See Letter 254, FK to Joseph Swan, 18 December 1929, below.
3. On 26 November 1929, Paul Douglas (1892–1976), later U.S. senator (Democrat, Illinois, 1949–1967), who was then teaching economics at the University of Chicago, had asked FK's advice about accepting the secretaryship of the NCLC. FK replied that she hoped he would accept and promised the NCL's close cooperation with the NCLC if he did so ("General Correspondence: Douglas, Paul H.," Box B12, NCL Records, DLC).
4. At a meeting of the NCLC on 16 December 1929, Abbott stated that most state child labor legislation limited employment only under the age of fourteen and that even this restriction was often ignored. Moreover, she noted, many children worked more than eight hours a day. The United States was "behind Great Britain in preventing interference with education by child labor," declared Abbott (*NYT,* 17 December 1929, 22).
5. Jeanie V. Minor (ca. 1871–1957) was paid by the NYCLC to work with the New York City Board of Health to enforce the state child labor law. With Dr. S. Josephine Baker of the Division of Child Hygiene of the state's Board of Health, Minor developed strict procedures for issuing working papers to children under the age of sixteen. On 18 December, FK wrote Minor a letter similar to this one to Alger (Felt, *Hostages of Fortune,* 102–103, 265n5; FK, New York, to Minor, 18 December 1929, "New York: Child Labor Committee, 1924–28," Box B7, NCL Records, DLC. See "Employment Certificates and the School-Leaving Age," Chapter 5 in Felt, for a history of child labor legislation in New York).
6. The NYCLC proposed a bill similar to the one outlined in FK's letter to Alger but the New York legislature defeated it in 1930. The legal age at which a minor could leave school was raised to sixteen in 1935 in New York State (Felt, *Hostages of Fortune,* 121–122, 126).

255. To Joseph R. Swan[1]

Mr. J. R. Swan
National Child Labor Committee
215 Fourth Avenue
New York City
[New York City]
December 18, 1929

My dear Mr. Swan

You are quite right. I am not a member of the National Child Labor Committee and never shall be until it acquires a vigorous, highly intelligent, widely respected executive.[2]

I disapprove of the cowardice of the Committee in yielding to the pressure of the propaganda of the National Association of Manufacturers in 1924, 1925 and 1926 as to the federal child labor amendment.[3]

Quite as vigorously I disapprove of the present subservience of the Committee to the National Association of Manufacturers as to the Program of the latter for establishing the 14th birthday and the 6th grade for children leaving school and going to work.

I have long considered the Committee an obstacle to progress and wish it would disband in the interest of the children.

These objections to the Committee and its present work apply only to recent years. I am proud of having been one of its founders with Dr. Adler and Mr. Edgar Gardner Murphy[4] and proud indeed to have helped in the creation of the Children's Bureau and the passage of the two federal child labor bills.

Yours sincerely

CC, "General Correspondence: 'S,'" Box B21, NCL Records, DLC

1. For information about Swan, see Letter 254, FK to George Alger, 18 December 1929, above.
2. For FK's resignation from the NCLC in 1919, see Letter 151, FK to NK, 18 October 1919, above.
3. See Letter 229, FK to Lillian Wald, 4 April 1927, above.
4. Felix Adler had chaired the NCLC in its early days. Edgar G. Murphy (1869–1913) founded the Alabama Child Labor Committee in 1901; he later helped found the NCLC and served as its first secretary (Felt, *Hostages of Fortune*, 45, 74; Goldmark, *Impatient Crusader*, 99, 89–92, 114–115).

256. To Norman Thomas

Mr. Norman Thomas
206 East 18th Street
New York City
[New York City]
February 5, 1930

Dear Mr. Thomas

I have the notice sent out February 4th warning me to be ready for the meeting on Tuesday evening, the 11th.[1]

I do not expect now to be in the city on that day and alas! I dare not take on my increasingly bent shoulders any new committee work for this winter, much as I should like to have a share in this particular research undertaking.

With congratulations on the successful luncheon when you ate up all the magistrates at one bite,[2] I am,

Yours sincerely

CC, "General Correspondence: 'T,'" Box B22, NCL Records, DLC

1. The notice was apparently an invitation to join a subcommittee of the LID, of which Thomas was executive director. FK had agreed in 1929 to serve on the LID's Board of Directors (Thomas, New York, to NK, 6 February 1929; FK to Thomas, 9 February 1929, "General Correspondence: 'T,'" Box B22, NCL Records, DLC).

2. FK probably referred to Thomas's speech at the LID meeting, "The People's Courts, How Can Justice Be Assured?" on 25 January 1930. Thomas attacked the bar association for "'its utter supineness'" and called for an investigation into the New York City judiciary (*NYT*: 22 January 1930, 6; 26 January 1930, 21).

257. To Elizabeth S. Magee

NATIONAL CONSUMERS' LEAGUE
156 FIFTH AVENUE
NEW YORK CITY

March 5, 1930

Dear Miss Magee

I am just back from Washington where, on Monday March 3rd, the Women's Joint Congressional Committee Sub-Committee on the Jones-Cooper Bill met, and later the whole representation of the Women's Joint Congressional Committee, eighteen persons representing eighteen organizations, a full roll call.[1]

Grace Abbott was invited to advise us and came. Everything that was said and done was confidential and there will be no newspaper releases, so I am writing you immediately because it is all urgent. My first act on returning was to draft a letter of which the enclosed is a copy to Hon. John G. Cooper of Ohio. His address is 2927 Macomb Street, Youngstown, Ohio.[2]

This letter is to ask you to discuss with Miss Gannett the feasibility of making Representative Cooper understand, that it is not a politically wise thing to repudiate a bill you have introduced in behalf of mothers and children.[3] What we think he needs to get:

A. Letters from his constituents (addressed to him in the House Office Building, Washington, D. C.) now in these days of primary elections, rebuking him for repudiating the Jones-Cooper Bill S.255 by introducing H.B.9888.

B. He should receive letters from Ohio citizens who are not his constituents rebuking him for disgracing Ohio by first introducing a valuable bill, then repudiating it, endangering not only the Sheppard-Towner work for the future but assuming part of the responsibility for the attempt to dismember the Children's Bureau by providing that its health work shall be transferred to the United States Public Health Service; and also

C. For leaving to the Children's Bureau only such vague duties under the single heading "Welfare" without definition, that Congress would be tempted to give the full amount proposed by H.~~B~~.***R***.9888 to the United

States Public Health Service for the duties assigned to it, but nothing to the Bureau for the vague idea of Welfare.

Please write me what you think of this plan. Mr. Cooper is receiving encouragement from the U.S.P.H.S. He is an administration Republican and an Honorary W.C.T.U. He is a railroad Brotherhood man.

Secretary Davis has publicly disapproved of H.R.9888.[4]

We are not publicly criticizing H.R.9888. We fear that would only help the U.S.P.H.S. Two years ago when the Manufacturers' Association published its education plan for juveniles, and I printed a large number of objections to it, the National Association of Manufacturers made some insignificant changes in their plan ***to meet my least important points,*** but kept the central evil.

We think the U.S.P.H.S. might adopt the same policy and fool people into thinking their bill all right ***because of a few minimal changes.***

We have now to find a good friend, who is a good fighter and will stick to his bill until it passes!

As soon as we get any news, we will let you know. Until then please think hard and give us the benefit thereof. ***If you think well of the suggestions about Mr. Cooper,—go ahead with them!***

Yours sincerely
F. Kelley

TLS, "General Correspondence: Magee, Elizabeth," Box B16, NCL Records, DLC

Enc: Letter to John G. Cooper, March __, 1930

1. Funding for the Sheppard-Towner Act lapsed on 30 June 1929, and despite vigorous efforts during the next year and a half, proponents failed to restore the program. Anticipating the end of funding, on 18 April 1929, Senator Wesley L. Jones (1863–1932; Republican, Washington, 1909–1932) had introduced S. 255, which would have extended Sheppard-Towner funding. The bill was referred to the Committee on Commerce (71st Cong., 1st sess., *Cong. Rec.,* 18 April 1929, 106). At its November 1929 meeting, the NCL resolved to work with the WJCC and to "strive by all other appropriate measures for prompt passage of this measure" (Lindenmeyer, *A Right to Childhood,* 103; FK to Hiram Johnson, 18 February 1930, "Sheppard-Towner Act: Correspondence, 1922–1931," Box C43, NCL Records, DLC). Members of the WJCC, the LWV, and the NCL and Julia Lathrop, Lillian Wald, Grace Abbott, and Alice Hamilton, among others, lobbied congressmen and President Hoover to support S. 255. Grace Abbott believed that there was enough support to move the bill through Congress, but it languished in committee because Hoover asked the chair not to act on it. The president wanted to dismantle federal funding for services to mothers and infants in favor of voluntary action at the local level, and he wanted to move the Children's Bureau into the Public Health Service and replace Grace Abbott as its director with the nation's surgeon-general. (FK, "Why the Children's Bill Did Not Pass"; Costin, *Two Sisters for Social Justice,* 166–168; NCL Board of Directors Minutes, 27 March 1930, 1–2, Box A2, NCL Records, DLC; Goldmark, *Impatient Crusader,* 110.)

2. Representative John G. Cooper (1872–1955; Republican, Ohio, 1915–1937) had himself been a child laborer; he began working in Youngstown steel mills at the age of thirteen. In 1919, the *New York Times* described him as a "union labor man" (28 September 1919, 3).

3. On 14 February 1930, Cooper introduced a bill (H.R. 9888) that he hoped would satisfy

the president and meet the demands of those who favored federal support for infant and maternal health, but it would have removed such work from the Children's Bureau. After Cooper's bill was referred to the Committee on Interstate and Foreign Commerce (71st Cong., 2nd sess., *Cong. Rec.*, 14 February 1930, 3706), FK warned in a *Survey* article that Cooper's bill would "disintegrate the Children's Bureau" if the bureau was removed from the Department of Labor and placed in the Public Health Service, where "children and their mothers would no longer occupy the center of this stage." She continued, "As the bill reads it is more like a head-on collision than a coordination." FK's enclosed letter to Cooper stated that despite his past "faithful interest" in maternity and infancy work, it was now "impossible to rely upon you as the consistent friend of the Children's Bureau." She concluded, "We deplore the necessity for this change but you have made it inevitable" (FK, "Don't Divide the Baby," 708; FK to Cooper, March 1930, copy, "General Correspondence: Magee, Elizabeth," Box B16, NCL Records, DLC). Later FK explained Cooper's reversal as due to pressure from the White House that "[a]s an Ohio Administration Republican he could not refuse" (FK, "Why the Children's Bill Did Not Pass," 176).

4. James J. Davis (1873–1947), who had been appointed to the Senate from Pennsylvania, was secretary of labor from 1921 to 1930 and had worked closely with Grace Abbott in the department of labor during that decade.

258. To John B. Kelley

[New York City]
March 11, 1930

Dear John

You are so hard to catch on the telephone that I am sending you this formal invitation.[1] Please be perfectly candid as I am in asking you.

Would you be interested to see and hear Al Smith performing at the Hotel Astor on April 7th at 7:00 P.M. on the occasion of the annual dinner of the Consumers' League of New York?[2]

This has nothing to do with our National dinner of last November. And I am afraid that my guests would hardly charm you.

Aside from Ko and Augusta [Kelley] I am asking Mrs. Morrill Goddard, Elisabeth Frank, Viola Conklin, Mr. and Mrs. Samuel Fels of Philadelphia and one or two others whom you do not know. It might even befall that Leo and Edith would be there. R.S.V.P.[3]

CC, FKP, NN

1. JK was living part of the year in his New York apartment and the remainder at FK's summer home, where he wrote FK that he hoped to write another book following *The Outsiders*, the book he self-published in 1926. He wanted her loans to him "to be on a business basis. . . . God bless your great generous heart, Dear Ma, for your kindness and bigness" (JK, [Brooklin, Maine], to FK, 8 September 1930, FKP, NN).

2. After his defeat in the presidential election of 1928, Al Smith retreated from politics and became president of Empire State, Inc., the company that built the Empire State Building. At the NCL's annual dinner, Smith walked a tightrope between his accomplishments as a progressive and his opposition to FK's legislative agenda. He pointed to his work on the

New York State Factory Investigating Commission in 1913 but spoke of the minimum wage "without directly declaring himself in favor of it." Instead, he said he saw no reason "why the State could not conduct a study of wage conditions" with the goal of raising wages "by means of publicity and the pressure of public opinion" (*NYT,* 8 April 1930, 30).

3. Apparently JK accepted the invitation, for FK wrote him that although she had to be in Washington, D.C., on 7 April 1930, "this is to beg you to go as though I were there and be even more genial than you always are!" (FK to JK, 5 April 1930, copy, FKP, NN). FK invited Jessamine R. Goddard, who had married newspaper editor Morrill Goddard in 1899; author Viola Conklin (b. 1849); laundry-soap manufacturer and Philadelphia civic leader Samuel S. Fels (1860–1950) and his wife Jennie May Fels, a member of the NCL Board of Directors; and Leo Mayer, a Harvard classmate of NK. Mayer and his wife Edith were among those who accepted FK's invitation (Edith Mayer, New York, to FK, 27 March 1930, FKP, NN). Molly Dewson presided at the dinner, which more than 400 people attended (*NYT,* 8 April 1930, 23).

259. To George McAneny[1]

Mr. George McAneny, President
The Regional Plan Association
130 East 22nd Street
New York City
156 Fifth Avenue, New York City
March 29, 1930

My dear Mr. McAneny

I have read with great interest the Regional Plan News. I am greatly interested in the work that has been done in behalf of the Regional Plan.[2] But I have lost all interest in the building of cities like Forest Hills, Sunnyside and Radburn.[3] I am in doubt whether the narrowmindedness of the aggregations of owners and tenants of such cities is not a serious social disadvantage.

If I am correctly informed, no Jew can be an owner, tenant or guest in Forest Hills to say nothing of the most cultivated or affluent Negro, and the same thing applies to Negroes in Radburn. I have never inquired about Jews there.[4]

One of my acquaintances tells me that because a Negro man was allowed to sleep in the basement of a house in Sunnyside three nights between jobs as a matter of convenience (although he was not eating with the family or dreaming of doing so) some Paul Pry called on the occupant of the house as a delegate from a group of neighbor tenants "to remonstrate against this invasion".

Whether planning extra-desirable dwellings and other surroundings for groups to which this narrowmindedness seems to be common is desirable, I am by no means clear.

Yours sincerely[5]

CC, "General Correspondence: Kelley, Florence," Box B14, NCL Records, DLC

1. McAneny (1869–1953), banker and publicist, had been active in New York City civic affairs since the 1890s.

2. At a conference on 22 March 1930, McAneny spoke of the need for a permanent city planning organization to work with those in the Regional Planning Association as the association developed zoning ordinances for New York's cities. He said that the movement of the population had been "guided only by individual discovery and effort with no 'concerted machine to direct it'" (*NYT,* 23 March 1930, II:1).

3. Forest Hills Garden on Long Island was a planned community funded by the Russell Sage Foundation in 1911. It was characterized by "remarkable visual unity" and "unusual community solidarity." Although it was designed to provide affordable housing for working families, an "amiable but costly rivalry" among homebuilders pushed the average income level of residents far higher than planners intended. The City Housing Corporation developed Sunnyside Gardens in Queens, New York, in 1924; it also developed Radburn, New Jersey, in 1927. (Newton, *Design on the Land,* 474–478, 489–495, quotes on 476 and 477; see also *NYT,* 21 February 1926, RE2 [Forest Hills]; 24 June 1924, XX4 [Radburn]; 26 January 1928, 22 [Sunnyside and Radburn].)

4. In 1932, both Sunnyside Gardens and Forest Hills were less than 10 percent Jewish (Wenger, *New York Jews and the Great Depression,* 82). Du Bois was turned down by the Russell Sage Foundation when he tried to buy a home in Forest Hills (Lovett, "Du Bois," 216).

5. George B. Ford, general director of the Regional Planning Association, replied to FK on behalf of McAneny, who was out of the country. He wrote that the association had not "the slightest racial prejudice in any of our interests" and that at least one "Negro" was to be on the board of the New York Housing Association. Ford concluded, "I think there is distinct hope for real broad mindedness in this question in the near future" (Ford to FK, 16 April 1930, "General Correspondence: Kelley Florence," Box B14, NCL Records, DLC).

260. To Elizabeth S. Magee

NATIONAL CONSUMERS' LEAGUE
156 FIFTH AVENUE, ROOM 1129
NEW YORK CITY

April 24, 1930

Dear Miss Magee

Mrs. Marconnier and I have read with pleasure and benefit your very interesting article for the Annals.[1]

My two major suggestions are: That the close is not up to the rest of the paper, as I have ventured to mark on page 7, and my second suggestion is that the treatment of the Manufacturers Association is too mild. Child labor is no longer a problem. It is a vast and growing evil.

The relation of the National Association of Manufacturers to it is permanently dynamic. The Association never rests. If it does not appear under its own full name, it works through its aliases, as the New York State Economic Conference, New York State Associat~~ioned~~***ed*** Industries,—and also all its state branches. In Massachusetts their branch has for several years prevented raising the school leaving age to fifteen years. In Wisconsin their state branch has, we understand, been instructed to push their National program.

There have been so many kindred interferences with child labor and compulsory education measures since the National Association of Manufacturers

Program appeared, that it is no longer a correct statement of the situation to say that it cannot yet be determined whether this is a maximum or minimum program. That was true in September 1927 when the Program was first issued. There has for many months been no doubt that it is, definitely and continuously, intended to bring down the standards of progressive states.[2]

I do not know what your limit of words is and I have, therefore, suggested the omission of several in case you are hampered when you wish more space for the next to the last paragraph of your article.

I am proud and happy that this article will appear in the Annals bearing signature of the Executive Secretary of the Consumers' League of Ohio.

Yours affectionately
Florence Kelley

Please ignore every suggested change that you do not like!

TLS, "General Correspondence: Magee, Elizabeth," Box B16, NCL Records, DLC

1. Emily Sims Marconnier was then an assistant at the NCL office and later directed the division of industrial relations at the New York State Department of Labor (*NYT,* 15 May 1954, 18). Magee had evidently sent FK a draft of her article, "Child Laborers' Gains and Losses since the War," which was published in the *Annals of the American Academy of Political and Social Science.*
2. Magee's article defended the child labor amendment and deplored the wide variation in state laws regarding child labor. Of the NAM program she wrote that since its 1927 publication, "no progress in raising standards . . . can be credited to the activity of the Association; moreover, state branches have openly opposed efforts to secure better laws" ("Child Laborers' Gains and Losses since the War," 60).

261. To Nicholas Kelley

MRS. FLORENCE KELLEY
NASKEAG, BROOKLIN
MAINE

July 5, 1930

Beloved Son

In spite of faithful efforts I have not been able to clear my mind of chagrin for my horrid mistake about the Penington, and the penalty I paid in losing half an hour with you. Everything else has been flawless except the heat of Thursday, already unbelievably more than a week ago.

The conference of the N.A.A.C.P. was by far the best yet held. It was a fitting coming of age party, and promises a lesson to Mr. Hoover in November wherever the Negro vote forms the balance of power. One reason of my hope that this may follow is the adoption of my resolution that the women of the auxiliaries to the branches be urged to make a house to house canvass, to assure the registration of Negro men and women in every district,—under the guidance of a highly competant man or woman to be added to the staff during this four months.[1]

It was amusing and encouraging that my brief speech in support of this preparatory measure was wired to two Washington papers by the correspondents in Springfield; and questions followed whether this was a serious move or merely convention oratory. Both were assured that it is the next step after the close of the convention. This getting down to brass tacks four months ahead of the Senatorial election is unparallelled in the history of the Association. I have not yet recovered from the excitement and exhilaration. We stayed over until it ended Tuesday night and started hither Wednesday morning.

The weather was perfect until the last half hour Thursday night when we had a mild shower between Blue Hill and Naskeag.

Today is exquisitely clear and cool and we are working on the porch in the place where Augusta photographed Miss Menah and me.

The United States Public Health Service is finally beaten. I have here received a copy of the bill introduced with the public official approval of President Hoover and Secretary [Ray] Wilbur. It is free from every fatally or very seriously injurious provision included in the series of its five predecessors. It is not likely to pass at this session, but we have great hopes of ***a*** changed spirit after November, in the White House.[2]

The play was obvious. These two dignitaries waited to see how the cat would jump in Denver, and the cat jumped unmistakably right for the mothers and babies. The new bill followed immediately.[3]

My hoped-for guest from Tennessee, Mrs. Trawick, from Nashville, has most unhappily gone over to the United States Public Health Service as a volunteer worker.[4] And she has cancelled her acceptance of my invitation for a visit this month. That grieves me because she is, otherwise, the most well-informed woman I have ever met from any southern state, beside having as much southern charm as Anne.[5]

Letters from the office report terrible heat on the days that we spent so comfortably in Springfield. The contrast between your temperature and ours is an ever-recurring grief year after year.

I hope your vacation may be longer this year.

You may be amused at Mr. Farrow's advertisement.

Your loving Ma[6]

TLS, FKP, NN

1. The NAACP's annual conference was held in Springfield, Massachusetts, on 25 June–1 July 1930. At the conference, FK advocated that NAACP branches work to defeat senators who had supported Hoover's (unsuccessful) Supreme Court nomination of John J. Parker, a North Carolina judge who had been quoted as saying "the participation of the Negro in politics is a source of evil and danger to both races" (*NYT*, 1 July 1930, 6 and 30 March 1930, 3). The senate rejected Parker's nomination in May 1930 (*NYT*: 8 May 1930, 1).

2. Kelley's optimism about the post-election political climate was based on the success of a June campaign by the WJCC to mobilize support for the Sheppard-Towner Act and the Children's Bureau (*NYT*, 12 June 1930, 14). In November 1930, this coalition succeeded in defeating President Hoover's efforts to use the White House Conference on Child Health and Protection to finalize public support for his plan to move the Children's Bureau into the Public Health Service, thereby ending its links with women's organizations. Yet the coalition did not succeed in restoring Sheppard-Towner funding (FK, "Why the Children's Bill Did Not Pass"; Costin, *Two Sisters for Social Justice,* 168–176; Goldmark, *Impatient Crusader,* 110–113). See also Letter 257, FK to Elizabeth Magee, 5 March 1930, above; and Letter 268, FK to Elizabeth Magee, 5 May 1931, below.

3. FK had recently told George Soule that the Denver meeting of the GFWC, which she had attended, was "virtually solid" in its support for keeping the Children's Bureau in the Labor Department (FK to Soule, 16 June 1930, copy, "Press and Periodicals: *New Republic,*" Box B20, NCL Records, DLC).

4. Mrs. Arch Trewick of Nashville was president of Tennessee's State Federation of Women's Clubs in 1933. In 1937, she was named the first director of health education of the Davidson County, Tennessee, Health Department.

5. Probably FK's longtime friend Anne Safford.

6. NK replied with family news and an expression of pleasure "that you had had so interesting a time among the colored brethren" (NK, New York, to FK, 11 July 1930, FKP, NN).

262. To Mabel Cory Costigan

[New York City]
September 23, 1930

Dear Mrs. Costigan

All your friends here are engaged in continuous Thanksgiving for the Colorado nomination![1]

Synchronizing with the success of Senator Norris, and the amazing majority of young Phil LaFollette, and the defeat of Cole Blease and Senator Ransdell, it all seems too good to be true in this year which began so discouragingly.[2]

There is accumulating evidence too in non-political fields, of quiet, continuous constructive work going on where we had almost ceased to look for it. For instance, last week I turned in for the Midmonthly October Survey, a criticism of the third tentative draft for a uniform Child Labor Law by the Commissioners for Uniform State Laws.[3] It is unbelievably better than any bill that I know anything about submitted hitherto by any national organization for adoption by the states.

This, of course, does not include the child labor amendment or the federal children's laws. Since, however, the Supreme Court condemns us to doing everything 44 times, this draft appears to be better worth the inordinate amount of effort than any previous sample. At the same time came Natalie Matthews' contribution to Mr. Hoover's White House Conference in the form of an enlightened discussion of hazardous occupations for children.[4]

And finally, I am laboring with a committee of the Taylor Society on a code covering all aspects of a well-conducted industrial establishment applying to men, women and children.[5] They will work over this two years before incurring publicity on their effort.

Success to your campaign!

Yours devotedly

CC, "General Correspondence: Costigan, Mr. and Mrs. Edward P.," Box B12, NCL Records, DLC

1. On 9 September 1930, Colorado Democrats nominated Edward Costigan for senator in a primary election (*NYT,* 11 September 1930, 3). He won the election and served in the U.S. Senate from 1931 until 1937.

2. In the August and September primary elections, George W. Norris was renominated for U.S. senator, while Senators Coleman Blease (1868–1942; Democrat, South Carolina, 1925–1931) and Joseph E. Ransdell (1858–1954; Democrat, Louisiana, 1913–1930) were defeated. Philip F. La Follette (1897–1965), son of Robert F. La Follette, won the Republican primary election for Wisconsin's governor (*NYT*: 17 August 1930, III:5; 10 September 1930, 1; 11 September 1930, 3; 17 September 1930, 3).

3. At its meeting in Chicago on 13 August 1930, the Conference on Uniform State Laws had adopted the draft of the commissioners. The draft was a decided step forward, wrote FK in her *Survey* article, but it had several serious weaknesses. She criticized the exclusion of all agricultural work in the legislation and the minimum age limit of fourteen (FK, "The Uniform Child Labor Law," 84–85).

4. Ellen Nathalie Matthews was director of the Industrial Division of the Children's Bureau. In 1930, she wrote the Children's Bureau publication *Children in Fruit and Vegetable Canneries: A Survey in Seven States.* The White House Conference on Child Health and Protection, announced in June 1929 by President Herbert Hoover and Secretary of the Interior Ray Wilbur, convened experts in Washington, D.C., to examine the status of children's health in the United States and recommend "what ought to be done and how to do it" after a survey was completed. It took place on 19–22 November 1930 (*NYT,* 20 June 1929, 24; Wilbur, "Children in a Modern World," 570).

5. The Taylor Society, to which FK belonged, promoted the application of scientific management principles to industrial work. It was one of several groups that influenced the industry codes of the controversial National Recovery Administration (1933–1935). FK had agreed to prepare a code that was "applicable to factories, large and small," she wrote NK. "I have had little to do with codes," she continued, "but a great deal to do with standards and I am tempted to commend, for introduction into this code, the cooperation between the Amalgamated Union and the organized manufacturers of men's garments, as a model for all branches of manufacture" (FK to NK, 14 July 1930, FKP, NN).

263. To Julia C. Lathrop

NATIONAL CONSUMERS' LEAGUE
156 FIFTH AVENUE, ROOM 1129
NEW YORK CITY

Election Day, [4 November], 1930

Dearest J. Lathrop

Last evening I dined at Miss Wald's, and their filing clerk fished out a mass of Congressional reports, bills, newspaper clippings, reprints of articles about the campaign from 1909 through 1912 which then culminated in the creation of the Bureau and your appointment.[1] Pertinent samples of these Miss Wald promised to mail to you this morning. I do not know where to look for anything comparable to that collection. She and I really concocted that phrase about the length, breadth and thickness of the duties of the Children's Bureau. I remember haggling with her about putting illegitimacy into the itemized list. At that time the itemized list seemed to me far more important than the generalized authorization to investigate everything appertaining to.

How different the experience has shown the case to be! L.D.W. received your inquiry about social research as a government service yesterday, and I found mine awaiting me at the office just now when I came in late after voting. I think the idea of a self-created committee for the purpose you sketch excellent statesmanship. Of course I would participate in calling it, and would attend and aid in its deliberations. I wonder whether, if enough of us assemble and take a lively part in the conference, that medical special session will really materialize?[2]

Yours devotedly
F. Kelley

TLS, Lathrop Papers, IRoC

1. Lathrop had been invited to speak at the White House Conference on Child Health and Protection and was seeking information from FK and Lillian Wald on the origins of the Children's Bureau. She wrote, "Anything as to how that comprehensive paragraph was obtained 'to investigate and report upon all matters pertaining to the welfare of children and child life among all classes of our people' I would like to have. One has to step softly on all this because as we both probably are well aware the parent [patent?] purpose of the Conference is to separate child welfare into certain component parts whereas the great wisdom of the committee was its broad definition of child welfare" (Julia Lathrop, Rockford, Ill., to FK, 29 October 1930, "General Correspondence: Lathrop, Julia C.," Box B15, NCL Records, DLC).

2. Subsequently Lathrop sent FK and Wald a series of questions she planned to distribute about forming a committee after the White House conference to discuss the topic of social research as a government service. She added that "medical men are to have a special session after the White House sanctioned by the Prest. & Interior Secretary Wilbur" (Lathrop to FK, 29 October 1930). In the end, illness prevented Lathrop from attending the conference (Julia Lathrop, Rockford, Ill., to FK, 12 November 1930, "General Correspondence: Lathrop, Julia C.," Box B15, NCL Records, DLC). FK told Elizabeth Magee that conferees should determine as much as possible from this "secret session of physicians" and "carry the news home with us." FK was "spending much energy on getting people to go and stay" after the conference so they could attend the physicians' session (FK to Magee, 6 November 1930, "General Correspondence: Kelley, Florence," Box B14, NCL Records, DLC). For FK's description of the opposition from physicians to the presence of women reformers at the conference, see Letter 264, FK to Grace Drake, 6 December 1930, below.

264. To Grace B. Drake

[New York City]
December 6, 1930

Dear dear Grace

I marvel that you care to give me a thought to say nothing of writing that enchanting letter with the best news of the year in it,

(a) that you feel better[1]
(b) that you are making a business of getting well
(c) that the wise men seem to have been really wise this time. This inference follows from (a) and (b).

The reason I did not come to see you either coming or going to and fro is that I have been skating on the thinnest of ice, which has fortunately held thus far and the worst strain is now over.

Every session of Mr. Hoover's child conference was worse than every other session from the point of view of the outrageous brutality of his sub-committee on the organization of government and of the larger committee of which it was a part. The first under the chairmanship of Dr. Haven Emerson, the second under that of Surgeon-General Hugh S. Cumming of whom I have just heard the cheerful news that his term of office will soon automatically end by reason of his age. I have hesitated about sending you the details.[2]

Since, however, the offenders were terribly punished in the most public way conceivable by the members of their own profession and by the denunciations of the press from Maine to California and from Oregon to Florida, I think you may be able to bear the strain.

Before the conference met on November 19th it published a volume of 600 pages bound in cloth and sent to members of the committees and to selected parts of the press, the mere negligible delegates whose role throughout was pitiable except as to numbers, received none; until they reached Washington stood from 3 ½ to 5 years in line and received unbound loose sheets containing material largely different from that contained in the bound copies, whence arose great confusion.

I missed the opening day, Wednesday, because of Florence's coming out party.[3] The circus began, however, on Thursday with a superb speech by the then Secretary of Labor, Mr. Davis. Knowing himself elected to the Senate and having no doubt that he would be seated he made all his swan song a superb address to a crowded audience of whom all but the administration seemed surprised and delighted at his positive attack on the proposal to transfer the Children's Bureau to the U.S. Public Health Service.[4] Usually when he has spoken with great positive conviction it has been in favor of making the deportation laws stronger or in some other way making life harder for his fellow immigrants to this country but that day he was so fine that no one could have wished for anything better.[5] At the end of his discourse, however, we were adjourned, all of us who were interested in the Bureau to a small unventilatable hall in the ground back of the Red Cross building.

On arriving there a dozen of us together found Dr. Emerson seated alone on a low platform capable of holding, by very careful placing, a maximum of six chairs and a diminutive table. He waved us away when we opened the door, shouted at us "this is a committee meeting, only members of the committee will meet" and rudely contradicted us that the committee had occurred the day before and this was to be a conference meeting which we should all attend throughout. At that moment his eye rested on Mary Anderson dragging a chair up the aisle. He leaped from his platform, ran to her, grabbed the chair out of her hands, shouted "this is for a man on the committee[.]"[6]

From that point on the President's conference was stormy and disillusioning. We adjourned at 12:30 for a luncheon, the substance of the speaking at which had to do with unemployment and Grace Abbott made a fine address on the effect of unemployment upon the children. That evening Dr. Emerson's Committee met and reaffirmed unanimously its recommendation for the transfer of its medical work from the Bureau. The protest continued throughout Friday morning and Saturday morning and at the closing session Senator [Ray] Wilbur announced that there would be no further discussion of the recommendation but it would go to a continuation committee yet to be appointed by the President.[7]

I am dictating in bed on Saturday morning, two weeks after that announcement by Secretary Wilbur.

I have just received a telegram from Washington saying that "The Senate voted December 4th to make Jones[–Cooper] Bill unfinished business on Monday."

The Women's Joint Congressional Committee has been polling the senate throughout the two weeks since the Conference ended. I believe that this telegram is a prophecy of favorable action on the same old bill which was introduced in April 1929 and has been held up by Mr. Hoover continuously while six other bills were introduced of which [not] one has yet come out of Committee in either House.[8]

Won't it be an irony if it turns out in the end that the Third White House Conference on Health and Protection of Children results in the re-establishment of the appropriation for the maternity and infancy bill to be carried on by the Bureau?

If you like the book of Bette which started toward you Thursday, just send a postal card and I will send you another by the same author called "Basquerie" which I am greatly enjoying while resting from two hectic months.[9]

Yours always devotedly, though inexpressively,

CC, FKP, NN

Note: The penciled address "Galen Hall Hotel[,] Atlantic City, N.J." is written across the top of the carbon.

1. Grace Drake wrote that although she had been "fearfully sick," she could now be outside four hours a day (Drake, Atlantic City, N.J., to FK, [28 November 1930], FKP, NN).

2. At the White House Conference on Child Health and Protection, the subcommittee of the conference's Committee on Public Health Organization voted overwhelmingly to transfer the Children's Bureau from the Labor Department to the Public Health Service. Grace Abbott was the only dissenter (*NYT,* 21 November 1930, 3). See Letter 261, FK to NK, 5 July 1930, below, for the retention of the Children's Bureau in the Labor Department. Haven Emerson (1874–1957) headed Columbia University's DeLamar Institute of Public Health (later the Mailman University School of Public Health) from 1922 to 1940. For the NCL's previous experiences with Cumming, see Letter 243, FK to Alice Hamilton, 20 June 1928; Letter 244, FK to Mabel Costigan, 30 June 1928; and Letter 246, FK to Alice Hamilton, 22 November 1928, all above.

3. In a letter to Albert and Esther Kelley, FK described in detail her granddaughter's party at Ko's home (FK, New York, to Albert and Esther Kelley, [ca. 16 December 1930], FKP, NN). In June 1930, Florence had graduated from The Baldwin School, a girls' preparatory school in Bryn Mawr, Pennsylvania. Later that summer FK wrote regarding Florence's decision to attend Smith College that she was "inclined to regret so able a girl's going to Smith," but after a friend persuaded her of the advantages of women's colleges, she realized that Florence would thus "escape being submerged in the mobs of half-prepared boys by entering a university as a Junior, after the incompetents have been more or less thoroughly winnowed out" (FK to NK, 15 August 1930, FKP, NN).

4. On 20 November, James J. Davis, vice-chairman of the White House children's conference, praised the work of the Children's Bureau since its founding. Arguing against its transfer, Davis said, "In research, in our popular education, in administrative demonstration, in co-operation with State and local agencies, the value of a unified approach to the problems of childhood has been demonstrated" (*NYT,* 21 November 1930, 3). Davis was in the last month of a nine-year term as U.S. Secretary of Labor; he had served under three presidents.

5. Davis had emigrated from South Wales with his parents in 1881, at the age of eight.

6. FK wrote in an article for *The Nation* that the White House conference had "served to reveal clearly at last President Hoover's long ill-concealed intent to dismember and destroy the federal Children's Bureau." She concluded, "The long-heralded conference has come and gone. It was stormy and disillusioning for committee members who had for months sacrificed time and strength to serve the children" ("Save the Children," 643). For more about the White House Conference on Child Health and Protection, see Letter 261, FK to NK, 5 July 1930, above.

7. The *New York Times* reported that the opposition to the Children's Bureau transfer "developed to a point which tonight threatened to distract attention from the purposes for which the conference was called." Emerson's announcement that the Committee on Public Health Organization had approved the subcommittee's vote on the transfer "transformed into a protest meeting the open session held today by the Public Health Section" (*NYT,* 22 November 1930, 6).

8. See Letter 257, FK to Elizabeth Magee, 5 March 1930, above.

9. Eleanor Mercein Kelly, *The Book of Bette: Recording Further Experiences of the Family Urruty among the Spains* (New York: Harpers, 1929) and *Basquerie* (New York: Harpers, 1927).

265. To Mrs. Wallace Grayston

[New York City]
December 23, 1930

My dear Mrs. Grayston

The three new ideas in legislation in which this organization is interested are compulsory unemployment insurance, the requirement that no chemical substances can be used in manufacture until it has first been examined by the federal Bureau of Standards and guaranteed non-injurious to people employed in using it or exposed to its poisons. This is intended to cover injuries to employes such as the hideous torture and death inflicted on workers with radium in making luminous objects (clocks, watches, etc.) or in the manufacture of paints and varnishes. And the third is the requirement that no newly introduced machine can be set up in any factory until it is first made safe and so certified by the U.S. Department of Labor.[1]

These three proposals, new in the sense that they have not yet been enacted into law in any state though all three are terribly needed in all the states.

If you will write to Professor John R. Commons of the Department of Economics, University of Wisconsin, Madison, Wisconsin, he can give you references with regard to the first.

The United States Public Health Service is in process of publishing its report of two years investigation into the use of radium and its effects upon the workers.[2]

The recommendation of the safeguarding of machines before they are allowed to be used is common to the reports of the factory inspectors and industrial commissioners of all the industrial states and can doubtless be found in such reports in the Huntington Public Library.

Yours very truly

CC, "Radium Poisoning: Correspondence, 1929–1947," Box C43, NCL Records, DLC

1. Mrs. Wallace Grayston had written the NCL: "Have a club paper, subject 'New Ideas in Legislation'—Can you send me any printed material that will be usable?" (Grayston, Huntington, Ind., to the NCL, 18 December 1930, "Radium Poisoning: Correspondence, 1929–1947," Box C43, NCL Records, DLC.)

2. In the spring of 1929, FK had written Alan Nevins, an editor at the *New York World*, stressing the need for continued widespread publicity in order to "force industrial diseases upon the list of compensable subjects." She was encouraged by Surgeon General Hugh Cumming's investigation, which had begun in February 1929, and hoped it would bring about "ways of making use of radium in industry safe." FK had been urging publication of Cumming's report for months (FK to Nevins, 25 March 1929; FK to Lewis R. Thompson, 15 September 1930, copy, "Radium Poisoning: Correspondence, 1929–1947," Box C43, NCL Records, DLC; *NYT*, 26 February 1929, 21). The final report was published as "Health Aspects of Radium Dial Painting. I. Scope and Findings"; "II. Occupational Environment"; "III. Measurements of Radioactivity in Workers;" "IV. Medical and Dental Phases," *Journal of Industrial Hygiene* 15 [September 1933]: 362–367, 368–382; [November 1933]: 433–446, 447, 465).

266. To Anthony F. Dirksen[1]

[New York City]
February 11, 1931

Mr. A. F. Dirksen, Secretary
Chicago Candy Association
35 East Wacker Drive
Chicago, Illinois
Dear Sir

Miss Mary Hillyer, Organizer of the Chicago Candy White List Committee, has asked me to write you in relation to your impression that I am a Russian and one of the country's leading Communists.[2]

If you would take the trouble to look in Who's Who in America, you would find my brief biography repeated in every edition since the first one issued, with all particulars as to the date and place of my birth, in Philadelphia, in the year 1859.

My father, William D. Kelley of Philadelphia, represented the fourth Congressional District of Pennsylvania in Congress, from 1860 to 1889 inclusive. His name appears officially in every edition of the Congressional Directory throughout those twenty-nine years.

My Quaker grandfather John Bartram,[3] the botanist, is commemorated in Philadelphia by Bartram Park which was his homestead when in the year 1732, the members of his Quaker meeting adopted a Minute: "It is not seemly that Friends hold other human beings as chattels." When the meeting adjourned they went home and set all their slaves free. This is a matter of history recorded in the annals of the Philadelphia Quaker Meeting. I am an active member of the meeting of the Religious Society of Friends at 15th Street and Stuyvesant Square, New York City[.][4]

I am also an active member of the Phi Beta Kappa Society, Cornell chapter, an eminently conservative body of citizens. This statement as to the Phi Beta Kappa Society can be verified from its records, I having been one of the first three Cornell students to whom keys were issued, in 1885.

I hold a card of invitation signed by President Hoover to attend the White House Conference on the Health and Welfare of Children, held in Washington last November.

I have never been a Communist and am not one now, quite the contrary.

This slander has been circulated industriously since 1924, by a body of libelers including the so-called Woman Patriots but really led by Cardinal [William H.] O'Connell of Boston.[5] It was started because of my advocacy of the federal Child Labor Amendment.

Because of your friendly interest in the work of the Candy White List Committee, in Chicago, I am writing these personal details in the interest of the Chicago Committee.

Yours very truly

General Secretary National Consumers' League

CC, "Candy White List Correspondence, 1928–1938," Box C1, NCL Records, DLC

1. Since 1926, Anthony F. Dirksen (c. 1894–1949) had been secretary of the Chicago Candy Association, a group of candy manufacturers (*Chicago Tribune,* 30 April 1949, A4). He was not listed in the first Candy White List of Chicago Committee for the White List in 1931 ("Minutes of the Meeting of the Executive Committee of the Combined Candy White List Committee," 5 February 1931, 3, "Minutes of Meetings, Executive Committee, 1929–32," Box C1, NCL Records, DLC).

2. In November 1930, NCL had sent Mary W. Hillyer, later a peace activist with the LID, to Chicago to organize local cooperation in establishing standards for candy manufacturers. Despite initial success in New York, the work in Chicago faced a challenge when some candy makers there spread rumors that FK was a communist in an attempt to undermine the work of the Candy White List by implying that "affiliations of the Consumers' League are therefore dangerous" ("Minutes of the Meeting of the Executive Committee of the Combined Candy White List Committee," 29 October 1931, 3, "Minutes of Meetings, Executive Committee, 1929–32," Box C1, NCL Records, DLC). Hillyer's work was funded by a grant from philanthropist Dorothy Whitney Elmhirst ("Secretary's Report," NCL Board of Directors Minutes, 4, Box A2; "Minutes of the Meeting of the Executive Committee of the Combined Candy White List Committee," 5 February 1931, 4, Box C1, "Minutes of Meetings, Executive Committee, 1929–32," both in NCL Records, DLC). For more about the NCL's work with the Candy White List, see Letter 244, FK to Mabel Costigan, 30 June 1928; Letter 247, FK to Presidents of State Consumers' Leagues, 10 January 1929; Letter 250, FK to Elizabeth Magee, 3 June 1929; and Letter 253, FK to Eleanor Roosevelt, 16 December 1929, all above.

3. John Bartram (1699–1777), Pennsylvania native and co-founder of the American Philosophical Society, earned an international reputation for his botanical research. He was FK's great-great-great-grandfather (see Sklar, *Florence Kelley and the Nation's Work,* 325n32).

4. The 15th Street Meeting House was the only Hicksite Quaker congregation in Manhattan (Barbour et al., *Quaker Crosscurrents,* 234).

5. See Letter 195, FK to Herbert Bayard Swope, 27 May 1924; Letter 217, FK to Paul Kellogg, 17 August 1926; and Letter 233, FK to Carrie Chapman Catt, 4 June 1927, all above.

267. To Robert La Follette, Jr.

[New York City]
March 10, 1931

Hon. Robert LaFollette
2244 Cathedral Avenue
Washington, D.C.

WOULD IT NOT BE FEASIBLE TO INCLUDE IN CONFERENCE[1] WALTER WHITE SECRETARY OF NATIONAL ASSOCIATION FOR ADVANCEMENT OF COLORED PEOPLE OR SOME EQUALLY DISTINGUISHED REPRESENTATIVE OF THE RACE

STOP IN ALL PROBLEMS OF EMPLOYMENT THE NEGROES INTEREST IS SO VITAL ESPECIALLY NOW STOP THE GROWING POLITICAL INDEPENDENTS OF THE RACE MAKES THEM ***HENCEFORWard a factor to be reckoned with.***

Florence Kelley[2]

TEL, FKP, NN

Note: Handwritten corrections not in FK's hand

1. Stating that "[i]n the midst of depression the nation is without effective political or economic leadership," George Norris, with Robert La Follette, Jr., Edward Costigan, and two other senators, had invited FK to a bipartisan conference in Washington, D.C., on 11–12 March 1931. The signers looked forward to "the formulation of a sound legislative program to be advanced at the next session of Congress." FK had immediately wired Norris, "PROUD TO BE ASKED WILL ATTEND CONFERENCE ELEVENTH AND TWELFTH" (Norris et al., Washington, D.C., to FK, 27 February 1931; FK to Norris, 28 February 1931, both in FKP, NN).

2. The conference, which the *New York Times* characterized as a "political revolt against existing economic conditions" made up of "progressive or left-wing members of both major political parties," adopted resolutions advocating studies of the current economic depression and (if conditions did not improve) congressional legislation "to prevent economic chaos and starvation." FK was quoted as finding the conference "very promising." Walter White was not among those listed as attending (*NYT:* 12 March 1931, 1, 21, 57 and 13 March 1921, 1).

268. To Elizabeth S. Magee

NATIONAL CONSUMERS' LEAGUE
156 FIFTH AVENUE
NEW YORK CITY

May 5, 1931

Dear Miss Magee

I cannot tell you how distressed I am to have missed you!

I hope you and your constituency will think well of the enclosed reprint.[1] I hope too that the approaching Board meeting will authorize a continuing campaign until the appropriation for the Sheppard-Towner work is restored.

Even the Quakers at their yearly meeting "deplored" "the second failure of Congress to re-establish the Sheppard-Towner fund."[2] I think we must do no less.

Yours devotedly
Florence Kelley

P.S. We have an edition of 2,500 reprints so please send names of any of your constituents who might be interested in it.

Colorado ratified the federal Child Labor Amendment the other day, making six states viz: Cal., Ariz., Ark., Montana, Wis., I think S. Dak or N. Dak was among the earliest[3]

TLS, "General Correspondence: Magee, Elizabeth," Box B16, NCL Records, DLC

1. FK apparently enclosed a copy of her article "Congress and the Children's Bureau," where she argued that if the administration of the Sheppard-Towner Act were to be shifted from the Children's Bureau in the Department of Labor to the U.S. Public Health Service, "the whole tempo and character of the work for maternity and infancy would almost inevitably be relaxed and its character changed, not for the benefit of mothers and children." Her article concluded, "Will the Hoover machine in the House kill the effort to restore the maternity funds?"

2. Both the Senate (on 10 January 1931) and the House (on 27 February with amendments) approved the Jones-Cooper bill (S. 255) providing funds for the Sheppard-Towner Act. However, the Senate could not agree on an amended bill before the 71st Congress adjourned on 3 March 1931 (71st Cong., 3rd sess., *Cong. Rec.*, 1913, 6301–6302, 7124–7126).

3. The Colorado legislature ratified the child labor amendment on 25 April (*NYT*: 26 April 1931, 22). No other states ratified it during FK's lifetime. But Grace Abbott and Francis Perkins persuaded President Franklin Roosevelt to include a child labor clause in the Fair Labor Standards Act of 1938, which limited the number of hours children under sixteen could work and stipulated that they could not work during school hours (Costin, *Two Sisters for Social Justice*, 157).

269. To Jane Addams

[New York City]
5-8-31

Dearest J. A.

I'm wondering what your next festivity will be.[1] I hope I may be eligible for it! It's rejuvenating for your Seniors to have the red letter days so close together!

The enclosed reprint is merely to keep you from getting too light minded.[2]

As always your devoted old
F. K.

ALS, JA Papers, PSC-P

1. On 2 May 1931, JA received the M. Cary Thomas award from Bryn Mawr College, which recognized the "eminent achievement" of an American woman. FK attended the ceremony, which featured speeches by Frances Perkins, John Dewey, and Grace Abbott (*NYT*, 3 May 1931, 16; Marion E. Park, Bryn Mawr, Pa., to FK, [18 April 1931], FKP, NN).

2. FK might have enclosed a copy of "Congress and the Children's Bureau." See Letter 268, FK to Elizabeth Magee, 5 May 1931, above.

270. To Frances Perkins

NATIONAL CONSUMERS' LEAGUE
156 FIFTH AVENUE
NEW YORK CITY

June 12, 1931

Dear Frances

I am leaving tonight for Minneapolis where I am to read a paper before the National Child Labor Committee meeting at the invitation of Mr. Dinwiddie, ***on June 16th***.[1]

So far as I have been able to learn the harvest of gains for the children this year with 44 legislatures in session is shockingly meager. So far as I know Pennsylvania enacting double compensation, and North Carolina forbidding girls under 18 to work between 9:00 at night and 6:00 in the morning, are the only important gains in the whole country.

This note is to beg you to wire me at ***collect***[2] the Minneapolis headquarters of the National Conference of Social Work, if you learn ***before*** June 16th, of any important measure beyond these two being actually signed by any governor, ***improving the condition of minor wage earners.***[3]

Yours sincerely, and as always, hopefully
F Kelley

TLS, Perkins Papers, NCC-RB

1. Courtenay Dinwiddie's (1882–1943) appointment as secretary of the NCLC in 1930 ended FK's conflict with the committee. Dinwiddie, an experienced child welfare worker from the New York City Department of Health, replaced Wiley Swift, who had resigned in the fall of that year (NCLC Press Release, "Executive Secretary Appointed by the National Child Labor Committee," 25 October 1930, Records of the NCLC, DLC; Trattner, *Crusade for the Children,* 184). Several months later, FK wrote Grace Abbott that she had "made peace" with the NCLC because Swift was no longer there. She solicited information from Abbott and from Ella Merritt in the Industrial Division of the Children's Bureau for her paper "The Child and the Machine," which she presented to a meeting of the NCLC that was held in conjunction with the National Conference of Social Work meeting in Minneapolis (14–20 June 1931). (FK, New York, to Abbott, 22 May 1931, Abbott Papers, ICU; FK, [New York], to Merritt, 18 May 1931, "Compensation for Injuries: General File, 1922–1923," Box C2; and FK to Merritt, 25 May 1931, "Child Labor: Amendment: Ratification, 1931–1938," Box C1, both in NCL Records, DLC.)
2. The word "collect" is handwritten above the line.
3. Perkins or one of her aides wired FK in Minneapolis "following changes made" and listed compensation awards, school-leaving ages, and ages at which children could work in factories for the states of Delaware, Michigan, New Jersey, North Carolina, Pennsylvania, Rhode Island, and Wisconsin (Perkins, New York, to FK, 15 June 1931, FKP, NN; Miss Miller, New York, to Miss Jurkowitz, [ca. 13 June 1931], Perkins Papers, NCC-RB). In her 16 June speech, later published in the NCLC proceedings, FK used some of this data to summarize the limited progress that had been made toward national standards for child labor. Only passage of the child labor amendment, she stressed, would stop the "sacrifice of minors and children to machines." She called for closer supervision of state child labor laws "until minors and machines in industry are forever separated" ("The Child and the Machine," in *Proceedings of the Twenty-Sixth Annual Conference of the National Child Labor Committee,* "National Child Labor Committee, 1922–31," Box C40, NCL Records, DLC).

Later, FK sent Perkins "heartfelt thanks" for the information that enabled her to finish for publication in the conference proceedings what had been "a sort of pipe-of-peace at the annual meeting" (FK to Perkins, 13 July 1931, Perkins Papers, NCC-RB). At the conference's closing session, speakers summarized their social welfare goals and called for "renewed inspiration" (*Minneapolis Tribune,* 20 June 1931, 1).

271. To Millie R. Trumbull[1]

Naskeag, Brooklin, Maine
July 10, 1931

Dear Millie Trumbull

Your letter of June 28th is a heartbreaking repetition of my experience with the Governor of Illinois in 1896.[2]

Profoundly as I hated and loathed that man, and burned with indignation against his lying perfidy, I cannot, now, even remember his name. He had called me to Springfield to consider with him in advance of the expiration of my term of office, the list of my subordinates in which he meant to make some changes. At the close of the interview I said to him "Your Excellency, although the subject has not been mentioned I assume that this means that you are about to re-appoint me." He said, "Certainly, why else should I consult you?"

A week later at midnight a Chicago reporter called me to the telephone from my bed where I was asleep to say:

"What do you think of your successor?" I said cheerfully "I am my own successor." He said, "Do you want to wait to see the truth in the morning papers or do you want me to tell you now?" And he told me that the most wretched of all my subordinates had been appointed and announced that afternoon as my successor.[3]

I do not see how this old Republic can go bumping along even as well as she does with such officials and such usages as we have had ever since its foundation.

I am interested to see that you speak of the factories wanting cheap hands in the fall. I wish we had any assurance that any factories anywhere, in this or other countries, will be wanting hands in the fall. For a year it has looked to me as though this is the worldwide breakdown of Capitalism, though not necessarily the arrival everywhere of Communism.

Have you read Norman Thomas' "America's Way Out"?[4]

Two years ago I joined the Taylor Society which exists to apply scientific management to industry. Three years ago a group of its ablest members formed the Cotton Textile Institute. They have been quietly and skillfully working to restore the cotton industry which had gone to pieces long before the panic of October 1929, and before the terrible strikes in the Carolinas and Virginia a year ago.

This year they have succeeded in getting 85 percent of the employing corporation including all the important ones to sign an agreement to abolish employment of women and girls at night. Ninety-seven percent of the 85 signing corporations have lived up to this agreement and the remaining 15 percent are almost all in North and South Carolina. This year the legislature in North Carolina passed a bill prohibiting employment of any girl below the age of eighteen years at night in a cotton mill. And there was a powerful movement in South Carolina headed by the president of the State Cotton Textile Association, for a sweeping bill prohibiting nightwork of women and youth. I am convinced that the men who have accomplished this exceedingly difficult voluntary work will not let go until the trade itself has brought its laggards up to the new standard.

What we had tried thirty years in vain to do through legislation the employers themselves have almost accomplished in three years.

And the wisest of them, Mr. Eben Whitman leading, are publicly out for the policy of legislation throughout the cotton textile area north and south.[5]

This is the only good thing that I know that this country owes to the depression. If immediate ruin did not stare the meaner manufacturers in the face days, and nights, and Sundays this miracle could never have occurred.

If you can afford the somewhat heavy dues of the Taylor Society I strongly recommend you to join it. Having begun as a small local group of engineers, it has become a worldwide group, still dominated by engineers but the most advanced of their profession with reformers and economists a lively minority. Their address is 29 West 39th Street, New York City.

If you give your title when you write to inquire about the dues, and state the length of your term of office, and say that I suggested that you apply for membership, you will I am certain, receive a cordial welcome unless, this being vacation, some stupid clerk is in charge of the office, while all of the heads are gone to Europe to attend various international conferences looking toward international peace in industry.

I want to write an article about you, and your work, and your retirement. This letter is really to beg you to send me everything that ought to go into an important Survey discussion, and a protest for appointment to office under civil-service principles in state offices as important as your own.

As a beginning I need to know the following points.

1. The date of your first appointment
2. The number of governors under whom you have served
3. The principal points that have favorably distinguished the Oregon law from other state laws
4. And, of course, most important, the present lapsed standards of enforcement.

There is a very valuable new book entitled "Social Welfare and Professional Education" by Edith Abbott.[6] In it she gives, for the first time so far as I know in any academic publication, full weight to enforcement as compared with the mere text of labor statutes. If you can get this book introduced in the Portland Public Library and in the state public library, you will be doing a real service!

Since the death of the Consumer's League of Portland (or Oregon) if it is dead, what group is there in the state interested in our general subjects?

1. How does the Oregon State Federation of Labor stand?
2. Is there a Portland Women's Club of any importance?
3. Has Dr. Vincent O'Hara been permanently silenced?[7]
4. Is there any equivalent for Rabbi Wise?[8]
5. Or any professor comparable to Mr. Foster, or Mr. Wood,[9] as they were in the palmy days of Reed College?

Yours still hopefully and always admiringly[10]

CC, FKP, NN

1. Millie Trumbull (b. 1866) had worked for twenty-eight years in Oregon state government, most recently as labor commissioner. She had corresponded with FK since 1905.

2. Trumbull recounted her dismissal from her position, a result of the Oregon legislature's passage of a bill consolidating the Departments of Child Labor and Industrial Welfare with the State Labor Bureau. Her successor, she wrote, "has no liking for the child labor duty" but sought the $50 monthly salary increase (Millie Trumbull to FK, 28 June 1931, FKP, NN).

3. John Altgeld's successor, John R. Tanner (1844–1901), governed Illinois from 1897 to 1901. Before he was appointed to succeed FK as chief factory inspector, Louis Arrington had worked at the Illinois Glass Factory. In a lengthy article, "Betrayed by Tanner," the *Chicago Times-Herald* had criticized Tanner's abrupt dismissal of FK and the deplorable conditions at the Illinois Glass Factory. In a report to Altgeld of 10 January 1895, FK had singled out the factory's child labor abuses. The *Times-Herald* praised her report because it had caused improvements, temporarily at least, at the factory (Sklar, *Florence Kelley and the Nation's Work,* 280–281, 286; Blumberg, *Florence Kelley,* 161–162; *Chicago Times Herald,* 6 September 1897, 5).

4. Norman Thomas, *America's Way Out* (New York: Macmillan, 1931).

5. FK expressed similar optimism about the elimination of night work for women and minors in the textile industry in the South in a *Survey* article. "Out of these distressing conditions [overproduction and high unemployment] re-enforced by depression," she wrote, "came a new willingness of the mill owners to adopt modern methods of management, looking towards stabilized economic and social conditions in the industry as a whole." She praised Eben Whitman (d. 1934), director of William Whitman, Inc., a company that owned textile mills in southern and northern states, for promoting the voluntary abolition of night work in southern mills. FK concluded, "Is not this success of cotton textiles aided by the [Cotton Textile] Institute a powerful argument for immediate extension of the same procedure to railroads, to coal, and to all other substandard areas of production and distribution?" (FK, "Ending Women's Nightwork in Cotton," 84–85; *NYT,* 1 May 1930, 19 and 28 February 1934, 19). For background on the NCL's involvement in the reform of the textile industry in the South, see Letter 252, FK to Roscoe Pound, 15 October 1929, above; and Storrs, *Civilizing Capitalism,* 64–68, 71–72.

6. FK congratulated Abbott on her "wonderful little book," *Social Welfare and Professional Education* (Chicago: University of Chicago Press, 1931) (FK, Brooklin, Me., to Abbott, 9 July 1931, Abbott Papers, ICU).

7. Father Edwin Vincent O'Hara (1881–1956) was a priest in Portland, Oregon, from 1905 to 1920. He chaired the Oregon Industrial Welfare Commission from 1913 to 1917 and in 1913 authored Oregon's minimum wage law for women.

8. Rabbi Stephen Wise (1874–1949) wrote Oregon's anti–child labor law and served on the state commission that administered it before he founded the Free Synagogue in New York City in 1907.

9. The first president of Reed College (1910–1919), William Trufant Foster (1879–1950), gave the faculty more power than was usually the case in academic institutions. He included Oregon's proposed minimum wage law as an issue for debate in his 1908 textbook *Argumentation and Debating*, which was used in over 100 colleges and universities across the country. Arthur Evans Wood (1881–1960), a member of Reed College's Sociology Department (1911–1915), helped write Oregon's minimum wage law in 1913 (Clark, *The Distinctive College*, 93–104).

10. FK subsequently asked Trumbull to serve—without pay—as secretary of the CL of Oregon (FK to Trumbull, 16 July 1931, copy, FKP, NN).

272. To Nicholas Kelley

[Naskeag, Brooklin, Me.]
July 22, 1931

Beloved Son

Thank you with all my heart for your letter of yesterday telling me that you wired the Phoenixville Bank to send in the check again; and that you paid the cost of protest.

I think the check must have been cashed or deposited on receipt irrespective of its date. And to my incurable chagrin, my salary check for July 15th [was?] not in the Irving Bank awaiting the arrival of Esther's on the 16th as dated. I should, of course, not have mailed a post-dated check. I cannot now explain to you what impulse made me do it.[1]

The weather was so hot and the New England roads are so bad outside of Massachusetts and Connecticut that, in spite of Miss Hansen's skillful and considerate driving, I arrived here so tired that I was not really rested for two full weeks.[2] We came on July 5th, Sunday afternoon, having followed a very beautiful route (including two hot nights and three short days at Old Bennington, with Miss [Helen Phelps] Stokes and Miss [Mary R.] Sanford; and several hours in the neighborhood of Bretton Woods and in sight of the Presidential Range. In the sixteen days, however, since our arrival there have been only four which could possibly be called clear. In all the rest there has been rain or fog or both.

I cannot remember whether I told you that I had inserted in the Intelligencer beginning with July 18th, a series of NOTICES that I shall welcome on Sunday afternoons throughout August beginning next Sunday, Members of the Religious Society of Friends and their friends for quiet meetings.[3]

I had mentioned this in advance to Bessie Balch and Mrs. Eaton. There were present last Sunday, as an experiment in advance of the date mentioned in the Intelligencer, Bessie, Helena Dudley, Mrs. and Miss Eaton and a neighbor of theirs, Mrs. Holden.[4] About the middle of the afternoon Mrs. [Jessamine] Goddard and Tiny walked in tremendously intrigued by what they discovered. Mrs. Goddard asked permission to come again.

Obviously it will be difficult to carry out the idea of Quiet Meetings. I borrowed the idea from Mrs. Magill to whom the Fifteenth Street Meeting (N.Y. City) recently sent greetings on the occasion of her 93rd birthday.[5] She has for years, welcomed friends on Sunday afternoons to her home in St. Petersburg, Fla.

I learned only recently that this is the 250th year since the founding of the first Meeting in this country, in Burlington, New Jersey. The Friend's Service Committee has sent out a notice to be read repeatedly in all meetings, urging Friends to use their vacation for making this a Friends' Year.

I posted arrows at both ends of the road that leads past Mr. Porter's land and my land, and ends at Henry Smith's and my corner. Naturally I posted them also at the entrance to my new road on which, three years ago, I spent a part of Mrs. [Mary Dana Hicks] Prang's bequest.

Amusingly enough the arrow at the Porter end attracted the attention of a regular contributor to the Baltimore Sun, who had twelve years ago reported one of our annual meetings in Philadelphia. Instantly she wrote volunteering to do a Sunday special article on the present status and aims of the League, and I have invited her for an interview next Saturday afternoon.[6] If she proves as intelligent as her letter indicated, I shall ask her also for next Sunday afternoon.

Professor Veblen's son with his wife, is nearby for the summer.[7] They are delightful people and I am inviting them also. Last Sunday was one of the four enchanting days, and the North porch proved a perfect place. Obviously the only difficulty will be in breaking up the meeting. I shall have to arrange with a confederate to do that not later than 5:30 daylight.

Are you planning for a meeting in your Meeting House this summer? I have to be back in New York on September 20th, but I could "come by" for any week-end that leaves time to reach New York on the 20th. If you have other plans don't give this a second thought![8] As you see from what precedes, I am not lacking Friends' meetings this summer.

Dear love to all the Sakonneteers,

Your immeasurably grateful,

P.S. Did you forward my letter to Esther? And, if so, what if anything did you tell her? I know you saved my face all that you possibly could.

CC, FKP, NN

1. NK assured FK that he had received her wire asking him to cover a $50 check that she sent to AK's wife, Esther King Kelley (NK, New York, to FK, 20 July 1931, copy, FKP, NN).

2. Helen R. Hansen had been FK's secretary since 1924 (FK to Hansen, 5 August 1924, "Plans to Curb the Supreme Court, Jan. 1, 1924–Aug. 1924," Box C40, NCL Records, DLC).

3. Such meetings had no liturgy and consisted only of spontaneous comments from those present who wished to speak.

4. Helena Dudley (1858–1932) directed the Denison Settlement House in Boston. Emily Lovett Eaton (b. 1874) had been president of the CL of Syracuse, New York.

5. Sarah Gardner Magill (d. 1934) was the widow of Swarthmore College president Edward H. Magill (*NYT,* 1 April 1934, 28).

6. FK's interview resulted in Susan Owen Watson's profile "A Guardian of Women in Industry," published in the Sunday magazine of the *Baltimore Sun* (13 September 1931, 7, 9).

Watson described FK as being "far from retirement" and "serene and confident" despite "forty years of pulling and tugging." She wrote that although FK's causes had endured numerous setbacks, she regarded the shorter women's work week, double compensation laws for child workers in seven states, and night work laws for women as significant achievements. Owens quoted FK as saying, "Reform comes slowly, almost imperceptibly. . . . It is like the tide. We know it is there, coming on, but we cannot see it" (7).

7. Mathematician Oswald Veblen (1880–1960), son of Andrew Veblen, a mathematics professor at State University of Iowa and nephew of Thorstein Veblen, married Elizabeth Richardson in 1908.

8. NK replied that he doubted the Friends would hold any meetings at Sakonnet that summer. In August he invited FK to join his family there in September (NK, New York, to FK, 27 July 1931, FKP, NN; and NK, New York, to FK, [21 August 1931?], FKP, NN).

273. To Lucy R. Mason[1]

Naskeag Brooklin Maine
8-7-31

Dear Lucy

1. I have worked faithfully and with keen pleasure over the ms. It will be of great and permanent value.[2]

For every time a southern state passes a [good?] bill we must add a few pages and print more copies.

2. The underlying plan, a permanent simultaneous illumination of the industrial legal status of the fourteen states, compared calmly with standards in force else where, has been sadly delayed.

Where have our minds all been?

Lucy Randolph Mason, ca. 1932. Courtesy of the Library of Congress, LC-USZ62-123747.

3. What exactly do you mean by code? A modification of the draft which the Taylor Society is far from ready to adopt?
adopt and promulgate?[3]

The thing itself can easily be imagined but the word is for our purposes far too new. We shou[l]d have to talk and write about definitions instead of about the work that so sorely needs to be done.

4. On the other hand, the truly new idea in the mss. is the Governors' Conference.[4] Should not the whole structure lead towards that as the next step?

Should it appear in the preface?

If so why?

5. Your letter of Aug. 4th is here referring to the Women's Bureau. I am anxious about your taking that Bureau seriously in matters of form because it is proverbially dull, and its reports are necessarily devoid of all sparkle and passion because they are official. It would be dreadful waste to subordinate your charm of expression to their leaden method!

6. Also! I am frightened at thought of your using material from the National Child Labor Committee because its editors are famous for garbling. Even the very great gain of substituting Mr. Courtenay Dinwiddie for Wiley Swift has not yet eradicated that.

I suggest, therefore, that if you use the proposed chart you submit it first to the Children's Bureau for criticism.[5]

7. I have examined the headings with care and have two comments: there should, I think, be two headings, nos 18 and 19
18 Limits of Hours of Labor of Men, and
19 Limits of Hours of Labor of Women[6]

The flat contradiction between the statements of fact should be resolved. Under the Oregon decision in the Bunting case, it has been untrue for several years, that the states can not limit the hours of labor of men, and you prove that they can and do limit them.

It is, however, so difficult to get them to do so, that it would be silly for women to take over the job. What wage earning men want for themselves, they are pretty well able to get either by statute or thru their organizations.[7]

Incidentally would it not be pleasanter reading if you varied the monotonous use of law by introducing statute wherever it is appropriate?

8. In the closing pages there is, I think, an undue optimistic note as to Southern industrial expansion.

If this depression continues world wide, and the disarmament conference fails as seems probable, under pressure of international fear of Russia, what assurance is there of markets for Southern products?[8]

And who are we to accept the shallow economists echoing Mr. Hoover?

We must go on basing our arguments, as always, on human need and on the experience and example of the Industrial World.

It is a superb piece of work and I am grateful for the opportunity to be even its carping critic!

Yours devotedly
Florence Kelley

ALS, FKP, NN

1. Lucy Randolph Mason (1882–1959) was general secretary of the Richmond, Virginia, YWCA from 1923 to 1932. With the NCL's financial support, Mason was appointed as lead organizer for the Southern Council for Women and Children in Industry. Although the NCL guaranteed Mason's salary for only three months in 1930, FK hoped that the Southern Council could keep Mason on its payroll for several more years. ("Report of the Secretary," NCL Council Minutes, 14 November 1930, 2–3, Box A8, NCL Records, DLC; Storrs, *Civilizing Capitalism,* 68–71.) Mason succeeded FK as general secretary of the NCL in September 1932.

2. In an earlier letter, FK had told Mason that the NCL would publish and cover the cost of her pamphlet *Standards for Workers in Southern Industry* (New York: National Consumers' League, 1931). She added that she would look at Mason's draft as soon as it arrived, even though "I seem utterly unable to get rested after the heat of July, and the long journeys to and from Minneapolis, and the final long drive . . . from New York to this extraordinarily restful place" (FK to Mason, 28 July 1931, FKP, NN).

The draft FK referred to has not survived, but the published pamphlet was the only reference source on the topic for the next five years and subsequent authors relied on it heavily, including Charles Pipkin (*Social Legislation in the South*) and Addison T. Cutler ("Labor Legislation in Thirteen Southern States").

3. Mason quoted from the draft of a proposed industrial code that mandated a shorter work week to achieve a "proper balance between production and consumption." The Taylor Society discussed this draft at its meeting in May 1931 (*Standards for Workers in Southern Industry,* 22).

4. The published pamphlet contains no reference to a governors' conference. Mason's draft probably referred to nascent proposals for cooperation among neighboring states in setting hours limits. Interstate competition among rival manufacturers constituted a major obstacle to state-by-state reform. In December 1932, the NCL began holding annual labor standards conferences attended by state and federal officials, union representatives, and reformers that fulfilled the objective of the earlier governor's conference idea.

5. Mason's work included numerous tables showing the components of southern states' child labor laws as well as which states had maximum hours laws and prohibited night work for women. Her published acknowledgments stressed that several southerners, including one Women's Bureau official, had shaped the pamphlet (*Standards for Workers in Southern Industry,* 3–4). Although Mason may have taken FK's suggestion to have the U.S. Children's Bureau double-check her data, in print she did not acknowledge FK's help with the pamphlet (see Storrs, *Civilizing Capitalism,* 137).

6. The published pamphlet explained that the 1917 Supreme Court ruling in the *Bunting v. Oregon* case did not fully resolve the constitutionality of labor laws for men, particularly in the case of laws mandating fewer than ten hours per day. It claimed that women had lower resistance than men to physical stress related to industrial work, but it emphasized social rather than biological justifications for women-only laws, such as men's exclusion of women from trade unions, the preference of unions for using contracts rather than laws to reduce members' hours, and the double burden of paid and unpaid labor for women (*Standards for Workers in Southern Industry,* 26–29).

7. The published pamphlet bears no trace of either the New South boosterism or the free-market optimism that FK objected to in Mason's draft. The final version quoted Tulane professor H. C. Nixon's comment that "'in the South . . . the coming of industry is late enough for a political sophistication to avoid many of the evils of the earlier industrial days in England and New England. . . . But at present it must be observed that political changes to meet political needs are far behind economic development in the South, and history is in danger of repeating itself'" (*Standards for Workers in Southern Industry,* 8).

8. The disarmament conference sponsored by the League of Nations was held in Geneva in February 1932. The *New York Times* reported concerns among conference planners about France's reluctance to reduce its arms and the worldwide economic depression (26 July 1931, 24).

274. To Albert and Esther Kelley

[Germantown, Pennsylvania]
October 21, 1931

Dear family:

Thanks to Dr. Wilmer I have grown strong enough to be allowed to dictate a little and this is one of the first letters. Last January, coming back from Florida, I spent a Sunday in Atlanta and acquired a terrible streptococcus infection.[1]

I am still recovering from it, having been disabled pretty completely all the year.

Even the tonic Maine air did not help.

On September 11 I started from Naskeag hither via Ko's, where I saw the whole delightful, happy, vigorous family together for three days. I arrived here the night of September 15 and told Dr. Wilmer this brief tale, leaving him to discover any other particulars. He and Dr. Lee and Dr. Cope, the Pathologist, now agree, after five and one-half weeks, that I am on the direct road to health in spite of a growth near the end of the colon.

At first there was talk of a prompt operation. Then immediate, extreme, intensive building up was substituted, and now the intruder is smaller and softer, and all thought of operation is abandoned.

Instead, however, I am to have two weeks of X-ray's every other day (three times a week). At the end of two weeks, there will be re-examination and further consultations.

I arrived here an almost total wreck. I had lost forty pounds. My haemoglobin was thirty-five. I had no reserve, nervous energy. In five days the haemoglobin rose to forty. At the end of the following week, it was fifty, then fifty-eight, and the report has not yet come in from yesterday's tests. It will probably register sixty-five. In the meantime, the red corpuscles have been increasing literally by millions, and I am now both a star patient and also an "encyclopedia patient." Dr. Wilmer suggests that, if the X-ray treatment meets their hopes, I may be at home before the end of three weeks.

I cannot tell you with what pride and affection he speaks of his experience with you. He was interested and happy to hear about Esther Jane and bids me greet you in this letter most cordially.[2]

Ko comes down every weekend. Last Saturday we drove together for two hours in an excellent car down the Wissahickon and down the Schuylkill to see the Art Gallery and then around and about during an entrancingly, lovely afternoon. He writes me every day items of unfailing interest to my incessant wonder.

The Board of the League has give me three months' vacation with pay and offered a second three months in case of any pretext whatever for it.[3] One by one the Board Members are coming over from New York to call upon me to my very great pleasure. This, however, has to be stopped, because of the X-ray treatment, requiring rest on the odd days when I do not receive it and being terribly fatiguing on the days when I do receive it.

My dear friends of the N.A.A.C.P. have sent me the most glorious floral exhibit ever beheld by me.[4]

With sentimental regrets I have had to give up my quarters at the Penington and all my possessions have been transferred to Ko's house, at the urgent entreaty of both Ko and Augusta. The latter is teaching daily professionally in a baby school in one of the modernized city primary schools under Mrs. Wesley Mitchell, who has transferred her energies from her own City and Country School to this public service.[5] The beginning of this experiment was delayed by reason of the infantile paralysis, and it is all still new and rather fatiguing for Augusta.[6] However, she is away from home from 8.30 A.M. to 4.00 or later P.M. Ko goes off at 6.00 A.M. for horseback riding, returning for breakfast, walking to the office and turning up for dinner at 7.40 P.M. It certainly does seem unreasonable to have only the two servants in that beautiful house all those hours every week day except Saturday.

We have all known each other long enough to be thoroughly convinced that the experiment is a safe one. If, however, I really should regain enough vigor to return to my old job, about which at this moment I feel very doubtful, I think I might perhaps go back to the Penington, because Ko's working hours and mine have always been irreconcilably different. However, the future will decide all that.

Whenever there is any real definite item of news, you shall have it. The reason you have heard nothing from me, in spite of your many delightful letters, is that I have had no secretary and have been too continuously exhausted to write even the shortest autographed notes. Dear love to Esther and Esther Jane and warmest thanks for your letters, so perfectly free from reproaches! You will, I am sure, be interested to know that one, dated September 8, with Birthday Greetings, arrived here on October 8, having been forwarded from the office instantly on its arrival there on October 7. The Postmark on the envelope tallied with your autographed date on the letter, and the mystery awaits your solution.

I was very thankful to get it even after a month in transit.

I wonder whether you noticed in a week day issue of the New York Times an item to the effect that Augustus Maverick Kelley had been awarded a $1,000 prize for his Greek Examination, which was a combination of the regular College Board exams and a special Harvard entrance exam, required by the donor of the prize, Jacob Gould Cooper. Augustus wrote one of the ten best examination papers. These were criticized by the College Board Committee on Greek and by the Harvard entrance examiners in Greek and then were turned over to the American Philological Society, which selected our little chap's as the best of the ten.[7] It is never to be forgotten that he will not be eighteen until Christmas.

I am sure you will be amused to know that, in order to avoid the annoyances of having the nurses waste their precious strength on my tangles, I cropped my hair at the end of the first week here to get rid of their insistent offers. I was utterly astounded to find that in cutting off the long hair, I had arrived at a complete undergrowth of brown with just here and there enough gray to save me from being accused of dyeing the remnant. When John came down to see me, he had been tremendously agitated, thinking how shattered I was going to look. With no expression on his face, except blank astonishment: "Why, Mother, that is the way I felt when I knocked on the door, and here you look like a rowdy boy", which is literally true when viewed from a sufficient distance to obscure the same old wrinkles. The discrepancy between my mop of hair and the wrinkles is grotesque.

More soon from your loving older sister.[8]

CC, FKP, NN

1. Harry B. Wilmer (1884–1943), associate professor of allergy at the University of Pennsylvania's medical school, also supervised treatment for allergies at Germantown Hospital. Earlier in the year, FK had complained to her brother and sister-in-law about the hazards of travel: "I am increasingly distrustful of railway trains both because of infections and of falls" (FK to Albert and Esther Kelley, 1 March 1931, FKP, NN). In May, perhaps aware of FK's poor health, the NCL Board had extended her usual vacation until 21 September 1931 (NCL Board of Directors Minutes, 28 May 1931, 2, Box A2, NCL Records, DLC).
2. Albert and Esther Kelley's daughter, Esther Jane, was born 28 July (AK to FK, 29 July 1931, FKP, NN).
3. The NCL Board approved this leave with pay at its 2 October meeting and appointed an executive committee to run the NCL in FK's absence (NCL Board of Directors Minutes, 2, Box A2, NCL Records, DLC).
4. FK wrote Walter White on 20 October, thanking him for the bouquet (FKP, NN).
5. Lucy Sprague Mitchell (1878–1967), a former Hull House resident, had organized the Bureau of Educational Experiments in 1916 (later the Bank Street College of Education) and chaired it from 1916 to 1954. She was part of a public school experiment, Little Red Schoolhouse, in New York City from 1924 to 1931.
6. Augusta Kelley's polio was apparently a mild case, for in the almost daily letters to FK from September 1931 to February 1932, NK referred only to Augusta's need for more rest than usual (FKP, NN).

7. FK summarized the *New York Times* account (20 September 1931, 18).
8. AK replied that he was sorry to learn of FK's suffering but he expressed optimism about her recovery under the care of Drs. Wilmer and Cope. He visited FK in November (AK, Bay Head, Fla., to FK, 25 October and 23 November 1931, FKP, NN).

275. To Emily Sims Marconnier

[Germantown, Pennsylvania]
October 30, 1931

Dear Emily:

I have written Judge Shientag direct and now find that I have not his address, so I am sending the letter to our office, trusting to you to forward it to him.

Mrs. Swope has never, so far as I know, taken any slightest active interest in the National League.[1]

If Miss [Molly] Dewson has been able to get some active help, it would be a great pity to distract Mrs. Swope's interest from the City League by offering her a position on our Board.

It is the best of news that Senator Costigan will address our meeting.[2] He has written me a lovely letter about it.

Now a few words about myself. I have been in hell since a week ago Monday, and I have to stick it out until a week from next Monday when the X-Ray treatment comes to an end. What they have done is to build me up for five weeks and then arrange to use what little strength I have acquired in that marvelously, intensive treatment to carry on a process more shattering and prostrating than I ever had imagination enough to conceive.

Fortunately my confidence in Dr. [Harry] Wilmer is unshaken, because I have before me the extraordinary results that he achieved for my brother, Albert. I will not waste the stenographer's precious time in telling you any more than this. It is the worst to date and, as to my impending escape, it is also the best.

I ought to have said, when speaking of Judge Costigan, that his return from the edge of the grave has been as wonderful as mine will be if it is ever achieved.

Love to Byrne and, as you well know, my undying devotion to you.

P.S. Please send me the exact title and address of our Philadelphia Branch and also the name and address of the Board Member who represents Philadelphia at our Board Meetings. I wish to acknowledge their lovely gift, but need these items before I can do so.

F.K.[3]

TL, FKP, NN

1. Marconnier told FK that as a sitting city court judge, Bernard Shientag had had to resign from the NCL Board because of its involvement in labor issues. FK's letter expressed her

regret over Shientag's resignation and thanked him for his "practicable and valuable advice." As a replacement for Shientag, Marconnier had suggested Mary Hill Swope, already an NCL Council member (Marconnier, New York, to FK, 29 October 1931; FK to Shientag, 30 October 1931, both in FKP, NN).

2. Costigan's secretary informed FK that he would speak at the NCL meeting on 24 November (Marguerite Owen, Washington, D.C., to FK, 27 October 1931, FKP, NN).

3. Presiding at the NCL annual meeting, John Lathrop, NK's Harvard classmate and minister of the First Unitarian Church in Brooklyn, described a recent visit to FK at the Germantown Hospital: "I can assure you that Mrs. Kelley is just as keenly interested now, even though she is obliged temporarily not to be in the midst of us. I am certain that her mind is at this very moment right here with us in our session." Edward Costigan closed his speech, "Government and Industry," with a tribute to FK, saying that his real reason for accepting the NCL's invitation to address them "was a desire here and everywhere else to pay tribute to the matchless individuality, the life-long public vision, the amazing humanitarian devotion and the wealth and splendor of mind and heart of the National Secretary of the Consumers' League" (NCL, "Thirty-Second Annual Luncheon Meeting," 24 November 1931, 3, 21, Box A8, NCL Records, DLC).

BIOGRAPHICAL DIRECTORY

ABBOTT, EDITH (1876–1957). Edith Abbott studied at the London School of Economics, where she was influenced by Beatrice and Sidney Webb, who argued that reform was more efficient than charity as a means of alleviating poverty. In 1908, she became the assistant to Sophonisba Breckinridge, director of the Chicago School of Civics and Philanthropy. Over the next two decades the two women helped establish and shape the field of social work, particularly with regard to comprehensive legislation that did not require means testing for the recipients of welfare benefits. She also worked in partnership with her sister Grace—Edith as the scholar and Grace as the implementer of knowledge. In 1920, she and Breckinridge transferred the School of Civics and Philanthropy to the University of Chicago, where in its new incarnation as the School of Social Service Administration, it became the first graduate school of social work. Edith became dean in 1924 and held the position until 1942. There she developed a curriculum that incorporated research from political science, economics, law, medicine, labor, and immigrant relations. Her influential *Public Assistance* (1941) advocated comprehensive social insurance.

ABBOTT, GRACE (1878–1939). Social worker Grace Abbott studied political science at the University of Chicago and planned to study law but instead joined the vibrant reform culture at Hull House. She and her sister Edith lived there for twelve years, during which time Grace participated in the Chicago garment workers' strike of 1910–1911, joined the successful campaign for woman suffrage in Illinois in 1913, and attended the International Congress of Women at The Hague with JA in 1915. From 1908 to 1917, she directed the Immigrants' Protective League, through which she and other social workers sought remedies for the exploitation of immigrants. In 1921, she became head of the U.S. Children's Bureau and administered the Sheppard-Towner Act. She was instrumental in defeating an attempt to transfer the Children's Bureau to the U.S. Public Health Service in 1930 and was an unofficial delegate to the League of Nations Advisory Committee on Traffic in Women and Children from 1922 to 1934. After she retired from the Children's Bureau in 1934, she helped draft the Social Security Act of 1935.

ADDAMS, JANE (1860–1935). JA graduated from Rockford Female Seminary in Illinois in 1881, then spent eight years fulfilling what she called "the family claim," traveling and seeking work commensurate with her talents. In London she learned of John Ruskin's philosophy and visited Toynbee Hall. In 1889, she and former Rockford Seminary classmate Ellen Gates Starr opened Hull House in a Chicago immigrant neighborhood. There JA gathered a network of talented women reformers that included FK, Alice Hamilton, Edith and Grace Abbott, Julia Lathrop, and Sophonisba Breckinridge. This network quickly expanded its mission to include improved sanitation, factory inspection laws, a juvenile court system, compulsory education laws, and child welfare policies and lobbying for reform at the local, state, and national levels to promote trade unions. The reform work of this cohort made Hull House the center of a large and growing women's movement for social reform between 1890 and 1930, which by 1910 was affiliated with more than 400 other social settlements. Sustained emotionally and financially by her life partner, Mary Rozet Smith, JA was by 1900 the best-known woman in American public life. Her many books reached national and international audiences and she wielded significant political power in American politics. In 1909, she was a co-founder of the National Association for the Advancement of Colored People, and in 1912, she supported Theodore Roosevelt's presidential bid with the Progressive Party. She served as president of the National American Woman's Suffrage Association from 1911 to 1914 and in 1913 attended the convention of the International Woman Suffrage Alliance in Budapest. A committed pacifist, she chaired the Woman's Peace Party in 1915 and was elected president of the International Congress of Women at The Hague that year. After World War I, she supported the League of Nations and was the co-founder and first president of the Women's International League for Peace and Freedom. Although she was harshly attacked in the U.S. for her pacifism during and after World War I, she became the first woman to receive the Nobel Prize for Peace in 1931.

ADLER, FELIX (1851–1933). Felix Adler was born in Germany and migrated as a child with his family to New York City. His father, Samuel Adler, was head rabbi of Temple Emanu-El of New York City (1857–1874), the leading Reform congregation in the United States. Felix Adler graduated from Columbia University in 1870 and then completed a doctorate at Heidelberg. In New York City in 1876, he founded the Ethical Culture Movement, a humanist faith open to all who believed in moral betterment. Through his Sunday lectures, Adler became one of the city's most prominent moral voices. Beginning in 1877, the New York Ethical Society sponsored visiting nurses in poor immigrant neighborhoods and a year later established free kindergartens. Adler married Helen Goldmark in 1880 and became a father figure for her younger sister, Josephine. In 1885, Adler organized the building of model tenements with low rents. He founded the Summer School of Applied Ethics, which, beginning in 1891, created a venue where many women reformers from Chicago, New York, and other cities first met one another. Adler helped FK and others organize the New York Child Labor Committee in 1902.

BAKER, NEWTON D. (1871–1937). Newton Baker earned a law degree at Washington and Lee University in 1894 and joined the reform culture of Cleveland, Ohio. As a member of the Democratic Party he enforced Ohio's child labor law and collaborated with the network of settlement house reformers centered on Goodrich House. He fought for such Progressive Era reforms as clean government and public ownership of streetcar franchises, serving as city solicitor (1901–1912) and mayor (1912–1916). He was president of the NCL from 1915 to 1922. In 1916, Wilson appointed him secretary of war. Serving in that position until 1921, he appointed FK secretary of the U.S. Board of Control of Labor Standards for army clothing (1917–1918), and oversaw the largest expansion of the U.S. military to date. After the war, he presided over a smooth demobilization of men and materiel. Although his formal relationship with the NCL ended in 1922, he continued to advise FK about legal matters. His postwar career as a corporate and patent attorney was punctuated with public service, as a member of the Permanent Court of Arbitration at The Hague in the 1920s and 1930s; as Protestant co-chair of the National Conference of Jews and Christians (1928–1937); and as an active supporter of the League of Nations. In his book *Progress and the Constitution* (1925), he characterized immigrants as the "mainstay of progress" who carried forward reforms that "the American part of the population was too conservative to effect." In the 1920s and 1930s he defended FK against slanderous attacks on her patriotism, calling her "the most patriotic, humane, and enlightened intellect" he had known.

BALCH, EMILY GREENE (1867–1961). After graduating from Bryn Mawr in 1889, Balch began her reform career with the Boston Children's Aid Society in the 1890s. In 1892, she met JA, Katharine Coman, and Vida Scudder at Felix Adler's Summer School of Applied Ethics. Four years later, she began a teaching career at Wellesley as an assistant in Coman's economics course. In 1903 she co-founded the Women's Trade Union League, and in 1911 she served in Massachusetts on the first minimum wage commission for women in the United States. Her pacifist beliefs led her to the International Congress of Women at The Hague in 1915. Upon her return to the United States she plunged more deeply into peace activism, particularly the more radical groups that emerged on the eve of World War I. Fired by Wellesley for her pacifism, she became a staff member of the newly founded Women's International League for Peace and Freedom in 1919, a position she held until her death, patiently building consensus among its diverse members. In 1946, she was awarded the Nobel Prize for Peace; she was the second woman to receive that honor.

BRANDEIS, LOUIS D. (1856–1941). Born into a secular Jewish family in Louisville that had emigrated from Germany in 1848, Louis Brandeis completed his secondary education at Dresden and earned a law degree at Harvard in 1877. He co-wrote "The Right to Privacy" in 1890, an article that established that important principle of twentieth-century jurisprudence. In his early career he practiced law privately and taught law at Harvard. The Homestead steel strike of 1892 clarified a growing interest in the labor movement that shaped his future career. He rose to national prominence with the brief in *Muller v. Oregon* (1908), prepared with Josephine Goldmark, his wife's sister and the NCL's research director. That brief, which overturned the court's laissez-faire decision in *Lochner v. New York,* consisted of a few paragraphs of legal argument and extensive sociological evidence about the effects of long hours on women's health. Known thereafter as the Brandeis brief, it established the precedent for the court's acceptance of sociological evidence, which later informed key court decisions, such as *Brown v. Board of Education* in 1954. Closely allied with Woodrow Wilson, Brandeis helped develop the Federal Reserve System and the Federal Trade Commission; in 1914, he was largely responsible for the clause in the Clayton Act, which legalized labor's right to organize. Wilson appointed him to the Supreme Court in 1916, where, with his elderly friend Oliver Wendell Holmes, he wrote many key dissenting opinions in favor of liberalizing constitutional interpretation. He supported many New Deal measures, including the Wagner Labor Relations Act and the Social Security Act. After retiring from the Court in 1939, he promoted the Zionist cause. At his death, he left one-quarter of his estate to Survey Associates, the company that published Paul Kellogg's *Survey* magazine.

BROOKS, JOHN GRAHAM (1846–1938). Descended from London dissenters who settled in Massachusetts in the 1630s, John Graham Brooks attended Oberlin College and Harvard Divinity School. In 1878, as a Unitarian minister in Roxbury he created a discussion group of working men. From 1882 to 1885, he studied labor problems in Europe, returning in 1891 for two years to study workmen's insurance in Germany for the U.S. department of labor. Brooks was an influential member of the American Economic Association, and in 1895 the AEA published his essay "The Papal Encyclical on the Labor Question." That year the American Academy of Political and Social Science published his book *The Future Problem of Charity and the Unemployed.* For the newly formed National Consumers' League in 1898 he wrote an influential pamphlet *The Consumers' League: The Economic Principles upon Which It Rests and the Practicability of Its Enforcement.* While president of the NCL, he authored several books, including *The Social Unrest: Studies in Labor and Socialist Movements* (1903); *As Others See Us: A Study of Progress in the United States* (1908); *The Conflict between Private Monopoly and Good Citizenship* (1909); *An American Citizen: The Life of William Henry Baldwin, Jr.* (1910); and *American Syndicalism: The I.W.W.* (1913). After he retired as president of the NCL in 1915, he held the title of honorary president until his death.

COMMONS, JOHN R. (1862–1945). John R. Commons was educated at Oberlin College and Johns Hopkins University in the 1880s, where he was strongly influenced by Richard T. Ely's critique of classical economics. His academic career in political economics at the University of Wisconsin was paralleled by a career in public life. Perhaps more than anyone else of his time, Commons showed that social scientific research could be used to shape government policy, a concept that became known as "the Wisconsin idea." He served with the U.S. Industrial Commission (1901), the National Civic Federation (1902–1907), various state and federal industrial commissions (1911–1915), and the Wisconsin Industrial Commission (1919–1945). From 1907 to 1911, he helped write public utility, workmen's compensation, and industrial commission laws in Wisconsin. In 1921, he drafted the first unemployment compensation bill in the United States. He helped organize the American Association of Labor Legislation in 1906. Many of his ideas were carried into the New Deal by students and others he had worked with.

COSTIGAN, EDWARD P. (1874–1939). Edward P. Costigan's family's wealth came from his father's investments in mining companies, but his career as an attorney focused on the rights of workers. He studied law in Utah and in 1899 earned a degree in economics at Harvard. He worked in Denver, Colorado, on many Progressive Era reforms, including the direct primary, civil service reform, and commission government. As the center of the Colorado Progressive Republican League that fought William Howard Taft in the presidential election of 1912, he supported Theodore Roosevelt's Bull Moose ticket. Costigan was counsel to the United Mine Workers during the Ludlow strike of 1914. He ran unsuccessfully for governor of Colorado in 1912 and 1914 on the Progressive Party ticket. Although his support of miners and his exposure of the illegal practices of the mining companies cost him political support, he was elected U.S. senator in 1930 as a Democrat and took many Progressive Era ideas to New Deal Washington, including federal relief for strikers, opposition to company unions, and public disclosure of income taxes paid by millionaires. He is best known for his tireless efforts to promote the Costigan-Wagner Anti-Lynching Bill. Health problems forced him to retire after one term. He and his wife Mable Cory Costigan were partners in reform until his death.

COSTIGAN, MABEL CORY (1873–1951). Mabel Cory Costigan moved easily from suffrage activism to political activism. In the early 1920s, she was active in the Conference for Progressive and Political Action, an organization of socialist labor and farmer activists who promoted third-party politics. Like her husband, whom she married in 1903, she was a vocal and highly visible supporter of the candidacy of Progressive Party candidate Robert La Follette in 1924; she campaigned for him in Rhode Island, Massachusetts, and New York, where she spoke to thousands of women workers. After 1920, she was nationally active in the League of Women Voters. In 1932, she joined Jeanette Rankin to lead a coalition of 3,000 women that pressured the Democratic and Republican parties to add peace planks to their platforms. Mabel Cory Costigan remained active in the NCL after FK's death.

DEWSON, MARY (Molly) (1874–1962). Reformer Molly Dewson's first job after graduating from Wellesley College in 1897 was as secretary of the Domestic Reform Committee of the Women's Educational and Industrial Union, Boston's largest social reform club. In that capacity, she conducted studies of the homes of working families; the result was her 1899 *Twentieth Century Expense Book,* a budgeting guide for homemakers. She came to national attention while working closely with FK and the NCL in 1911 as executive secretary of the Massachusetts Minimum Wage Investigative Committee.

Her report to the Massachusetts legislature led to the first minimum wage law in the United States. She and her life partner, Polly Porter, aided Red Cross relief efforts in France after World War I. As research secretary for FK at the NCL, a position she held from 1919 to 1924, she focused on state minimum wage laws for women and children. After leaving the NCL, she actively advanced the NCL's agenda as president of the New York Consumers' League until 1931. In her campaign for Franklin Roosevelt in 1932, she successfully mobilized women voters on his behalf and rose to prominence as head of the Women's Division of the Democratic National Committee (1933–1937). Dewson used this position to create a powerful network of women party leaders that helped secure Frances Perkins's appointment as U.S. secretary of labor in 1933. In 1935, she helped draft the Social Security Act, and in 1937, she became one of the three members of the newly created Social Security Board.

DOCK, LAVINIA LLOYD (1858–1956). Lavinia Dock was born into a family of Pennsylvania Germans whose landed property made it unnecessary for her to work for a living or to marry. None of her five sisters married. By the time she took up residence at the Henry Street Nurses Settlement in 1896, she had already become a leader in nursing education, having acquired her own education at Bellevue Hospital in New York City, which introduced Florence Nightingale's professional principles to the United States, and having taught at Johns Hopkins Hospital in Baltimore and Cook County Hospital in Chicago. In 1890 she authored *Materia Medica for Nurses,* which for decades remained the standard text for nursing education. After moving to the Henry Street settlement, she taught graduate nursing courses at Teachers College, Columbia University, and worked with trade unionists like Leonora O'Reilly, but her main work lay in writings that promoted professional nursing standards, especially (after 1900) as contributing editor of the *American Journal of Nursing,* and (in 1899) as co-founder and secretary of the International Council of Nurses. With Adelaide Nutting of Johns Hopkins she wrote the four-volume *History of Nursing* (1907–1912), which documented the loss of nurses' status when men took over the medical profession in the seventeenth century. Arrested for trying to vote in 1896, in 1907 Lavinia Dock became a full-time suffragist, joining the Equality League of Self-Supporting Women, founded that year by Harriot Stanton Blatch with an agenda adopted from the British suffrage movement. In 1915 she left Henry Street and moved to Washington, D.C., where she worked with Alice Paul and the militant National Woman's Party.

DU BOIS, WILLIAM EDWARD BURGHARDT (1868–1963). Born to a middle-class, mixed-race family in Great Barrington, Massachusetts, W. E. B. Du Bois graduated from Fisk University in Nashville in 1888, where he learned about the harsh realities of racism. After further graduate study in Berlin, he became the first African American to complete a PhD at Harvard in 1895; his dissertation on the suppression of the slave trade is still regarded as a key historical study. Invited by the University of Pennsylvania to conduct survey research on African Americans in Philadelphia, he wrote *The Philadelphia Negro: A Social Study* (1899), a path-breaking investigation based on interviews in 2,500 households. He conducted similar work for the U.S. Bureau of Labor in Virginia in 1897. That year, Du Bois began teaching at Atlanta University, where he offered courses about the social and economic conditions of African Americans that were modeled on his survey work. In 1903, he emerged as a national figure with the publication of his *Souls of Black Folk,* a lyrical work that explored African American culture and called for a civil rights alternative to Booker T. Washington's agenda of black economic advancement without civil rights. When this call made his presence a liability to Atlanta University, he moved north and organized a group of black ministers who created the Niagara Movement in 1905 and sought to generate support for black civil rights. Lacking funding, that movement failed, but in 1909 with the help of Mary White Ovington (the only white person in the Niagara Movement) and other white women in the social settlement movement, he drew together at Lillian Wald's Henry Street Settlement a group, including FK, that founded the National Association for the Advancement of Colored People and obtained funding for its publication, *The Crisis,* with Du Bois as editor. From 1910 until FK's death in 1931, Du Bois served with her on the board of the NAACP, forging a friendship that he warmly commemorated at her memorial service. As editor of *The Crisis,* Du Bois campaigned for black civil rights, woman suffrage, and federal laws to repress lynching in the Jim Crow South. Visits to Liberia (1923) and the Soviet Union (1926) deepened his knowledge of and interest in Pan-Africanism and Marxist thought, which eventually precipitated a conflict with the NAACP in 1934 that forced him to resign. An ardent internationalist, he was a member of the U.S. delegation to the UN's founding conference in 1945. In 1947, he wrote *An Appeal to the World,* a militant protest against racism in the United States as a violation of international human rights agreements. In 1950, he helped found the Peace Information Center, which endorsed the Stockholm Peace Appeal that called for the banning of nuclear weapons. Du Bois was awarded the International Peace Prize from the World Council of Peace in 1953. In 1961, he joined the Communist Party and emigrated to Ghana, where he lived until his death.

EDSON, KATHERINE PHILIPS (1870–1933). Born in Ohio, Edson moved to Los Angeles in 1900, a decade after she married in Chicago. Like many of FK's reform colleagues, her family had ties to New England traditions, including support for women's rights and higher education for women. In Los Angeles she joined the Friday Morning Club, a powerful women's club that became the means by which she entered local and state politics. In 1911, she was a central figure in the successful adoption of a woman suffrage amendment to the California constitution. In 1912, she was elected to the Los Angeles Charter Revision Commission and became the first woman elected to the executive committee of the National Municipal League. She campaigned actively for the election of Progressive Republican Hiram Johnson as governor in 1910, and he appointed her to the state Bureau of Labor Statistics in 1912. In that capacity she studied minimum wage legislation for women, which had been passed in Australia and Massachusetts, and in 1913 her bill passed the California state legislature, establishing an Industrial Welfare Commission empowered to set minimum wages, maximum hours of work, and other working standards. Johnson promptly appointed her to the commission and she served until 1931, focusing primarily on the enforcement of the state's minimum wage law. After the U.S. Supreme Court ruled the minimum wage law of Washington, D.C., unconstitutional, she successfully continued to enforce California's law and even expanded it to include additional industries. Ill health forced her to decline an appointment in the administration of President Franklin D. Roosevelt. After her death, the League of Women Voters created a redwood grove park named for her in northern California.

ELY, RICHARD T. (1854–1943). Political economist Richard T. Ely graduated from Columbia University in 1876 and completed a Ph.D. at the University of Heidelberg in 1879 with Karl Knies, a leading exponent of the German school of historical economics. A Christian Socialist, Ely helped found the American Economic Association in 1885 to advance a moral perspective on the social question. In 1892, unhappy at Johns Hopkins University, he moved to the University of Wisconsin with his pupil, John Commons. There, in a trial staged by the university trustees, he denied that he was a socialist. In 1906, with John Commons he helped found the American Association for Labor Legislation. Ely wrote pioneering studies of the labor movement and socialism and trained many students who later became nationally known, including Woodrow Wilson, Albion Small, Edward A. Ross, and John R. Commons. His major works, which include *Property and Contract in Their Relations to the Distribution of Wealth* (1914), argued that the premises of laissez-faire economics were false and that the state should enact legislation that protected workers and redressed the imbalance in wealth and opportunity.

ENGELS, FREDERICK (1820–1895). Frederick Engels was the eldest son of a successful Westphalia textile manufacturer. As a soldier in Berlin he encountered the radical thought of Hegel, Rabbi Moses Hess, and Henri Saint-Simon. His work for his father's firm in Manchester, England, in the 1840s, and the misery he witnessed in the textile district further radicalized him. His influential *The Condition of the Working Class in England in 1844*, which in 1887 FK translated into English and published for the first time in the United States, launched a lifelong intellectual partnership with Karl Marx. They co-authored *The Communist Manifesto* for Germany's Communist League on the eve of the 1848 revolution. Engels managed the family's Manchester textile plant successfully from 1850 to 1870 and was able to support Marx and his family, who fled from Germany after the failure of the revolution. After Marx died in 1883, Engels devoted much of his time to editing and publishing volumes two and three of Marx's *Capital*; he was at work on volume four when he died.

FRANKFURTER, FELIX (1882–1965). Felix Frankfurter emigrated with his parents from Austria to the United States to escape anti-Semitism in 1894. He graduated from City College of New York in 1902, then from Harvard Law School. After working in Washington, D.C., he returned to Harvard in 1914 as the first Jewish faculty member of its law school. During World War I, he returned to Washington as a special assistant to Secretary of War Newton Baker. At Baker's urging, he became legal counsel to the president's Mediation Commission, where he supported the labor movement in key strikes. From 1916, he provided legal counsel to the NCL. Protecting civil liberties became a theme of his career, and he helped found the American Civil Liberties Union in 1920. Returning to Harvard after the war, he taught innovative classes and trained many attorneys who contributed to New Deal legislation. Frankfurter and his former students helped draft the Social Security Act and the Fair Labor Standards Act. In 1939, President Roosevelt appointed him to the Supreme Court, where he served until 1962. He helped the Warren court assemble a unanimous opinion in *Brown v. Board of Education* in 1954.

GOLDMARK, JOSEPHINE (1877–1950). Josephine Goldmark graduated from Bryn Mawr College in 1898 and pursued graduate studies at Barnard College for a year thereafter. After her father died in 1881, Felix Adler, the husband of her older sister and the founder of the Ethical Culture Movement, became the main influence in her life. Another older sister, Alice, married Louis Brandeis. Initially she was a volunteer assistant to FK at the NCL and from 1903 to 1917 was the league's publications secretary. In 1907, she compiled the evidence included in the NCL's brief in *Muller v. Oregon.* Working closely with Louis Brandeis, she authored most of what came to be called the Brandeis brief, which she later expanded into her 1912 book *Fatigue and Efficiency: A Study in Industry.* Drawing on factory inspectors' and public health reports in the United States and Germany, she summarized scientific arguments for protective labor legislation in the brief and the book. Other works published under her supervision include the NCL's *Child Labor Legislation Handbook* (1907) and *Handbook of Laws Regulating Women's Hours of Labor* (1912), both of which became blueprints for reform legislation during and after the Progressive Era. In 1912, she served on the committee that investigated the Triangle Shirtwaist Company fire in New York City. In the 1920s, Goldmark investigated nursing education for the Rockefeller Foundation, and her *Nursing and Nursing Education in the United States* (1923) generated sweeping reform in that field. During those years she also worked with the NCL's campaign to secure legislative protection for workers who used radium paint to make instrument dials. She became assistant director of social research for the Russell Sage Foundation and during World War I served as executive secretary of the Committee on Women in Industry, which later became the U.S. Women's Bureau. In 1936 she authored *Democracy in Denmark.* Her biography of FK, *Impatient Crusader,* was published in 1953.

GOLDMARK, PAULINE (1874–1962). Pauline Goldmark graduated from Bryn Mawr in 1896. In 1900, she traveled throughout New York State giving lectures about the evils of sweatshop labor to Political Equality Clubs. It was she who introduced her sister Josephine to FK. She was the first full-time secretary for the Consumers' League of New York (1899–1907), from which base she produced documentary evidence on sweatshop work as early as 1903 that New York factory inspectors used in court cases. With her sister Josephine, she assisted Louis Brandeis in the preparation of the

Brandeis brief in 1906. In 1911, she did survey work for the New York State Factory Investigating Committee for its reports to the state legislature, and throughout that decade she regularly lobbied the state legislature to pass protective labor legislation for women and child laborers. In the 1910s, she served as vice chairman of the New York Child Labor Committee and as a member of the industrial board of the New York State Labor Department. She became vice president and research secretary of the NCL in 1917 and served as a director of the NCL from 1921 to 1926 and 1928 to 1931. During the 1920s and 1930s, she consulted with American Telephone and Telegraph on the conditions of labor for its women workers.

GOMPERS, SAMUEL (1850–1924). Labor leader Samuel Gompers immigrated to the United States from England with his family at the age of thirteen. He worked in the cigar industry, beginning as a tenement worker with his father and entering a succession of factories as a skilled worker. He joined the Cigarmakers International Union in the 1860s, a base from which he and his friend Adolph Strasser created a model of unionization that future craft unions would emulate, featuring higher dues, sick relief, a strike fund, and unemployment compensation. Responding to the 1885 New York court decision *In Re Jacobs,* which overturned legislation that his union had obtained to prohibit the manufacture of goods in tenements, Gompers decided to pursue labor's goals through direct negotiation with employers rather than through labor legislation. In 1886, he founded the American Federation of Labor, an organization that focused on achieving benefits for skilled workers and shunned involvement with the needs of unskilled workers and with socialist third parties. In an effort to offset intense employer resistance to unionization, he allied his movement with the National Civic Federation in the 1910s. By 1920, the AFL had four million members.

HAMILTON, ALICE (1869–1970). After Alice Hamilton earned an M.D. at the University of Michigan in 1893, she studied in Germany and at Johns Hopkins University. During her first job at the Women's Medical School of Northwestern University, she lived at Hull House, where she started a well-baby clinic and became a close friend and the personal physician of JA. Her work with JA, FK, and Julia Lathrop in Chicago shaped her views on social reform and helped her become the founder of industrial medicine. In 1910, the governor of Illinois appointed her to the first survey in the United States on the extent of industrial disease caused by lead, arsenic, brass, carbon monoxide, cyanides, and turpentine. She was a special investigator for the federal Bureau of Labor Statistics from 1911 to 1920, experience that became the basis for the landmark text *Industrial Toxicology* (1934), which she co-authored. In 1919, she was the first woman to be appointed to the faculty at Harvard Medical School, where her work shaped the field of occupational health over the next twenty-six years. A member of the health committee of the League of Nations and an advocate of birth control, she served as a consultant to Frances Perkins's Department of Labor in the 1930s. There she participated in a survey that prompted the passage of Pennsylvania's first workers' compensation law for occupational diseases. She served as president of the NCL from 1944 to 1949.

HARRIMAN, FLORENCE HURST (1870–1967). Although Florence "Daisy" Harriman was not college-trained, she had a long career as an activist, researcher, and diplomat. She began her reform efforts as a suffragist. In the 1910s, she worked for the National Civic Federation, which sent her to the South to survey the conditions of women and child workers. She served on the Commission on Industrial Relations (1913–1916), the first woman to do so. This experience radicalized her and precipitated a break with the Civic Federation. In the 1920s, she was the chair of the NCL's Campaign Committee to Oppose the ERA. Harriman was deeply committed to Democratic Party politics. She co-founded the Women's National Democratic Club in 1922 and was its president for eight years. For thirty-two years she was the District of Columbia's woman delegate to the Democratic National Committee. In 1937, Franklin Roosevelt appointed her as ambassador to Norway, where she provided the first on-site reporting to the United States of the Germans' invasion of that country. She was a longtime supporter of the League of Nations and pushed for a greater U.S. commitment to the United Nations after World War II.

KELLEY, ALBERT BARTRAM (1870–1932). FK's younger brother, Bertie, or Bert, attended the University of Pennsylvania in 1888 and 1898. He was employed throughout his career as an insurance agent in Philadelphia, New York City, Cincinnati, and later Panama City, Florida. He married Marianna ("Polly") Parrish (1874–1965), a descendant of Lucretia Mott, in April 1904. They had three children, Martha ("Patsy") (b. 1906), Albert B. (b. 1909), and Joseph (b. 1911). AK divorced Marianna Kelley in October 1927. He married Esther King in 1929, and they had a daughter, Esther Jane, born in 1931.

KELLEY, ANN VALENTINE (b. ca. 1899). Born in Richmond, Virginia, Ann Valentine married John Kelley in August 1920. Although based in New York City, they spent a great deal of time on John's yacht, the *Diablesse,* which they sailed across the Atlantic and around the Caribbean several times. Ann Kelley divorced JK in June 1927 and remarried later that year.

KELLEY, AUGUSTA MAVERICK (1885–1989). A native of San Antonio, Texas, Augusta Maverick, FK's daughter-in-law, was the daughter of George M. and Mary V. Maverick. (A cousin, Samuel Maverick, originated the term "maverick" because he did not brand his cattle. The term later acquired political meaning as a person who did not follow party policy.) Augusta Maverick married Nicholas Kelley in June 1909. Except for the years 1918–1921, the Kelleys lived in and around New York City. They had three children, Nicholas, Jr. (1910–2002), Florence (1912–1997), and Augustus (1913–1999).

KELLEY, CAROLINE BONSALL (1829–1906). After the death of her parents, Caroline Bonsall, FK's mother, was adopted by Elizabeth and Isaac Pugh and lived with them in Germantown along with Isaac's sister, woman's rights and antislavery leader Sarah Pugh. CBK married WDK in 1854 and they had eight children. No daughter except FK lived beyond the age of six. After the death of her husband, CBK lived in Philadelphia, Pennsylvania; Waverly, Massachusetts; and White Plains, New York.

KELLEY, JOHN BARTRAM (1888–1968). With his sister MK, JK attended the Hillside Home School in Hillside, Wisconsin, in the 1890s and various schools in New York City and Massachusetts. After working as a hotel clerk and laborer, first on a ranch and later with the United States Reclamation Service, he enrolled as a special student at Harvard in 1908. He was dismissed from Harvard in June 1910. JK then worked as a journalist in Portland, Oregon, and a miner in Ontario, Canada. About 1919 he took up sailing, which became an important part of his life. He always aspired to be a writer and in 1926 self-published his book, *The Outsiders*. After his marriage to Ann Kelley ended in the summer of 1927, he divided his time between New York City and FK's home in Brooklin, Maine.

KELLEY, MARGARET DANA (1886–1905). MK, FK's daughter, was educated at the Hillside Home School in Hillside, Wisconsin, and at Ferry Hall in Lake Forest, Illinois. In 1904–1905 she attended Brookline High School while boarding with Elizabeth Glendower Evans in Cambridge. She had completed her first week at Smith College when she died suddenly of a heart attack on 28 September 1905.

KELLEY, NICHOLAS (1885–1965). FK's oldest child "Ko" was educated at the Lewis Institute in Chicago and the Sachs Collegiate Institute in New York City. He received his B.A. from Harvard in 1906 and his LL.B. from Harvard in 1909. He married Augusta Maverick in 1909 and they had three children, Nicholas, Jr.; Florence; and Augustus. NK practiced law in New York City until July 1918, when he became a member of the war loan staff at the U.S. Treasury Department and subsequently assistant secretary in charge of foreign business. In June 1920, he was appointed assistant secretary of the treasury. Leaving that position in April 1921, he returned to New York City to practice law in the firm of Larkin, Rathbone and Perry, later Kelley, Drye, Newhall, Maginnes and Warren. NK served on a number of boards, including the Henry Street Settlement, Fisk University, Swarthmore College, and the Legal Aid Society.

KELLEY, WILLIAM DARRAH (1814–90). Primarily self-taught, WDK, FK's father, worked as an apprentice for a Philadelphia jeweler from 1828 to 1835. While working as a jeweler in Boston in 1835 he became active in the Democratic Party. Returning to Philadelphia in 1840, he read law and passed the Pennsylvania bar in 1841. WDK served as judge of the common pleas court for Philadelphia from 1846 to 1856. He was elected to the U.S. Congress as a Republican in 1861 and served in the House of Representatives until his death in 1890. While in Congress WDK actively supported antislavery and civil rights, including woman suffrage, as well as a strong protective tariff.

KELLEY, WILLIAM DARRAH, JR. (1857–1942). FK's older brother, Will, or Billy, attended the University of Pennsylvania, class of 1876. He left Philadelphia for Chattanooga, Tennessee, where his employment included managing an investment securities firm and practicing law. He married Caroline Tyler (d. 1946) and had two children, William Darrah Kelley, III, and Emily.

KELLOGG, PAUL UNDERWOOD (1879–1958). After a brief stint as a journalist in Michigan, Paul Kellogg entered Columbia University in 1901. He attended the New York Charity Organization Society's Summer School of Philanthropy the following summer, where he met Edward T. Devine, editor of the Charity Organization Society magazine *Charities*. Devine promptly added Kellogg to his staff. In 1907–1908, Kellogg oversaw the Pittsburgh Survey, funded by the Russell Sage Foundation, the most comprehensive social survey of its time. The volumes of the survey, which focused on labor conditions in industry, the human cost of industrial accidents, and the experience of women and immigrant workers, among other topics, set a standard for sociological analysis that influenced scholarship and journalism for decades. In 1909, he returned to the Charity Organization Society, where he edited its reorganized magazine, newly named *Survey*, becoming editor-in-chief in 1912. Under his leadership, *Survey* helped shape social policy and the field of social work on issues that included protective labor legislation, workers' compensation, factory regulation, and social insurance. In the 1930s, Kellogg helped shape the Social Security Act as a member of the Advisory Council to the Committee on Economic Security.

LATHROP, JULIA C. (1858–1932). For ten years after she graduated from Vassar, Julia Lathrop worked as a secretary in her father's law office. In 1890, at age thirty-two, she joined JA and Ellen Gates Starr at Hull House, where she stayed for twenty years. During that time, she contributed to *Hull-House Maps and Papers* (1895) and worked as an inspector for the Illinois Board of Charities. In 1901, she resigned from the board to protest the political patronage that put unqualified people in civil service social work positions. Two years later, her commitment to proper training of social workers was expressed in her work with Graham Taylor to construct the curriculum that in 1908 became the Chicago School of Civics and Philanthropy. She worked closely with Edith Abbott and Sophonisba Breckinridge to build the research department there. In 1912, she was appointed head of the federal Children's Bureau. Under Lathrop's leadership, the bureau studied maternal mortality, nutrition, and illegitimacy; established a birth registration process; and organized a national conference on child welfare standards. In 1921, Lathrop and her reform network successfully ushered the Sheppard-Towner Act through Congress. Although legislators cut the funding for this program of federal funding for mothers and infants later in the decade, the Sheppard-Towner program provided a model that was more fully realized in the welfare state construction of the New Deal years. After leaving the Children's Bureau in 1921, Lathrop served as president of the Illinois League of Women Voters and as assessor on the Child Welfare Commission of the League of Nations.

LIPPMANN, WALTER (1889–1974). Walter Lippman studied philosophy, sociology, and economics at Harvard University with philosophers William James and George Santayana and British socialist Graham Wallas. He left Harvard in 1910 a few weeks shy of earning his master's degree to begin a career as a journalist, where he soon was appointed as assistant to muckraking journalist Lincoln Steffens. His early writings drew the attention of Herbert Croly, who hired him as editor of his new magazine, the

New Republic. Lippmann's career was marked by ambivalence toward reform. After an early embrace of socialism, he renounced that movement and argued that only experts were qualified to organize society. After helping Woodrow Wilson draft his Fourteen Points, he denounced the League of Nations. After initially supporting the New Deal, he turned against it in the mid-1930s. Yet his writings provoked serious thought about the nature and organization of U.S. society by exploring issues such as the role of public opinion in political decision making and Keynesian economics. Toward the end of his life he became an elder statesman of the antiwar movement and a fierce opponent of Lyndon Johnson's conduct of the Vietnam War.

LLOYD, HENRY DEMAREST (1847–1903). Henry Demarest Lloyd was educated at Columbia College and Columbia Law School. After being admitted to the New York bar in 1869, he joined New York's Mugwump reform circles. In 1872, Lloyd moved to Chicago to work as financial editor for the *Chicago Tribune* and soon thereafter married Jessie Bross, the well-educated, warm-hearted daughter of the *Tribune*'s publisher. His career as a muckraking journalist achieved national prominence in 1881 with the publication in the *Atlantic Monthly* of "Story of a Great Monopoly," which exposed the ruthless semi-legal methods of the Standard Oil Company. His radical views precipitated his departure from the *Tribune* in 1885, and henceforth his wife's independent income supported their family. Further radicalized by the execution of the Haymarket anarchists in 1887, he published a series of books that profoundly influenced FK's generation of reformers: *A Strike of Millionaires against Miners* (1890), *Wealth against Commonwealth* (1894), and *Labour Copartnership* (1898). Just before his death he worked with attorney Clarence Darrow and labor leader John Mitchell to defend the United Mine Workers in their anthracite strike of 1902 against the Pennsylvania coal trust; the case set a precedent for compulsory arbitration.

PAUL, ALICE (1885–1977). After graduating from Swarthmore College in 1905, Alice Paul began her career as an investigator for the New York Charity Organization Society. In 1906, she traveled to London to study social work at the Woodbridge Settlement for Religious and Social Study and the London School of Economics. In London, she joined the Women's Social and Political Union just at the moment when that group left the suffragist mainstream within the Liberal and Labour parties and began to pursue militant tactics designed to win the attention of the Conservative Party. Paul was arrested and engaged in a prison hunger strike but was not force fed. She returned to the United States in 1910 and three years later began to introduce there protest tactics that she had learned in England, founding the Congressional Union in 1914, which became the National Woman's Party in 1916. Leaders in the National American Woman's Suffrage Association disapproved of the NWP's militant tactics, and differences deepened after 1920, when Paul sought to promote sex equality through an Equal Rights Amendment to the U.S. Constitution, a step that leaders in the mainstream of the suffrage movement believed would imperil hard-won legislation that benefited working women. The debate over the ERA in the 1920s highlighted these contrasting views. Paul earned a Ph.D. in law from American University in 1928 and continued to advocate the passage of the ERA until her death.

PERKINS, FRANCES (1882–1965). Frances Perkins studied chemistry and physics at Mount Holyoke College, graduating in 1902. While a student, she organized a chapter of the NCL on campus. She taught for five years after graduating, including three years in Chicago, where she became a part of the settlement house culture of Hull House and Chicago Commons. In 1909, she was awarded a fellowship from the Russell Sage Foundation to study at the New York School of Philanthropy, and she completed an M.S. in sociology and economics at Columbia. She immediately began working for the New York City Consumers' League, succeeding Pauline Goldmark as executive secretary. In 1912, in the aftermath of the Triangle Shirtwaist Company fire, she left the NCL to become the investigating secretary of the State Factory Investigating Commission. In 1919, Governor Al Smith named her to the Industrial Commission of the State of New York, which she began to chair in 1926. In New York State, she participated in a dense network of women reformers that included Eleanor Roosevelt, FK, Molly Dewson, and the Goldmarks. Governor Franklin Roosevelt appointed her head of the state labor department in 1929, where she administered workmen's compensation, expanded factory inspection, and worked to abolish child labor. At the urging of Dewson, JA, and Grace Abbott, Franklin Roosevelt appointed her secretary of labor in 1933, a post she held until 1945. She shaped the Social Security Act and the Fair Labor Standards Act in the 1930s and persuaded Franklin Roosevelt to bring the nation into the International Labour Organization.

SMITH, MARY ROZET (1868–1934). Mary Rozet Smith's wealthy parents prepared her for a life of leisure at Miss Kirkland's School for Girls. Yet her search for a purposeful life carried her to Hull House, where her friend Jennie Dow taught kindergarten. Smith visited the settlement during its first year and soon thereafter she replaced Ellen Gates Starr in JA's affections and became JA's life partner. Her steady financial contributions kept the settlement in the black during its first decade after JA's own resources were depleted. Smith also participated in the life of settlement, especially in clubs and classes for children. Although her family made extensive claims on her attention and resources, she crafted a joint life for herself and JA that centered on JA's reform career, providing the emotional support that enabled JA to participate so creatively in public life. She traveled extensively with JA and was an integral part of JA's network of women reformers.

WALD, LILLIAN D. (1867–1940). After graduating from the New York Hospital School of Nursing in 1891, Lillian Wald enrolled briefly in the Woman's Medical College of the New York Infirmary but chose nursing instead. She began by teaching home nursing to immigrants on the Lower East Side of Manhattan and quickly decided that home health care was the field she wanted to pursue. With funding from benefactors, she and her friend Mary Brewster purchased the house that later became Henry Street Settlement. Although unaware of JA's Hull House at the time she started Henry Street, Wald soon became fast friends with JA and the two settlements were the cornerstones of a thriving settlement house movement during the Progressive Era. Like Hull House, the Henry Street Settlement became a locus of social change; it was the site of the National Negro Conference in 1909, which became the founding meeting of the NAACP. Wald used her settlement to launch the Visiting Nurses Service, which by 1903 had eighteen district nursing service centers that provided health care to 4,500 clients. The Visiting Nurses Service grew rapidly and was a model for similar programs across the country; Wald's service developed the field of public health nursing. Her work with the Visiting Nurses Service awakened her to the gaps in public policy that affected her immigrant neighbors; she participated in campaigns to eradicate tuberculosis, improve housing, and enact wage and hours legislation. With FK and others she founded the National Child Labor Committee and with FK generated the idea that led to the creation of the federal Children's Bureau. As World War I approached, she helped organize and was president of the American Union Against Militarism and was a member of the Woman's Peace Party. After World War I, despite intense personal attacks during the Red Scare, she helped found the Women's International League for Peace and Freedom.

WISCHNEWETZKY, LAZARE (ca. 1860–ca. 1920). LW was born in Taganrog, Russia, a Black Sea seaport 400 miles east of Odessa. Although FK later referred to his ethnicity as Jewish, this identity seems not to have been a factor in their relationship. They met when both were studying at the University of Zurich, he as one of a large group of Russian medical students that included many women. FK and LW's shared interest in government and law brought them together in the classes of Professor Julius Platter in 1882–1883, and almost certainly she attended meetings of the exiled German Social Democratic party in his company. Although FK initially rejected his proposal to marry, they were married in a civil ceremony on 14 October 1884. Their three children, Nicholas, Margaret, and John, were born in 1885, 1886 and 1888. Lazare never succeeded in establishing a medical practice after he moved with FK to New York City in 1886. He began beating her in 1891, and she fled with the children to Chicago in late December that year. LW lost a court challenge to FK's custody of the children in 1892, and they were divorced in 1900. Letters from NK to FK referred to LW after 1910, when LW was apparently still living in New York City and NK provided him with an income.

BIBLIOGRAPHY

PRIMARY SOURCES

Archival Collections

Bentley Historical Library, University of Michigan, Ann Arbor, Michigan
Frank Addison Manny Papers, 1868–1954
Chicago Historical Society, Chicago, Illinois
City Club of Chicago Records, 1903–1978
Elmer L. Andersen Library, Social Welfare History Archives, University of Minnesota, Minneapolis, Minnesota
Paul U. Kellogg Papers, 1891–1952
Franklin D. Roosevelt Presidential Library and Museum, Hyde Park, New York
Papers of Eleanor Roosevelt
Glenn G. Bartle Library, State University of New York at Binghamton
Minutes of the Meeting of the [NAACP] Board of Directors, 1909–1959
Historical Society of Pennsylvania, Philadelphia, Pennsylvania
Correspondence of William Darrah Kelley, 1814–1890
Howard Colman Library, Archives, Rockford College, Rockford, Illinois
Julia C. Lathrop Papers
The Huntington Library, Art Collections and Botanical Gardens, San Marino, California
Papers of Clara Dorothy Bewick Colby, 1882–1914
Illinois State Archives, Springfield, Illinois
John Peter Altgeld Correspondence, 1893–1897
International Institute of Social History, Amsterdam, Netherlands
Karl Marx/Friedrich Engels Papers
Library of Congress, Manuscript Division, Washington, D.C.
League of Women Voters (U.S.) Records, 1884–1986
Papers of Newton Diehl Baker, ca. 1898–1962
Papers of Carrie Chapman Catt, 1848–1950
Papers of Felix Frankfurter, 1846–1966

Papers of Robert M. La Follette, 1879–1910. Unpublished microfilm also at the State Historical Society of Wisconsin.
Papers of the NAACP
Papers of Elizabeth Cady Stanton, 1814–1946
Papers of Theodore Roosevelt, 1759–1993
Records of the National American Woman Suffrage Association, 1839–1961. Unpublished microfilm.
Records of the National Consumers' League, 1882–1986. Unpublished microfilm.
Records of the National Child Labor Committee, U.S., 1904–1953
Records of the National Woman's Party, 1850–1975
Records of the Women's Joint Congressional Committee

Louis D. Brandeis School of Law, University of Louisville, Louisville, Kentucky
Papers of Louis Dembitz Brandeis

Martin P. Catherwood Library, Kheel Center, Cornell University, Ithaca, New York
Amalgamated Clothing Workers of America Records, 1914–1980
American Association for Labor Legislation Records, 1905–1943
Papers of I. M. Rubinow, 1895–1936

Michigan Historical Library, University of Michigan, Ann Arbor, Michigan
Frank Addison Manny Papers, 1868–1954

Moorland-Spingarn Research Center, Manuscript Division, Howard University, Washington, D.C.
Joel Elias Spingarn Papers, 1875–1939

National Archives at College Park, College Park, Maryland
Records of the Children's Bureau, 1912–69, RG 102

New York Public Library, Manuscripts and Archives Division, New York, New York
Florence Kelley Papers, 1832–1967
Lillian Wald Papers, 1889–1957

New York State Archives, Albany, New York
Correspondence of the New York State Factory Investigating Commission, 1912–1916

New York State Library, Manuscripts and Special Collections, Albany, New York
New York Child Labor Committee, Records, 1903–1941

Rare Book & Manuscript Library, Columbia University, New York, New York
Kelley Family Papers, 1681–1936
Papers of Randolph Silliman Bourne, ca. 1910–1966
Papers of Frances Perkins, ca. 1895–1965
Papers of Lillian D. Wald, 1895–1936

Schlesinger Library, Radcliffe Institute for Advanced Study, Cambridge, Massachusetts
Hamilton Family Papers, 1818–1976
Papers of Mary Anderson, 1918–1960
Papers of John Graham Brooks, 1845–1938
Papers of Molly Dewson, 1893–1962
Papers of Josephine Clara and Pauline Dorothea Goldmark, 1886–1962
Papers of the Women's Trade Union League and Its Principal Leaders, 1855–1964
Records of the Consumers' League of Massachusetts, 1891–1955

State Historical Society of Wisconsin, Archives Division, Madison, Wisconsin
Victor Berger Papers
Richard T. Ely Papers
Henry Demarest Lloyd Papers, 1847–1903
Sterling Memorial Library, Yale University, New Haven, Connecticut
William Kent Family Papers, 1768–1961
Swarthmore College Peace Collection, Swarthmore, Pennsylvania
Jane Addams Papers, 1838–1935
UCLA Library, Department of Special Collections, Los Angeles, California
Katherine Philips Edson Papers, 1870–1933
University of Chicago Library, Special Collections, Archives, Chicago, Illinois
Edith and Grace Abbott Papers, 1870–1967
W. E. B. Du Bois Library, Special Collections and Archives, University of Massachusetts, Amherst, Massachusetts
W. E. B. Du Bois Papers, 1803–1999
Western Michigan University Archive & Regional History Collections, Kalamazoo, Michigan
Caroline Bartlett Crane Collection, 1843–1945
Yale University Library, Manuscripts and Archives, New Haven, Connecticut
Walter Lippmann Papers, 1900–1974

Published Microfilm

Boehm, Randolph, August Meier, and Mark Fox, eds. *Papers of the NAACP.* Frederick, Md.: University Publications of America, 1982.
Bryan, Mary Lynn McCree, ed. *The Jane Addams Papers.* Ann Arbor, Mich.: University Microfilms International, 1984.
Haggerty, Donald L. *National Woman's Party Papers: The Suffrage Years, 1913–1920.* Bethesda, Md.: University Publications of America, ca. 1981.
Ham, Gerald F., ed. *Papers of Henry Demarest Lloyd.* Madison: State Historical Society of Wisconsin, 1971.
James, Edward T. *Papers of the Woman's Trade Union League and Its Principal Leaders.* Woodbridge, Conn.: Research Publications, 1979.
Lillian Wald Papers, 1895–1936. Woodbridge, Conn.: Research Publications, 1991–
National Woman's Party Papers, 1913–1974. Sanford, Calif.: Microfilming Corporation of America, 1977–1979.
Papers of Carrie Chapman Catt. Washington, D.C.: Library of Congress Photoduplicating Service, 1983.
Papers of Louis Dembitz Brandeis. Frederick, Md.: University Publications of America, 1984.
Papers of W.E.B. Du Bois. Ann Arbor, Mich.: University Microfilms International, 1979.
Records of the Children's Bureau, 1912–1969. Alexandria, Va.: Chadwyck-Healey, 1988.
Richard T. Ely. Madison, Wis.: State Historical Society of Wisconsin, 1981. Exclusive distribution by Chadwyck-Healey.
Victor L. Berger Papers. Wilmington, Del.: Scholarly Resources, 1994.

Journals Consulted

American Labor Legislation Review
Annals of the American Academy of Political and Social Science
Atlantic Monthly
Charities and Commons
Equal Rights
Life and Labor Bulletin
Monthly Labor Review
New Republic
Proceedings of the National Conference of Charities and Corrections
Social Service Review
Survey
The Crisis
The Nation
Woman Citizen
Woman Patriot

Oral Histories

Gluck, Sherna Berger. "Interview with Jesse Haver Butler." 1/15/1973. Women's History: Suffragists. *The Virtual Oral/Aural History Archive, California State University, Long Beach.* Available at http://www.csulb.edu/voaha.

Descriptions of Archival Collections

"Inventory of the League of Women Voters of Pikes Peak Region Records." *Rocky Mountain Online Archive.* Available at http://rmoa.unm.edu.

Articles

Addams, Jane. "The Subjective Necessity for Social Settlements." In Addams, *Philanthropy and Social Progress.* New York: Thomas Y. Crowell, 1893.

"An Election Issue—Mothers." *Woman Citizen* 11 (August 1926): 25.

Andrews, John. "Secretary's Report: Proceedings of Business Meeting." *American Labor Legislation Review* 6 (March 1916): 104–105.

Beyer, Clara M. "What Is Equality?" *The Nation* 116 (21 January 1923): 116. Reprinted as Document 24 in Kathryn Kish Sklar with Kezia Procita and Jess Segal, "Who Won the Debate over the Equal Rights Amendment in the 1920s?" *Women and Social Movements in the United States, 1600–2000* Vol. 4 (2000).

Black, Ruby A. "Equal Rights at the Industrial Conference." *Equal Rights* XII (30 January 1926): 402–403. Reprinted as Document 10 in Kathryn Kish Sklar with Kezia Procita and Jess Segal, "Who Won the Debate over the Equal Rights Amendment in the 1920s?" *Women and Social Movements in the United States, 1600–2000* Vol. 4 (2000).

Bradley, Phillips. "The Farm Bloc." *Journal of Social Forces* 3 (May 1925): 714–718.

Brandeis, Elizabeth. "Labor Legislation." In *History of Labor in the United States.* Vol. 3, *Labor Legislation,* ed. John R. Commons et al. New York: Macmillan, 1935.

———. "Minimum Wage Legislation." In *History of Labor in the United States.* Vol. 3, *Labor Legislation,* ed. John R. Commons et al. New York: Macmillan, 1935.

Brandeis, Louis D., and Josephine Goldmark. *The People of the State of New York, against Charles Schweinler Press, a Corporation, Defendant. A Summary of "Facts of Knowledge" Submitted on Behalf of the People in Support of Its Brief on the Law.* New York: B. H. Tyrell, 1914.

Bureau of Statistics of Labor of Illinois [Florence Kelley]. "The Sweating System of Chicago," in *Seventh Biennial Report, 1892.* Springfield, Ill.: H. W. Rokker, 1893. Reprinted as Document 1 in Kathryn Kish Sklar and Jamie Tyler, "How Did Florence Kelley's Campaign against Sweatshops in Chicago in the 1890s Expand Government Responsibility for Industrial Working Conditions?" *Women and Social Movement in the United States, 1600–2000* Vol. 2 (1998).

Catt, Carrie Chapman. "Poison Propaganda." *Woman Citizen* (31 May 1924): 14, 32–33.

Chamberlain, J. P. "The United States and the International Labor Organization." *American Labor Legislation Review* 13 (June 1927): 171–175.

Chamberlain, Mary. "The Women at Zurich." *Survey* 42 (14 June 1919): 426–428.

Chase, Lucetta C. "The Social Program of the General Federation of Women's Clubs: One Index of Fifty Years of Progress." *Social Forces* 1 (May 1923): 465–469.

Cline, Leonard. "The War on the Peace Seekers." *New Republic* 39 (2 and 9 July 1924): 149–150, 184–185.

"Common Welfare." *Survey* 35 (9 October 1915): 36.

Commons, John R. "The International Association for Labor Legislation." *Charities and the Commons* 20 (12 September 1908): 687–689.

"Consumers' Leagues in Germany and America." *American Food Journal* 7 (15 June 1912): 52.

"Conventions of the International Labor Conference." *Survey* 43 (20 December 1919): II:288.

Creel, George. "How 'Tainted' Money Taints." *Pearson's* (March 1915): 289–297.

Cutler, Addison. "Labor Legislation in Thirteen Southern States." *Southern Economic Journal* 7, no. 3 (1941): 297–316.

Dock, Lavinia. "The Right to Differ." *Survey* 49 (15 January 1923): 530.

[Du Bois, W. E. B.]. "Education." *The Crisis* 36 (April 1929): 132.

———. "Message to the American People." *The Crisis* (August 1929): 265.

Edson, Katherine. "Student Nurses and the Eight-Hour Law in California." *Survey* 31 (24 January 1914): 499–500.

"The General Welfare." *Survey* 56 (15 June 1926): 366–367.

Hamilton, Alice, and Jane Addams. "After the Lean Years: Impressions of Food Conditions in Germany after the Peace Was Signed." *Survey* 42 (6 September 1919): 793–797.

Hart, Jerome A. "The Sand Lot and Kearneyism." In Hart, *In Our Second Century, From an Editor's Note-Book.* San Francisco: Pioneer Press, 1931.

Heaton, Herbert. "'Social Justice' Motive in Creating International Labor Standards." *American Labor Legislation Review* 17 (June 1927): 166.

Herron, Belva M. "Factory Inspection in the United States." *American Journal of Sociology* 12, no. 4 (January 1907): 487–499.

Hershaw, L. M. "Disfranchisement in the District of Columbia." *The Crisis* (August 1915): 183. Reprinted as Document 16J in Kathryn Kish Sklar and Chelsea Kuzma, "How Did the Views of Booker T. Washington and W. E. B. Du Bois toward Woman Suffrage Change, 1900–1915?" *Women and Social Movements in the United States, 1600–2000* Vol. 2 (1998).

Johnson, F. Ernest. "Facing Industrial Facts in the Churches." *Survey* 54 (15 April 1925): 100.

Johnson, Marjorie Daw. "Chickens to Moscow." *American Heritage* (June/July 1978): 64–67.

Kelley, Florence. "As Others See Us." *Charities and the Commons* 21 (7 November 1908): 178–179.

———. "A Burglar Four Years Old in the Memphis Juvenile Court." *Survey* 32 (20 June 1914): 318–319.

———. "Can the Leopard Change Its Spots?" *Survey* 52 (2 November 1927): 289.

———. "The Case for the Minimum Wage: Status of Legislation in the United States." *Survey* 33 (6 February 1915): 487–489.

———. "A Challenge to Social Workers." *Survey* 42 (19 September 1919): 896–897.

———. "Child Labor." In *Fifth Annual Report of the Bureau of Labor Statistics of the State of Connecticut for the Year Ending November 30, 1889*. Hartford: Case, Lockwood & Brainard, 1890.

———. "Child Labor and Woman Suffrage." *Outlook* 82 (March 1906): 622.

———. "Child Labor in Massachusetts." *Survey* 58 (15 April 1927): 119.

———. "Child Laborers' Gains and Losses since the War." *Annals of the American Academy of Political and Social Science* 151 (September 1930): 55–61

———. "Children's Compensation for Industrial Accidents." *Survey* 56 (1 June 1926): 323–325.

———. "The Condition of Europe." *Survey* 42 (5 July 1919): 528–529, 558.

———. "Congress and the Babies." *Survey* 46 (14 May 1921): 200.

———. "Congress and the Children's Bureau." *Survey* 65 (15 February 1931): 544.

———. "The Consumer and the Near Future." *Survey* 42 (5 April 1919): 5–7

———. "Don't Divide the Baby." *Survey* 63 (15 March 1930): 708.

———. "An Effective Child Labor Law." *Annals of the American Academy of Political and Social Science* 21 (1903): 438–444.

———. "Ending Women's Nightwork in Cotton." *Survey* 67 (15 October 1931): 84–85.

———. "Evils of Child Labor." *Frank Leslie's Illustrated Newspaper* 60 (1 March 1890): 84.

———. "Die Fabrik-Gesetzgebung der Vereinigten Staaten." ("Factory Legislation in the United States") *Archiv für Soziale Gesetzgebung und Statistik* 38 (1895): 192–209.

———. "Factory Inspection in Pittsburgh." *Charities and the Commons* 21 (6 March 1909): 1105–1116.

———. "Handbook of Child Labor Legislation." *Charities* 12 (16 January 1904): 79.

———. "I Go to Work." *Survey Graphic* 58 (1 June 1927): 271–274, 301. Reprinted in Florence Kelley, *Notes of Sixty Years: The Autobiography of Florence Kelley*, ed. Kathryn Kish Sklar. Chicago: C. H. Kerr, 1986.

———. "International Commission on Child Labor Laws." *Survey* 31 (25 October 1913): 86.

———. "Leisure by Law for Women." *Social Service Review* 2 (March 1928): 24–36.

———. "The Maine State Convention." *The Suffragist*, 18 September 1915, 3, 8.

———. "The Manufacturers' Plan for Child Labor." *Survey* 59 (15 October 1927): 70–72

———. "The Manufacturers' Program Won't Do." *Survey* 60 (15 June 1928): 344–345.

———. "Measuring the Health of Working Children." *Child Labor Bulletin* 7 (February 1919): 4.

———. "Minimum Wage Boards." In *Proceedings of the National Conference of Charities and Correction*, 148–156. Fort Wayne, Ind.: National Conference of Charities and Corrections, 1911.

———. "Minimum-Wage Laws." *Journal of Political Economy* 20 (December 1912): 999–1010.

———. "Minimum Wage Protest." *Survey* 42 (12 April 1919): 83.

———. "My Philadelphia." *Survey* (1 October 1926): 7–11, 50–57. Reprinted in Florence Kelley, *Notes of Sixty Years: The Autobiography of Florence Kelley*, ed. Kathryn Kish Sklar. Chicago: C. H. Kerr, 1986.

———. "The New Woman's Party." *Survey* 45 (5 March 1921): 827–828.

———. "Our Newest South." *Survey* 62 (15 June 1929): 342–344.

———. "Progress of Labor Legislation for Women." In *Proceedings of the National Conference of Social Work Held in Washington, D.C.* Chicago: University of Chicago Press, 1923.

———. "Ein Ruckblick auf den Pullman-Strike." ("Looking Back on the Pullman Strike") *Sozial-politisches Centralblatt* 4, no. 5 (1894): 55–57.

———. "Save the Children." *The Nation* 131 (10 December 1930): 643–644.

———. "A Skeleton in Industry's Closet." *Survey* 59 (15 January 1928): 523–525.

———. "The Sterling Discrimination Bill." *The Crisis* 26 (October 1923): 252–253.

———. "The Sweating System." In Residents of Hull-House, *Hull-House Maps and Papers*. New York: T. Y. Crowell, 1895.

———. "Thirty Years of the Consumers' League." *Survey* 60 (15 November 1929): 210–212.

———. "Twenty-Five Years of the Consumers' League Movement." *Survey* 35 (27 November 1915): 212–214.

———. "The Uniform Child Labor Law." *Survey* 65 (15 October 1930): 84–85.

———. "Wage Earning Women in War Time: Textiles." *Journal of Industrial Hygiene* 1 (October 1919): 261–282.

———. "Die weibliche Fabrikinspektion in der Vereinigten Staaten." ("Women Factory Inspectors in the United States") *Archiv für Soziale Gesetzgebung und Statistik* 11 (1897): 128–142.

———. "What Kind of Equality for Women?" *The Nation* 124 (2 March 1927): 237.

———. "White Child Slavery: A Symposium." *The Arena* 1 (December 1889): 589–603.

———. "Why Let Children Die?" *Survey* 44 (19 June 1920): 401.

———. "Why the Children's Bill Did Not Pass." *American Labor Legislation Review* 21 (June 1931): 175–179.

———. "The Women's Congress at Vienna." *Survey* 46 (1 September 1921): 627–629.

Kelley, Florence, and Alzina Stevens. "Wage Earning Children." In Residents of Hull-House, *Hull-House Maps and Papers.* New York: T. Y. Crowell, 1895.

Kelley, William Darrah. *The Enforcement of the Fourteenth Amendment Essential to the Prosperity of the South: Speech of Hon. William D. Kelley, of Pennsylvania, in the House of Representatives, March 29, 1871.* Washington, D.C.: Congressional Globe, 1871.

Kellogg, Paul. "Letting George Do It." *Survey* 33 (13 February 1915): 541–542.

———. "The Pittsburgh Survey." *Charities and the Commons* 21 (2 January 1909): 517–526.

[Key Men of America]. *The Common Enemy* N.p.: 1927.

Lindsey, Benjamin. "Judge Lindsey on Colorado Politics." *Charities and the Commons* 21 (31 October 1908): 145–146.

Lloyd, Henry D. "The Populists at St. Louis." *Review of Reviews* 14 (September 1896): 303.

Mackenzie, Frederick. "The Challenge to Autocracy." *Survey* 42 (13 September 1919): 853.

Magee, Elizabeth. "Child Laborers' Gains and Losses since the War." *Annals of the American Academy of Political and Social Science* 151 (September 1930): 57–61.

Marx, Karl. "The *Kölnische Zeitung* on the Elections." *Neue Rheinische Zeitung,* no. 210, 1 February 1849. In *Karl Marx/Frederick Engels: Collected Works,* 8:286–289, available online at www.marxists.org/archive/marx/works/1849/02/01.htm.

Maxwell, Lucia. "Spider Web Chart: The Socialist-Pacifist Movement in America Is an Absolutely Fundamental and Integral Part of International Socialism." *Dearborn Independent* 24 (22 March 1924). Reprinted in Kathryn Kish Sklar and Helen Baker, "How Did Women Peace Activists Respond to 'Red Scare' Attacks during the 1920s?" *Women and Social Movements in the United States, 1600–2000* Vol. 2 (1998).

"Money for Education." *The Crisis* 36 (September 1929): 314, 317.

"Mrs. Kelley Looks Ahead." *Survey* 63 (15 December 1929): 326.

"The National Child Labor Meeting." *Charities and the Commons* 17 (January 1907): 519–520.

National Commission on the Observance of International Women's Year. *The Spirit of Houston: The First National Women's Conference: An Official Report to the President, the Congress and the People of the United States.* Washington, D.C.: National Commission on the Observance of International Women's Year.

"Nominations for the Board of Directors." *The Crisis* 12 (December 1915): 86.

"The Parting Shot." *American Food Journal* 7 (15 April 1912): 20.

"Porcupine Fire, 11 July 1911." In *SOS! Canadian Disasters.* Available online at http://www.collectionscanada.gc.ca/sos/002028–4100–e.html.

"Reclassification Endangered." *Woman Citizen* 8 (29 December 1923): 20.

Reed, Anna Y. "Child-Labor Legislation: A Point of View." *Elementary School Journal* 23, no. 4 (December 1922): 276–282.

Rogers, Lindsay. "First and Second Sessions of the Sixty-Eighth Congress." *American Political Science Review* 19, no. 4 (1925): 761–772.

Rubinow, Isaac M. "Health Insurance: The Spread of the Movement." *Survey* 36 (15 July 1916): 407–409.
Smith, Geddes. "Behemoth Walks Again." *Survey* 56 (15 June 1926): 360.
Stanton, Elizabeth Cady. "War or Peace, Competition or Co-operation?" *Commonwealth* 5 (21 May 1898): 3–7.
Swift, Wiley. "The Child Labor Position." *Survey* 59 (15 October 1927): 72–73.
Tawney, R. H. "The Assessment of Wages in England by the Justices of the Peace." In *R. H. Tawney: The American Labour Movement and Other Essays,* ed. J. M. Winter. New York: St. Martin's Press, 1979.
———. "The Minimum Wage in Great Britain." *New Republic,* 28 June 1922.
Tcherkesoff, W. *Concentration of Capital: A Marxian Fallacy.* 1902; reprint, London: Freedom Press, 1911.
"Towards the Peace That Shall Last." *Survey* 33, part 2 (6 March 1915): 1–8.
Van Kleeck, Mary. "How the United States Can Aid the International Labor Organization through Research." *American Labor Legislation Review* 17 (June 1927): 170.
"Wages and Hours of Union Hotel and Restaurant Employees." *Monthly Labor Review* 37 (August 1933): 350–354.
Warren, Bentley W. "Destroying Our 'Indestructible States.'" *Atlantic Monthly* 133 (March 1924): 370–378.
Webb, Sidney. "The Economic Theory of a Legal Minimum Wage." *Journal of Political Economy* 20 (December 1912): 973–998.
"We Come of Age." *Crisis* 11 (November 1915): 25–28.
"Whistling in the Dark." *American Food Journal* 7 (15 July 1912): 73.
Wilbur, Ray L. "Children in a Modern World: The White House Conference on Child Health and Protection." *Survey* 63 (15 February 1930): 570.
"Women of the World." *Survey* 46 (16 April 1921): 75.
Zeisler, Sigmund. "Reminiscences of the Anarchist Case." *Illinois Law Review* 21, no. 3 (1926): 224–250.

Books and Pamphlets

Addams, Jane. *Democracy and Social Ethics.* New York: Macmillan, 1902.
———. *Peace and Bread in Time of War.* New York: Macmillan, 1922.
Anderson, Mary. *Woman at Work.* Minneapolis: University of Minnesota Press, 1951.
Anthony, Susan B., and Ida Husted Harper, eds. *History of Woman Suffrage.* Vol. 4. Rochester, N.Y.: Susan B. Anthony, 1902.
Beasley, Maurine H., Holly C. Shulman, and Henry R. Beasley, eds. *The Eleanor Roosevelt Encyclopedia.* Westport, Conn.: Greenwood Press, 2001.
Berge, George W. *The Free Pass Bribery System.* Lincoln, Neb.: Independent Publishing Co., 1905.
Beyer, Clara M. *History of Labor Legislation for Women in Three States.* Washington, D.C.: GPO, 1932.
Bisno, Abraham. *Abraham Bisno, Union Pioneer: An Autobiographical Account of Bisno's Early Life and the Beginnings of Unionism in the Women's Garment Industry.* Madison: University of Wisconsin Press, 1967.

Brandeis, Louis D., and Josephine Goldmark. *Women in Industry: Decision of the United States Supreme Court in Curt Muller vs. State of Oregon: Upholding the Constitutionality of the Oregon Ten Hour Law for Women and Brief for the State of Oregon.* New York: National Consumers' League, [1908].

Breckinridge, Sophonisba P. *Women in the Twentieth Century: A Study of Their Political, Social and Economic Activities.* 1933; reprint, New York: Arno Press, 1972.

Carroll, Mollie Ray. *Labor and Politics: The Attitude of the American Federation of Labor towards Legislation and Politics.* Boston: Houghton Mifflin, 1923.

Cole, G. D. H. *A Short History of the British Working-Class Movement, 1789–1927.* Vol. 3, *1900–1927.* London: Allen & Unwin, 1932.

Commons, John R., and Allen B. Forsberg. *Unemployment Compensation and Prevention.* Washington, D.C.: Distributed by the Committee on Women in Industry, National League of Women Voters, 1924.

Constantine, J. Robert, ed. *Letters of Eugene V. Debs.* Vol. 1. Urbana: University of Illinois Press, 1990.

Erickson, Ethel L. *The Employment of Women in Offices.* Women's Bureau Bulletin no. 120. Washington, D.C.: GPO, 1934.

Ffrench, Charles. *Biographical History of the American Irish in Chicago.* Chicago: American Biographical Publishing, 1897.

Fink, Gary M., ed. *Biographical Dictionary of American Labor Leaders.* Westport, Conn.: Greenwood Press, 1984.

Fitch, John A. *The Steel Workers.* New York: Russell Sage Foundation, 1911.

Frankfurter, Felix, Mary W. Dewson, and John R. Commons. *State Minimum Wage Laws in Practice.* [New York]: National Consumers' League, 1924.

Gille, Frank H. *Encyclopedia of Ohio.* St. Clair Shores, Mich.: Somerset Publishers, 1982.

Goldmark, Josephine. *Child Labor Legislation: Schedules of Existing Statutes and the Standard Child Labor Law.* Philadelphia: American Academy of Political and Social Science, 1908.

———. *Impatient Crusader: Florence Kelley's Life Story.* Urbana: University of Illinois Press, 1953.

Gordon, Ann D., ed. *The Selected Papers of Elizabeth Cady Stanton and Susan B. Anthony.* Vol. 1. New Brunswick, N.J.: Rutgers University Press, 1997.

Gordon, Mildred J. *The Development of Minimum-Wage Laws in the United States, 1912 to 1927.* Women's Bureau Bulletin no. 61. Washington, D.C.: GPO, 1928.

Grossman, James R., Ann Durkin Keating, and Janice L. Reiff, eds. *The Encyclopedia of Chicago.* Chicago: University of Chicago Press, 2004.

Haferbecker, Gordon M. *Wisconsin Labor Laws.* Madison: University of Wisconsin Press, 1958.

Hamilton, Alice. *Exploring the Dangerous Trades.* Boston: Little, Brown, 1943.

Hardin, James N., ed. *Dictionary of Literary Biography.* Vol. 66, *German Fiction Writers, 1885–1913.* Detroit, Mich.: Gale Research Co., 1988.

Harper, Ida Husted, ed. *History of Woman Suffrage.* Vol. 5. New York: National American Woman Suffrage Association, 1922.

———. *History of Woman Suffrage.* Vol. 6. New York: National American Woman Suffrage Association, 1922.

House Journal of the Legislature of the State of Nebraska. Lincoln, Neb.: Jacob North & Company, 1907.

Illinois Fact Book and Historical Almanac 1673–1978. Comp. John Clayton. Carbondale, Ill.: Southern Illinois University Press, 1970.

Johnson, Tom. *My Story.* New York: Huebsch, 1911.

Kaufman, Stuart B., ed. *Samuel Gompers Papers.* Vol. 2. Urbana, Ill.: University of Illinois Press, 1987.

Kelley, Florence. *Our Toiling Children.* Chicago: Woman's Temperance Publication Association, 1889.

———. *Some Ethical Gains through Legislation.* New York: Macmillan, 1905.

———. *Twenty Questions about the Federal Amendment Proposed by the National Woman's Party.* New York: National Consumers' League, 1922.

———. *Women in Industry: The Eight Hours Day and Rest at Night, Upheld by the United States Supreme Court.* National Consumers' League Women in Industry Series No. 13. New York: National Consumers' League, May 1916.

Kelley, Florence, and Marguerite Marsh. *Labor Legislation for Women and Its Effects on Earnings and Conditions of Labor.* Philadelphia, Pa.: N.p., 1929.

Laws, Annie. *History of the Ohio Federation of Women's Clubs for the First Thirty Years, 1894–1924.* Cincinnati: Ebbert & Richardson, 1925.

Laws, Joint Resolutions, Appropriations and Memorials Passed at the Thirtieth Session of the Legislative Assembly of the State of Nebraska. Lincoln, Neb.: Woodruff-Collins, 1907.

Link, Arthur S., ed. *Papers of Woodrow Wilson.* Vols. 37, 38, 40. Princeton, N.J.: Princeton University Press, 1981.

MacKenzie, Norman Ian, and Jeanne MacKenzie, eds. *The Diary of Beatrice Webb.* Vol. 3. Cambridge, Mass.: Belknap Press of Harvard University Press, 1984.

Marquis, Albert N., ed. *Who's Who in Chicago: The Book of Chicagoans, 1926.* Chicago: A. N. Marquis, 1926.

Mason, Lucie. *Standards for Workers in Southern Industry.* New York: National Consumers' League, 1931.

Marx, Karl, and Frederick Engels. *Letters to Americans, 1848–1895: A Selection.* Ed. Alexander Trachtenberg. New York: International Publishers, 1953.

Nathan, Maud. *The Story of an Epoch-Making Movement.* Garden City, N.Y.: Doubleday, Page, and Company, 1926.

National Congress of Mothers and Parent-Teacher Associations. *Triennial Hand-Book 1908–1911.* n.p., n.d.

National Consumers' League. *Children's Compensation for Industrial Accidents; How the States Love Their Children.* NCL Pamphlet no. 1. New York: National Consumers' League, 1926.

National Consumers' League. *Children's Compensation for Industrial Injuries; What Price Children?* NCL Pamphlet no. 2. New York: National Consumers' League, 1926.

Ovington, Mary White. *How the National Association for the Advancement of Colored People Began.* New York: NAACP, 1914.

Peabody, Francis G. *Jesus Christ and the Social Question: An Examination of the Teaching of Jesus in Its Relation to Some of the Problems of Modern Social Life.* New York: Macmillan, 1900.

Proceedings of the Friends' General Conference, Held at Toronto, Canada, 1904. Philadelphia: Friends' General Conference, 1904.

Report of the Committee on Manufactures on the Sweating System. Washington, D.C.: GPO, 1893. Reprinted as Document 6 in Kathryn Kish Sklar and Jamie Tyler, "How Did Florence Kelley's Campaign against Sweatshops in Chicago in the 1890s Expand Government Responsibility for Industrial Working Conditions?" *Women and Social Movement in the United States, 1600–2000* 2, no. 0 (1998).

Robins, Margaret Dreier. *Need of a National Training School for Women Organizers, the Minimum Wage, Industrial Education: Presidential Address to the Fourth Biennial Convention, National Women's Trade Union League, St. Louis, June 2, 1913.* Chicago: National Women's Trade Union League, 1913.

Sandeen, Eric J., ed. *Letters of Randolph Bourne: A Comprehensive Edition.* Troy, N.Y.: Whitson Pub. Co., 1981.

Sumner, Helen L. *Child Labor Legislation in the United States.* Washington, D.C.: GPO, 1915.

Urofsky, Melvin I., and David W. Levy, eds. *Letters of Louis D. Brandeis.* Vols. 3 and 4. Albany, N.Y.: SUNY Press, 1973.

U.S. Children's Bureau. *The Promotion of the Welfare and Hygiene of Maternity and Infancy: The Administration of the Act of Congress of November 23, 1921, for the Period March 20, 1922 to June 20, 1923.* Washington: GPO, 1924.

Walling, William English. *Socialism As It Is: A Survey of the World-Wide Revolutionary Movement.* New York: Macmillan, 1912.

Webb, Sidney, and Beatrice Webb. *Industrial Democracy.* London: Longmans, Green, 1897.

WILPF. *Report of the International Congress of Women: Zurich, May 12 to 17.* Geneva, Switzerland: WILPF, [1919].

Winslow, Mary N. *Effects of Labor Legislation on the Employment Opportunities of Women.* Women's Bureau Bulletin no. 65. Washington, D.C.: GPO, 1928.

Woods, Robert Archey, and Albert J. Kennedy. *Handbook of Settlements.* New York: Charities Publication Committee, 1911.

Zonta Club Manual. [Chicago, Ill.]: Zonta International, 2003.

SECONDARY SOURCES

Articles and Web Sites

Applebaum, Harvey M. "Miscegenation Statutes: A Constitutional and Social Problem." *Georgetown Law Journal* 53 (1964): 49–91.

Boris, Eileen. "On the Importance of Naming: Gender, Race, and the Writing of Policy History." *Journal of Policy History* 17, no. 1 (2005): 72–92.

———. "'Social Responsibility on a Global Level': The National Consumers' League, Fair Labor, and Worker Rights at Century's End." In *A Coat of Many Colors: Immigration, Globalism, and Reform in the New York City Garment Industry,* ed. Daniel Soyer, 211–233. New York: Fordham University Press, 2005.

Brito, Patricia. "Protective Legislation in Ohio: The Inter-War Years." *Ohio History* 88 (Spring 1979): 173–197.

Bulmer, Martin, Kevin Bales, and Kathryn Kish Sklar. "The Social Survey in Historical Perspective." In *The Social Survey in Historical Perspective, 1880–1940,* ed. Martin Bulmer, Kevin Bales, and Kathryn Kish Sklar. Cambridge: Cambridge University Press, 1991.

Braitman, Jacqueline R. "A California Stateswoman: The Public Career of Katherine Philips Edson." *California History* 65 (June 1986): 82–95.

Carle, Susan D. "Race, Class and Legal Ethics in the Early NAACP, 1910–1920." *Law and History Review* 20 (Spring 2002): 97–146.

Currarino, Rosanne. "The Politics of 'More': The Labor Question and the Idea of Economic Liberty in Industrial America." *Journal of American History* 93, no. 1 (2006): 17–36.

Doak, Melissa, Rebecca Park, and Eunice Lee. "How Did Gender and Class Shape the Age of Consent Campaign within the Social Purity Movement, 1886–1914?" *Women and Social Movements in the United States, 1600–2000* 4, no. 0 (2000).

Fettig, David. "F. Augustus Heinze of Montana and the Panic of 1907." *The Region* (August 1989), available online at http://minneapolisfed.org/pubs/region/89–08/REG898C.cfm.

Fineman, Martha. "Feminist Theory and Law." *Harvard Journal of Law and Public Policy* 18, no. 2 (1995): 349–369.

Fink, Leon. "Labor, Liberty, and the Law: Trade Unionism and the Problem of the American Constitutional Order." *Journal of American History* 74, no. 3 (1987): 904–925.

Forbath, William E. "Caste, Class, and Equal Citizenship." *Michigan Law Review* 98, no. 1 (1999): 1–91.

Fraser, Nancy, and Linda Gordon. "Contract versus Charity: Why Is There No Social Citizenship in the United States?" In *The Citizenship Debates: A Reader,* ed. Gershon Shafir. Minneapolis: University of Minnesota Press, 1998.

Goldin, Claudia. "The Work and Wages of Single Women: 1870 to 1920." *Journal of Economic History* 40, no. 1 (1980): 81–89.

Gordon, Linda. "What's New in Women's History." In *Feminist Studies/Critical Studies,* ed. Theresa de Lauretis. Bloomington: Indiana University Press, 1986.

Griffith, Robert. "Prelude to Insurgency: Irvine L. Lenroot and the Republican Primary of 1908." *Wisconsin Magazine of History* (Autumn 1965): 16–28.

Hall, Jacquelyn Dowd. "Disorderly Women: Gender and Labor Militancy in the Appalachian South." *Journal of American History* 73 (1986): 354–382.

Held, Virginia. "Rights." In *A Companion to Feminist Philosophy,* ed. Alison M. Jaggar and Iris Marion Young. Oxford: Blackwell, 1998.

Hagemann, Gro. "Protection or Equality? Debates on Protective Legislation in Norway." In *Protecting Women: Labor Legislation in Europe, the United States, and Australia, 1880–1920,* ed. Ulla Wikander, Alice Kessler-Harris, and Jane Lewis. Urbana: University of Illinois Press, 1999.

Hixson, William B., Jr. "Moorfield Storey and the Defense of the Dyer Anti-Lynching Bill." *New England Quarterly* 42, no. 1 (1969): 65–81.

Howe, Renate. "A Paradise for Working Men but Not for Working Women: Women's Wage-work and Protective Legislation in Australia. 1890–1914." In *Protecting Women: Labor Legislation in Europe, the United States, and Australia, 1880–1920*, ed. Ulla Wikander, Alice Kessler-Harris, and Jane Lewis. Urbana: University of Illinois Press, 1999.

Judt, Tony. "The Social Question Redivivus." *Foreign Affairs* 76, no. 5 (September/October 1997): 95–117.

Kerr, Thomas J. "The New York Factory Investigating Commission and the Minimum Wage Movement." *Labor History* 12, no. 3 (1971): 373–391.

Kessler-Harris, Alice. "The Paradox of Motherhood." In Kessler-Harris, *Gendering Labor History*. Urbana: University of Illinois Press, 2007.

Kiss, Elizabeth. "Justice." In *A Companion to Feminist Philosophy*, ed. Alison M. Jaggar and Iris Marion Young, 487–499. Oxford: Blackwell, 1998.

Koven, Seth, and Sonya Michel. "Womanly Duties: Maternalist Politics and the Origins of Welfare States in France, Germany, Great Britain, and the United States, 1880–1920." *American Historical Review* 95, no. 4 (October 1990): 1076–1108.

Laughlin, Kathleen. "How Did State Commissions on the Status of Women Overcome Historic Antagonisms between Equal Rights and Labor Feminists to Create a New Feminist Mainstream, 1963–1973?" *Women and Social Movements in the United States, 1600–2000* 9, no. 3 (2005).

Littleton, Christine. "Reconstructing Sexual Equality." *California Law Review* 75, no. 4 (1987): 1279–1337.

———. "Review: Whose Law Is This Anyway?" *Michigan Law Review* 95, no. 6 (1997): 1568.

LoCasto, Anissa Harper, and Kathryn Kish Sklar. "Pacifism vs. Patriotism in Women's Organizations in the 1920s: How Was the Debate Shaped by the Expansion of the American Military?" *Women and Social Movements in the United States, 1600–2000* 2, no. 0 (1998).

Lovett, Robert Mors. "Du Bois." *Phylon* 2, no. 3 (1941): 214–217.

Maver, Irene. "No Mean City: 1914 to 1950s." 2004. www.theglasgowstory.com/story.php.

Mayeri, Serena. "How and Why Was Feminist Legal Strategy Transformed, 1960–1973?" *Women and Social Movements in the United States, 1600–2000* 11, no. 1 (2007).

McGuire, John T. "Making the Case for Night Work Legislation in Progressive Era New York, 1911–1915." *Journal of the Gilded Age and Progressive Era* 5, no. 1 (January 2006): 47–70.

Messer-Kruse, Timothy. "Technology and the Decline of Child Labor: The Impact of the Owens Bottle Machine Reconsidered." *Labor: Studies in Working-Class History of the Americas* 5, no. 1 (2008): 23–45.

Oestricher, Richard. "Urban Working-Class Political Behavior and Theories of American Electoral Politics, 1870–1940." *Journal of American History* 74, no. 4 (1988): 1257–1286.

Perrin, Thomas. "Swope of Hull-House: The Influence of Settlement Life on Gerard Swope." N.d. Part of Urban Experience in Chicago: Hull-House and Its Neighborhoods, 1889–1963, available online at http://www.uic.edu/jaddams/hull/urbanexp/index.htm.

Prasch, Robert E. "American Economists and Minimum Wage Legislation during the Progressive Era: 1912–1923." *Journal of the History of Economic Thought* 20, no. 2 (1998): 161–175.

Rauchway, Eric. "A Gentlemen's Club in a Woman's Sphere: How Dorothy Whitney Straight Created the New Republic." *Journal of Women's History* 11 (June 1999): 60–85.

Schofield, Ann. "Rebel Girls and Union Maids: The Woman Question in the Journals of the AFL and IWW." *Feminist Studies* 9, no. 2 (1983): 335–358.

Schroedel, Jean Reith, and Bruce Snyder. "People's Banking: The Promise Betrayed?" *Studies in American Political Development* 8 (Spring 1994): 173–193.

Skerrett, Ellen. "The Irish of Chicago's Hull-House Neighborhood." *Chicago History* 30 (Summer 2001): 22–63.

Sklar, Kathryn Kish. "The Consumers' White Label of the National Consumers' League, 1898–1918." In *Getting and Spending: American and European Consumption in the Twentieth Century*, ed. Susan Strasser, Charles McGovern, and Matthais Judt. New York: Cambridge University Press, 1998.

———. "Florence Kelley Tells German Readers about the Pullman Strike, 1894." *Mid-America* 82, nos. 1–2 (2000): 127–139.

———. "'The Greater Part of the Petitioners Are Female': The Reduction by Statute of Women's Working Hours in the Paid Labor Force, 1840–1917." In *Worktime and Industrialization: An International History*, ed. Gary Cross. Philadelphia: Temple University Press, 1988.

———. "The Historical Foundations of Women's Power in the Creation of the American Welfare State, 1830–1930." In *Mothers of a New World: Maternalist Politics and the Origins of Welfare States*, ed. Seth Koven and Sonya Michel. New York: Routledge, 1993.

———. "Hull-House Maps and Papers: Social Science as Women's Work in the 1890s." In *The Social Survey in Historical Perspective, 1880–1940*, ed. Martin Bulmer, Kevin Bales, and Kathryn Kish Sklar. Cambridge: Cambridge University Press, 1991.

———. "'Some of Us Who Deal with the Social Fabric': Jane Addams Blends Peace and Social Justice, 1907–1919." *Journal of the Gilded Age and Progressive Era* 2 (January 2003): 80–96.

———. "Two Political Cultures in the Progressive Era: The National Consumers' League and the American Association for Labor Legislation." In *U.S. History as Women's History: New Feminist Essays*, ed. Linda Kerber, Alice Kessler-Harris, and Kathryn Kish Sklar. Chapel Hill: University of North Carolina Press, 1995.

———. "Who Funded Hull House?" In *Lady Bountiful Revisited: Women, Philanthropy, and Power*, ed. Kathleen D. McCarthy. New Brunswick, N.J.: Rutgers University Press, 1990.

———. "Why Were Most Politically Active Women Opposed to the ERA in the 1920s?" In *Rights of Passage: The Past and Future of the ERA*, ed. Joan Hoff Wilson. Bloomington: Indiana University Press, 1986.

Sklar, Kathryn Kish, and Kari Amidon. "How Did Women Activists Promote Peace in Their 1915 Tour of Warring European Capitals?" *Women and Social Movements in the United States, 1600–2000* Vol. 2 (1998).

Sklar, Kathryn Kish, and Helen Baker. "How Did Women Peace Activists Respond to 'Red Scare' Attacks during the 1920s?" *Women and Social Movements in the United States, 1600–2000* Vol. 2 (1998).

Sklar, Kathryn Kish, and Jill Dias. "How Did the NWP Address the Enfranchisement of Black Women, 1919–1924?" *Women and Social Movements in the United States, 1600–2000* Vol. 1 (1997).

Sklar, Kathryn Kish, with Kezia Procita and Jess Segal. "Who Won the Debate over the Equal Rights Amendment in the 1920s?" *Women and Social Movements in the United States, 1600–2000* Vol. 4 (2000).

Sklar, Kathryn Kish, and Jamie Tyler. "How Did Florence Kelley's Campaign against Sweatshops in Chicago in the 1890s Expand Government Responsibility for Industrial Working Conditions?" *Women and Social Movement in the United States, 1600–2000* Vol. 2 (1998).

Swensen, Rolf. "Pilgrims at the Golden Gate: Christian Scientists on the Pacific Coast, 1880–1915." *Pacific Historical Review* 72 (May 2003): 229–263.

Thane, Pat. "Visions of Gender in the Making of the British Welfare State: The Case of Women in the British Labour Party and Social Policy, 1906–1945." In *Protecting Women: Labor Legislation in Europe, the United States, and Australia, 1880–1920,* ed. Ulla Wikander, Alice Kessler-Harris, and Jane Lewis. Urbana: University of Illinois Press, 1999.

University Archives and Records Center, University of Pennsylvania. "Women at Penn: Distinguished Early Graduates, Faculty, and Benefactors of the University." Available at www.archives.upenn.edu/histy/features/women/biog.html.

Walling, William English. "The Founding of the N.A.A.C.P." *The Crisis* 36 (July 1939): 226.

Werum, Regina. "Elite Control in State and Nation: Racial Inequalities in Vocational Funding in North Carolina, Georgia, and Mississippi, 1918–1936." *Social Forces* 78, no. 1 (1999): 145–186.

Books and Dissertations

Abell, Aaron. *American Catholicism and Social Action: A Search for Social Justice.* South Bend, Ind.: University of Notre Dame Press, 1963.

Addams, Jane. *My Friend, Julia Lathrop.* New York: Macmillan, 1935.

Archer, Robin. *Why Is There No Labor Party in the United States?* Princeton, N.J.: Princeton University Press, 2007.

Barbour, Hugh, Christopher Densmore, Elizabeth H. Moger, Nancy C. Sorel, Alson D. Van Wagner, and Arthur J. Worrall. *Quaker Crosscurrents: Three Hundred Years of Friends in the New York Yearly Meetings.* Syracuse, N.Y.: Syracuse University Press, 1995.

Beaver, Daniel R. *Newton D. Baker and the American War Effort, 1917–1919.* Lincoln: University of Nebraska Press, 1966.

Benson, Susan Porter. *Household Accounts: Working-Class Family Economies in the Interwar United States.* Ithaca, N.Y.: Cornell University Press, 2007.

Bickers, Robert. *Britain in China: Community, Culture and Colonialism, 1900–1949.* Manchester: Manchester University Press, 1999.

Bionaz, Robert. "'Streetcar City': Popular Politics and the Shaping of Urban Progressivism in Cleveland, 1880–1910." Ph.D. diss., University of Iowa, 2002.

Blumberg, Dorothy Rose. *Florence Kelley: The Making of a Social Pioneer.* New York: A. M. Kelley, 1966.

Bondfield, Margaret. *A Life's Work.* London: Hutchinson, 1948.

Bredbenner, Candice Lewis. *A Nationality of Her Own: Women, Marriage, and the Law of Citizenship.* Berkeley: University of California Press, 1998.

Brody, David. *Labor Embattled: History, Power, Rights.* Urbana: University of Illinois Press, 2005.

———. *Labor in Crisis: The Steel Strike of 1919.* Urbana: University of Illinois Press, 1987.

Brown, Victoria Bissell. *The Education of Jane Addams.* Philadelphia: University of Pennsylvania Press, 2004.

Bryan, Mary Lynn McCree, and Allen F. Davis, eds. *100 Years at Hull-House.* Bloomington: Indiana University Press, 1990.

Butler, Amy E. *Two Paths to Equality: Alice Paul and Ethel M. Smith in the ERA Debate, 1921–1929.* Albany: State University of New York Press, 2002.

Card, David, and Alan B. Krueger. *Myth and Measurement: The New Economics of the Minimum Wage.* Princeton, N.J.: Princeton University Press, 1995.

Carlson, Peter. *Roughneck: The Life and Times of Big Bill Haywood.* New York: W. W. Norton, 1983.

Clark, Burton R. *The Distinctive College: Antioch, Reed & Swarthmore.* Chicago: Aldine, 1970.

Clemens, Elisabeth S. *The People's Lobby: Organizational Innovation and the Rise of Interest Group Politics in the United States, 1890–1925.* Chicago: University of Chicago Press, 1997.

Cobble, Dorothy Sue. *Dishing It Out: Waitresses and Their Unions in the Twentieth Century.* Urbana: University of Illinois Press, 1991.

———. *The Other Women's Movement: Workplace Justice and Social Rights in Modern America.* Princeton, N.J.: Princeton University Press, 2004.

Cohen, Lizabeth. *A Consumers' Republic: The Politics of Consumption in Postwar America.* New York: Knopf, 2003.

Conable, Charlotte Williams. *Women at Cornell: The Myth of Equal Education.* Ithaca, N.Y.: Cornell University Press, 1977.

Costin, Lela B. *Two Sisters for Social Justice : Biography of Grace and Edith Abbott.* Urbana: University of Illinois Press, 1983.

Cott, Nancy. *The Grounding of Modern Feminism.* New Haven, Conn.: Yale University Press, 1987.

Crocker, Ruth. *Mrs. Russell Sage: Women's Activism and Philanthropy in Gilded Age and Progressive Era America.* Bloomington: Indiana University Press, 2006.

Daniels, Doris Groshen. *Always a Sister: The Feminism of Lillian D. Wald.* New York: Feminist Press, 1989.

Davis, Allen F. *American Heroine: The Life and Legend of Jane Addams.* New York: Oxford University Press, 1973.

Dawley, Alan. *Struggles for Justice: Social Responsibility and the Liberal State.* Cambridge: Belknap Press, 1991.

DeBenedetti, Charles. *The Peace Reform in American History.* Bloomington: Indiana University Press, 1980.

Destler, Chester M. *Henry Demarest Lloyd and the Empire of Reform.* Philadelphia: University of Pennsylvania Press, 1963.

Dimand, Robert W., Mary Ann Dimand, and Evelyn L. Forget, eds. *A Biographical Directory of Women Economists.* Cheltenham, UK: Edward Elgar, 2000.

Diner, Steven J. *A Very Different Age: Americans of the Progressive Era.* New York: Hill and Wang, 1998.

Draper, Hal. *The Marx-Engels Chronicle.* New York: Schocken Books, 1985.

Dublin, Thomas. *Immigrant Voices: New Lives in America, 1773–1986.* University of Illinois Press, 1993.

Dubofsky, Melvyn. *We Shall Be All: A History of the Industrial Workers of the World.* New York: Quadrangle, 1969.

Duffus, R. L. *Lillian Wald: Neighbor and Crusader.* New York: Macmillan, 1938.

Dye, Nancy Schrom. *As Equals and as Sisters: Feminism, Unionism, and the Women's Trade Union League of New York.* Columbia: University of Missouri Press, 1980.

Evans, Richard. *Comrades and Sisters: Feminism, Socialism and Pacifism in Europe, 1870–1945.* Sussex: Wheatsheaf Books, 1987.

Evans, Sara. *Personal Politics: The Roots of Women's Liberation in the Civil Rights Movement and the New Left.* New York: Knopf, 1979.

Felt, Jeremy P. *Hostages of Fortune: Child Labor Reform in New York State.* Syracuse, N.Y.: Syracuse University Press, 1965.

Filippelli, Ronald L., ed. *Labor Conflict in the United States: An Encyclopedia.* New York: Garland, 1990.

Fink, Leon. *Workingmen's Democracy: The Knights of Labor and American Politics.* Urbana: University of Illinois Press, 1983.

Foner, Philip S. *History of the Labor Movement in the United States.* Vol. 2. New York: International Publishers, 1955.

Fones-Wolf, Ken. *Trade Union Gospel: Christianity and Labor in Industrial Philadelphia, 1865–1915.* Philadelphia, Pa.: Temple University Press, 1989.

Forbath, William E. *Law and the Shaping of the American Labor Movement.* Cambridge, Mass.: Harvard University Press, 1991.

Forgacs, David, ed. *An Antonio Gramsci Reader: Selected Writings, 1916–1935.* New York: Schocken Books, 1988.

Foster, Carrie A. *The Women and the Warriors: The U.S. Section of the Women's International League for Peace and Freedom, 1915–1946.* Syracuse, N.Y.: Syracuse University Press, 1995.

Fraser, Steven. *Labor Will Rule: Sidney Hillman and the Rise of American Labor.* New York: Free Press, 1991.

Freyer, Tony. *Regulating Big Business: Antitrust in Great Britain and America, 1880–1990.* Cambridge: Cambridge University Press, 1992.

Garvey, Ellen Gruber. *The Adman in the Parlor: Magazines and the Gendering of Consumer Culture, 1880s to 1910s.* New York: Oxford University Press, 1996.

Geidel, Peter. "Alva E. Belmont: A Forgotten Feminist." Ph.D. diss., Columbia University, 1993.

Gettleman, Marvin E. *An Elusive Presence: The Discovery of John H. Finley and His America.* Chicago: Nelson-Hall, 1979.

Glickman, Lawrence B. *A Living Wage: American Workers and the Making of Consumer Society*. Ithaca: Cornell University Press, 1997.

Glickman, Rose L. *Russian Factory Women: Workplace and Society, 1880–1914*. Berkeley: University of California Press, 1984.

Graves, Pamela M. *Labour Women: Women in British Working-Class Politics, 1918–1939*. Cambridge: Cambridge University Press, 1994.

Green, Jim. *Death in the Haymarket: A Story of Chicago, the First Labor Movement, and the Bombing that Divided Gilded Age America*. New York: Pantheon, 2006.

Greene, Julie. *Pure and Simple Politics: The American Federation of Labor and Political Activism, 1881 to 1917*. New York: Cambridge University Press, 1998.

Hall, Jacquelyn Dowd, James Leloudis, Robert Korstad, Mary Murphy, Lu Ann Jones, and Christopher B. Daly. *Like a Family: The Making of a Southern Cotton Mill World*. Chapel Hill: University of North Carolina Press, 1987.

Hall, Kermit. *Oxford Companion to the Supreme Court of the United States*. New York: Oxford University Press, 1992.

Harbaugh, William H. *Lawyer's Lawyer: The Life of John W. Davis*. New York: Oxford University Press, 1973.

Harrison, Dennis Irven. "The Consumers' League of Ohio: Women and Reform, 1909–1937." Ph.D. diss., Case Western Reserve University, 1975.

Hart, Vivien. *Bound by Our Constitution: Women, Workers, and the Minimum Wage*. Princeton, N.J.: Princeton University Press, 1994.

Hewett, Waterman Thomas. *Cornell University: A History*. 4 vols. New York: University Publishing Society, 1905.

Hilts, Philip J. *Protecting America's Health: The FDA, Business, and One Hundred Years of Regulation*. Chapel Hill: University of North Carolina Press, 2003.

Hoffman, Beatrix. *The Wages of Sickness: The Politics of Health Insurance in Progressive America*. Durham: University of North Carolina Press, 2001.

Hoff-Wilson, Joan, ed. *Rights of Passage: The Past and Future of the ERA*. Bloomington: Indiana University Press, 1986.

Hyman, Paula E., and Deborah Dash Moore, eds. *Jewish Women in America: An Historical Encyclopedia*. New York: Routledge, 1997.

Jablonsky, Thomas J. *The Home, Heaven, and Mother Party: Female Anti-Suffragists in the United States, 1868–1920*. Brooklyn: Carlson, 1994.

Johnson, Kimberley S. *Governing the American State: Congress and the New Federalism, 1877–1929*. Princeton, N.J.: Princeton University Press, 2007.

Kapp, Yvonne. *Eleanor Marx*. Vol. 1, *Family Life*. New York: Random House, 1972.

Kellogg, Charles Flint. *NAACP: A History of the National Association for the Advancement of Colored People*. Baltimore, Md.: Johns Hopkins University Press, 1967.

Kessler-Harris, Alice. *Out to Work: A History of Wage-Earning Women in the United States*. New York: Oxford University Press, 1982.

———. *In Pursuit of Equity: Women, Men, and the Quest for Economic Citizenship in 20th-Century America*. New York: Oxford University Press, 2001.

Kolko, Gabriel. *Railroads and Regulation, 1877–1916*. Princeton, N.J.: Princeton University Press, 1965.

Lagemann, Ellen Condliffe. *A Generation of Women: Education in the Lives of Progressive Reformers.* Cambridge, Mass.: Harvard University Press, 1979.

Leach, William. *True Love and Perfect Union: The Feminist Reform of Sex and Society.* New York: Basic Books 1980.

Lefaucheux, Marie-Hélène. *Women in a Changing World: The Dynamic Story of the International Council of Women since 1888.* London: Routledge & Kegan Paul, 1966.

Lehrer, Susan. *Origins of Protective Labor Legislation for Women, 1905–1925.* Albany, N.Y.: SUNY Press, 1987.

Lemons, J. Stanley. *The Woman Citizen.* Urbana: University of Illinois Press, 1973.

Levine, Lawrence. *Highbrow/Lowbrow: The Emergence of Cultural Hierarchy in America.* Cambridge: Harvard University Press, 1988.

Lewis, David Levering. *W. E. B. Du Bois: Biography of a Race.* New York: Henry Holt, 1993.

Lief, Alfred, ed. *The Dissenting Opinions of Mr. Justice Holmes.* New York: Vanguard Press, 1929.

Lindenmeyer, Kriste. *A Right to Childhood: The U.S. Children's Bureau and Child Welfare, 1912–46.* Urbana: University of Illinois Press, 1997.

Linn, James Weber. *Jane Addams: A Biography.* New York: Appleton, 1938.

Loth, David. *Swope of G.E.: The Story of Gerard Swope and General Electric in American Business.* New York: Simon and Schuster, 1958.

Loughran, Miriam E. "The Historical Development of Child-Labor Legislation in the United States." Ph.D. diss., Catholic University of America, 1921.

MacLaury, Judson. *History of the Department of Labor, 1913–1988.* Washington, D.C.: U.S. Department of Labor, 1988.

Magat, Richard. *Unlikely Partners: Philanthropic Foundations and the Labor Movement.* Ithaca, N.Y.: Cornell University Press, 1999.

Marchand, C. Roland. *The American Peace Movement and Social Reform, 1898–1918.* Princeton, N.J.: Princeton University Press, 1972.

Marshall, Susan. *Splintered Sisterhood: Gender and Class in the Campaign against Woman Suffrage.* Madison: University of Wisconsin Press, 1997.

Marshall, T. H. *Citizenship and Social Class, and Other Essays.* Cambridge: Cambridge University Press, 1950.

Martin, Rose L. *Fabian Freeway: High Road to Socialism in the U.S.A., 1884–1966.* Chicago: Heritage Foundation, 1966.

Mattson, Kevin. *Creating a Democratic Public: The Struggle for Urban Participatory Democracy during the Progressive Era.* University Park, Pa.: Pennsylvania State University Press, 1998.

McCormick, Richard L. *From Realignment to Reform: Political Change in New York State, 1893–1910.* Ithaca, N.Y.: Cornell University Press, 1979.

McGerr, Michael E. *A Fierce Discontent: The Rise and Fall of the Progressive Movement in America, 1870–1920.* New York: Free Press, 2003.

McGuire, John T. "'A Catalyst for Reform: The Women's Joint Legislative Conference and Its Fight for Labor Legislation in New York State, 1918–1933." Ph.D. diss., Binghamton University, 2000.

Montgomery, Maureen. *"Gilded Prostitution": Status, Money, and Transatlantic Marriages, 1870–1914*. London: Routledge, 1989.

Mott, Frank Luther. *A History of American Magazines*. 5 vols. Cambridge, Mass.: Harvard University Press, 1938–1968.

Mullendore, William Clinton. *History of the United States Food Administration, 1917–1919*. Stanford, Calif.: Stanford University Press, 1941.

Muncy, Robyn. *Creating a Female Dominion in American Reform, 1890–1935*. New York: Oxford University Press, 1991.

Murphy, Paul L. *World War I and the Origins of Civil Liberties in the United States*. New York: Norton, 1979.

Neilson, Kim E. *Un-American Womanhood: Antiradicalism, Antifeminism, and the First Red Scare*. Columbus: Ohio State University Press, 2001.

Neuzil, Mark. *Mass Media & Environmental Conflict: America's Green Crusades*. Thousand Oaks, Calif.: Sage, 1996.

Newton, Norman T. *Design on the Land: The Development of Landscape Architecture*. Cambridge, Mass.: Belknap Press of Harvard University Press, 1971.

Nordin, Dennis S., and Roy V. Scott. *From Prairie Farmer to Entrepreneur: The Transformation of Midwestern Agriculture*. Bloomington: Indiana University Press, 2005.

Pedersen, Susan. *Eleanor Rathbone and the Politics of Conscience*. New Haven: Yale University Press, 2004.

Pfannestiel, Todd J. *Rethinking the Red Scare: The Lusk Committee and New York's Crusade against Radicalism, 1919–1923*. New York: Routledge, 2003.

Pipkin, Charles. *Social Legislation in the South*. Southern Policy Paper No. 3. Chapel Hill: University of North Carolina Press, 1936.

Preston, William, Jr., *Aliens and Dissenters: Federal Suppression of Radicals, 1903–1933*. Urbana: University of Illinois Press, 1994.

Rader, Benjamin G. *The Academic Mind and Reform: The Influence of Richard T. Ely in American Life*. Lexington: University of Kentucky Press, 1966.

Randall, Mercedes M. *Improper Bostonian: Emily Greene Balch*. New York: Twayne, 1964.

Rauchway, Eric. *Murdering McKinley: The Making of Theodore Roosevelt's America*. New York: Hill and Wang, 2003.

Rodgers, Daniel T. *Atlantic Crossings: Social Politics in a Progressive Age*. Cambridge: Harvard University Press, 1998.

Rose, Stephen J., and Heidi I. Hartmann. *Still a Man's Labor Market: The Long Term Earnings Gap*. Washington, D.C.: Institute for Women's Policy Research, 2004.

Ross, B. Joyce. *J. E. Spingarn and the Rise of the NAACP, 1911–1939*. New York: Atheneum, 1972.

Salvatore, Nick. *Eugene V. Debs: Citizen and Socialist*. Urbana: University of Illinois Press, 1982.

Sanders, Elizabeth. *Roots of Reform: Farmers, Workers, and the American State, 1877–1917*. Chicago: University of Chicago Press, 1999.

Schmidt, Gertrude. "History of Labor Legislation in Wisconsin." Ph.D. diss., University of Wisconsin, 1933.

Schneirov, Richard, Shelton Stromquist, and Nick Salvatore, eds. *The Pullman Strike and the Crisis of the 1890s: Essays on Labor and Politics.* Urbana: University of Illinois Press, 1999.

Sicherman, Barbara, ed. *Alice Hamilton: A Life in Letters.* Cambridge, Mass.: Harvard University Press, 1984.

Sklar, Kathryn Kish. *Florence Kelley and the Nation's Work: The Rise of Women's Political Culture, 1830–1900.* New Haven, Conn.: Yale University Press, 1995.

———, ed. *Notes of Sixty Years: The Autobiography of Florence Kelley.* Chicago: C. H. Kerr, 1986.

Sklar, Kathryn Kish, Anja Schüler, and Susan Strasser, eds. *Social Justice Feminists in the United States and Germany: A Dialogue in Documents, 1885–1933.* Ithaca, N.Y.: Cornell University Press, 1998.

Skocpol, Theda. *Protecting Soldiers and Mothers: The Political Origins of Social Policy in the United States.* Cambridge: Harvard University Press, 1995.

Soldon, Norbert C. *Women in British Trade Unions, 1874–1976.* Dublin: Gill and Macmillan, 1978.

Steel, Ronald. *Walter Lippmann and the American Century.* Boston: Little, Brown, 1980.

Steinberg, Ronnie. *Wages and Hours: Labor and Reform in Twentieth-Century America.* New Brunswick: Rutgers University Press, 1982.

Storrs, Landon R. Y. *Civilizing Capitalism: The National Consumers' League, Women's Activism, and Labor Standards in the New Deal Era.* Chapel Hill: University of North Carolina Press, 2000.

Strom, Sharon Hartman. *Beyond the Typewriter: Gender, Class, and the Origins of Modern American Office Work, 1900–1930.* Urbana: University of Illinois Press, 1992.

Stuart, Amanda Mackenzie. *Consuelo and Alva Vanderbilt: The Story of a Daughter and a Mother in the Gilded Age.* New York: HarperCollins, 2005.

Tax, Meredith. *The Rising of the Women: Feminist Solidarity and Class Conflict, 1880–1917.* New York: Monthly Review Press, 1980.

Thompson, E. P. *The Making of the English Working Class.* London: V. Gollancz, 1963.

Torpey, John. *The Invention of the Passport: Surveillance, Citizenship, and the State.* Cambridge: Cambridge University Press, 2000.

Trattner, Walter I. *Crusade for the Children: A History of the National Child Labor Committee and Child Labor Reform in America.* Chicago: Quadrangle Books, 1970.

Tuttle, William M., Jr. *Race Riot: Chicago in the Red Summer of 1919.* New York: Atheneum, 1970.

Waldron, Jeremy, ed. *Theories of Rights.* London: Oxford University Press, 1984.

Unger, Nancy C. *Fighting Bob LaFollette: The Righteous Reformer.* Chapel Hill: University of North Carolina Press, 2000.

Ware, Susan. *Beyond Suffrage: Women in the New Deal.* Cambridge, Mass.: Harvard University Press, 1981.

———. *Partner and I: Molly Dewson, Feminism, and New Deal Politics.* New Haven, Conn.: Yale University Press, 1987.

Wedin, Carolyn. *Inheritors of the Spirit: Mary White Ovington and the Founding of the NAACP.* New York: John Wiley, 1998.

Wenger, Beth S. *New York Jews and the Great Depression: Uncertain Promise.* New Haven, Conn.: Yale University Press, 1996.

Wesser, Robert F. *Charles Evans Hughes: Politics and Reform in New York, 1905–1910.* Ithaca, N.Y.: Cornell University Press, 1967.

White, G. Edward. *Justice Oliver Wendell Holmes: Law and the Inner Self.* New York: Oxford University Press, 1993.

Wilson, Jan Doolittle. *The Women's Joint Congressional Committee and The Politics of Maternalism, 1920–1930.* Champaign, Ill.: University of Illinois Press, 2007.

Woloch, Nancy. *Muller v. Oregon: A Brief History with Documents.* Boston: Bedford/St. Martin's, 1996.

Young, Louise. *In the Public Interest: The League of Women Voters, 1920–1970.* New York: Greenwood, 1989.

Zipser, Arthur, and Pearl Zipser. *Fire and Grace: The Life of Rose Pastor Stokes.* Athens: University of Georgia Press, 1989.

INDEX

KATHRYN KISH SKLAR is distinguished professor of history and co-director of the Center for the Historical Study of Women and Gender at SUNY, Binghamton. She is the author of *Women's Rights Emerges within the Anti-Slavery Movement: A Short History with Documents, 1830–1870*; *Florence Kelley and the Nation's Work: The Rise of Women's Political Culture, 1830–1900*; and *Catharine Beecher: A Study in American Domesticity.*

BEVERLY WILSON PALMER is a research associate at Pomona College. She is the editor of *Selected Letters of Charles Sumner*; *Selected Papers of Thaddeus Stevens*; *Selected Letters of Lucretia Coffin Mott*; and *A Woman's Wit and Whimsy: The 1833 Diary of Anna Cabot Lowell Quincy.*

The University of Illinois Press
is a founding member of the
Association of American University Presses.

Composed in 10.5/12.5 Adobe Minion
with Scala Sans display
by Jim Proefrock
at the University of Illinois Press
Designed by Copenhaver Cumpston
Manufactured by Sheridan Books, Inc.

UNIVERSITY OF ILLINOIS PRESS
1325 South Oak Street
Champaign, IL 61820-6903
www.press.uillinois.edu